P9-DUQ-378

Encyclopedia of Alzheimer's Disease

ALSO BY ELAINE A. MOORE

Autoimmune Diseases and Their Environmental Triggers
(McFarland, 2002)

WITH LISA MOORE

Graves' Disease: A Practical Guide
(McFarland, 2001)

Encyclopedia of Alzheimer's Disease

With Directories of Research, Treatment and Care Facilities

Elaine A. Moore
with Lisa Moore

Illustrations by MARVIN G. MILLER

McFarland & Company, Inc., Publishers
Jefferson, North Carolina, and London

This book is intended as an educational resource and not as a substitute for treatment. Before making any therapeutic changes, the procedures and therapies described in this book should be discussed with a medical professional.

Library of Congress Cataloguing-in-Publication Data

Moore, Elaine A., 1948–
Encyclopedia of Alzheimer's disease ; with directories of research, treatment, and care facilities / Elaine A. Moore ; with Lisa Moore ; illustrations by Marvin G. Miller.
p. cm.
Includes bibliographical references and index.

ISBN 0-7864-1438-3 (illustrated case binding : 50# alkaline paper) ∞

1. Alzheimer's disease—Encyclopedias. 2. Alzheimer's disease—Directories. I. Moore, Lisa, 1973– . II. Title.
[DNLM: 1. Alzheimer Disease—Directory. 2. Alzheimer Disease—Encyclopedias—English. WT 13 M821e 2002]
RC523.M665 2003 616.8'31'003—dc21 2002012202

British Library cataloguing data are available

Manufactured in the United States of America

McFarland & Company, Inc., Publishers
Box 611, Jefferson, North Carolina 28640
www.mcfarlandpub.com

To Marie Pacer and to everyone
who helped in her care, especially Ken, Bob, Laurie, John,
Nora, Richard, Joyce, Scott, Dawn, Valerie, Brett,
Lisa, Jessie, Joey, Marie, Annette, Gerry,
Virgie, Irene, Amy and Johnny

Contents

Preface

Nearly one hundred years ago, in Germany, Dr. Alois Alzheimer encountered a middle-aged female patient with a progressive form of dementia. Finding no medical references for this disorder, Dr. Alzheimer became intrigued. After her death, at autopsy, he found the woman's brain atrophied and riddled with plaque deposits. Puzzled, Dr. Alzheimer continued researching this disorder, but he never found the answers he sought. For the next half-century, its incidence rose with each generation, but researchers learned little about the origins of this condition, which eventually became known as Alzheimer's disease.

Thanks to tremendous advances in the field of neurology, the genetic and environmental causes of Alzheimer's disease are no longer the mystery they were for Dr. Alzheimer. Furthermore, many new therapies such as cholinesterase inhibitors have been shown to slow disease progression as well as manage symptoms. Clinical trials suggest that vaccines may soon be used as a preventative measure. Dietary supplements, herbal medicines, antioxidant vitamins, stress reduction and other aspects of holistic healing are also known to reduce symptoms and offer protective benefits.

The *Encyclopedia of Alzheimer's Disease* is a comprehensive reference guide intended for anyone involved in the care, treatment, and day-to-day concerns of patients with Alzheimer's disease and related disorders. It is also intended for anyone who is interested in learning more about the genetic and environmental factors that contribute to both early onset and late onset Alzheimer's disease.

A progressive neurological disorder that affects about 35 percent of the elderly population, Alzheimer's disease is the most common cause of dementia and one of the leading causes of death in the elderly. Characterized by early symptoms of confusion and short-term memory impairment, Alzheimer's disease arises from a constellation of specific cellular and biochemical changes that destroy brain cells. As a consequence, the cellular connections that govern thinking, learning, and memory are disrupted.

When we first decided to write an Alzheimer's disease reference book, we envisioned creating an encyclopedic list, detailing everything that is currently known about dementia. Having an intimate connection to Alzheimer's disease, we have witnessed firsthand how patients and their relatives often walk away from doctor's appointments with more questions than answers. Both patients and family members frequently want to know more about the prognosis of this disease and they want to know the reasons why it may have developed. They also want to know how the diagnosis of Alzheimer's disease was made and what other conditions might cause similar symptoms. Our goal in writing this book was to answer these and related questions and provide a general resource for all patient concerns.

As we began compiling information, we soon realized, however, that an ordinary encyclopedic approach would fail to help anyone who needed to find a nearby research center or a local long-term or day care facility, particularly one in another part of the country. To facilitate finding such information, we added three major sections to the book: Long-Term and Day Care Treatment Centers; Research Facilities; and Resources.

In the encyclopedia part of this volume, we have tried to cover the many topics relevant to an understanding of the development, care, and treatment of Alzheimer's disease. In doing so, we included many cross-references designed to serve people with little knowledge of Alzheimer's disease as well as those with greater knowledge. For instance, readers searching for a basic understanding of Alzheimer's disease can explore general topics such as "Alzheimer's disease" or "Brain changes in Alzheimer's disease." Those looking for specific topics, such as neurotransmitters, can look under this specific subject heading.

In instances where the encyclopedia includes similar or related topics, we have listed them as cross-references at the end of individual entries. For instance, at the end of the entry describing the "Diagnosis of Alzheimer's Disease," the reader is directed to also see specific diagnostic criteria, such as the "DSM IV Diagnostic Criteria."

Following the encyclopedia is a representative list of long-term and day care treatment facilities that have specifically noted that they care for Alzheimer's disease patients. We listed these entries by state and city, although space prohibited us from including very small towns. With each entry, we've added helpful information, such as the size of the facility, its certifying agencies and primary insurance carriers, and whether it offers provisions for day care and home health care.

Because many nursing homes care for Alzheimer's disease patients but do not specifically advertise as such, we may have failed to list some facilities that do indeed care for Alzheimer's disease patients. And because policies at nursing homes often change over time, we advise calling prospective nursing homes and verifying information before arranging to visit specific facilities. Further information on nursing homes can be found on the Internet, with state listings linked to the Medicare web site (http://www.medicare.gov) and in the reference section of most public libraries. Here you will find Medicare and Medicaid listings of nursing homes and helpful reference books such as the HCIA-Sachs guide to nursing homes, which is updated annually.

Nursing home directors can also provide needed information to help with your search for a home. We would like specifically to thank Sandy Clarke, director of Namaste Alzheimer's Center in Colorado Springs, Colorado, for her generous sharing of information. We would also like to thank Namaste for allowing Elaine to work as a volunteer while researching gerontology in the graduate sociology program at the University of Colorado.

We suggest making at least two personal visits before selecting a long-term care facility. These visits provide an opportunity to observe both the staff members and the residents and how they relate to one another. When visiting nursing homes, family members should make sure that the safety and well-being of patients are top priorities and that there is sufficient staff to take care of the individual needs of all patients. The institution should also be clean, organized, secure, and cheerful.

It is also important to consider what features of a nursing home would be most appreciated by patients and what extra amenities might be most attractive. Even patients in the late stages of Alzheimer's disease have likes and dislikes and the capacity for enjoyment. As an example, some nursing homes have greenhouses and gardens and some allow visits from family pets. If these are particularly attractive features, they should be taken into consideration during the process of selecting a long-term or day care facility.

The next section, on research facilities, lists the many government and university affiliated research centers in the United States that specialize in Alzheimer's disease research. Most of these centers conduct clinical trials, and different centers usually focus on specific aspects of Alzheimer's disease. Because some of the newer experimental therapies are designed to prevent further deterioration as well as reduce symptoms, all Alzheimer's disease patients can benefit from participating in these programs. Most programs are geared toward outpatients but some university programs are affiliated with specific nursing homes.

The final section (before the index), Resources, lists a wide selection of available books, journals, national and local organizations, Internet sources, support groups, and government resources. The State Ombudsman listing provides contact information for anyone who needs help locating a suitable nursing home. The state ombudsman programs are also instrumental in resolving problems with nursing homes should they occur.

Belonging to a support group, whether online or a local chapter of the Alzheimer's Association, is well worth the time and effort. We personally found the Rocky Mountain Chapter of the Alzheimer's Association to be a tremendous resource. Like many people we've met, we benefited from the support, educational materials, and respite care which they provided, but most of all, we found comfort in learning how well many other people cope and in realizing that we were not alone in our challenge. From others we learned many suggestions and became empowered through education.

With the many great advances in Alzheimer's disease today, knowledge is especially empowering. It is important for Alzheimer's disease patients and their family members to know that there are many treatments today that not only ameliorate but also help prevent symptoms. While changes may not become apparent overnight, recent studies have demonstrated beneficial effects from herbs, dietary changes, hormones, stress reduction, and anti-inflammatory agents.

Today, Alzheimer's disease is not the bleak disorder it was a decade ago. Alzheimer's disease and related disorders are now easier to diagnose, and, with early diagnosis, easier to treat and sometimes keep from progressing. It is important for caregivers to be aware of all available treatments, both conventional and holistic, which offer hope for Alzheimer's disease. Numerous resources, including opportunities for respite care, are now available for caregivers. Studies show that caregivers who are given training and support are better equipped to care for Alzheimer's disease patients, and trained caregivers are able to provide home care for longer periods of time.

The Encyclopedia

A2M. A2M is a possible susceptibility gene for Alzheimer's disease located on chromosome 12. [A2M was discovered by Rudolph Tanzi, a geneticist from Harvard University. It appears to control the rate at which neurons produce beta amyloid protein.]

Abeta (Aβ). Abeta (Aβ) is an acronym for β-amyloid protein, a characteristic feature of the senile plaque deposits seen in the brain of patients with Alzheimer's disease. *See* Amyloid beta protein.

Aβ 42. Aβ 42, a form or subtype of Aβ ending at amino acid 42, is the earliest species of Aβ deposited in the neuritic plaques riddled through the brain of Alzheimer's disease patients. These plaques are almost exclusively composed of Aβ 42. Shifts in the metabolic pathways that produce Aβ 42 are suspected of influencing Alzheimer's disease development. Laboratory tests for Aβ 42 are available, but their use as a diagnostic marker for Alzheimer's disease has not been established. Aβ 42 is decreased in the spinal fluid of patients with Alzheimer's disease, presumably because of its aggregation in brain lesions. (Check, William, Ph.D. "Puzzling out a role for Alzheimer's tests," *CAP Today, In the News*, publication of the College of American Pathologists, June 1998)

Abstract reasoning. Abstract reason is tested by asking the patient to explain a few common proverbs, such as "The early bird catches the worm." The answers are then evaluated in terms of relevance. A tendency to interpret these sayings in literal, concrete terms may indicate organic brain disease, schizophrenia, or mental retardation. However, a limited education can also cause patients to offer literal explanations.

Acetyl-L-Carnitine (ALCAR). The dietary supplement acetyl-L-carnitine (ALCAR) is reported to offer benefits in Alzheimer's disease treatment. While a daily dose of 500 mg to 1,000 mg is generally recommended, the amount needed for improvement in Alzheimer's disease has not yet been determined. In several studies, acetyl-L-carnitine was found to enhance cellular adenosine triphosphate (ATP) production (the body's source of energy), and to prevent pesticide-induced injury in rats.

Furthermore, ALCAR has been reported to reduce production of mitochondrial free radicals, help maintain transmembrane function, and enhance electron transfer. The National Institute of Health is currently doing clinical trials using ALCAR. Side effects of this supplement include increased appetite, body odor, and rashes. (Brooks, J. et al., "Acetyl L-carnitine slows decline in younger patients with Alzheimer's disease: a reanalysis of a double-blind placebo-controlled study using the trilinear approach,"

International Journal of Psychogeriatrics, June 1998; 10#(2): 193–203; Perlmutter, David, "Functional Therapeutics in Neurodegenerative Disease," Physicians Committee for Responsible Medicine website: http://www.pcrm.org/health/Preventive_Medicine/alzheimers.html)

Acetylcholine. The first neurotransmitter discovered, acetylcholine is a messenger chemical produced by the nervous system. Neurotransmitters are chemicals that allow cells to communicate with one another. This communication is necessary for thought and learning processes.

Acetylcholine levels are consistently decreased in the brains of Alzheimer's disease patients, with the amount of this reduction correlating to disease severity. Acetylcholine reduction is a secondary event, resulting from the destruction of neurons in the parts of the forebrain rich in acetylcholine. The enzyme choline acetyltransferase (CAT), which synthesizes or produces acetylcholine, is reduced by up to 90 percent in Alzheimer's disease patients.

Acetylcholine is found at the neuromuscular junction (which connects nerve cells to muscle cells) in autonomic ganglia and at parasympathetic nerve endings. In the neuromuscular junction, the endings of motor neurons release acetylcholine. Acetylcholine diffuses across the cleft between neuronal endings and muscle fibers and attaches to receptor molecules in the muscle fiber membrane, initiating permeability changes and consequent depolarization. Without acetylcholine, the nervous system cannot communicate with muscle cells.

Acetylcholine is produced by cholinergic neurons, which are concentrated in certain areas of the nervous system, particularly the basal forebrain and the striatum. The physiological action of acetylcholine is different at central and peripheral nerve endings. In the peripheral nervous system, its action is brief and spatially precise. In the central nervous system, its actions are slower and more diffuse.

Acetylcholine also helps brain cells communicate with each other by facilitating communication from the basal forebrain to the cerebral cortex and hippocampus, aiding the learning and memory processes. In addition, acetylcholine regulates sleep and facilitates higher cognitive functions. Acetylcholine deficiency can predispose a person to a wide range of neurological diseases, including Alzheimer's disease and stroke. The effect of acetylcholine is limited by the enzyme acetylcholinesterase and by the number of protein receptors able to bind with acetylcholine. Normally, acetylcholinesterase destroys any acetylcholine remaining after it is initially used.

In the early stages of Alzheimer's disease, a select group of neurons become deficient in acetylcholine. Studies indicate that there is a dramatic loss of acetylcholine in the cortex and hippocampal formation of Alzheimer's patients. The hypothesis that memory and cognitive deficits are caused by decreased acetylcholine activity in the brain has shaped pharmacological research. Drugs that block or inhibit acetylcholinesterase increase the amount of acetylcholine available for neurotransmission. Although acetylcholine deficiency is still considered an important step in the pathogenesis of Alzheimer's disease, the fundamental basis of the neuronal degeneration is thought to be more significant.

Acetylcholine receptor, muscarinic 1-5 *see* Muscarinic acetylcholine receptor

Acetylcholine receptor, neuronal nicotinic *see* Nicotinic acetylcholine receptor

Acetylcholinesterase. Acetylcholinesterase, which is also known as cholinesterase, is an enzyme that destroys the neurotransmitter acetylcholine after it has been used. Normally present in the body, acetylcholinesterase limits the amount of acetylcholine present in the circulation. An increase in acetylcholinesterase causes a reduction in available stores of acetylcholine. Drugs designed to inhibit the production of acetylcholinesterase cause a rise in the body's levels of available acetylcholine.

Acetylcholinesterase inhibitors. Acetylcholinesterase inhibitors, which are also

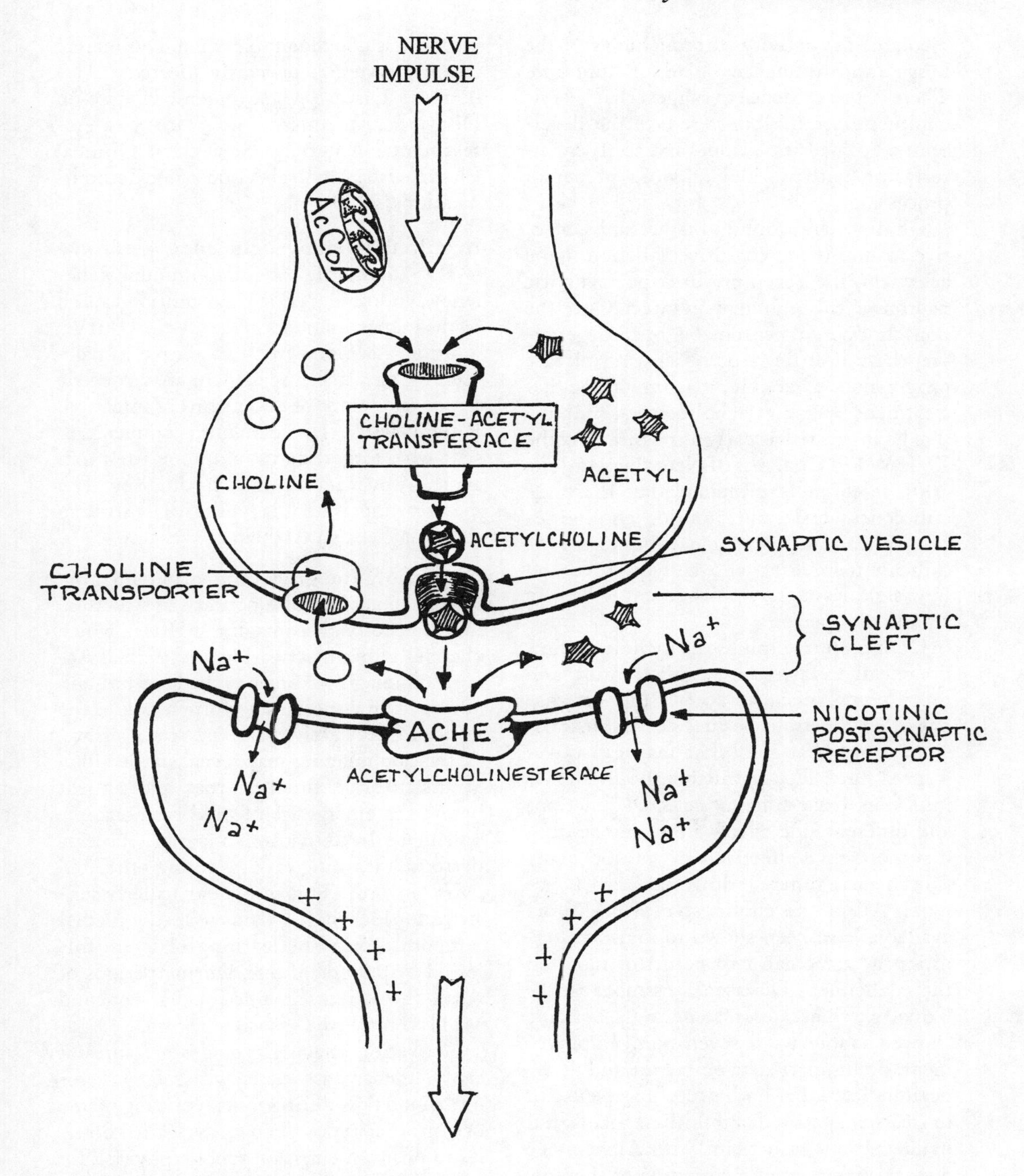

Acetylcholine (illustration by Marvin G. Miller).

known as cholinesterase inhibitors, are a class of drugs widely employed in the treatment of Alzheimer's disease. Introduced in the early to mid–1990s, acetylcholinesterase inhibitors are designed to improve cognitive function. Acetylcholinesterase is an enzyme present in the brain that hydrolyzes or breaks down the neurotransmitter acetylcholine. Acetylcholinesterase also inhibits dopamine release in cells in the substantia nigra, mediates the activity of bronchioles in the lungs, and influences bladder function. There is also evidence to suggest that acetylcholinesterase inhibitors reduce the development of neuritic plaques indirectly by interfering with normal amyloid precursor processing.

Cholinesterase inhibitors are only effective in improving cognitive function if the acetylcholine receptors and postsynaptic neurons in the brain remain intact. Once the non-cholinergic neurons begin to degenerate, there is little hope of slowing disease progression. Therefore, it is important that treatment with acetylcholinesterase inhibitors be instituted as early as possible. At the XVII World Congress of Neurology in June 2001, researchers explained that there are still controversies surrounding cholinesterase inhibitors, particularly because it is difficult to predict who will improve and how significant the improvement will be in a particular person.

Cholinesterase inhibitors include tacrine, donepezil, rivastigmine, galantamine and metrifonate. Because acetylcholinesterase has other functions besides nerve transmission, drugs that inhibit it may cause unwanted side effects. Available cholinesterase inhibitors have different selected functions and different side effects so while one drug may not prove effective or have too many side effects, a different drug may prove beneficial. All of the cholinesterase inhibitors available have been shown to improve cognition by a median two points or more on the Alzheimer's Disease Assessment Scale-Cognitive Subscale. In some trials, patients showed as much as a seven-point improvement. Preliminary data on tacrine and donepezil indicate that both drugs may be useful in treating apathy, disinhibition, pacing and hallucinations in patients with Alzheimer's disease. After about six months of therapy, nearly all patients begin to regress. However, the rate of decline is slower after treatment than before treatment.

Not all Alzheimer's patients respond to cholinesterase inhibitors. It is reported that only 25–30 percent of patients show improvement. Some researchers suspect that response is dependent on which cholinergic receptor system is primarily affected. ("Alzheimer's Disease Management: Update on Diagnosis, Treatment, and Outcomes, Assessment," American Society of Clinical Pharmacists, Medical Association Communications, 2000)

Acquired immune deficiency syndrome (AIDS) dementia. Acquired immune deficiency syndrome (AIDS), a condition caused by the human immunodeficiency virus (HIV), is often associated with cognitive impairment. Cognitive impairment may precede the development of other signs of infection. Patients with AIDS dementia complex present with forgetfulness and poor attention, typically over several months duration. The memory impairment is typically less striking than that seen in Alzheimer's disease.

Activation Imaging. Activation imaging refers to a method of functional or structural magnetic resonance imaging (MRI) in which changes in brain activation are studied. Activation imaging compares the level of brain activity while subjects perform a task to the level of brain activity in the resting state. Activation imaging may reveal subtle alterations in brain function that may appear before the emergence of mild memory impairment. In activation imaging, subjects perform a learning task involving unrelated pairs of words. This test is particularly sensitive for identifying damage to the medial temporal lobe. The learning tests are followed by periods of rest. During periods of recall, the patients are told the first word and asked to recall the associated word.

Activation imaging provides measures of signal intensity associated with relative cerebral blood flow during tasks requiring memory or other types of cognitive skills. Similar to positron emission topography (PET), activation imaging has the advantage of producing more detailed pictures in less time and does not subject the patient to radiation.

Activities of daily living (ADL). The term "activities of daily living" (ADL) refers to activities such as bathing, eating, grooming, toileting, and dressing that are part of one's personal self-care. People with dementia may not be able to perform these functions without assistance. Clinicians often measure a person's ADL to see if these functions have improved in response to different therapies.

Activity as a form of therapy. Activities offer stimulation and an opportunity to learn new tasks. Activities are beneficial in that they help sustain social skills, and they encourage hand-eye coordination. Patients with Alzheimer's disease, whether cared for at home or in institutional settings, benefit from a variety of activities, including crafts, music groups, shopping trips, exercise, small discussion groups, games such as bingo, and field trips to fairs, festivals and community events. Other recommended activities include reading, puzzles and card playing. Individuals with Alzheimer's disease frequently enjoy personal hobbies such as sorting beads or rearranging their possessions. As long as these activities are not disruptive, they should be encouraged.

Acupuncture. Small studies have shown that transcutaneous electrical nerve stimulation (TENS), a form of acupuncture, may improve memory and daily living skills in patients with Alzheimer's disease. Further studies are needed to confirm these findings. ("Alzheimer's Disease, Nutrition and Dietary Supplements," *Intellihealth*: http://www.intelihealth.com/IH/ihtIH/WSIHW000/8303/29429.html.)

Acute illness. Acute illnesses are illnesses that emerge suddenly and are of short duration. Unlike chronic illnesses, which persist indefinitely, acute illnesses, such as muscle sprains, are self-limiting.

Acute organic brain syndrome. Acute organic brain syndrome is a general term used to describe sudden-onset cognitive dysfunction characterized by symptoms of memory impairment and disorientation, which may progress to delirium. The prevalence of this disorder increases with age and commonly occurs in the presence of pneumonia, systemic infections, congestive heart failure, high fever, fluid and electrolyte imbalances, stroke, the postoperative state, and intoxication with drugs or alcohol. Other common clinical features include a depressed or fearful mood, apathy, irritability, impaired judgment, suspiciousness, delusions, hallucinations, and combative, uncooperative, or frightened behavior. Alzheimer's disease is the most common cause of organic brain syndrome, but in Alzheimer's disease, dementia is not acute. Rather, symptoms progress slowly over time and do not improve. In acute organic brain syndrome, symptoms subside as the underlying abnormalities are corrected.

AD7c. AD7c is a protein found in neuronal threads. A laboratory test to measure levels of AD7c in spinal fluid is available, but its use as a diagnostic marker for Alzheimer's disease has not yet been established.

Administration on Aging (AoA). The Administration on Aging (AoA) is a branch of the National Institute of Health. The AoA supports numerous studies on Alzheimer's disease and provides educational and support resources for the elderly. The AoA works with the Health Care Financing Administration, the Health and Human Services Department of the Inspector General, the Department of Justice, Medicare contractors, health care providers and others to develop programs that train volunteer retired professionals such as doctors, nurses, accountants, attorneys and teachers to serve as resources and educators for older people in their communities.

Adult day care centers. Adult day care is a service offered through many nursing homes, senior service centers and a number of nonprofit agencies. The center providing adult day care may provide transportation as an additional service. Patients at adult day care centers participate in various activities, and they receive meals as well as their medications if arranged. Adult day care provides respite for caregivers of dementia patients, and patients benefit from the stimulation and the interaction with others. Adult day care and respite care are often available through community groups, sometimes on a sliding fee schedule. Some insurance policies cover day care.

Advance directives. Advance directives (advance care planning directives) are care provisions written and signed in advance of their need that are available in the event the patient later becomes incompetent to make these decisions. Advance directives include the following points: whether and when cardiopulmonary (CPR) and do not resuscitate (DNR) orders should be withheld or put into place, the circumstances under which other-life-supporting measures, such as feeding tubes, antibiotics, hospitalization and surgical procedures, would be desired, and who should be legally designated as durable power of attorney for health care decisions and to assist the physician and family in determining what the patient's wishes would have been in case the patient becomes unable to indicate this. With good advance care planning, patients have communicated with their physician, and understand their diagnosis, prognosis and the likely outcomes of the care directives they have mandated. Advance care directives should also include appropriate contingency plans to ensure that the patient's preferences are honored.

A written legal document called an advance directive (living will or durable power of attorney) can be used to list all the provisions of one's advance care directive. Advance care directives are documented when patients are admitted to a hospital or long-term care facility. Advance care directives ensure that a patient's decisions are honored.

Adverse reaction. An adverse reaction refers to undesirable effects caused by therapeutic intervention. This term usually refers to the adverse effects of medications. In controlled trials conducted before drugs are put on the market, drugs are evaluated for a number of different adverse effects.

Advisory Panel on Alzheimer's Disease. The Advisory Panel on Alzheimer's disease is an organization established by congressional mandate for the purpose of evaluating the accessibility of long-term care services for Alzheimer's disease patients.

Advocacy. Because patients with Alzheimer's disease may eventually lose their ability to make decisions, it's important at the time of diagnosis for the patient and his or her family to arrange for an advocate who can make decisions for the patient, including those regarding living wills and trusts, power of attorney and guardianship. The determination of power of attorney or guardianship is fundamental to making economic or ethical decisions regarding patient care. Many patients with mild cognitive impairment are legally competent to execute a valid power of attorney, giving another person the power to make decisions regarding his or her health and estate. Guardianship must be imposed upon a patient who has become incompetent to render informed consent.

Affect. Affect refers to an individual's outwardly or externally expressed emotion. This may or may not be appropriate to the individual's reported mood and content of thought. For example, a patient who appears angry when relating a happy event would be described as having an inappropriate affect. Affect may be referred to as flat. This means that the patient's expression is absent or neutral. A flat affect may be caused by neuroleptic drugs, and is occasionally seen in schizophrenia. A labile affect is one characterized by rapid fluctuations between manifestations of happiness, sadness, and other emotions. Labile affect is often seen in patients with organic brain disorders.

Affective disorders. Affective disorders are defined by the American Psychiatric Association as mood disorders. Depression and euphoria are the primary symptoms of affective disorders, but not the only ones. Other symptoms include insomnia, anorexia, melancholia, suicidal thoughts, and feelings of worthlessness or being a bother to others. Euphoria is often associated with symptoms of hyperactivity and flight of ideas. Affective disorders are characterized by prolonged disturbances of mood, accompanied by a full or partial manic or depressive syndrome not due to any other physical or mental disorder.

Afferent nerve fibers. Afferent, or sensory, nerve fibers are nerve fibers originating in the posterior root of the spinal cord and are situated in a welling in the posterior root called the posterior root ganglion. Afferent fibers carry nervous impulses back to the nervous system, transmitting information about sensations of touch, pain, temperature, and vibration.

Age. Alzheimer's disease is very rarely seen in younger patients (early-onset Alzheimer's disease). Most cases are late-onset, with the incidence of developing it increasing with advancing age. Up to the age of 65, Alzheimer's disease develops in only 1 person in 1000. However, approximately 5 percent of people older than 65 are affected, and although there are reports that 25–45 percent of individuals older than 85 are affected by dementia, statistics show that 20 percent of people older than age 80 develop Alzheimer's disease and 26 percent of people older than age 85 develop Alzheimer's disease. (Munoz, David and Howard Feldman, "Causes of Alzheimer's Disease," *Canadian Medical Association Journal*, 2000 162; 65–72)

Age-associated memory impairment. While it has long been suspected that memory loss is a normal part of aging, researchers at Washington University's Alzheimer's Disease Research Center conducted studies that prove otherwise. The results of their research indicate that individuals who show signs of age-associated memory impairment eventually go on to develop dementia, suggesting that these symptoms may represent a dementia prodrome rather than a benign variant of aging. (Department of Neurology and the Alzheimer's Disease Research Center, Washington University, St. Louis Missouri, 2001.)

Agency for Health Care Policy and Research (AHCPR). The Agency for Health Care Policy and Research in Silver Spring, Maryland, is a federal organization dedicated to improving the access, quality, effectiveness and outcome of health care. AHCPR Publications, including "Alzheimer's Disease: Availability of Specialized Nursing Home Programs, Intramural Research Highlights," and "NMES: National Medical Expenditure Survey, Number 1, Publication 91-0100," are available free of charge by calling the Publications Clearinghouse at 1-800-0358-99295 or by ordering online at http://www.ahcpr.gov/gils/00000408.htm.

Agency for Healthcare Research and Quality. The Agency for Healthcare Research and Quality works to improve the quality, appropriateness, and effectiveness of health care, and to improve access to health services. One of its chief responsibilities is the dissemination of research-based information to medical practitioners, consumers and other healthcare professionals. The agency funds a number of research projects and sponsors 12 Evidence-Based Practice Centers to aid clinicians, health plans and health insurance purchasing groups.

Aggression. Aggression refers to hostile, injurious or destructive behavior or outlook especially when caused by frustration.

Aging process. Aging is the major risk factor of Alzheimer's disease in the general population. The aging process also causes certain changes that contribute to the development of Alzheimer's disease in genetically susceptible individuals. Some pathogenic factors directly associated with aging include oxidative damage from free radicals and mutations in messenger RNA. Some of the histological changes seen in the brains of patients with Alzheimer's disease, such as beta amyloid plaque formation, are also seen in the elderly, although to a lesser extent.

Agitation. Agitation refers to an incessant condition of being bothered, disturbed or troubled. Agitation is characterized by an inability to sit still or concentrate.

Agnosia. Agnosia is a condition characterized by the inability to recognize objects when using a given sense such as sight, even when that sense is intact. Agnosia is derived from the Greek word for lack of knowledge. A person with visual agnosia would not be able to recognize objects by sight although he may be able to recognize them by hearing. In neuropsychological testing, visual, auditory, and tactile recognition abilities are measured in a test of cerebral cortex function.

Agraphia. Agraphia is a condition of expressive writing dysfunction, indicating a lesion at the posterior-frontal area of the brain. Patients with agraphia are unable to express themselves in writing.

Aisen, Paul. Paul Aisen, M.D., is the Director of the Department of Neurology, Georgetown University Medical Center in Washington, DC.

Akathisia. Akathisia is a condition of restlessness in which patients cannot sit still and feel compelled to walk or pace. Akathisia can occur as a side effect of neuroleptic drugs.

Alexia. Alexia is a condition of visual receptive aphasia, indicating parietal-occipital disease. Patients with alexia are unable to understand written words.

Allele. An allele is one of the two forms of a gene. The Apolipoprotein E gene has three forms, or alleles, known as 2, 3, or 4. Individuals have 2 alleles for each gene, one from each parent.

Alpha lipoic acid. Alpha lipoic acid is a naturally occurring anti-oxidant that is also available as a dietary supplement. Alpha lipoic acid has been reported to offer neuroprotection in neurodegenerative diseases. It demonstrates excellent blood-brain barrier penetration and acts as a metal chelator for ferrous iron, copper and cadmium and also participates in the regeneration of endogenous antioxidants, including the body's natural stores of vitamins E and C and glutathione. (Perlmutter, David, "Functional Therapeutics in Neurodegenerative Disease," Physicians Committee for Responsible Medicine: http://www.pcrm.org/health/Preventive_Medicine/alzheimers.html)

Alpha secretase enzyme. Alpha secretase in an enzyme found in nerve cells that competes with beta secretase in splicing amyloid precursor protein. When alpha secretase makes the first cut in the precursor protein, another enzyme, gamma secretase, produces a second cut that results in an innocuous protein fragment known as P3. When beta secretase makes the first cut, beta amyloid protein is produced. For this reason, alpha secretase is considered protective against the development of Alzheimer's disease.

Alpha synuclein. Alpha synuclein is a protein that builds up in the brains of individuals with Parkinson's disease. In studies, mice with both beta amyloid and alpha synuclein deposits develop Lewy body dementia and movement problems sooner than mice with only alpha synuclein. (Proceedings of the National Academy of Sciences 2001, 10.1073)

Aluminum deposits. Early research suggested a causative association between aluminum deposits and Alzheimer's disease. However, the matter is still up for debate. A number of studies have failed to establish a definitive connection. When aluminum is injected into an animal brain, it produces an acute encephalopathy accompanied by neuronal inclusions that resemble neurofibrillary tangles. These aluminum-induced tangles are now known to be of a different composition when compared to the neurofibrillary tangles characteristically seen in Alzheimer's disease. However, a number of studies have found that increased levels of aluminum in drinking water are associated with Alzheimer's disease, and aluminum plays a pivotal role in beta amyloid production. References for related articles can be found at the Natural Medical Protocols web site: http://www.natmedpro.com/nmp/RefsAlzheim.htm

One reason aluminum is suspected of contributing to Alzheimer's disease is the dementia commonly seen in dialysis patients who are exposed to aluminum as part of their treatment. The acute encephalopathy of dialysis patients has indeed been traced to the aluminum in dialysis water, confirming that aluminum is neurotoxic for humans if it reaches the brain, but, neither the clinical syndrome nor the pathological changes in dialysis patients resemble those seen in Alzheimer's disease. Furthermore, a number of studies of aluminum in tap water, the ingestion of antacids containing aluminum, and workers exposed to aluminum dust and fumes show no increased risk of developing Alzheimer's disease.

Although ingestion has not been proven to contribute to Alzheimer's disease development, studies show that the concentration of aluminum in the brains of individuals with Alzheimer's disease is high and its distribution is non-uniform. Therefore, the problem is suspected by some researchers to be one of faulty metabolism, rather than increased ingestion, of aluminum.

Researchers at the University of Tennessee in Knoxville hypothesize that a critical mass of metabolic errors co-localized in specific areas of the brain is essential to produce Alzheimer's disease. Aluminum is a known neurotoxin, which has been shown to participate in formulating this critical mass by interfering in the metabolism of glucose and iron, and by proteolytic processing of beta-amyloid precursor protein. (Joshi, Jayant et al. "Iron and Aluminum Homeostasis in Neural Disorders," *Environmental Health Perspectives* 102, Supplement 3, September 1994)

Alz-50. Alz-50 is an antigen seen in increased levels in neurons of patients with Alzheimer's disease. Alz-50 is a suspected marker for neurons that will eventually exhibit tangles. Antibodies to Alz-50 react with the brain tissue of Alzheimer's disease patients. As a reagent, Alz-50 is used as a monoclonal antibody to help stain autopsy specimens in an effort to help diagnose Alzheimer's disease.

Alzheimer, Alois (*b.* Markbreit, Germany, 1864; *d.* Frankfurt am Main, Germany, 1915). Excelling in science, Alois Alzheimer studied medicine in Berlin, Tubingen, and Wurzburg where he graduated in 1887. He began work in the state asylum in Frankfurt am Main primarily studying the cortex of the human brain. He eventually created a brain research laboratory at the Munich Medical School.

Alzheimer published many papers on brain disease, and in 1906 he presented a lecture that made him famous. In this lecture, Alzheimer described a woman with an unusual disease, exhibiting symptoms of memory loss, disorientation, hallucinations, and premature death at age 55. At autopsy, the woman's brain was found to have deposits of plaque and neurofibrillary tangles. Alzheimer attributed her symptoms to a disease of the cerebral cortex, and Dr. Kraepelin, a renowned neurologist, named the disease after Alzheimer. Alzheimer was appointed to chair the department of psychology at the Friedrich-Wilhelm University in 1913, and developed a severe cold complicated by endocarditis, from which he never fully recovered.

Alzheimer Research Forum. The Alzheimer Research Forum in an Internet organization devoted to advances and news about Alzheimer's disease. http://www.alzforum.org/members/

Alzheimer's Association. The Alzheimer's Association, which is also known as The Alzheimer's and Related Disorders Association, is the largest national voluntary health organization committed to finding a cure for Alzheimer's and helping those affected by the disease. The twin goals of the association are protecting individuals with dementia who participate in research and encouraging dementia research to go forward. One or more chapters of the national organization are located in almost every city in the United States. Chapters regularly sponsor educational activities that are open to the public. The Alzheimer's Association uses a two-person logo symbolizing help and hope for those impacted by the disease. The Alzheimer's Association also sponsors an annual National Alzheimer's Disease Education Conference where researchers can exchange ideas on practical yet innovative approaches to Alzheimer's care.

Alzheimer's disease (AD). Alzheimer's disease (AD) is a chronic, progressive neurodegenerative disorder characterized by impairment of memory, thinking, behavior, and emotion. AD is the most common cause of dementia, and it is the fourth leading cause of death in the United States. One of the most prominent symptoms of AD is that patients forget things that they have just said or done, although they remember events from the past clearly. Other common symptoms include confusion, poor judgment, agitation, withdrawal, and hallucinations. In its early stages, AD is characterized by progressive loss of memory and orientation with preservation of motor, sensory, and linguistic abilities. It eventually evolves into global impairment that affects multiple cognitive functions.

Alzheimer's disease has a mean life expectancy of 8–10 years after onset of symptoms, with a range of 1–25 years. Three distinct stages occur in this disease, with the last stage ending in death, usually from secondary causes. Symptoms in the three stages may overlap, and individual symptoms and their severity may vary from patient to patient. Although the clinical signs of AD are generally predictable, there are no definitive clinical signs or laboratory tests available to diagnose AD. The customary clinical practice is to exclude other causes of dementia and give the patient a diagnosis of probable Alzheimer's disease. A definitive diagnosis can only be made by brain biopsy or autopsy.

The gross pathology of the brain in Alzheimer's disease is characterized by diffuse atrophy, particularly in the areas of the brain known as the cortex and hippocampus. Over time, patients with AD experience a progressive loss of nerve cells in both the gray matter of the brain and in the hippocampus, which governs memory. Pathological changes seen at autopsy include premature, severe diffuse atrophy of brain tissue, particularly in the frontal lobes. Neuropathological hallmarks of the brain tissue in AD include senile (neuritic) plaques, neurofibrillary tangles, and neuronal loss throughout the cerebral cortex. Additional pathology includes granulovacuolar changes and accumulation of lipofuscin. Loss of cholinergic neurons leads to deficiencies of the neurotransmitter acetylcholine. These features are also found to a lesser extent in the normal aging population.

There are three distinct types of Alzheimer's disease: 1) a sporadic disorder that accounts for about 75 percent of all cases; typically develops in patients older than 65, with chances of developing it increasing with age; 2) a familial disorder that accounts for about 25 percent of all cases; most familial disorders are late-onset, developing in individual older than 65; less than 5% of all instances of Alzheimer's disease are early-onset familial with the mean age of onset usually before age 65; early onset familial Alzheimer's disease (EOFAD) can be further divided into subsets depending on the causative gene; 3) a disorder that accompanies Down's Syndrome and represents less than 1 percent of all cases of Alzheimer's disease. Alzheimer's disease is also known as senile dementia/Alzheimer's type, diffuse brain atrophy and primary degenerative dementia. *See also* Diagnosis, Epidemiology, Etiology (Causes), Stages, and Symptoms.

Alzheimer's Disease Anti-inflammatory Prevential Trial (ADAPT). The Alzheimer's Disease Anti-inflammatory Prevential Trial (ADAPT) is a National Institutes of Health funded project designed to evaluate the use of anti-inflammatory agents to protect the brain and prevent the onset of Alzheimer's disease in first-degree relatives of patients with Alzheimer's disease. Information on this study can be found on the Internet at www.2stopAD.org.

Alzheimer's Disease Assessment Scale Cognition Component (ADAS-Cog). The Alzheimer's Disease Assessment Scale (ADAS-Cog) developed by Rosen, Mohs and Davis is a well-validated multi-item test battery administered by a psychometrician (technician trained to perform tests used in psychological evaluation). The ADAS-Cog is a reliable instrument for measuring changes in memory and cognition. It evaluates 11 items, including aspects of memory, attention, praxis, reason and language and takes about 30 minutes.

The worst possible score is 70. Higher scores reflect poorer performance, and positive numerical changes from baseline score during clinical trials represent a worsening in cognitive ability. Elderly, normal adults may score as low as 0 or 1 unit, but individuals without dementia may score higher.

The ADAS-Cog score is reported to deteriorate at a rate of about 2 to 10 units per year for untreated patients with mild to moderate dementia. The ADAS-Cog is a useful tool in diagnosing dementia and in assessing the efficacy of therapeutic agents.

Alzheimer's Disease Centers of the NIA. The National Institutes of Aging Division of the National Institutes of Health has created 30 federally funded Alzheimer's Disease Centers that are located throughout the country. The centers specialize in Alzheimer's disease research. Each center specializes in one particular area of expertise, and all the centers work together, sharing data and coordinating their efforts.

Alzheimer's Disease Clinical Trials Database. The Alzheimer's Disease Clinical Trials Database is a joint effort of the Food and Drug Administration and the National Institute on Aging, which lists about 5,000 clinical studies primarily sponsored by the National Institutes of Health. Here you can find comprehensive trial information, learn how to sign up for specific trials, receive updates and get information on drug development.

Alzheimer's Disease Cooperative Study (ADCS). The Alzheimer's Disease Cooperative Study (ADCS), established by the National Institute of Aging (NIA) in 1991, is a national consortium of 83 ADCS medical research centers and clinics in the United States and Canada coordinated by the University of California, San Diego (UCSD). The ADCS consortium was first organized under a cooperative agreement between NIA, the National Institutes of Health and UCSD. During its first decade, the ADCS established a network of leading researchers who have carried out 13 clinical trials [involving 2,500 participants] for promising new therapies. Previous studies have investigated the use of vitamin E, selegiline, and estrogen therapy. Current projects include clinical trials involving the effects of a cholesterol-lowering statin drug, antioxidant therapy, valproic acid therapy, and a high dose vitamin regimen. The ADCS is also developing evaluation tools for Alzheimer's disease prevention research.

Alzheimer's Disease Cooperative Study–Clinical Global Impression of Change (ADCS-CGIC). Introduced by the National Institute on Aging's Alzheimer's Disease Cooperative Study in 1996, the ADCS-CGIC is a neuropsychiatric evaluation tool for assessing the efficacy of treatment. The ADCS-CGIC consists of three parts, including a semi-structured baseline interview administered to both the patient and an informant with knowledge of the patient's condition, a follow-up interview after treatment, administered to both the patient and informant, and a clinician's rating interview based on his impressions of the interviews, administered before and after treatment.

The ADCS-CGIC evaluates 15 parameters related to cognition, behavior, social skills and daily functioning. The global rating is based on the second interview and is graded by a 7-point scale: 1 = very much improved, 2 = much improved, 3 = minimally improved, 4 = no change, 5 = mild worsening, 6 = moderate worsening, 7 = marked worsening. (Schneider, L.S., Jason Olin, et al. "Validity and Reliability of the Alzheimer's Disease Cooperative Study-Clinical Global Impression of Change," *Alzheimer Disease: From Molecular Biology to Therapy*, edited by R. Becker and E. Giacobine. Boston: Birkhäuser Publishing, 1996, 425–429.)

Alzheimer's Disease Demonstration Grants to States (ADDGS) Program. Administered through the Administration of Aging Division of the U.S. Department of Health and Human Services, The Alzheimer's Disease Demonstration Grants to States (ADDGS) Program is an award of more than $8 million in grants. The awards were given to 25 states in 2000 and 2001 to develop effective models of intervention to serve persons with Alzheimer's disease and their families and caregivers. The goal of this program is to expand the availability of diagnostic and support services for individuals with Alzheimer's disease and their families and caregivers. The program also aims to improve the responsiveness of home and community-based care for individuals with Alzheimer's disease. The primary focus of the program is areas that are hard-to-serve, including rural areas. Detailed information about the state programs, including family education and outreach information in several languages can be found at http://www.aoa.gov/alz.

Alzheimer's Disease Education and Referral (ADEAR) Center. The Alzheimer's Disease Education and Referral (ADEAR) Center operated by the National Institute of Aging provides information to health professions and the public on Alzheimer's disease and other conditions of memory impairment. (800)-438-4380, http://www.alzheimers.org.

Alzheimer's Disease International. Alzheimer's Disease International is a worldwide confederation of Alzheimer's disease associations. The international groups provide advice, training, educational support, advocacy, informational brochures and helplines.

Alzheimer's Disease Research Program. The Alzheimer's Disease Research (ADR) Program, which began in 1985, currently funds 22 outstanding biomedical researchers in the United States, Canada, and Europe. Alzheimer's Disease Research invites applications for both Standard Awards and Pilot Project Awards. For further information contact the American Health Assistance Foundation.

***Alzheimer's Disease Review*.** The *Alzheimer's Disease Review* is a medical journal that focuses on studies pertaining to Alzheimer's disease. While this journal has ceased publication, its archives are available through www.coa.uky.edu/ADReview and review articles are being published in the *Journal of Alzheimer's disease.*

Alzheimer's Family Relief Program. The Alzheimer's Family Relief Program offered by the American Health Assistance Foundation is a financial assistance program, which can help to meet the cost of Alzheimer's patient care.

Ambulation. Ambulation refers to the ability to walk without assistance. Patients with intact ambulation are said to be ambulatory.

American Association of Homes and Services for the Aging. The American Association of Homes and Services for the Aging is a non-profit organization that sponsors the Continuing Care Accreditation Commission, a group that inspects and certifies care facilities for the elderly. This agency also aids individuals in locating housing, adult day care, companion services and assisted living or nursing home care. Financial assistance that is available depends on the type of service, your local community and the type of insurance that you have. (800) 272-3900, http://www.aahsa.org/public.alzheim.htm.

American Health Assistance Foundation. The American Health Assistance Foundation (AHAF) is a non-profit charitable organization dedicated to funding research on Alzheimer's disease, providing educational resources about Alzheimer's disease to the public, and providing emergency financial assistance to Alzheimer's disease patients and their caregivers. 16825 Shady Grove Road, Suite 140, Rockville, Maryland 20850, (800) 437-2423, http://www.ahaf.org.

***American Journal of Alzheimer's Disease*.** The *American Journal of Alzheimer's Disease* is a medical publication dedicated to the management and treatment of patients with Alzheimer's disease. Subscription information and a cumulative subject index of past articles can be found at http://www.alzheimersjournal.com.

Amino acids. Amino acids are chemical molecules, or building blocks, that form protein. Some amino acids also have the ability to act as neurotransmitters. Amino acids are made of nitrogen and carbon units bonded together to form various shapes and sizes with specific properties. Some amino acids also contain sulfur. Humans possess about 20 different types of naturally occurring amino acids, which are supplied by animal or plant proteins. The most important of these are glutamate and its derivative gamma-aminobutyric acid (GABA).

Some amino acids are altered slightly before they can be used as neurotransmitters. For instance, the amino acid tyrosine, which is found in cheese, is converted into at least two neurotransmitters, dopamine and norepinephrine. Tryptophan, an amino acid found in high concentrations in milk and turkey, is converted into the neurotransmitter serotonin. When a large amount of tyrosine is consumed, tryptophan absorption is inhibited since tyrosine and tryptophan compete for absorption sites in the gut.

Used as therapy the amino acid 5-hydroxytryptophan has been used in doses of 800 mg daily to raise serotonin levels in patients with Alzheimer's disease, and up to 4 grams of tyrosine have to been used to raise dopamine levels. Both of these therapies are reported to offer some benefits for patients with Alzheimer's disease.

Ampalex *see* CX 516

AMY 117. AMY 117 is a protein found in the areas of the brain affected by Alzheimer's disease. AMY 117 forms plaques that resemble beta amyloid so closely that it can only be differentiated with sophisticated techniques.

Amygdaloid nucleus (amygdala). The amygdaloid nucleus (amygdala) of the brain's limbic system is an almond-shaped area situated partly anterior and partly superior to the tip of the inferior horn of the lateral ventricle. Destruction of the amygdaloid nucleus and its surrounding area in patients with aggressive behavior results in a decrease in aggressiveness, emotional instability and restlessness.

Amyloid. Amyloid is a type of protein primarily composed of amyloid beta-peptide that is encoded within the larger beta amyloid precursor protein gene on chromosome 21 from which it is derived.

Amyloid angiopathy. Amyloid angiopathy is a cerebrovascular condition that almost invariably accompanies Alzheimer's disease. In this condition, the same amyloid protein deposits found in senile plaques also form deposits in the blood vessels serving the brain, reducing blood flow and inducing clot formation. Studies indicate that APOE gene polymorphism is a risk factor, influencing hemorrhage in cerebral amyloid angiopathy.

Amyloid beta (β) peptide (Abeta). Amyloid beta peptides are harmless fragments derived from the proteolytic process (enzyme degradation) of amyloid precursor protein (APP).

Amyloid beta (β) peptide antibody. Amyloid beta (β) peptide antibodies are naturally occurring antibodies that target and destroy beta amyloid protein. Amyloid beta peptide is produced by normal cells and can be detected in the plasma and cerebrospinal fluid. In studies, mice immunized with amyloid beta vaccines (to stimulate production of amyloid beta antibodies) or administered antibody to amyloid beta, showed dramatically reduced plaque deposits, neuritic dystrophy and reactive gliosis by astrocytes.

Amyloid Beta Protein. Amyloid beta protein, which is also known as β-amyloid, A beta, Aβ or beta amyloid protein (BAP), is a generic name for a class of sticky proteins found in the brains of patients with Alzheimer's disease. Amyloid beta protein consists of 38 to 43 amino acids. Several genes influence the type or specific amino acid sequence of beta amyloid protein that is formed. The longer forms, particularly those that end in 42 amino acids, have an increased propensity to aggregate into polymers and plaque deposits. These forms are also most likely to produce neuronal damage.

Amyloid beta protein in blood vessels is produced by smooth muscle cells. Derived from amyloid precursor protein (APP), amyloid beta protein has a molecular weight of 4 kD. A peptide protein, it is comprised of 11–15 amino acids of the transmembrane domain and 28 amino acids of the extracellular domain of APP.

Amyloid beta protein forms plaques on the outsides of brain cells. These plaques are found outside nerve cells surrounded by the debris of dying neurons. These plaques grow so dense that they trigger an inflammatory reaction from immune system cells located in the brain. This immune response destroys brain cells.

Amyloid beta protein is a subunit protein or fragment derived from its precursor, amyloid precursor protein (βAPP), by a mechanism known as proteolytic processing. More precisely, beta amyloid is formed by nerve cells when the enzymes beta and gamma secretase cause APP to split into uneven fragments. The slightly longer variant is directly toxic to nerve cells. Among other things, BAP appears to stimulate the release of oxygen free radicals, triggering a destructive biochemical cascade in the brain.

β-amyloid is produced by all cell types and is not unique to neurons. In fact, Aβ is produced and secreted as a soluble peptide protein during normal cell metabolism. The amyloid beta protein deposits seen in Alzheimer's disease are identical to the amyloid beta protein produced in the brain cells of normal individuals. Amyloid beta protein may have either neurotrophic or neurotoxic effects depending on neuronal age, protein concentration, and the presence of fetal or adult neurons. Neurotrophic effects may reside in the first 28 residues of Aβ since there is evidence of neurite outgrowth and neuronal survival in these forms. However, there is much evidence for the neurotoxic effects of Aβ. Aβ causes increases in intracellular calcium, induces apoptosis, activates microglia, enhances oxidative damage and enhances the vulnerability of neurons to excitotoxicity and hypoglycemic damage. Neurotoxicity appears to be dependent on the length and aggregation of the amyloid beta fragment, with some fragments influencing hydrogen peroxide accumulation in cells, resulting in free radical-induced lipid peroxidation and cell death.

Amyloid beta protein tends to aggregate and form diffuse deposits as well as amyloid cores in the brain of patients with Alzheimer's disease. Senile neuritic plaques in Alzheimer's disease consist of beta amyloid cores surrounded by activated microglia, fibrillary astrocytes and dystrophic neuritis (neurites and axonal terminals). The type of amyloid beta protein seen in senile neuritic plaques exerts neurotoxic effects, causing neuronal degeneration. Deposits of amyloid beta protein are thought to be an early and obligatory event, preceding the development of tau-positive paired helical filaments, the substances that make up neurofibrillary tangles. However, amyloid beta protein deposits are also seen in normal aging, suggesting that it is the maturation or density of plaque deposits, or shifts in the pathways that produce or remove Aβ, that are critical to Alzheimer's disease development.

High levels of beta amyloid are also associated with reduced levels of the neurotransmitter acetylcholine and are suspected of disrupting channels that carry the elements sodium, potassium and calcium. These elements serve the brain as ions, producing electric charges that must fire regularly in order for signals to pass from one nerve cell to another. If the channels that carry ions are damaged, the resulting imbalance can interfere with nerve function and signal transmission.

Although it was once thought to be metabolically inert, beta amyloid is now known to damage neuronal processes, place them at risk for injury and stimulate cell death by apoptosis in response to excitotoxins. In nonneuronal cells, amyloid beta can also affect signal transduction processes.

Amyloid hypothesis. The notion that Alzheimer's disease is directly caused by increased beta amyloid protein formation is known as the amyloid hypothesis.

Amyloid plaques. Amyloid plaques are deposits or aggregates of beta amyloid protein found on the nerve cells of patients with Alzheimer's disease. Amyloid plaque may occur as diffuse deposits or in the amyloid core of senile neuritic plaque formations. *See* Senile neuritic plaques.

Amyloid Precursor Protein (APP). Amyloid precursor protein (APP) is the parent protein from which beta amyloid protein is derived. By a splicing or proteolytic process, APP is broken down into fragments. Depending on which secretase enzymes initiate the process, beta amyloid protein may be a harmless peptide chain or a longer form with

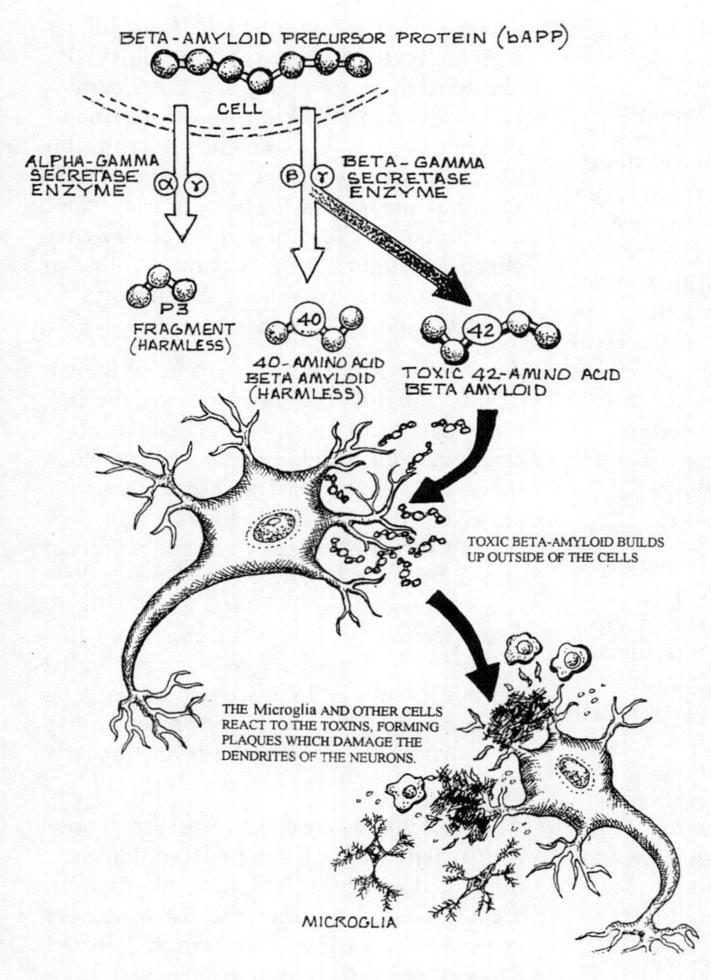

Amyloid Plaque Formation (illustration by Marvin G. Miller).

more amino acids and more propensity to damage neurons and form plaque. Recent studies indicate that a defect in APP rather than beta amyloid protein may be the underlying cause of Alzheimer's disease.

Amyloidosis. Amyloidosis is the generic term used to describe a number of diseases, including Alzheimer's disease, that have abnormal deposits of amyloid fibrils and plaques in specific organs. These abnormal plaque deposits eventually lead to organ failure. In systemic amyloidosis there is widespread distribution of amyloid deposits in several different organs of the body.

AN-1792 Vaccine. AN-1792 is a synthetic form of the 42 amino acid beta amyloid protein. AN-1792 has been formulated into a vaccine intended to reduce symptoms in Alzheimer's disease by preventing or reversing amyloid plaque formation, neuritic dystrophy, synaptic loss and gliosis. Currently the focus of clinical trials, AN-1792 works by inducing the production of antibodies to beta amyloid protein, the substance present in the plaque deposits characteristically seen in the brain of patients with Alzheimer' disease. AN-1792 was made by combining a synthetic version of beta amyloid protein with a stimulant that provokes the immune system into targeting and clearing beta amyloid plaques from the brain.

Developed by Ireland's Elan Corporation at its San Francisco branch, in conjunction with Wyeth Ayerst Laboratories in New Jersey, AN-1792 has already been proven to be safe for humans and successful in studies using mice. AN-1972 contains an enzyme derived from brain plaque. This enzyme is recognized by the immune system as a foreign substance. Similar to the mechanism behind vaccines offering protection against infectious agents, the immune system reacts in an immune response intended to protect the body from this foreign molecule. In this immune response, antibodies against this substance are produced. These antibodies target the amyloid plaque deposits, reversing the brain changes that contribute to symptoms in Alzheimer's disease. Clinical trials involving 375 patients in the United States and Europe began in the fall of 2001 (Berenstein, Seth. "Alzheimer's Vaccine Tested," July 23, 2001, *The Denver Post* via Knight Ridder News Service).

Angiography. Angiography is an imaging technique used to detect blood vessel abnormalities. Cerebral angiography is used to detect and diagnose space-occupying lesions such as tumors, hematomas, or abscesses. Cerebral angiography is performed under general anesthesia, with the patient in the supine position using contrast dye. Cerebral angiography is an invasive technique with a morbidity of 0.5 to 2.5 percent. (Snell, Richard, M.D. *Clinical Neuranatomy for Medical Students*, Third Edition. Boston: Little, Brown and Company, 1992.)

Animal models. Animal models are used to determine the etiology, or underlying causes, of diseases and to assess treatment. In animal model studies, animals (usually mice or rats) are subjected to certain factors, including environmental agents, to determine if disease symptoms develop under similar conditions to those seen in humans with the disease. In animal treatment models, animals are subjected to drugs and other therapies to determine if symptoms of disease are reversed and to assess the therapies for potential signs of toxicity.

Anomia. Anomia is a condition characterized by problems with names. Patients with anomia frequently confuse the names of relatives, for example, substituting daughter for mother or father for husband.

Anorexia. Anorexia is a prolonged loss of appetite. A common symptom of Alzheimer's disease, anorexia may lead to nutrient deficiencies and wasting away.

Anosmia. Anosmia is an inability to smell. There are several causes, some due to neuropathology, such as tumors of the base of the frontal lobe or pituitary area, arteriosclerosis, cerebrovascular disease, meningitis, hydrochephalus, and post-traumatic brain syndrome. *See* Odor identification test.

Anthocyanins. Anthocyanins are potent antioxidants found in fruit, vegetables and red wines. In many countries anthocyanin products are used as medications. In 2001, researchers at Michigan State University identified the presence of three anthocyanins and plant chemicals known as bioflavinoids in tart cherries. These compounds inhibit Cyclooxygenase 1 and 2 enzymes and prevent inflammation in the body. Their actions are similar to those of ibuprofen. Twenty cherries contain 25 mg of anthocyanins, an amount sufficient to inhibit the enzymes responsible for inflammation.

Antibodies. Antibodies are proteins known as immunoglobulins produced by the immune system to help protect against infectious agents. Antibodies are produced when individuals are exposed to infectious agents or given vaccines that contain specially treated forms of infectious agents. Serum and cerebrospinal fluid from some Alzheimer's disease patients contain an antibody that specifically recognizes amoeboid microglial cells. Studies suggest that microglial antibodies may be indicative of an ongoing degenerative process. Their presence may have diagnostic potential even in the early stages of Alzheimer's disease.

Anti-inflammatory drugs. Anti-inflammatory drugs, including non-steroidal anti-inflammatory drugs (NSAIDs) and steroids, are often used to treat the inflammatory process associated with Alzheimer's disease. Studies indicate that non-steroidal anti-inflammatory agents offer therapeutic value in Alzheimer's disease by preventing the production of amyloid beta protein. However, corticosteroids used long-term may actually cause memory loss and, unlike NSAIDs, do not appear to affect prostglandins, substances that appear to be related to the development of Alzheimer's disease.
Although researchers once suspected that anti-inflammatory drug worked by inhibiting cyclooxygenease (COX) enzymes, it is now known that certain anti-inflammatory agents, particularly ibuprofen, reduce levels of amyloid-beta 42, a protein incriminated in the formation of plaque deposits. Indomethacin and sulindac are also effective in reducing levels of amyloid-beta 42 when high doses are used. (Greenwell, Ivy. "New

light on how ibuprofen protects against Alzheimer's disease," *Life Extension*, February, 2002, 23.)

Antioxidant therapy. Antioxidant vitamins and minerals function to prevent damage associated with free radicals, ions that lack coupling molecules. Free radicals are responsible for oxidative cell death associated with amyloid beta protein, hydrogen peroxide, and the excitatory amino acid glutamate. Many antioxidants, particularly vitamins E and C, have been shown to protect neurons from this damage. A placebo-controlled clinical trial of vitamin E (at a high dose of 2000IU daily), the drug selegiline, or both, found that treatment with either compound delayed disease progression in patients with moderately severe Alzheimer's disease. Combinations of different antioxidants are currently undergoing clinical trials.

Apathy. Apathy is a lack of feeling or emotion characterized by withdrawal and an inability to react with feeling to one's environment. Apathy is a common symptom in Alzheimer's disease and may be confused with depression. An apathetic person lacks emotions, motivation, interest, and enthusiasm while a depressed person is generally very sad, tearful, and hopeless.

Aphasia. Aphasia is a condition of an inability to use language. Aphasia is caused by destruction of the cells of the brain in areas that govern language. The two most common types of aphasia are Broca's aphasia and Wernicke's aphasia. Most neurological patients have some intact communication function. In tests used to evaluate aphasia, certain areas of dysfunction are diagnostic for certain conditions. Auditory receptive aphasia is associated with lesions at Wernicke's area of the temporal lobe, whereas visual receptive aphasia (alexia) indicates a lesion at the parietal-occipital area. Expressive speaking aphasia is associated with a lesion at Broca's area of the frontal lobe, whereas expressive writing aphasia (agraphia) is located with a lesion at the posterior frontal area. Global aphasia, which involves both expressive and receptive aphasias, indicates extensive lesions of Broca's area, Wernicke's area, the parietal-occipital area, and the posterior frontal area.

Aphasia-agnosia-apraxia syndrome *see* Pick's disease

Apolipoprotein A (APOA). Apolipoprotein A (APOA) is a protein normally found in the body. Apolipoprotein A is produced in the small intestine and liver and helps prevent coronary heart disease because of its ability to clear cholesterol from the body. APOA is also thought to help reduce levels of beta amyloid. According to a study funded by the U.S. Public Health Service, increasing APOA levels may help prevent or delay the dementia associated with Alzheimer's' disease. Some foods, including fruits, soybeans, coconut oils, and some wines and teas can stimulate cells to produce more APOA.

Apolipoprotein E (APOE). Apolipoprotein E (APOE) is a naturally occurring protein found in the body. APOE is produced primarily by the liver, but is also produced by cells in the brain and adrenal glands and by macrophage cells in the circulation. In the brain, APOE is produced and secreted by astrocytes in the hippocampus. Research suggests that APOE is involved in cholinergic synaptic remodeling following injury to neurons in the entorhinal cortex. As both a free and a bound protein, APOE circulates between the cells of the brain and also within some neurons, suggesting multiple metabolic functions.

The APOE gene on chromosome 19 is associated with the development of Alzheimer's disease. APOE has three allelic variants, APOE2, APOE3, and APOE4. Everyone inherits one allele for APOE from each of their parents resulting in five common genotypes—2/3, 3/3, 2/4, 3/4 and 4/4. The APOE 4 allele is strongly associated with Alzheimer's disease and may represent an important risk factor for the disease.

Overall, APOE4 may account for more than 60 percent of all cases of late onset Alzheimer's disease. People who carry it do not necessarily develop Alzheimer's disease, but if they do, their brains appear more riddled with plaques and tangles than the brains of Alzheimer's patients with slightly different versions of the APOE gene. APOE4 also appears to have a broad impact on the well being of nerve cells. People who are homozygous for APOE4, meaning they carry two identical alleles or copies of APOE4 have more difficulty recovering from strokes and traumatic head injuries, and they're more likely to sustain brain damage during cardiovascular surgery.

Allele 4 of the APOE gene has a dose-related effect on risk and the age of onset for late-onset familial Alzheimer's diseases as well as sporadic cases of the early onset form, whereas allele 2 appears to offer protection. The alleles apolipoprotein E 2, 3, and 4 all have different binding strengths. The APOE4 allele appears to promote the binding of amyloid beta protein, facilitating the formation of plaque deposits. An immunoreactive form of APOE has been found in the neurons containing neurofibrillary tangles in patients with Alzheimer's disease. Studies are being conducted to see what role APOE has in the abnormal phosphorylation of tau protein.

Patients with alleles e4/e4 have a 95 percent chance of developing Alzheimer's disease by 80 years of age, and patients with the rare e2/e2 rarely develop Alzheimer's disease. Although the presence of the APOE4 allele may be associated with cognitive decline in older persons, the APOE genotype alone is not considered useful in predicting whether an individual will develop Alzheimer's disease.

In one study, both the magnitude and the extent of brain activation during memory-activation tasks in regions affected by Alzheimer's disease, including the left hippocampal, parietal, and prefrontal regions, were greater among the carriers of the APOE4 allele than among carriers of the APOE3 allele. During periods of recall, individuals with the APOE4 allele had a greater average increase in signal intensity in the hippocampal region and a greater number of activated regions throughout the brain. Longitudinal assessment after two years indicated that the degree of baseline activation correlated with degree of decline in memory.

APOE is found in the cytoplasm of neurons. It regulates neurite outgrowth and sprouting of dorsal root ganglia neurons in vitro. It also appears to be involved in mobilization and redistribution of cholesterol in repair, growth, and maintenance of myelin and neuronal membranes during development or following injury. APOE, along with the more benign amyloid P and glycosaminoglycans may act as chaperones that mediate β-pleated amyloid formation from amyloid beta protein. APOE is found in senile plaques, vascular amyloid deposits and neurofibrillary tangles (NFTs). APOE is also present in hippocampal neurons in Alzheimer's disease even in the absence of NFTs. The APOE domain exhibits an isoform-specific association in that the E4 isoform segregates with a higher risk of the disease. Peptides derived from the receptor binding domain of apolipoprotein E have also been found to be toxic to neurons.

Recent studies indicate that patients with E4 are more likely to respond to drug treatment designed to reduce beta-amyloid formation than patients without E4. Results of the Nun Study show that individuals without the E4 allele are more likely to maintain high levels of cognitive function in old age. (Bookheimer, Susan, et al. "Patterns of Brain Activation in People at Risk for Alzheimer's Disease," *New England Journal of Medicine*; 343 (7): 450. Sabbagh, Marwan, et al. "β-Amyloid and Treatment Opportunities for Alzheimer's Disease," *Alzheimer's Disease Review*, 3:1–19 1998.)

Apolipoprotein E Genotype. The apolipoprotein E gene on chromosome 19 is linked to Alzheimer's disease. Specifically, the apolipoprotein E 4 allele has been found to increase the risk for Alzheimer's disease in genetically diverse populations in Asia, the Americas and Europe. However, the risk is lower in Africans and African-Americans.

Aolipoprotein E plays a role in the transport and redistribution of lipids and is implicated in the growth and repair of injured neurons in the nervous system. Everyone inherits one allele for APOE from each of their parents resulting in five common genotypes—2/3, 3/3, 2/4, 3/4 and 4/4. Two common polymorphisms of this gene exist, resulting in three isoforms, APOE e2, e3, and e4. The APOE4 allele is over-represented in Alzheimer's disease. APOE4 homozygotes (patients having both 2 copies of e4) have a 95 percent chance of developing Alzheimer's disease by age 80. These individuals may have a reduced ability to suppress amyloid fibril formation and an increased susceptibility for amyloid beta protein production. Besides its association with Alzheimer's disease, the epsilon 4 allele of apolipoprotein E is associated with higher lipid concentrations and higher risk of cardiovascular disease.

Several studies suggest that the APOE 4 allele is also present in greater frequency in persons with Lewy body disease, dementia pugilistica, and Pick's disease. Although the frequency of Alzheimer's disease is relatively similar in most populations, the allele frequencies vary significantly in different racial and ethnic groups. In some populations, the APOE 2 allele may increase risk for Alzheimer's disease.

Because Alzheimer's disease develops in the absence of the APOE 4 allele and because many people with this allele do not develop Alzheimer's disease, genetic testing for this allele is not recommended for use as a predictive genetic test. Testing for the APOE genotype would be helpful, however, in diagnosing early-onset dementia when diagnosis is uncertain. (Farrer, Lindsay, Ph.D. "Statement on Use of Apolipoprotein E Testing for Alzheimer Disease," American College of Medical Genetics, Bethesda, MD 1995.)

Apolipoproteins. Lipoproteins are lipid substances normally present in the body. High density lipoproteins (HDLs) can be divided into subtypes apolipoprotein A, B, C and E. The major apolipoprotein, apolipoprotein A-1, sets the plasma level of HDL and appears to confer protection against the development of atherosclerosis. Higher levels of Apolipoprotein A-1 are associated with a low tendency toward developing congestive heart disease. All of the apolipoprotein subtypes have distinct roles and contribute to the body's total lipoprotein level.

Apoptosis. Apoptosis is a term referring to programmed cell death. All of the body's cells, including neurons or brain cells, have a certain life span. Apoptosis may be disrupted in two major ways, each of which is associated with different types of disease. Inappropriate activation of apoptosis leads to disorders such as the wide array of neurodegenerative conditions associated with pathological cell loss. Inappropriate apoptosis or extended cell survival leads to diseases associated with excessive accumulation of cells. Examples include cancer, chronic inflammatory conditions and autoimmune diseases.

An increasing body of indirect evidence suggests that neuronal cell apoptosis may be triggered by amyloid β deposits and other neurotoxic abnormal protein structures or aggregates such as those seen in Alzheimer's disease. Proteolytic enzymes called capases are critical to the control of apoptosis. Researchers are currently working on developing therapeutic agents that inhibit capases, reducing accelerated apoptosis in neurodegenerative diseases.

Apoptosis-Related Gene 3 (ALG-3). The Apotosis-Related Gene 3 (ALG-3) codes for a partial complementary DNA that is homologous to the familial Alzheimer's gene STM2 and rescues cells from normal pathways of apoptosis.

Appearance. Appearance is often relevant to the diagnosis of mental disorders. Patients with Alzheimer's are often poorly groomed and sometimes dirty. It is not unusual for patients with Alzheimer's to adapt unusual modes of dress such as many layers of clothing or wear clothing inappropriate for the season or temperature.

Apraxia. Apraxia is a condition characterized by the inability to perform an action, even though the muscles required are perfectly capable of performing the action in a different context. An apraxic patient might be unable to touch her nose with her index finger when asked to do so by an examiner, even if the examiner performed the motion. However, the same patient could perform the movement if their nose itched. Apraxia often accompanies certain forms of aphasia and is caused by damage or injury to areas of the brain associated with motor skills and cortical motor integration. Apraxia is derived from the Greek word for lack of action.

Arachnoid mater. The arachnoid mater is a delicate impermeable membrane that covers the spinal cord and lies between the pia mater internally and the dura mater externally. The arachnoid mater is separated from the pia mater by a wide space known as the subarachnoid space, which is filled with cerebrospinal fluid.

Archicortex. The archicortex refers to the area of the cerebral cortex that covers the hippocampal formation.

Aricept *see* Donepezil hydrochloride

Arnold Pick's disease *see* Pick's disease

Art therapy. Art therapy is a form of therapy in which patients are encouraged to draw, color, or paint as a creative outlet. Art therapy is included as an activity in many nursing homes and adult day care programs.

Ashwaganda (Withania somnifera). Ashwaganda (Withania somnifera) is an herbal preparation that is reported to offer benefits for patients with Alzheimer's disease. Ashwaganda reduces inflammation, reduces free radical damage, and enhances the effect of the neurotransmitter acetylcholine. Inflammation, free radical damage, and low acetylcholine levels are all considered contributing factors for the development of Alzheimer's disease.

Assisted living. Assisted living, which is also known as residential care, is a housing option for older adults who are able to live alone but need some assistance with personal care. In many assisted living communities, residents may opt to have one or more meals provided by the facility. If the need for care increases, some assisted living facilities require that the resident transfer to a nursing home. Check with your local Area Agency on Aging to see if there are any subsidized assisted living facilities in your area.

Assisted-living costs. Costs for assisted living residences range from less than $1,000 monthly to more than $3,000 monthly, depending on the services and accommodations offered. The facility's charges reflect the number of services to which the resident has access, such as meals, help administering medications and laundry services. In addition to basic charges, there may be extra charges for some services. The cost may also vary according to the size of the room or apartment provided.

In some states, funds are available for those who cannot afford assisted living. In those states, the service components of assisted living may be paid by Medicaid if the state has applied for and been approved under a home and community-based waiver. The waiver is for persons who are determined to be eligible for nursing home care. The resident may then use Supplemental Security Income (SSI) to pay for the room and board costs. (American Associations of Homes and Services for the Aging)

Assisted-living facility. In assisted living facilities, residents live in private apartments, usually with kitchenettes and bathrooms in complexes that have staff available to help residents eat, bathe and dress. In some facilities, meals, housekeeping, laundry and transportation are provided. Although medical care is not provided, the staff will often supervise medications. Assisted living facilities do not have to follow the stringent guidelines required by long-term care facilities. Some facilities charge extra for minor assistance and as needs increase, a home health aide may be necessary. Furthermore, facilities in many states can evict residents with little notice as their level of care increases.

Up to one-half of all patients in assisted living facilities are reported to have dementia. One-quarter of all assisted living facilities in the U.S. offer special wings or pods for individuals with Alzheimer's disease and other forms of dementia. The annual cost of a private room in an assisted living facility is about $27,000, less than two-thirds the cost of a nursing home. Long-term care insurance policies generally help pay for assisted living. It is important when selecting an assisted-living facility to find out what provisions they have for patients who may eventually require full-term care and to know what safeguards the facility has in place to protect patients who may be inclined to wander from the facilities.

Astrocytes (Astroglial cells). A type of neuroglial cell found in the brain, astrocytes produce proteins that promote neuronal growth or survival and growth factors that stimulate the growth of microglial cells. Microglia, in turn, produce mitogens that activate astrocytes. Astrocytes also offer protection to neurons under attack by inflammatory cells.

With branching processes that extend in all directions, astrocytes may be fibrous or protoplasmic. Fibrous astrocytes are primarily found in the white matter, where their processes travel between nerve fibers. Protoplasmic astrocytes are primarily found in the gray matter, where their processes pass between the nerve cell bodies.

Many of the terminal processes of astrocytes link to blood vessels, netting capillaries into clusters and forming the glial limiting membranes of the central nervous system. Astrocytic processes are also found near the initial segment of most axons.

Astrocytes form a supporting framework for nerve cells and nerve fibers. By covering the synaptic contacts between neurons they may play a role in insulating axon terminals and preventing them from influencing other neurons. Astrocytes may also form barriers for neurotransmitters, and they are known to act as immune system scavengers, engulfing and destroying damaged neurons. Astrocytes store glycogen within their cytoplasm. In response to norepinephrine, the glycogen can be broken down into glucose and released to surrounding neurons.

At Home Assisted Living. A brainchild of Sunrise Assisted Living, an industry founder 20 years ago, at home assisted living provides the services of assisted living in a person's own home. Special services include

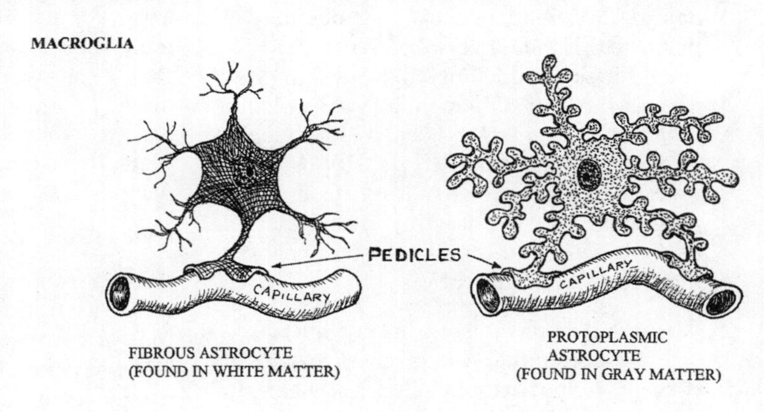

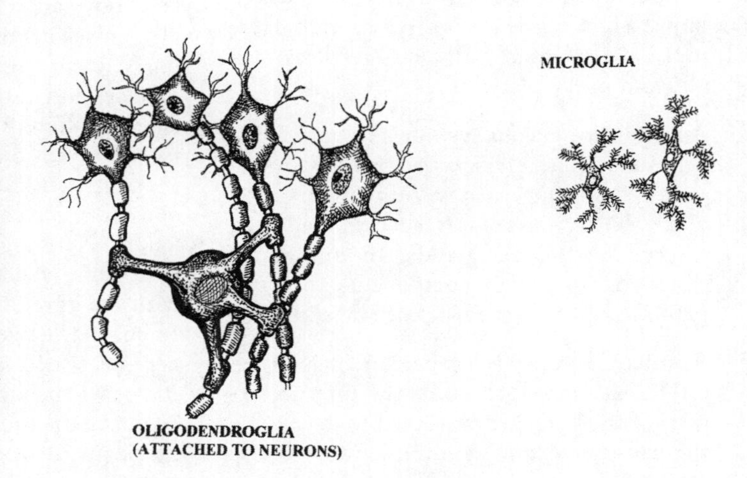

Astrocytes and Microglial Cells (illustration by Marvin G. Miller).

emergency response buttons and devices that store medications and remind patients to take their medications at the right time. If the patient does not comply, an alarm is sounded at the main Sunrise offices.

Ataxia. Ataxia is a disturbance of voluntary movement frequently seen in cerebellar disease. In individuals with ataxia, the muscles contract irregularly and weakly. Tremor may occur during fine movements such as writing and shaving. Muscle groups fail to work together and there is decomposition of movement. When asked to touch the tip of his nose with index finger, the patient fails to make contact.

Atherosclerosis. Atherosclerosis is a an inflammatory condition causing plaque deposits within blood vessels. When these lesions block blood flow to the brain they cause symptoms of dementia. While plaque build-up is seen in the normal elderly population, it is an increased density or accumulation of plaque that leads to disease. Atherosclerosis is caused by a combination of cholesterol and immune system changes that result in inflammation.

Atrophy. Atrophy is a condition of increased cell destruction that results in a shrinkage of tissue. Cerebral atrophy is typically seen in patients with Alzheimer's disease and it is also seen in the normal elderly population. However, in Alzheimer's disease, cerebral atrophy is associated with neurofibrillary tangles and senile plaques.

Autonomic nervous system. The autonomic nervous system refers to the part of the nervous system concerned with the innervation of involuntary structures, such as the heart, smooth muscles, and glands. The autonomic system has two major components: the sympathetic and the parasympathetic systems.

Autopsy. Autopsy is a procedure performed after death in which all of the internal organs of the body are examined to determine the cause of death. A brain autopsy is the final confirmation of an Alzheimer's disease diagnosis. If other forms or causes of dementia are also present, an autopsy will reveal this. A brain autopsy involves removal and examination of brain tissue for the characteristic structures, senile plaques and neurofibrillary tangles typically associated with Alzheimer's disease. Arrangements for autopsy should be made no less than 30 days prior to death. The cost of the autopsy may be reduced if the brain is donated for research.

Brain autopsy in Alzheimer's disease consists of an examination of the tissue. A microscopic count of the number of silver-staining (argyrophilic) plaques and neurofibrillary tangles is performed and compared to the number normally seen for the patient's age group. The National Institutes of Health has established minimal criteria for the pathologic diagnosis of Alzheimer's disease. For patients less than 50 years old, more than 2 neorcortical plaques plus more than 2 neurofibrillary tangles/any 20X magnified field are diagnostic for Alzheimer's disease, whereas in patients older than 75 years, more than 15 neocortical plaques are diagnostic.

Avlosulfon *see* Dapsone

Axon. Axons are long processes or neurites that arise from the central cell body of neurons or nerve cells. Axons are the main way by which neurons transmit or pass on information to other neurons. Axons generally arise from a small conical elevation on the cell body called the axon hillock. Occasionally, however, axons may arise from the proximal part of a dendrite. Axons have smooth surfaces and, although their diameter varies among different neurons, individual axons have uniform diameters.

Axons tend to branch away from the cell body, forming collateral branches along their length. Near the point at which they terminate, axons generally form profuse branches with enlarged distal ends called terminals. Axons may be very short, particularly in the nervous system or they may be long, for instance when extending from a peripheral receptor in the toe to the spinal cord. The initial segment arising from the axon hillock is the most excitable part of the axon and it is the site at which an action potential originates (*see* Excitation of nerve cells).

Ayurveda. Ayurveda is an ancient medical tradition with roots in India. Ayurveda uses herbs to treat dementia. Winter cherry or Ashwaganda (*Withania somnifera*) demonstrates antioxidant and anti-inflammatory properties in laboratory studies and it enhances the tolerance of stress in animals. Brahmi (*Herpestis monniera*) improves motor skills as well as the ability to learn and retain information.

Babinski's sign. Normally, in response to stroking the sole of the foot, the big toe flexes and the other toes fan out. This is known as Babinski's sign. Absence of Babinski's sign is indicative of upper motor neuron lesions.

BACE1 enzyme. The BACE1 enzyme has been implicated as the enzyme responsible for the destructive plaques found in the brains of Alzheimer's disease patients. BACE1 begins the process that cleaves or snips amyloid precursor protein, forming beta amyloid protein fragments that aggregate to form plaques. Therapies that inhibit BACE1 are being studied for their role as treatment agents in Alzheimer's disease. ("Scientists Zero In on Enzyme at Work in Alzheimer's Disease, NIA News, February 26, 2001)

Balanced Budget Refinement Act. The Balanced Budget Refinement Act of 1999 requires Medicare to pay for skilled nursing care following hospitalization. In October 2001 the amount of Medicare payments for skilled nursing facilities increased by 2.1 percent following guidelines proposed by the Balanced Budget Act. Payment will increase again in 2002, which will bring it to its full payment rate.

Baltimore Longitudinal Study of Aging (BLSA). The Baltimore Longitudinal Study of Aging (BLSA), which started in 1958, is America's longest running scientific study of human aging.

Baptist. Baptist is a term used to describe scientists who adhere to the theory that the formation of beta amyloid plaque deposits is the underlying disease mechanism in Alzheimer's disease. The debate between the Baptists and Tauists has subsided in recent years with the realization that both plaques and tangles may be the result rather than the cause of cellular changes in Alzheimer's disease.

Basal forebrain. The basal forebrain is a loosely used term that refers to the area at and near the inferior surface of the telencephalon, between the hypothalamus and the orbital cortex. Rich in cholinergic neurons, the basal forebrain reaches the surface of the brain in the anterior perforated substance, extending superiorly into the septal area.

Basal ganglia. The basal ganglia are a group of nuclei that form part of each cerebral hemisphere. Internally located, they are only visible in surgical sections of the hemispheres. The major basal ganglia are the caudate and lenticular nuclei.

Basal nuclei. The term basal nuclei refers to a collection of masses of gray matter located within each cerebral hemisphere. The three main basal nuclei include the corpus striatum, the amygdaloid nucleus and the claustrum.

Bazelon Center and Fund. Founded in 1972, the Bazelon Center for Mental Health Law is a nonprofit national legal advocacy organization for people with mental disabilities. The Center works to protect patients' rights and promote their access to needed services. The Fund, established in 1905, works with decision makers in the public and private sectors, using litigation, policy analysis, coalition building and technical support for local advocates to advance and protect the rights of adults and children with mental illness or developmental disabilities who rely on public services and to ensure their equal access to health and mental health care, education, housing, and employment. Bazelon Center for Mental Health Law, 1101 Fifteenth Street, NW, Suite 1212, Washington, DC 20005-5002, (202) 467-5730, www.bazelon.org.

Beck Anxiety Inventory (BAI). The Beck Anxiety Inventory (BAI) is a 21-item self-administered evaluation tool that measures symptoms associated with anxiety. Initially used on cancer patients, it can be used in any disorder in which emotional symptoms occur.

Beck Depression Index (BDI). The Beck Depression Index (BDI) is a widely used evaluation tool that measures the severity of depression by evaluating 21 symptoms. A short form of the BDI (BDI-SF) consisting of 13 items is also used.

Behavioral and Social Research Program (BSR). The federal government's Behavioral and Social Research Program (BSR) supports behavioral and social research and training on aging processes. The BSR supports numerous activities related to Alzheimer's disease including research on reducing the burden of care for caregivers and multidisciplinary studies on the design and effectiveness of special care units.

Behavioral Pathology in Alzheimer's disease (BEHAVE-AD). The Behavioral Pathology in Alzheimer's disease (BEHAVE-AD) test is an evaluation tool used to evaluate emotional changes such as agitation in patients with Alzheimer's disease. This test, which provides a global rating of non-cognitive symptoms, is designed for use in assessing the efficacy of prospective clinical drugs.

Behavioral Rating Scale for Dementia. The Behavioral Rating Scale for Dementia is a questionnaire given to a patient informant by a trained interviewer. The questions focus on behavioral changes observed within the previous month. This assessment tool offers insight into the psychopathology of patients with dementia, including an evaluation of mood disorders, agitation, aggression, and psychotic symptoms.

Benton Visual Retention Test. The Benton Visual Retention Test is a neuropsychological test used to test memory and recall. Patients are shown pictures and later asked to recall what they saw. The test cutoff score is 6 or less. The Benton test assesses visual perception, visual memory and visuoconstructive abilities. There are three forms of the test, each consisting of 10 designs.

Beta (β) Amyloid precursor protein (βAPP). Beta (β) Amyloid precursor protein (βAPP) is a transmembrane glycoprotein isoform or subtype of amyloid precursor protein (APP). βAPP can be between 695 and 770 amino acids long. βAPP is found on the cell surface of neurons where it matures. Its expression is stimulated by endogenous factors such as cytokines, growth factors, estrogens, head trauma and excitotoxicity. Increases in βAPP occur at the same time as neuronal differentiation. The cloning of the gene mutation coding for βAPP on chromosome 21 led to an understanding of the role of genes in conferring susceptibility to Alzheimer's disease. Beta APP may exist in different isoforms derived from alternative mRNA gene splicing. The gene products of Beta APP are expressed in different tissues, with the highest concentrations occurring in the brain.

Although the precise biological role of βAPP remains unclear, scientists have found that many kinds of cells and tissues produce βAPP. βAPP runs through the outer cell membrane, with a short piece jutting into the cell and a longer piece extending into the extracellular space (outside of the cell). Beta APP can be broken down or proteolyzed in two different ways resulting in extracellular secreted C-terminal truncated molecules or the beta-amyloid peptide product. The β-amyloid peptide is snipped out of the section of βAPP that spans the cell membrane.

Beta (β) amyloid protein (BAP). Beta amyloid protein (BAP) is a short 40–42 amino acid fragment of the transmembrane protein, β Amyloid precursor protein (β APP). It is the primary component of the senile plaques seen in the brain of patients with Alzheimer's disease and is thought to contribute to neuronal death. *See also* Amyloid beta protein and Senile neuritic plaque

Beta secretase (BACE). Beta secretase is an enzyme found in nerve cells that is essential for the production of beta amyloid protein.

Beta amyloid protein is the primary constituent of the plaques responsible for neuronal death in the brains of individuals with Alzheimer's disease. Along with gamma secretase, beta secretase splices its precursor protein into uneven fragments, one of which results in a toxic version of beta amyloid protein. Inside nerve cells, beta secretase competes with an enzyme known as alpha secretase, an enzyme that may offer protection against Alzheimer's disease. Therapies including vaccines designed to inhibit beta secretase are currently being developed.

Beta-2 microglobulin. Beta 2 microglobulin is a precursor protein that breaks down into Abeta 2 M, a peptide increased in the amyloid disorder chronic hemodialysis arthropathy. Increased serum levels of beta-2 microglobulin result from reduced clearance by the kidneys. Alterations to beta-2 microglobulin may facilitate protein aggregation and fibril formation in neurons.

Binswanger's disease. Binswanger's disease is a rare form of vascular dementia distinct from Alzheimer's disease associated with stroke-related cerebral lesions in the brain. The trademark of this disease is damage to blood vessels in the white matter of the brain, particularly in the regions of the pons, basal ganglia and thalamus. These changes are discernible with magnetic resonance imaging (MRI) studies.

Patients with Binswanger's disease experience loss of memory and cognition and often show signs of hypertension, stroke, blood abnormalities, disease of the large blood vessels in the neck and disease of the heart valves. Other common symptoms include urinary incontinence, difficulty walking, Parkinsonian-like tremors, and tremors. However, not all patients have these symptoms, and symptoms are often transient. Sometimes, symptoms resolve and patients return to their pre–Binswanger selves. Symptoms generally occur after age 60. While treatment revolves around reducing blood pressure, there are reports of aspirin showing favorable results.

Bleomycin hydrolase. The gene for the enzyme bleomycin hydrolyase has been found to have an association with late onset Alzheimer's disease independent of that of the APOE 4 gene. This enzyme is suspected of playing a role in the formation of amyloid deposits in the brains of Alzheimer's patients.

Blessed, G. Blessed and his associates were the first to make the observation that most cases of dementia are caused by Alzheimer's disease. This initial observation was published in the *British Journal of Psychiatry* in 1968.

Blessed Dementia Rating Scale. The Blessed Dementia Rating Scale is a neuropsychiatric evaluation tool employing informant-based ratings of daily living skills in patients with dementia.

Blessed Test. The Blessed Test is a quick test of cognitive ability. The test assesses activities of daily living and evaluates memory, concentration and orientation.

Blood brain barrier. The blood brain barrier is a membrane separating the blood and the central nervous system. The strength of the barrier varies in different regions of the brain, and its permeability to various substances is variable and dependent on the size of the molecules. The barrier is almost impermeable to plasma proteins and other large organic molecules, whereas gas molecules, glucose, certain minerals, and water pass through freely.

Normally, the blood brain barrier protects us from potentially harmful substances. Certain drugs, however, especially lipid-soluble substances, are more readily able to enter the brain.

Board-and-care homes. In some communities, board-and-care homes provide another housing option for patients with dementia, especially those in the early stages who can no longer live independently. These homes are typically large homes that have been converted to provide accommodations for up to 20 residents. Residents generally share bathrooms, kitchens, living rooms and porches. Most of these facilities retain staff that are trained to help with personal care and meal preparation. In some facilities, meals are provided. If the need for care increases, residents may be required to transfer to a nursing home.

Boston Naming Test (BNT). The Boston Naming Test, or BNT, is a psychological test used to measure language function, including naming ability. Developed by Kaplan, Goodglass, and Weintraub in 1983, the BNT is a confrontation-naming task, which presents line drawings of objects or actions and requires that the subject provide a word corresponding to each of the pictures.

Bovine spongiform encephalopathy (BSE). Bovine spongiform encephalopathy, a new variant of Cruetzfeldt-Jakob disease commonly known as mad cow disease, is a disorder associated with the consumption of meat infected with prions. Gerald Wells and John Wilesmith of the Central Veterinary Laboratory in Weybridge, England, first recognized BSE in 1986, although there are early reports of its existence dated from 1980. The brains of animals affected by BSE are characteristic of prion disease. The brain tissue is riddled with holes, leading to severe neuronal loss, necrosis of the cerebral cortex, and ataxia. BSE has been traced to animal feed supplemented with meat and bone offal from contaminated dead sheep that might have been suffering from another type of prion spongiform encephalopathy, sheep and goat scrapie.

Braak and Braak Staging *see* Neuropathological staging of Alzheimer's disease

Brain. The brain is a central nervous system organ that lies in the cranial cavity. It is continuous with the spinal cord. Like the spinal cord it is surrounded by three meninges, the dura mater, the arachnoid mater, and the pia mater.

Brain anatomy. The human brain contains three basic components: the hindbrain or rhombencephalon at the top of the spinal cord, the midbrain or mesencephalon and the forebrain or prosencephalon. Human brain development begins at about 14 days after conception. Cell division continues until about the eighth week when the three basic components of the brain appear. The first weeks and months of fetal development are associated with rapid nerve cell development and differentiation. Cells with specialized functions migrate to specific areas of the brain. This migration affects how neurons differentiate into specialized cells.

Brain imaging. Brain imaging is traditionally divided into 1) structural imaging (computed tomography or CT scan) and magnetic resonance imaging (MRI), techniques which reflect the anatomy of the brain; 2) functional imaging (single-photon emission tomography or SPECT and positron emission tomography or PET, techniques which assess cerebral function in relative or absolute terms. Sometimes, structural and functional imaging are combined into innovative techniques such as functional MRI.

Brain in Alzheimer's disease. Gross examination of the brain in Alzheimer's disease shows a variable degree of cortical atrophy (shrinkage of the cerebral cortex). There is a characteristic widening of the cerebral folds or sulci that is most pronounced in the frontal, temporal, and parietal lobes. When atrophy is significant, there is a compensatory enlargement of the ventricles secondary to loss of tissue or parenchyma.

Microscopic examination of the brain in Alzheimer's disease reveals nerofibrillary tangles, senile plaques, activated microglial cells, neuropil threads and amyloid angiopathy (deposits of beta amyloid protein in the blood vessels of the brain). A loss of neurons and synapses is prominent in specific areas, primarily the entorhinal and hippocampal areas, and in the neocortex. Tangles may not be involved in the cell loss of the neocortex. Synaptic loss can be measured in the cortex and hippocampal areas and occurs between and within areas of neuritic plaque.

All of these changes may be seen in patients without dementia although to a lesser degree and the distribution of these changes is markedly different. However, the diagnosis of Alzheimer's disease is based on a clinical correlation between the patient's neuro-

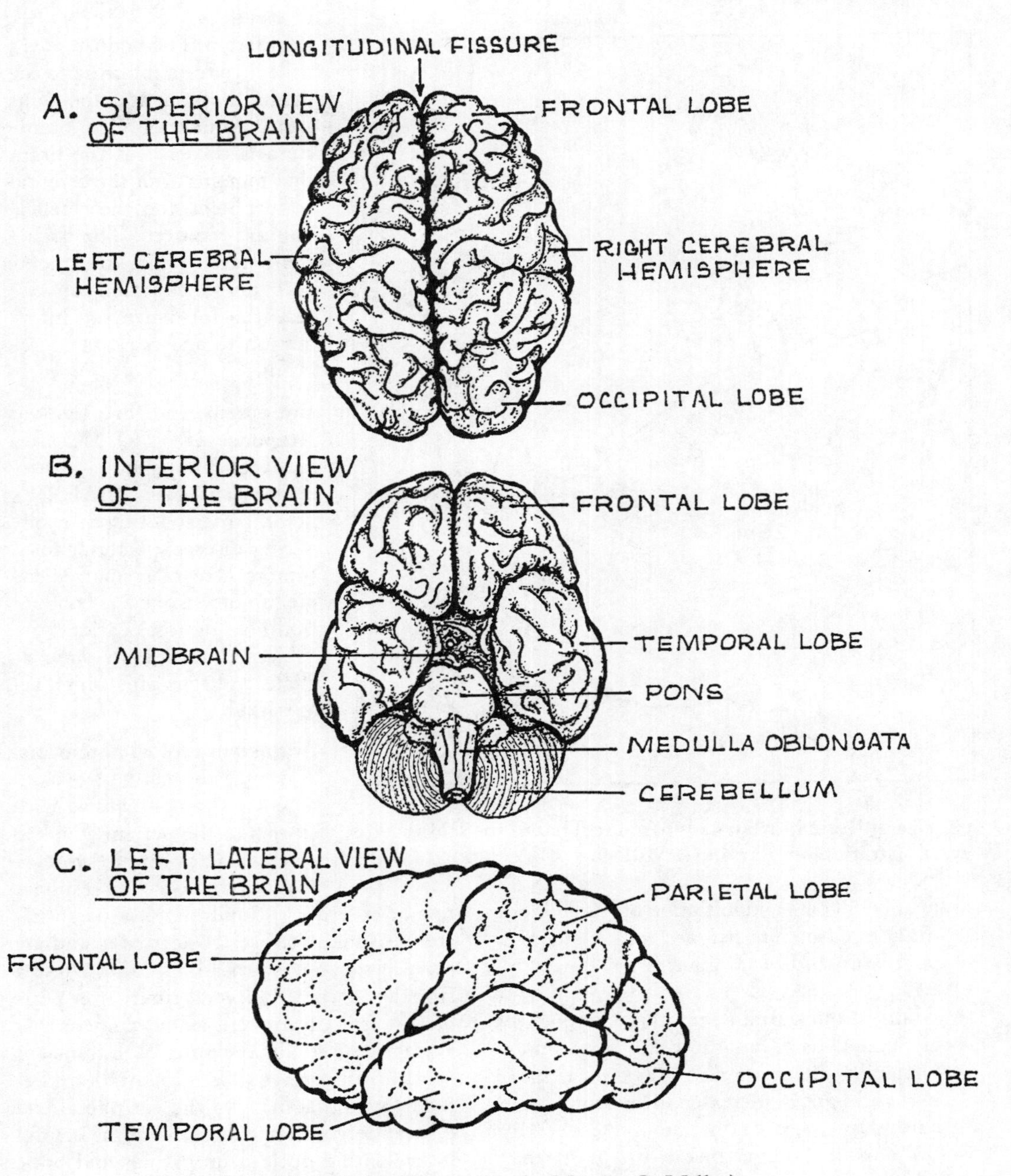

The Adult Brain (illustration by Marvin G. Miller).

logic or mental status and the frequency of plaques and tangles in the brain.

Brain injuries. Traumatic brain injury and Alzheimer's disease share similar clinical and pathological features that suggest common neurodegenerative mechanisms, including increases in amyloid precursor protein (APP), amyloid beta protein and tau protein. A dramatic increase in APP occurs in the first and third days after traumatic brain injury. It is suspected that injury-induced alterations in APP expression and processing may result in increased deposits

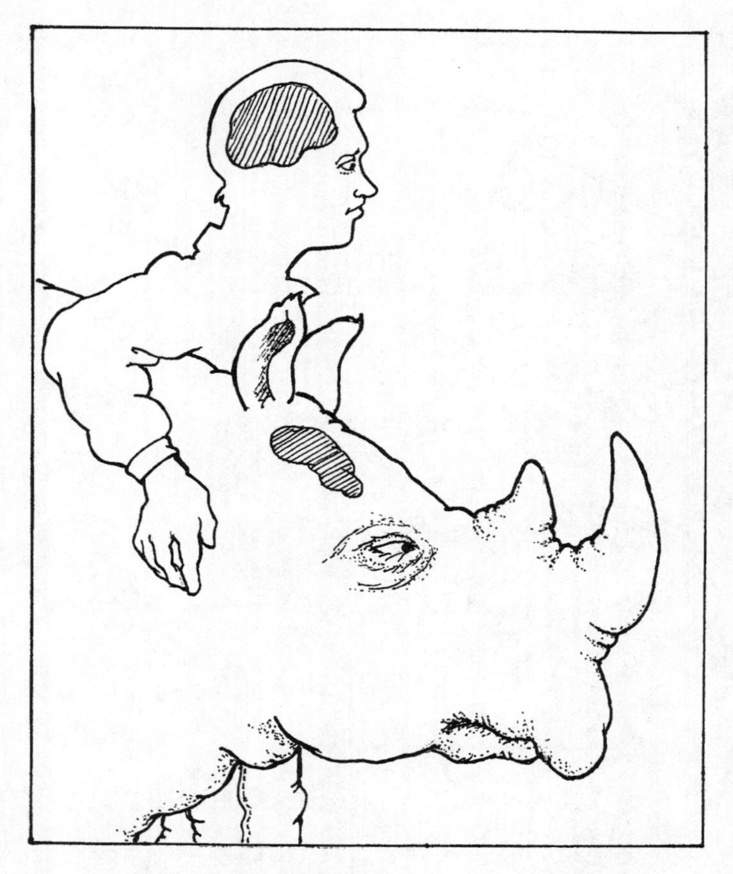

Size of Brain in Man Compared to That of the Rhinoceros (illustration by Marvin G. Miller).

of amyloid beta and initiation of Alzheimer's disease pathogenesis. *See also* Dementia pugilistica and Head injuries.

Brain tumors. Brain tumors are frequently associated with organic brain syndromes. Generally, there are also major focal findings and signs of increased intracranial pressure. However, brain tumors, especially those in the "silent" area of the brain, may present exclusively as a change of personality and intellectual decline. Subtle focal findings can usually be demonstrated on the neurologic examination, but they are occasionally lacking. (DeKosky, S. "Over-expression of Amyloid Precursor Protein After Traumatic Brain Injury in Rats and in Human Head-Injured Patients." [University of Pittsburgh] 2001.)

Brainstem. The brainstem is a collective term referring to the medulla oblongata, the pons and the midbrain. The brainstem is the part of the brain that remains after the cerebral hemispheres and the cerebellum are removed. The brainstem plays a major role in cranial nerve function and is essential for conveying information to and from the cerebrum.

Brainstem Auditory Evoked Responses (BAER). Measurement of brainstem auditory evoked responses (BAER) is helpful in diagnosing demyelinating disease, posterior fossa tumors, cerebellar pontine angle tumors, stroke and conduction hearing loss. Patients are subjected to sounds such as clicks and tone pips which act as stimuli.

Brainstem evoked potentials. The measurement of evoked potentials is noninvasive with no risk to the patient. Evoked potentials are minute voltage changes that occur in response to a brief sensory stimuli. Evoked potentials are measured from scalp electrodes and are time-related to sensory stimuli. In the test, a stimulus is repeated several times after periods of rest. A computerized instrument that averages the results measures each transient evoked response. Evoked potential studies reflect neural activity of the peripheral and central nervous systems. This test is helpful in evaluating optic neuropathies and optic nerve lesions.

Brief Cognitive Rating Scale. The Brief Cognitive Rating Scale is an extension assessment tool of the Global Deterioration Scale (GDS), a global assessment tool for evaluating one's individual course of Alzheimer's disease. The Brief Cognitive Rating Scale consists of measures derived from

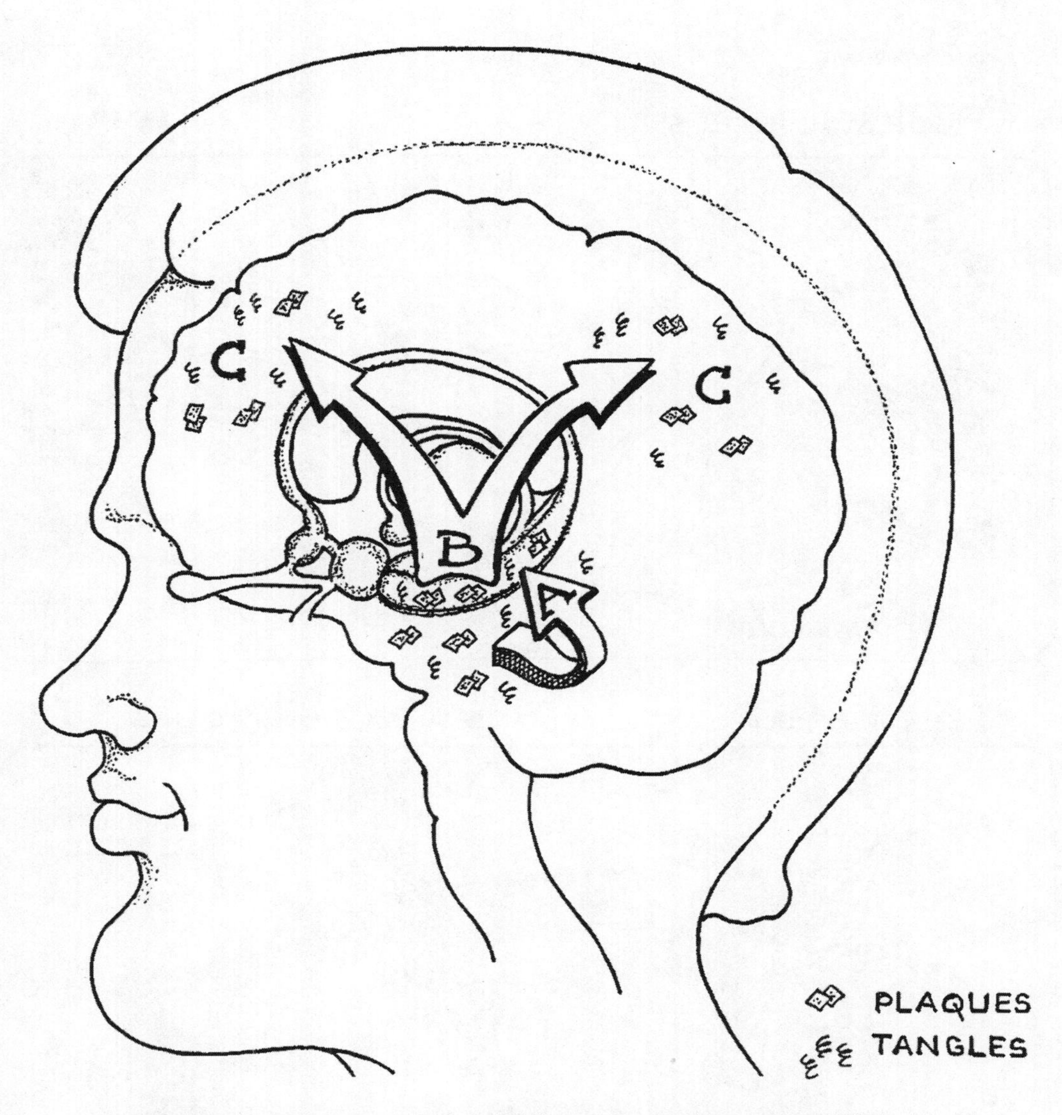

The Brain in Alzheimer's Disease (illustration by Marvin G. Miller).

Alzheimer's begins slowly by spreading clumps of tangled fibers and amyloid plaques throughout the message centers of the brain. The plaques and fibers then disrupt and damage the neurons in the brain. As the affected neurons stop communicating with each other, reasoning and memory diminish, and the brain atrophies. (A) Amyloid plaques and neurofibrillary tangles first develop in the entorhinal cortex, which is the area for memory processing and is responsible for retrieving old memories and making new ones. (B) The tangles and plaques next begin moving up into the hippocampus, where the more complex memories of objects and events are formed. (C) In the last stages the plaques and tangles enter the neocortex, or top of the brain. This area is responsible for commanding all behavior after sorting through the information and stimuli it has received.

and designed to be optimally concordant with the GDS. This tool is useful in the further guiding of staging assignments and predicting further deterioration.

Bright light therapy. In a number of studies, bright light therapy has been used to eliminate agitation, particularly sundowning, in patients with Alzheimer's disease. Bright light therapy is currently being eval-

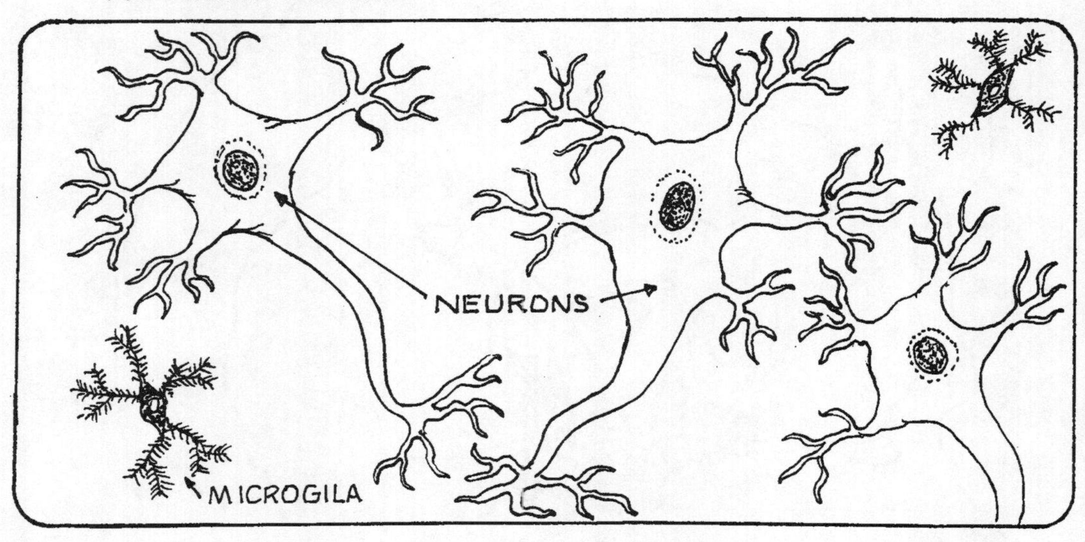

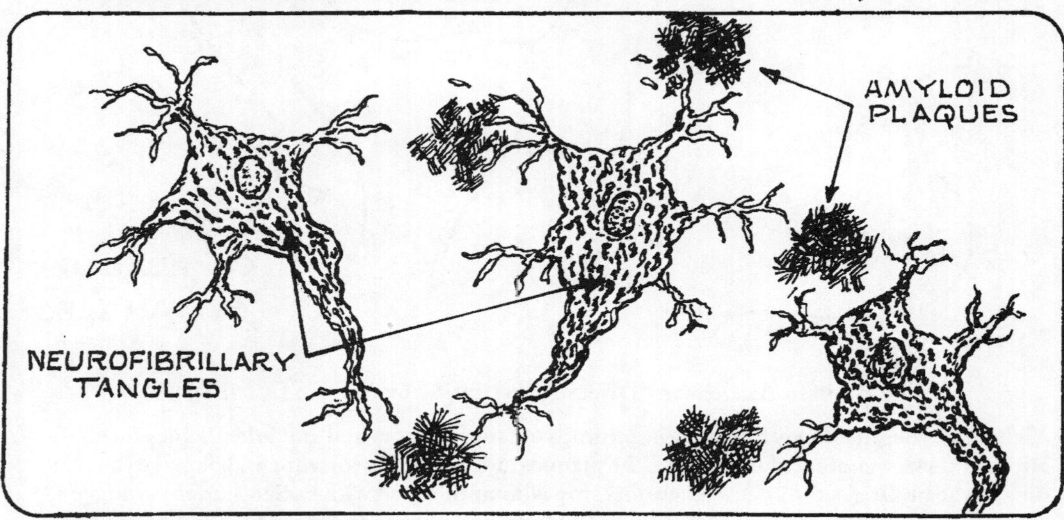

Brain Cells in Normal and Alzheimer's Disease Brain (illustration by Marvin G. Miller).

uated by researchers at Harvard University and at the Centre de sant Elisabeth-Bruyere Health Centre in Ottawa, Ontario, Canada, through a grant from the National Institutes of Aging. The contact person for this study is Virginia Bove, Staff Assistant: (617) 855-3293. (Satlin, M.D., Andrew, et al. "Bright light treatment of behavioral and sleep disturbance in Alzheimer's disease patients," *American Journal of Psychiatry*, 1992 149: 1028–1032.)

Broca's aphasia. Individuals who sustain damage to Broca's area have difficulty producing language, a condition known as Broca's aphasia. This conditions is also called non-fluent, motor, or expressive aphasia.

Broca's area. Broca's area refers to the left inferior frontal region of the brain. Damage to Broca's area causes an inability to use language (aphasia). Individuals who have damage in this area produce few written or spoken words. They tend to leave out all but the most meaningful words in a sentence and to speak or write in a telegraphic matter. Despite their difficulties in producing words, Broca's aphasics have relative little difficulty comprehending language because the affected area of the brain contains the motor programs for the generation of language.

Buschke-Fuld Selective Reminding Test. The Buschke-Fuld Selective Reminding test is a verbal memory task used to evaluate learning and memory. This test is included in neuropsychological evaluations.

Busipirone (Buspar). Busipirone (Buspar) is a partial 5-hydroxytryptamine (serotonin) agonist, which has anti-anxiety activity and few adverse side effects. Studies of busipirone used in patients with Alzheimer's disease showed an overall reduction of agitated behaviors, although the intensity of these effects varied among subjects.

CADASIL (Cerebral Autosomal Dominant Arteriopathy with Subcortical Infarcts and Leukoencephalopathy) *see* Vascular dementias

Calcium. Many facets of brain metabolism are dependent on the mineral calcium. Amyloid beta protein, which is increased in patients with Alzheimer's disease, disturbs calcium metabolism and increases the calcium concentrations of neurons. This may activate enzymes and cause the production of the abnormal phosphorus metabolism that leads to neurofibrillary tangles and directly damages the mitochondria of neurons.

The abnormal calcium regulatory system in Alzheimer's disease may cause too much calcium to build up in brain cells, which leads to neuronal cell death.

Calcium channel blockers. Calcium channel blockers are drugs that block the entry of calcium into cells, thereby reducing activities that require calcium such as neurotransmission. Generally used for certain heart conditions, calcium channel blockers are being studied for their potential role in treating Alzheimer's disease.

California Verbal Learning Tests. Psychological test used to measure verbal memory. Patients are subjected to a verbal list of words which they are asked to remember. Patients are tested to see how many words they recall at different times after hearing the words.

Cambridge Examination for Mental Disorders of the Elderly (CAMDEX). The Cambridge Examination for Mental Disorders of the Elderly (CAMDEX) is a standardized instrument or evaluation tool used to help determine the date of onset of dementia. Three questions are used to help determine the age of onset.

Cambridge Neuropsychological Test Automated Battery (CANTAB). The Cambridge Neuropsychological Test Automated Battery (CANTAB) is a neuropsychological evaluation tool used to assess cognitive deficits in humans with neurodegenerative disease or brain damage. It consists of 13 interrelated computerized tests of memory, attention and executive function, administered via a touch sensitive personal computer screen. The tests are language and largely culture free and have shown to be highly sensitive in the early detection and routine screening of Alzheimer's disease.

Canadian Study of Health and Aging (CSHA). The Canadian Study of Health and Aging (CSHA) is a multicenter epidemiologic study of dementia and other health problems in elderly people in Canada conducted between 1992 and 1997. In the first phase of the study, 14,206 subjects 65 years old or older were randomly selected from throughout Canada, and 10,263 subjects agreed to participate. Subjects were interviewed and assessed with the Modified Mini-Mental State Examination. In the second phase of the study, this cohort was reevaluated. The data from this study is widely used in epidemiological studies of Alzheimer's disease.

Capases. Capases are proteolytic enzymes that help control apoptosis, the programmed death of cells. Capases function to reorganize dying cells by facilitating safe clearance by immune system cells known as phagocytes. Increased capase activity is suspected of contributing to the neuron destruction seen in Alzheimer's disease. Researchers are currently working on capase inhibitors, drugs with the potential of blocking capase activity.

Carbamazepine (Tegretol). The anticonvulsant carbamazepine (Tegretol) is sometimes used to treat symptoms of agitation in Alzheimer's disease patients.

Caregiver Bill of Rights. Caregivers have the right to receive adequate training in caregiver skills along with accurate, understandable information about the needs of the patients they are caring for. Caregivers have the right to appreciation and emotional support for their decision to accept the challenge of providing care. Caregivers have a right to protect their assets and financial future without severing their relationship with the patients under their care. Caregivers have a right to receive respite care during emergencies and so that they may attend to their own personal needs. Caregivers have a right to provide care at home for as long as they are able and find care alternatives when they are no longer able to provide care. Caregivers have the right to temporarily alter their premises to provide safe housing for those under their care.

Caregiver training. Caregiver training is provided free of charge by the Alzheimer's Association and through local community services. Research shows that caregivers who are given training are better able to provide home care for longer periods of time. Caregiver training also provides information for helpful community services that can help with home care when caregivers must be away, such as respite care assistance programs.

Caregivers. About 80 to 90 percent of the 4 million Americans with Alzheimer's disease are cared for at home by family caregivers, and this number is expected to grow. Potential stressors associated with this care include managing behavioral disturbances, attending to physical needs, and providing constant vigilance. The effects of these stressors can be catastrophic. Family caregiving has been associated with increased levels of depression and anxiety, poorer self-reported physical health, compromised immune function, and increased mortality.

As the disease progresses, caregivers often find themselves cut off from social activities. Feelings of resentment may arise, especially after the patient's behavior deteriorates. Studies show that caregivers who work full-time may end up using an average of three weeks vacation time to help with the special needs of those in their care, and one-fifth of caregivers will quit their jobs to provide this care. Caregivers can take advantage of programs such as support groups, adult day care, and respite care. Sometimes, local agencies will provide weekly nursing services to help with the burden of caring for a patient with dementia at home.

High levels of burden experienced by caregivers are associated with increasing distress, poor physical health, and greater use of healthcare, which can have a negative impact for Alzheimer's disease patients. Caregivers of Alzheimer's patients are reported to experience more depression than other caregivers. It is also reported that caregivers who are more burdened or stressed are more likely to place patients in institutions at earlier stages of dementia. In one report, a high percentage of spousal caregivers scored high on evaluations for depression. Behavioral problems in dementia patients are reported as being closely linked to stress in the caregiver.

Patients with mild to moderate Alzheimer's disease require, on average, 3 to 3.5 hours of caregiver time daily while severely demented patients may require 8 hours or more of caregiver time daily. In one study, 50 percent of caregivers who received intensive caregiver training were still managing patients in the home after 4 years, whereas only 8 percent of caregivers who had no training were still providing home caregiving.

Researchers have examined a number of

psychosocial interventions aimed at alleviating distress associated with dementia caregiving. Resources for Enhancing Alzheimer's Caregiver Health (REACH) has developed a number of intervention strategies to help caregivers. *See* REACH.

Carnitine *see* Acetyl L-Carnitine

Casein kinase-1 (CK-1). Casein kinase-1 (CK-1) is an enzyme found in high concentrations in patients with Alzheimer's disease. Researchers from the National Institutes of Health found a high level of CK-1 in the nerve cells inside cellular sacs called vacuoles. These vacuoles had previously been associated with brain changes known as granulovacuolar degeneration.

The research, led by Dr. Jeffrey Kuret of Ohio State University, suggests that CK-1 may be involved in the process by which tau protein is phosphorylated and found in the plaques, tangles and granuovacuolar degeneration seen in the brains of patients with Alzheimer's disease. Not only does this discovery offer insight into the disease process, it can be used as a diagnostic marker for Alzheimer's disease. ("Normal Cellular Enzyme Becomes Marker for Alzheimer's Disease." The National Institute on Aging of the National Institutes of Health Press Release, October 1, 1999. Online at http://www.nih.gov/nia/new/press/CK-1.NIH.htm)

Catecholamines. Catecholamines are neurotransmitters that structurally have one amine group. Derived from the amino acid tyrosine, catecholamines include norepinephrine and dopamine. Neurons that produce catecholamines are primarily found in the brainstem and forebrain. Despite their restricted origins, catecholamines have far-reaching effects. Terminals for catecholamines are found in glands, smooth muscle and widespread areas of the brain.

Cathepsin D inhibitors. The precursor protein Beta APP can result in several different isoforms depending on how it is spliced. In Alzheimer's, beta APP is spliced to form increased amounts of beta amyloid peptide fragments ending in the amino acid 42. These peptides accumulate and represent the main components of senile plaques. The acid protease cathepsin D has similar properties to the beta secretase enzyme that facilitates the increased production of beta amyloid fragments. Research is directed toward drug therapy to block cathepsin D in an effort to simultaneously block beta secretase activity.

Causes of Alzheimer's disease. There are several schools of thought regarding the causes of Alzheimer's disease. While it is widely accepted that increased production of beta amyloid protein leads to Alzheimer's disease, alterations in tau protein and amyloid precursor protein, decreased permeability of the blood brain barrier, altered brain glucose metabolism, genetic mutations, defects in the cholinergic system, and the binding of toxic metals to amyloid beta protein are also suspected of playing a causative role. Many researchers today suspect that Alzheimer's is caused by a combination of genetic and environmental factors and that these variations account for the many variations or subtypes of Alzheimer's disease that exist.

Cells. Cells are the basic building blocks of human tissue. The brain is primarily composed of central nervous system cells known as neurons and immune system cells known as microglia.

Centella asiatica. *Centella asiatica*, the herb commonly known as gotu kola, has long had the reputation of improving memory. In Ayurvedic and traditional Chinese medicine, gotu kola has long been used to boost memory, stall memory loss and support healthy blood vessels. Gotu kola appears to enhance blood flow and increase the tone of blood vessels. For Alzheimer's disease, 200 mg of the freeze-dried herb or 400–500 mg of the crude herb are used three times daily. (Duke, James A. *The Green Pharmacy.* Emmaus, PA: [Rodale Press,] 1997. "Gotu kola," Whole Health MD.com Supplements, http://www.wholehealthmd.com/refshelf/substances_view/0,1525,10031,00.html.)

Center for Mental Health Services (CMHS). The Center for Mental Health Services (CMHS) is a service of the federal government which focuses on the diagnosis and treatment of mental illness.

Centers for Medicare & Medicaid Services (CMS). Formerly known as the Health Care Financing Administration, the Centers for Medicare & Medicaid Services (CMS) regulate government health insurance. With the name change, there is an increased emphasis on responsiveness to the people served by these programs. CMS provides health insurance for more than 74 million Americans through Medicare, Medicaid, and SCHIP. Individuals under these plans receive their benefits through a fee-for-service delivery system or through managed care plans. The CMS also provides technical assistance to the Public Health Service and other agencies to coordinate delivery and funding of the Department of Health and Human Services' maternal and child health care programs. Information on their programs is available at *http://www.hcfa.gov/* and http://www.medicare.gov.

Central Nervous System (CNS). The central nervous system (CNS) consists of the brain and the spinal cord. The CNS is an intricate system linking the brain and the body's network of nerves. While generally shielded from the blood and lymphatic systems, the CNS is intimately linked to the immune and endocrine systems, with each of these systems influencing functions in the other systems. The interior of the central nervous system is organized into gray and white matter.

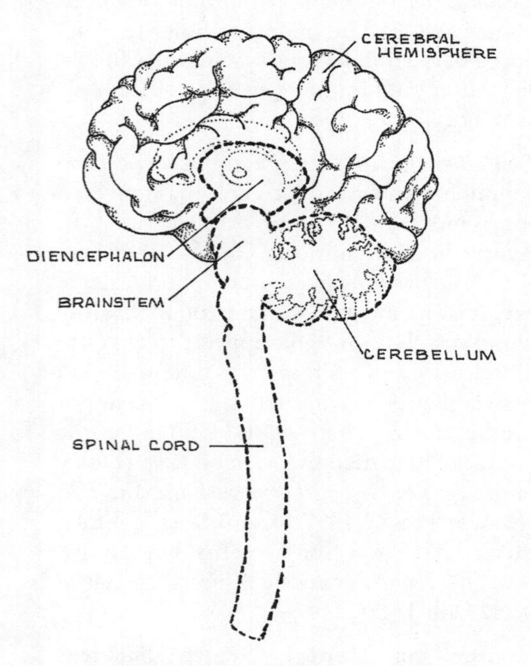

Central Nervous System (illustration by Marvin G. Miller).

Central sulcus. The surface or outer regions of the cerebral cortex are thrown into folds or gyri, which are separated from one another by fissures known as sulci. The sulci conveniently are used to divide the hemispheres of the brain into distinct sections or lobes. The central sulcus indents the hemisphere near its midpoint. The gyrus that lies in front of the central sulcus contains the motor cells that initiate movement for the opposite side of the body.

Cerebellar ataxia. Cerebellar ataxia is a gait disturbance detected during neuropsychological testing. The gait is staggering, unsteady, and wide-based with exaggerated difficulty on the turns. The patient cannot stand steadily with feet together, whether eyes are open or closed.

Cerebellum. The cerebellum is a highly developed area of the hindbrain associated with thinking, speaking, memory and emotions. The cerebellum lies within the posterior or rear cranial fossa posterior to the pons and the medulla oblongata. The cerebellum consists of two hemispheres connected by a median portion known as the vermis. The cerebellum is connected to the midbrain, pons, and medulla by processes known as peduncles.

Afferent nerve fibers enter the cerebellum through all three pairs of cerebellar peduncles and terminate as mossy fibers in the cerebellar cortex. The large Purkinje cells of the cerebellum link the cortex to the intracerebellar nuclei.

The main function of the cerebellum is to coordinate all reflex and voluntary muscular activity. It regulates muscle tone, maintains normal body posture and permits voluntary

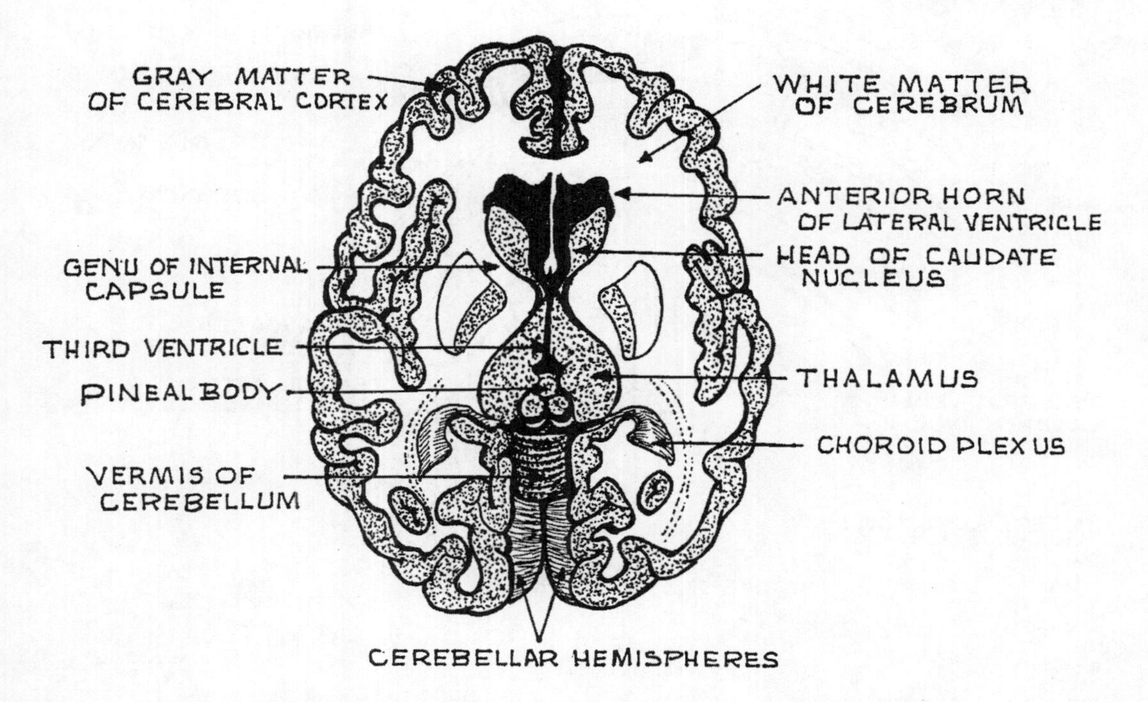

Gray and White Matter of the Brain (illustration by Marvin G. Miller).

movement. The cortex of the cerebellum does not vary between regions, either in its microscopic appearance or in its functions. The cerebellar hemispheres are linked by nervous pathways to their respective sides of the body. Thus, a lesion affecting the left cerebellar hemisphere would cause symptoms, such as gait impairment, in the left side of the body. Signs of cerebellar dysfunction include hypotonia, alteration of gait, ataxia, dysdiadochokinesis, nystagmus, dysarthia and disturbances of reflexes.

Cerebral atrophy. Cerebral atrophy is the shrinking of brain tissue due to neuronal damage or degeneration.

Cerebral blood flow studies. Cerebral blood flow, or blood flow within the brain, can be measured by the injection or inhalation of radioactive krypton or xenon. Normal cerebral blood flow is 50 to 60 ml/100 grams of brain per minute. Patients with Alzheimer's disease experience reduced blood flow velocity (BFV) values in their middle cerebral artery, which can be further demonstrated on MRI. The greatest reductions in blood flow were related to the greatest amounts of cerebral atrophy.

Cerebral circulation. The brain is supplied with arterial blood from two internal carotid arteries and two verterbral arteries, which unite anteriorly to form the basilar artery. The most important factor in moving blood through the brain is the arterial blood pressure. Arterial blood pressure is reduced or inhibited by raised intracranial pressure, increased blood viscosity or thickness and narrowing of the blood vessels. Cerebral blood flow, however, generally remains constant despite changes in the general blood pressure unless the arterial blood pressure becomes very low.

Cerebral cortex. The cerebral cortex refers to the surface layer of gray matter cushioning the cerebrum. The cerebral cortex is primarily involved in the coordination of sensory and motor information.

Representing approximately 80 percent of the human brain, the cerebral cortex refers to the expanded or surface portion of the

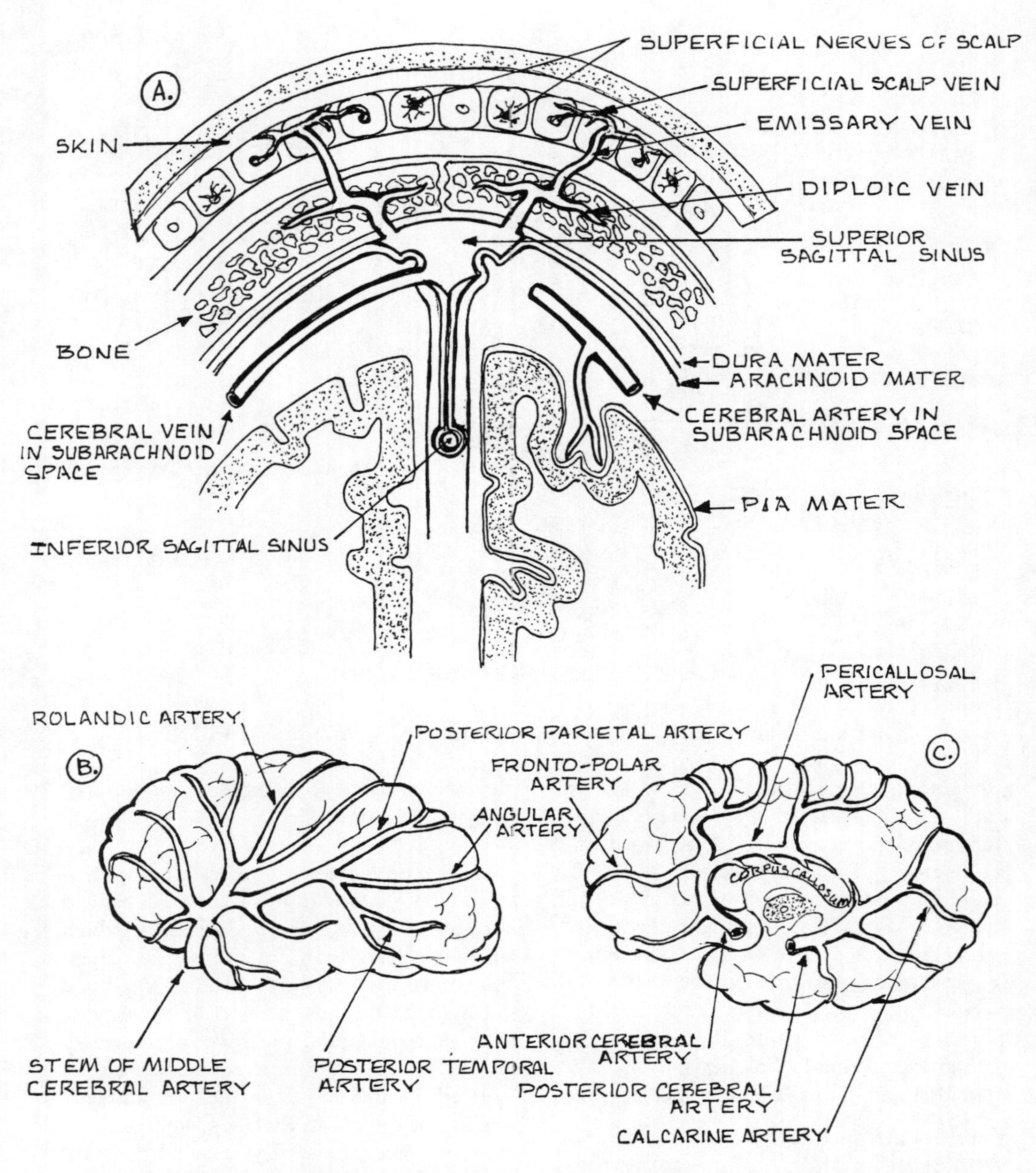

Cerebral Blood Vessels (illustration by Marvin G. Miller).

cerebral hemispheres. The cerebral cortex consists of a sheet of neurons and their interconnections, which extend to about 2.5 square feet in area. This thin layer contains about 30 billion neurons, interconnected by 100,000 km of axons and dendrites. One of the most striking changes in evolution is the tremendous increase in the size of the cerebral hemispheres and the even greater increase in the area of cerebral cortex on their surfaces.

The cortex is composed of gray matter,

which is thrown into folds, or gyri, separated by closely set transverse fissures known as sulci. Only about one-third of the cortex lies exposed. The remaining two-thirds form the walls of the sulci. The cortex is thickest over the crest of a fold and thinnest in the depth of a sulcus.

The neurons which form the cerebral cortex are located immediately below the bones of the skull, arching from just behind the forehead and over the top and sides, back to where the back of the head meets the neck. Like all gray matter, the cerebral cortex consists of a mixture of nerve cells, nerve fibers, neuroglia, and blood vessels. The nerve cells present include: pyramidal cells, stellate cells, fusiform cells, horizontal cells of Cajal and cells of Martinotti. These cells vary in size and the types of neurites or processes they contain.

The cerebral cortex can also be divided into layers that differ in the type of cells they are primarily composed of. The most superficial layer is known as the molecular or plexiform layer. This layer contains large numbers of synapses between neurons.

The cerebral cortex is the most complex region of the brain. It has many specialized regions and lobes that control particular functions, such as word association and reflection. For instance, widespread lesions of the frontal lobe might cause symptoms and signs indicative of loss of attention span or changes in social behavior. Widespread degeneration of the cerebral cortex causes symptoms of dementia. Basic aspects of perception, movement and adaptive response to the outside world also depend on the cerebral cortex.

The cerebral cortex in Alzheimer's disease, studied by electron microscopy, reveals innumerable, non-compacted deposits of beta amyloid protein containing few or no surrounding dystrophic neurites or glial cells. With recent studies indicating that certain neurons in the cerebral cortex involved with higher learning are capable of regeneration, therapies designed to stimulate neurogenesis are under investigation. *See* Neocortex.

Cerebral hemispheres. The cerebral hemispheres dividing the cerebrum in the forebrain are separated by a deep midline sagittal fissure known as the longitudinal cerebral fissure. The fissure contains the fold of the dura mater, the falx cerebri and the anterior cerebral arteries. In the depths of the fissure, the corpus callosum connects the hemispheres across the midline. A second horizontal fold of dura mater called the tentorium cerebelli separates the cerebral hemispheres from the cerebellum.

In order to provide maximal surface area for the cerebral cortex, the surface of each hemisphere is thrown into folds or gyri, which are separated from each other by fissures known as sulci. The hemispheres are further divided into lobes, which have names corresponding to the cranial bones under which they lie. The primary lobes are the frontal,

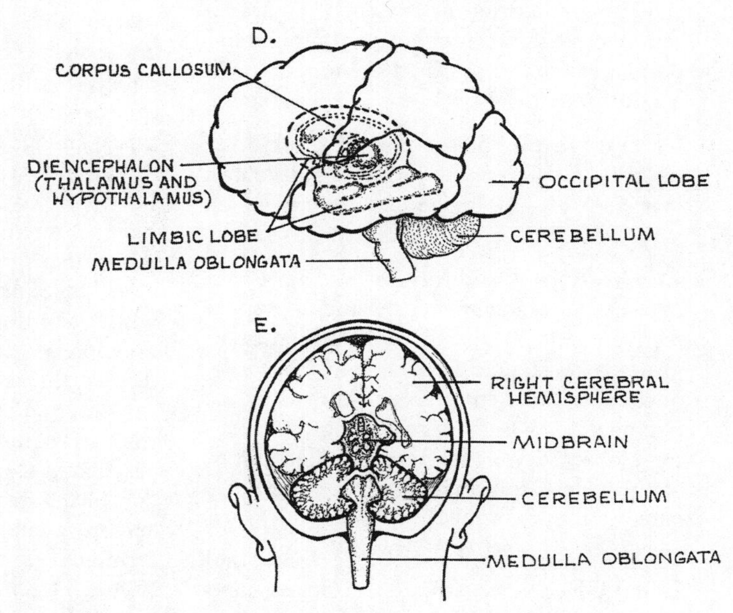

Hemispheres and Lobes of the Brain (Cerebellum/Cerebral Hemisphere) (illustration by Marvin G. Miller).

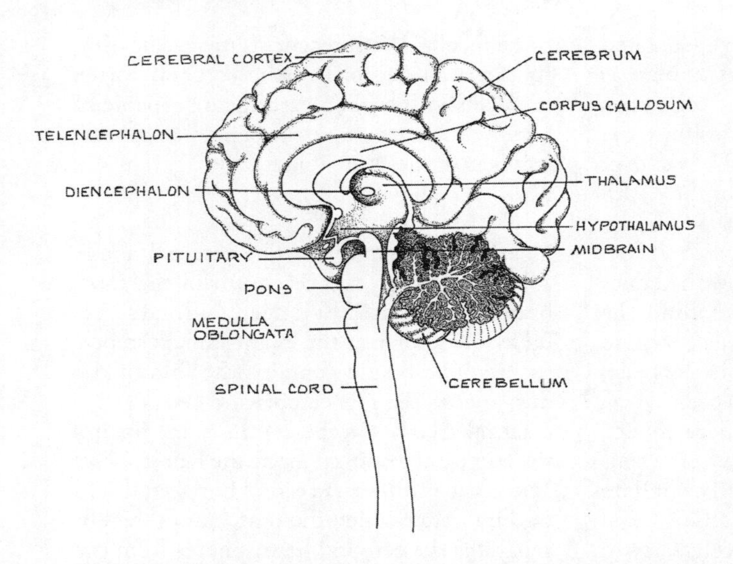

Midsagittal Section of the Brain (illustration by Marvin G. Miller).

parietal, temporal and occipital lobes. The gyri that lie anterior to the central sulcus in each hemisphere initiate movement in the opposite side of the body.

Cerebral ischemia. Impairment of blood flow to the brain results in a lack of oxygen causing a condition of ischemia. Neuronal function ceases after about one minute and permanent changes occur after about 4 minutes of ischemia.

Cerebral thrombosis. Cerebral thrombosis refers to the presence or formation of a blood clot in vessels supplying the cerebrum, which may result in a cerebral accident or stroke.

Cerebrolysin. Cerebrolysin (Ebewe Pharmaceutical) is a neurotrophic and neuroprotective agent produced from purified brain proteins by standardized enzymatic breakdown. Cerebrolysin contains biologically active peptides which exert nerve growth factor-like activity on neurons from dorsal root ganglia. Cerebrolysin is currently being evaluated in clinical trials.

Cerebrospinal fluid (CSF). Cerebrospinal fluid (CSF) is a normally clear, colorless fluid that surrounds the brain and spinal cord. CSF is withdrawn during lumbar punctures and evaluated when certain conditions such as encephalitis or subarachnoid bleeding are suspected.

Cerebrovascular disease. Cerebrovascular disease, which is also known as vascular disease, refers to the dysfunction of any of the blood vessels supplying the cerebrum. The severity of the condition is largely dependent on the size of the affected blood vessel. Infarcts to large vessels may result in ischemia (decreased blood supply to brain) whereas infarcts to small capillaries lead to microinfarcts, which, over time, may cause tissue injury. Affected vessels may be narrowed or they may be prone to spasm.

Infarcts or injuries to the cerebrovascular system cause neurodegenerative changes that may be confused with Alzheimer's disease. Chronic cerebrovascular disease, however, is commonly associated with an increased magnetic resonance imaging (MRI) signal in the periventricular white matter. This pattern often follows the general distribution of the deep border zone territory seen in the small vessels, particularly microangiopathy of hypertension, lipohyalinosis, and amyloid angiopathy.

Patients with Alzheimer's disease may have co-existing cerebrovascular disease. Several postmortem studies of suspected Alzheimer's patients show that co-existing vascular lesions are common. Furthermore, while neuroimaging studies, such as MRI, are more sensitive for detecting Alzheimer's disease, the neuropathological exam, including psychometric testing, is more sensitive than neuroimaging for detecting cerebrovascular disease. Because many treatments are able to reverse symptoms associated with cerebrovascular disease, it is important to determine if cerebrovascular disease is present. (Chui, Helen, et al. "Differentiating Alzheimer Disease and Vascular Dementia: Reframing the Question," *Alzheimer Disease: From Molecular Biology to Therapy.* Edited by R. Becker and E. Giacobine. Boston: Birkhäuser Publishing, 13–17 [1996.])

Cerebrovascular system. The cerebrovascular system refers to the cerebrum and the blood vessels that support it.

Cerebrum. The cerebrum or telencephalon, along with the diencephalons, makes up the forebrain. The cerebrum can be divided into left and right sides, which are known as the cerebral hemispheres.

Certificate in Dementia Care. Certificates in dementia care are awarded to caregivers who take 32 hours of coursework through the Alzheimer's Learning Institute of the Alzheimer's Association. The course must be completed within 18 months and is available to professional caregivers including RNs, LPNs, CNAs, personal care providers, social workers, activity directors, activity assistants, administrators, and special care coordinators. Typical course classes cover special concerns of teamwork in a dementia care environment, interpreting behavior, successful communication, sexuality and intimacy, assessment and documentation, activities, and disease progression.

Chelation therapy. In chelation therapy, chelating agents, such as ethylenediaminetetraacetic acid (EDTA) are used to remove excess or harmful metals from the body. Garry F. Gordon, M.D., co-founder of the American College of Advancement in Medicine, reports that chelation therapy can benefit memory in patients with Alzheimer's-like dementia by improving blood flow to the brain. For senile dementia, Dr. Charles Farr, co-founder of the American Board of Chelation, recommends using 10 to 15 chelation therapies alternating with intravenous hydrogen peroxide. (http://www.alternativemedicine.com)

Some researchers report that the binding of transition metals to amyloid peptide, rather than the peptide itself, is the cause of neurotoxicity in Alzheimer's disease. In June 2001, Ashley Bush at Massachusetts General and fellow researchers described how the copper/zinc chelator clioquinol cut Abeta deposits in the brain by half in mice without any apparent effects. This approach follows the concept that chelating copper and zinc should be able to break up plaques since these metals are shown to potentiate Abeta aggregation and toxicity. While these findings are undergoing further studies, they add support to chelation therapy.

Chlamydia pneumoniae. In one study, *Chlamydia pneumoniae,* a bacterium that generally causes respiratory infections, has been found in the parts of the brain affected by late-onset Alzheimer's disease but not in unaffected parts. The presence of the bacterium may have been the result of Alzheimer's disease or it may be a causative agent. More studies are being undertaken to clarify the role of this bacterium.

Chlorpromazine (Thorazine). Chlorpromazine (Thorazine) is a major tranquilizer used for the manifestations of psychotic disorders.

Choline. The amino acid choline is one of the building blocks of both acetylcholine and lecithin. Lecithin contains the amino acids choline and inositol. Researchers have tried using choline and lecithin supplements as well as choline-rich foods to increase acetylcholine levels in individuals with Alzheimer's disease. Although preliminary reports were encouraging, recent studies have failed to prove conclusively that supplemental choline results in significant memory improvement. Still, many herbal products sold as memory aids contains significant amounts of choline. Foods that contain choline include brazil nuts, horehound, ginseng, eggs, English pea, mung beans, fava beans, fenugreek, and dandelion. (Duke, James A. *The Green Pharmacy.* Emmaus, PA: Rodale Press. 1997.)

Cholinergic basal forebrain. The cholinergic basal forebrain is the area in which cholinergic neurons are concentrated. *See* Basal forebrain.

Cholinergic hypothesis. The cholinergic hypothesis refers to the theory that the destruction of cholinergic neurons is the primary mechanism leading to Alzheimer's disease.

Cholinergic neuronal pathways. Neurons at the basal forebrain provide most of the cholinergic innervation to the cortex. These neurons are preferentially affected by neurofibrillary tangles, which are responsible for the cholinergic neurotransmitter deficits. Drugs known as cholinesterase inhibitors, such as donepezil, are used to correct these deficits and increase cholinesterase levels.

Cholinergic system. The cholinergic system refers to the neurons in the brain that use acetylcholine to communicate. There are two main clusters of cells in the cholinergic system: cholinergic cells in the pedunculopontine region of the brainstem, which innervates the thalamus and basal ganglia, and cholinergic cells in the basal forebrain, which innervates regions of the cortex with cholinergic prominence. While patients with Alzheimer's disease experience a loss of cholinergic neurons in the basal forebrain, the cholinergic neurons found in the brainstem are not affected. The basal forebrain's cortical cholinergic system mediates attentional processes. Researchers at Ohio State University have postulated that dysfunctions in the excitability of these cholinergic neurons underlie the impaired attentional processing that contributes to the cognitive deficits seen in Alzheimer's disease.

The cholinergic system plays a role in emotion and non-cognitive behavior and may be involved in neuropsychiatric symptoms in Alzheimer's disease. Presynaptic neurons in the basal forebrain that produce the neurotransmitter acetylcholine in their axons transmit impulses to postsynaptic neurons. Deficits in acetylcholine or its failure to bind to receptors disrupt cholinergic activity in the brain. The amount of acetylcholine available for neurotransmission depends on the enzymes choline acetyltransferase and acetylcholinesterase (AChE).

Choline acetyltransferase catalyzes the synthesis of acetylcholine by transferring an acetyl group from acetyl-coenzyme A and combining it with choline. The newly synthesized acetylcholine molecules are then stored in specialized vesicles in the endings of presynaptic cholinergic neurons in the brain. In response to an incoming nerve impulse, calcium-activated movement of the vesicles releases their contents into the synaptic cleft. Here, most of the acetylcholine molecules rapidly bind to post-synaptic membrane receptors on neurons. Any remaining acetylcholine is quickly inactivated by the enzyme acetylcholinesterase. After the nerve impulse is transmitted, the receptor sites are vacated and used acetylcholine is also inactivated or hydrolyzed by acetylcholinesterase.

The cholinergic neurons in the basal forebrain and the brainstem act via two distinct mechanisms: the muscarinic and nicotinic systems.

Cholinesterase. Cholinesterase is an enzyme present in the brain, plasma and skeletal muscles that regulates levels of acetylcholine. There are two types of cholinesterase, acetylcholinesterase (AChE) and butyrylcholinesterase (BuChE), which is also known as pseudocholinesterase.
Both cholinesterase enzymes have multiple functions. AChE is involved in the development of certain pathways in the brain and inhibits dopamine release in the substantia nigra. BuChE has primary effects on butyrylcholine, although, like AChE, it hydrolyzes the neurotransmitter acetylcholine. Since both enzymes have multiple effects, the long-term effects and safety of cholinesterase inhibitors depends on how these other enzyme systems are affected.

Cholinesterase inhibitors *see* Acetylcholinesterase inhibitors

Chorea. Chorea is a disorder characterized by quick, jerky, irregular movements, including swift grimaces and sudden movements of the head or limbs.

Choroid plexus. The choroids plexuses are the areas of the brain found within the lateral, third, and fourth ventricles that produce cerebrospinal fluid.

Chromosomes. The entire genetic component of a human being is packed into 23 pairs of chromosomes. Chromosomes are H-shaped structures located inside the cell nucleus. Each chromosome contains the DNA for thousands of different genes. Genes are short pieces of DNA that tell the body's cells what proteins to produce and how to act or appear. Chromosomes 1, 14, 19 and 21 are associated with genetic mutations that are responsible for certain disease states, including Alzheimer's disease.

Chromosome 1. A mutation to the presenilin-2 gene on chromosome 1 is responsible for approximately 1 percent of all cases of Alzheimer's disease. The age of onset for this mutation is the late 40s to early 50s.

Chromosome 10. Researchers have found a susceptibility locus for Alzheimer's disease on chromosome 10 independent of the apolipoprotein E gene.

Chromosome 14. A mutation to the presenilin-1 gene on chromosome 14 is responsible for approximately 4 percent of all cases of Alzheimer's disease. The age of onset for this mutation is 28 years to 50 years.

Chromosome 19. A mutation to the Apolipoprotein E4 (APOE4) gene on chromosome 19 is the genetic mutation responsible for most cases of Alzheimer's disease. The APOE4 allele is associated with both early and late-onset Alzheimer's disease.

Chromosome 21. A mutation to the amyloid precursor protein (APP) gene on chromosome 21 is responsible for less than 1 percent of all cases of Alzheimer's disease. The age of onset for this mutation is 45 years to 65 years.

Circadian rhythm. Circadian rhythm refers to the normal peak and flow of the body's hormones and other chemicals in relationship to the time of day. Thyroid hormones, for instance, normally are released at their highest concentrations during the night. Disruption of circadian rhythm is related to a number of different illnesses. Researchers at Harvard University, through a grant from the National Institute on Aging, are currently conducting studies to see if disruption of circadian rhythm contributes to the development of Alzheimer's disease, and they are evaluating bright light therapy. The contact person for this study is Virginia Bove, Staff Assistant, (617) 855-3293.

Circumscribed brain atrophy *see* Pick's disease

Citicoline. Citicoline is a substance currently being investigated as a therapeutic agent in Alzheimer's disease. Citicoline affects the cholinergic system and increases the production of nerve growth factor. Citicoline has proven beneficial in the past for treating head injury and stroke.

Cleveland Scale for Activities of Daily Living. The Cleveland Scale for Activities of Daily Living is a global assessment tool used for documenting functional deficits such as the ability to bathe, dress and eat. This evaluation tool is helpful in determining disease staging and projecting the expected rate of disease progression in individuals with Alzheimer's disease. This tool can also be used to measure response to various therapeutic interventions.

Clinical Dementia Rating Scale (CDRS). The Clinical Dementia Rating Scale (CDRS) is an evaluation tool used to distinguish normal brain aging from progressive Alzheimer's disease by dividing Alzheimer's disease into 5 distinct stages. The CDRS also includes additional semistructured evaluation tools, such as a "sum of boxes," for further guiding staging assignments. One study has found that the CDRS was more sensitive and reliable than psychometric measures for tracking dementia progression relevant for clinical trials or responses to therapy.

Clinical Global Impression (CGI). Clinical Global Impression (CGI) is a neuropsychiatric evaluation tool. While it has been used to assess the efficacy of therapy in clinical trials, this tool has shown little sensitivity for evaluating treatments for Alzheimer's disease. This tool is a measurement of overall cognitive ability.

Clinical Global Impression of Change scale (CGIC). Clinical Global Impression of Change is a neuropsychiatric evaluation tool given at different times in order to determine alterations in mental status in response to treatment modalities. Patients and informants familiar with their condition are interviewed to assess changes in cognitive function over time. The unstructured format of the CGIC makes it less reliable than other evaluation tools. To address past concerns related to this tool, the National Institute on Aging's Alzheimer's Disease Cooperative Study combines the CGIC with other measures when conducting clinical trials.

Clinical trials. The purpose of clinical trials is to improve the understanding of certain conditions and to evaluate the benefits and risks of new therapeutic agents. Patients participating in a clinical trial for neurological conditions continue to receive medical care, routine laboratory tests and other diagnostic tests from their primary physicians. The patient's primary physician and the sponsoring agency simultaneously evaluate test results. For a listing of organizations that recruit for clinical trials, see the resource section.

Clinical trials that are continuing or being initiated in a 5 year effort supported by the National Institute of Aging include trials for: vitamin E and donepezil, cholesterol lowering statin therapy, high-dose folate/B6/B12 supplements, hormone replacement therapy, herbal medicine, the anticonvulsant valproate, and indole-3-proprionic acid antioxidants.

According to one study, patients who participate in clinical trials are less likely to need nursing home placement than patients at a similar stage of disease who do not participate in trials. This may be due to the benefits of increased interaction and attention that patients in clinical trials experience. Alternately, it could be because the caregivers of Alzheimer's disease patients who encourage participation in clinical trials may be more involved and concerned with the individuals' care. (Albert, S.M. et al. "Participation in Clinical Trials and Long-Term Outcomes in Alzheimer's Disease." *Neurology*, 49, 1997: 38–43.)

Clinician Interview Based Impression of Change (CIBI). The Clinician Interview Based Impression of Change (CIBI) is a tool used in evaluating mental status. The CIBI is a clinician's or physician's assessment of global change over time in response to therapy.

Clinician Interview Based Impression of Change with Caregiver Input (CIBIC Plus). The Clinician Interview Based Impression of Change with Caregiver Input (CIBIC Plus) is an assessment tool based on both an evaluation by a physician and input given by the patient's primary caretaker. Because mental status may vary from day to day, with alternating periods of lucidity, input from a caregiver offers a wider view of one's impairment and insight into daily living skills.

The CIBIC Plus is scored as a seven point categorical rating, ranging from a score of 1, indicating "markedly improved," to a score of 4, indicating "no change," to a score of 7, indicating "markedly worse."

Clioquinol. Clioquinol is a drug long used as an antiamoebic agent. It was withdrawn in 1971 because of its likely association with cases of subacute myelo-optic neuropathy mostly occurring in Japan. Researchers at Massachusetts General have shown that clioquinol is an effective chelator for zinc and copper. In studies with mice, clioquinol was shown to reduce Abeta production in half.

Clock Draw Test. The clock draw test is a neuropsychological evaluation tool best used in combination with other cognitive assessment tools. There are variations of the test, but its main focus is asking the patient to draw the face of a clock with all the numbers. The patient is then asked to draw the hands set at a certain time. The test assesses cognitive or visuospatial impairment.

Clozapine. Clozapine is an anti-psychotic medication occasionally used to manage symptoms in Alzheimer's disease. Side effects include sedation, ataxia, falls, delirium and bone marrow suppression, making this drug an unlikely first choice for patients with dementia.

Clusterin (apolipoprotein J). Clusterin or apolipoprotein J is a multifunctional protein present in the brain, which is associated with aggregated amyloid beta peptide in the senile and diffuse plaques of Alzheimer's disease. Clusterin is reported to enhance the oxidative stress caused by amyloid beta. Enhanced neurotoxicity has been observed in the highly aggregated amyloid deposits.

Cochrane Dementia Group registry of clinical trials. The Cochrane Collaboration is a nonprofit organization named after Archie Cochrane, a British physician who alerted other physicians that there was a need for ready access to evidence from randomized controlled clinical trials. The Cochrane Collaboration developed into an international organization which conducts systematic reviews of randomized controlled trials in all areas of health, including clinical trials related to dementia. Reviews of studies involving dementia are listed in the Cochrane Dementia Group registry of clinical trials.

Coenzyme Q-10 (Co-Q-10). Coenzyme Q-10 (Co-Q-10) is a substance known to enhance the bio-availability of other nutrients. A potent antioxidant, Co-Q-10 has free-radical scavenging properties and helps transport electrons into cell mitochondria where they are used for energy production. Idebenone is a form of Co-Q-10 with increased blood-brain barrier penetration.

Coexisting illness. Coexisting illnesses are illnesses that exist in addition to the patient's primary disorder. Patients with Alzheimer's disease frequently have coexisting illnesses, such as hypertension or diabetes. The effects of therapy on both disorders need to be considered. Certain drugs used to treat coexisting illnesses may have adverse effects on cognition. Drugs that are likely to be offenders include anticholinergics, antihypertensives, antidepressants, antianxiolytics and antipsychotics. Even over-the-counter medications, such as cough and cold preparations, have the potential to impair memory. If a new medication is introduced or its dosage is increased and new dementing symptoms appear, consideration should be given to stopping the drug to see if it is responsible for the change in symptoms.

Cognex *see* Tacrine hydrochloride

Cognitive ability. Cognitive ability refers to the intact function of thought processes, such as learning, comprehension, memory, reasoning and judgment. Cognitive ability also refers to one's ability to logically deal with problems and to communicate.

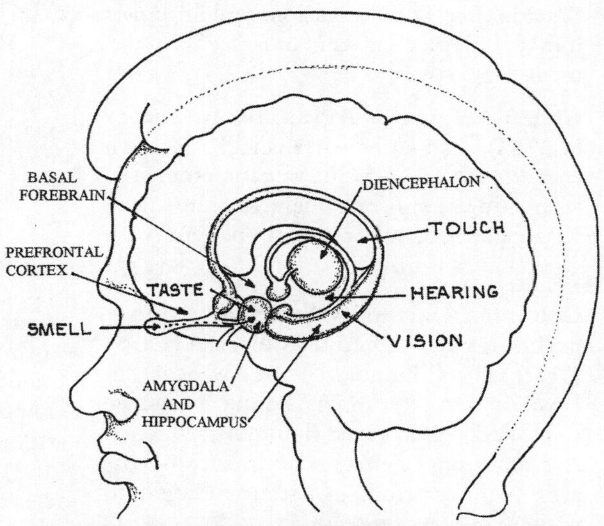

STIMULUS RECEIVED BY THE CEREBRAL CORTEX IS RELAYED BY THE AMYGDALA AND HIPPOCAMPUS TO THE DIENCEPHALON. THE INFORMATION IS NEXT TRANSMITTED TO THE PREFRONTAL CORTEX AND THE BASAL FOREBRAIN. WHERE IT IS TRANSMITTED BACK TO THE SAME SENSORY AREA THAT FIRST RECEIVED THE INFORMATION. SOME MEMORY MAY BE STORED IN THE CEREBRAL CORTEX DURING THIS PROCESS.

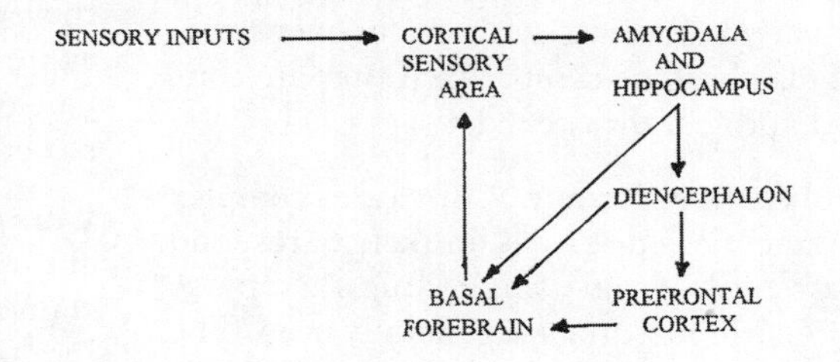

Learning/Thought Process (illustration by Marvin G. Miller).

Cognitive assessment. Cognitive ability is assessed by a number of different neuropsychological tests, including tests for verbal recall, visuospatial ability, praxis and orientation. These tests measure judgment, reason, logic and general intelligence. Because ethnic and cultural differences can affect some of these test results, a wide panel of tests offer a more accurate representation of cognitive ability. *See also* Neuropsychological tests.

Cognitive impairment. Cognitive impairment refers to a reduction in the ability to extract, process, retain, and retrieve thoughts. Cognitive impairment results from dysfunction or loss of the neurons responsible for cognition. Cognitive impairment may be temporary or transient as a result of injury, the side effects of medications or delirium or it may be permanent as in most forms of dementia.

Cohen-Mansfield Agitation Inventory (CMAI). The Cohen-Mansfield Agitation Inventory (CMAI) is an evaluation tool used to measure emotional behavior and neuropsychiatric manifestations in patients with Alzheimer's disease.

Columbia University Scale for Psychopathology in Alzheimer's disease (CUSPAD). The Columbia University Scale for Psychopathology in Alzheimer's disease (CUSPAD) is an evaluation tool used to assess emotional behavior and neuropsychiatric manifestations in patients diagnosed with Alzheimer's disease.

Combativeness. Combativeness is a form of aggressive behavior in which those affected are inclined to initiate fights, both physical and verbal. Patients with Alzheimer's disease may become combative if they are confused and feel threatened.

Combination therapy. A disease as complex as Alzheimer's disease is unlikely to respond satisfactorily to one single drug therapy. A combination of drugs is generally used. The drugs most often used are: acetylcholinesterase inhibitors, inhibitors of beta-amyloid formation or deposition, neuronal growth factors, anti-inflammatory agents, estrogens, and neuroprotective agents including antioxidants.

Preliminary research findings presented at the annual meeting of the American Geriatrics Society in May 2001 suggest that a combination of the cholinesterase inhibitors donepezil and rivastigmine may be effective in improving cognitive function among patients with Alzheimer's disease. The study, which was conducted by J.R. Shua-Hain, M.D. and colleagues at Meridian Hospitals Corporation of New Jersey, involved reducing the dose of donepezil from 10 mg to 5 mg daily and adding an initial dose of 1.5 mg rivastigmine once daily. After three days with no side effects, rivastigmine was increased to 1.5 mg twice daily. Improvement was seen mostly in improved linguistic skills and functional performance.

Commissures. Commissures are nerve fibers of different diameters found in the white matter of the brain. Commissures are supported by neuroglial cells. The corpus callosum is the largest commissure of the brain, connecting the two cerebral hemispheres.

Communication. People with dementia eventually lose their language abilities and their ability to communicate. When first losing language skills, patients may rely more on other senses such as touch and sight. It is important that patients with dementia continue to have regular checkups for hearing and vision and that hearing aids and spectacles are of the right prescription. Caregivers should speak clearly and slowly and make eye contact, making sure they have the patient's attention before speaking. While patients may no longer understand language, they will still understand hugs, smiles and expressions of gratitude and appreciation. Cueing and memory aids can be used to help patients with impaired language skills.

Competence. Competence refers to one's ability to act in a specific capacity. For instance, individuals with Alzheimer's disease lose their mental competence.

Complement. Complement is an immune system chemical released during the immune response. There are several different types of complement, which are released in a cascade, initiated by the release of complement 1, or C1. According to one hypothesis, inflammation in Alzheimer's disease is triggered by the activation of C1. Activation of the complement system is a powerful immune system effector mechanism. It can initiate the production of other pro-inflammatory factors such as tumor necrosis factor (TNF) and contribute to neurodegeneration in Alzheimer's disease.

Computed axial tomography (CAT scan). Computed axial tomography is a CT scan performed on a specific axial plane; used as a synonym for CT scan.

Computed tomography (CT scan). Computed tomography is a diagnostic imaging technique introduced in 1980 used to determine structural anatomy. Computed tomography relies on the same principles as conventional x-rays. CT enabled clinicians to exclude intracranial lesions or tumors as a cause of dementia, and is the procedure of choice for visualizing the characteristic structural changes of Alzheimer's disease, such as increased ventricular size and the presence of cortical atrophy. Brain CT scans, particular views of the medial temporal lobe, are able to differentiate changes in the normal aging brain from those seen in Alzheimer's disease. This accuracy increases when a functional imaging technique such as SPECT is combined with CT.

In CT, structures in the brain are distinguished from one another by their ability to absorb x-rays. The x-ray tube emits a narrow beam of radiation as it passes in a series of scanning movements through a 180-degree arc surrounding the patient's head. The resulting x-ray images are fed to a computer which processes the information and displays it on a terminal screen. The sensitivity of the CT head scan is so precise that the gray matter of the cerebral cortex, white matter, internal capsule, corpus callosum, ventricles and subarachnoid spaces can all be recognized. By using a contrast dye, changes in blood flow can also be examined.

When it was introduced CT caused a rise in diagnostic accuracy of Alzheimer's disease from 43 percent to 70 percent. Before probable diagnoses were confirmed in postmortem examination. CT replaced invasive methods of pneumoencephalography and cerebral angiography, a procedure used sparingly in the elderly because of its associated morbidity. However, single CT scans, whether analyzed qualitatively or quantitatively, cannot distinguish Alzheimer's disease from normal elderly adults because of the overlap seen in brain atrophy in both groups. Serial quantitative CT scans of lateral ventricular volume, however, have been shown to demonstrate a distinct difference in patients with Alzheimer's disease when compared to normal elderly subjects.

Confrontations. Patients with Alzheimer's often become involved in confrontations with their caregivers. Caregivers are reminded to not draw attention to failure and avoid confrontation by staying calm. Conflict causes unnecessary stress for both the patient and the caregiver. Patients with dementia invariably forget things or deny that they have done something wrong. Often, they accuse others of taking their possessions when they have hidden their possessions and forgotten where they put them. They may become defensive, making the situation worse. Caregivers are reminded that it is the fault of the disease, not the person. Experts suggest that caregivers nip confrontations in the bud by distracting the patient, giving them tasks to do such as folding towels or dusting furniture. Another suggestion is changing the scenery by taking the patient for a walk or car ride.

Confusion Assessment Method Diagnostic Algorithm (CAM). The Confusion Assessment Method Diagnostic Algorithm (CAM) is an evaluation tool used to measure confusion. CAM includes 4 features: acute onset and fluctuating course, inattention, disorganized thinking, and altered level of consciousness.

Consortium to Establish a Registry for Alzheimer's Disease (CERAD). CERAD is a standardized clinical and neuropsychological evaluation tool consisting of the verbal fluency test, Boston Naming Test, Mini-Mental Status Examination, ten-item word recall, constructional praxis, and delayed recall of praxis items. Testing usually takes 20–30 minutes and is useful in assessing and tracking cognitive decline.

CERAD was established in 1986 in an effort to develop standard methods to evaluate persons with Alzheimer's disease and to gather clinical, neuropsychological and neuropathological information about this disorder. CERAD also evaluates informant-based ratings of emotional and behavioral status collected by 30 Alzheimer's disease research centers in the United States. This information is analyzed for the purpose of standardizing and testing the reliability of commonly used brief assessment instruments so that it can provide accurate tools for use in epidemiologic surveys, dementia registries, and research protocols, including clinical trials, for Alzheimer's disease.

CERAD's clinical assessment protocol was designed to provide clinicians with the minimum information necessary to make a confident diagnosis of Alzheimer's disease. Tools used in this protocol include interviewing procedures for both patients and informants, a general physical and neurological examination including a structured assessment for extrapyramidal dysfunction, and brief cognitive scales. Global dementia severity can then be staged according to the Clinical Dementia Rating. Diagnosis is aided by the use of the NINCDS/ADRDA criteria.

CERAD neuropsychological measures are able to effectively distinguish cases with mild probable Alzheimer's disease from patients without dementia and education-matched control subjects. (Morris, John C. "Clinical and Neuropathological Findings From CERAD." *Alzheimer Disease: From Molecular Biology to Therapy,* edited by R. Becker and E. Giacobini. Boston: Birkhauser, 1996. 7–12.)

Constructional Praxis. Constructional praxis is a neurospsychological assessment tool. Patients are given tasks such as building with blocks. This test evaluates cognitive function by evaluating all aspects of motor planning, including the ability to perform tasks in logical steps that lead to completion.

Continuing Care Accreditation Commission (CCAC). The Continuing Care Accreditation Commission (CCAC), founded in 1985, is the nation's only accrediting body for continuing care retirement communities. Sponsored by the American Association of Homes & Services for the Aging (AAHSA), CCAC is an independent entity that accredits only those organizations that pass its inspections.

Continuing Care Communities. Continuing care communities (CCRCs), which originated in the 1980s, are communities that offer several different types of care in one area or community. This allows residents the ability to move to units, including rooms in a nursing home, if the need arises. A CCRC may offer residents the use of apartments, small homes, or structured "life-care" facilities. Fees are based on the amount of care that residents require, with complete or life-care being the most expensive. Ninety-four percent of CCRCs are managed by nonprofit groups. The average fee is about $110,000 for a two-bedroom apartment, although the rates may be triple at more luxurious communities. There are also monthly fees, averaging $2,000, for a two-bedroom unit, which can rise each year.

Advantages include the nursing care that is provided and the flexibility of being able to move to units providing full care if the need arises. Because all housing units are in the same general location, spouses remain nearby if one of them needs to enter a nursing home in the CCRC.

Disadvantages include the forfeiting of entry fees if the arrangement does not prove satisfactory. And while early communities occasionally went bankrupt, state laws ensure that CCRCs keep larger cash reserves. Still it is a good idea to ask the facility for its latest audit report or check with the state insurance commission, which generally regulates CCRCs. It is also important to check on the availability of the type of housing you initially need and to find out the policy regarding admission to the nursing home if the need should arise and the facility is full.

Continuum of Care. Continuum of care refers to the care services available to individuals throughout the course of their care. Changes to care can be made as disease symptoms progress or improve, but the course of care is still continuous.

Copper. Copper is a mineral found in inverse relation to zinc in the body. Results of the Nun Study show an association between high serum copper levels and Alzheimer's disease development. (Tully, C.L. et al. "Serum Zinc, Senile Plaques, and Neurofibrillary Tangles: Findings from the Nun Study." *Neuroreport*, 1995:6 (16), 2105–2108.)

Cornell Scale for Depression. The Cornell Scale for Depression is a neuropsychological evaluation test which has proven to be sensitive, reliable and valid for assessing depression in patients with Alzheimer's disease.

Corpus callosum. The corpus callosum is the largest commissure or fiber bundle of the brain, connecting the two cerebral hemispheres. The corpus callosum is further divided into the rostrum, the genu, the body and the spenium. Most fibers within the corpus callosum interconnect symmetrical areas of the cerebral cortex. Because it transfers information from one hemisphere to another, the corpus callosum is essential for learned discrimination, sensory experience and memory.

Cortex. The cortex, or neomammalian area of the brain, the most developed of the brain's areas, is responsible for our lower functions and associations, abstract thinking, and planning abilities.

Cost of care. The cost of Alzheimer's disease is tremendous with expenditures for medical care, long-term care, home care, and lost productivity amounting to approximately $100 billion annually. Most of these costs are borne by family caregivers. The Alzheimer's Association reports that the annual cost of nursing home care is approximately $42,000, not counting lost wages. With variations in different parts of the country, the cost may exceed $70,000 annually.

Corticosteroid therapy *see* Prednisone

Cranial nerves. Twelve pairs of cranial nerves extend from the lower surface of the brain through openings or foramina in the skull to the periphery of the body.

Cranium. The cranium, or skull, is the bony outer covering housing the brain.

Creutzfeldt-Jakob disease (CJD). Creutzfeldt-Jakob disease (CJD), a neurological disorder caused by an infectious agent known as a prion, results in a type of dementia that may be confused with Alzheimer's disease. Its onset is subacute rather than chronic. It causes other neurologic abnormalities besides organic brain syndrome, such as myoclonic jerks (muscle twitches), extrapyramidal findings, and visual disturbances. The hallmark of CJD is a spongiform change of the gray matter with slight involvement of the white matter. When examined by electron microscopy, the brain tissue in CJD appears vacuolated. The vacuoles contain vesicles and membranous debris.

Creutzfeldt-Jakob disease (CJD) is classified as a form of spongiform encephalopathy. The first cases of Creutzfeld-Jakob disease were reported in 1920 by Drs. Hans Gerhard Cretuzfeldt and Alfons Jakob. CJD appears to be more prevalent in Sephardic Jews and in families from Chile and Slovakia, and it generally presents as a type of dementia between the fifth and seventh decades of life. Either injection of human pituitary-derived growth hormone (commonly given to children with growth disorders in the 1970s and 1980s) or grafting tissue surrounding the human brain can transmit this disease to humans. CJD can also be transmitted by corneal transplantation, the implantation of dura mater, and contaminated brain electrodes and surgical instruments.

CJD can occur in multiple forms including sporadic, iatrogenic, or familial. Sporadic CJD is a rare, poorly understood disorder whereas iatrogenic forms occur as a result of contamination with infected tissue. Familial CJD stems from a genetic mutation in the prion protein gene. New variant CJD (nvCJD) was recognized in 1996 in the United Kingdom, where the deaths of 48 from nvCJD patients had been documented by 2000. Cases of nvCJD have also been reported in the United States as a result of eating elk contaminated with wasting disease. *See also* Prions.

Critically attained threshold of cerebral hypoperfusion (CATCH). The critically attained threshold of cerebral hypoperfusion (CATCH) hypothesis points to reduced cerebral blood flow as a contributing factor for the develop of both early and late-onset forms of Alzheimer's disease. This viewpoint is supported by the fact that chronic cerebral hypoperfusion (reduced blood flow) can affect metabolic, anatomic and cognitive function adversely. In addition, therapies aimed at improving or increasing cerebral blood flow often show benefits in patients with Alzheimer's disease. According to this theory, advanced aging in patients with vascular risk factors can result in the CATCH syndrome. This, in turn, triggers defects in the brain's blood circulation that impair neuronal cell function. According to this theory, this results in a cascade of events that ultimately lead to the development of Alzheimer's disease. (de la Torre, J.C. "Critically attained threshold of cerebral hypoperfusion: the CATCH hypothesis of Alzheimer's pathogenesis." *The Neurobiology of Aging*, Aug 2000: 21 (2), 331.)

Crystallin, Alpha B. Alpha beta crystalline is a heat shock protein whose expression is elevated in Alzheimer's disease for reasons that are unclear. Heat shock proteins are produced in response to stress and by infectious agents. Normally, heat shock proteins play a valuable role in chaperoning toxins from the body. However, increased amounts can cause immune system changes that lead to inflammation.

Cueing. Cueing or priming refers to prompts, hints, and other information used to help patients with dementia remember words or tasks. Cueing can involve the use of pictures, lists or simple one word reminders.

Cyclooxygenase (COX)-2. Cyclooxygenase-2 (COX-2) is an enzyme released during the inflammatory response. In neuronal activities, it helps the body produce chemicals known as prostglandins. Prostglandins are oxygenated unsaturated cyclic fatty acids that have a variety of hormone-like actions, such as muscle relaxation. Prostglandins also increase levels of the excitotoxin glutamate, which is a powerful neurotoxin.

COX-2 is upregulated or over-expressed in the Alzheimer's disease brain. Studies indicate that COX-2 overstatement causes neuronal cell cycle dysregulation in a murine model of Alzheimer's disease neuropathology. Preliminary evidence utilizing this model suggests that neuronal over-expression of COX-2 increases beta-amyloid peptide neurodegeneration, increases the susceptibility of excitotoxic lesions, and is associated with an age-dependent accumulation of brain microglia. Drugs designed to inhibit the action of cyclooxygenase may offer therapeutic benefits in patients with Alzheimer's disease. Inhibition of neuronal COX-2 by drug therapy may control microglial responses, demonstrating a neuron-to-glia interaction that may be mediated by oxidants generated by COX.

Cyclooxygenase 2 (COX-2) inhibitor. Cyclooxygenase (COX-2) inhibitors are anti-inflammatory drugs that inhibit the production of COX-2, a natural substance activated by inflammatory stimuli. Selective COX-2 inhibitors are currently undergoing clinical trials. Studies at the University of Michigan of Ann Arbor have detected the presence of natural COX inhibitors in tart cherries.

Cyclooxygenases. Cyclooxygenases are enzymes that convert acids in the body into prostglandins. The most important of these compounds are cyclooxygenase 1 (COX-1) and cyclooxygenase 2 (COX-2).

Cytochrome-c oxidase. Cytochrome-c oxidase is an enzyme necessary for proper functioning of cell mitochondria. Deficiencies of cytochrome oxidase (complex IV) activity in the cerebral cortex and platelets have been reported in patients with Alzheimer's disease. Alzheimer's disease has specifically been linked to mitochondrial anomalies affecting cytochrome-c oxidase, and these anomalies may contribute to the abnormal production of free radicals. Free radicals are known to damage neurons. Free radicals are a normal part of aging and also occur in oxidative stress. Studies show that oxidative stress is increased in Alzheimer's disese patients.

Cytokines. Cytokines are immune system chemicals, such as the interferons, interleukins and various growth factors that modulate the immune response. In response to an immune system threat, glial cells in the brain come to the rescue and release cytokines. As chemical messengers, cytokines in the brain contribute to the inflammation and tissue injury seen in many of the neurodegenerative disorders. Specifically, beta amyloid inflames surrounding microglial cells. These cells release inflammatory cytokines, nitric oxide, and other neurotoxins that can destroy nearby neurons. The cytokine transforming growth factor-β (TGF-beta) is suspected of contributing to the development of Alzheimer's disease.

CX516 (Ampalex). CX516 (Ampalex) is an investigative drug produced by Cortex Pharmaceuticals that regulates receptors on which the excitotoxins glutamate and aspartame accumulate. Because these compounds are powerful nerve toxins, CX516 shows promise in that it reduces their concentrations. CX516 functions as a novel AMPA receptor mediator. It facilitates the function of a subtype of glutamate receptor by increasing the amount of current flow that takes place when glutamate binds to the AMPA receptor. Currently undergoing clinical trials for Alzheimer's disease, CX516 is also used for the treatment of schizophrenia, and is reported to improve memory performance in healthy elderly subjects.

D'Adamio, Luciano, M.D., Ph.D. Dr. Luciano D'Adamio is a Professor of Immunology at Albert Einstein College of Medicine in New York City. While working as a principal investigator at the Laboratory of Cellular and Molecular Immunology Division of the National Institute of Allergy & Infectious Diseases in Bethesda, Maryland, Dr. D'Adamio isolated the Familial Alzheimer's Disease (FAD) Presenilin-2 (PS-2) gene and proved that the PS-2 gene could inhibit apoptosis of autoreactive cells in the thymus by cell membrane death receptors. At Albert Einstein, Luciano continues his research involving the processing of Amyloid βPP, the third FAD gene known to date.

Dapsone (Avlosulfon). Dapsone (Avlosulfone), produced by Immune Network, Incorporated, is an anti-infective agent used to treat leprosy. Because dapsone-treated leprosy patients have a lower prevalence of Alzheimer's disease than the general population, dapsone is being investigated in clinical trials for its use as a therapeutic agent in Alzheimer's disease.

Dehydroepiandrosterone (DHEA) sulfate. Dehydroepiandrosterone (DHEA) sulfate is a naturally occurring hormone that declines with aging. In one study, 50 healthy subjects and 24 Alzheimer's patients were evaluated for levels of DHEA and cortisol. The ratio of DHEA sulfate to cortisol was significantly lower in the patients with Alzheimer's disease, particularly the female patients in the study. (Schwartz, A. "Biological role of dehydroepiandrosterone." *Gerontologist*, 1992: 32 (3), 425. Carlson, Linda E. and Barbara B. Sherwin. "Relationships among cortisol (CRT) dehydroepiandrosterone-sulfate (DHEAS), and memory in a longitudinal study of healthy elderly men and women." *Neurobiology of Aging:* 20 (3), 315–324.)

DeKosky, Steven T., M.D. Dr. Steven T. DeKosky of the University of Pittsburgh is Director of the Alzheimer's Disease Research Center and Director of the Division of Geriatrics and Neuropsychiatry. He is also a practicing neurologist. His clinical research includes differential diagnosis, neuroimaging, genetic risks of Alzheimer's disease and trials of new medications. His basic research centers on structural and neurochemical changes in human brains in dementia.

Dr. DeKosky, who is listed in "Best Doctors in America," also chairs the National Medical and Scientific Advisory Council for, and is Vice Chairman of, the Board of Directors of the Alzheimer's Association. He also chairs the Professional Advisory Board of the Greater Pittsburgh chapter of the Alzheimer's Association and was a Founding Member of the Lexington-Blue Grass Chapter of the Alzheimer's Association.

Delirium. Delirium is an acute condition characterized by a reduced ability to maintain attention to external stimuli and confusion or disorganized thinking, as indicated by rambling, irrelevant, or incoherent speech. The essential features of delirium include global cognitive impairment, abnormal psychomotor activity and a disturbance of the sleep-wake cycle.

Delirium is one of the most frequent forms of psychopathology seen in hospitalized elderly persons. The elderly are uniquely prone to developing delirium. Delirium can be precipitated by many different illnesses and by therapeutic amounts of many different medications. Certain acute and life-threatening illnesses such as myocardial infarction or pneumonia may initially present as delirium. The DSM-III 1987 criteria for delirium include two of the following symptoms:

1) reduced level of consciousness (e.g., difficulty staying awake during an examination)
2) perceptual disturbances (e.g., misinterpretations, illusions or hallucinations)
3) disturbance of sleep-wake cycle with insomnia or daytime sleepiness
4) increased or decreased psychomotor activity
5) disorientation to time, place or person
6) memory impairment (e.g., inability to learn new material, such as the names of unrelated objects after five minutes or to remember past events, such as historical events)

Delirium differs from dementia in the onset and duration of cognitive impairment and level of consciousness. The onset of cognitive impairment in delirium is typically hours or days, and it lasts days to weeks. Furthermore, patients with delirium shows signs of either diminished alertness (hypo-alertness) or intensified alertness (hyper-alertness). Patients with delirium show limited ability to extract, process and retain and recall information. The level of consciousness in delirium tends to fluctuate. (Goodwin, Donald and Samuel Guze. *Psychiatric Diagnosis.* Fourth Edition. New York: Oxford University Press, 1989)

Delusions. Delusions are false beliefs regarding the self, or persons or objects outside the self that persist despite facts to the contrary; from the word delude, which means to mislead the mind or its judgment.

Dementia. Dementia is a chronic brain disorder characterized by decline of memory and disorientation in comparison with previous normal cognitive function. A diagnosis of dementia is based on a history of decline in performance and by abnormalities noted during clinical examination and neuropsychological testing. The criteria established by the NINCDS-ADRDA state that confirmation of dementia should be based on measurable abnormalities in two or more aspects of cognition. The term dementia is used to describe a number of different physical disorders of the brain arising from different causes.

Dementia is usually progressive, irreversible and ultimately fatal. Alzheimer's disease is the most common cause of dementia, accounting for about 60 percent of the irreversible cases. Dementia can also result from a number of different degenerative diseases, vascular disorders, traumas, infectious agents, toxic compounds, space-occupying lesions and other disorders.

Degenerative disorders that can cause dementia include Alzheimer's disease, Pick's disease, Huntington's disease, progressive supranuclear palsy, some cases of Parkinson's disease, cerebellar degenerations, some cases of amyotrophic lateral sclerosis (ALS), Parkinson-ALS dementia complex of Guam and other island areas, and rare genetic and metabolic diseases (Hallervorden-Spatz, Kufs', Wilson's, late-onset metachromatic leukosdystrophy, adrenoleukodystrophy).

Vascular dementia can be caused by multi-infarct dementia, cortical micro-infarcts, lacunar dementia, Binswanger disease, hydrocephalus, and cerebral embolic disease.

Anoxic dementia, which is caused by a lack of oxygen to the brain, can result from cardiac arrest, severe cardiac failure, and carbon monoxide poisoning. Traumatic dementia can occur as a result of dementia pugilistica (boxer's dementia) and head injuries (both open and closed).

Infectious dementia can occur a result of acquired immune deficiency syndrome (AIDS), opportunistic infections, Creutzfeldt-Jakob disease (subacute spongiform encephalopathy), progressive multifocal leukoencephalopathy, post-encephalitis dementia, herpes encephalitis, bacterial meningitis or encephalitis, brain abscess, parasitic encephalitis, neurosyphilis, and fungal meningitis or encephalitis.

Autoimmune disorders that may cause dementia include Behcet's syndrome, systemic lupus erythematosis (SLE), vasculitis, and some cases of multiple sclerosis (MS).

Space-occupying lesions that can cause dementia include chronic or acute subdural hematoma, primary brain tumors and metastatic tumors, including carcinoma, leukemia, lymphoma and sarcoma.

Toxic forms of dementia include alcoholic dementia, carbon monoxide poisoning, metallic dementia (caused by lead, mercury, arsenic, manganese, etc.) and organic poisons, including solvents and insecticides. A number of drugs may cause dementia when used in high doses, including sedatives, hypnotics, anti-anxiety medications, anti-hypertensives, anti-arrhythmics, anticonvulsants such as phenobarbital, anti-psychotics, digitalis and derivatives and drugs with anticholinergic side effects.

Psychiatric disorders that may progress to dementia include depression, anxiety, psychosis and sensory deprivation.

Nutrient deficiencies that may cause dementia include pellagra (vitamin B6 deficiency), thiamine deficiency (Wernicke-Korsakoff syndrome), cobalmin deficiency (vitamin B12 deficiency and pernicious anemia), folate deficiency, and Marchiafava-Bignami disease.

Other disorders that may cause dementia include myxedema coma, epilepsy, post-traumatic stress disorder, some cases of Whipple disease, heat stroke, hyperthyroidism, hypothyroidism, hypoglycemia, hypernatremia (high blood sodium), hyponatremia (low blood sodium), hyperlipidemia (high blood lipids), hypercapnia (excess carbon dioxide), kidney failure, liver failure, Cushing syndrome, Addison's disease and hypopituitarism. (Katzman, R. et al. "Accuracy of Diagnosis and Consequences of Misdiagnosis of Disorders Causing Dementia." Washington, DC: Office of Technology Assessment, U.S. Congress, 1986.

Dementia pugilistica (DP). Dementia pugilistica (DP) is a neurological disorder also known as Punch Drunk or Boxer's Syndrome because of its association with brain injuries. Researchers at the University of Pennsylvania's Center for Neurodegenerative Disease Research conducted a study comparing the brains of patients with DP to the brains of Alzheimer's disease patients. In their report, published in the June 2001 issue of the international neurology journal *Acta Neuropathologica*, the researchers wrote that their findings suggest that brain injury can cause DP by activating mechanisms similar to the ones that cause tau lesions in Alzheimer's disease. This suggests that head injury can increase susceptibility to Alzheimer's disease in later life.

Dementia Trialists' Collaboration. The Dementia Trialists' Collaboration evaluates data from clinical trials and determines the benefits or pitfalls of the therapies studied in the trials. Reviewers randomly select trials for inclusion and then evaluate individual patient data.

Dendrite. Dendrites are short processes arising from the cell body of neurons that receive information and conduct it toward the cell body. Dendrites, which may be referred to as neurites or nerve fibers, are necessary for learning.

The diameter of dendrites tapers the further away they extend from the cell body. Dendrites often branch profusely, causing large numbers of small projections called dendritic spines. Having cytoplasm similar to that of the cell body, dendrites are often considered extensions of the cell body, allowing for the reception of axons from other neurons. Dendrites conduct the nerve impulse toward the cell body.

Dentate nucleus. Masses of gray matter are embedded in the white matter of the cerebellum. The largest of these areas is known as the dentate nucleus.

Deoxyribonucleic acid (DNA). Deoxyribonucleic acid (DNA) is a chain of nucleotides (cytosine, guanine, adenine or thymine) linked with ribose sugar molecules. DNA forms the base of genetic material. Specific patterns of nucleotides (the composition of the molecules and how they arre strung together) represent particular genes.

Depression. Depression may be confused with dementia in that many of the symptoms are the same, including loss of interest in hobbies and community activities, apathy, weight loss, and sleep disorders. In some cases, depression coexists with dementia. Depression is more likely to occur in mild to moderate Alzheimer's disease as opposed to severe Alzheimer's disease. This may be because severely affected patients are unable to communicate their symptoms. Other symptoms of depression include dysphoric mood, loss of appetite, fatigue, irritability, insomnia and agitation.

Major depression with dementia that sometimes occurs in the elderly may be an early sign of Alzheimer's disease, preceding diagnosis by two years or less. Some experts believe that disease progression may even be delayed by treating such patients with both an antidepressant and a more specific therapeutic agent such as donepezil. Apathy may sometimes be confused with depression. Apathy is more commonly seen than depression in Alzheimer's disease. Apathy is characterized by a lack of emotions, motivations and interest rather than sadness, which is a symptom of depression.

Caregivers should be alert for symptoms of melancholia or depression including crying, complaining or suicidal ideation. Depression may contribute to impaired activities of daily living, and a sudden impairment of activities of daily living may suggest coexisting depression. Patients exhibiting symptoms of depression should be considered for a trial of antidepressants even if they do not meet the full diagnostic criteria for major depression because depression in patients with advanced Alzheimer's disease may present with atypical symptoms, including mood swings, impatience, and aggression.

Treatment of depression in elderly patients with Alzheimer's disease is usually initiated with selective serotonin reuptake inhibitors (SSRIs), such as fluoxetine or sertraline. These drugs may have cognitive-enhancing effects and are considered to be the treatment of choice for depression in Alzheimer's disease. Although these drugs have a low incidence of side effects, they should be started at low dosages and increased slowly. Older medications, such as the tricyclic antidepressants (amitriptyline, nortriptyline, imipramine, desipramine) often cause anticholinergic side effects that may impair cognition or cause urinary retention, constipation and orthostatic hypotension. Thus, they are usually contraindicated in Alzheimer's disease. (Evans, M.D., Rebecca and Martin Farlow, M.D. "Drug Therapies for Alzheimer's Disease," *Home Healthcare Consultant*, 2000. Online at http://www.mmhc.com/hhcc/articles/HHCC9905/Evans.html)

Desferrioxamine. Desferrioxamine is an iron chelating agent used to reduce toxic accumulations of iron and aluminum in the brains of Alzheimer's disease patients. Originally used to treat dementia in dialysis patients caused by aluminum toxicity, desferrioxiamine has been shown to improve cognitive function in some patients with Alzheimer's disease.

DHA *see* Docosahexaenoic acid

Diabetes *see* Insulin

Diagnostic and Statistic Manual of Mental Disorders, 4th Edition, revised (DSM-IV-R). The Diagnostic and Statistic Manual of Mental Disorders, 4th Edition, revised (DSM-IVR) in 2000 is the current edition of the official diagnostic manual of the American Psychiatric Association. *See* DSM IV Diagnostic criteria for Alzheimer's dementia.

Diagnostic criteria for Alzheimer's disease. There are no simple blood or imaging tests that are routinely used to diagnose Alzheimer's disease. However, advances in positron emission tomography (PET) testing are enabling physicians to diagnose Alzheimer's disease accurately and at earlier stages. The essential elements supporting diagnosis include an acquired decline in cognitive functions, an impairment of daily living activities, and a progressive disease course combined with imaging tests that show the characteristic brain changes seen in Alzheimer's disease.

General diagnostic criteria include: dementia established by exam and objective testing, memory impairment and at least one other cognitive function such as language, progressive worsening of memory and one other cognitive function, no disturbance in consciousness, onset between age 28 and 90, and absence of another brain disorder or systemic disease that might cause dementia. Diagnosis may be supported by one of the following criteria: loss of motor skills, diminished activities of daily living and altered patterns of behavior, family history of dementia, and imaging tests that support a diagnosis consistent with cerebral atrophy.

The American Academy of Neurology guidelines for a diagnosis of Alzheimer's disease include: a careful clinical history which includes the onset of symptoms and their progression, a mental status examination such as the Mini-Mental Status Examination (MMSE), a neurological examination, neuroimaging tests such as CT or MRI (to see if there is evidence of silent stroke, tumors, subdural hematoma), and basic laboratory tests to rule out other causes of dementia, such as vitamin B12 deficiency or thyroid dysfunction.

When symptoms alone are being considered, observation over time is often required before diagnosis of Alzheimer's disease can be certain. A significant association with the e4 allele of the apolipoprotein E gene supports the diagnosis of Alzheimer's disease in patients with dementia. However, this test is neither fully specific nor sensitive. The clinical diagnosis of Alzheimer's disease (prior to autopsy confirmation) is reported to be correct about 80–90 percent of the time. While tests for AD7c and amyloid beta 42 are available, they are best performed on spinal fluid and their use as diagnostic markers has not been established.

A definitive diagnosis can only be made at autopsy. Characteristic brain changes are seen post-mortem, including neuronal cell death, brain shrinkage, microscopic Aβ-amyloid neuritic plaque deposits and intraneuronal neurofibrillary tangles. The plaque deposits stain positive with Aβ-amyloid antibodies and negative for prion antibodies. The numbers of plaques and tangles exceed those found in age-matched controls without dementia.

Cultural variables, including languages, social customs, traditions and the quality and quantity of education must all be taken into consideration when tests for cognitive ability are evaluated. Existing test batteries yield high false-negative results among educated individuals and false-positive results among the very elderly and illiterate. One study, the Age-Associated Dementia project, conducted by the World Health Organization (WHO), indicated that the following criteria are reliable for diagnosing Alzheimer's disease: the DSM-III-R, IVD10 and NINCDS-ADRDA.

The diagnosis of probable Alzheimer's disease is supported by deficits in two or more areas of cognition, progressive worsening of memory, no disturbances of consciousness, onset between the ages of 40 and 90 (most commonly after age 65), absence of other systemic disorders, and associated symptoms of depression, insomnia, incontinence, delusions, verbal outbursts, sexual disorders and weight loss. Features that make a diagnosis of Alzheimer's unlikely include sudden, apoleptic onset, and focal neurology findings such as sensory loss, incoordination and visual field deficits, seizures, and gait disturbances early in the course of the illness.

Early diagnosis is important because research indicates that current medication and care options are effective in people with mild to moderate symptoms. While there is currently no cure for Alzheimer's disease, medication can improve certain cognitive functions, including memory and thought. Early reports from clinical trials suggest that vaccines may be effective in breaking down amyloid deposits and reversing damage. *See also* NINCDS-ADRDA Criteria for Alzheimer's disease, Laboratory tests, Differential diagnosis, Diagnostic and Statistic Manual of Mental Disorders, 4th Edition, revised (DSM-IV-R), Metabolic causes of dementia, and Positron emission tomography.

Dick, Malcolm Boyne, Ph.D. Dr. Malcolm Boyne Dick is a doctor of cognitive psychology and an expert in the treatment, diagnosis and possible preventative measures associated with Alzheimer's disease. Dr. Dick maintains an office at the Institute for Brain Aging and Dementia at the University of California at Irvine.

Diencephalon. The diencephalon, the central part of the forebrain, consists of a dorsal thalamus and a ventral hypothalamus as well as an epithalamus and subthalamus. Accounting for only about 2 percent of the weight of the brain, the diencephalon is very important for many of the body's primary functions. The diencephalon consists of the third ventricle and the structures that form its boundaries. The inferior surface of the dienchephalon is the only area exposed to the surface in the intact brain.

Diet and Nutrition. Foods high in citrulline, such as watermelon, have been found to inhibit nitric oxide production, reducing free radical formation, offering protection against Alzheimer's disease. Diets high in antioxidants, including red wine and fish, have also been shown to have a protective effect.

Dietary restriction. Dietary restriction refers to reduced calorie intake with maintained nutrition. In many studies dietary restriction has been found to extend the life span of rodents and prevent the neuronal degeneration characteristically seen in Alzheimer's disease. Specifically, it increases resistance of neurons, preventing dysfunction and degeneration and improves behavioral outcome in experimental models of Alzheimer's disease and other age-related neurodegenerative disorders.("Neuroprotective strategies for Alzheimer's disease." *Life Extension*, Medical Updates, January 2002: 73. Excerpted from *Experimental Gerontology*, 2000: 35 (4), 489–502.)

Differential diagnosis. Dementia can occur from other causes besides Alzheimer's disease. The differential diagnosis of dementia should emphasize potentially treatable disorders that may cause, or exacerbate, dementia. Differential diagnosis is based on the knowledge of the salient features of Alzheimer's disease and a recognition of conditions that can mimic this disease.

Although reversible disorders are uncommon, their importance justifies a thorough evaluation of each patient. Before a diagnosis of Alzheimer's disease can be made other causes of dementia must be ruled out, especially treatable forms of cognitive decline such as cerebrovascular events, nutritional disorders, neoplastic disorders, genetic disorders, depression, chronic drug intoxication, chronic central nervous system infection, infectious processes, thyroid disease including Hashimoto's encephalopathy, toxic conditions, vitamin deficiencies (especially B12 and thiamine), and normal pressure hydrocephalus.

Other degenerative disorders associated with dementia such as fronto-temporal dementia, Picks disease, Parkinson's disease, diffuse Lewy body disease, Creutzfeldt-Jakob disease, and CADASIL may also be confused with Alzheimer's disease. Computerized topography and magnetic resonance imaging studies are valuable for identifying other causes of dementia, such as neoplasms or brain tumors, normal pressure hydrocephalus, and cerebral vascular disease.

Prior to arriving at a diagnosis of Alzheimer's disease, doctors should conduct a diagnostic work-up that either rules out these other disorders or shows that one or more of these conditions may be contributing to the dementia. The history should include the nature of the patient's symptoms, their onset, progression and any interference with work or family life. It should also include questioning of prior conditions, current medications, and psychiatric problems. The physical examination should include an evaluation for major relevant medical conditions, including stroke, cancer, hypertension nutritional disorders, and thyroid disorders. *See* Metabolic causes of dementia.

Diffuse Lewy body dementia (DLBD). Diffuse Lewy body dementia (DLBD) is a neurological condition clinically and pathologically distinct from Alzheimer's disease. DLBD is associated with a more profound and more generalized cholinergic deficit than Alzheimer's disease. In addition to parkinsonian symptoms, patients may experience delusions and visual hallucinations. The disease course tends to be more rapid than what is typically seen in Alzheimer's disease. Many subjects progress from symptom onset to death within 3 to 4 years. In clinical trials, the anticholinergic medication rivastigmine caused a reduction of parkinsonian symptoms and an increase in cognitive function as measured by neuropsychiatric testing. (Fallow, M.D., Martin "Therapeutic Advances for Alzheimer's Disease and Other Dementias." *Medical Education Collaborative*, 2001. http://www.medscape.com/Medscape/Neurology/TreatmentUpdate/1999/tu03/pnt-tu03.html)

Digital Subtraction Angiography (DSA). Digital subtraction angiography (DSA) is a computer-assisted imaging procedure used to visualize the blood vessels within and supplying the brain as well as other vascular abnormalities. The image produced by DSI is enhanced by the elimination of surrounding and interfering structures. DSA is used to diagnose arteriosclerotic disease, vascular lesions and tumors and other space occupying lesions.

Dignity. Caregivers are reminded of the importance of treating Alzheimer's disease patients with respect and dignity. Patients with Alzheimer's disease still have feelings and they often become frustrated as they begin to struggle with everyday tasks. Maintaining dignity is important for Alzheimer's disease patients.

Disability Assessment for Dementia (DAD). The Disability Assessment for Dementia (DAD) is a global assessment tool used for documenting functional deficits such as the ability to bathe, dress and eat. The DAD is useful in predicting the individual disease course and expected disease progression in patients with Alzheimer's disease.

Disorientation. Patients with dementia frequently become disoriented to person, place and time. *See also* Orientation.

Distraction. Distraction refers to divergence of attention, inability to pay attention, or mental derangement. Patients in any of the stages of Alzheimer's disease may experience distraction.

Do not resuscitate (DNR) orders. As part of an advanced directive or a living will, do not resuscitate (DNR) orders are care directives prohibiting caregivers from using life-prolonging measures, such as cardiopulmonary resuscitation (CPR), to patients who would not survive without them. According to the Department of Medicine at West Virginia University in Charleston, only about 15 percent of hospitalized patients survive and are discharged after CPR. And as many as half of CPR patients suffer fractured ribs, fractured sternum, aspiration pneumonia, hemorrhage, or pulmonary edema. Patients are presumed to consent to CPR unless they have a signed DNR order, a living will, or a medical power of attorney indicating that the patient would not wish to receive CPR.

While laws may vary by state, in general, a DNR order may be written by any attending physician who shares primary responsibility for the patient. Informed consent of the patient or his surrogate is required. DNR orders may be written for a child, if a parent and two physicians agree. If the patient is incapacitated and there is no appointed surrogate, a physician may write a DNR order with the concurrence of a second examining physician.

A patient or surrogate may revoke a DNR order by a written or verbal request to any healthcare provider. The healthcare provider must immediately notify the attending physician, who must immediately cancel the order. When patients are transferred to other facilities, such as to a hospital from a nursing home, the DNR order should accompany the patient and will remain in effect until new orders are issued. DNR orders do not apply to patients who experience a cardiac or respiratory arrest as a result of a trauma situation.

A physician may ethically cancel CPR or refuse to initiate it when it is not medically appropriate, will likely not be successful or if it will likely harm the patient with no likely benefit. However, if the patient or family reasonably requests that the physician perform CPR, he may be legally challenged if he declines to initiate or continue CPR.

Docosahexaenoic acid (DHA). Docosahexaenoic acid (DHA) is an omega 3 essential fatty acid. DHA is the primary structural fatty acid in the gray matter of the brain and retina of the eye. DHA is important for mental and visual function. The average diet is low in DHA due to low consumption of red meats, animal organ meats, and eggs. Because of its importance as a neurotrophin, DHA is added to infant formula in England. In the United States, DHA is available as a dietary supplement.

Donepezil hydrochloride. The cholinesterase inhibitor donepizil hydrochloride (Aricept or E2020) is the drug most commonly used in the treatment of Alzheimer's disease. Approved by the FDA in 1996 for treatment of mild to moderate Alzheimer's disease, donepezil inhibits the breakdown of the chemical acetylcholine without causing the changes in liver enzymes seen with tacrine hydrochloride. Aricept is used in the management of patients with mild to moderate symptoms of Alzheimer's disease, although it does not stop or slow down the disease's progression. The usual dosage is 5 mg to 10 mg taken once daily.

Side effects, which include diarrhea, vomiting, muscle cramps, nausea, fatigue, insomnia and anorexia, are generally mild and decline with continued use of the drug. Less common side effects include abnormal dreams, constipation, dizziness, drowsiness, fainting, frequent urination, weight loss headache, joint pain, stiffness or swelling, mental depression and unusual bleeding or bruising.

Rare side effects include black, tarry stools, bloating, bloody or cloudy urine, blurred vision, burning, prickling or tingling sensations, cataracts, chills, clumsiness or unsteadiness, confusion, cough, decreased or painful urination, dryness of mouth, eye irritation, fever, flushing of skin, changes in blood pressure, hives, hot flashes, increased sexual desire, increased heart rate, urinary incontinence, agitation, abnormal crying, aggression, delusions, irritability, nervousness, nasal congestion, pain in chest, upper stomach or throat, shortness of breath, sneezing, and tremor.

Symptoms of overdose include convulsions, increased sweating, increased watering of mouth, increased muscle weakness, low blood pressure, severe nausea and vomiting, slow heartbeat and troubled breathing.

Dopamine. Dopamine is a catecholamine neurotransmitter derived from the amino acid tyrosine. The neurons that produce dopamine are known as dopaminergic neurons. Dopaminergic neurons are primarily located in the compact part of the substantia nigra and in the adjacent ventral tegmental area as well as the hypothalamus, the retina and the olfactory bulb. Dopamine is instrumental for movement and it is also involved in motivation and cognition. Deficiencies of dopamine are part of the underlying pathology in Parkinson's disease.

Doppler imaging. Doppler imaging is a noninvasive diagnostic test in which a Doppler ultrasonic probe is employed. Doppler imaging is used to diagnose abnormalities of carotid blood flow, ulcerative plaques and carotid artery occlusive disease.

Down's Syndrome. Less than 1 percent of all cases of Alzheimer's disease are associated with Down's Syndrome, which is also known as trisomy 21. However, essentially all patients with Down's Syndrome develop the neuropathological hallmarks of Alzheimer's disease (neurofibrillary tangles and plaque deposits) after age 35. If they are carefully tested, more than half of these individuals show clinical evidence of cognitive decline. The incidence of Alzheimer's disease in the Down's Syndrome population is estimated to be three to five times greater than in the general population. It is recommended that individuals with Down's Syndrome be tested at age 30 to provide a baseline assessment of psychological performance. If the tests show deterioration, further tests must be done to rule out diseases that present similar symptoms.

The presumed explanation for this association is the lifelong over-expression of the amyloid precursor protein (APP) gene on chromosome 21 and the resultant overproduction of Aβ-amyloid, particularly Aβ42, in the brains of persons who are trisomic, having an extra copy for this gene. Neuropathological studies have shown that amyloid beta deposition occurs in Down's Syndrome at a very young age (20–30 years). However, research in this area is lacking because of a paucity in obtaining brain tissue from patients with both disorders. The co-existence of Alzheimer's disease is responsible for the sharp decline in survival of Down's Syndrome patients older than 45 years.

Driving. As soon as Alzheimer's disease is diagnosed, the patient should be prevented from driving. A Swedish study reported that over half of elderly people involved in fatal accidents had some degree of neurological impairment. Even in the early stages of Alzheimer's disease patients may lose their way home and experience other problems when driving. Judgmental deficits associated with dementia, visual field defects after stroke or other brain injury or delayed reflexes contribute to increased likelihood of collisions or loss of control.

Drug interactions. Many drugs, both over-the-counter and prescription, are known to interfere with the metabolism of other drugs. It is important to advise the patient's doctor of all medications, even herbs, administered to patients with Alzheimer's disease.

Drug therapy. Drug therapy refers to the use of oral or intravenous medications to help control or alleviate symptoms of disease. *See* Treatment in Alzheimer's disease.

Drug toxicity. Many toxic drug metabolites produce a reversible delirium and rarely dementia. Older persons may be more susceptible than younger persons to drug side effects on cognition. This is due to many factors, including altered drug kinetics and the use of multiple medications. A typical presentation is the rapid worsening of dementia following the administration of a new drug or following the reinstitution of a previous medication that the patient has not taken for some time. Psychotropic medications, including neuroleptics and sedative-hypnotics, and cardiovascular medications, especially antihypertensives, are common offending agents.

DSM IV Diagnostic criteria for Alzheimer's Dementia. The following diagnostic criteria are listed in the Diagnostic and Statistic Manual of Mental Disorders published by the American Psychiatric Association:

A. The development of multiple cognitive deficits manifested by both
   1) memory impairment (impaired ability to learn new information or to recall previously learned information)

2) one (or more) of the following cognitive disturbances: aphasia (language disturbance) or apraxia (impaired ability to carry out motor activities despite intact motor function)
3) amnesia (failure to recognize or identify objects despite intact sensory function)
4) disturbance in executive functioning (such as planning, organizing, sequencing, abstracting)

B. The cognitive deficits in Criteria A1 and A2 each cause significant impairment in social or occupational functioning and represent a significant decline from a previous level of functioning.

C. The course is characterized by gradual onset and continuing cognitive decline.

D. The cognitive deficits in Criteria A1 and A2 are not due to any of the following:
1) other central nervous system conditions that cause progressive deficits in memory and cognition (e.g. cerebrovascular disease, Parkinson's disease, Huntington's disease, subdural hematoma, normal-pressure hydrocephalus, brain tumor)
2) systemic conditions known to cause dementia (e.g., hypothyroidism, vitamin B12 deficiency, niacin deficiency, hypercalcemia (high blood calcium level), neurosyphilis, HIV infection)

E. The deficits do not occur exclusively during the course of a delirium.

F. The disturbance is not better accounted for by another Axis I disorder (e.g., Major Depressive Disorder, Schizophrenia) (Diagnostic and Statistical Manual of Mental Disorders IV TR- Text Revision, Washington, DC: American Psychiatric Press, 2000.)

Dura mater. The dura mater is a thick, dense, strong, inelastic fibrous membrane that encloses the spinal cord and the brain. Adhering firmly to the inner surface of the skull, the dura mater is often described as consisting of an outer layer, the cranial dura mater, and an inner layer known as the meningeal dura. The dura mater extends along each nerve root of the spinal cord and becomes continuous with the connective tissue surrounding each spinal nerve. The inner surface of the dura mater is in contact with the arachnoid mater of the brain. No space exists on either side of the dura under normal circumstances since one side is attached to the skull and the other side adheres to the arachnoid.

Durable power of attorney. A durable power of attorney is a legal document that allows an individual (the principal) an opportunity to authorize an agent to make legal decisions in the event the person is no longer to make decisions for themselves.

Durable power of attorney for health care. A durable power of attorney for health care is a legal document that allows an individual to appoint an agent to make all decisions regarding health care, including choices regarding health care providers, medical treatment and end-of-life decisions.

Dysarthria. Dysarthria occurs in cerebellar disease as a result of loss of voluntary movement affecting the muscles of the larynx. Speech is jerky and the syllables are often separated from one another or slurred. Speech may also be explosive.

Dysdiadochokinesis. Dysdiadochokinesis, a sign of cerebellar disease, is the inability to perform alternating movements regularly and rapidly. On the side where cerebellar lesions occur, the movements are slow, jerky and incomplete.

Dysphasia. Dysphasia is the inability to find the right word or the loss of the power to use or understand language as a result of injury or disease affecting the brain.

Early onset familial Alzheimer's disease (EOFAD). Early onset familial Alzheimer's disease (EOFAD) refers to families in which multiple cases of Alzheimer's disease occur with the mean age of onset occurring before age 65. Age of onset is usually in the 40's or early 50s although onset in the late 20s and early 60s has been reported. EOFAD represents about 5 to 10 percent of all cases of Alzheimer's disease. Prevalence in the general population has been reported to be 41.2 per 100,000 persons. Sixty-one percent of patients with EOFAD have been found to have a positive family history, and 13 percent met stringent criteria for autosomal dominant inheritance occurring in three generations. EOFAD causes symptoms identical to those seen in other forms of Alzheimer's disease. The distinguishing characteristics are age of onset and family history. Only about 120 families worldwide are currently known to carry the mutations for EOFAD.

At least three subtypes of EOFAD have been identified based on the causative genes on chromosomes 14, 21 and 1. Because patients with apparent EOFAD have been reported to have no involvement with these three genes, it is suspected that other genetic associations exist. The most common responsible mutations are in the presenilin 1 gene on chromosome 14. Mutations to this gene account for 30 to 50 percent of all EOFAD.

AD1 represents 10–15 percent of all EOFAD. It is associated with the gene symbol APP on chromosomal locus 21q21.3-q22. The normal gene product is amyloid precursor protein. Three different mutations at codon 717 of the APP gene have been reported.

AD3 represents 20–70 percent of all EOFAD. It is associated with the gene symbol PSEN1 or PS-1 found on chromosomal locus 14q24. The normal gene product is presenilin 1. Typically, PS-1 mutations are found in patients with age of onset between 30 and 50.

AD4 is a rare form of EOFAD. It is associated with the gene symbol PSEN2 or PS-2 on chromosomal locus 1q31-q42. The normal gene product is presenilin 2. Typically, PS-2 mutations are found in patients with age of onset between 50 and 70. Both PS-1 and PS-2 mutations show overproduction of the longer forms of amyloid beta protein and increased serum levels of Aβ42. Testing for the responsible gene mutations is not necessary for diagnosis because the disease occurs so early it identifies itself. However, detecting the presence of an autosomal dominant Alzheimer's disease gene can be informative for other family members. (Bird, M.D., Thomas University of Washington Medical Center, Seattle, 1996. *Alzheimer Overview,* July 2000 revision, National Institutes of Health.)

Echoencephalography (ECHO) scan. An echoencephalogram (ECHO) is a simple diagnostic test that uses pulsating ultrasonic waves to indicate deviation of the midline structures of the brain. A probe with a transducer and ultrasonic beam is placed over the midaxis, which is on the temporal bones of the skull. The bones of the skull act as reflectors, helping project images of the spaces between the ventricles. If the ECHO shifts because of an abnormal focus, this suggests a space-occupying lesion. ECHO scans have largely been replaced by computed axial tomography (CAT) scans.

Echolalia. Echolalia is characterized by repetition of anything spoken to the person, as if echoing the person who is speaking to them. Echolalia is commonly seen in Pick's disease.

Eden alternative. The Eden alternative refers to a concept used in nursing homes, which emphasizes the placement of pets, plants, and other homelike amenities in patient rooms to help patients adapt and not feel displaced.

Efferent nerve fibers. Efferent nerve fibers carry nerve impulses away from the nervous system. Efferent fibers transmit impulses to muscles and glands.

Efficacy of treatment. Efficacy of treatment refers to the power of a particular treatment to produce its intended effects.

EGb 761. EGb 761 is an extract of the herb *Ginkgo biloba* used in Europe to alleviate symptoms of cognitive dysfunction. In clinical trials, Egb 761 has been proven to be safe and appears capable of stabilizing, and, in a substantial number of cases, improving the cognitive performance and the social functioning of patients with dementia for 6 months to 1 year. These changes were measured by the ADAS-Cog. While modest, these changes were of sufficient magnitude to be recognized by the caregivers of patients who participated in the studies. (Le Bars, P. et al. "A placebo-controlled, double-blind, randomized trial of an extract of Ginkgo biloba for dementia. North American Egb Study Group." *JAMA*, Oct. 1997: 278 (3),70)

Eldepryl *see* Selegiline

Elder Books. Elder Books, in Forest Knolls, California, is a publishing company dedicated to publishing practical hands-on guidebooks for family and professional caregivers of persons with Alzheimer's disease. Elder Books also offers a workshop, Activities in Action, designed to help caregivers enhance quality of life for Alzheimer's patients through the use of simple, stimulating activities. http://www.elderbooks.com.

Elder law attorneys. Elder law attorneys are lawyers who specialize in laws pertaining to the elderly and the protection of their assets. The Alzheimer's Association provides guidance in finding elder law attorneys in your area.

Eldercare Locator. The Eldercare Locator division of the Administration on Aging provides help locating needed resources for the elderly. (800) 677-1116 Monday to Friday, 9 A.M. to 8 P.M., Eastern Standard Time.

Electroencephalogram (EEG). An electroencephalogram (EEG) is a diagnostic technique used to measure changes in brain wave activity. While not as specific as MRI for diagnosing Alzheimer's disease, EEG is helpful in ruling out other causes of dementia. The EEGs of patients with severe dementia may reveal significant abnormalities whereas mild cases of dementia show only slight abnormalities. Generally, in the later stages of Alzheimer's disease, there is progressive slowing of the EEG tracing with decreased alpha and beta activity although there is increased activity of the delta and theta waves. Some researchers also report that Alzheimer's patients exhibit dominant occipital alpha wave activity, increases of theta power, and decreased EEG coherence. The type of EEG modality may also affect the results. Computerized quantitative EEG appears to be more sensitive than traditional EEG tracing procedures that are manually calculated.

According to current theory, a normal EEG pattern in an individual with severe dementia is likely to be indicative of Alzheimer's disease since most other conditions that result in dementia, including delirium, show abnormal EEG patterns even when there are only mild clinical symptoms. The EEG pattern is also useful in ruling out Creutzfeldt-Jakob disease and epilepsy because they both cause characteristic changes easily seen on an EEG. In Huntington's disease, there is low-amplitude background activity. In cerebrovascular dementia, 75 percent of individuals have been found to have focal abnormalities, including lateralized slow, sharp, or spike waves, whereas in frontal lobe dementia, the EEG is generally normal.

Encephalitis. Encephalitis is a condition of brain inflammation. Encephalitis may be caused by bacterial or viral infections, toxins or autoimmunity.

Encephalopathy. Encephalopathy is a condition marked by brain inflammation resulting from exposure to environmental substances including infectious agents and organic solvents. Toxic encephalopathy may cause transient symptoms such as the reversible symptoms of acute ethyl alcohol (ethanol) poisoning or permanent residual cognitive impairment which occurs after an overwhelming acute exposure capable of causing coma or death. Long-term toxin exposure resulting in encephalopathy differs from Alzheimer's disease in that there is an absence of naming problems (anomia) and lack of progression to dementia.

End of life care. End of life care refers to the final services of care provided by physicians, nursing homes, hospices, hospitals and other care providers. These providers are required to follow individual state guidelines and regulations defined by legislative enactments, case law and organizational policies and protocols. Adherence to these guidelines is monitored through risk managers and legal counsel.

Specifically, policies for end of life care focus on advance care planning directives such as health care proxies, do-not-resuscitate orders and living wills. Ethically, patients or their legal representatives have a right to ask for effective pain relief and palliative care, and legally, they have a right to choose or refuse treatment with full knowledge of the benefits or risks.

End of life decisions *see* Advance directives

Endoplasmin-reticulum associated binding protein (ERAB). Endoplasmin-reticulum associated binding protein (ERAB) is a protein present in the areas of the brain affected by Alzheimer's disease. ERAB appears to combine with beta amyloid, which in turn attracts new beta amyloid from outside the cells. High concentrations of ERAB are also suspected of enhancing the nerve-destructive power of beta amyloid.

Entorhinal cortex. The entorhinal region of the cerebral cortex links the hippocampus to the rest of the brain. In Alzheimer's disease, the entorhinal cortex is the first brain structure to suffer neuronal damage. Damage in this region is evident long before an individual develops perceptible memory loss. As the damage eventually spreads to the hippocampus, the memory deficit becomes more pronounced.

Environmental factors. Environmental factors are causes of disease that originate outside of the body. External factors include contaminated food, chemical toxins, head injuries, atmospheric particles and pollutants, infectious agents, and stress.

For years scientists have suspected that the environment plays a role in neurodegenerative diseases, including Alzheimer's disease. The fact that identical twins may not both develop Alzheimer's disease is proof that more than genes play a role. Scientists are currently studying the environmental toxins that are related to the chronic death of neurons, the cells that serve as information transmitters and processors in the brain.

According to current theory, the effects of environmental agents may take years to show up. This latent period makes establishing causal relationships difficult. The body's nervous system also has an amazing ability to heal. After a stroke, for example, surviving neurons sprout and establish new connections in an effort to keep the brain in balance. With age, however, this compensatory mechanism declines and the effects of environmental agents become more severe.

In addition, the association between the HLA 2 allele and early onset Alzheimer's disease suggests immune system involvement. This is further supported by the presence of immune system chemicals known as cytokines in the brains of patients with Alzheimer's disease. The immune system initiates an immune response and produces these chemicals in response to environmental factors. Furthermore, several studies show a decreased prevalence of Alzheimer's disease among patients taking anti-inflammatory drugs on a long term-basis.

Although no environmental factors responsible for the development of Alzheimer's disease have been convincingly identified, certain environmental factors are associated with disease development. These factors include low education, head trauma, smoking, arterial disease, diabetes and menopause. Results from the Nun study also indicate that a number of environmental factors, including emotional distress, low verbal skills, low anti-oxidant levels, abnormal zinc metabolism, elevated homocysteine levels and high copper levels may also contribute to the development of Alzheimer's disease. And some, but not all, studies on people exposed to intense electromagnetic fields have reported a higher incidence of Alzheimer's disease. Some researchers believe that magnetic fields may interfere with the concentration of calcium inside cells or cause increased production of beta amyloid.

Gary Oberg, M.D., past president of the American Academy of Environmental Medicine, warns that "Toxins such as chemicals in food and tap water, carbon monoxide, dies, fumes, solvents, aerosol sprays, and industrial chemicals can cause symptoms of brain dysfunction which may lead to an inaccurate diagnosis of Alzheimer's disease or senile dementia." (Oberg, M.D., Gary "Causes of Alzheimer's Disease and Other Forms of Senile Dementia." http://www.Alternative Medicine.com) *See also* Nun's study.

Enzymes. Enzymes are bodily proteins that function to catalyze specific bodily processes.

Ependyma. Ependyma are neuroglial cells that line the cavities of the brain and the central canal of the spinal cord. Ependyma form a single layer of cells with microvilla and hair-like protrusions known as cilia which aid in the movement of cerebrospinal fluid.

Ependymomas. Ependymomas are brain tumors that originate in the ependymal cells lining the fourth ventricle of the brain. Ependymomas may invade the cerebellum and produce the symptoms and signs of cerebellar deficiency. Tumors in this region may also compress the vital nuclear centers situated beneath the floor of the ventricle, causing cardiac (heart) irregularities.

Epidemiology. Epidemiology refers to the incidence of disease in different populations. Worldwide, approximately twenty million people are suffering from Alzheimer's disease, four million of these people residing in the United States alone. As the lifespan increases, the number is predicted to rise, multiplying threefold by the year 2050.

Prevalence estimates suggest that Alzheimer's disease affects about 10 percent of persons over the age of 65, making it one of the most common chronic diseases in older persons. Other than age, there are no well-documented risk factors for Alzheimer's disease. Persons with lower educational attainment may be at greater risk, as they are more susceptible to many other common chronic diseases.

Nearly all patients who inherit Down's Syndrome develop Alzheimer's disease if they live into their 40s. Women under the age of 35, but not older mothers, who give birth to children with Down's Syndrome are also at much higher risk for developing Alzheimer's disease.

Alzheimer's disease is rare in West Africa, but African-Americans have four times the risk as white Americans. Hispanics are twice as likely to develop Alzheimer's disease than whites. Alzheimer's disease occurs less in the Native American Crees and Cherokees and in Asians than in the general American population. While Alzheimer's disease occurs less often in Japan, a study of Japanese men indicated that their risk is increased if they move to America.

Researchers at the University of Pittsburgh also report that certain villages in rural India boast the lowest reported prevalence of Alzheimer's disease in the world. This population is also reported to have a low frequency of the apolipoprotein E4 gene variant. Other proposed causes for the low rates of Alzheimer's disease in India and Nigeria include better vascular health, indicated by lower blood pressure, cholesterol and body weight. ("What is Alzheimer's Disease? An overview of Alzheimer's Disease and its causes." Well Connected, 1999, Nidus Information Services reprinted in WebMD Health: http://my.webmd.com/content/article/1680.50324)

Eptastigmine (MF-201). Eptastigmine (MF-201) is a long-acting cholinesterase inhibitor currently being evaluated for use as a therapeutic agent in Alzheimer's disease.

Ergoloid mesylate (Hydergine). Ergoloid mesylate (Hydergine) is one of the first drugs approved by the Food and Drug Administration (FDA) for use in treating dementia. Although Hydergine was once popular in treating Alzheimer's disease because it increases oxygen flow to the brain, it has fallen out of favor. Studies have been conflicting on its benefits.

Estrogen. Animal models have shown that chronic estrogen deficiency affects behavior and cognitive function. This deficiency has been associated with decreased cholinergic activity and is improved with estrogen replacement. Estrogen is thought to modulate multiple neurotransmitters within the brain, increasing the survival of cholinergic neurons and increasing levels of choline acetyltransferase. Estrogen has also been shown to stimulate neurite growth and synapse formation and improve regional blood flow in the brain. Estrogen may also play a role in modulating gene expression.

Estrogen replacement therapy. At least ten controlled trials conducted between 1952 and 2000 have assessed estrogen's role on cognitive function. Most trials did not control for related variables such as depression and education. Eight studies showed that estrogen improved cognitive function in at least one test parameter. In the first long-term study of its kind, researchers at the NIA have found that estrogen replacement therapy improves blood flow to the brain. Overall, the women in the study using estrogen scored higher on memory tests. However, the largest published trials (Polo-Canola, 1998 and Aleve's de Mores, 2001) did not show improvement in any cognitive parameter studied. Although more trials are in progress, several epidemiological studies suggest that the use of estrogen in post-menopausal women may delay the onset or risk of Alzheimer's disease. (Green, Robert M.D. "Is the Concept of a Neuroprotective Drug Viable for Dementia?" *Medscape*, September 9, 2001. "Study Suggests ERT Stimulates Blood Flow to Key Memory Centers in the Brain," NIA News, June 27, 2000)

Ethics committees. Most hospitals and nursing home facilities have ethics committees composed of physicians, social workers and nurses to determine if the care and treatment of a particular patient is being administered in accordance with ethical guidelines.

Ethnicity. Ethnicity refers to the risk of developing disease for different ethnic groups. *See* Epidemiology

Etiology of Alzheimer's disease. The etiology, or causes, of Alzheimer's disease include genetic and environmental factors. Like heart disease, Alzheimer's disease is related to a number of different causes. For instance, the genes associated with early-onset Alzheimer's disease cause changes that lead to the formation of beta amyloid protein plaque deposits in the brain. However, it is clear that genes in and of themselves are not enough to cause most instances of Alzheimer's disease. A number or researchers, for example, believe that elevated cholesterol levels contribute to both heart disease and Alzheimer's disease. Researchers at New York University's Nathan Kline Institute have shown how mice on high-fat diets have an increased rate of beta amyloid production in their brains. Other environmental causes include head injuries and heavy metals.

Excitation of nerve cells. When nerve cells are excited or stimulated by electrical, mechanical or chemical means, the cell membrane changes, allowing more sodium ions to enter or diffuse into the cell cytoplasm. This caused the cell membrane to become depolarized, resulting in a brief action potential which allows potassium ions rather than sodium ions to enter the cell. This action potential is conducted along neurites as nerve impulses. Nerve impulses are followed by brief non-excitable states known as refractory periods. The greater the excitatory stimulus, the stronger the impulse.

Excitotoxicity. Excitotoxicity refers to the toxic over-activation of glutamate receptors in neurons in the brain. Excitotoxicity is an important mechanism leading to neuronal cell death in many disease states, including Alzheimer's disease. There is some evidence that glial cells, particularly oligodendrocytes, are also damaged by excitotoxins.

Excitotoxins. Excitotoxins are chemical neurotransmitters, such as glutamate, that stimulate neurons. Excitotoxins primarily work by opening calcium channels on certain types of receptors. When excitotoxins are introduced at high concentrations or for extended periods of time, excess calcium enters the cells. This initiates a cascade of cell destruction mediated by free radical production and the release of an enzyme known as phospholipase C. This enzyme breaks down some of the fatty acids that make up the protective cell membrane. This releases an amino acid called arachidonic acid, which further injures the cells and causes the production of two other enzymes, lipoxygenase and cyclo-oxygenase. Some of the chemical reactions produced by these processes result in rapid cell death.

Two excitotoxins that have been linked to the development of Alzheimer's disease include monosodium glutamate and aspartame. According to Dr. Russell Blaylock, Alzheimer's disease is a classic case of excitotoxin damage. One reason is that beta amyloid protein makes glutamate receptors more receptive to the effects of excitotoxin-induced neuronal cell death. (Blaylock, Russell L. M.D. *Excitotoxins: The Taste That Kills*. Sante Fe, NM: Health Press, 1994. 133–190.)

Exelon *see* Rivastigmine

Exercise. Several studies conducted by the Society for Neuroscience indicate that exercise benefits the brain, particularly the hippocampus. In one study, adult mice with access to running wheels doubled the number of new brain cells produced in the hippocampus. In another study, voluntary physical activity alone was enough to cause neuronal growth, which was evidenced by improved performance on memory and learning tasks. Overall, the studies suggest that an active lifestyle helps maintain brain function and that specialized exercise regimens may help repair damaged or aged brains.

Exocytosis. Exocytosis refers to the process in which the neurotransmitter necessary for nerve impulses is discharged in to the synaptic cleft.

Falx cerebelli. The falx cerebelli of the brain is a small triangular process of dura mater, received into the posterior cerebellar notch. Its base is attached, above, to the under and back part of the tentorium.

Falx cerebri. The falx cerebri is a sickle-shaped fold of the dura mater situated in the midline between the two cerebral hemispheres. The falx cerebri is a strong, arched process which descends vertically in the longitudinal fissure between the cerebral hemispheres. It is narrow in front, where it is attached to the crista galli of the ethmoide, and broad behind, where it is connected with the upper surface of the tentorium cerebelli. Its upper margin is convex, and attached to the bioregion of the inner surface of the skull it contains the superior sagittal sinus. Its lower margin is free and concave, and contains the inferior sagittal sinus. The falx cerebri helps to limit movement of the brain within the skull.

Familial Alzheimer's disease (FAD). Approximately 4–8 percent of all cases of Alzheimer's disease are familial. Although one third of people with Alzheimer's disease have an affected relative, only a small percent of these people have familial Alzheimer's disease (FAD). Symptoms of FAD are identical to those seen in sporadic cases. However, patients with FAD have a family history or a genetic makeup consistent with FAD, which is entirely inherited. FAD may occur as early-onset or late-onset varieties. *See* Early-onset familial Alzheimer's disease and Late-onset familial Alzheimer's disease. (Munoz, David. "Causes of Alzheimer's Disease." *Canadian Medical Association Journal*; 2000 162; 65–72.)

Familial fatal insomnia. Familial fatal insomnia is a prion disease that starts with protracted insomnia which progresses to dementia, with sufferers unable to differentiate reality from dreams. Death typically occurs between seven and 15 months after the onset of symptoms.

Feeding problems. Patients in the early stages of dementia may no longer be able to choose nutritional food. It's important to ensure that patients living alone have nutrient rich meals available. In the later stages of dementia, patients may lose interest in eating and become difficult to feed, often refusing or spitting out food. While it is important to encourage dementia patients to maintain skills such as feeding themselves, this may necessitate having someone sit with them and ensure that they are eating. On occasion patients may have to be spoon-fed.

Studies indicate that tube feedings do not prolong life and frequently cause discomfort and medical complications. Alternatives to tube feeding include changing the consistency of food to pureed or liquid forms, adding thickening agents if aspiration is a problem, employing favorite foods and abandoning dietary restrictions that may no longer be necessary.

Financial burden. The financial burden of Alzheimer's disease is impressive. In 1991, the estimated cost of caring for an individual with Alzheimer's disease was $47,000 annually. The combined direct and indirect cost including medical care, loss of productivity, resource loss and family care for all patients with Alzheimer's disease in the United Stats are estimated at $100 billion per year. As the population ages, the number of people with Alzheimer's is expected to increase dramatically.

Financial capacity. Financial capacity is significantly impaired in the earliest stages of Alzheimer's disease. Patients with mild Alzheimer's disease demonstrate deficits in more complex financial decisions and show impairment in most financial activities. Patients with moderate Alzheimer's disease show severe impairment in all financial abilities and activities. Researchers at the Department of Neurology at the University of Alabama at Birmingham have developed a Financial Capacity Instrument to be used as a tool for assessing domain-level financial activities and task-specific financial abilities in patients with dementia. It is important that patients with Alzheimer's disease be relieved of managing financial activities when they are no longer capable of doing so.

Financing long-term care. Long-term care, whether it is provided by a nursing home or a home care agency, may be paid for through personal funds, private insurance, public assistance or a combination of these. Typically, long-term nursing home residents pay for the first months or years of care with their personal funds or with long-term care insurance. When these funds are depleted, the Medicaid program pays for life-time nursing home care. For patients requiring short nursing home care, Medicare and other insurance programs usually cover the costs. For patients younger than 65, Social Security may cover the first two years of care and then Medicaid kicks in. Medicare does not typically pay for nursing home care, other than for temporary care following hospitalization.

Folic acid deficiency. Folic acid or folate is a B vitamin. Folic acid deficiencies can lead to deficiencies of vitamin B 12, causing symptoms of dementia. While folate can correct vitamin B 12 deficiencies in blood levels, the changes in the brain are not necessarily corrected. For this reason folic acid and vitamin B 12 should be taken together. Furthermore, high amounts of folate in the absence of adequate B12 can provoke or worsen neurological conditions.

A recent long-range Swedish study (Kungsholmen Project) of persons 75 years old and older, which was published in the May 8, 2001, issue of *Neurology*, suggests that more than half of those in this age group have low levels of vitamin B12 and folic acid, and that low levels of either of these two vitamins are related to an increased risk of developing Alzheimer's disease.

Food and Drug Administration (FDA). The Food and Drug Administration (FDA) is the department of the federal government that conducts research and develops standards on the composition, quality and safety of drugs, cosmetics, foods, and food additives. The FDA is responsible for evaluating and regulating clinical trials on the experimental drugs and biological products intended for therapies in Alzheimer's disease.

Forebrain *see* prosencephalon

Fourth ventricle. The fourth ventricle, situated in the posterior cranial fossa, refers to the cavity of the hindbrain. Lined with ependymal cells, the fourth ventricle houses portions of the choroid plexus, and consequently, is filled with cerebrospinal fluid.

Free radicals. Free radicals are unstable chemical molecules that bind to other molecules in a process known as oxidation. Oxidation is a normal bodily process that enables us to utilize energy from food. Oxidation generates free radicals naturally. Free radicals are highly reactive compounds that take electrons from other molecules in an effort to stabilize themselves. In doing so, they produce more free radicals. Brain cells of Alzheimer's disease patients are suspected of being more susceptible to the effects of oxidative stress and subsequent cell death related to increased monoamine oxidase (MAO) activity.

When the body experiences prolonged exposure to free radicals due to oxidative stress, it can no longer neutralize them. Free radicals cause damage by affecting DNA and triggering other harmful processes. Free radicals play a role in many serious disorders including coronary artery disease and cancer. Many researchers think that free radicals released when beta amyloid breaks into protein contribute to the development of Alzheimer's disease. In response to oxidation the immune system initiates an inflammatory response. During this process, harmful chemical molecules and chemicals are released. In particular cyclooxygenase is released, which increases levels of the excitotoxin glutamate.

Neurons, the nervous system cells that make up the bulk of brain tissue, are extremely sensitive to attacks by destructive free radicals. Furthermore, lesions typically seen in the brains of Alzheimer's disease patients are associated with attacks by free radicals with consequences including damage to DNA, protein oxidation, lipid peroxidation, advanced glycosylation end products, and metal accumulation (iron, copper, zinc and aluminum). These metals have catalytic activity that perpetuate the production of free radicals.

Furthermore, beta amyloid is aggregated and produces more free radicals when it is in the presence of free radicals. Beta amyloid toxicity is eliminated by free radical scavengers known as antioxidants. Also, apoplipoprotein E is subject to attack by free radicals, and the resulting peroxidation is associated with Alzheimer's disease. Antioxidants are substance such as vitamin E that neutralize free radicals.

Friends Life Care at Home. Based in Blue Bell, Pennsylvania, Friends Life Care at Home provides the lifetime care services of a continuing care community within the person's own home. Financing this care can be arranged through an insurance plan. Members sign up while they are still healthy and are guaranteed future care, including subsidized meals delivered to their door, daily visits by a registered nurse if needed, and home health care, including assistance with bathing, provided by a nurse's aide. Because care is provided at home, the fees are much less than those of other facilities. For its most comprehensive plan, the initial fee is $21,150, and there is a $350 monthly payment. Additional services are planned in the Maryland and Washington, D.C., areas.

Frontal cortex. The frontal area of the cortex is the area where memories are permanently stored after they are processed in the hippocampus. Individuals with Alzheimer's disease as well as the normal elderly experience age-related withering of this region. This explains why elderly people who do not have Alzheimer's disease may also show signs of short-term memory loss.

Frontal lobe. The frontal lobe refers to the front or central area of each cerebral hemisphere. The frontal lobe is nearly completely devoid of granular layers and is characterized by the prominence of its pyramidal nerve cells.

The frontal lobe may be divided into front (anterior) and back (posterior) sections with their own specialized functions. The posterior region, known as the motor area, primary motor, area or Brodmann's area, produces isolated movements in the opposite side of the body when stimulated. The primary auditory area, the taste area and the sensory speech area of Wernicke can be found within the motor regions of the frontal lobe.

Frontotemporal lobe dementia (FTD). Frontotemporal lobe dementia (FTD) is a disorder accounting for nearly 20 percent of all cases of dementia. Like Alzheimer's disease, FTD is also associated with deposits of tau protein, and some cases of frontotemporal dementia are familial. One of the genes associated with frontotemporal dementia lies on chromosome 17, home of the tau gene. In recent years, twenty different mutations to these gene have been described. Semantic dementia is a rare form of FTD.

Errors in the tau gene may interfere with the way tau protein binds to the tubular backbone of cells or they may cause an imbalance in the types of tau protein produced. Both of these situations would cause a buildup of excess free tau, the protein that accumulates in the neurofibrillary tangles seen in both frontotemporal dementia and Alzheimer's disease. Twenty-five percent of patients with FTD are reported to have a pathologic accumulation of hyperphosphorylated protein in their brain cells.

Another similarity to Alzheimer's disease is the presence of reactive glial cells. However, the pattern in frontotemporal lobe dementia is different as is the neuronal outcome. Unlike the brain in Alzheimer's disease, the brain in frontotemporal dementia is characterized by altered apoptosis and cell death in astrocytes and possibly microglia.

Most cases of FTD are diagnosed in individuals in their 40s through 60s. Early symptoms in FTD are changes in personality and behavior. Memory is generally unaffected in the early stages of the diseases. Although it is difficult to diagnose FTD, it is important to differentiate it from Alzheimer's disease because cholinesterase inhibitors do not help in FTD and may make symptoms worse. The Alzheimer's Association also sponsors local FTD support groups in some areas.

Functional loss. Functional loss in Alzheimer's disease can be assessed by a number of evaluation tools such as the Instrumental Activities of Daily Living (IADL). A characteristic pattern of progressive functional losses has been described as existing at 16 successive levels in Alzheimer's disease. Clinicians can use knowledge of these levels to help diagnose and stage Alzheimer's disease, identify any excess functional disabilities that may be adding to morbidity but which may be capable of being corrected, help in tracking the disease course in Alzheimer's disease.

Gait alterations. Gait refers to a person's manner of walking. Normally, gait or movement is performed voluntarily with precision and economy of effort. In disorders affecting the cerebellum, alteration of gait may occur. The head is often rotated and flexed and the shoulder on the side of the lesion is lower than that of the normal side. The patient assumes a wide base when standing and appears stiff-legged to compensate for the loss of muscle tone. When walking, the individual may lurch and stagger toward the affected side. In later stages of Alzheimer's disease, patients often have "reduced gait," meaning that their ability to lift their feet as they walk has diminished. Gait evaluation is part of the neurological examination.

Galantamine hydrobromide (Reminyl). Galantamine hydrobromide (Reminyl) is an acetylcholinesterase inhibitor approved for use in Alzheimer's disease. Galantamine has a dual mode of action in that it is able to modulate the nicotinic receptor and strengthen the ability of some neurons to receive chemical message. Galantamine is effective for treating patients with Alzheimer's disease who also have cerebrovascular disease or probable vascular disease. Galantamine is reported to improve all major cognitive and non-cognitive measures in Alzheimer's disease as well as cerebrovascular disease, including vascular dementia. According to Dr. Gary Small, a medical advisor to Jansen Pharmaceuticals, the developer of galantamine, clinical trials lasting one year showed that Reminyl can delay the emergence of debilitating behavioral disturbances associated with Alzheimer's disease, including agitation, aggression, delusions, hallucinations, and the lack of inhibition for at least five months.(Downs, Peter. "New Alzheimer's Drug: Is It Any Better Than the Others?" CBS Health Watch, July 23, 2001. http://cbshealthwatch.netscape.com/cx/viewarticle/401765.)

Gamma-aminobutyric acid (GABA). Gamma-aminobutyric acid is an amino acid that acts as a neurotransmitter. GABA is the major transmitter for brief, point-to-point, inhibitory synaptic events in the central nervous system.

Gamma secretase. Gamma secretase is an enzyme directly responsible for the increased production of beta amyloid protein found in the brain of patients with Alzheimer's disease. The genes presenilin 1 and presenilin 2 exert tight control over gamma secretase. Individuals with early onset Alzheimer's disease frequently have mutations to these genes, and these mutations are associated with increased production of beta amyloid protein by gamma secretase and an enhanced penchant for making the more toxic version of beta amyloid protein. One aim of therapy, including vaccine therapy, is the inhibition of gamma secretase.

Gamma secretase inhibitors. Gamma secretase inhibitors are substances that inhibit gamma secretase, an enzyme that contributes to the development of beta amyloid protein. Researchers at the Washington University School of Medicine have discovered that these compounds also prevent certain immune system cells from being produced. These findings were presented in the June 19, 2001, issue of the *Proceedings of the National Academy of Sciences*. Gamma secretase inhibitors are currently being studied for their role as a therapeutic agent in Alzheimer's disease. Because gamma secretase is necessary for many bodily functions including cell production, it may have side effects that prohibit its use.

Ganglia. Ganglia are fusiform swellings of nerve fibers. Each ganglion is surrounded by a layer of connective tissue that is continuous with the cell body.

Genes. Genes are the basic units of heredity. Genes are sections of DNA coding for a particular trait.

Genes in Alzheimer's disease. Scientists have identified four genetic mutations associated with Alzheimer's disease. Analysis of the biochemical effects of these genes indicates that they all influence the breakdown of β-amyloid precursor protein (APP), causing the accumulation of beta amyloid protein deposits. The first three genes listed are only seen in the early-onset varieties of Alzheimer's disease. These mutations enhance the proteolytic processing of β-APP, causing overproduction and accumulation of the neurotoxic derivative, amyloid- β-peptide.

1) the β-amyloid precursor protein (APP) gene on chromosome 21; mutations in this gene account for less than 1 percent of Alzheimer's disease; onset of symptoms in people with this gene occurs between ages 45 to 65. Several point mutations in this gene are sufficient to cause early-onset autosomal dominant familial Alzheimer's disease. Some mutations increase the production of β-amyloid, while others favor the formation of long (42 amino acid) forms of β-amyloid, which aggregate more readily than the shorter (40 amino acid) forms.
2) the presenilin-1 gene on chromosome 14; accounts for approximately 4 percent of cases; onset ranges from age 28 to 50.
3) the presenilin-2 gene on chromosome 1; accounts for about 1 percent of cases; onset in the late 40s and 50s.
4) the APOE4 gene on chromosome 19; unlike the other three genes which occur only in early onset Alzheimer's disease, the APOE4 gene occurs in both early onset and late onset Alzheimer's disease. The APOE4 gene is known to reduce the clearance of amyloid beta protein, resulting in an accumulation of this neurotoxin protein. The APOE 4 gene is not as damaging as the early onset mutations. Many people who inherit this gene will never develop the disease even in their 90s. There may be other genes not yet identified that cause an increased risk of developing Alzheimer's disease, and there may be other genes that offer protection against disease development.

Genetic counseling. Genetic counseling refers to the process of providing individuals and families with information on the nature, inheritance and implications of genetic disorders to help them make informed medical and personal decisions.

First-degree relatives of individuals with sporadic Alzheimer's disease have about a 20 percent lifetime risk of developing Alzheimer's disease. Presumably, when several family members have Alzheimer's disease, the risk is further increased. Early-onset familial Alzheimer's disease is inherited in an autosomal dominant manner. Offspring of individuals with the early-onset form of the disease have a 50 percent chance of inheriting this gene, making their risk of developing early-onset Alzheimer's disease 50 percent.

Genetic mapping. Genetic mapping refers to a study of all of the genes in the human body and their properties.

Genetic mutations. Genetic mutations are changes occurring in the DNA of genes. Three specific genetic mutations have been discovered in patients with Alzheimer's disease. These are mutations in the amyloid precursor protein gene, influencing how it is spliced, and two mutations termed presenilin 1 (PS1) and presenilin 2 (PS2). Although these mutations are clearly associated with Alzheimer's disease, they occur very infrequently.

Another form of genetic mutation that is considered an early predisposing factor for Alzheimer's disease is trisomy of the 21st chromosome, which results in Down's Syndrome. Although the relationship between Alzheimer's disease and Down's Syndrome is not clearly understood, it is known that amyloid precursor protein is encoded in the long arm of chromosome 21.

Genetic testing. Currently, outside of research trials, tests are only available for presenilin-1, a gene associated with early-onset Alzheimer's disease. A significant association with the e4 allele of apolipoprotein E, a polymorphism associated with both early-onset and late-onset Alzheimer's disease, supports the diagnosis of Alzheimer's disease in patients with dementia, but this test in neither fully specific nor sensitive.

Results of testing at-risk asymptomatic (having no clinical symptoms) adults can only be interpreted after an affected family member's disease-causing mutation has been identified. Testing of asymptomatic at-risk individuals with equivocal symptoms is predictive rather than diagnostic testing. The National Society of Genetic Counselors does not recommend testing children at risk for adult onset disorders in the absence of symptoms because it removes their choice in knowing this, raises the possibility of stigmatization within the family and other social settings, and could have serious educational or career implications.

Several recent studies indicate that genetic testing for Apolipoprotein E may be appropriate for patients suspected of having Alzheimer's disease because patients with the APOE4 allele may respond better to certain therapies, such as protease inhibitors.

Genetics of Alzheimer's disease. Most cases of Alzheimer's disease are caused by a complex interaction of genes that confer susceptibility in combination with environmental factors, including infections and head injuries. Alzheimer's disease occurring in patients younger than 60 is associated with three distinct gene mutations. A common polymorphism in another gene, the apolipoprotein E gene, confers susceptibility in patients with both early-onset and late-onset Alzheimer's disease. Most incidences of Alzheimer's disease are late-onset, occurring in patients older than 60. In older patients, genes appear to cause susceptibility to Alzheimer's disease, but one can have the associated gene without ever developing Alzheimer's disease. *See* Genes in Alzheimer's disease for a list of the genes associated with Alzheimer's disease.

Geriatric Depression Scale. The Geriatric Depression Scale is a neuropsychiatric evaluation tool developed by Yesavage in 1983. This tool is primarily used to diagnose depression in the elderly.

Gerontology. Gerontology is the scientific field dealing with the study of the aging population and their special problems.

Gerstmann-Straussler-Scheinker Disease. Gerstmann-Straussler-Scheinker disease or syndrome is a condition caused by transmissible spongiform encephalopathies or prions. This disease characteristically causes a lack of muscle coordination and a destruction of brain tissue.

Ginkgo biloba. Ginkgo biloba is a herb used for a wide variety of conditions associated with aging, including memory loss and poor circulation. For centuries, extracts from the leaves of the ginkgo biloba tree have been used in Chinese herbal medicine for a variety of medical conditions including dizziness, inflammation, memory impairment and reduced blood flow to the brain. Because of its antioxidant properties, ginkgo biloba is reported to prevent damage caused by free radicals.

Having properties of a blood thinner or anticoagulant, gingko is thought to improve blood flow to the brain by dilating blood vessels. A daily dose of 240 milligrams of a standardized gingko biloba extract is approved for use in Alzheimer's disease in Germany. The two primary ingredients in ginkgo include glycosides and terpenes. Studies indicate that ginkgo biloba may slightly improve the memory of persons with Alzheimer's disease, although it's unclear if the improvement is significant.

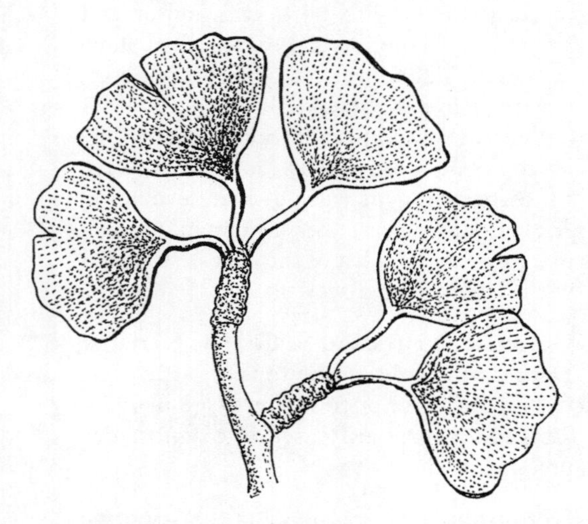

Ginkgo biloba leaves (illustration by Marvin G. Miller).

Side effects include allergic skin reactions and headaches. In large doses exceeding 240 milligrams daily, ginkgo may cause diarrhea, irritability and restlessness. Because of its anticoagulant properties, ginkgo should not be taken in conjunction with anticoagulant medications, such as coumadin, and it should not be used by individuals taking aspirin, vitamin E or other non-steroidal anti-inflammatory drugs. Ginkgo is also reported to be potentially harmful if taken with tricyclic antidepressant medications, including amitriptyline (Elavil).

Extracts of ginkgo biloba leaf, particularly Egb 761, have also been found to have a profound inhibitory influence on monoamine oxidase-B. Ginkgo biloba is also known to be involved in the reduction of inflammation, reduction of oxidative stress, membrane protection, and neuro-transmission modulation. In a study published in the *Journal of the American Medical Association*, conducted by Le Bars and co-workers, 202 subjects were given ginkgo biloba and evaluated for 52 weeks. In the treatment group, a substantial number of patients either stabilized or demonstrated improvement in cognitive performance as measured by psychometric testing.

The National Institute on Aging and the Office of Alternative Medicine, both at the National Institutes of Health, are currently funding studies on ginkgo biloba involving 3,000 individuals. To date, all trials have shown positive results. (Duke, James A. 1997, *The Green Pharmacy*. [Emmaus, PA:] Rodale Press 1997. Perlmutter, David. "Functional Therapeutics in Neurodegenerative Disease," Physicians Committee for Responsible Medicine website: http://www.pcrm.org/health/Preventive_Medicine/alzheimers.html.) *Also see* Egb 761.

Glial cells. The primary cells of the brain are neurons and glial cells (glia). There are approximately 100 billion neurons in the human brain and several times that many glial cells. Glial (from the word "glue") cells make up approximately 90 percent of the brain's cells. Glia beneficially modulate the function and viability of neurons.

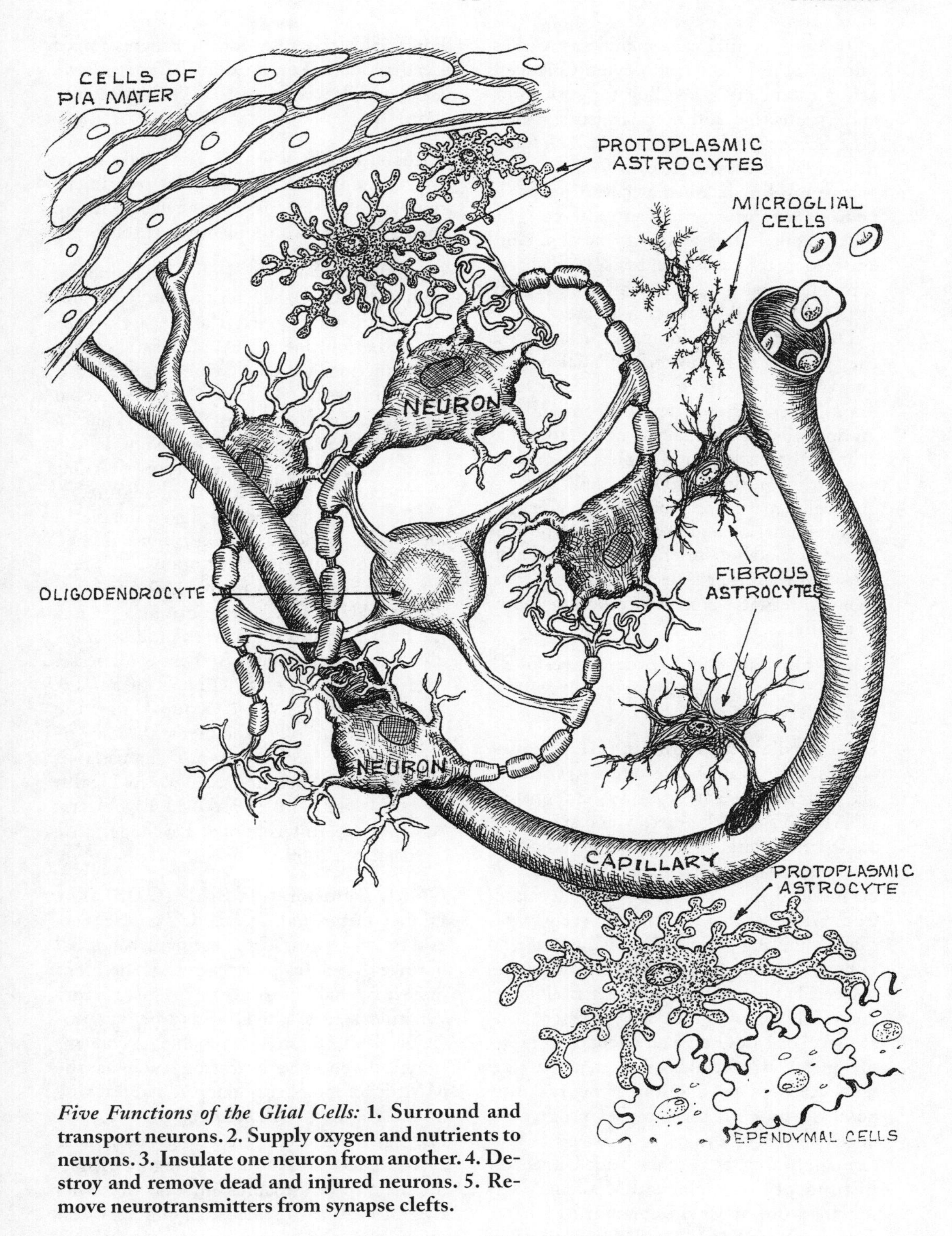

Five Functions of the Glial Cells: **1. Surround and transport neurons. 2. Supply oxygen and nutrients to neurons. 3. Insulate one neuron from another. 4. Destroy and remove dead and injured neurons. 5. Remove neurotransmitters from synapse clefts.**

Glial Cells of the Brain (illustration by Marvin G. Miller).

The brain's glial cells include astrocytes, microglia, and oligodendrocytes. Glial cells act as caretakers, providing support, guidance, protection and nourishment for neurons. Schwann cells, a type of glial cell found in peripheral nerves, help to form the protective myelin sheath that covers axons. In neurodegenerative diseases, altered glial function, including reactivity, is seen. Generalized reactive astrocytosis is observed throughout pathologically affected regions of the brain in Alzheimer's disease.

During fetal development, neurons use the supporting framework of glial cells to help them migrate to other areas of the brain. After neuronal development and migration, glial cells remain although they may change their shape and molecular properties. At birth, there are about half as many glial cells as neurons. There are two distinct types of functional glial cells. One type controls the metabolism and function of neurons and the other type coats the neuronal axons with a fatty protective covering known as myelin.

Glial fibrillary acid protein (GFAP). GFAB is a protein produced by nervous system cells.

Glial fibrillary acid protein (GFAP) antibodies. GFAP antibodies are autoantibodies targeting the nervous system protein GFAB. GFAP antibodies, which are associated with several different nervous system diseases, including Alzheimer's disease, may be induced by exposure to toxic levels of lead. GFAP autoantibodies are seen in patients suffering from senile dementias and in healthy, aging people. Because of the suspected involvement of environmental pollutants such as lead in the development of neurological diseases, some researchers postulate that metal-induced alterations in neural proteins leads to production of neural antibodies, which, in turn, causes progressive degeneration of the nervous system. (Waterman, Stacey, et al, New York University Institute of Environmental Medicine, Nelson Institute of Environmental Medicine, Tuxedo, New York. "Lead Alters the Immunogenicity of Two Neural Proteins. A Potential Mechanism for the Progression of Lead-induced Neurotoxicity." *Environmental Health Perspectives*, 102(12) [1994,]: 1052–1056)

Gliosis. Proliferation of glial cells in an effort to replace damaged or destroyed neurons. In reactive gliosis, astrocytes fill in the spaces previously occupied by neurons.

Global assessments. Global assessments, such as the Global Deterioration Scale and the Clinical Dementia Rating, are procedures that outline the characteristic cognitive, functional, and behavioral course of individual cases of Alzheimer's disease. Global outlines are useful in providing clinicians a rapid and comprehensive overview of the disease course and in identifying features that occur out of sequence or prematurely.

Global assessments are also valuable in identifying generally benign, normal aged subjective forgetfulness as opposed to features consistent with incipient Alzheimer's disease. These assessments can also project the final stages of the disease process in individuals with incipient Alzheimer's disease. (Reisberg, Barry, et al. "Report of an IPA Special Meeting Work Group Under the co-sponsorship of Alzheimer's Disease International, the European Federation of Neurological Societies, the World Health Organization, and the World Psychiatric Association." International Psychogeriatric Association, 2000.)

Global Deterioration Scale (GDS). The Global Deterioration Scalde (GDS) is an evaluation tool used to distinguish normal brain aging from progressive Alzheimer's disease by dividing Alzheimer's disease into 7 distinct stages. The GDS as a staging procedure is considered as reliable as conventional psychometric testing such as the MMSE for long-term longitudinal tracking of the course of Alzheimer's disease. The GDS also has a semi-structured component available for further guiding staging assignments. These measures include the Brief Cognitive Rating Scale and a number of assessments for documenting functional deficits such as activities of daily living.

Glutamate. Glutamate is an amino acid that acts as an excitatory neurotransmitter. Having excitatory properties, glutamate induces activity, or "firing," of neurons. Normally, glutamate helps send signals along nerve neuronal pathways and promotes learning, memory, and other cognitive functions. Glutamate also controls the flow of calcium ions into neurons through the methyl-D-aspartate-regulated channel.

Glutamate is the major neurotransmitter for brief, point-to-point excitatory synaptic events in the central nervous system, similar to the action of acetylcholine in the peripheral nervous system. In the presence of excess glutamate, however, too much calcium is able to enter neurons. According to one theory, glutamate would therefore cause the generation of free radicals that could be neurotoxic, causing the neurodegeneration seen in Alzheimer's disease.

The damage or neurotoxicity caused by glutamate starts with an excess of glutamate in the spaces between neurons, where it binds to and overstimulates receptors for N-methyl-D-aspartate (NMDA). A protein receptor, NMDA normally resides on cell surfaces. When NMDA receptors become overexcited, a cascade of events is initiated that eventually results in nerve cell death. Stroke, trauma and various forms of dementia are related to glutamate–NMDA excitotoxicity. Drugs such as memantine, which block NMDA receptors, are routinely used in Europe for the treatment of neurodegenerative disorders.

Glutathione. Glutathione is a naturally-occurring antioxidant, which is also sold as a dietary supplement. Glutathione specifically works on cerebral mitochondria, maintaining both vitamins E and C in their reduced state and removing potentially damaging peroxides. It also inhibits the production of nitric oxide. Patients with Parkinson's disease have been found to have profoundly decreased brain levels of glutathione, and the use of glutathione as a therapy for this disorder is currently under investigation. The body's production of glutathione may be increased by the use of vitamins C and E, silymarin (milk thistle), alpha lipoic acid, L-cysteine, L-methionine, L-glutamine, reducing xenobiotic challenges and reducing drug challenges that induce cytochrome P450 enzymes.

Glyceryl-phosphorylcholine. Glycerylphosphorylcholine is a substance used as a drug in Europe and Japan to correct cognitive impairment associated with degenerative brain disease.

Glycosaminoglycans (GAGs). Glycosaminoglycans (GAGs), formerly known as mucopolysaccharides, are congestive mucinous sugar polymer components such as hyaluronic acid. Glycosaminoglycans are found in the senile neuritic plaques that riddle the brains of patients with Alzheimer's disease. GAGs are thought to be critical for the assembly of components that make up senile plaques. Researchers are working on a compound that protects glycosaminoglycans from proteolysis. The sulfated GAGs resulting from proteolysis have an affinity for beta amyloid. Preventing proteolysis would effectively reduce the formation of the fibrils that ultimately lead to neuronal cell death.

Goldsmith, Harry S., M.D. Dr. Harry Goldsmith is a pioneer in the use of omentum implantation as a therapy for Alzheimer's disease and stroke. Currently at the University of Nevada, Dr. Goldsmith has been perfecting this treatment since the 1960s. One of his patients was featured on the Channel 2 nightly news in Southern California in 2000. *See* Omentum.

Gotu kola *see* Centella asiatica

Granulovacuolar degeneration. Granulovacuolar degeneration, one of the characteristic brain changes seen in Alzheimer's disease, refers to the formation of small (5 μm in diameter), clear holes or vacuoles. These are seen in the cytoplasm of neurons in postmortem brain biopsies. Each granuovacuolar degeneration contains an argyrophilic granule. Hirano bodies are elongated, glassy, eosinophilic bodies consisting of paracrystalline arrays of beaded filaments. The chemical compound actin is the major constituent of Hirano bodies. Both granulovacuolar degeneration and Hirano bodies are commonly seen in the pyramidal cells of the Hippocampus in patients with Alzheimer's diseases and other neurodegenerative disorders. Their significance is unclear.

Gray matter. The gray matter that makes up the interior of the central nervous system consists of nerve cells and the proximal or end portions of their processes embedded in neuroglia. The gray matter consists of a mixture of nerve cells including their dendrites, neuroglia and blood vessels. The nerve cells are multipolar and the neuroglia forms an intricate network around neurons. The abundance of blood vessels causes the characteristic pink-gray color of gray matter.

On cross-section of the spinal cord, the gray matter is seen as an H-shaped pillar with anterior and posterior gray columns, or horns, united by a thin gray commissure containing the small central canal. The amount of gray matter present in the spinal cord at any level is related to the amount of muscle innervated at that level.

Specific areas of gray matter are often called nuclei, particularly if the contained cell bodies are functionally related. An area where gray matter forms a surface covering on some part of the central nervous system is referred to as a cortex.

Grooved Pegboard Test. The grooved pegboard test is a psychological test used to measure visuomotor coordination.

Guarana. Extracts of the plant compound guarana are being studied for their use as a therapy in Alzheimer's disease. This herb has antioxidant properties and is reported to reduce production of beta amyloid protein.

Haldol *see* Haloperidol

Hallervorden-Spatz disease. Hallervorden-Spatz disease is a rare, inherited neurological movement disorder characterized by progressive nervous system degeneration. Symptoms may develop as early as childhood and include slow writhing, distorting muscle contractions of the limbs, face or trunk, involuntary muscle spasms, muscle rigidity, ataxia, confusion, disorientation, seizures, stupor, and dementia. Other less common symptoms include painful muscle spasms, speech difficulties, mental retardation, facial grimacing, and visual impairment. Symptoms vary among those with this disorder, and death usually occurs within 10 years from the onset of symptoms.

Hallucination. Hallucination refers to the perception of something (visual image or sound) with no external cause, usually arising from a central nervous system disorder or in response to drugs.

Haloperidol (Haldol). Haloperidol (Haldol) is a major tranquilizer indicated for the management of psychotic disorders and severe behavior problems, including combativeness. Haldol is contraindicated and not recommended for patients with severe toxic central nervous system depression, Parkinson's disease or who are in comatose states. Side effects include a syndrome characterized by potentially irreversible, involuntary, dyskinetic movements and a potentially fatal symptom complex sometimes referred to as Neuroleptic Malignant Syndrome (NMS). Symptoms of NMS include hyperexia (fever), muscle rigidity, altered mental status including catatonic signs, and evidence of autonomic instability (irregular pulse or blood pressure, tachycardia, increased sweating and renal failure). Haldol decanoate is a long-acting form of haloperidol.

Harry, Jean, Ph.D. Jean Harry is head of the neurotoxicology group at the National Institutes of Environmental Health Sciences. Her work focuses on the intricate role between neurons and glial cells and the role of this relationship in causing neurodegenerative disease.

Hashimoto's encephalitis. Hashimoto's encephalitis is a form of encephalitis caused by an autoimmune process. In this disorder, which occurs more often in women than men, the thyroid autoantibodies responsible for Hashimoto's thyroiditis (autoimmune hypothyroidism) attack brain cells. Symptoms of this disease include dementia, myoclonus (erratic or jerking muscle contractions), ataxia (inability to coordinate muscles), epileptic seizures, disturbances of consciousness, and personality change or psychotic phenomena.

According to researchers, it is unclear whether the cerebral manifestation of Hashimoto's thyroiditis represents an autoimmune reaction against a shared antigen or if cerebral autoimmune vasculitis co-exists with the thyroiditis. Test results suggest the presence of a chronic inflammatory process. Unlike other causes of dementia, Hashimoto's encephalitis responds to steroid treatment. It is important to differentiate Hashimoto's encephalitis from Alzheimer's disease since with treatment, Hashimoto's encephalitis is a reversible condition, although patients may still experience impaired cognitive abilities. Hashimoto's encephalitis is suspected when thyroid autoantibodies in serum are raised and blood tests reveal clinical or subclinical hypothyroidism. In doubtful cases, fine needle biopsy of the thyroid gland reveals characteristic cellular changes. (Seipelt, M. et al. "Hashimoto's encephalitis as a differential diagnosis of Creutzfeldt-Jakob disease." *J Neurol Neurosurg Psychiatry*, 1999, 66: 172–176).

Head injuries. Blows to the head due to falls or injuries may injure the scalp, the skull and the brain. Severe blows to the head may even change the shape of the skull at the point of impact or cause the skull to be fractured. A severe, localized blow will produce local indentation and splintering of bone. Repeated blows, such as occur in boxing, result in a series of fractures.

Brain injuries can occur as a result of displacement and distortion of the neuronal tissues at the moment of impact. Floating in cerebrospinal fluid, the brain is capable of a certain amount of movement, although movement is limited by cerebral veins and other structures. Blows on the front or back of the head are more likely to cause displacement of the brain as well as stretching and distortion of the brainstem. Blows to the side of the head produce less cerebral displacement although they may cause considerable rotation of the brain. Brain lacerations are very likely to occur when the brain is forcibly thrown against the sharp edges of the skull bones.

A sudden severe blow to the head, for instance, as a result of an automobile accident, can cause brain damage at both the point of impact and at the pole of the brain opposite the point of impact where the brain is thrown against the skull wall. This is referred to as a contrecoup injury. In head injuries, cranial nerves and blood vessels may be damaged, reducing blood flow to the brain and causing intracranial hemorrhage. Individuals with a history of traumatic injury and the APOE4 genotype have demonstrated an increased risk for developing Alzheimer's disease.

An analysis of head injuries among World War II veterans links serious head injury in adulthood with Alzheimer's disease in early life. Researchers at Duke University in a study funded by the NIA looked at military records of male Navy and Marine veterans who were hospitalized during their period of service with a diagnosis of head injury or an unrelated condition. ("New Study Links Head Injury, Severity of Injury with Alzheimer's Disease," *NIA News*, October 23, 2000). *See also* Brain injuries.

Health Care Financing Administration (HFCA). The Health Care Financing Administration, an agency that manages government health insurance, is now known as the Centers for Medicare & Medicaid Services (CMS). *See* Centers for Medicare & Medicaid Services.

Health care proxy. A health care proxy is someone that a patient or his or her representatives have legally appointed to make health care decisions for them in the event they are unable to make their own decisions.

Health Insurance Portability and Accountability Act of 1996 (HIPAA). The Health Insurance Portability and Accountability Act implements the civil monetary penalties which can be assessed for Medicare fraud.

Health maintenance organization (HMO). Health maintenance organizations

(HMOs) are insurance groups that offer lower cost health care by using a select group of health care providers [exclusively]. Patients may only consult these providers, usually for a small fee or co-payment.

Health Security Plan. The Health Security Plan guarantees comprehensive health benefits for all American citizens and legal residents, regardless of health or employment status. The plan empowers each state to set up one or more health alliances that contract with health plans and bargain on behalf of area consumers and employers. Each state plan must meet national standards for coverage and quality. The Health Security Plan provides that elderly and disabled Americans receive outpatient prescription drug benefits under Medicare and expanded access to home and community based long-term care services. This plan aims to cut the projected growth in health care costs by increasing competition in health care, reducing administrative costs, and imposing budget discipline.

Heavy metals. Heavy metals refer to metals high in molecular weight such as antimony, arsenic, bismuth, lead, and mercury.

Helping Our Mobile Elderly (H.O.M.E.). Helping Our Mobile Elderly (H.O.M.E.) is a model project providing residential care in a small home-like settings for women with memory loss due to Alzheimer's disease and other brain disorders. H.O.M.E., which is an independent non-profit organization licensed by the State of California, has demonstrated its ability to provide life-enhancing care with minimal physical or chemical restraints and few acute hospitalizations. The Alzheimer's Association has featured H.O.M.E.'s philosophy in a new document called "Key Elements of Dementia Care."

Herbal therapy. In several major studies, herbal therapy has proven effective in reducing symptoms of Alzheimer's disease. The herbs most commonly used are ginkgo biloba, guarana (*Paullinia cupana*), gotu kola (*Centella asiatica*), huperzine, and rosemary (*Rosmarinus officinalis*). Other herbs reported to have benefits include Asian ginseng (*Panax ginseng*), American ginseng (*Panax quinquefolium*), Nicotine (*nicotiana tobaccum*), Snowdrop (*Galanthus nivalus*), Sage (*Salvia officianalis*), Lemon balm (*Melissa officinalis*), Bitter Melon, Cat's Claw and Peony (*Paeonia suffruticosa*).

Herpes Viruses. Studies show that a high proportion of the brains of Alzheimer's disease patients and of age-matched healthy people contain latent Herpes Simplex Virus 1 (HSV 1). Researchers in Bristol, UK, have shown that the combination of HSV1 in the brain along with the apolipoprotein E 4 allele is a strong risk factor for developing Alzheimer's disease. Dr. David Perlmutter and others have also conducted research that supports this.

Individuals who die of Alzheimer's disease have been found to have a very high gene penetration of apolipoprotein E4 and a chronic infection with herpes simplex Type 1 (cold sores). These findings suggest that the virus harbored in the brain tissue reactivates periodically, causing more damage, and eventually Alzheimer's disease in carriers of the apolipoprotein E4 allele. (Itzhaki, R.F., G.K. Wilcock and W Lin. "Herpes Viruses, Alzheimer's Disease and Herpes Simplex Encephalitis," Molecular Neurobiology Lab. UMIST, Manchester M 60, Grenchay Hospital, Bristol BS16 1LE, UK. Itzhaki, R.F., et al. "Herpes simplex virus type 1 in brain and risk of Alzheimer's Disease," *Lancet* 349, 241–244).

Hindbrain *see* Rhombencephalon

Hippocampus. The hippocampus refers to a specific region of the brain's mesial temporal lobe memory system. Alzheimer's disease is characterized by the death of nerve cells in this key memory center of the brain. The region primarily affected in Alzheimer's disease encompasses two paired structures symmetrically set on both sides of the brain: the seahorse-shaped hippocampus, which seems to be resting on the enthorhinal cortex, a cortical region which links the hippocampus to the rest of the brain. New memories reside in this region temporarily

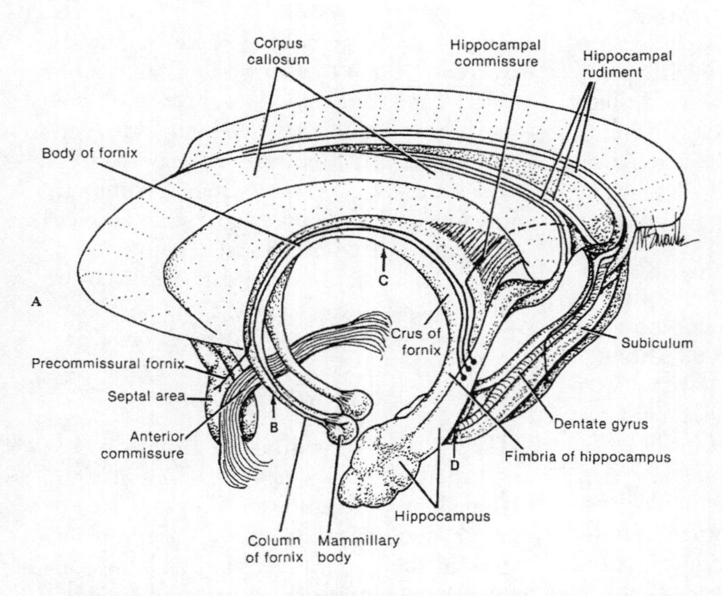

Hippocampus (from *The Human Brain*, 3rd ed., by John Nolte [St. Louis: Mosby Year Book, 1993]; reprinted with permission from Mosby Year Book, Inc.).

before they are eventually filed in the frontal cortex. If the circuitry in this region is damaged, these memories are lost. Alzheimer's disease wipes out new memories as well as the ability to learn.

Anatomically, the hippocampus is a curved elevation of gray matter that extends throughout the entire length of the floor of the inferior horn of the lateral ventricles. The hippocampus is part of the limbic system, a cluster of nuclei in the lower region of the forebrain. The hippocampus interacts with the cerebral cortex in determining emotions and processing memories. The hippocampus is responsible for modulation and storage of newly acquired data. It is affected in the earliest stages of Alzheimer's disease, with cell destruction accelerating proportionately to disease progression.

Damage to the hippocampus results in changes in autonomic and endocrine functions as well as behavior, memory and learning. However, there is not one precise general function related to neuronal damage in the hippocampus. The hippocampus is a major part of the medial temporal lobe. When parts of the medial temporal lobe are surgically removed, patients exhibit problems learning new information although they may be able to learn new tasks.

Several researchers have reported that a linear loss of volume of specific hippocampal brain regions correlates with the clinical changes seen in Alzheimer's disease. These volume changes are accompanied by changes in the percentages of neurons with neurofibrillary changes and with neuronal loss. In magnetic resonance imaging (MRI) studies, bilateral volumetric hippocampal atrophy has been found to be a highly sensitive indicator of early Alzheimer's disease. In one study, this measurement afforded a greater than 95 percent accuracy rating in correctly classifying Alzheimer's disease although researchers concluded that differentiation from other causes of temporal lobe pathology may be limited.

Hirano bodies. Hirano bodies are elongated, glassy, eosinophilic (stain with eosin) bodies consisting of crystalline arrays of beaded filaments, primarily composed of actin. Hirano bodies are found most commonly in the hippocampal pyramidal cells of patients with Alzheimer's disease and other neurodegenerative disorders. They are of unknown significance. Hirano bodies were first described by Hirano in Sommer's sector of the hippocampus in Guam amyotrophic lateral sclerosis (ALS)-parkinsonism-dementia complex. As an age-related change, Hirano bodies begin to appear during the second decade and occur in small numbers up to the sixth decade at which time they markedly increase. Their concentrations are much higher in individuals with Alzheimer's disease.

Histology. Histology is the study of tissue cells. Histological changes seen in the brains of individuals with Alzheimer's disease include neuronal loss in the nucleus basalis of

Meynert, hippocampus, and association cortex; neuronal degeneration, dendritic pruning, synaptic loss, presence of neurofibrillary tangles containing paired helical filaments, and the presence of senile plaques. Additional histological changes include granulovacuolar changes and accumulation of lipofuscin granules.

HLA 2. HLA are human leukocyte antigen markers for immune system genes found on the short arm of chromosome 6. Although HLA antigens are commonly associated with autoimmune disease development, the HLA 2 allele is associated with an earlier age of onset in individuals who develop Alzheimer's disease. This association also suggests that inflammation, a common immune system effect, may play a role in autoimmune disease development.

Hoarding. Hoarding refers to collecting and putting things away in a guarded manner. Alzheimer's disease patients may fear that others are stealing their possessions. This causes them to hoard certain items, although they are likely to forget where they have hidden these items.

Home and Community Based Programs. The goal of home and community based care is for people to be able to live as independently as possible for as long as possible. Home and community based programs include: adult day care services, clinical drug trials, driving assessment programs, transportation services, attorneys, free legal services and insurance counseling, meal programs, assisted living and residential care facilities, in-home agencies, and short-term respite care facilities. These programs are generally sponsored by a combination of local and federal government agencies. Information on local programs is available through the Alzheimer's Association or community based social service departments.

Home based care *see* **Friends Life Care at Home**

Home care. Of the 4 million Americans affected with Alzheimer's disease, it is estimated that 80 percent of these individuals are living at home and are being cared for by family caregivers. However, home care may also be provided by licensed home care agencies. Generally, Medicare will pay for some homecare services, including nursing care and physical therapy. Home care services also may assist with housekeeping, shopping, and other household chores that are too difficult for patients with dementia. These services may also be paid for or partially subsidized by local, county, or state programs or by private insurance.

Home Care Accreditation Program. Established in 1988, the Joint Commission's Home Care Accreditation Program accredits organizations that offer a variety of services in the patient's or client's home. Inspectors conduct surveys before the service provider receives accreditation. The length of the survey and its costs are dependent on the type of services provided, the volume of services provided and the organizational structure of the service provided.

Home Health Care. Home health care services are medical services provided by hospitals and home care agencies. Services include phlebotomy for laboratory testing, assistance with wound care, intravenous medications, and assistance with bathing. Home health care agencies can also provide respite care for patients with dementia if their caretaker is away.

Insurance companies generally pay for the services provided by home health care. Medicare and Medicaid cutbacks have reduced the amount of home care that they will provide, but in most instances they will provide limited home health care for patients with dementia who are able to live at home. Health care, which is generally provided by nurse's aides, includes assistance with bathing, laundry, and meal preparation. If private agencies provide home care, there may be a minimum requirement of three to four hours, which may be more time than is needed. See also Medicare HMOs.

Homocysteine. The amino acid homocysteine has been found to be elevated in patients with both heart disease and Alzheimer's disease. In ADCS clinical trials, researchers evaluated the effects of homocysteine reduction related to high dose supplements of folate, vitamin B6, and vitamin B12. Results indicate that patients with mild to moderate dementia and elevated plasma homocysteine levels respond well to vitamin substitution when assessed with the MMSE exam. However, patients with severe dementia and normal plasma homocysteine levels showed no signs of improvement. The study concluded that plasma homocysteine may be the best marker for detecting treatable vitamin deficiencies in patients with dementia.

Hormone replacement therapy (HRT) *see* Estrogen; Clinical trials; Estrogen replacement therapy

Horsebalm *see* Monarda

Huntington's chorea. Huntington's chorea, or disease, a form of severe dementia, is a condition characterized by quick, jerky, irregular movements. Patients with this disorder experience degeneration of the neurons that produce the neurotransmitters GABA, acetylcholine and P-substance. This results in an overactivity of the dopamine-secreting neurons of the substantia nigra region of the brain. Huntington's disease is caused by a dominant gene located on chromosome 4. A strong association between affective disorder and Huntington's disease suggests that affective disorder may be an early manifestation of Huntington's disease.

Huperzine A. Herbal extract derived from Chinese club moss (*Huperzia serrata*) widely used to treat fever. *Huperzia* is also an alternate name used for some of the *Lycopodium* club mosses. Studies indicate that huperazine, like the prescription drug tacrine, inhibits the breakdown of the neurotransmitter acetylcholine. People with Alzheimer's disease generally have low levels of acetylcholine. The National Institutes of Health is currently planning to use Huperzine A in clinical trials. Memory-enhancing effects have been reported in scopolamine-impaired rats. Currently used in China to treat dementia. (James A. Duke, *The Green Pharmacy*, 1997, Emmaus, PA, Rodale Press.)

Hydergine *see* Ergoloid mesylate

Hydrocephalus. Hydrocephalus is a condition characterized by an abnormal increase in the volume of cerebrospinal fluid within the skull. Hydrocephalus generally develops as a result of a blockage of the foramina in the roof of the fourth ventricle in the brain. Hydrocephalus may occur as a congenital defect or it may be caused by adhesions that develop during meningitis. Hydrocephalus may occur due to displacement of the medulla oblongata by a tumor.

In normal pressure hydrocephalus, patients show signs of gait disturbance, dementia and incontinence. The onset usually occurs over several months, although the onset may be acute. Compared to Alzheimer's disease, the dementia is mild and the gait is severe, although in some cases the dementia may be more pronounced. Brain scans typically demonstrate hydrocephalus with enlargement of ventricles out of proportion to sulci. Other clinical signs include motor signs preceding cognitive dysfunction, short duration of dementia prior to surgery, and known causes such as traumatic or spontaneous subarachnoid hemorrhage, meningitis or partial obstruction.

Hydrogen peroxide. Theories supporting the claim that beta amyloid protein is the major culprit in Alzheimer's disease lend themselves to the hypothesis that beta amyloid increases production of hydrogen peroxide within neurons. According to this theory, hydrogen peroxide contributes to free radical oxidative damage and neuronal cell death.

Hypertension. Chronic hypertension, a condition of high blood pressure, increases the risk for mental impairment, including reduced short-term memory and attention, Alzheimer's disease, and dementia. Studies indicate, however, that controlling blood pressure may ward off memory impairment. Treating hypertension can reduce the risk of dementia in elderly patients with elevated systolic pressure.

Hypothalamus. The hypothalamus located in the forebrain forms the lower part of the lateral wall and floor of the third ventricle. The hypothalamus has a controlling influence on the autonomic nervous system and appears to integrate the autonomic and neuroendocrine systems. The hypothalamus is regarded as a higher nervous center for the control of lower autonomic centers in the brainstem and spinal cord. Nerve cells in the hypothalamus produce and release many releasing factors that control or inhibit many of the body's hormones. The hypothalamus also helps control emotions and behaviors by processing information received from other areas of the body.

Ibuprofen. Ibuprofen is a non-steroidal anti-inflammatory drug. Recent studies show that the use of ibuprofen may protect against Alzheimer's disease, specifically by inhibiting the formation of beta amyloid protein 42. Research shows that taking as little as 800 mg of ibuprofen daily reduces the risk of contracting Alzheimer's disease without serious side effects. In one study, anti-inflammatory drugs slashed the incidence of Alzheimer's disease by 75 percent. In another study, ibuprofen was shown to have a neuroprotective effect. (Greenwell, Ivy. "New light on how ibuprofen protects against Alzheimer's disease." *Life Extension*, February 2002, 23.)

Idebenone. Idebenone is a form of Co-Q-10 with increased blood-brain barrier penetration. Idebenone has been reported to increase levels of nerve growth factor in the body, suggesting its value as an alternative therapy for Alzheimer's disease.

Imaging studies. Imaging studies involve the process of producing an image of the body's parts by radiographic (X-ray) or related techniques.

Immobility. In the late stages of Alzheimer's disease, many patients become immobile, apparently forgetting how to move. Immobility may weaken muscles to the point where patients become entirely wheelchair bound or bedridden. Bedsores may become a problem. Frequent washing of bed linens and moving the patients every two hours during the day can help prevent bedsores. Lotions to soothe dry skin also offer benefits. Patients should be encouraged to move and exercises can be administered to the legs and arms to help maintain flexibility. One study reported that 62 percent of patients with mild to moderate dementia reported having joint pain yet few patients with severe dementia receive pain medication although there is no evidence that they are not experiencing pain.

Immune system. The immune system is a constellation of organs and blood cells that work together to protect us from disease. Immune system organs include the bone marrow, lymph glands, spleen, appendix, tonsils, and adenoids. The key players of the immune system are white blood cells, primarily lymphocytes and macrophages. Immune system cells travel to locations in the body where they perceive a foreign threat, usually an infectious agent or an allergen. Here they release factors that result in inflammation. Immune system cells also produce antibodies to fight the foreign agent during a subsequent attack.

Inanition. Inanition is a condition of exhaustion caused by a lack of food and water. Inanition may eventually lead to death in patients with Alzheimer's disease.

Incidence. The incidence of Alzheimer's disease is estimated at 0.5 percent per year at age 65 and 8 percent per year after the age of 85. Alzheimer's disease is estimated to affect 4 million people in the United States.

Incontinence. Incontinence, which may be urinary or fecal, refers to the inability of the body to control evacuative functions. Incontinence is commonly seen in the later stages of Alzheimer's disease. Incontinence is one of the main reasons patients are moved into nursing home settings. When the patient first shows signs of incontinence the doctor should be notified so he can check for evidence of urinary tract infection. Urinary incontinence may be controlled for some time by limiting liquid intake in the evening and reminding the patient to use the bathroom.

Independence. Patients with dementia are encouraged to remain independent for as long as possible. This helps maintain self-respect and decreases the burden for the caregiver. Patients who are able to still shop and perform other tasks away from their home should always carry proper identification, including information about where they live. Patients should be encouraged to eat with proper utensils and write their name so that these skills are not readily lost. Patients should not be discouraged from keeping pets since pets can provide companionship and purpose. If the patient cannot look after his or her pet, caregivers should make arrangements so that the person can still see the pet on a regular basis.

Indiana Alzheimer Disease National Cell Repository. The Indiana Alzheimer's Disease National Cell Repository sponsored by the federal government gathers family history information and genetic material from families with histories of Alzheimer's disease. This information is available to researchers worldwide.

Indole-3-Proprionic Acid (IPA). Indole-3-proprionic acid (IPA) is a highly potent, naturally occurring antioxidant. Research indicates that IPA has the ability to inhibit the action of the enzymes that contribute to beta amyloid plaque deposits in Alzheimer's disease. ADCS clinical trials are currently evaluating the safety and tolerability of IPA in patients with Alzheimer's disease.

Infection related dementia. Dementia can result from infection with a number of different agents including the retrovirus, human immunodeficiency virus (HIV), which causes acquired immune deficiency syndrome (AIDS). Bacterial and viral forms of meningitis, especially cryptococcal meningitis, can present as dementia, although there are almost always other associated signs and symptoms such as severe headache. Syphilis, resulting from the infectious agent *Treponema pallidium*, also causes a form of dementia as it forms brain abscesses. Creutzfeldt-Jakob disease also causes a form of dementia related to a slow virus known as a prion. *See also* Acquired immune deficiency syndrome related dementia and Cretuzfeldt-Jakob disease.

Inflammation. Inflammation is a process initiated by the immune system. In a reaction known as the inflammatory response, white blood cells, particularly microglial cells, cluster or aggregate at the point of injury or threat by foreign organisms. Activation of microglial cells is necessary for chronic inflammation. In addition, during the immune response, immune system cells release neurotoxic chemicals such as cytokines and complement. Cytokines regulate the severity of the inflammation. Complement cascades into a number of compounds that sustain the inflammatory process.

Studies of the brain in patients with Alzheimer's disease show evidence of inflammation within or adjacent to neuritic plaques. Multiple cytokines have been detected in these lesions, and there is also evidence of other immune system chemicals known as complement, indicating activation of the complement cascade. Research is currently underway regarding the beneficial effects of anti-inflammatory medications.

In one study of identical twins, it was found that the only significant difference in pairs where one twin developed Alzheimer's disease was the use of anti-inflammatory medications by the twin who was not afflicted. Since identical twins have identical genes, this shows that more than genes are at stake in the development of Alzheimer's disease.

Other evidence for the role of inflammation in the pathogenesis (disease process) of Alzheimer's disease include the presence of activated microglial cells and reactive astrocytes. These cells are known to produce cytokines and complement. The white matter of patients with Alzheimer's disease has been found to contain a high concentration of activated microglial cells, especially in relation to plaque and its amyloid and also in

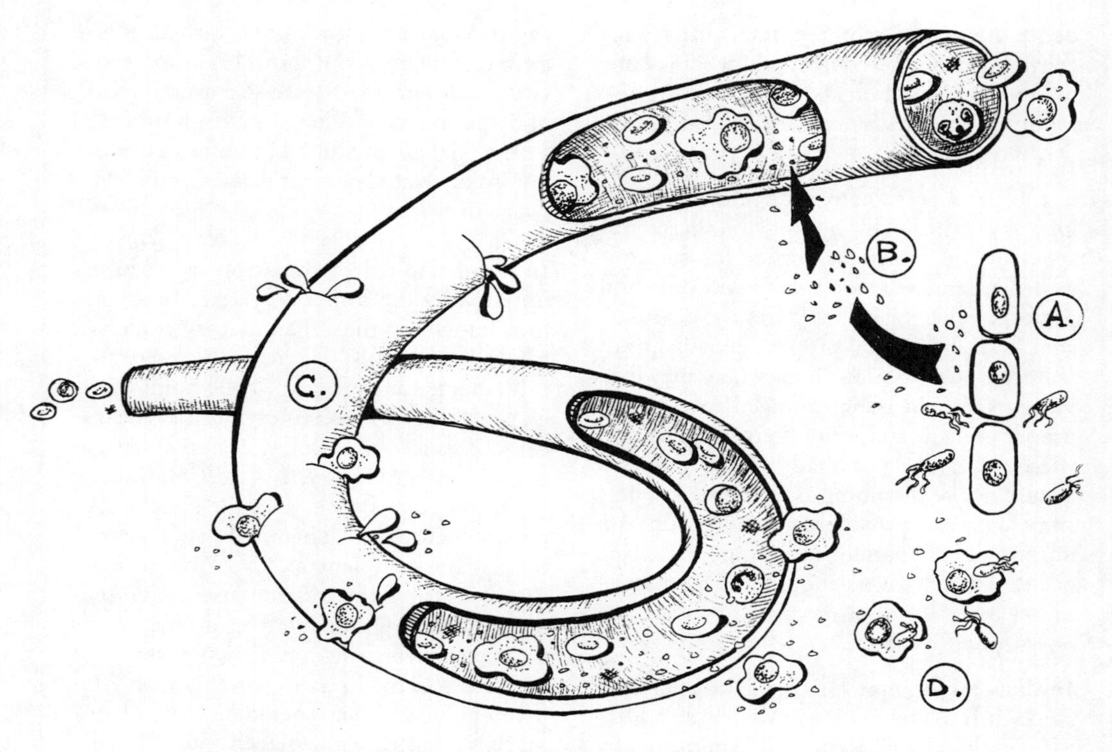

Inflammation Response (illustration by Marvin G. Miller).

A. **Bacteria or other irritants invade and damage tissue**
B. **Chemicals, such as histamines and cytokines, are released by tissue cells and enter blood vessels**
C. **The blood vessel wall becomes more elastic and permeable, allowing fluid and activated macrocytes to enter the affected area.**
D. **Phagocytes cells attack the bacteria; serum complement and other protein molecules enter the affected area**
E. **Secondary inflammatory reaction follows, including heat, swelling and pain**

the neurophil between plaque deposits. *See* Anti-inflammatory drugs.

Informant Questionnaire on Cognitive Decline in the Elderly (IQCODE). The Informant Questionnaire on Cognitive Decline in the Elderly (IQCODE) is a neuropsychiatric evaluation tool. It consists of a questionnaire administered to a proxy or informant and measures the fall from higher to lower intellectual level.

Inheritance. Two-thirds of people with Alzheimer's disease do not have a family history of it. One-third of Alzheimer's disease patients have a close relative (parent or sibling) with the disorder. Having a family history of Alzheimer's does not include grandparents with the disease or parents if they developed Alzheimer's disease after age 65. Patients without a family history have the same risk factors, depending on their age, as the general population. People with a family history may have an increased risk of inheriting Alzheimer's disease but this is difficult to prove unless there are other blood relatives who are affected. Even in these patients, the risk of inheriting familial Alzheimer's disease is low and reported to be less than one percent.

Instrumental Activities of Daily Living (IADL). The Instrumental Activities of

Daily Living (IADL) is a global assessment tool used for documenting functional deficits such as the ability to bathe, dress and eat. By assessing how individuals with Alzheimer's disease are able to manage activities of daily living, evaluators can determine the disease stage and predict one's individual disease course. In conjunction with a carefully documented history, the IADL can be useful in documenting the presence of functional deterioration.

Insulin. Insulin is a hormone produced by the islet cells of the pancreas. Insulin regulates blood glucose (sugar) levels. Patients with insulin dependent diabetes are unable to produce sufficient insulin. There are many studies examining the relationship between diabetes and Alzheimer's disease. While there is no consensus of agreement, it is known that increased insulin is a characteristic finding in the early stages of Alzheimer's disease. When this results in a normal or slightly increased blood sugar, memory is enhanced because glucose utilization in the hippocampal formation and increased formation of acetyl coenzyme A is promoted. This results in increased formation of the neurotransmitter acetylcholine, which is deficient in Alzheimer's disease. However, a chronic severe high blood sugar can impair memory. This is seen in the later stages of Alzheimer's disease, when reduced insulin levels are common. While changes in insulin levels and blood glucose levels appear to be a part of the mechanism in dementia, overall, most studies show a low incidence of diabetes in patients with Alzheimer's disease. (Michel, Jean-Pierre, et al. "Diabetes and Dementia: A Retrospective Neuropathologic Study of Old Diabetics Compared to Non-Diabetic Controls." *Alzheimer Disease: From Molecular Biology to Therapy*, edited by R. Becker and E. Giacobine. Boston: Birkhäuser Publishing, 1996, 3–46.)

Integrins. Integrins are a family of extracellular matrix (ECM) receptors that adhere to ECM proteins such as fibronectin and laminin. Researchers at the Utah School of Medicine in Salt Lake City, Utah, injected human integrin genes into adenoviruses and infected dorsal root ganglion neurons of adult rats with this virus to cause gene mutations. The mutated cells experienced cell growth and pronounced improvement. Researchers are currently repeating their studies in other types of central nervous system neurons to see if there are therapeutic applications for Alzheimer's disease.

Interleukin 1 (IL-1). Interleukin 1 (IL-1) is an inflammatory cytokine produced during the immune response. Microglia in the brain produce IL-1 during their response to beta amyloid deposits. IL-1 initiates a cascade of cell destruction and upregulates expression and processing of βAPP. Over-expression of IL-1 in Alzheimer's disease sets in motion a self-propagating cascade of cellular events known as the cytokine cycle, which correlates with formation of neuritic beta amyloid plaques and with progression of neurofibrillary tangles. Other consequences include the production of S-100 beta, a protein which induces intraneuronal free calcium concentrations, which are neurotoxic.

Studies in Italy suggest that there is either a linkage dysequilibrium with an unknown locus relevant to Alzheimer's disease on chromosome 2q or that IL-1 polymorphisms contribute to neurodegenerative processes in the pathology of Alzheimer's disease.

Internal capsule. The internal capsule is a compact band of white matter composed of ascending and descending nerve fibers that connect the cerebral cortex to the brainstem and spinal cord. The internal capsule is often involved in vascular brain disorders. Even small hemorrhages may cause clots that destroy immediate neural tissue and compress or destroy surrounding nerve fibers.

International Classification of Diseases, 10th revision (ICD-10). While the criteria of the National Institute of Neurological and Communicative Disorders and Stroke and the DSM-III-R are generally used to diagnose Alzheimer's disease, the International Classification of Diseases, 10th revision (ICD-10) is generally used to define subcategories of vascular dementia and other dementias.

Interview for Deterioration in Daily Living Activities in Dementia (IDDD). The Interview for Deterioration in Daily Living Activities in Dementia (IDDD) is a global assessment tool used for documenting functional deficits such as the ability to bathe, dress and eat. It is a useful tool in predicting one's individual disease course and expected rate of disease progression for patients with Alzheimer's disease.

Intracranial area of the brain. The intracranial area of the brain is the area situated or occurring within the cranium.

Iron deposits. Redox-active iron deposits have been found in the senile plaques and neurofibrillary tangles seen in the brain of patients with Alzheimer's disease. Iron has long been known to catalyze free radical formation, and free radical oxidation is also linked to the development of Alzheimer's disease. Increased levels of the iron binding protein melanotransferrin seen in Alzheimer's disease patients indicate that iron metabolism in the brains of these patients may be impaired.

Researchers at the University of Tennessee in Knoxville have shown that iron interacts with oxygen to produce free radicals. These radicals oxidatively modify proteins and make them more susceptible to proteolysis, damage DNA and peroxidize lipids. Beta-amyloid production is also increased in the presence of iron. (Joshi, Jayant et al. "Iron and Aluminum Homeostasis in Neural Disorders." *Environmental Health Perspectives* 102, Supplement 3, September 1994.)

Desferrioxamine, an iron-chelating agent, as well as anti-inflammatory drugs and estrogens, have been found to have antioxidant effects, reducing iron concentrations and offering a therapeutic role in the prevention of Alzheimer's disease.

Ischemia. Ischemia is a condition of localized tissue anemia or lack of blood circulation due to obstruction of the inflow of arterial blood. Ischemia is caused by the narrowing of arteries by spasm or disease.

Ischemia Scores. Ischemia scores (Rosen Modification) are used to evaluate if cognitive impairment is related to ischemia or dementia. In Alzheimer's disease, Ischemia Scores are less than 4, with higher scores relating to ischemia.

Joint Commission on Accreditation of Healthcare Organizations (JCAHO). The Joint Commission is a private, nonprofit organization dedicated to improving the quality of care in organized healthcare settings. JCAHO evaluates, accredits, consults, and sets standards for long-term care facilities, home care agencies, hospices, hospitals, and other healthcare delivery systems. Accreditation surveys assess the organization's compliance with applicable safety and other standards and provide guidance for the organization to improve its future delivery of care.

Journal of Alzheimer's Disease. The international medical publication *Journal of Alzheimer's Disease* is a peer-reviewed journal published by IOS press. Its goals are to facilitate progress in understanding the etiology, pathogenesis, epidemiology, genetics, behavior, treatment, and psychology of Alzheimer's disease. The journal publishes research reports, reviews, short communications, book reviews and letters to the editor. For more information see http://www.j-alz.com.

Judgment. In neuropsychological exams, judgment is tested by a series of questions designed to show how well the patient perceives the circumstances of the situation described. Questions include asking the patient what he or she would do if he or she lose their credit cards. Judgment is poor in organic brain disease, mental retardation, and psychotic states.

Keepsake Program. The Keepsake Program provides answers to questions about memory changes caused by aging. The program hosts free educational seminars that explain normal forgetfulness as well as the changes that occur in Alzheimer's disease and related disorders. The program also discusses information about available resources in your community provided by the Alzheimer's Association and community services. Information can be obtained from local Alzheimer's Association chapters.

Ketoglutarate dehydrogenase enzyme complex (KGDHC). The ketoglutarate dehydrogenase enzyme complex (KGDHC) is a mechanism involved in normal metabolism. Abnormal oxidative processes, including a reduction in activity of the ketoglutarate dehydrogenase enzyme complex, is seen in the brains of Alzheimer's disease patients. The decline in KGDHC activity correlates with the degree of dementia.

Khacaturian, Zaven, Ph.D. Dr. Zaven Kacaturian is the director of the Alzheimer's Association's Ronald & Nancy Reagan Research Institute.

Kinases. Kinase are protein enzymes involved in many of the body's processes. In Alzheimer's disease, altered activity of kinases, particularly cyclin-dependent kinase 5 (cdk5) are thought to be responsible for the aberrant phosphorylation of microtubule associated proteins. Therapy geared toward reducing the activity of these kinases would reduce this process. This is one of the primary focuses in Alzheimer's disease research.

Korean ginseng. The herb Korean ginseng has been reported to improve cognitive function in healthy persons when used at a dose of 100 mg taken twice daily. It has also been used for Alzheimer's patients although there is no clinical research for this use.

Korsakoff's syndrome (Korsakoff's psychosis). Korsakoff's syndrome is a form of dementia caused by thiamine (vitamin B1) deficiency. Thiamine deficiency is caused by alcoholism, malnutrition or malabsorption of nutrients. It may also be precipitated by administration of carbohydrates to patients with marginal thiamine stores. Korsakoff's syndrome presents with an anterograde amnesia in which the patient is unable to learn new information. Classically, this condition develops in the wake of an acute Wernicke's encephalopathy (inflammation in Wernicke's region of the brain) with confusion, ophthalmoplegia (visual disturbance) and ataxia. However, many patients with Korsakoff's syndrome do not present with Wernicke's encephalopathy.

Patients with Korsakoff's psychosis may have relatively intact intelligence but an inability to form new memories. They typically make up answers as they go along, concealing to some extent the memory loss.

Kunitz protease inhibitor (KPI) domain. Amyloid precursor protein (APP) has several different isoforms it can take. Certain of these isoforms contain a Kunitz protease inhibitor (KPI) domain. This molecule regulates the clotting cascade, a biological mechanism that leads to normal blood clotting. Isoforms with the KPI domain may primarily function to regulated clotting within the brain. Normal processing of APP includes cleavage of a peptide bond in the middle of the amyloid beta sequence. This prevents the potential formation of insoluble aggregates of amyloid beta protein.

The development of amyloid deposits in Alzheimer's disease is thought to arise from abnormal processing of the APP molecule in such a way that increased amounts of amyloid beta protein are formed. Tissue cultures of neurons show that amyloid beta protein has both toxic and trophic effects.

Laboratory tests. There are no laboratory tests routinely used to diagnose Alzheimer's disease. A test for the apolipoprotein E4 allele can be used to suggest Alzheimer's disease in cases of early-onset dementia, although the presence of the E4 allele is not evidence of Alzheimer's disease.

Laboratory tests are helpful, however, in ruling out other causes of dementia. The most frequently ordered tests include: vitamin B12 level to rule out B12 deficiency, T4 or TSH levels to rule out hypothyroidism, RPR and FTA to rule out syphilis, and a thyroglobulin antibody titer to rule out Hashimoto's encephalopathy.

In addition, chemical profiles are also frequently ordered to role out chronic metabolic disturbances, including diabetes and dehydration. A ceruloplasmin level may be used to rule out Wilson's disease and a drug screen may be performed to rule out drug toxicity. A complete blood count (CBC) is used to rule out chronic infections and anemia, and a heavy metal screen can be performed to rule out lead, mercury, arsenic and copper poisoning. Also, an HIV test is often used to rule out HIV encephalopathy. A sedimentation rate and an autoantibody panel may be performed to rule out inflammatory and autoimmune conditions.

Laisure, Linda. Linda Laisure is the founder and director of H.O.M.E (Helping Our Mobile Elderly), a model project providing residential care in a small home-like setting. A specialist in gerontology with a certificate from the University of California at Los Angeles, Laisure has presented at the American Society on Aging Conference for the past 10 years and was speaker at the National Conference on Residential Care in 1992.

Language. Language refers to the ability of the brain to elaborate sounds used for communication and to produce mental images of sounds as part of the thinking process. Sounds are trapped in the back of the brain near the primary auditory cortex. The frontal speech area of the brain elicits these sounds and articulates them into speech. As the link between human thought and communication, language is dependent on memory.

Both normal aging and dementia are associated with many language changes, including both linguistic knowledge and performance. In diagnosing dementia, language changes associated with aging, such as a reduction in naming ability, must be considered. Studies show a significant decline in naming ability for the general population at about age 70. Age-related language problems have been found to be caused by a reduction of retrieval skills rather than a loss of knowledge. In several studies, cueing or priming resulted in an improved performance.

A number of studies indicate that patients with Alzheimer's disease have a mixture of lexical, semantic and pragmatic language problems. While these changes are seen in all stages of the disease, the degree of language impairment appears to correlate with the severity of dementia. The major language impairments in Alzheimer's disease include: difficulties with naming, auditory and written comprehension, speech and no change in syntax, repetition abilities or articulation. Naming deficits are considered one of the earliest signs of Alzheimer's disease with nouns being particularly affected. (Melvod, Jais et al. "Language During Aging and Dementia." *Clinical Neurology of Aging, Second Edition.* New York: Oxford University Press, 1994, 329–343.)

Late-onset familial Alzheimer's disease (LOFAD). Late-onset familial Alzheimer's disease (LOFAD) is a complex disorder that may involve multiple susceptibility genes. Many families have multiple affected members, most or all of who experience the onset of dementia after the age of 60–65 years. Disease duration is typically 8–10 years, but ranges from 2 to 25 years. Although no one gene is responsible for this disorder, several genetic associations have been made.

A well-documented association of LOFAD with the e4 allele of Apolipoprotein E chromosomal locus 19q13 has been made. APOE e4 appears to affect the age of onset by shifting the onset age toward an earlier age. Two common polymorphisms of this gene exist, resulting in three isoforms APOE e2, 23, and e4. The most common isoform in the general population is APOE3. In clinical series, the APOE4 allele is over-represented in LOFAD.

There is also evidence that a region on chromosome 12 may contain a susceptibility gene for LOFAD and an association with the alpha2 macroglobulin gene has been made.

The usefulness of APOE testing remains unclear since the e4 allele may be found in individuals with no signs of dementia. Presence of an e4 allele in an individual with dementia increases the probability that Alzheimer's disease is the cause. However, a three-generation family history with close attention to the history of individuals with dementia is sufficient to support a diagnosis of LOFAD.

Late-Stage Alzheimer's Disease. The late-stage of Alzheimer's disease refers to the terminal or final stage of Alzheimer's disease, which can last for several months up to a year or longer. In this stage, symptoms are severe, and patients can no longer care for themselves in a life-sustaining manner. For family caregivers, the terminal phases of dementing illness can be challenging. In this stage, the patient has few or no verbal abilities, may not recognize family members or caregivers, may become incontinent and usually non-ambulatory (unable to walk without assistance), and may demonstrate agitated behavior. It is recommended that patients make advance directives before they reach this stage.

Lateral sulcus. The lateral sulcus of the cerebral hemisphere is a deep cleft found mainly on the inferior and lateral surfaces of the brain.

Lawton and Brody Scale for Instrumental Activities of Daily Living (IADL). The IADL, designed by M. P. Lawton and E. M. Brody, describes activities of daily living that are impaired in neurodegenerative diseases. An assessment of IADL can be performed periodically to evaluate disease progression or response to treatment. Activities included in the IADL include the ability to use the telephone, shop independently, prepare and serve adequate meals, maintain housekeeping skills, do personal laundry, travel independently, take appropriate medications and handle finances.

Lewy bodies. Lewy bodies are inclusions found within the cytoplasm of neurons. Lewy bodies are more frequently seen as a spheroid with a dense central core and a less dense surrounding area, although in nerve cell processes they may be elongated. Lewy bodies are primarily seen in idiopathic parkinsonism and less frequently in postencephalitic parkinsonism, Hallervorden-Spatz disease, progressive supranuclear palsy, and with aging and Alzheimer's disease. Large numbers in the cerebral cortex represent diffuse Lewy body dementia.

Lewy body dementia. Lewy body dementia is the second most common form of degenerative dementia, accounting for up to 25 percent of cases of dementia in the elderly population. Lewy body dementia is being diagnosed more frequently and is characterized by fluctuating cognitive impairment, alterations of alertness or attention span, spontaneous parkinsonism and recurrent visual hallucinations. Variations or subtypes of this disease exist, with variations in symptom severity. Patients with Lewy body dementia show a reduction in pre-synaptic cholinergic transmission from the basal forebrain as well as deficits in cholinergic transmission from brain stem nuclei.

Accurate diagnosis of this condition is important as the management of psychosis and behavioral disturbances is complicated by the sensitivity to neuroleptic medications exhibited by patients with this disorder. Evidence indicates that patients with this disorder also respond well to cholinergic enhancers. Neuroimaging findings show a preservation of medial temporal lobe structures although there is a similarity to Alzheimer's disease in the distribution pattern of white matter observed on MRI. On SPECT exam, patients with Lewy body dementia exhibit a greater degree of occipital hypoperfusion when compared to patients with Alzheimer's disease. Lewy body disease may overlap with both Alzheimer's disease and with the dementia associated with Parkinson's disease. (Barber, R., et al. "Dementia with Lewy bodies: Diagnosis and Management." *International Journal of Geriatric Psychiatry*, Dec 2001, S12-S18.)

Lewy body variant of Alzheimer's disease. Although Lewy bodies are regarded as hallmarks of Parkinson's disease, these neuronal inclusions are also seen in the brains of individuals with clinical and pathological features of Alzheimer's disease. These cases are said to be Lewy body variants of Alzheimer's disease. There is considerable overlap of symptoms in diffuse Lewy body dementia and Alzheimer's disease although Lewy body dementia patients do not have the characteristic senile plaques and neurofibrillary tangles seen in Alzheimer's disease.

Life prolonging interventions. Life prolonging interventions are treatments such as cardiopulmonary resuscitation (CPR) that, if withheld, would likely result in death.

Life sustaining treatment. Life sustaining treatment is treatment that slows the dying process and includes feeding, hydration, and medications.

Limbic system. The limbic system includes a group of structures within the brain associated with emotion, behavior, drive and memory. Anatomically, the limbic structures include the subcallosal, the cingulated, and the parahippocampal gyri, the hippocampal formation, the amygdaloid nucleus, the mammilary bodies and the anterior thalamic nucleus.

Lipid peroxidation. Lipid peroxidation is a free radical-related process that occurs as a part of the body's normal metabolism. Lipid peroxidation associated with inflammation may cause cellular damage as a result of oxidative stress. The accumulation of products of lipid peroxidation, including lipid hydroperoxides and aldehydes, has been reported in the brains of patients with Alzheimer's disease.

Lipofuscin. Lipofuscin is a yellowish-brown pigment found in various parts of the body. The amount of lipofuscin within the body increases with age. Lipofuscin granules are present in the cytoplasm of neurons, possibly as a harmless metabolic by-product.

Living trust. A living trust is a legal document allowing an individual (the grantor or trustor) to create a trust and appoint someone else as trustee (usually a trusted individual or a bank representative). The trustee has authority to carefully invest and manage the grantor's assets.

Living will. A living will is a legal document that expresses an individual's decision on the use of artificial life support systems.

Lobar distribution. Lobar distribution refers to cellular differences such as atrophy seen in the lobes of the brain. Abnormalities of lobar distribution are commonly associated with and helpful in diagnosing neurodegenerative disorders. For instance, studies of lobar distribution in Alzheimer's disease are characterized by temporoparietal predominance whereas loss of deep nuclear structures such as selective early loss of caudate mass or signal abnormality in the striatum are seen in Huntington's chorea or Creutzfeldt-Jakob disease.

Lobar sclerosis *see* Pick's disease

Logical Memory Delayed Recall. A section of the Wechler memory scale test, the measurement of logical memory delayed recall is used to assess dementia.

Long-term care. Long-term refers to the care needed for patients suffering from a chronic condition or illness that limits their ability to carry out basic self-care tasks. Long-term care often involves the most intimate aspects of living including feeding and personal care. According to the Family Caregiver Alliance (FCA), an estimated 12.8 million Americans of all ages need long-term care. Approximately 57 percent of these people are aged 65 and older. The most severely disabled population, those who need substantial help carrying out 3 or more self-care tasks, comprise approximately 5.1 million Americans. Many long-term care options exist, including nursing homes, senior services, homecare, live-in help, senior housing with services, subsidized senior housing, assisted living residential care, and board-and-care homes.

Most people who need long-term care live at home or in community settings, not in institutions. About 2.4 million Americans live in institutions such as nursing homes. The General Accounting Office reports that public and private spending on long-term care services in 1993 was estimated to exceed $108 billion. About $70 billion of this money was paid by federal and state government funds, primarily Medicaid. Most of the remaining $38 billion was paid by individuals and their families. It's estimated that the number of older people requiring long-term care may as much as double over the next 25 years. (GAO/HEHS-95-26, November 7, 1994. *Long-Term Care: Diverse, Growing Population Includes Millions of Americans of All Ages*, U.S. General Accounting Office)

Long-term care insurance. Long-term care insurance is private insurance taken out before it is needed that may pay for some or all of nursing home care costs, depending on the particular coverage. Typically, there is a limit on the fees paid daily and the duration of the coverage. For instance, a policy may pay up to $160 daily for five years. Some long-term care insurance policies also cover home care services. For most people, long-term care coverage is only affordable if the policy is purchased when they are in their fifties or sixties. By age 70, the cost for a new policy is generally prohibitive. Many companies sell long-term policies but these companies may not be in business when they are needed. Make sure there are provisions for this possibility. Local agencies dedicated to the needs of the aging population can help provide assistance and advice for older adults seeking insurance.

In general long-term care insurance is appropriate for people who have significant financial assets that they would like to protect. Typically, policies have a waiting period of 6 months before they will pay for nursing home care. If a family expects to use up all their financial resources during this period, they will then qualify for Medicaid. In this case, long-term insurance would not be helpful.

Lumbar puncture. Lumbar puncture (spinal tap) is a medical procedure used to withdraw a sample of cerebrospinal fluid for laboratory testing or to inject drugs, including anesthetic agents. To rule out other causes of dementia a lumbar puncture may be performed to look for signs of chronic meningitis, syphilis multiple sclerosis, and other inflammatory diseases.

M266. M266 is a monoclonal antibody which binds to Abeta, drawing it out of the brain and reducing plaque formation. Researchers at Eli Lilly and Company in Indianapolis are currently evaluating M266 for its role as a therapy in Alzheimer's disease.

Mad cow disease *see* Bovine spongiform encephalopathy

Magnesium. The mineral magnesium is essential for many of the body's metabolic processes, including more than 300 different enzyme reactions. Low magnesium levels are associated with neurodegenerative conditions, perhaps because of the resulting free radical production.

Magnesium levels in the brain can be extremely low even when plasma or blood levels of magnesium are normal. This can happen when the brain is exposed to toxic metals since there is competition for entry into brain cells. Magnesium is depleted within the hippocampus of patients with Alzheimer's disease. Some researchers say it is the low levels of magnesium, rather than the high levels of aluminum, that are responsible for dementia. Normally, magnesium is transported throughout the body, linked to the protein albumin. It's thought that the type of albumin that serves this purpose has more of an affinity for aluminum.

Magnesium deficiency occurs in alcoholism, chronic diarrhea, malabsorption syndromes, chronic use of diuretics, diabetes, and in a high percent of patients undergoing heart surgery.

Magnetic resonance imaging (MRI). Magnetic resonance imaging (MRI) is a diagnostic technique that uses the magnetic properties of the hydrogen nucleus excited by radio-frequency radiation. In this procedure, radiation is transmitted by a coil surrounding the head. The excited hydrogen nuclei emit a signal that is detected as induced electric currents in a receiver coil. MRI is used to demonstrate atrophy or deterioration of brain cells. MRI in older patients with normal cognition may show medial temporal atrophy and thus indicate the possibility of future decline, whereas cerebral atrophy is seen after a substantial proportion of neural cells have died. Coronal T1-weighted spin echo sequences from MRI of the brain are used in the diagnostic protocol set up by CERAD. This MRI assessment protocol is used to rate atrophy (both focal and global), white matter abnormalities, and areas of cerebral infarction or hemorrhage.

MRI can easily distinguish gray and white matter because gray matter contains more hydrogen in the form of water than white matter. Because MRI provides better differentiation between gray and white matter, it can provide more information than computed tomography. Providing better anatomical resolution, MRI has shown that atrophy of the hippocampus is a hallmark of Alzheimer's disease and can be seen in the very early stages of the disease. Longitudinal studies have shown that dilation of the peri-hippocampal fissure can predict the diagnosis of Alzheimer's disease with over 90 percent accuracy.

MRI studies of the entorhinal cortex, the banks of the superior temporal cortex, and the anterior cingulate indicate that these areas show reduced volume changes before the hippocampal area. Researchers in Boston found that they could identify people who would develop Alzheimer's disease over time based on measurements of these brain regions with 93 percent accuracy.

Visual ratings of MRI scans of the entorhinal cortex are particularly useful for differentiating Alzheimer's disease from normal aging. Subcortical white-matter lesions (leukoariois) are related to age whereas lesions around the ventricular system appear to be associated with cognitive decline and are found in Alzheimer's disease.

Functional MRI is a similar technique that creates real-time images of active brain regions by measuring oxygen metabolism. In a normal elderly person doing a memory task, a computer enhanced image shows that the memory centers of the brain are activated. In a person with Alzheimer's disease, the pattern is disturbed. The memory centers of the hippocampus and entorhinal cortex fire weakly and at the wrong time. (NIA News, March 29, 2000)

Magnetic resonance spectroscopy (MRS). Magnetic resonance spectroscopy (MRS) is an advanced imaging technique capable of measuring changes in brain metabolism. MRS produces spectra of relatively weak magnetic signals from nuclei of phosphorus, carbon, or hydrogen not associated with water. These spectra provide information about chemical compounds and the energy state within specific regions of the brain. MRS has the ability to measure the concentrations of various neurotransmitters and brain metabolites and metabolite fluxes through brain compartments. Alterations of cerebral metabolites can help in the diagnosis and response to therapy in many different neurological disorders, including Alzheimer's disease.

Malnutrition. Malnutrition is a condition of nutrient deficiency caused by poor diet, the inability to properly absorb nutrients (malabsorption), chronic diarrhea, or the chronic use of diuretics or laxatives. Specific nutrient deficiencies, such as vitamin B1 and B12 and magnesium deficiencies may contribute to the development of neurodegenerative disorders.

Malnutrition may also occur in patients with Alzheimer's disease due to improper or poorly supervised diets. Malnutrition may cause a worsening of dementia and contribute to death.

Managed care. Managed care refers to health care provisions and guidelines established by insurance providers, including the federal government, which are based on patient diagnosis. As of 2000, 31 states had Medicaid managed care plans for at least some individuals in the public mental health system. However, the term "managed care" has different meanings for medical providers and insurance companies.

The American Medical Association defines managed care as "those processes or techniques used by any entity that delivers, administers and/or assumes risk for health care services in order to control or influence the quality, accessibility, utilization or costs and prices or outcomes of such services provided to a defined enrollee population."

The Health Insurance Association of America (HIAA) defines managed care as "systems that integrate the financing and delivery of appropriate health care services to covered individuals through the use of four elements: arrangements with selected providers to furnish a defined set of health care services to members; explicit standards for choosing those providers; formal programs for ongoing quality assurance and utilization review; and significant financial incentives for members to use the plan's providers and procedures." However, the HIAA's qualifications of incentives to use the plan's providers and procedures may prohibit those insured from using providers outside of the plan.

Managed care is designed to achieve cost efficiency while protecting medical consumers. The expansion of managed care to people on federal medical assistance (Medicaid) has been controversial. According to a report by the Milbank Memorial Fund, positive effects include: increased access, decreased use of inappropriate inpatient care, an expanded array of services, more flexibility in service delivery, more consistency in clinical decision making, more focused, goal-directed treatment and increased emphasis on accountability and outcomes.

Problems include: an incentive in a risk-based contract to under-treat, particularly to underserved, people with serious disorders, an undue focus on acute care and neglect of rehabilitation and other services associated with significant long-term payoff in improved functioning, potential difficulties created by Medicaid managed care contracts in serving the non–Medicaid population, frequent billing difficulties, initial payment difficulties, difficulties ensuring, quality and consistent outcomes across regions. ("Effective Public Management of Mental Health Care: Views from States on Medicaid Reforms That Enhance Service Integration and Accountability." New York, Milbank Memorial Fund in conjunction with the Bazelon Center for Mental Health Law, [2000.])

Massage Therapy and Physical Therapy. The loss of communication skills causes frustration in Alzheimer's disease patients. Massage and physical therapy are forms of touch therapy that can cross these communication barriers. In one study, people with Alzheimer's disease who received hand massages and were spoken to in a calm manner had a reduction in pulse rate and in inappropriate behavior. Some nursing homes have incorporated massage therapy into their scope of services. Healthcare professionals speculate that massage may offer benefits because of its relaxing effects and because it provides a form of social communication and a moderate form of exercise. ("Alzheimer's Disease, Nutrition and Dietary Supplements," *Intellihealth*, http://www.intelihealth.com/IH/ihtIH/WSIHW000/8303/29429.html)

Medicaid. Medicaid is a joint federal and state program that helps older people and those with disabilities pay for medical expenses that they can no longer afford. Medicaid will help pay for nursing home care and for some community services, usually limited home health, hospice, and personal care, with the amount of services determined by the state in which you live.

Most nursing homes participate in the Medicaid program. Medicaid typically pays 60 percent of all nursing home bills nationwide. In a few states, Medicaid may also pay for other long-term care options, including assisted living care, board-and-care homes, and some community-based services. To qualify for Medicaid, most people must contribute a substantial amount of their income, for instance, a social security check, before the state will pay for the balance. Widowed and single people must spend down their assets, owning no more than about $2,000 before their coverage starts. To do this, most people must sell their homes unless they can establish that they will eventually be able to move back home. For individuals with living spouses, many assets, including the residence and some income, are exempt. A resident's spouse is allowed to keep their home, car, clothing and generally up to $80,000 in assets such as stocks, bonds, pension and annuity income, and savings and bank accounts. The exact amounts vary by states.

Penalties for divesting assets in an attempt to qualify for Medicaid are high, and residents may be disqualified for Medicaid benefits if they are found to have divested assets. Some attorneys specialize in arranging assets advantageously to help people qualify for Medicaid. Medicaid is careful in only allowing admission to nursing homes that are appropriate for dementia patients. The nursing home's social worker will help prospective residents determine if they are eligible.

Medical ethics. Medical ethics is a branch of medicine that focuses on the ethical ramifications of patient care, ensuring that treatment is in the patient's best interest. Most healthcare providers have medical ethics boards that review patient care directives.

Medical problems. Individuals with Alzheimer's disease are at increased risk for developing certain other medical problems. They suffer from an increased incidence of neurologic complications, infections, hip fractures and malnutrition. These patients have been shown to have an increased risk for stroke, myoclonus, urinary tract infections and aspiration pneumonia.

Medicare. Medicare is the federal government's health insurance plan for the elderly. Medicare underwrites health insurance for persons 65 and older and some persons with disability. Medicare also covers limited nursing home care, limited home health and hospice care. Medicare will only cover nursing home care under certain circumstances, including short-term stays following hospitalization. Medicare may also cover home or inpatient hospice care during the last 6 months of life. If the resident qualifies, Medicare covers the bill of nursing home care for the first 20 days. After that, residents are required to make a co-payment of about $96 daily for a maximum of about 100 days. Many supplemental Medicare plans will cover this co-payment. When coverage runs out, the resident may use Medicaid or private payment. However, not all nursing homes are Medicare certified although they may be Medicaid certified. If you plan on using short-term Medicare coverage, make sure the nursing home you select is Medicare certified.

A 50-state analysis of Medicare spending sponsored by the Alzheimer's Association and released in April 2001 projects that the price tag for Medicare beneficiaries with Alzheimer's disease will grow by 54.5 percent by 2010 with an increase from $31.9 billion in 2000 to $49.3 billion by 2010. And patients with Alzheimer's disease make up only 10 percent of the Medicare population, although between 2010 and 2050 the number of Americans with Alzheimer's disease is expected to swell from an estimated 5.5 million to an estimated 14 million. (Levine, Jeff. "Alzheimer's Disease Could Bankrupt Medicare," WebMD, April 2001)

Medicare HMOs. Medicare HMOs, which are also known as social HMOs or SHMOs, are federally funded programs that provide home-care aides, home medical supplies, and other home-based medical services. Medicare HMOs can also arrange to send Alzheimer patients to adult day care. The idea behind SHMOs is that it is far less expensive to care for patients in their own home than in a nursing home. The services that they provide make this possible. Four SHMOs located in various parts of the country serve approximately 80,000 Medicare recipients. See also SCAN Health Plan of Long Beach, California.

Medicare Payment Advisory Commission (MedPAC). The Medicare Payment Advisory Commission (MedPAC) was established in 1997 by the merger of the Physician Payment Review Commission and the Prospective Payment Assessment Commission. Created by congressional mandate, MedPAC's 15 members review payment policies and make congressional recommendations by March 1 of each year. They also evaluate current Medicare policies and send a report of their findings to Congress each June. MedPAC holds regular meetings that are open to the public.

Medications that may cause or worsen cognitive impairment. Medications that may cause or worsen cognitive impairment include: antiarrhythmic agents for the treatment of heart rhythm disturbances, antibiotics, anticholinergic agents, anticonvulsants, antidepressants, antiemetics, antihistamines/decongestants, antihypertensive agents, antimanic agents, antineoplastic agents, antiparkinsonian agents, corticosteroids, histamine H2-receptor antagonists, immunosuppressive agents, muscle relaxants, narcotic analgesics, radiocontrast agents, sedatives, and overdoses of nonsteroidal anti-inflammatory agents. (Sloane, Philip. "Advances in the Treatment of Alzheimer's Disease." *American Family Physician*, November 1, 1998). *See also* Treatment of Alzheimer's disease.

Medulla oblongata. The medulla oblongata or myelencephalon, a cone-shaped tissue, situated in the hindbrain, connects the pons superiorly and the spinal cord inferiorly. A median fissure is present on the front or anterior surface flanked by swellings known as pyramids. Olives, arising from olivary nuclei, are situated behind the pyramids. Posterior to the olives are the inferior cerebellar peduncles, which connect the medulla to the cerebellum.

Mega, Michael, M.D., Ph.D. Dr. Michael Mega is the director of the Memory Disorder and Alzheimer's Disease Clinic and assistant professor at the University of California at Los Angeles School of Medicine.

Melancholia. Melancholia is a mental condition characterized by extreme depression, bodily complaints, and often hallucinations and delusions.

Melanin. The pigment melanin is found in various parts of the body. Melanin granules are scattered throughout the cytoplasm of certain neurons, particularly those found in the substantia nigra region of the midbrain. Their presence is thought to be related to ability of these cells whose neurotransmitter is dopamine to produce compounds known as catecholamines.

Melatonin. Melatonin is a natural-occurring hormone involved in regulation of sleeping and waking. It is also sold as a dietary supplement. Melatonin, a potent antioxidant which is secreted by the pineal gland, had free-radical scavenging properties, and it has been demonstrated to increase gene expression for antioxidant enzymes. Levels of melatonin are high in children and decline with aging. The Alzheimer's Disease Cooperative Study is currently evaluating the use of melatonin for sleep disturbances in Alzheimer's disease.

Memantine. Memantine, a N-methyl-d-aspartate (NMDA) receptor antagonist, is reported to improve functioning in patients with advanced Alzheimer's disease. Derived from the anti-influenza drug amantadine, memantine blocks the overstimulation of the NMDA receptor caused by the excitotoxin glutamate. Memantine blocks the NMDA receptor, protecting neurons from excessive stimulation by the neurotransmitter glutamate without upsetting glutamate's normal role in brain function.

In 28-week trials conducted at New York University, patients showed a one point decline compared with a 5.86 decline on control subjects using placebos. Memantine has been used as a therapeutic agent for Alzheimer's and other degenerative diseases in Europe since 1980. Studies of memantine as a therapy for both vascular dementia and Alzheimer's disease show a favorable response in more than 70 percent of subjects.

Side effects, although rare, are related to the ability of memantine to indiscriminately shut down normal signaling systems, including those required for mental functioning. Other side effects observed in patients with dementia treated with memantine include vertigo, restlessness, hyperexcitation and fatigue. Parkinsonian patients using 30mg/day of memantine have experienced nervous energy, emotional agitation, confusion, dizziness and stomach upset. The effects appear to be increased in patients with AIDS dementia and in patients taking antidepressant medications. Memantine is scheduled to approved in the United States in 2005. *See also* glutamate. ("Needless Brain Wasting," *Life Extension*, July 2001, 65–68)

Memorial Delirium Assessment Scale (MDAS). The Memorial Delirium Assessment Scale (MDAS) is a neuropsychiatric evaluation tool which measures awareness, disorientation, short-term memory impairment, impaired digit span, shift attention, disorganized thinking, perceptual disturbance, delusions, psychometric activity and disorder of arousal. The MDAS is used to aid in the diagnosis of delirium.

Memory. Memory is the process or power of recalling or reproducing what has been learned or retained, especially through associative mechanisms. Memory also refers to the store of things learned in the past either through activity or experience and recalled through repetition or recognition. Memory can be subdivided into immediate, short-term, recent and remote memory. Serially subtracting numbers from a list is a function of immediate memory. Short-term memory can be tested by showing or reciting a list of three objects and having the person repeat this list 15 minutes later. Recent memory refers to recall of events occurring in past days or weeks or months. Remote memory refers to recall of events occurring many years in the past. In patients with dementia, recent memory is usually more severely impaired than remote memory.

Memory aids. Memory aids are techniques and tools used to help patients with short-term memory impairment although they are not as helpful in the later stages of dementia. Message boards, large clocks, lists and instruction sheets can be used to remind patients of mealtimes and other activities. Caregivers are encouraged to keep familiar objects in their usual places, make sure clocks and watches are accessible and show the correct time, indicate dates on calendars, use message boards, leave notes when they are away indicating when they will return, and display photographs of family members and close friends that are clearly labeled. Research suggests that gently encouraging patients to use their brain may help them as long as they are not overwhelmed or pushed.

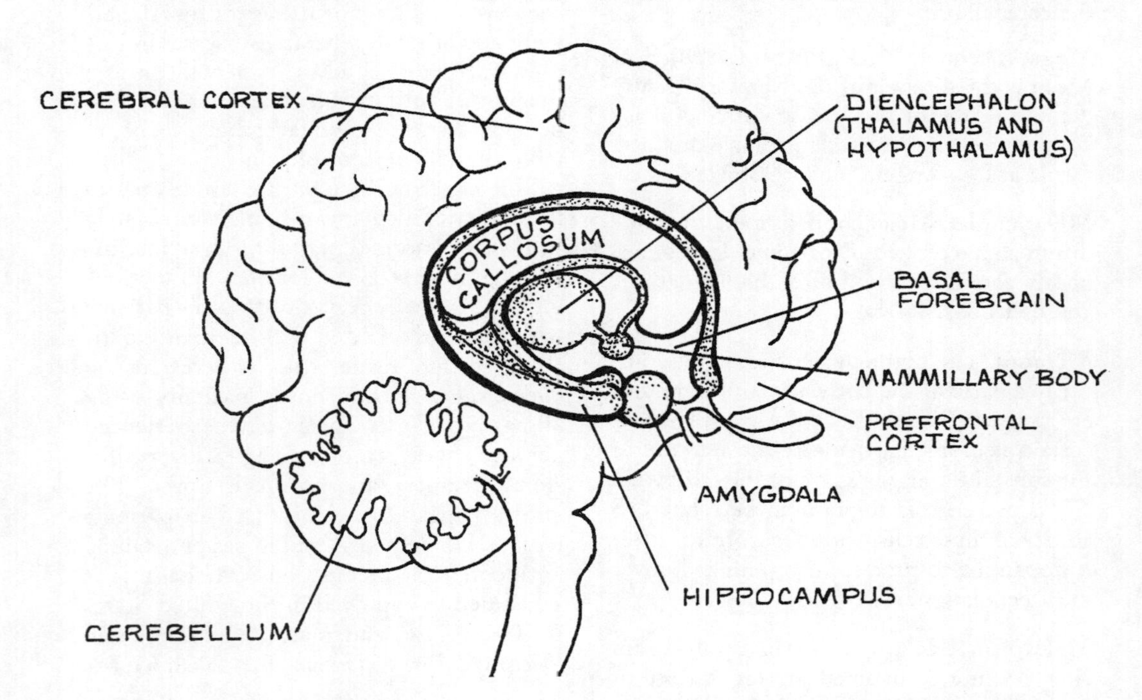

The Memory Center of the Brain (illustration by Marvin G. Miller).

- **The Cerebral Cortex is involved in conscious thought and language**
- **The Basal Forebrain is important in memory and learning and consists of numerous neurons containing acetylcholine**
- **The Hippocampus is essential for memory storage**

Memory impairment. Memory impairment refers to the diminished ability to process, reproduce, or recall what has been learned and retained.

Meninges of the brain. Three meninges or membranes surround the brain: the dura mater, the arachnoid mater, and the pia mater.

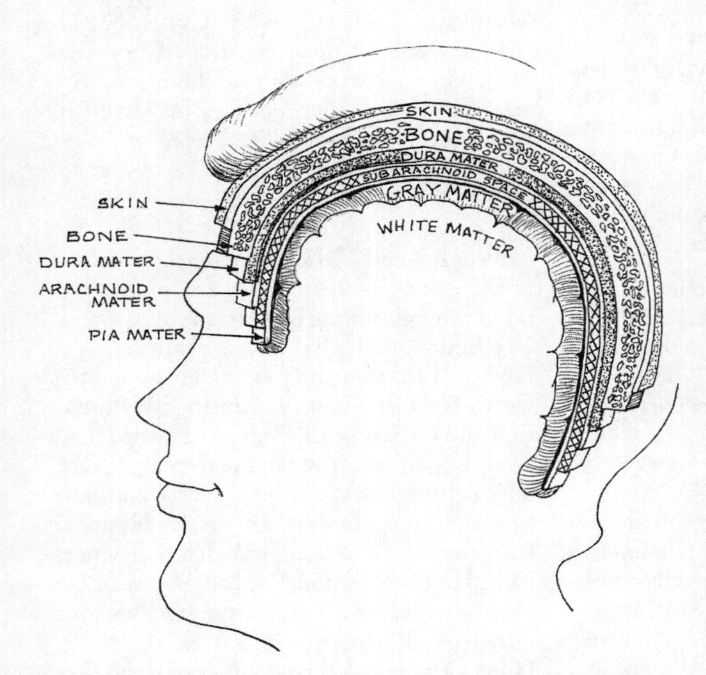

Protective Layers of the Brain (Dura Mater, Pia Mater, Arachnoid Mater) (illustration by Marvin G. Miller).

Meningitis. Meningitis is a condition caused by inflammation of the meninges of the brain, causing headache over the entire head and back of the neck. Meningitis is usually of a bacterial or viral origin.

Mercury. Studies of brain tissue from Alzheimer's disease patients show high concentrations of mercury. Patients with amalgam dental fillings, which are primarily made of mercury, are reported to have a higher incidence of Alzheimer's disease. Amalgam fillings also contain silver, tin, copper and zinc.

Mesencephalon. The mesencephalon or midbrain is a narrow part of the brain about 0.8 inches long connecting the forebrain to the pons and cerebellum of the hindbrain. The narrow cavity of the midbrain consists of a cerebral aqueduct, which connects the third and fourth ventricles. The tectum refers to the part of the midbrain that lies posterior to the cerebral aqueduct.

Mesial temporal lobe. The mesial temporal lobe refers to the area of the temporal lobe situated in, near, or directed toward the median plane of the body, compared to the distal part, which is furthest away from the body.

Metabolic causes of dementia. A number of different medical conditions are well-known for causing organic brain syndrome. One of the most common causes is untreated hypothyroidism that has progressed to myxedema or total thyroid failure. However, the autoantibodies responsible for autoimmune hypothyroidism (Hashimoto's thyroiditis) may target brain rather than thyroid tissue, causing dementia in the absence of thyroid dysfunction.

Similar cases are seen with disorders of calcium metabolism, especially hypercalcemia, and also with electrolyte imbalance. Chronic liver and renal disease are frequently associated with an organic brain syndrome. However, it would be unusual for organic brain syndrome to emerge in these conditions without evidence of the primary disorder. Repeated episodes of hypoglycemia can also cause dementia, although in this case, the history is usually clearly episodic rather than gradual or sporadic.

Pernicious anemia, which can be diagnosed by a decreased vitamin B 12 level, can cause an organic brain syndrome even without hematologic or other neurologic findings. Korsakoff's syndrome, due to thiamine (vitamin B1) deficiency, presents with a type of amnesia in which the patient is unable to learn new information. Vascular dementia is caused by any of the syndromes resulting from brain damage due to diminished oxygen reserves, including ischemia, anoxia, or hypoxia. CADASIL is another cause of vascular dementia. *See* Vascular dementia.

Metabolism. Metabolism is the process of building up and breaking down of chemical foods within the body. Digestion is an example of metabolism. The products of metabolism are known as metabolites. For instance, drugs known as phenothiazines are metabolized by the body, forming hundreds of different chemical metabolites. Changes in metabolism of the brain have been seen in many neurological disorders including stroke, alcoholism and Alzheimer's disease.

Metalloproteinases. Metalloproteinases are enzymes that facilitate the binding of metals such as copper and aluminum to proteins, including amyloid beta protein. Therapies that inhibit metalloproteinases are currently being evaluated.

Metals *see* Minerals

Metrifonate. Currently under consideration by the FDA as a treatment for Alzheimer's disease, metrifonate has a 30 year record of safety and tolerability. Introduced in the 1960s, it was originally used as treatment for schistosomiasis. Although it is not a cholinesterase inhibitor, it is gradually converted in the body to a phosphate compound that acts as a long-inhibitor of both cholinesterase enzymes. Metrifonate produces a stable inhibition of acetylcholinesterase that is longer-lasting than that observed with either Tacrine hydrochloride or donepezil hydrochloride.

In one study involving 4 different randomized, 12-week long, placebo-controlled trials at 120 ambulatory clinics, metrifonate given at doses of 30 to 80 mg daily was found to safely improve the cognitive performance of patients with mild to moderate Alzheimer's disease, not only relative to placebo, but, at doses of 60 to 80 mg daily, also relative to baseline performance levels. This is the first such finding for an acetylcholinesterase inhibitor. Metrifonate also stands out in that is has been demonstrated to have the capacity to improve not only cognition, but also psychiatric and behavioral disturbances, the ability to conduct activities of daily living, and global functioning of patients with mild to moderate Alzheimer's disease. Side effects were primarily of a gastrointestinal nature and included diarrhea and nausea. (Farlow, M.D., Martin R., and Pamela A. Cyrus, M. D. "Metrifonate Improves the Cognitive Deficits of Patients with Alzheimer's Disease Relative to Placebo Treatment and to Baseline Performance *The Annals of Long-Term Care* 2000. Online at http://www.mmhc.com/nhm/articles/NHM9909/farlow.html)

Microglial cells. Microglia are the smallest of the neuroglial cells. They are found scattered throughout the central nervous system. The brain's micloglial cells are immune system cells that become activated by neurotoxins and other injuries, causing inflammation and initiating an immune response that, according to some researchers, results in the destruction of neurons. Jean Harry and Jau-Shyong Hong, researchers at the National Institutes of Environmental Health Sciences (NIEHS) are currently studying reactive gliosis in experiments conducted with in vitro (outside of the body) cell cultures. Hong's experiments have supported the theory that overactive microglia kill neurons, and that, in contrast, cells known as astroglia produce proteins that promote neuronal growth or survival. On exposure to amyloid beta peptide fragments, microglia exhibit scavenger cell activity, engulfing exposed neurons.

Harry suspects that specific patterns of neurodegeneration may be due to signaling interactions that occur between the brain's neural and glial cells. Her work focuses on the effects of environmental chemicals on this interaction. ("Environmental Toxins and The Brain," NIEHS News, 1996; *Environmental Health Perspectives* 104 (8), 5)

Although microglial cells in the brain do have a role in the development of Alzheimer's disease, Tony Wyss-Coray and colleagues at the Gladstone Institute of Neurological Disease at the University of California, San Francisco, found that in the presence of increased Transforming Growth Factor Beta-1 (TGF-b1), microglial clear away beta amyloid. Their study, which was published in the May 2000 issue of *Nature Medicine*, reports that the molecules produced by TGF-b1 have a potential role in the treatment of Alzheimer's disease. (Franzen, Harald. "Molecule Helps Brain Cells Clear Alzheimer's Plaques." *Scientific American*, Medicine, May 1, 2000)

Microtubule-associated protein tau (MAPT). Microtubule-associated protein tau includes a number of different proteins that bind the microtubule structure of neurons and stable their polymerized structure. In Alzheimer's disease, a hyperphosphorylated form of tau protein is responsible for the defective microtubules that lead to neuronal degeneration.

Midbrain *see* mesencephalon

Milbank Memorial Fund. The Milbank Memorial Fund is an endowed national foundation that has contributed to innovation in health and social policy since 1905. The Fund supports nonpartisan analysis, study, research and communication on significant issues in health policy. 645 Madison Avenue, New York, NY 10022, (212) 355-8400, *www.milbank.org*.

Mild cognitive impairment (MCI). Mild cognitive impairment (MCI) is a condition characterized by isolated lapses in short-term memory, normal function in other cognitive domains, and normal basic activities of daily living. Once thought to be manifestation of the normal aging process, mild cognitive impairment is considered to be the earliest stage of Alzheimer's disease. Dr. John Morris and other researchers at the Washington University School of Medicine in St. Louis, Missouri, report that the key here is repeated lapses in memory. A temporary period of mild cognitive impairment can occur as a result of taking too much of certain medicines, a blow to the head or the lassitudes of depression. But when repeated problems of short-term memory occur, this is likely to be an early stage of Alzheimer's disease. In this early stage, magnetic resonance scans of the brain reveal that the hippocampus is somewhat smaller than normal or it may even be shrunken in appearance.

Research at the Mayo Clinic in Rochester indicates that patients with MCI progress to Alzheimer's disease at a rate of 10 to 15 percent each year, while normal control subjects progress at a rate of 1 to 2 percent each year. Mayo Clinic researchers describe MCI as a state that may be transition between normal cognitive abilities and clearly recognizable Alzheimer's disease. In psychometric screening, patients with MCI may show only slight deviations from normal. Generally they have scores of 24 or higher (out of 30) on the Mini-Mental Status Exam.

Patients with greater cognitive impairment, positive tests for the apolipoprotein E 4 allele, and hippocampus atrophy on MRI are predictors of a more rapid disease progression. (Waldemar, M.D., Gunhild. "New Perspectives in Dementia." XVII World Congress of Neurology, June 17, 2001.)

Minerals. Minerals are chemical elements or compounds that result from the inorganic processes of nature. A number of minerals are involved in the normal metabolic functions of the brain, and a number of mineral imbalances have been suspected of contributing to the development of Alzheimer's disease.

While early studies suggested that an increased ingested of aluminum was responsible for the development of Alzheimer's disease, this has turned out to be untrue. However, because nerve cells grow but do not regenerate, the brain is the organ best suited for the accumulation of metabolic errors over an extended period of time. Researchers at the University of Tennessee in Knoxville have proposed that imbalances in both aluminum and iron contribute to but do not initiate Alzheimer's disease. (Joshi, Jayant G., et al. "Iron and Aluminum Homeostasis in Neural Disorders." *Environmental Health Perspectives 102*, Supplement 3, September 1994)

Results of the Nun's Study indicate that

alterations in the normal balance of copper and zinc are also associated with the development of Alzheimer's disease.

Mini Mental Status Examination (MMSE). The Mini Mental Status Examination (MMSE) is the most widely used evaluation tool used to measure the severity of dementia. Patients with mild dementia have a score of 22–30, with moderate dementia a score of 11–21 and severe dementia 0–10. Patients with dementia generally have scores below 30.

The MMSE includes assessments of orientation, memory, attention and calculation, language, ability to follow commands, reading comprehension, ability to write a sentence, and ability to copy a drawing.

Some researchers have suggested using a cutoff score of 23 or less for the presence of dementia in individuals with at least 8 years of education. It's been noted that education, occupation, and cultural and background factors can strongly influence MMSE scores. In one study, normal farmers were found to score an average of more than 2 points lower on the MMSE than normal white-collar workers. The MMSE also permits considerable flexibility in administration, and the mode of administration has also been found to influence the score.

Mitochondria. Mitochondria are cellular component found in the cell cytoplasm that have recently been found to have their own DNA. Mitochondria also produce enzymes essential for energy metabolism. Mitochrondrial dysfunction is related to a number of different diseases. In Alzheimer's disease, mitochondrial dysfunction is related to the toxic effects of excitatory neurotransmitters, primarily glutamate. These excitatory neurotransmitters stimulate specific neuronal receptors, which, when altered by defective mitochondrial energy production, cause a self-perpetuating cascade of events that ultimately result in neuronal cell death.

Normally, with adequate mitochondrial energy production, a normal transmembrane potential exists. This transmembrane potential has a profound effect on the activity of the NMDA receptor for the excitatory neurotransmitter glutamate. Normally, this receptor is blocked by magnesium ions. However, when mitochondrial activity is depressed, alterations in the transmembrane potential reduce this magnesium block. This allows glutamate to react with the NMDA receptor, causing an influx of calcium in the neuron. It is the influx of calcium into the cell which initiates the cascade of events leading to neuronal cell destruction.

Mitochrondrial DNA polymorphisms. Polymorphisms to mitochondrial DNA are linked to many diseases, including Alzheimer's disease. The mitochondrial dysfunction caused by these polymorphisms leads to excessive free-radical production and oxidative tissue damage, which is confined to the brain.

Mixed forms of dementia. Mixed forms of dementia are conditions in which more than one form of dementia is present. Examples include Lewy body dementia or vascular dementia occurring in individuals with coexisting Alzheimer's disease.

Modified Mini–Mental State Examination. The Modified Mini–Mental State Examination is a screening test for cognitive impairment on which scores range from 0 to 100 with lower scores indicating greater impairment. Scores of less than 78 suggest cognitive impairment.

Modified Scales of Psychological Development (M-OSPD). The Modified Scales of Psychological Development (M-OSPD) is an evaluation tool used to diagnose dementia. Developed in 1994, the M-OSPD assesses dementia severity in ranges where the MMSE scores are low or at bottom.

Molecular genetics. Molecular genetics refers to the study of the structure and function of particular genes. The molecular genetics of Alzheimer's disease involves mutations of several different genes, particularly those influencing amyloid precursor protein and its processing, immune system genes, neurotransmission, the immune system, neurotrophic factors, and signal transduction.

Monarda. *Monarda* includes various species of the herb commonly referred to as horsebalm. Horsebalm is rich in carvacrol, a compound found by Austrian scientists to help inhibit the breakdown of acetylcholine. Horsebalm also contains the compound thymol, which also prevents the breakdown of acetylcholine. Of importance, horsebalm has the ability to cross the blood-brain barrier. Normally, this barrier acts as a protective mechanism, preventing toxic drugs from directly injuring brain tissue. In the case of horsebalm, this ability is a benefit because of the possibility that it could directly influence acetylcholine levels in the brain when added to shampoo. (Duke, James A. *The Green Pharmacy.* Emmaus, PA: Rodale Press, [2000] 1997.)

Monoamine oxidase (MAO). The naturally occurring enzyme monoamine oxidase (MAO) catalyzes the oxidation of dopamine to an aldehyde compound, dihydroxyphenylacetaldehyde, with formation of hydrogen peroxide. Without sufficient glutathione peroxidase enzymes to break down this substance, excess hydrogen peroxidate combines with ferrous iron forming ferric iron and the highly reactive hydroxyl radical which is responsible for free radical damage to the body. Inhibiting MAO with drugs such as Selegiline may offer benefits in many of the neurodegenerative disorders including Alzheimer's disease.

Monoamine oxidase inhibitor (MAO inhibitor). Monoamine oxidase inhibitors are drugs that inhibit the production of monoamine oxidase, which reduces free radical production. Selegeline, a potent inhibitor of a type of MAO known as MAO_B, delays the need for dopamine replacement therapy in patients with Parkinson's disease. Selegeline is also being evaluated for its ability to improve cognitive defects in Alzheimer's disease. Extracts of ginkgo biloba have also been found to inhibit MAO. (Perlmutter, David. "Functional Therapeutics in Neurodegenerative Disease." Physicians Committee for Responsible Medicine website, http://www.pcrm.org/health/Preventive_Medicine/alzheimers.html)

Monoclonal Antibody Therapy. Monoclonal antibodies are laboratory produced protein antibodies that have a single, selected specificity. Monoclonal antibodies are capable of reacting with and destroying certain antigens or proteins in the body that are associated with disease. Monoclonal antibodies are currently being used to treat a variety of cancers and autoimmune disease. They are also being evaluated for their role in the treatment of Alzheimer's disease.

Monosodium glutamate (MSG). Monosodium glutatamate is a flavor enhancer added to many foods. Monosodium glutamate, like the artificial sweetener aspartame, is also an excitotoxin capable of destroying neurons in the hypothalamus. In 1968, Dr. Olney of Washington University in St. Louis, Missouri, found that MSG causes widespread destruction of neurons in the hypothalamus and other areas of the brain adjacent to the ventricular system. He found the damage to be most severe in the brain of the newborn. As a result, MSG was voluntarily removed from baby foods in 1969. Both glutamate and aspartame can cause neurons to become extremely excited. If given in large enough doses, they can cause these cells to degenerate and die, generally within two hours. (Blaylock, M.D., Russell L. *Excitotoxins, the Taste That Kills.* Sante Fe, NM: Health Press, 1994, 33–57.)

Mood. Mood is a conscious state of mind or predominant emotion, including feelings such as well-being, mania and depression.

Morrison-Bogorad, Marcelle. Marcelle Morrison-Bogorad is the Director of Neurosciences at the U.S. National Institute of Aging in Bethesda, Maryland.

Mortality. According to the National Center for Health statistics, there were 22,725 deaths attributed to Alzheimer's disease in 1998, making Alzheimer's disease the 9th Cause of Death Rank Among Americans Ages 65 years and older. (National Vital Statistics Reports, Vol. 48, No. 11, U.S. Department of Health and Human Services, Hyattsville, MD). In 1998, Alzheimer's disease was ranked 12th for all causes of death. In

1999, the number jumped, moving into the 9th place for all causes of death, due mainly to the inclusion of death formerly classified as "presenile dementia." The 44,507 deaths from Alzheimer's disease in 1999 surpassed the totals for other major causes of death, including motor vehicle accidents and breast cancer. ("Mortality declines for several leading causes of death, 1999," Press Release of U.S. Department of Health and Human Services, June 26, 2001.)

Dementia is known to shorten life expectancy; previous estimates of median survival after the onset of dementia have ranged from 5 to 13 years. According to a 2001 report published by The Clinical Progression of Dementia Study Group, previous studies may not consider patients with rapidly progressive illness who were not yet officially diagnosed with dementia. After adjustment for length bias, the median survival for dementia was reported to be 3.1 years for subjects with probable Alzheimer's disease, 3.5 years for subjects with possible Alzheimer's disease, and 3.3 years for subjects with vascular dementia. Overall, a younger age at the onset of dementia was associated with longer survival. The level of education was not associated with survival. (Wolfson, Ph.D., Christina, et al. "A Reevaluation of the Duration of Survival after the Onset of Dementia." *The New England Journal of Medicine,* 344 (15), April 12, 2001, 1111–1116.) The Center for Disease Control statistics for mortality can be found online at http://www.cdc.gov/nchs.

Motor fibers. Motor nerve fibers are efferent nerve fibers that transmit impulses from the central nervous system to muscles, causing them to contract. Their cells of origin lie in the anterior gray horn of the spinal cord.

Multi-infarct dementia (MID). There is no absolute way of differentiating multi-infarct dementia (MID) from Alzheimer's disease. A significant number of patients, particularly elderly patients, have elements of both disorders, making complete differentiation sometimes impossible. However, because infarcts may affect any part of the brain, symptoms do not follow a pattern as they do in Alzheimer's disease. On average, MID patients live several years less than Alzheimer's disease patients due to their propensity for heart attacks and severe strokes.

In multi-infarct dementia, the patient characteristically shows a stepwise deterioration in neurologic function with a background of risk factors for cerebrovascular disease, particularly hypertension. Multi-infarct dementia is usually accompanied by other focal signs in addition to mental decline. Minor focal abnormalities might be found in the neurologic examination and imaging procedures, particularly MRI, may show signs of numerous small infarcts.

The history in Alzheimer's disease is generally that of a gradual progressive dementia with a normal general neurologic examination and an imaging procedure that shows evidence of cerebral atrophy. The medical history is generally negative.

Multiple Sclerosis (MS). Multiple sclerosis is an inflammatory disease characterized by destruction of the protective myelin sheath that covers nerve axons. The inflammatory reaction in MS primarily occurs within the white matter of the central nervous system. Approximately 1 million individuals are affected worldwide, with about 300,000 of them living in the United States. Women with MS outnumber men by 2:1 and symptoms usually commence in early adulthood. Paralysis, sensory disturbances, uncoordination, and visual impairment are common features. The exact cause of MS in unknown but most cases have an autoimmune origin, and MS is considered an autoimmune disorder.

Muscarinic receptors. Acetylcholine reacts with post-synaptic muscarinic receptors in the hippocampus and temporal cortex. Muscarinic receptors are not affected in Alzheimer's disease.

Music therapy. For centuries, music has been used as a form of therapy. On August 1, 1991, the U.S. Senate Special Committee on Aging met with music therapists, doctors, musicians, nursing home residents and family members of Alzheimer patients to hear testimony on the benefits of music therapy for the elderly. Dr. Oliver Sacks, a renowned neurologist, stated that music is a lifeline for Alzheimer's patients, because meaningful music does for them what their damaged brains can no longer do—organize and make incoming stimuli comprehensible, allowing them to "hold themselves and their worlds together."

As Dr. Sacks explained, Alzheimer's disease patients do not lose their personalities or their minds, just their access to them. Music helps sort through this confusion. Music therapy is used to improve physical, psychological, cognitive and social functioning and is reported to cause significant increases in levels of melatonin, norepinephrine and epinephrine in Alzheimer's disease patients. (U.S. Senate Special Committee on Aging, "Forever Young: Music and Aging," August 1, 1991, Serial No. 102-9. U.s. Government Printing Office Washington, DC: 1992; Alzheimer's Ease htttp:www.nh.ultranet.com/~akzease/thewayfull.html)

Mutations. Mutations are changes that occur in genes. Genes are composed of proteins, and proteins are composed of amino acids. A difference in one amino acid or a rearrangement of the amino acid sequence causes a gene mutation. Mutations are permanent and can be passed on from generation to generation. Some mutations alter specific attributes or characteristics, which can cause disease or disease susceptibility. Mutations in the presenilin genes are involved in the etiology of the majority of cases of familial early-onset Alzheimer's disease. Mutations in Alzheimer's disease are generally dominant, meaning that they predominate over their partner allele.

Mycoplasma fermentans. Mycoplasma is an infectious agent distinct from bacteria and viruses. *Mycoplasma fermentans* is thought to occur as a mutated form of the *brucellosis* bacteria. While most people harbor traces of this infectious agent, it is usually innocuous. However, according to the Consumer Health Organization of Canada, one out of 300,000 people with mycoplasma develop Alzheimer's disease depending on their genetic predisposition. (Scott, Donald, *Consumer Health Organization of Canada Newsletter*, 2000, June; vol. 23).

Myelencephalon *see* medulla oblongata

Myelin basic protein (MBP). Myelin basic protein is the primary constituent of the protective myelin sheath that covers nerve axons. Myelin basic protein is also expressed within the nervous system in locations outside of the myelin sheath and it may be found in the thymus and other lymphoid tissues. In patients with multiple sclerosis, myelin basic protein is one of the major targets of the inflammatory immune response.

Myelin basic protein (MBP) antibodies. MBP antibodies are autoantibodies that destroy the protective myelin covering of nerve axons, interfering with the proper transmission of nerve impulses. Toxic concentrations of lead are associated with the development of MBP antibodies. MBP antibodies are seen in multiple sclerosis, amyotrophic lateral sclerosis (ALS) and Alzheimer's disease. Although Alzheimer's disease primarily affects neurons, there is secondary involvement of myelin.

Myelin sheath. The myelin sheath is a protective segmented, discontinuous layer or covering found on nerve axons, which is essential for the normal transmission of nerve impulses. The myelin sheath is destroyed or demyelinated in both multiple sclerosis and Alzheimer's disease.

Myelinated nerve fibers. Myelinated nerve fibers are processes surrounded by myelin sheaths. The myelin sheath is not formed by the neuron but by supporting cells (oligodendrocytes in the central nervous system and Schwann cells in the peripheral nervous system).

Myoclonus. Myoclonus is a condition of uncontrolled muscle twitches.

N-acetylcysteine (NAC). The supplement N-acetylcysteine (NAC) has been reported to prevent apoptotic death in nerve cells and protect mitochondria proteins (cell components responsible for energy production) from free radical damage in aged mice, slowing age-related memory loss. The antioxidant properties and probable action on mitochondrial bioenergetic ability in the synaptic terminals may explain these effects. NAC has also been reported to inhibit the production of nitric oxide. (*Brain Research*, 2000, vol 855(1); 100–106).

Naproxen. Naproxen is a non-steroidal anti-inflammatory agent (Aleve, Anaprox, Naprosyn) which inhibits prostaglandin production. Naproxen is currently being evaluated for its use in treating Alzheimer's disease.

National Alzheimer's Coordinating Center (NACC). The National Alzheimer's Coordinating Center at the University of Washington in Seattle is a coordinating agency sponsored by the National Institute on Aging. The Center facilitates collaborative research among the 30 Alzheimer's Disease Centers, evaluating data and making it available to researchers and the public.

National Center on Caregiver Division. Initiated by a grant from the Archstone Foundation and managed by the Family Caregiver Alliance, the National Center on Caregiver Division, established in July, 2001, is an organization dedicated to empowering caregivers. Its objectives are to develop and disseminate information about best practices for caregiving at the state and national levels, to provide assistance to policy makers, to deliver high quality consumer information to caregivers, and to provide quality information for media researching caregiver issues. For more information, see the Family Caregiver Alliance under Caregivers in the Resource Section.

National Citizens' Coalition for Nursing Home Reform. The National Citizens' Coalition for Nursing Home Reform is a national advocacy group that works to define and improve the quality of long-term care. Their web site offers links to a number of affiliated state advocacy groups. http://www.ncnhr.org

National Institute of Allergy and Infectious Disease (NIAID). The Clinical Immunology Division of the National Institute of Allergy and Infectious Diseases division of the National Institutes of Health is conducting research in the area of vaccines for Alzheimer's disease.

National Institute of Mental Health (NIMH). The National Institute of Mental Health (NIMH) is the division of the National Institutes of Health dedicated to mental disorders. The NIMH conducts and supports research to learn more about the causes, prevention, and treatment of mental and emotional illnesses, including multiple aspects of Alzheimer's disease.

National Institute of Mental Health (NIMH) Alzheimer's Disease Genetics Dataset. The NIMH's Alzheimer's disease genetics dataset is an initiative that serves as a national resource of demographic, clinical and genetic data from people with Alzheimer's disease.

National Institute of Neurological and Communicative Disorders and Stroke (NINDS). NINDS is the Federal Government's principal agency for research on the causes, prevention, detection and treatment of neurological diseases and stroke. The NINDS also studies Alzheimer's disease and works on research geared toward developing new medications for Alzheimer's disease and other neurological disorders.

National Institute on Aging (NIA). The National Institute on Aging (NIA) is a branch of the National Institutes of Health. The NIA is the federal government's principal agency for conduction and support of biomedical, social and behavioral research on the aging process. The NIA maintains an Office of Biological Resources and Resource Development dedicated to research in diseases that target the elderly population. The NIA also supports the NIA Aging Cell Repository located at the Cornell Institute for Medical Research in Camden, New Jersey. The repository maintains skin fibroblast cultures from documented Alzheimer's cases and from individuals who are at high risk. The repository also has prepared DNA from many of the cell lines, including the Characterized Alzheimer's Disease mutation DNA panel. The NIA also supports a Geriatrics Program that supports research and research training directed at the pathology and treatment of age-related diseases.

National Institutes of Health (NIH). The National Institutes of Health is a constellation of federally sponsored agencies dedicated to advances in the prevention, diagnosis and treatment of diseases.

National Library of Medicine (NLM). The National Library of Medicine (NLM) is the world's largest research library in a single scientific and professional field. The NLM's database includes references to more than 9 million medical articles published in 3900 biomedical journals. The NLM can be accessed free on the Internet.

National Senior Citizens Law Center (NSCLC). The National Senior Citizens Law Center (NSCLC) advocates nationwide to promote the independence of low-income elderly individuals, as well as persons with disabilities, with particular emphasis on women and racial and ethnic minorities. As a national support center, the NSCLC advocates through litigation, legislative and agency representation and assistance to attorneys and paralegals in field programs.

Nefiracetam. Nefiracetam is a chemical compound that enhances the activity of nicotinic acetylcholine receptors by interacting with a protein kinase C pathway, which accelerates acetylcholine turnover and release. Nerifacetam is currently undergoing clinical trials for Alzheimer's disease.

Neocortex. The cerebral cortex does not have a uniform structure. Almost all the cortex that can be seen from the outside of the brain is composed of neocortex. The prefix "neo" refers to the common notion that the neocortex first appeared late in vertebrate evolution. The neocortex accounts for more than 90 percent of the total cortical area in man. The remainder is made up of paleocortex and archicortex. The two principal neuronal cell types in the neocortex are stellate cells and pyramidal cells.

Neomammalian brain *see* Cortex

Neostigmine. Neostigmine is a drug used to inhibit the action of the enzyme acetylcholinesterase. This potentiates the activity of the neurotransmitter acetylcholine.

NeoTrofin (AIT-082). NeoTrofin (AIT-082) is a stimulant of endogenous neurotropic factors. Neotrofin is capable of stimulating nerve growth factor, causing neuronal regeneration. This drug is currently in phase 3 of clinical trials. NeoTrofin acts at the site of heme oxygenase to generate carbon monoxide and by activation of guanylyl cyclase induces a cascade of biochemical reactions through the second messenger system leading to the production of mRNA for neurotrophins. *See* Neurotrophins.

Nerve cell *see* Neuron

Nerve fibers. Nerve fibers are the processes (axons and dendrites) that project from the body of nerve cells. Bundles of nerve fibers in the central nervous system are known as nerve tracts.

Nerve growth factor (NGF). Nerve growth factor (NGF) is a chemical substance normally produced by the body that helps promote nerve growth and offers protection from damage. Therapies that are able to increase levels of NGF are being studied for their role in the treatment of Alzheimer's disease. Levels of NGF are increased by idebenone, a form of coenzyme–Q-10 that readily crosses the blood brain barrier. By increasing levels of NGF, vulnerable cholinergic neurons may be preserved. Cerebrolysin is another agent showing promise. Produced from purified brain proteins, cerebrolysin mimics one of the natural nerve growth factors. In one study, more than 60 percent of subjects treated with cerbrolysin reported improved memory and concentration.

Nerve impulses. The nerve impulse begins at one spot on either a dendrite or axon. The axon acts as a semi-permeable membrane, keeping sodium ions on the outside of the cell body and chloride and potassium ions on the inside. This produces a net positive

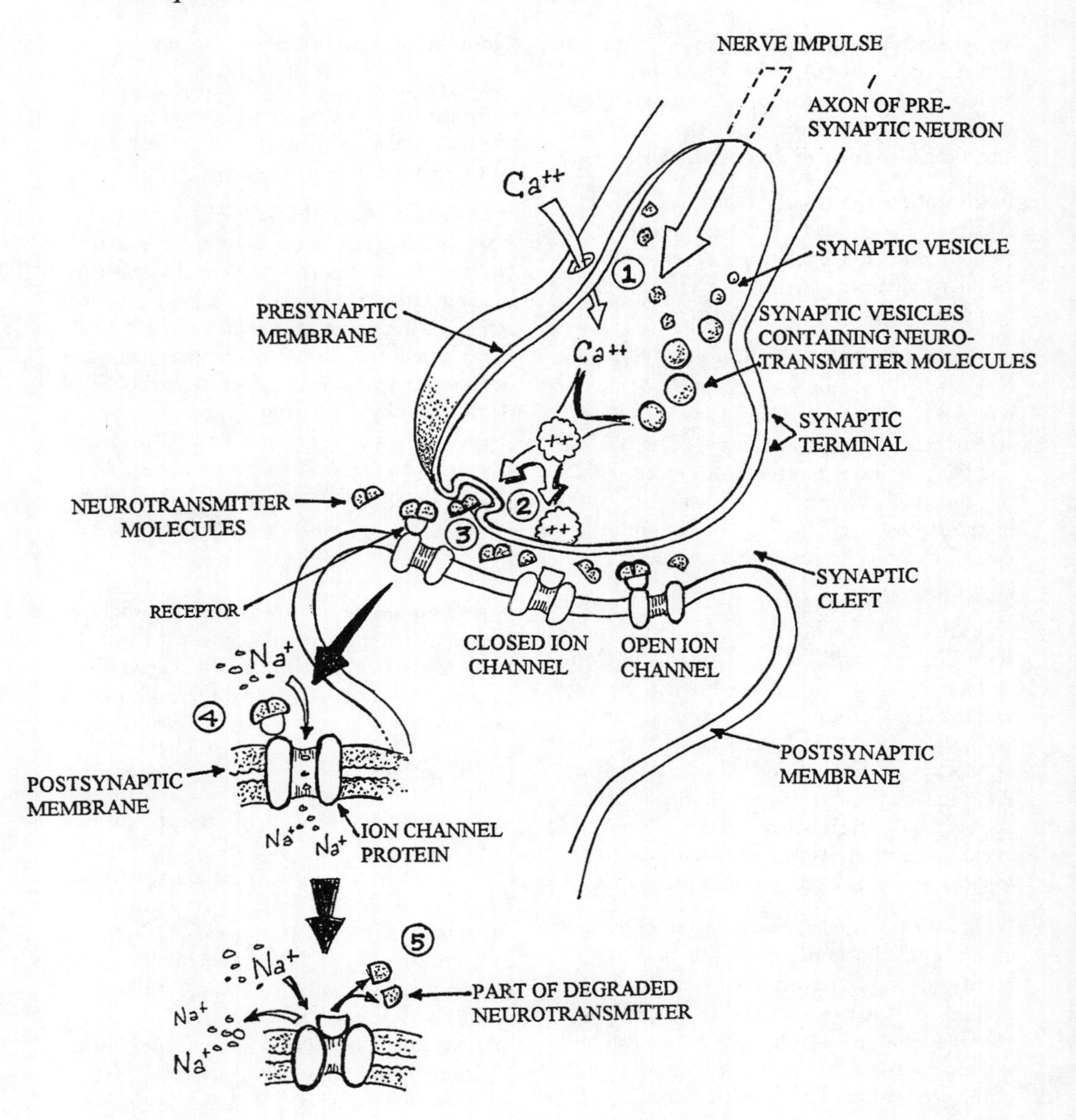

Transmission of Nerve Impulses (illustration by Marvin G. Miller).

1. Nerve impulses trigger an influx of calcium ions; calcium causes synaptic vesicles to fuse with the Pre-synaptic membrane.
2. The synaptic vesicle releases neurotransmitter molecules into the synaptic gap; these molecules bind to receptors on the post-synaptic membrane of neurons specific for this neurotransmitter.
3. When the neurotransmitter binds to its receptor, the ion channel opens, allowing ions to enter. This changes the voltage of the post-synaptic membrane and transmits the impulse.
4. The neurotransmitter molecules are broken down by enzymes and the ion channel closes.

charge on the outside of the axon and a net negative charge on the inside. When a site on the axon is stimulated, sodium rushes into the interior of the nerve fiber, depolarizing the axon. This is called the axon potential. The rushing of sodium into the interior of the nerve fiber continues down the axon until it reaches the end of the fiber. While there is an electric current generated, the impulse serves as a chemical message. A gap or synapse must be bridged in order for this chemical message to reach the next neuron down the line.

Nervous system. The nervous system, together with the endocrine or glandular system, controls the functions of the body. The nervous system is composed of specialized cells which receive sensory stimuli and transmit them to effector organs. The nervous system is divided into two major components, the central nervous system and the peripheral nervous system.

Neural thread protein (NTP). Neural thread proteins are protein molecules, such as myelin basic protein, that are produced by brain cells. Nymox Pharmaceutical Corporation has developed a test called AlzheimAlert to measure concentrations of neural thread protein (NTP) in urine. This protein is found in higher amounts on the urine of patients with Alzheimer's disease. However, this protein may be increased in other conditions. Nymox offers this test through its Clinical Reference Laboratory in Maywood, New Jersey.

Neurites. Neurites are the nerve fiber processes, both axons and dendrites, that extend from the cell body of neurons. Neurites are responsible for both receiving and transmitting information.

Neuritic plaque *see* Senile plaque

Neurodegenerative disease. Neurodegenerative diseases affect the gray matter of the brain. Neurodegenerative diseases are characterized principally by the progressive loss of neurons with associated changes in white matter tracts. In these disorders, the pattern of neuronal loss is selective, affecting one or more groups of neurons, while leaving others intact. Also, neurodegenerative diseases appear to emerge without any clear inciting event in patients who have shown no previous indications of neurologic deficits. Neuropathologic findings differ greatly. In some disorders, there are intracellular abnormalities with some degree of specificity such as the neurofibrillary tangles seen in Alzheimer's disease. In other disorders, there may only be loss of the affected neurons. Generally, neurodegenerative diseases are grouped according to the anatomic regions of the brain that are primarily affected.

The major neurodegenerative diseases affecting the cerebral cortex are Alzheimer's disease and Pick's disease. Their principal clinical manifestation is dementia, a condition characterized by progressive loss of cognitive function independent of the state of dementia. Gross examination of the brain shows a variable degree of cortical atrophy or shrinkage with widening of the cerebral sulci that is most pronounced in the frontal, temporal and parietal lobes. With significant atrophy, there may be an compensatory enlargement of the ventricles due to loss of tissue cells.

Neurofibrillary tangles (NFTs). Neurofibrillary tangles (NFTs) are one of the characteristic brain findings seen in individuals with Alzheimer's disease. In Alzheimer's disease, NFT clusters are found inside neurons in the hippocampus and neocortex. NFTs resemble pairs of threads wound around each other in a helix. Thus, the tangles are known as paired helical filaments or PHFs.

These tangles consist of an abnormal (containing too much phosphorus/protein molecule) form of a protein called tau. Normally, tau is significant because it binds to a protein named tubulin, which in turn forms structures known as microtubules. Microtubules are important in that they run through cells, imparting support and shape. Microtubules also provide routes that allow for the flow of nutrients through nerve cells. The abnormal tau isolated from the brain of patients with Alzheimer's disease causes a

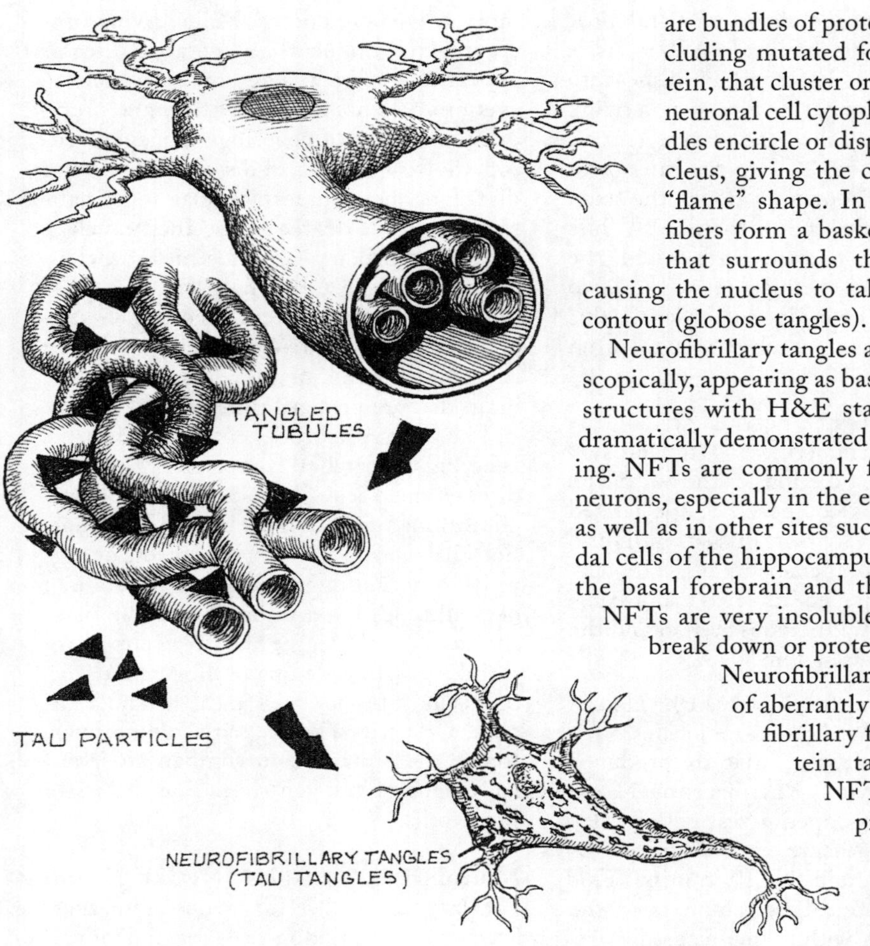

Neurofibrillary Tangles in the Neuron Cell (illustration by Marvin G. Miller).

Top: **Microtubules provide structural support and routes of transport for nutrients and other elements needed by the neuron; *middle:* Microtubules are constructed of a protein called tubulin. The protein tau binds readily to the tubulin in the microtubules; *bottom:* During Alzheimer's Disease, either the tau produced is altered or the tubulin-tau binding process changes. As a result the microtubules become distorted and twisted due to the faulty binding process. This distortion of the tubules disrupts the neurons' ability to function and transport material properly.**

breakdown of microtubule assembly. Thus, while neurons are degenerating because of their damaged microtubule systems, the abnormal tau continues to accumulate and form PHFs.

NFTs represent the damaged remains of the microtubule support structures. NFTs are bundles of protein filaments, including mutated forms of tau protein, that cluster or aggregate in the neuronal cell cytoplasm. These bundles encircle or displace the cell nucleus, giving the cell an elongated "flame" shape. In some cells, the fibers form a basket weave pattern that surrounds the cell nucleus, causing the nucleus to take on a rounded contour (globose tangles).

Neurofibrillary tangles are visible microscopically, appearing as basophilic fibrillary structures with H&E staining. They are dramatically demonstrated with silver staining. NFTs are commonly found in cortical neurons, especially in the entorhinal cortex, as well as in other sites such as the pyramidal cells of the hippocampus, the amygdala, the basal forebrain and the raphe nuclei. NFTs are very insoluble and difficult to break down or proteolyze.

Neurofibrillary tangles consist of aberrantly phosphorylated fibrillary forms of the protein tau. Structurally, NFTs are composed predominantly of paired helical filaments (PHFs) along with some straight filaments that appear to have the same composition as the helical filaments. Other antigens besides tau that have been found in paired helical filaments include microtubule associated protein (MAP2), ubiquitin and amyloid beta peptide. PHFs are also found in the dystrophic neurites that form the outer portions of neuritic plaques and in axons coursing through the gray matter of the brain.

The presence of NFTs signifies the failure of the neuron to properly maintain its cytoskeleton, which is required to support the complex branching shape of its numerous processes. Although plaques are occasionally seen in the brain of normal elderly people, neurofibrillary tangles are not seen in normal aging. Patients with Alzheimer's disease have an increased number of NFTs and their architectural distribution promotes and defines the stages of the disease. The development of NFTs contributes to the death of neurons which characterize the brain in Alzheimer's disease.

The areas of the brain preferentially affected by NFTs, such as the hippocampus, determine the specific symptoms. For example, NFTs frequently destroy areas of the hippocampus that are involved in processing experiences before storing this information as permanent memories. Symptoms of impaired short-term memory seen in the early stages of Alzheimer disease are a direct result. This also explains why memories from earlier times remain intact.

Neurofibrillary tangles have also been associated with other neurologic disorders including postencephalitic Parkinson's disease, progressive supranuclear palsy, dementia pugilistica (type of dementia resulting from repeated head blows), subacute sclerosing disorders, amyotrophic lateral sclerosis (ALS)/Parkinsonism dementia complex of Guam, panecephalitis and early onset epilepsy.

While there is debate as to which comes first, the NFTs or the plaques, dementia in Alzheimer's disease is generally thought to be better correlated with NFT pathology than with plaque deposits.

A compound capable of increasing tau phosphatase activity would inhibit the hyperphosphorylation of tau protein and prevent the formation of NFTs. Studies are being conducted to develop such compounds. Another therapeutic approach would be the use of compounds capable of breaking the abnormal phosphate bounds. (Bouras, Constantin, et al. "Regional Distribution of Neuropathological Changes in Alzheimer's Disease." *Alzheimer Disease: From Molecular Biology to Therapy*, Edited by R. Becker and E. Giacobine. Boston: Birkhäuser Publishing, 1996, 25–29.)

Neurogenesis. Neurogenesis refers to the regeneration of neurons. For years, researchers thought that human neurons could not regenerate. In 1998, researchers discovered that certain hippocampal neurons have the ability to regenerate and did so when exposed to hippocampal dependent learning tasks.

Neuroglia. Neuroglia refers to the specialized non-excitable cells that make up the central nervous tissue. Neuroglia are generally smaller than neurons and outnumber them by 5–10 times. Comprising about half of the total volume of the brain and spinal cord, neuroglia form the supporting framework or scaffolding of neurons. Neuroglial cells include: astrocytes, oligodendrocytes, microglia, and ependyma.

Neuroleptic medications. Neuroleptic agents, such as thioridazine, haloperidol, and loxapine, are sometimes beneficial in reducing symptoms of anxiety and agitation in patients with Alzheimer's disease. The more potent neuroleptics are generally reserved for the acutely and uncontrollably agitated patient. It is important in using these drugs to be aware of side effects such as increased confusion and extrapyramidal signs.

Neurological disorder. Neurological disorders refer to conditions associated with disturbance in the structure or function of the nervous system resulting from developmental abnormalities, disease, injury or toxins.

Neurologist. A neurologist is a physician who specializes in the field of neurology. Neurologists diagnose and treat patients with neurodegenerative diseases and with disorders caused by nervous system injury or trauma.

Neurology. Neurology is the scientific study of the nervous system, including the brain, especially in respect to its structure, functions and abnormalities.

Neuroma. Neuromas are tumors or masses growing from a nerve and usually consist of nerve fibers. Neuromas may also occur as masses of nerve tissue in an amputation stump, resulting from the abnormal regrowth of severed nerves.

Neuromodulator. Neuromodulators are substances, generally polypeptide chemicals that potentiate or inhibit the transmission of a nerve impulse but are not the actual means of transmission.

Neuromuscular junction. The area where nerve fibers meet muscle fibers is known as the neuromuscular junction. In smooth muscle, a single neuron can exert control over a large number of muscle fibers.

Neuron destruction. Central nervous system neurons destroyed by trauma or disease ordinarily do not regenerate. The first reaction of a neuron to injury is loss of function. Whether the cell recovers or dies depends on the severity and duration of the damage. Typically, the injured nerve cell becomes swollen and the nucleus becomes distorted. Immune system cells known as phagocytes engulf and remove cells that are injured beyond repair. In Alzheimer's disease, several different mechanisms contribute to neuronal destruction.

Neuronal degeneration. Many neurons degenerate during fetal development probably due to their failure to establish adequate functional connections. After birth, a continuous number of neurons gradually degenerate and die. By old age, most individuals have lost about 20 percent of the neurons they were born with. This may account for some of the loss of central nervous system efficiency typically seen in the elderly.

Neurons. The brain is composed of two basic cell types, neurons and glial cells. There are about 100 billion neurons in the human brain and several times that many glial cells. Neurons contain cell bodies or perikaryons and extensions or processes (axons and nerve fibers). Located in the brain, spinal cord and ganglia, neurons vary in size from 4 microns to 100 microns in diameter. Their length varies from several millimeters to several feet. Neurons can transmit nerve signals to and from the brain at a rate of 200 mph.

The nerve cell body of neurons consists of a mass or microtubule of cytoplasm surrounding a centrally located large cell nucleus. The region in the granular cytoplasm next to the axon is called the axon hillock. Nissl substance, a compound found in the cytoplasm is responsible for producing protein and distributing it to the axon and dendrites. In damaged or fatigued neurons, Nissl substance clusters to the periphery or edge of the cell membrane. Neurofibrils are numerous parallel fibrils that run through the cytoplasm and aid in cell transport. The neurofibrils may form bundles of microfilaments. The external membrane of the cell body is composed of loosely arranged protein layers situated between a fatty lipid layer. The lipid layer allows carbohydrates and minerals to enter the cell as needed. The permeability of the membrane to potassium ions is much greater than it is for sodium ions.

Each neuron evolves as a round cell body, or soma, that migrates to specific locations during development. Here, neurons grow projections known as axons and dendrites. Each neuron has one axon and about 100,000 dendrites. Neurons send out axons and dendrites in all directions through which they can communicate with other axons and dendrites. These connections intertwine, but do not touch, to form an interconnected tangle with 100 trillion constantly changing connections. The space or gap between these projections is known as a synaptic cleft or synapse. A single neuron may communicate across 100,000 different synapses.

Neurons may be unipolar, bipolar, or multipolar depending on the number of neurites arising from the cell body. Neurons may also be classified as pseudopolare (spelling cells or interneurons). Pseudopolare cells form all the neural wiring within the central nervous system. These cells have two axons, one which communicates with the spinal cord, the other which communicates with skin or muscle cells. Unipolar neurons have a single process or neuron, whereas bipolar neurons

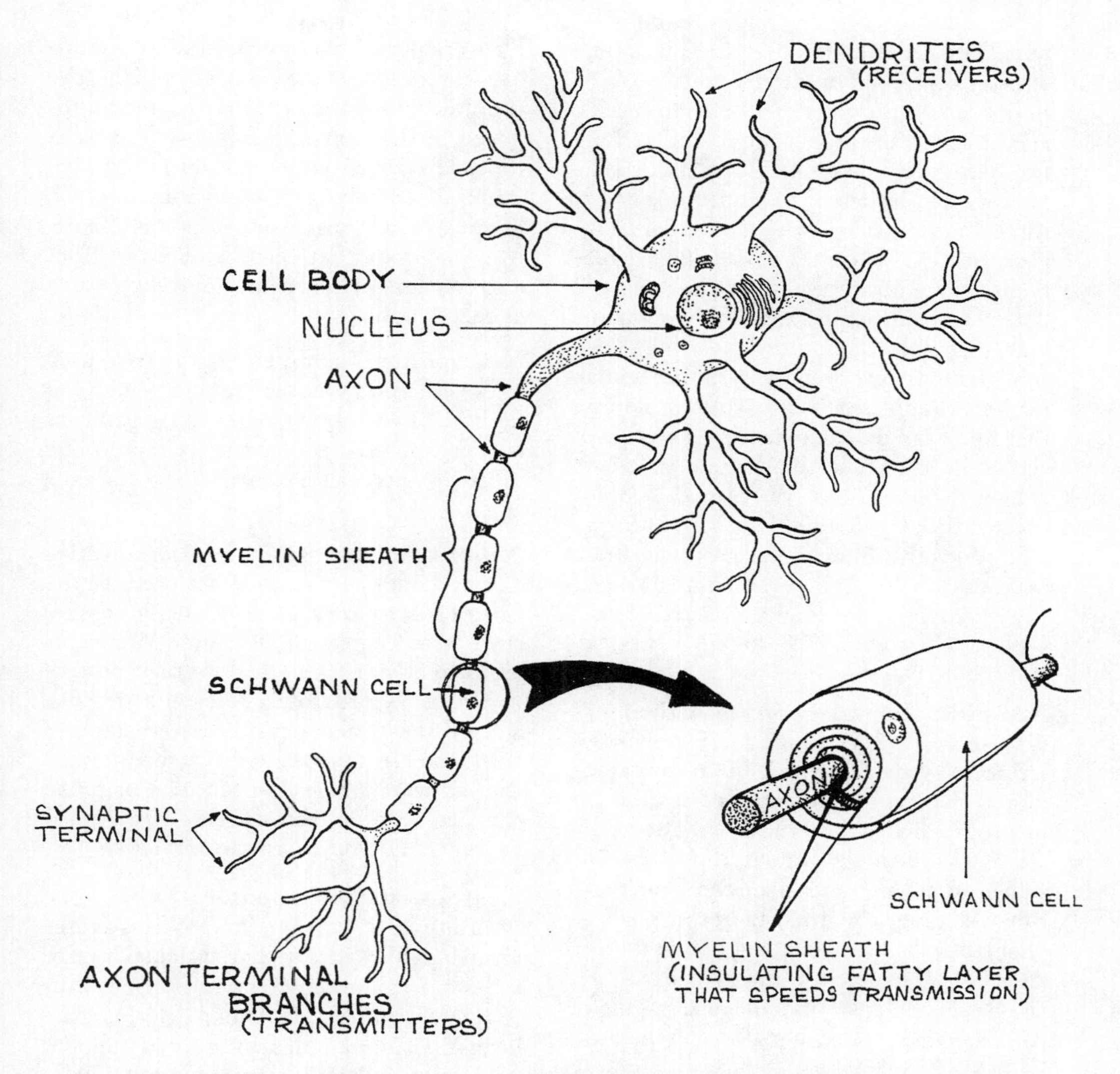

Neurons with Processes (Axons and Dendrites) (illustration by Marvin G. Miller).

have projections at each end, and multipolar neurons have one axon and many dendrites. Most vertebrate neurons are multipolar. By size, neurons may be classified into Golgi type 1 neurons with axons up to 1 meter or longer in length, and Golgi type II neurons with short axons that terminate near the cell body.

Not all neurons fire or produce action. Some neurons are inhibitory—they stop other neurons from firing. Still others modulate and modify the action of the primary neurons. Everything in the brain is very carefully regulated, right down to the subcellular level. Some single brain cells may connect to thousands of other neurons. However, for neurons to function, they must be able to transport materials between the cell body and synapses. For this transport, an intact microtubule system is essential.

Thus, neurons may also be classified according to their connections. Sensory neurons are either directly sensitive to various stimuli, such as temperature and touch, or they are capable of receiving director connection from non-neuronal receptor cells. Motor neurons act directly on muscles or glands, and interneurons connect other neurons. The central nervous system is almost entirely composed of interneurons.

In Alzheimer's disease, neurons in specific areas, such as the hippocampus and neocortex, become dysfunctional. Specifically, the microtubule system of these neurons is disrupted and replaced by neurofibrillary tangles with characteristic paired helical filaments. This injury eventually leads to cell death, leaving behind neuronal fragments known as "tombstones" or "ghost cells." Although it has long been thought that human neurons cannot regenerate, studies indicate that hippocampal neurons from a section of the brain known as the dentate gyrus are able to do so. (Gibbs, W. Wayne. "Dogma Overturned, Upending a long-held theory, a study finds that humans can grow new brain neurons throughout life—even into old age." *Scientific American: Science and the Citizen* Online. November 1998. http://www.sciam.com/1998/1198kssue/1198infocus.html)

Neuropathological staging of Alzheimer's disease. In 1992, H. Braak and E. Braak described a system in which the neuropathological changes in Alzheimer's disease occur in progressive stages, based on the alterations found in the hippocampus. For instance in stage I and II of the Braak and Braak staging, abnormal tau protein phosphorylation is increased long before there is any clinical evidence of disease. (Braak, H. and Braak, E. "Neuropathological staging of Alzheimer-related changes." *Acta Neuropath.* 1992, 82: 239–259.)

Neuropathology. Neuropathology refers to pathology or disease occurring in the central nervous system. While some of the neuropathological changes seen in Alzheimer's disease also occur in the normal non-demented elderly population, the density and distribution of the principal lesions found in Alzheimer's disease are significantly different.

Neuropathy. Neuropathy is an abnormal and usually degenerative state of the nervous system, including its nerves. The term neuropathy is also used to refer to a systemic condition, such as muscular atrophy, that stems from a neuropathy.

Neuropeptides. Neuropeptides are chemicals composed of amino acids which have the ability to act as neurotransmitters. Produced in the central nervous system, neuropeptides, such as somatostatin and substance P, control many bodily functions such as muscle relaxation and blood pressure. Most neurons that contain neuropeptides also contain classical neurotransmitters such as acetylcholine.

Neuropraxia. Neuropraxia is the term used to describe a transient or temporary injury to peripherally nerves. The resulting paralysis is incomplete and recovery is rapid. The most common cause of neuropraxia is pressure.

Neuroprotective agents. Neuroprotective agents are subjects designed to preserve the function of neurons. Neuroprotective agents such as nerve growth factor and vitamin E are currently being studied for their protective roles. Neuroprotective agents are considered the Alzheimer's disease therapy of the future. In contrast to drugs that prevent the pathways that lead to neurodegenerative changes, neuroprotective agents are designed to protect neurons from this assault.

Neuropsychiatric inventory (NPI). The Neuropsychiatric Inventory or NPI is a caregiver-based inventory that evaluates twelve symptoms commonly seen in patients with Alzheimer's disease, including delusion, hallucinations, agitation, depression, dysphoria, euphoria or elation, anxiety, apathy, irritability and disinhibition, night-time behavior disturbances, eating disturbances and abnormal motor or movement behavior. The NPI is commonly used to evaluate response to drug therapy, with favorable results causing a four point increase in the score.

Neuropsychologic symptoms in Alzheimer's disease. Neuropsychologic symptoms in Alzheimer's disease include symptoms of memory loss and impairment of judgment, language, learning, abstract thinking, and visual-spatial coordination skills.

Neuropsychological Tests. Neuropsychological tests refer to a wide array of procedures used to objectively assess neuropsychological or neurobehavioral performance, including cognitive, adaptive and emotional behaviors. Neuropsychological tests include full-scale verbal and performance parameters of intelligence quotient (IQ). Tests are used to measure various parameters, including verbal and non-verbal memory, remote memory, mood, affect, visuomotor coordination, visuospatial planning and organization, cognitive function, language function, attention and spontaneous speech. Tests are usually conducted over a period of 6 to 10 hours. A clinical neuropsychologist administers and evaluates the tests. Progressive dementing processes such as Alzheimer's disease and multi-infarct dementia are associated with marked worsening of performances on serial neuropsychological assessments. Neuropsychological tests are used to assist in diagnosing the presence or absence of organic brain lesion, assist in determining if the brain dysfunction is localized (focal) or diffuse, describe the effects of an identified lesion on cognition and behavior and assist in planning treatment.

Neuroscience and Neuropsychology of Aging (NNA) Program of the NIA. The Neuroscience and Neuropsychology of Aging (NNA) Program, which is sponsored by the National Institute on Aging, supports extramural research and training to further the understanding of the aging of the nervous system. An important component of this program is the support of basic, clinical and epidemiological studies of Alzheimer's disease and related dementia of aging. For more information, contact NNAquery@EXMUR.NIA.NIH.GOV.

Neurotoxin. Neurotoxins are substances with the ability to injure or destroy neurons or brain cells. In Alzheimer's disease amyloid β protein is known to exert neurotoxic effects. Biological neurotoxins include a diverse family of bacterial, animal and plant derived chemicals.

Neurotransmitters. Neurotransmitters are chemical messenger molecules that allow individual neurons to communicate with one another and also with muscles and other cells. While there are some instances in which neurons are directly connected or coupled, allowing ionic currents to flow between neurons, in most cases neurons communicate with each other by releasing neurotransmitters, typically at specialized sites known as synapses.

Neurotransmitters, which are sometimes called neuromodulators or neurohormones, excite or inhibit the cellular functions of neurons during synaptic communication. Neurotransmitters are necessary for transmitting impulses at the presynaptic axon to the postsynaptic axon. Once stimulation or inhibition has taken place, the neurotransmitter is broken down by an enzyme or it is taken up by the presynaptic axon terminal. For example, the neurotransmitter acetylcholine is broken down by the enzyme acetylcholinesterase. Mitochondria within the presynaptic vesicles provide energy for the synthesis of new transmitter substance, which is stored in prepackaged aliquots.

Most neurons produce and release only one type of neurotransmitter at their nerve endings. However, a few neurons release an excitor neurotransmitter, such as glutamate, at one synapse, and a neuropeptide at another synapse. Different neurons may produce and release different neurotransmitters. For example, acetylcholine is widely used by neurons in the central and peripheral nervous system, whereas dopamine is produced by neurons in a part of the brain known as the substantia nigra. While the list of neurotransmitters is likely to grow, current neurotransmitters include acetylcholine, norepinephrine, epinephrine, dopamine, glycine, serotonin, gamma-aminobutyroic acid (GABA), enkephalins, substance P, and glutamic acid.

Neurotransmitters are released from their nerve endings during the nerve impulse. Once in the synaptic cleft they achieve their potential by briefly raising or lowering the resting potential of the post-synaptic membrane. Many drug therapies revolve around changing the concentrations of neurotransmitters. For instance, the benzodiazepine drugs such as diazepam (Valium) bind to

GABA receptors and increase the effects of GABA released at nerve synapses. While l-dopa is beneficial in restoring levels of dopamine in patients with Parkinson's disease, attempts to raise the acetylcholine level in patients with Alzheimer's disease have not been as successful since multiple transmitter systems are affected. For example, cortical somatostatin-containing interneurons are affected as much as cholinergic neurons.

While deficiencies of acetylcholine are one of the best known chemical aberrations seen in Alzheimer's disease, other neurotransmitters not related to the cholinergic system, including serotonin, GABA, somatostatin, and norepinephrine, are also reduced in Alzheimer's disease. These deficiencies may also contribute to cognitive dysfunction.

Neurotrophic factors. Neurotrophic factors are proteins such as nerve growth factor, that promote nerve cell growth and survival.

Neurotrophins. Neurotrophins are substances, such as the essential fatty acid docosahexaenoic acid (DHA), which provide nutrition to nerves.

Nicotinamide adenine dinucleotide (NADH). The naturally occurring substance nicotinamide adenine dinucleotide (NADH), which is also sold as a dietary supplement, has been reported to improve cognitive function in patients with Alzheimer's disease when administered at a dose of 5 mg given twice daily. (Perlmutter, David. "Functional Therapeutics in Neurodegenerative Disease," Physicians Committee for Responsible Medicine website, http://www.pcrm.org/health/Preventive_Medicine/alzheimers.html)

Nicotine. Nicotine is a basic drug that acts on receptors in the cholinergic system in the brain that are depleted. Some studies suggest that nicotine may protect nerve cells and help prevent the formation of beta amyloid protein. Unlike the chemicals released in cigarette smoke, nicotine itself does not cause cancer. However, in high doses it acts like a poison and has long been used as an insecticide. Researchers are investigating nicotine-like drugs that may protect nerve cells without causing side effects.

Nicotinic acetylcholine receptor. The nicotinic receptor is one of the two main categories of receptors that the body has for acetylcholine. The nicotinic acetylcholine receptor is a specialized ion channel that plays an important role in learning, memory, stress response and survival. Ion channels function as portholes in cell membranes, regulating the flow of current to cells. These channels are influenced by both the neurotransmitter acetylcholine and exogenous sources of nicotine. These channels, in turn, regulate neuronal activity in a region of the brain known as the hippocampus. Research in this area indicates that nicotinic ligands, substances that bind to the nicotinic receptor, may be useful in preventing neurological disorders such as Alzheimer's disease, depression, epilepsy, and Parkinson's disease. It's known that individuals with Alzheimer's disease have fewer nicotinic receptors in their cerebral cortex. ("A New Side of the Nicotinic Receptor." *Environmental Health Perspectives.* 1998; 106 (4): Forum)

NINCDS-ADRDA Criteria for Alzheimer's disease. The National Institute of Neurological and Communicative Disorders and Stroke (NINCDS) and the Alzheimer's Disease and Related Disorders Association (ADRDA) have established criteria to aid in the diagnosis of patients with Alzheimer's disease. The NINCDS-ADRDA criteria require unmistakable deterioration in at least two cognitive domains relative to the patient's previous level of function. This is determined by a history of intellectual decline and must be documented by formal mental status testing. The NINCDS-ADRDA criteria for dementia do not require that the loss of cognitive function be severe enough to interfere with impaired social and occupational functioning as dictated by some other criteria.

The terms benign senescent forgetfulness and age-associated memory impairment have been proposed to refer to some persons with evidence of cognitive impairment who do not meet present clinical criteria for dementia. (Bennett, David and Jacob Fox. "Alzheimer's Disease and Other Dementias." *Neurology for the Non-Neurologist*, Third Edition, 1994. [edited by William J. Weiner.] Philadelphia: J.B. Lippincott, 195–196.)

Nitric oxide (NO). Nitric oxide (NO) is a gaseous neurotransmitter which acts as the primary vasodilator (dilates or relaxes blood vessels) in the brain. Nitric oxide is formed when the amino acid L-arginine is oxidized to citrulline by the action of the enzyme nitric oxide synthase. Although nitric oxide is a free radical due to its unpaired electron, it does not appear to cause any damage by itself, with the exception of damage to mitochondrial complex I. However, when combined with the superoxide anion, the potent oxidant peroxynitrite is formed. Peroxynitrite has been implicated in neuronal cell damage, including DNA strand breaks, DNA deamination, and damage to mitochondrial complexes.

In the hippocampus, NO and another gaseous neurotransmitter, carbon monoxide, serve as retrograde messengers that produce activity-dependent presynaptic enhancement during long-term potentiation. Long-term potentiation, which can last hours or days, refers to prolonged changes in a target neuron resulting from intense but brief trains of stimuli delivered to a presynaptic neuron.

Nitric oxide synthase. Nitric oxide synthase is an enzyme used in the production of nitric oxide. Nitric oxide synthase is heavily concentrated in the hippocampus. Neuronal nitric oxide synthase is activated by a calcium-dependent mechanism, but it can also be stimulated by the cytokine IL-1 beta. Elevated levels of nitric oxide synthase can result in excess amounts of nitric oxide, which may contribute to the pathogenesis of Alzheimer's disease. Therapies, such as arginine analogues, intended to inhibit nitric oxide synthase are currently being researched.

NMDA (N-methyl-d-aspartate) receptor. The NMDA receptor is the most common of the three types of glutamate receptors found on neuron membranes in the brain. A component of the excitatory pathway, the NMDA (N-methyl-d-aspartate) receptor is stimulated by the excitatory neurotransmitter glutamate. Enhanced NMDA receptor sensitivity to glutamate can result from an altered electrochemical gradient caused by dysfunctional mitochondria, which occurs in Alzheimer's disease and is thought to be due to decreased mitochondrial energy production. The net result is excess glutamate, a neurotransmitter, which is thought to be toxic to neurons.

Some researchers explain that the excitotoxins aspartame and monosodium glutamate can cause excess stimulation of the NMDA receptor. It is postulated that excess excitation of the NMDA receptor destroys it, rendering this transduction system ineffective. The NR receptor is also known to weaken with age.

Protective agents that inhibit the release of glutamate or the stimulation of the NMDA receptor include the anticonvulsant medications gabapentin, lamotrigene, muscarinic receptor antagonists, GABA receptor antagonists, alpha 2-receptor antagonists, diphenylhydantoin, carbamazepine, the NMDA antagonists remacemide and memantine, and Huperzine A. *See also* Excitotoxins.

Noncognitive behavioral abnormalities. The original patient described by Dr. Alois Alzheimer in 1907 was remarkable for both her progressive cognitive impairment and for a number of non-cognitive behavioral abnormalities. The presence of these non-cognitive behavioral symptoms has become as much a part of the symptomology of Alzheimer's disease as the cognitive decline and often precipitate institutionalization. These non-cognitive symptoms include apathy, hyperexcitability, delusions, hallucinations, depression, agitation, and hostility. A number of studies consistently suggest that the presence of psychotic symptoms in Alzheimer's disease is associated with an accelerated deterioration of cognitive function.

Although antipsychotic drugs were once used to treat these symptoms, studies have found that at recommended doses they are only modestly helpful when compared to placebos. At higher doses, these drugs cause increased sedation which has been found to result in unsteady gait and a higher incidence of falls.

Nonsteroidal anti-inflammatory drugs (NSAIDs). Non-steroidal anti-inflammatory drugs (NSAIDs) are compounds distinct from steroids that effectively inhibit the inflammatory process. NSAIDs inhibit cyclooxygenases and thus inhibit synthesis of prostaglandin signals for IL-1 production, although they have little effect on complement. Nevertheless, evidence indicates that low doses of NSAIDs may suffice to achieve a neuroprotective effect that appears to require sustained exposure, most likely for several years before the onset of dementia, to produce effects. Short-term incidence studies suggest that NSAIDs can prevent incident Alzheimer's disease if exposure predates disease onset by several years.

Norepinephrine (Noradrenaline). Norepinephrine is a catecholamine neurotransmitter derived from the amino acid tyrosine. Neurons containing norepinephrine as their neurotransmitter are called noradrenergic neurons. Noradrenergic neurons are found only in the pons and medulla. All areas of the cerebral cortex appear to receive some noradrenergic innervation. The actions of norepinephrine are nearly silent during sleep and become activated during wakefulness, becoming most active in situations that are startling or call for watchfulness. Thus, the primary role of norepinephrine appears to be one of maintaining attention and vigilance.

Normal pressure hydrocephalus (NPH). Normal pressure hydrocephalus (NPH) is a clinical syndrome characterized by the gradual onset of a cluster of gradually worsening symptoms, including gait apraxia, dementia and incontinence. First described by Solomon Hakin in 1964, NPH may also present with more overt psychiatric symptoms such as mania or depression. Other neurological features such as speech impairment may also develop. Diagnosis is made with computed tomography imaging or magnetic resonance imaging. These studies commonly show increased ventricular size and a reduction of both white matter in the areas surrounding the ventricles and gray matter in the cortical regions. Even in the absence of these changes, patients with the classical symptoms of NPH should be evaluated further. An abnormal cerebrospinal fluid absorption pathway is suspected of being the underlying cause of NPH because when the volume of spinal fluid is reduced, patients often improve.

Alzheimer's disease, Binswanger's disease and NPH may all cause dementia and dilated cerebral ventricles. Imaging studies may fail to distinguish if the dilation is from cerebral atrophy (Alzheimer's or Binswanger's) or from NPH. Patients with NPH, however, generally exhibit gait disturbances and incontinence before cognitive impairment. NPH may be precipitated by subarachnoid hemorrhage, infection, central nervous system trauma and neoplasm.

Novartis Foundation for Gerontology. The Novartis foundation for Gerontology is dedicated to promoting healthy aging. The Alzheimer's disease center funded by this organization provides educational support related to Alzheimer's disease. http://www.halthandage.com/Home/gm=20!gc=11!=2!gid2=81.

Nucleus basalis of Mynert. The nucleus basalis of Meynert is the area of the neocortex rich in cells that produce acetylcholine. It is one of the earliest areas affected in Alzheimer's disease.

Nun study. The Nun Study of 2,500 Catholic nuns (School Sisters of Notre Dame) living in convents throughout the Midwest has provided researchers with insight into the many factors that contribute to the development of Alzheimer's disease. In a number of published reports and one popular book, DH Snowdon and his colleagues from the Sanders-Brown Center on Aging of the College of Medicine at the University of Kentucky in Lexington described their findings.

From the Nun Study, Snowdon et al. showed that the presence of cerebral infarcts, even if small and scarce, raised the risk of dementia as much as 20 times for those with brain lesions similar to those seen in Alzheimer's disease. Infarcts unrelated to Alzheimer's disease-type lesions were found to be associated with few cognitive effects. Other factors related to the development of Alzheimer's disease included low serum folate levels, high copper levels, greater functional dependence on others, increased weight loss in old age and a lower number of positive emotions. This study suggests that careful monitoring and treatment of hypertension and other vascular risk factors along with a healthy diet and exercise plan could potentially reduce the incidence of dementia.

Of interest, researchers also showed that the nuns who retained the highest levels of cognitive ability throughout their life were least likely to have the APOE4 allele. *See* also Writing study. (Snowdon, Ph.D.,David. *Aging with Grace: What the Nun Study Teaches Us About Leading Longer, Healthier and More Meaningful Lives.* New York: Bantam Publishing, 2001)

Nursing home accreditations. Federal and state nursing home inspections are a matter of public record. When evaluating nursing homes, request their most recent state survey, although if it is more than 6 months old, circumstances may have changed since the report. Government inspections, including Medicaid and Medicare inspections, occur at least annually and are designed to insure that minimum federal and state requirements are met regarding the building, sanitation, safety features, adequate staffing and administration. Another report worth viewing is the "quality indicators" report, which is available for all Medicare and Medicaid certified nursing homes. This report lists all problems experienced by residents at the facility, including weight loss, dehydration, skin breakdown, falls, fractures and behavioral problems. Scores for each nursing home are compared or ranked to those of other homes in the state.

All nursing homes are licensed by the state in which they are located. Homes that receive Medicaid or Medicare reimbursement must also be certified by the state agency responsible for nursing home regulation. See resource section for a listing of state licensure and certification programs for assistance in helping choose a nursing home.

Nursing home costs. Before making any arrangements for nursing home care, it is important to completely understand all the financial arrangements of the home you have selected. Nursing homes charge a basic daily or monthly rate.

Besides the daily or monthly fee, the nursing home may charge extra for physician's fees, medications, laundry, special feeding, frequent linen changes, or special supplies such as wheelchairs and walkers and physical therapy.

Many residents or their families pay for nursing home care out of their private funds. Long-term care insurance policies can be used to help defray these costs. Others whose finances are depleted rely on Medicaid to cover the costs of their nursing home care. To find out whether a resident is financially eligible for Medicaid, call the Department of Social Services in your area. For information regarding Medicare, call the Social Security Administration. However, Medicare pays for very little nursing home care, and it never pays for long-term nursing home care. Veterans of the United States armed forces should also check with the Veterans Administration to see if they are eligible for nursing care benefits.

Nursing homes generally ask for financial disclosure to help determine the appropriate payment mechanism. Admissions personnel will assist families in determining what information is necessary and what forms need to be filed to expedite placement. Because some nursing homes have waiting lists, it is a good idea to complete paperwork in advance in the event that an emergency placement becomes necessary. (American Association of Homes and Services for the Aging)

Nursing home facilities. Most nursing homes in the United States are owned and operated by for-profit corporations. Others are owned and operated by not-for-profit organizations, including churches and fraternal groups. In addition, a small number of facilities are operated by government agencies or the Veteran's Administration.

Nursing home options. Nursing homes have changed in recent years, both in the multi-tiered levels of care that they provide and in their individual philosophies. Resident-Centered care facilities are moving away from the institutionalized settings of the past and offering individualized holistic care. No two nursing homes are alike today. It is important to explore all of the nursing homes in your area before deciding on which one is most suitable for your family member. The one closest to home may not be the best when it comes to personalized care and activities that encourage residents to maintain their skills.

Several factors must be considered when choosing a nursing home, including inspection reports (*See* Nursing home accreditations) and the type of insurance plans they are accredited to accept. The environment must also be carefully observed. Odor is a key indicator of quality. The facility should be clean, odor-free, spacious, and quiet with a pleasant atmosphere. The building should be well-lighted with ample windows so that residents do not feel contained. The building must be safe so that residents cannot escape from the grounds, but there should be adequate escape routes in the event of a fire. If there are multiple stories, see if there are adequate elevators that function properly.

The staff should be clean and well-groomed, and the turnover rate should be low. Nurses should be trained in geriatric care and at least some of the staff should have advanced training in caring for Alzheimer's disease patients. During your visit, observe the residents to see if they are involved in activities or given opportunities for socialization. See what policy the nursing home has if you intend to arrange occasional home visits or want to have a pet visit.

Check to see if staffing is adequate. One national advocacy organization recommends that the ratio of licensed practical nurses (LPNs) to patients be 1:15 on days, 1:25 on evenings and 1:35 on the night shift. There should also be a sufficient number of nurses' aides (1:5 on days, 1:10 on evenings, and 1:15 on nights) and registered nurses (RNs) working in supervisory capacities. The nursing home you select should pay their workers salaries equivalent or higher than other nursing homes in the area.

Find out if there are hidden charges (*see* Nursing home costs) and ask if the facility provides services such as barber and beauty shops, religious services, or routine dental care. Find out in an advance deposit is required and the terms for its refund. Find out how long the current owner of the facility has operated it. Facilities with long-term ownership offer greater stability.

Find out if all residents have roommates, and, if so, find out the guidelines used when roommates do not get along. Find out if there are resident and family councils established to help solve problems as they arise. Ask if food can be brought in from the outside and find out what happens if the resident has special food needs. Find out if physical restraints are used, and, if so, find out what circumstances mandate their use. Find out how often patients are bathed. Ask if side-rails are routinely used on beds. Their use is generally not recommended because they are associated with a higher rate of injuries. Find out what areas patients are allowed to wander in and inquire if they have ever had problems with patients wandering away from the facility. Find out if there are night call lights or lights that can be pulled in case of an emergency. Find out when visiting hours are and see if additional visits can be arranged as new residents become accustomed to their new facility.

When you select a nursing home, find out how much clothing you'll need to bring and how much closet space is allocated for patients. Find out how the facility would like you to label the residents' personal items. Find out if there are any limitations on what you can bring to make rooms more homelike. And be sure to let staff members know what name the resident prefers to use and any special needs they may have.

Nutrient deficiencies. Studies show that brain thiamine (vitamin B1) levels are decreased in patients with Alzheimer's disease, and 25 percent of Alzheimer's disease patients have lower levels of vitamin B12. Deficiencies in both of these nutrients can contribute to symptoms of dementia. Studies also show that 50 percent of institutionalized patients suffer from protein malnutrition. (Folstein, M. "Nutrition and Alzheimer's Disease." *Nutrition Reviews*, 1997, vol 55 (1): 23–25.)

Nystagmus. Nystagmus refers to loss of voluntary movement of the ocular movements. A sign of cerebellar disease, nystagmus is characterized by rhythmical oscillation of the eyes.

Occipital lobe. The occipital lobe of the cerebrum is bounded anteriorly by the parietal and temporal lobes on both the lateral and medial surfaces of each hemisphere.

Odor Identification Test. Studies funded by the NIA and the NIMH suggest that a simple odor identification test may help doctors predict which individuals with mild cognitive impairment will go on to develop Alzheimer's disease. Study participants were exposed to a 15 to 20 minute scratch and sniff test using distinct smells such as methanol, peanuts and soap. After smelling the odor, participants were asked to pick what it was from 4 alternative choices. None of the participants who scored well on the test developed Alzheimer's within 20 months. However, 19 of 47 subjects who had difficulty identifying the odors, although they reported having no trouble identifying odors, went on to develop Alzheimer's disease during the follow up period. ("Odor Identification Test May Help Predict Alzheimer's Disease." NIA NEWS, August 28, 2000).

Olanzopine (Zyprexa). Olanzoprine (Zypexa) is an atypical antipsychotic medication, which effectively reduces symptoms of psychosis and aggression in patients with Alzheimer's disease while posing a very low risk for side effects. In one study, following a double-blind, 6-week exposure to 1 mg–10 mg olanzapine daily, patients improved significantly on the primary efficacy measured by psychometric tests used to determine Agitation/Aggression, Delusions and Hallucinations. Symptoms which emerged during treatment included sleepiness, accidental injury and rash. Measures of agitation and psychosis improved significantly at 5 mg daily versus placebo. Results were less apparent at 10 mg/daily and not evident at 15 mg daily. (Street, J.S. et al. "Long-term efficacy of olanzapine in the control of psychotic and behavioral symptoms in nursing home patients with Alzheimer's dementia." *International Journal of Geriatric Psychiatry*, 2001, December; 16 (1):62–70)

Older Americans Act. The Older Americans Act offers a form of federal assistance that pays for some supportive services including home health care. The Administration on Aging (AoA) is the primary federal group that ensures that provisions of the Older American Act are carried out. Programs established by the Act are often a combination of federal and State Units on Aging initiatives. This results in a wide variation of programs and services from state to state although the AoA awards state grants to ensure that all states comply with the Act. The Act is a plan ensuring community-based services, supportive services and centers, long-term care ombudsman programs and services for the special needs of Alzheimer's disease patients.

A primary purpose of the Act is to encourage and assist state and area agencies on aging to develop greater capacity and foster the development and implementation of comprehensive and coordinated systems to serve the elderly. The Act defines three essential services, including information and assistance, transportation and case management. The Act also mandates nutrition programs, including congregate and home-delivered nutrition services and programs for minorities, including American Indians, Alaska natives and Native Hawaiians.

Oligodendrocytes. Oligodendrocytes are neuroglial cells frequently found in rows along myelinated nerve fibers and cell bodies. With small cell bodies and only a few delicate processes, oligodendrocytes are responsible for the formation of the myelin sheath of nerve fibers in the central nervous system. Age-related alteration is oligodendrocytes may contribute to dysfunctional axon connections leading to cognitive deficits even in the absence of neuron loss. Age-related alterations include changes, such as the presence of inclusion bodies, in their internal structure and also their processes.

Olmstead Decision, American with Disabilities Act. In July 1999, the Supreme Court issued the Olmstead Decision, which interpreted Title II of the Americans with Disabilities Act and its implementing regulating, requiring states to administer their services, programs and activities "in the most integrated setting appropriate to the needs of qualified individuals with disabilities."

Ombudsman. An ombudsman is a consumer advocate who investigates nursing home complaints and attempts to resolve problems. Your local ombudsman may also be able to help you in your selection of a good nursing home. A list of contact information by state for the ombudsman program can be found in the resource section.

Omentum. The omentum is a pocket of fat and blood vessels that lies like a blanket covering the intestines. Dr. Harry Goldsmith, a researcher at the University of Nevada, has found that the omentum can be used to provoke new blood vessel growth in areas of the body lacking blood flow. Besides promoting angiogenesis or new blood vessel growth, omentum also increases choline acetyltransferase, the enzyme necessary for the synthesis of acetylcholine in the brain.

In the late 1970s, Goldsmith successfully implanted omentum into stroke patients. In studies he conducted in 1993, Goldsmith implanted omentum into a man who had Alzheimer's disease for nine years. A single photon/positron emission computed tomography can (SPECT) showed that blood flow had increased dramatically after the operation, and the man's personal physician reported that his patient was remarkably improved. Among the areas of improvement noted were judgment, confusion, naming, and gait. Although the patient died of other causes two years later, an autopsy showed that in the area where the omentum had been placed, the number of senile plaques were greatly reduced.

In the procedure used by Dr. Goldsmith, the omentum is brought up through the neck and placed over the brain. The omentum remains attached to its original blood supply. According to Goldsmith, keeping the omentum attached to its blood supply prevents problems associated with transposing only a piece of it onto the brain. Besides its ability to stimulate blood vessels, the omentum contains numerous nerves and neurochemicals that help nerves grow, such as fibroblast growth factor (FGF). FGF has been shown to provoke the growth of new brain cells in areas of the brain affected by Alzheimer's disease. The omentum also appears to maintain dopamine, serotonin and norepinephrine when implanted into the brain. ("An Exiting New Treatment for Alzheimer's Disease." *Life Extension*, August, 2000, 63–65)

Omnibus Reconciliation Act (OBRA) regulations. The Omnibus Reconciliation Act (OBRA) provides regulations with clear recommendations for the treatment of behavioral, cognitive, and affective symptoms in elderly patients with Alzheimer's disease. These regulations help in determining the specific symptoms likely to respond to specific pharmaceutical therapies. These regulations also set guidelines for the amount of time a specific drug should be given before its efficacy can be determined. In long-term care settings, treatment is monitored to ensure that it conforms to OBRA regulations.

Opiod peptides. Opiod peptides are naturally occurring as well as synthetic chemicals of the opiod family. Duke University's Jau-Shyong Hong and the NIEHS's Jean Harry are currently researching the effects of opiod peptides on neurodegeneration caused by microglia. In a different study, researchers demonstrated that chronic exposure to morphine inhibited neuronal growth in the adult hippocampus. (Eisch, A., et al. "Opiates inhibit neurogenesis in the adult rat hippocampus." Proceedings of the National Academy of Sciences, June 6, 2000.)

Organic brain syndrome. Organic brain syndrome is a term commonly used for patients with impaired memories.

Organic solvents. Organic solvents refers to a class of chemicals such as naptha, toluene, xylene, chloroform and hexane used in industries such as painting and cleaning. Organic solvents can cause transient symptoms such as inebriation, dizziness, headache and nausea. Used chronically, organic solvents may cause symptoms of encephalopathy, including poor attention, mood changes, memory problems and delirium.

Orientation. Patients being assessed for mental status are generally evaluated for orientation of time, place and purpose. To be disoriented for time, the patient should be off by more than one day of the week and more than several days off the current date. Misidentifying the relationship of relatives is a sign of disorientation to place. For instance, patients with Alzheimer's disease may say that their doctor is their son.

Oxford Universities Scale for the Psychopathological Assessment of Dementia (MOUSEPAD). The Oxford Universities Scale for the Psychopathological Assessment of Dementia (MOUSEPAD) is an evaluation tool used to assess emotional changes and neuropsychiatric manifestations in patients diagnosed with dementia.

P97. P97 is a molecule isolated by Korean researchers that is found in higher concentration in the blood of people with Alzheimer's disease than in normal people, according to the results of one study. If other studies confirm this finding, this test could be used as a diagnostic tool for Alzheimer's disease and as a diagnostic marker for assessing a favorable response to therapy. (Moyer, Paula. "New Blood Test May Help Diagnose Alzheimer's Disease, Eventual Goal: Treatment Before Symptoms Develop," *WebMD Health*, May 17, 2000)

Pacing. Patients with Alzheimer's disease often pace or wander aimlessly, especially in the evening hours. Pacing should be allowed as it is a reflection of the body's natural reaction to dealing with stress and agitation. Pacing is often triggered by an internal stimulus such as pain, hunger or boredom or some environmental distraction such as noise or temperature.

Paclitaxel (Taxol). Paclitaxel (Taxol), a drug used for ovarian and breast cancer, may slow nerve degeneration and is under investigation as a therapeutic agent for Alzheimer's disease. Paclitaxel has the ability to bundle the microtubule protein, possibly protecting it from the aberrant phosphorylation seen in Alzheimer's disease.

Pain. While Alzheimer's disease is not generally associated with pain, patients with this disorder may not be able to convey their pain. Caregivers must be alert for signs such as holding one's head or favoring one leg or arm, and they must be on the alert for falls and other injuries.

Paleocortex. The paleocortex refers to the surface cortex covering some restricted parts of the base of the telencephalon. The paleocortex is thought to be of ancient origin compared to the neocortex.

Paleomammalian brain. The paleomammalian brain refers to the region of the brain descending upward from the reptilian brain. The paleomammalian brain, which includes the limbic system, promotes survival and refines and coordinates movement. This area is also associated with the development of the apparatuses for memory and emotions that stem from the body's internal regulatory system.

Palliative care. Palliative care, also known as comfort care, focuses on quality of life for individuals with a progressive disease. The goal of palliative care, rather than offering a cure, is to provide comfort, control of pain, and a reduction of symptoms associated with one's illness. It includes the management of psychological, social and spiritual challenges that affect the patient. Palliative care is also used to support the family of a person with a progressive life-limiting disease.

Paranoia. Paranoia refers to psychosis characterized by systematized delusions of persecution or grandeur usually without hallucinations; a tendency on the part of an individual or group toward excessive or irrational suspiciousness and distrustfulness of others.

Parasympathetic nervous system. The parasympathetic functions of the autonomic nervous system are involved with conserving and restoring energy. Parasympathetic nerves slow the heart rate, increase peristalsis in the intestine, and increase glandular activity.

Parietal lobe. The parietal lobe found in each cerebral hemisphere occupies the area posterior to the central sulcus and superior to the lateral sulcus. The cortical areas of the parietal lobe can be divided into several distinct somesthetic areas and the outer layer of Baillarger. The cortical areas of the parietal lobe receive sensations from the pharyngeal region including the tongue and jaws, the face, fingers, hands, arm, trunk, thigh, and enable one to recognize objects placed in hand without the aid of vision.

Parkinson's disease (Parkinsonism). Parkinson's disease is a disorder associated with neuronal degeneration in the substantia nigra and other areas of the brain. This results in a reduction of the neurotransmitter dopamine, which leads to hypersensitivity of the dopamine receptors in the post-synaptic neurons in the corpus striatum. Signs and symptoms of this disorder include tremor, postural disturbances, cogwheel rigidity and bradykinesis, marked by difficulty in initiating and performing new movements. Consequently, movements are slow, the face is expressionless, and the voice is slurred and unmodulated.

Parkinson's disease (Parkinsonism) is the most common disease involving the basal ganglia. The symptoms are variable in relative severity and onset and usually include tremor, rigidity and difficulty moving. The tremor is a resting tremor, characteristically involving the hands in a "pill-rolling" movement, which diminishes during voluntary movement and increases during emotional stress. The rigidity is caused by increased tone in all muscles, although strength is nearly normal and reflexes are not particularly affected. The rigidity may be uniform throughout the range of movements imposed by an examiner and are often referred to as plastic or lead-pipe rigidity. Alternately, the rigidity may be interrupted by a series of brief relaxations referred to as cogwheel rigidity.

Rigidity in Parkinsonism is quite distinct from spasticity. Patients with spasticity exhibit muscle tone that is increased selectively in the extensors of the leg and the flexors of the arm and can be overcome by force.

Difficulty in movement (bradykinesia or slow movement and hypokinesia or few movements) shows up as decreased blinking, an expressionless face, and the absence of the arm movements normally associated with walking. Parkinson gait is characterized by stooped posture, with the hips and knees slightly flexed. Steps are short and often shuffling, with decreased arm swings. Patients often turn around stiffly.

The underlying defect in Parkinsonism is damage to the dopaminergic neurons (neurons that secrete the neurotransmitter dopamine) in the basal ganglia of the substantia nigra. While it has long been suspected that environmental agents were responsible for this damage, in recent years, pesticides have been pinpointed as the major culprit. The decreased dopamine levels caused by this damage cause the symptoms of Parkinsonism.

Alzheimer's disease and Parkinson's disease are distinct neurological disorders, but up to one-third of Alzheimer patients develop Parkinson's and some Parkinson's patients develop signs of Alzheimer's disease. To study the connection, researchers from the University of California San Diego's departments of neurosciences and pathology in collaboration with researchers from the Gladstone Institute of Neurological Diseases at the University of California San Francisco have developed strains of mice with the same protein abnormalities seen in these two disorders. In Alzheimer's disease, amyloid precursor protein (APP) accumulates in brain cells, whereas alpha-synuclein (SYN) is known to accumulate in patients with Alzheimer's disease.

When both proteins were increased in the studies with mice, symptoms of both Alzheimer's disease and Parkinson's disease intensified. In addition, increased levels of the breakdown product of APP, amyloid beta, enhanced the accumulation of SYN in brain cells. Drugs aimed at preventing the accumulation of these proteins could offer improvement for both disorders. (Nolte, John. *The Human Brain, An Introduction to its Functional Anatomy*, Third Edition, 1993. St. Louis: Mosby Year Book. "Alzheimer's and Parkinson's Proteins Create a Destructive Team." Sept 26, 2001, *Science Daily Magazine*)

Pathology. Pathology refers to the study of the essential nature of diseases, especially the structural and functional cellular changes that contribute to disease development. The pathology of Alzheimer's disease involves the destruction of neurons in certain areas of the brain, a loss of synaptic connections and an alteration in the neurotransmitters that allow neurons to communicate with one another and process information.

Peripheral nervous system. The peripheral nervous system consists of the cranial and spinal nerves and their associated ganglia. The nerve fibers, or axons, of the peripheral nervous system conduct information to and from the central nervous system. Although they are surrounded by fibrous sheaths, nerve fibers have little protection and are commonly damaged by trauma.

Perlmutter, David, M.D. Dr. David Perlmutter is a neurologist and Alzheimer's disease researcher. He has proposed a model of Alzheimer's disease that involves genetics, environmental agents, nutrition, lifestyle and infection. Dr. Perlmutter theorizes that many exposures can initiate an upregulation of the immune system. This immune response releases inflammatory cytokines which, in turn, upregulate the expression of the immune inducible form of nitric oxide synthase. This sets forth a destructive cascade of metabolic steps that eventually result in neuronal cell death.

Environmental agents responsible for this cascade include enteric bacteria, toxic metals, pesticides, food and environmental antigens, and stress responses mediated through the pituitary-thyroid-adrenal axis and chronic infection.

Personality changes. Personality changes are often seen in Alzheimer's disease. According to researchers at the University Memory and Aging Center in Cleveland, in some cases, personality changes occur before any cognitive changes become apparent. Personality changes range from apathy and indifference to marked agitation and include irritability, suspiciousness, aggressiveness, fearful behavior, drastically inappropriate behavior, heightened anger, hostility, mood swings, childish impulsiveness, paranoia, and overt sexuality or promiscuousness.

Phenserine. Phenserine, a phenylcarbamate of physostigmine, is a reversible acetyl-selective cholinesterase inhibitor currently being evaluated in clinical trials for Alzheimer's disease. In studies of rates with lesions of the forebrain cholinergic system, an injection of phenserine were found to significantly decrease the levels of secreted beta-amyloid precursor protein in the rats' cerebrospinal fluid.

Phosphatidylserine. Phosphatidylserine is a naturally occurring substance that promotes cell health and boosts the activity of acetylcholine and other brain chemicals. Phosphatidylserine is available as a dietary supplement widely used in Europe and Japan to correct cognitive impairment associated with degenerative brain disease. Sold as a health food supplement in the United States, it can be found in many preparations designed to improve memory naturally. A typical dose is 200 milligrams taken twice daily. Phosphatidylserine enhances both neuronal and mitochondrial stability and activity. In addition, it reduces mitochondrial free-radical production.

Researchers at Stanford University School of Medicine evaluated a group of 149 patients with age-associated memory impairment who were given 100 mg of phosphatidylserine or a placebo twice daily. Actual improvement based on psychometric testing was seen in a majority of treated patients, specifically those who had scored above the range of cognitive performance associated with dementing disorders such as Alzheimer's disease, but who were performing in the low normal range for persons of the same age. (Perlmutter, David. "Functional Therapeutics in Neurodegenerative Disease." Physicians Committee for Responsible Medicine website, http://www.pcrm.org/health/Preventive_Medicine/alzheimers.html.)

Phosphorylation. Phosphorylation is a process in which phosphorus molecules in the form of phosphate ions bind to other molecules. In Alzheimer's disease, aberrant or abnormal phosphorylation of tau protein leads to a cascade of events resulting in the death of brain cells known as neurons. This abnormal tau protein contains 5 to 9 moles of phosphate for each mole of protein, whereas normal tau contains 2 to 3 moles of phosphate for each mole of protein.

This increased phosphorylation is known as hyperphosphorylation. Before the microtubule structure is permanently damaged, neuronal plasticity occurs. In neuronal plasticity, the rigid neuron structure becomes flexible and dendritic processes are impaired.

One of the causes of aberrant phosphorylation of tau protein is a defect in the normal activity of enzymes known as kinases. Changes in the activity of kinases are thought to be due to altered patterns of apoptosis, which are under genetic regulation.

Physostigmine. Physostigmine is a carbamate compound similar to the cholinesterase inhibitor rivastigmine. Physostigmine is reported to be useful in reducing delusions and agitation.

Physostigmine salicylate (Synapton). Physostigmine salicylate available in the sustained-release compound Synapton is a cholinesterase inhibitor used in the treatment of Alzheimer's disease. Cholinesterase inhibitors delay the intrasynaptic degradation of the neurotransmitter acetylcholine, thereby increasing its effects. Small but reliable improvement in memory performance has been noted after administration of physostigmine salicylate although the side effects of this drug, which include nausea, vomiting, diarrhea, flushing, sweating and bradycardia) limit its use. There is evidence, however, that long-term use retards the deterioration in cognitive function over time even in patients who fail to improve during short-term trials of the drug. (Tariot, Pierre, M.D., et al. "Treating Alzheimer's Disease, Pharmacologic options now and in the near future." *Postgraduate Medicine*, vol 101 (6), June 1997)

Phytochemicals. Phytochemicals, which are also known as nutraceuticals, are naturally occurring chemicals found in plants that have medicinal properties.

Pia mater. The pia mater is a vascular membrane that closely covers the spinal cord. The pia mater extends along each nerve root and becomes continuous with the connective tissue surrounding each spinal nerve.

Pick's disease. Pick's disease is a neurodegenerative disorder of the cerebral cortex that results in a dementia characterized by progressive impairment of intellect and judgment and transitory aphasia. Pick's disease results from disease-related changes in brain tissue, including shrinking of the brain tissues and the presence of abnormal bodies (Pick bodies) in the nerve cells of the affected areas of the brain. Pick's disease is also known as aphasia-agnosia-apraxia syndrome, Arnold Pick's disease, cerebral atrophy, circumscribed brain atrophy, lobar sclerosis and presenile dementia.

Pick's disease affects about 1 out of every

100,000 people. It affects both sexes although it is more common in women. It may occur as early as 20 years old, but usually begins between the ages of 40 and 60 years. The average age of onset is 54 years. Pick's disease is suspected of being a dominant hereditary disorder. Risk factors include having a personal or family history of Pick's disease or senile dementia.

Movement and coordination difficulties may be one of the earliest symptoms. Other symptoms include mood and personality changes, loss of initiative, flat affect, impaired judgment, excessive manual exploration of the environment, withdrawal from social interaction, decreased ability to function in self-care, repetition of anything spoken to the person (echolalia), incomprehensible speech, aphasia, inability to comprehend speech, poor enunciation, decreased reading and writing abilities, loss of cognitive skills, weakness, increased muscle tone, urinary incontinence, and progressive dementia.

Diagnosis is based on neurologic exam and testing to rule out other conditions. Temporal and frontal lobe signs are most common, with resulting behavioral and language changes. An electroencephalogram shows nonspecific changes in electrical activity, although a head CT scan shows atrophy (loss of tissue mass) of affected areas of the brain.

Far less common than Alzheimer's disease, Pick's disease results in distinct brain changes. The brain in Pick's disease invariably exhibits a pronounced, although frequently asymmetric atrophy of the frontal and temporal lobes with conspicuous sparing of the posterior two-thirds of the superior temporal gyrus. Only rarely is there involvement of either the parietal or occipital lobe.

Brain atrophy can be severe, reducing the gyri to a thin wafer, which can be observed on gross examination as a "knife–edge" appearance. This pattern of lobar atrophy is often prominent enough to distinguish Pick's disease from Alzheimer's disease from a gross or direct observation of the brain. Besides the localized cortical atrophy, the caudate and putamen also show signs of atrophy.

When examined microscopically, neuronal loss is most severe in the outer three layers of the cortex and may be severe enough to superficially resemble another disorder, laminar necrosis. Some of the surviving neurons, called Pick cells, exhibit characteristic swelling. These cells may also contain Pick bodies, which are cytoplasmic, round to oval, filamentous inclusions that stain weakly with eosin but dramatically with silver stains. Structurally, they are composed of neurofilaments, endoplasmic reticulum, and paired helical filaments similar to those seen in Alzheimer's disease. Unlike the neurofibrillary tangles of Alzheimer's disease, however, Pick bodies do not survive the death of their host neuron and do not remain as markers of disease.

Although there is no cure for Pick's disease, treatment, similar to that used in Alzheimer's disease, is used in an effort to improve cognitive function and reduce further deterioration. Behavior modification may also be used to help control unacceptable behavior.

Pillaging. Pillaging, or stealing, is commonly seen in patients with Alzheimer's disease. Some patients with Alzheimer's disease become inordinately fond of hiding their possessions, and sometimes they confuse their own possessions with those of others. In nursing homes, this may be a problem as patients will sometimes wander into the rooms of others to pillage items. The problems of pillaging can be managed by supervision, understanding, keeping valuables locked up, and gentle admonitions.

Plaque. Plaque refers to deposits of protein and other substances that interfere with normal cell function. Plaque deposits in the brain are one of the characteristic signs of Alzheimer's disease. *See* Senile neuritic plaque.

Platelet activation studies. Platelets, or thrombocytes, are blood components distinct from blood cells that are involved in the clotting process. Derived from the megakaryocyte cell line, platelets are normally found in the blood. Studies have shown that blood platelets are abnormally highly activated in Alzheimer's diseases. Clues to this mechanism may enable researchers to find out why the neurons in Alzheimer's disease become abnormal.

Blood platelets secrete both amyloid precursor protein (APP) and beta amyloid protein, components of the cortical plaques associated with Alzheimer's disease. While platelets are normally activated at a rate of about 0.5 percent, Alzheimer's disease patients show rates 30 to 50 percent higher than the baseline rate. Researchers at the University of Miami made this discovery report that a test for platelet activation can serve as a diagnostic marker when combined with other parameters such as clinical symptoms and genetic studies.

Some researchers think that platelet abnormalities contribute to thrombosis or clot formation, causing ministrokes and other cerebrovascular abnormalities that may be connected to Alzheimer's disease. (Sevush, S. and L. Horstmann. "Platelet Activation Observed in Alzheimer's Patients." *Medical Tribune, Family Physician Edition*, 1998, June 18139 (12): 31.

Pons. The pons, or bridge, a section of the hindbrain, is situated on the anterior or front surface of the cerebellum, inferior to the midbrain and superior to the medulla oblongata. The anterior of the pons is covered by transverse fibers that connect the two cerebellar hemispheres.

Porteus Mazes. The Porteus Mazes Test is a mental status evaluation tool used to measure planning ability. While memory deficit is usually the first prominent complaint in Alzheimer's disease, attention, planning and abstract reasoning are also affected.

Positron emission tomography (PET) scan. Positron emission tomography (PET) is an imaging technique that provides a direct measure of the brain's metabolic activities. Specifically, PET identifies changes in cell metabolism, particularly the utilization of glucose and oxygen. PET scans have the advantage of providing numerical values for regional cerebral metabolic rates, making them useful in differentiating Alzheimer's disease from vascular dementia, multiple infarct dementia, Pick's disease, Huntington's disease, and depression. Patterns of impairment characteristically seen in Alzheimer's disease include temporoparietal and frontal hypometabolism with relative sparing of the visual and sensorimotor cortex. These changes are often asymmetric.

Glucose metabolism is determined by using 18-F-fluorodeoxyglucose (FDG-PET). In Alzheimer's disease, FDG-PET shows decreased accumulation in the neocortical association areas, but sparing of the basal ganglia, thalamus, cerebellum, and the primary sensory and motor cortex. The classic pattern is biparietal temporal hypometabolism. The extent of this reduced glucose metabolism correlates well with the severity of the cognitive impairment. PET studies performed in middle-aged persons with normal cognition who have the APOE4 allele have identified parietal, temporal and prefrontal deficits in glucose metabolism. PET scans of people with Alzheimer's disease show less baseline neural activity than those of age-matched controls. PET has also elucidated blood-brain barrier integrity, dopamine metabolism, and specific receptors in brains of Alzheimer's disease patients.

Besides assessing glucose metabolism, some PET techniques involve using the isotype O15 in cases of suspected dementia. With this technique, patients with Alzheimer's disease exhibit diminished oxygen consumption in the fronto-temporal-parietal lobes. In severe disease the frontal lobes are primarily affected.

However, PET scans cannot differentiate familial from sporadic Alzheimer's disease. Some studies indicate that reductions in mean PET measures of regional brain metabolism are more severe in patients who have more severe dementia. Cognitive defects have also been demonstrated to be associated with specific metabolic deficits, making PET an excellent tool for correlating brain metabolism with cognitive deficits. For instance, patients scoring low on tests such as visual recall that reflect right neocortical function exhibited functional asymmetry with altered metabolism in the right hemisphere.

A consortium of PET centers worldwide has provided their brain imaging and autopsy data from 138 dementia patients. Autopsy confirmation of Alzheimer's disease was obtained in 70 percent of the cases. PET had a sensitivity of 94 percent and specificity of 78 percent for detecting the presence of neurodegerative disease. The sensitivity of PET for detecting Alzheimer's disease was 94 percent, and specificity was 73 percent, demonstrating the good correlations between PET imaging and brain autopsy.

In a related study of 129 cognitive impaired subjects, PET scan accurately identified 87 percent of subjects with mild to moderate dementia and 96 percent of subjects with severe dementia. In another study, PET scan was shown capable of identifying patients with mild cognitive impairment who went on to develop Alzheimer's disease. These patients showed greater metabolic reduction in the posterior association cortex on the initial PET scan compared with those subjects who did not progress to a diagnosis of probably Alzheimer's disease. (Edward, Coleman, M.D., R. "Positron Emission Tomography in the Evaluation of Dementia." presented at the 48th Annual Meeting of the Society of Nuclear Medicine, June 23, 2001.)

In January 2001, researchers at the University of California–Los Angeles announced that they have developed a variation of PET testing which is presumably more capable of accurately diagnosing Alzheimer's disease in its early stages. This test combines PET imaging with the injection of a chemical tracer and identifies the specific lesions seen in Alzheimer's disease.

Postsynaptic vesicles. Depolarization of the presynaptic endings of neuronal processes causes a release of neurotransmitter into the synaptic cleft. Some of the neurotransmitter molecules then bind to receptors in waiting or postsynaptic vesicles. Transmitter-receptor binding causes some change in the postsynaptic neuron, such as rapid opening of an ion channel or a slower cascade of biochemical events that culminates in an electrical or similar charge.

Preclinical phase of Alzheimer's disease. The preclinical phase of Alzheimer's disease refers to the time frame when pathological changes can be seen in brain tissue although there are no symptoms of cognitive impairment. Depression may be a hallmark of the preclinical phase.

Prednisone. Prednisone is a synthetic glucocorticoid steroid used as an anti-inflammatory agent. Prednisone suppresses both the acute phase inflammatory response and the complement cascade. In pilot studies involving 138 patients, prednisone showed no improvement over a 16-month period. Compared to the placebo group, patients on prednisone showed moderate to severe problems. (*Nia News*. Alzheimer's disease research update, February 8, 2000).

Prenatal genetic testing. It is possible to perform prenatal diagnosis of early-onset familial Alzheimer's disease by analyzing fetal DNA extracted from cells obtained by chorionic villus sampling at about 10–12 weeks gestation or amniocentesis at 16–18 weeks gestation. These samples can be tested for mutations in the presenilin 1 (PSEN 1) gene for those families in which a disease-causing mutation has been identified in an affected family member.

Presenile dementia. Presenile dementia occurs to dementia occurring in individuals younger than 50 years of age. *See also* Early-onset familial Alzheimer's disease and Pick's disease.

Presenilin genes. The genes for presenilin are associated with Alzheimer's disease. Chromosome 14 linkage has been reported in a number of autosomal dominant early-onset pedigrees of familial Alzheimer's disease. The chromosome 14 gene called S182, AD2, or presenilin 1 (PS-1), encodes a predicted membrane-spanning protein whose function and possible interactions with β APP are unclear. According to one current theory, mutations to PS-1 may affect Golgi or membrane traffic permitting β APP to enhance production of amyloid beta protein. Over 30 different mis-sense mutations and one deletion mutation in the coding region of 10 axons of the PS-1 gene have been identified in over forty families. PS-1 is reported to have more than 40 sites of mutations, with most mutations leading to amino acid substitutions. Two exon deletion and two truncation mutations have also been reported.

The presenilin 2 (PS-2 or STM2 gene), on chromosome 1, codes for a membrane protein with amino acids similar to that of PS-1. PS-2 is also linked to familial Alzheimer's disease. While PS-1 mutations are associated with early onset FAD (ages 30–50), PS-2 mutations are association with familial forms of Alzheimer's disease occurring in individuals aged 50–70 years. Two sites of PS-2 mutations have been identified.

Presenilin therapy. Presenilin is a protein containing two aspartate amino acids aligned in strategic positions suggesting that they could act as protease enzymes capable of splitting other proteins. Both gamma and beta secretase promote formation of beta amyloid protein, whereas alpha secretase promotes binding of a harmless peptide fragment.

Recent studies suggest that presenilins may either have gamma secretase activity or they may be part of a group of proteins that is complexed together to influence gamma secretase cleavage of amyloid precursor protein. Presenilin may also be involved in trafficking amyloid precursor protein, thereby promoting its splicing into beta amyloid protein. In addition, the protein nicastrin has been found to bind to presenilin. This protein appears to facilitate the formation of beta amyloid protein. In studies where PS-1 has been activated or removed, levels of secreted beta amyloid protein are markedly reduced. Therapies designed to reduce presenilin are being evaluated for their role in reducing Abeta production.

Presynaptic vesicles. Presynaptic vesicles, which are found near the ending of neuronal processes, contained pre-packaged amounts of neurotransmitter. Depolarization of the presynaptic ending causes some of the presynaptic vesicles to merge with the presynaptic membrane and dump their contents into the synaptic cleft. Neurotransmitter molecules then diffuse across the synaptic cleft.

Prevalence. Alzheimer's disease is the most common cause of dementia in North America and Europe. Prevalence increases with increasing age. Approximately 10 percent of all persons over the age of 70 years have significant memory loss and more than half of these individuals have Alzheimer's disease. The prevalence of dementia in individuals over the age of 85 years is estimated to be 30 to 50 percent with approximately 20 percent of individuals older than 80 having Alzheimer's disease.

Studies have shown that the prevalence of Alzheimer's disease doubles every five years, with 3 percent of 65 to 74 year olds affected. Approximately 47 percent of those aged 85 and older may become affected. According to the United Nations Department of International Economics and Social Affairs, more than 7 million people in North America and Europe have been diagnosed with dementia.

Primary Progressive Aphasia. Primary progressive aphasia (PPA) is a form of dementia that can occur before the age of 65. Individuals with PPA have impaired language functions, including difficulty with speaking, reading, writing, speaking and understanding speech.

Principal. Principal refers to the patient or individual signing the power of attorney to authorize another individual to legally make his or her decisions.

Prions. Prions are infectious agents composed of nude (without any type of nuclear or cytoplasmic membrane) polypeptide proteins devoid of genetic material. Capable of multiplying rapidly, prions can cause neurodegenerative disorders in humans and domestic animals. Distinct from viruses, bacteria, fungi and parasites, prions do not use the nucleic acid template DNA-RNA for reproduction, a mechanism ordinarily common to all living things. Infected prions can damage brain tissue through a process of vacillation, making neurons appear like sponges with pitted holes, thus the diseases they cause are known as spongiform encephalopathy.

To prevent the possible dissemination of human prion infections like Creutzfeldt-Jakob disease (CJD), the FDA has implemented guidelines for blood banks. Blood banks now permanently defer donors who have been diagnosed with CJD, donors who have received a dura mater transplant or human pituitary-derived growth hormone, donors who have traveled in the United Kingdom between 1980 and 1996, and donors who have injected bovine insulin since 1980.

Extremely hardy prions can survive the pressurized steam of autoclaves, filtration, extreme heat, radiation, formaldehyde and decades of freezing.

Program for All-Inclusive Care for the Elderly (PACE). The PACE program is a federal health insurance program that serves the frail elderly and features a comprehensive service that integrates Medicare and Medicaid financing. States that elect to cover PACE services as a State Plan option must enter into a program agreement with a PACE provider and the Department of Health and Human Services.

Progressive Deterioration Scale (PDS). The Progressive Deterioration Scale (PDS) is an evaluation tool that measures quality of life changes. The PDS is helpful in evaluating responses to therapy.

Progressive supranuclear palsy (PSP). Progressive supranuclear palsy (PSP) is a rare brain disorder that causes serious and permanent problems with control of gait and balance. The most obvious is an inability to aim the eyes properly or blurry vision. This occurs because of lesions in the area of the brain that coordinate eye movements. Patients also show alterations of mood and behavior, including depression, apathy and progressive mild dementia. Symptoms can vary, and this disease may be confused with Parkinson's disease, Alzheimer's disease and prion diseases. The key to diagnosis is the identification of early gait disturbances and difficulty with eye movement.

Propentofylline. Propentofylline is a medication with nerve-protective properties that may enhance metabolism in the brain. The drug appears to improve symptoms and slow disease progression. Propentofylline is also thought to have a number of neuroprotective effects, including the ability to facilitate the release of nerve growth factor and decrease levels of damaging cytokines, free radicals and glutatmate. Propentofylline is being evaluated as a therapy in both Alzheimer's disease and vascular dementia. Because of its theorized mode of action, Propentofylline may slow disease progression as well as reduce symptoms of dementia.

Prosencephalon. The prosencephalon or forebrain is the third major section of the brain at the furthest or highest point from the spinal cord. The prosencephalon consists of the diencephalons (between brain), which is the central part of the forebrain, and the telencephalon, or cerebrum.

Prostate apoptosis response-4 (Par-4) protein. Prostate apoptosis response-4 (Par-4) protein is a protein compound found in the areas of the brain affected by Alzheimer's disease. Par-4 is suspected of causing nerve cells to self-destruct.

Protein kinases. Protein kinases are enzymes responsible for the phosphorylation (addition of phosphorus molecules) of hydryoxyl side chains on proteins. Protein kinases accomplish this by catalyzing the transfer of phosphate ions from adenosine triphosphates, ATP, the body's energy source derived from food. In Alzheimer's disease, disturbances to the balance of kinase and phosphatase activities may lead to the inappropriate hyperphosphorylation of various proteins, including tau protein.

Pseudodementia. Pseudodementia is a rare syndrome of depression with impaired cognition in which treatment of the depression relieves the cognitive deficit.

Psychologist, clinical. Clinical psychologists are scientists with doctoral degrees in the field of psychology who have been trained to treat patients with psychological disorders.

Psychology. Psychology is the scientific study of the mind and behavior.

Psychosis. Psychosis is a general term for a state of mind or mental disorder characterized by defective or lost contact with reality. Psychotic patients may have hallucinations, delusions or other severe thought processes.

Psychotropic agent. Psychotropic agents are medications designed to change psychological behavior. The mode of these agents varies, and specific agents are selected on the basis of clinical symptoms. For instance, patients showing signs of apathy and depression are likely to be prescribed antidepressant medications.

Pupil Dilation Test. Pupil dilation using an acetylcholine receptor test is used to measure the cholinergic neuronal system in an effort to help diagnose Alzheimer's disease. In this test, a single drop of 0.01 percent solution of tropicamide (an acetylcholine receptor antagonist) is placed in one eye and a drop of water in the other. Hypersensitivity to antagonists of acetylcholine neurotransmission is measured by an increase in pupil size. This test has been reported to distinguish Alzheimer's disease with an accuracy rate of 95 percent.

Quetiapine fumarate. Quetiapine fumarate is an anti-psychotic medication currently being studied for use in patients with dementia. In one study using flexible doses of quetiapine, 15 percent of subjects withdrew over 1 year because of adverse experiences or co-existing illnesses. Side effects were mild and typically transient. Thirty percent of subjects experienced sedation, 15 percent developed orthostatic hypotension (low blood pressure on rising), and 12 percent experienced dizziness. Encouraging behavioral effects were observed in patients with dementia. (Tariot, M.D., Pierre N., et al. "Pharmacologic Therapy for Behavioral Symptoms of Alzheimer's Disease. *Clinics in Geriatric Medicine*, volume 17 (2): 359–376 [2001.])

Radionuclide Brain Scan. A radionuclide scan or brain scan is a diagnostic procedure in which a small amount of a radioisotope is administered intravenously to measure the tissue uptake of the isotope. A brain scan is used to detect the presence of a space-occupying intracranial lesion. The scan cannot determine if the lesion is due to a tumor, hematoma, abscess or vascular malformation. Patients should be apprised that scanning is done by a large overhanging machine that emits a ticking sound as the machine moves. Other than the intravenous administration of the radioisotope, the procedure is painless.

Rapid eye movement (REM). Rapid eye movement (REM) is a mentally active period during which dreaming occurs. Rapid eye movement during this period is a reflection of increased brain activity. REM accounts for about 25 percent of the sleep cycle. The non–REM portion can be divided into 4 different stages. In each stage, brain waves become progressively larger and slower, and sleep becomes deeper. After reaching the deepest period, stage 4, the pattern reverses and sleep becomes lighter until REM sleep, the most active period, occurs. This cycle typically occurs about once every 90 minutes in humans.

REACH *see* Resources for Enhancing Alzheimer's Caregiver Health

Receptor. Receptors are protein molecules found on the surface or nucleus of cells that react with substances, including hormones, neurotransmitters and drugs, and cause reciprocal physiological actions. Free nerve endings can also act as receptors, reacting to sensations such as pain, touch, pressure, cold and heat.

Recombinant DNA technology. Recombinant DNA technology refers to the artificial rearrangement of DNA. In this process segments of DNA from one organism are incorporated into the genetic makeup of another organism. Using these techniques, researchers can study the actions and functions of specific genes.

Reflex disturbances. In cerebellar disease, movement of the tendon reflexes is extended. Because of loss of influence on the stretch reflexes, the movement consists of a series of flexion and extension movements with the leg moving like a pendulum. Reflex testing is a well-known, sensitive indicator of nervous system integrity. Reflex changes occur in the later stages of Alzheimer's disease and other cerebral degenerative diseases.

Some researchers have noted that the overt occurrence of a continuous sucking, licking or grasping in cerebral degenerative diseases. Signs of dysfunction of the plantar extensor reflex differentiates Alzheimer's disease patients. Those with these overt reflexes may have deficiencies in basic activities of daily living but are not yet incontinent as opposed to permanently incontinent Alzheimer's disease patients who are deficient in activities of daily living, but are still ambulatory. It appears that these neurologic reflexes emerge at a certain stage of Alzheimer's disease just as they disappear in certain stages in the course of infancy. Reflex testing has the advantage of not being influenced by education and cultural factors. (Reisberg, Barry, et al. "Report of an IPA Special Meeting Work Group Under the Co-sponsorship of Alzheimer's Disease International, the European Federation of Neurological Societies, the World Health Organization, and the World Psychiatric Association." International Psychogeriatric Association, 2000.)

Remacemide. The drug Remacemide is a NMDA antagonist. By inhibiting the neurotransmission of glutamate in the brain, remacemide offers protection against neuronal destruction. Excess glutamate is thought to be toxic to neurons, and elevated levels of glutamate have been associated with various neurodegenerative disorders, including Alzheimer's disease.

Reminyl *see* Galantamine hydrobromide.

Repetitive behavior. Patients with Alzheimer's disease exhibit repetitive behavior, often repeating the same questions, pacing, and performing repetitive activities, such as cleaning the same item.

Reptilian brain. The reptilian brain refers to the base of the brain where the necessary command centers for living, including sleep and waking, respiration and temperature regulation, are located.

Research. The Alzheimer's Association supports many types of research on Alzheimer's disease. All patients with Alzheimer's disease should be allowed to enroll in research efforts particularly when there is a potential benefit or therapeutic value for the individual. Regardless of the particular program, patients should have access to an available proxy, such as a family member or caregiver, who can decide if the research protocol is in the patient's best interest. All research projects should have Institutional Review Boards that oversee the projects and evaluate potential risks.

Resident-Centered Care. Nursing home philosophy, advocates decision-making by residents, rather than having the staff make all decisions. In Resident-Centered care, the staff focuses on the individual needs of the patients and offers holistic care for those who are terminally ill.

Resources for Enhancing Alzheimer's Caregiver's Health (REACH). REACH is a unique, 5-year program sponsored by the National Institute on Aging and the National Institute for Nursing Research. REACH grew out of a National Institutes of Health (NIH) initiative that acknowledged the well-documented burdens associated with caring for dementia patients, as well as the emergence in the literature of promising dementia caregiver interventions.

In 1995, NIH funded six intervention sites and a coordinating center to develop interventions for family caregivers of individuals with moderated degrees of impairment. Each of these sites investigated a different intervention, although there were some items common to all groups, and all of the sites included substantial minority participation. The following caregiver interventions were investigated: 1) home-based behavioral skills training and problem solving, 2) telephone-based system offering voice mail support and advice, 3) training in behavior and stress management provided through a primary care setting 4) home-based, family-focused multisystem intervention with computer-telephone integration, 5) group-based coping skills training and enhanced support, and 6) home-based environmental and behavioral skills training.

Respite care. Respite care refers to temporary home-care. Respite care can be provided by volunteers through some local Alzheimer's Associations and as a paid service by home-care nursing services.

Resveratrol. Resveratrol is a plant chemical known as a flavinoid found in red wine and grape juice. Because of its antioxidant properties, resveratrol is suspected of offering therapeutic benefits in Alzheimer's disease. Clinical studies show that individuals who drink a small glass of red wine daily have a reduced incidence of Alzheimer's disease.

Retention and Immediate Recall. The cognitive skill of retention and immediate recall can be tested by giving the patient a list of words, including dates, addresses, and objects. The patient should repeat the words at the time the examiner recites them to verify that the words have been heard. Three to 5 minutes later the patient should be asked to repeat the words. If the answers are wrong, the examiner attempts to determine if the subject is aware that he or she is wrong or if they are attempting to contrive answers.

Normally, subjects recall the words correctly. Poor recent memory is characteristic of organic brain disease. Poor remote memory is seen in psychiatric and severe emotional disorders.

Rey-Osterreith complex figure. The Rey-Osterreith complex figure is used as a psychological profile test to measure visuo-spatial planning and organization and nonverbal memory.

Rhombencephalon. The rhombencephalon, or hindbrain, is the first major division or section of the brain found in ascending order from the spinal cord. The rhombencephalon consists of three major sections: the myencephalon or medulla oblongata, the metencephalon or pons, and the cerebellum.

Rifamycin (rifampicin). The antibiotic rifampicin, which is widely used is the treatment of tuberculosis and leprosy, has been found to prevent the aggregation and neurotoxicity of amyloid beta protein in test tube studies. This inhibitory activity is attributed to the naphthohydroquinone structure, which acts as a free radical scavenger.

Risk factors. Multiple studies have been conducted to help determine which patient groups may be at highest risk for developing Alzheimer's disease. Risk factors are not causes of disease but factors that make people more susceptible to developing a certain disease. This does not mean they will develop the disease. Knowing what factors confer risk can enable these populations to seek preventative measures. The most reproducible risk factors for Alzheimer's disease include: increasing age, family history of dementia in a first degree relative before age 65, Down's syndrome in a first degree relative and the APOE-e4 allele. Approximately 50 percent of all patients with a first degree relative with Alzheimer's disease will develop this disorder if followed into the 80th decade. This represents a 2–4 fold increase compared to age-matched controls.

Some researchers also consider the female gender a risk factor since women are 2 to 3 times more likely than men to develop Alzheimer's disease, with a lifetime risk of 1 in 3 women at age 65. Studies indicate that 50–70 percent of all women older than 80 years are affected.

A history of head trauma has been associated with an increased risk of developing Alzheimer's disease. Head circumference and brain size have been inversely associated with Alzheimer's disease. Smaller brain size has also been associated with an earlier disease onset. Low intelligence and limited education have also been associated with an increased risk of Alzheimer's disease. *See also* Nun studies and Writing studies.

Risperidone (Risperdal). Risperidone (Risperdal) is one of the newer atypical antipsychotic medications used to treat verbal or physical aggression and wandering. Risperidone appears to significantly decrease symptoms of psychosis and aggression while posing a very low risk for severe side effects.

Two large, multicenter trials have been completed in nursing home patients with fairly severe dementia. The first trial, using doses ranging from 0.5 mg to 2mg daily, showed beneficial effects on both psychosis and aggression. The second study used doses of 1.1 mg to 1.2 mg daily and compared risperidone to haloperidol. While effects were comparable, the tolerability of risperidone appeared to be better with low risk of dose-related parkinsonism and sedation.

Rivastigmine. Rivistagmine (Exelon), a drug commonly used for the treatment of mild to moderate Alzheimer's disease, is a carbamate compound that acts as a cholinesterase inhibitor, with selective action in the cortex and hippocampus. Formerly known as ENA 713, rivastigmine is an intermediate-acting inhibitor. Its effects are reversible after an intermediate length of time, and as the disease progresses and the brain's concentration of acetylcholine diminishes, the drug is less effective. The daily dose is generally 3 mg to 12 mg taken twice daily in divided doses taken in the morning and evening.

Side effects, which may be significant, include nausea, vomiting, loss of appetite and weight loss. Less common side effects include high blood pressure, runny nose, slow heartbeat and fainting. Rare side effects include aggression, irritability, nervousness, seizures, trembling and difficulty urinating.

Rivastigmine may also increase the effects of neuromuscular blocking agents used in surgery to relax muscles. Rivastigmine may also cause some people to become dizzy, clumsy, or unsteady. This drug should not be stopped abruptly. Stopping or decreasing the dose by a large amount may cause mental or behavioral changes.

An overdose of rivastigmine may lead to seizures or shock. Some signs of an overdose include large pupils, irregular breathing, fast or weak pulse, severe nausea and vomiting, increasing muscle weakness, greatly increased sweating and greatly increased watering of the mouth.

Rofecoxib (Vioxx). Rofecoxib (Vioxx) is a drug approved by the FDA for relief of the signs of osteoarthritis. A selective COX-2 inhibitor, rofecoxib is undergoing clinical trials for its use in Alzheimer's disease.

Rosemary (*Rosmarinus officinalis*). Herb containing a number of different antioxidants, most notably, rosmarinic acid, that helps reduce free radicals. Rosemary also contains several compounds that are reported to inhibit the breakdown of acetylcholine. Rosemary has long been used as a memory booster. Rosemary can be drank as a tea. Alternately, it can be used as an essential oil added to bathwater, but not directly to skin. Duke, James A. *The Green Pharmacy.* [Emmaus, PA:] Rodale Press, Emmaus, PA, 1997.

Routines. Caregivers are reminded of the importance routines play in reducing the decisions patients with Alzheimer's disease must make. Routines provide security for patients with dementia. Daily routines which keep the patient active help them sleep at night and regular toileting may reduce the chance of accidents. Keeping keys and other possessions in one place, even wearing them on a safety pin over clothing, can prevent confusion and frustration.

S-adenosylmethionine (SAMe). S-adenosylmethionine (SAMe) is a naturally occurring compound available as a dietary supplement that increases the body's levels of serotonin, melatonin, and dopamine. Clinical studies indicate that patients with Alzheimer's disease and depression have decreased levels of SAMe in their brain tissues. Although there are reports of improvement in Alzheimer's disease using SAMe, more studies are needed to determine the safety and effectiveness of this supplement for dementia patients.

Safe Return Program. Safe Return is the only nationwide identity program for people with Alzheimer's disease who wander. Sponsored by the Alzheimer's Association, the program includes identification products like wallet cards and clothing tags, a national photo/information database, wandering behavior education, training for families and caregivers, and a 24-hour toll free emergency crisis line.

To register, a person with dementia or their caregiver fills out a form, supplies a photo, and chooses the type of ID product the registrant will wear or carry. If a person is later reported missing, Safe Return immediately alerts local law enforcement agencies and helps in distributing and faxing photo flyers to law enforcement personnel and hospitals. Since 1993, the program has helped to locate and return more than 2,700 registrants to their families. Details can be obtained through the national Alzheimer's Association office or through local Alzheimer's Association chapters. *See* Resource Section.

Safety. Caregivers are reminded to keep the home and surroundings as safe as possible. As dementia progresses, loss of physical coordination and memory increases the chances of injury. Common hazards include loose or worn carpets and throw rugs, polished floors, loose stair railings and clutter. Patients who have a tendency to wander must be properly supervised regardless if they live at home or in an assisted living facility. Patients with a tendency to pace should be encouraged to take supervised walks. Physical activity may also help patients sleep better at night.

St. George-Hyslop, Peter, M.D., D.Sc. Dr. Peter St George-Hyslop is Assistant Professor, Department of Medicine, Division of Neurology and Director of the Center for Research in Neurodegenerative Disease at the University of Toronto. The recipient of numerous medical awards, including an Award for Medical Research from the Metropolitan Life Foundation, he is a member of the American Society for Clinical Investigation where he is well known for his research into Alzheimer's disease.

Sandoz Clinical Assessment-Geriatric (SCAG). The SCAG is a neuropsychological assessment tool which has been largely replaced by the cognitive testing sections of the Alzheimer's Disease Assessment Scale (ADAS-Cog). The SCAG is reported to have limited utility because of its lack of sensitivity and its limited scope. Evaluations are best made in patients with either mild or severe dementia and only one or two categories of symptoms. SCAG does not encompass behavioral disorders, altered mood states and impaired cognitive function.

SCAN Health Plan of Long Beach, California. The SCAN Health Plan, a social HMO, provides half the cost of adult day care and medical services for Alzheimer's patients who are able to live at home. The adult day care center charges $40 a day and SCAN pays half of this and also provides medical supplies costing $100/month. Caseworkers regularly visit the home to help with household problems.

Secretase enzymes. Secretase enzymes are naturally occurring chemicals that act as proteases (break down protein molecules). Both beta and gamma secretase cleave amyloid precursor protein (APP) in a way that results in the neurotoxic form of amyloid beta protein. Alpha secretase cleaves APP in a way that results in harmless amyloid beta peptides. Drugs are currently being studies that would inhibit beta or gamma secretase or cause increased production of alpha secretase.

Selective Serotonin Reuptake Inhibitors (SSRI's) Selective Serotonin Reuptake Inhibitors, SSRIs, are a class of drugs, such as fluoxetine (Prozac) that are commonly used as antidepressants. SSRIs are psychoactive drugs and may impair judgment, thinking, and motor skills.

Selegiline hydrochloride (Eldepryl, Atapryl). Selegiline, a drug commonly known as l-deprenyl, is sold under the brand names Atapryl and Eldepryl. Primarily used for the treatment of Parkinson's disease, selegiline is an inhibitor of the enzyme monoamine oxidase (MAO) type B. In addition, it also increases dopamine activity in the brain. In the central nervous system MAO compounds are used in the catabolism of catecholamines and serotonin. Because elevated levels of MAO-B are also found in patients with Alzheimer's disease, long-term inhibition with selegiline may have anti-neurotoxic properties.

Side effects include vitamin K deficiency, which has been associated with a necrotizing form of enterocolitis. At least 3–5 weeks should elapse between the discontinuation of fluoxetine (Prozac) and the initiation of MAO inhibitors such as selegiline. Selegiline should not be used in patients undergoing therapy with opiod narcotics, including meperidine (Demerol). Severe agitation, hallucinations, and death have occurred with concomitant administration of selegiline and meperidine.

Selegiline is currently being studied in clinical trials for its benefits in Alzheimer's disease. Studies thus far have found that mental deterioration from Alzheimer's disease was slowed by an average of 7 months by either selegiline or high doses (2,000 I.U. daily) of vitamin E. (Hingley, Audrey. "Alzheimer's: Few Clues on the Mysteries of Memory." The Food and Drug Administration. *FDA Consumer Magazine*, May/June, 1998. Online at http://www.fda.gov/fdac/featires/1998/398_alz_html)

Senile dementia / Alzheimer's type (SDAT). Before today's sophisticated imaging techniques became available, there were few diagnostic tools to aid in the diagnosis of Alzheimer's disease. When patients died and were autopsied, many were found to have other forms of dementia besides Alzheimer's disease. Because of this, patients suspected of having Alzheimer's disease were given the diagnosis of senile dementia/Alzheimer's type. With modern imaging techniques and the ability to rule out other causes of dementia, however, a diagnosis of Alzheimer's disease is generally 90 percent accurate, and this term is not used as often as it was in the past. *See* Alzheimer's disease.

Senile (neuritic) plaque. Senile or neuritic plaques are neurotoxic protein deposits found in excess amounts in the brains of patients with Alzheimer's disease. Senile neuritic plaques are complex extracellular (located in the spaces outside of cells) lesions composed of a central deposit or core of beta amyloid protein surrounded by activated microglia, fibrillary astrocytes, and dystrophic neurites (dendrites and axonal terminals). Microscopically viewed, neuritic plaques are focal, spherical collections of dilated, tortuous, silver-staining neuritic processes known as dystrophic neurites surrounding a central amyloid core. Often, a clear halo surrounds these components. Neuritic plaques range from 20 to 200 μm in diameter.

Dystrophic neurites are swollen, distorted neuronal processes. Complex sugar polymer components known as glycosaminoglycans are critical for the formation of plaque, acting as the glue for the assembly of these deposits. Senile plaques are often surrounded by microglial cells and reactive astrocytes.

The amyloid core consists of β-amyloid, a predominantly 42kDa protein derived from its precursor amyloid precursor protein by a mechanism known as proteolytic processing. β-amyloid is produced by all cell types and is not unique to neurons. Other components of senile plaque include al-1-antichymotrypsin, glycosaminoglycans and apolipoprotein E.

In Alzheimer's disease, plaques can be found in the hippocampus and amygdala as well as in the neocortex. Similar to the invasions of NFTs, there is usually relative sparing of primary motory and sensory cortices. In some patients there are also diffuse plaques that lack the surrounding neuritic reaction. Diffuse plaques are found in superficial portions of the cerebral cortex as well as in basal ganglia and cerebellar cortex. When diffuse plaques are found in the cerebral cortex, they usually appear to be centered on small vessels or on clusters of neurons. These lesions, which generally occur along with senile plaques, are thought to possibly represent an earlier disease stage.

In the fifth decade of life, many individuals begin to develop senile plaque deposits in their cerebral cortex. By the eighth decade of life, approximately 75 percent of the population is affected by these plaques. The density of these plaques does not increase with age, suggesting that plaque forms quickly. Initially, plaques begin as innocuous deposits of non-aggregated, beta amyloid protein free of neurotoxic effects. However, in some individuals these deposits transform into the neurotoxic senile plaques associated with Alzheimer's disease. It is suspected that a certain enzyme, butyrcholinesterase, plays an essential role in this maturation process.

The distribution and chemical composition of senile neuritic plaques and neurofibrillary tangles are similar in normal elderly people and those with Alzheimer's disease. After a certain density of these lesions is reached, symptoms of Alzheimer's disease develop. Among people with Alzheimer's disease, this level varies depending on genetic and environmental risk factors, as well as co-morbid brain pathology.

In postmortem examination, the plaques should stain positively with A-amyloid antibodies and negative for prion antibodies. The numbers of plaques and tangles must exceed those found in age-matched controls for a diagnosis of Alzheimer's disease.

Senility. Senility refers to the physical and mental bodily changes or infirmities associated with aging.

Senior Medicare Patrol Project. The United States Department of Health and Human Services, through the Administration on Aging, has created 52 Senior Medicare Patrol Project Grants. Senior volunteers undergo several days of training reviewing health care benefit statements and outlining the steps seniors can take to protect themselves. Volunteers work in local senior centers and other places to assist seniors with questions about their benefits and billing problems.

Sentinel Event Alert. A sentinel event alert refers to a medication, condition, or flaw in nursing care that leads to the injury or death of patients. Sentinel event alerts are monitored by accreditation agencies including the Joint Commission on Accreditation of Hospitals to determine the cause of the alert and how it can be corrected.

Sequencing. Sequencing refers to the human behavior of doing things in a logical, predictable order.

Serotonin. Serotonin, or 5-hydroxytryptamine, is a monoamine (having one amine group in its structure) neurotransmitter derived from the amino acid tryptophan. Neurons that produce serotonin are primarily found in the region of the brainstem known as the Raphe nuclei. The actions of serotonin are widespread, with firing rates fluctuating between sleep and wakefulness. Serotonin is involved in arousal, mood and pain control. Studies of postmortem brain tissue from Alzheimer's disease patients show a distinct deficit of serotonin. In several small studies, drugs such as Trazodone, which are known to increase serotonin level, were found to be effective in reducing agitation.

Seven Minute Screen. The Seven Minute Screen, developed by researchers at the University of Vermont, is a test used to help identify patients who should be evaluated for Alzheimer's disease. The Seven Minute Screen, which takes an average of seven minutes and 42 seconds to complete, consists of four sets of questions that focus on orientation, memory, visuospatial skills and expressive language. These are the areas must likely to reveal deficiencies related to Alzheimer's disease.

The test may be administered by a nurse practitioner, physician assistant, or other trained office personnel. Orientation is tested by asking the subject to identify the present month, date, year, day of the week and time of day. The degree of error is graded. A one day error in date is scored as one, while a one month error is scored as 5.

To test memory, subjects are asked identify 16 items drawn on four cards. They are given clues or hints from the tester. After successful identification, the card is hidden and the subject is asked to recall the item after being given the clue. The subject is then distracted by being asked to state the months of the year backwards. The subject is then asked to recall the 16 items.

Visuospatial skills are tested by showing the subject two-dimensional visual images such as a clock with different times. To test expressive language or verbal fluency, the subject is asked to name as many animals as possible within one minute.

In studies, individuals with Alzheimer's disease had significantly worse scores on each of the four tests, and 92 percent of individuals with Alzheimer's disease were correctly identified. (Solomon, P.R., W.W. Pendlebury. "Recognition of Alzheimer's disease: the 7 minute screen." *Family Medicine*, 1998, vol 30, 265–271.)

Severe Impairment Battery. The Severe Impairment Battery developed by Saxton in 1990 is an evaluation tool for assessing dementia. This series of tests is found to be reliable in gauging the severity of dementia in patients with low scores on the Mini Mental Status Examination.

Sexuality. Patients with dementia are still sexual beings although they may no longer remember how to arouse their partners or remember what is appropriate behavior. In many cases Alzheimer's patients become uninhibited sexually. At the same time their physical condition and indifference to grooming may make sexual activity despairing for the caregiver spouse. Other patients may lose complete interest in sex.

Shadowing. Shadowing refers to following, mimicking, and interrupting behaviors that people with dementia may experience.

Single-nucleotide polymorphisms (SNPs). Single-nucleotide polymorphisms are common, single base-pair variations of DNA.

Single photon/positron emission computed tomography (SPECT). Single photon/positron emission computed tomography (SPECT) is an imaging technique capable of assessing function in relative or absolute terms. SPECT studies of the brain involve the administration of compounds that are normally distributed in the brain according to cerebral blood flow. Thus, a relative measure of cerebral activity can be assessed in different regions of the brain. SPECT usually measures blood flow but it can also image muscarinic and dopamine receptors. In Alzheimer's disease, temporoparietal hypoperfusion is usually seen, with frontal lobe blood flow sometimes also being diminished. When present in sufficient magnitude, temporal lobe dementia is generally present. SPECT is also used to assess the response to drug therapy.

Skilled nursing care. Skilled nursing care is a level of care that includes ongoing medical or nursing services.

Sleep disturbances. Sleep disturbances typically seen in dementia include increased difficulty falling asleep, frequent awakenings, and decreased total sleep time. Studies indicate that there is a rough relationship between the severity of dementia and the magnitude of the sleep disorder. Management of sleep disturbances includes an avoidance of caffeine and other stimulants, an adherence to a regular sleep-wake cycle, and enhanced activity or exercise during the day. Benzodiazepine medications, such as diazepam (Valium) and lorazepam (Ativan) are widely used but are associated with significant side effects. Antidepressant medications, particularly Trazodone (Desyrel), are also commonly used because of the association between sleep disorders and depression.

In one study, changes in sleep structure, especially REM sleep, and in EEG activation were studied in relation to the cholinergic deficit seen in Alzheimer's disease. Only REM sleep was reduced when compared to control subjects. REM is associated with EEG slowing, and Alzheimer's disease patients showed increased EEG activation.

Smoking. The effects of cigarette smoking on Alzheimer's disease are unclear, although one recent study found that the risk of dementia is significantly increased in smokers. Factors that cause increased risk of heart disease, including smoking, have also been found to cause an increased risk for developing Alzheimer's disease. The specific effects of nicotine from smoking, however, remain unclear.

Social HMOs (SHMOs) *see* Medicare HMOs

Social Security Benefits. People under the age of 65 of who have Alzheimer's disease may qualify for Social Security disability payments (SSDI). After 24 months on SSI, the disabled person would then be covered by Medicare.

Spearman's rank order correlation coefficient. Spearman's rank order correlation coefficient is a system used to evaluate results of paired word testing.

Special care units (SCUs). Special care units (SCUs) are designated areas in residential care facilities or nursing homes that care specifically for the special needs of patients with Alzheimer's disease.

SPECT *see* Single photon/positron emission computed tomography scan

Spinal Cord. The spinal cord is a grayish-white structure extending along the back of the body from the foramen magnum in the middle portion of the skull to the lower border of the first lumbar vertebra, a region in the lower back. The spinal cord is situated within the verterbral canal of the vertebral column. It is surrounded by three meninges,

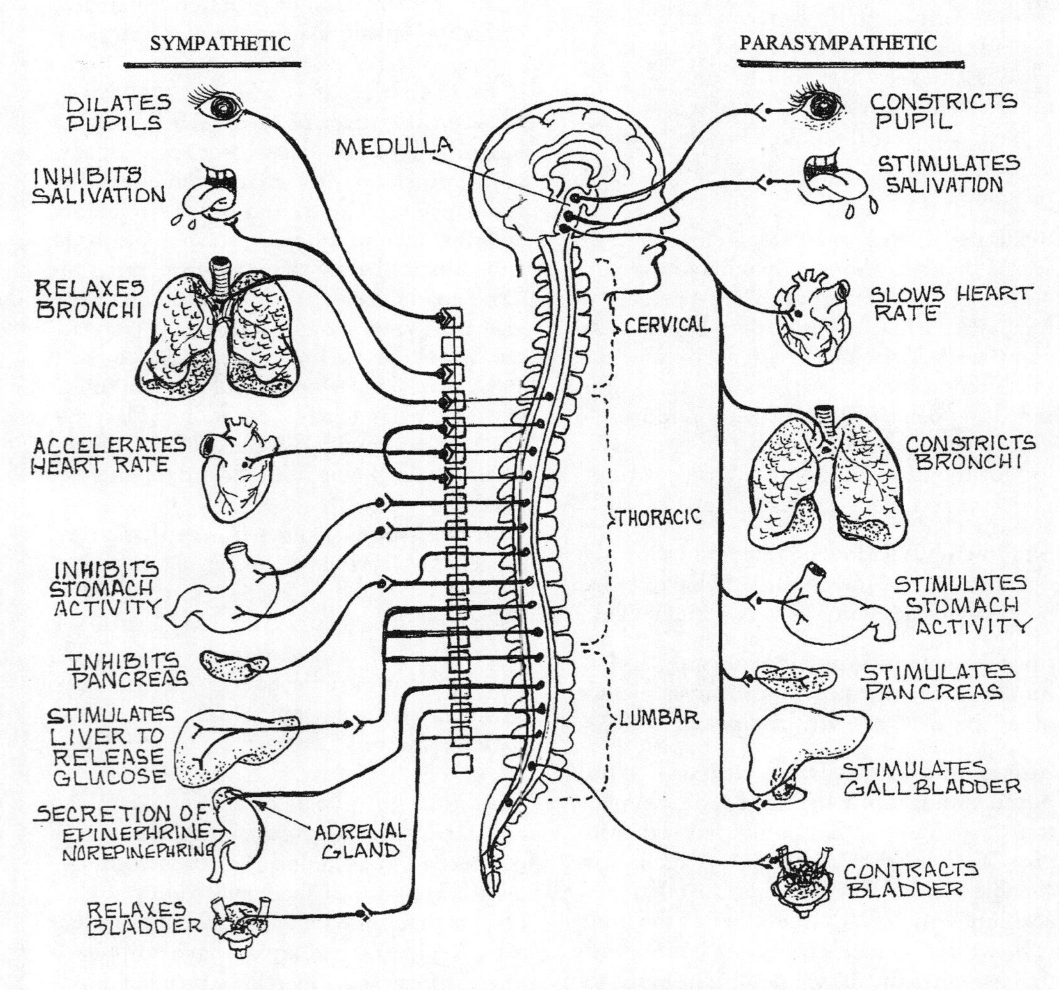

Spinal Cord and Central Nervous System (illustration by Marvin G. Miller).

or protective layers: the dura mater, the arachnoid mater and the pia mater. The spinal cord is further protected by cerebrospinal fluid which surrounds the spinal cord in an area known as the subarachnoid space.

The spinal cord is—for the most part—cylindrical. However, there are fusiform enlargements in the cervical region of the neck and at the lumbosacral region of the lower back. The entire length of the spinal cord is attached to pairs of spinal nerves by motor roots anteriorly and sensory roots posteriorly.

The spinal cord is composed of an inner core of gray matter surrounded by an outer covering of white matter. The gray matter is composed of columns or horns united by a thin gray commissure containing the central canal. The white matter consists of anterior (front), lateral (side) and posterior (rear) columns of tissue.

Spinal nerves. Thirty-one pairs of spinal nerves extend from the spinal cord through spaces between the vertebra of the spine. The spinal nerves are named after the regions of the vertebral column with which they are associated: cervical, thoracic, lumbar, sacral and coccygeal.

Sporadic Alzheimer's disease. Sporadic Alzheimer's disease, as opposed to the familial type, is the primary category of Alzheimer's disease, representing approximately 75 percent of all cases. Patients with sporadic Alzheimer's disease have a negative family history for this disease. Onset in sporadic Alzheimer's disease can occur at any time during adulthood.

Stages of Alzheimer's Disease. While the predominant symptoms of Alzheimer's disease vary from patient to patient, certain characteristic behavioral changes occur over a time frame that can be generally broken down into three stages. However some of these symptoms may appear in any of the stages. Furthermore, in all stages, short lucid periods can occur. The typical clinical duration of Alzheimer's disease is 8–10 years with a range of 1 to 25 years.

1) Early Stage (2 to 4 years)—characterized by short term memory loss that may be subtle with patient attempting to cover up by using lists and notes; declining interest in environment, people, and present affairs; vague uncertainty and hesitancy in initiating actions, particularly those involving new situations; difficulty in making decisions; shows signs of depression and aggression; poor work performance by the end of this stage with patients often being dismissed from their jobs. In the early stage, patients may exhibit difficulties with language, become disoriented in time, and become lost in familiar places. They may also lack initiative and motivation and lose interest in hobbies and activities. At this stage the dementia is often overlooked and may be incorrectly diagnosed as old age. Because onset is gradual, it is difficult to sometimes determine exactly when the disease process began.
2) Middle Stage (2 to 12 years)—characterized by progressive memory loss, hesitation in responding to questions; signs of memory loss such as difficulty following simple instructions or doing simple calculations; can no longer manage to live alone without problems; is unable to cook, clean or shop; may experience hallucinations and episodic bouts of irritability and unprovoked aggression; evasiveness, anxiety, and agitated movement including night activity due to disturbances of the sleep-wakefulness cycle; misplaces bills, documents, keys; loses way home in familiar surroundings; forgets to pay bills, lets household chores slip and newspapers pile up; neglects to dispose of garbage; forgets to take medications; loses possessions and then claims they were stolen; neglects personal hygiene (bathing, shaving, dressing), adopts a bizarre mode of dress such as

many inappropriate layers of clothing; loses social graces, which may result in social isolation for the patient and his family. Diagnosis is often made in this stage, with the person having increasing difficulty in coping with day-to-day living.

3) Final Stage (up to a year)—characterized by marked loss of weight due to disinterest in eating or inability to hold utensils; patients in this stage typically become totally dependent and inactive and often require 24-hour nursing care; unable to communicate verbally or in writing; no recognition of family and close friends; incontinence of urine and feces; possibility of major seizures; infantile gestures such as grasping; snout and sucking reflexes are readily elicited; inability to stand and walk, becomes bedridden or confined to a wheelchair; increasing degrees of physical disability; death is usually caused by aspiration pneumonia, inanition or malnutrition.

State policies on mental health care. Policies regarding provisions for mental health care, including long-term care and day care, are determined by individual states. As of 2001, 31 states had elected to participate in at least some Medicaid-sponsored managed care programs. States that have sought to move away from public bureaucracies have favored using for-profit-out-of-state vendors, hoping the influences of corporate business can improve outdated systems. States with these contracts report success both in holding down costs and in expanding access while securing consumer satisfaction. Still other states have created their own managed care systems or modified public programs, combining them with existing county-based systems or community mental health boards.

Cost control is always an issue although it may arise in different contexts. Some states feel that efficiency of a particular program and integration of state and local systems make one program more attractive than another. States have been motivated to shift to managed care so that they may exert more control over the providers and managers of control. With a government contract in hand, state officials can require accountability, demand or improve performance and become eligible for incentives and participation in innovative programs.

Each state makes its own decision regarding the specific populations that will be covered in a Medicaid managed care arrangement.

Statins. Statins refer to a class of cholesterol-lowering drugs. Studies indicate that cholesterol plays a role in Alzheimer's disease development. In ADCS clinical trials, patients with mild or moderate Alzheimer's disease taking statins are being studied and compared to patients of similar age and disease progression who are not taking statin medications.

Stem cells. Stem cells are early primitive embryonic cells that differentiate to form all of the cell types in the human body, depending on the body's needs. The process of differentiation allows some cells to become brain cells, whereas others become blood or liver cells. In embryos less than 4 days old, the stem cells are called totipotent stem cells because they have total potential to form all of the cells needed to sustain life. Implanted into a woman's uterus, these cells could form a complete human being.

After 4 or 5 days, the cells are pluripotent. They still have the potential to differentiate into virtually every cell in the body, but they can no longer form an entire human being. As the cells continue to divide into more cells, they become multipotent. Multipotent stem cells can form many, but not all, types of cells.

Stem cells are found in both embryos, infants, children and adults. While embryonic stem cells offer a wealth of possibilities, most adult stem cells are multipotent and can form only a limited number of cell types. There are other disadvantages to using adult stem cells, including the fact that they are hard to identify and take a long time to grow in tissue cultures.

When transplanted into the human body,

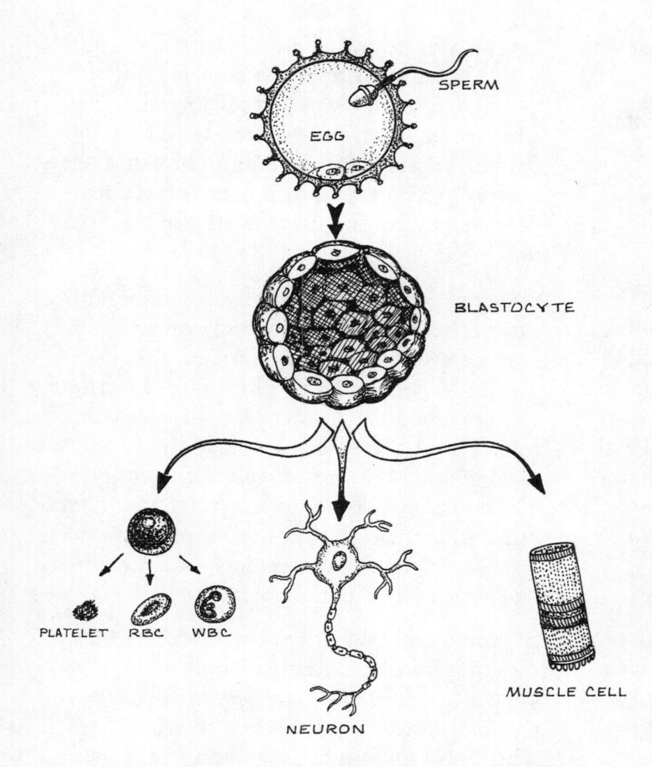

Stem Cell Differentiation (illustration by Marvin G. Miller).

The origin of the stem cell is thought to arise from either the fertilized egg, or the inner cell mass of the blastocyte (hollow sphere of cells created following several divisions of the egg cell). Stem cells differentiate into many unique types of cells including blood, tissue, nerve, and muscle cells.

stem cells are able to form whatever cell type is needed. In other words, stem cells can differentiate and form new brain cells or new kidney cells. In experiments, stem cells have been shown to work just like this. However, because stem cells are immortal and do not have a programmed cell death, many researchers think that they are more likely to eventually become cancerous. If stem cells prove to be safe and effective, they may one day be used to treat neurodegenerative diseases such as Alzheimer's disease. Now that neurons in the human adult brain are known to regenerate, stem cell therapy seems a likely therapy. The feasibility of neuron grafting in general is currently being explored in animal models.

Stress. Stress is a physical, chemical or emotional factor that causes bodily or mental tension, which, when chronic, is known to contribute to the development of many diseases. Although stress is inevitable and involves any change, it is one's reaction to stress that can cause problems. Both aging and stress are chronic negative regulators of neurogenesis (regeneration of neurons) in humans. One of the major effects of stress is impaired hippocampal-dependent learning. Stress also causes immune system changes that may promote inflammation, which is thought to be a factor in the development of Alzheimer's disease.

Stroke. Stroke or cerebral accident is a condition of sudden diminution or loss of consciousness, sensation, or voluntary movement caused by rupture or obstruction (such as due to a blood clot) of an artery of the brain. *Also See* multi-infarct dementia.

Stroop Color Interference Test. The Stroop Color Interference Test is a mental status evaluation tool used to measure attention to a complex set.

Subarachnoid space. The subarachnoid space, which completely surrounds the brain, is the interval or space between the arachnoid mater and pia mater. The space is filled with cerebrospinal fluid and contains the large blood vessels of the brain.

Subdural hemorrhage. Subdural hemorrhage refers to intracranial bleeding resulting from tearing of the superior cerebral veins of the brain. The cause is usually a blow to the front or back of the head. This results in excessive front-back displacement of the brain within the skull. When the vein is torn, even under low pressure, blood begins to accumulate in the potential space between the dura and the arachnoid spaces. Clots can form (subdural haematoma). Subdural clots can increase rapidly causing acute symptoms.

Subsidized senior housing. Many federal and state programs are set up to pay for a portion of the cost of housing for older and disabled adults with low and moderate incomes. In subsidized senior housing, residents live in their own apartments within a senior housing complex. Some of these facilities provide assistance with shopping, laundry, and transportation needs. Individuals may hire a home health care agency to help with their medical needs. In some communities, resources are available to help with the cost of home health care. Other communities offer services such as Meals-On-Wheels to help the elderly and disabled.

Substance P. Substance P, a neuropeptide found in the axons of some neurons, is associated with pain and temperature. Substance P is released from terminals of electrically stimulated primary sensory neurons by a mechanism that depends on the presence of calcium. Substance P is destroyed by a neutral metallopeptidase enzyme known as substance P degrading enzyme.

Substantia nigra. The midbrain can be divided into two halves called the cerebral peduncles. Each of these is divided into an anterior portion known as the crus cerebri and an anterior portion known as the tegmentum. The crus cerebri and the tegmentum are separated by a pigmented band of gray matter known as the substantia nigra. The substantia nigra is a large motor nucleus composed of medium-size neurons with many processes. These neurons contain inclusion granules of melanin pigment within their cytoplasm. The substantia nigra is associated with muscle tone and has connections extending to the cerebral cortex, the spinal cord, the hypothalamus and the basal nuclei.

Sundowning. Sundowning is a term used to describe the restlessness and agitation dementia patients experience during the late afternoon or evening hours.

Sunrise Assisted Living's "At Home" Assisted Living Program. Sunrise Assisted Living was founded in 1981 by Paul and Terry Klaasen in response to their difficulties finding suitable care for Terry's mother. They modeled Sunrise after senior homes Paul had remembered seeing in Holland. At Sunrise, seniors live in a comfortable residential environment with all the services they need.

Support group. Support groups are organizations dedicated to the education and support of patients, their families and caregivers. Whether local groups or Internet sources, support groups play an invaluable role. The Alzheimer's Association supports local chapters in most areas of the country. There are no costs and most groups meet once a month. The purpose of support groups is for family members to share with one another in a confidential setting.

Suspiciousness. Patients with Alzheimer's disease often become suspicious when they are confused. Frequently, they misplace possessions and accuse others of stealing them. This behavior is more common in the early stages of Alzheimer's disease.

Sympathetic nervous system. The sympathetic role of the autonomic nervous system prepares the body to handle emergencies. It accelerates the heart rate, causes constriction of peripheral blood vessels and raises the blood pressure. The sympathetic nervous system also elicits a redistribution of blood flow, causing blood to leave the skin and intestines and move to the brain, heart and skeletal muscles.

Symptoms. The most common initial symptom of Alzheimer's disease is memory impairment. Important tasks are left undone and possessions may be misplaced. The major symptoms in Alzheimer's disease include: 1) problems with intellect, such as impaired memory, judgment and abstract thinking 2) orientation problems, including not knowing what day or time it is or who they are 3) problems with language and communication, and 4) changes in personality including anxiety, irritability, and agitation. Other symptoms commonly seen include mood disturbances, depression, social withdrawal, lack of initiative, altered perception, hallucinations, wandering, verbal and physical aggression, apathy, altered sleep patterns and vegetative behaviors such as lack of appetite.

The onset of symptoms may be almost imperceptible but will typically progress, becoming serious within a few years time. After the memory disorder becomes apparent, disorders of cognition, such as the inability to balance a checkbook, will emerge. Other common symptoms include confusion in following directions, getting lost while driving a car, and frightening lapses of memory such as leaving on a gas stove, may also occur.

In the later stages of the disease, the patient with Alzheimer's disease experiences difficulty communicating. Reading and writing also become impaired and activities of daily living, such as bathing and dressing, are usually neglected. Agitation, hallucinations, delusions, and violent outbursts may occur at any time during the course of the illness. Previous personality traits are often exaggerated or they may be completely obscured by new behavior patterns. A general physical decline is not seen until the latest stages of the illness. *See also* Warning signs, and Diagnosis.

Synapse. The nervous system consists of large numbers of neurons that are linked together to form functional conducting pathways. Where two neurons or a neuron and a skeletal muscle cell come into close proximity and communicate with one another, their communication occurs over a site or bridge known as a synapse. Axons and dendrites communicate with one another by sending chemical messengers across synapses. The synaptic cleft or synapse refers to the space or gap between the neurons' axons and dendrites where functional communication occurs. Under physiological conditions, communication takes place in one direction only.

Synapses may be either chemical or electrical. Most synapses are chemical, in which a chemical substance known as a neurotransmitter passes across the narrow space between cells and attaches to a protein receptor. Chemical synapses may excite (stimulate) or inhibit other cells. Electrical synapses are ordinary gap junctions between two neurons which permit the spread of activity between one neuron and another, ensuring that a group of neurons performing together will function as a group.

The surfaces of the terminal axon expansion and the neuron are referred to, respectively, as pre-synaptic and post-synaptic membranes.On the pre-synaptic side, the presynaptic terminal contains many small vesicles that contain the neurotransmitter. The vesicles fuse with the pre-synaptic membrane and discharge the neurotransmitter in the synaptic cleft by a process of exocytosis.

Synaptic loss is commonly seen in the hippocampus and neocortex of patients with

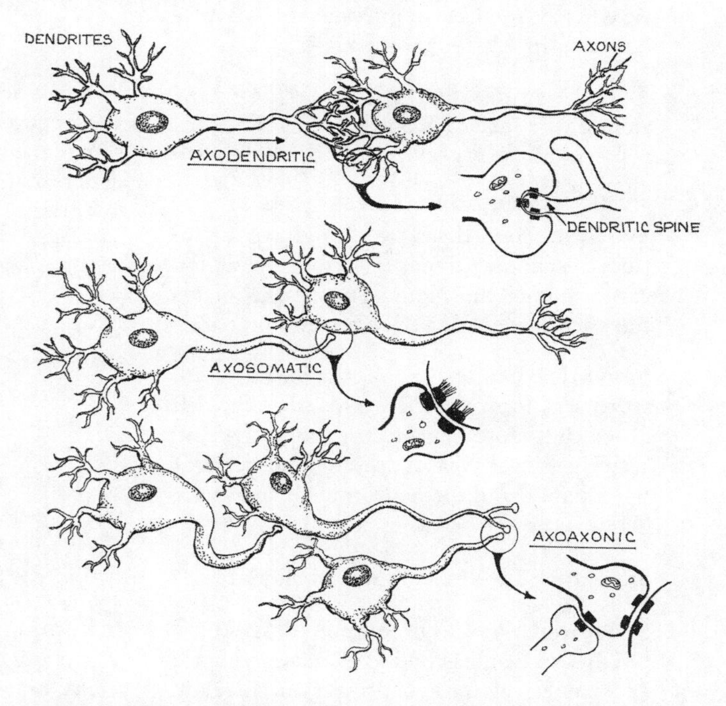

Chemical Synapses (illustration by Marvin G. Miller).

Alzheimer's disease. This loss, which can be measured by measuring synaptic density, correlates with disease severity. The immediate cause of dementia in Alzheimer's disease is a loss of these synapses, which results in cerebral disconnections and the inability to process thoughts.

Synaptic connections. Axons connect to other axons through chemical messages sent through synaptic connections. These connections are necessary for the survival of individual neurons. Neurons that fail to receive synaptic signals from their target cells undergo cell death. As the brain matures, the synaptic connections are modified by use. In the absence of proper stimulation, the number of synaptic connections are reduced and neurons die. With enriched experiences and stimulation, neural synapses sprout new branches and connections. Surviving neurons fire quick responses across synapses. The more firing (such as repetition in learning) across a specific connection, the stronger the connection.

Synaptic density. Measurements of synaptic density are used to measure the synaptic loss seen in Alzheimer's disease.

Synaptic spines. Synaptic spines are extensions of the surface of a neuron that form receptive sites for synaptic contact with afferent nerves.

Synaptic strengths. The strength of a particular synapse. Synaptic strength, which varies among the many synapses, regulates the effectiveness of a particular connection.

Synaptic vesicles. Synaptic vesicles are small sacs located at the ends of nerve cell axons that store neurotransmitters. During activity the vesicles release their contents at the synapse, and the neurotransmitter stimulates receptors on other cells.

Synapton *see* Physostigmine salicylate

Synaptophysin. The compound synaptophysin can be measured to evaluate synaptic density. Levels of synaptophysin correlate well with cognitive function.

Tacrine hydrochloride (THA). Tacrine hydrochloride or THA (brand name Cognex) is a drug known as a reversible cholinesterase inhibitor commonly used in the treatment of Alzheimer's disease. The first cholinesterase inhibitor to receive FDA approval for treatment of mild to moderate Alzheimer's disease, tacrine is given in daily doses ranging from 10 mg to 640 mg. Because the drug is short-acting, it is usually given 4 times daily. Tacrine works by blocking the enzyme acetylcholinesterase, an enzyme that breaks down acetylcholine, therefore prolonging the period of time that neurons are exposed to acetylcholine.

Although widespread degeneration of multiple neuronal systems eventually occurs in patients with Alzheimer's disease, early changes in this disease selectively involve neuronal pathways that project from the basal forebrain to the cerebral cortex and hippocampus. These changes result in deficiencies of cortical acetylcholine that ultimately account for some of the symptoms associated with mild to moderate dementia. Tacrine acts by elevating acetylcholine concentrations in the cerebral cortex by slowing the degradation of acetylcholine released in cholinergic neurons that are still intact. While it does not improve function in damaged neurons, tacrine helps preserve functional neurons. However, there is no evidence that tacrine alters the course of the underlying disease process in Alzheimer's disease.

Presumably, tacrine elevates acetylcholine concentrations in the cerebral cortex by slowing the degradation of acetylcholine that is released by still intact cholinergic neurons. While tacrine does not alter the course of the underlying dementing process, it can reduce mild symptoms. As the disease progresses and fewer cholinergic neurons remain functionally intact, the effects of tacrine may diminish.

Side effects include elevation of liver enzymes, nausea, vomiting, diarrhea, indigestion, myalgia (muscle pain), and anorexia. The major disadvantage of tacrine is that patients must be closely monitored for liver damage. Also, because elevated levels of acetylcholine can exacerbate bladder outflow problems, aggravate obstructive pulmonary disease and increase the risk of gastric acidity and gastrointestinal bleeding, patients must be under close medical supervision. Cimetidine (Tagamet) may cause higher blood levels of tacrine, which may increase the chance of side effects. Tacrine may cause higher blood levels of theophylline, which may increase the chance of side effects from this drug.

According to the results of one study, tacrine has no effect on women with the APOE4 gene although it did help those who carried the APOE2 or APOE3 alleles. Because both cigarette smoking and tacrine both have effects on liver function, smokers have lower rates of tacrine absorption. Tacrine should be prescribed carefully in patients with a history of abnormal liver function tests.

A report published by the Dementia Trialists' Collaboration in JAMA (JAMA, Nov. 28, 1998; 280(20): 1777–1782) found that cholinesterase inhibition with tacrine appears to reduce deterioration in cognitive performance during the first 3 months and increase the odds of global clinical improvement. Effects observed on measures of behavioral disturbance were of questionable significance, and functional autonomy was not significantly affected.

In one clinical trial, more than 80 percent of patients without the APOE4 allele responded well to tacrine. Of the patients with the APOE4 gene, 60 percent of patients were unchanged or worse after 30 weeks. The results of this study indicate that patients not carrying APOE4 respond better to tacrine than those carrying APOE4. The results indicate that there is a genotype-dependent difference in the way individuals with Alzheimer's disease respond to cholinesterase inhibitors and that the APOE4 genotype influences the function and integrity of the cholinergic system. (Poirer, Judes, Isabelle Aubert, et al. "Apolipoprotein E4 and Cholinergic Activity in Alzheimer's Disease," *Alzheimer Disease: From Molecular Biology to Therapy*, edited by R. Becker and E. Giacobini. Boston: Birkhäuser Publishing, 1996, 55–60.)

Tau protein. Tau protein is a normal brain constituent. Specifically, tau is a microtubule-associated protein that is involved in microtubule assemble and stabilization. In adult human brain, six tau isoforms are produced from a single gene by alternative mRNA splicing. These isoforms differ from each other by variations in their amino acid structures.

Tau isolated from the brains of patients with Alzheimer's disease contains higher concentrations of the amino acids serine and heroine phosphate than tau in normal brains. This "hyper-phosphorylation" of tau may lead to the abnormal conformation characteristic of Alzheimer's disease. Conformational changes in tau are among the first detectable changes in the neurons of the hippocampus in the brains of Alzheimer's disease patients.

One of the pathologic hallmarks of Alzheimer's disease is the presence of neurofibrillary tangles, intraneuronal deposits of paired helical filaments (as well as fewer straight filaments) made of hyperphosphorylated tau and ubiquitin. Both of these elements are increased in the spinal fluid of patients with Alzheimer's disease. Besides Alzheimer's disease, other conditions, such as the frontotemporal dementias, are associated with abnormal deposits of tau.

Although tau protein is elevated in the spinal fluid of patients with Alzheimer's disease, measurements of its concentration are not routinely performed because their diagnostic significance remains unclear. Tau is also increased in conditions associated with rapid destruction to the central nervous system, such as acute strokes, trauma and encephalitis. Tau is also elevated in the spinal fluid of 20 to 40 percent of patients with frontal lobe dementia and a number of patients with vascular dementia. (Check, William, Ph.D. "Puzzling out a role for Alzheimer's tests." *CAP Today*, In the News, publication of the College of American Pathologists, June 1998.)

Tauists. Scientists who adhere to the theory that tau protein formation is responsible for the development of Alzheimer's disease.

Taxol *see* Paclitaxel

Tela choroidea. The tela choroidea is a two-layered fold of pia mater. On either side of the midline the tela choroidea projects downward through the roof of the third ventricle to form the choroids plexuses of the third ventricle.

Telencephalon *see* Cerebrum

Telomerase. Telomerase is a specialized form of reverse transcriptase, an enzyme which facilitates messenger RNA. Telomerase has been proposed to possess anti-aging properties. Specifically, its catalytic subunit is active in neurons throughout the brain during development, but is absent from neurons in the adult brain. This subunit of telomerase also exhibits neuroprotective properties in experimental models of neurodegenerative disorders. That suggests that inducing telomerase in neurons may protect against age-related neurodegeneration. ("Neuroprotective strategies for Alzheimer's disease." *Life Extension*, Medical Updates, January 2002, 73, excerpted from Experimental Gerontology, 2000, 35(4), 489–502)

Temporal lobe. The temporal lobe of each cerebral hemisphere occupies the area inferior the lateral sulcus. The lateral surface of the temporal lobe can be further divided into three gyri or folds, the superior, the middle and the inferior temporal gyri.

Tentorium cerebelli. The tentorium cerebelli of the brain is an arched lamina, elevated in the middle, and sloping downward toward the circumference. It covers the superior surface of the cerebellum and supports the occipital lobes of the brain. Its anterior border is free and concave and bounds a large oval opening, the incisura tontorii, for the transmission of the cerebral peduncles.

Terminal Illness. Terminal illnesses refer to disorders for which there is no cure. Terminal disorders eventually lead to death.

Testosterone. Testosterone, like estrogen, has recently been found to be beneficial in reducing the amount of plaque formation by altering the mechanism in which beta peptides are produced from A beta precursor protein (beta APP). Increasing evidence indicates that testosterone increases the secretion of the non-amyloidogenic APP fragment, spAPP alpha, and decreases the secretion of A beta peptides from nerve cells. This result raises the possibility that testosterone supplementation in elderly men may be protective in the treatment of Alzheimer's disease. (Proceedings of the National Academy of Sciences of the United States of America, 2000; vol 97 (3): 1202–1205; Hammond, J, et al. "Testosterone-mediated Neuroprotection through the Androgen Receptor in Human Primary Neurons." Journal of Neurochemistry, June 2001, 77(5): 1319–1326).

Texas Functional Living Scale (TFLS). The Texas Functional Living Scale (TFLS) is a new performance-based measure of functional abilities with an emphasis on instrumental activities of daily living skills. Introduced by researchers at the University of Texas Southwestern Medical Center in Dallas, the procedure is brief and weighted toward the ability to perform cognitive tasks, rather than informant-based.

Thal, Leon, M.D. Doctor Leon Thal is chair of the Department of Neurosciences at the University of California San Diego School of Medicine and principal investigator of the Alzheimer's Disease Cooperative Study (ADCS) consortium.

Thalamus. The thalamus is a large egg-shaped mass of gray matter that forms the dorsal portion of the forebrain. The anterior end of the thalamus forms the posterior boundary of the interventricular foramen.

Third ventricle. The third ventricle, an area of the brain derived from the forebrain vesicle, is a narrow cleft that separates the two thalami.

Thyroid disease. Thyroid diseases have long been associated with Alzheimer's disease. The autoimmune hyperthyroid disorder, Graves' disease, is reported to occur more often in patients with a family history of Alzheimer's disease. (Riddha Arem, M.D.,

The Thyroid Solution, New York, 1999) While the reasons for this relationship are unclear, both disorders are associated with deficiencies of B vitamins, increased levels of glycosaminoglycan, and a suspected causative relationship with the excitotoxins monosodium glutamate and aspartame. Most patients with Graves' disease go on to develop autoimmune hypothyroidism or Hashimoto's thyroiditis, which is also associated with Alzheimer's disease.

Acquired cerebellar ataxia has been described in patients with hypothyroidism and is typically reversible by thyroid hormone replacement therapy. The cerebellar dysfunction is attributed to metabolic and physiological effects related to thyroid hormone deficiency. Even when thyroid function is corrected, patients with thyroid autoantibodies may develop Hashimoto's encephalopathy or Hashimoto's associated ataxia, conditions in which thyroid antibodies attack neurons rather than thyroid cells. (Selim, M., and D. Drachman, "Ataxia associated with Hashimoto's disease" progressive non-familial adult onset cerebellar degeneration with autoimmune thyroiditis." *J Neurol Neurosurg Psychiatry*, Jul 2001; 7 (1): 81–87)

Hyperthyroidism is rarely associated with dementia. One elderly patient with dementia, who was diagnosed with possible Alzheimer's disease on the basis of SPECT, was found to have Graves' disease. When therapy with beta blockers and anti-thyroid drugs was instituted, his memory improved and his initial uptake defect in the temporoparietal region also responded to therapy. (T. Fukui, et al. "Hyperthyroid dementia: clinicoradiological findings and response to treatment." *Journal of Neurological Science*, Feb 2001; 184(1): 81–88.)

One earlier study involving medical record reviews determined that for hypothyroidism, there was a slight positive association for Alzheimer's disease, whereas patients with Graves' disease had a negative association for Graves' disease. (Yoshimasu, F., et al. "The association between Alzheimer's disease and thyroid disease in Rochester, Minnesota." *Neurology*, Nov 1991; 41(11): 1745–1747.)

Touch therapy. Alzheimer's disease patients have the need for touch, love and companionship. Touch can convey care, compassion, and reassurance. Because touch is so important, some institutions use touch therapy as part of their healing philosophy. In touch therapy, caregivers touch patients in their course of administering therapy.

Toxins. Toxins are environmental substances, including drugs, chemicals and infectious agents, capable of causing harm to the body. During fetal development, toxins can affect the migration of neurons, disrupting normal brain function.

Toxins can also injure brain cells and disrupt the brain's chemical messengers after birth. Scientists theorize that environmental exposures have a latent effect on the brain, causing a noticeable degeneration years later.

Trailmaking B. The Trailmaking B test is a mental status evaluation tool used to measure attention to a complex set.

Transcutaneous electrical nerve stimulation (TENS). Transcutaneous electrical nerve stimulation (TENS) is a well-known treatment that uses low-level electrical pulses to suppress chronic pain. Several studies utilizing this therapy have demonstrated improvement in memory and functioning in Alzheimer's patients. An experimental surgical technique being tested on animals employs small plastic implants in the brain that release a powerful nerve growth factor that may prevent neuronal destruction.

Transforming Growth Factor Beta-1 (TGF-β1). Transforming growth factor beta-1 (TGF-β1) is a cytokine suspected of playing a central role in the development of Alzheimer's disease. Released during the immune response, TGF-β1 regulates beta amyloid precursor protein synthesis and processing, plaque formation, astroglial and microglial response, and neuronal cell death. Its role in influencing amyloid beta protein production has long been thought to directly contribute to the pathological changes in Alzheimer's disease. However, researchers at the Gladstone Institute of Neurological

Disease in San Francisco have found that increased levels of TGF- β1 cause the production of molecules that destroy beta amyloid. Mice genetically engineered to produce increased levels of both beta amyloid and TGF- β1 were found to have 75 percent fewer plaques and 60 percent lower beta-amyloid levels. (Franzen, Harald. "Molecule Helps Brain Cells Clear Alzheimer's Plaques." *Scientific American*, Medicine, May 1, 2000)

Traumatic head injury. Traumatic head injuries are listed as a risk factor for Alzheimer's disease. *See* Brain injuries and Head injuries.

Treatment in Alzheimer's disease. Treatment options in Alzheimer's disease are diverse. Neurologists such as Harvard University's Dr. Kenneth Kosik report that controlling symptoms will likely require more than one drug therapy.

In general, there are four therapeutic approaches to treating Alzheimer's disease: 1) the relief of behavioral symptoms associated with dementia, including depression, agitation and psychosis 2) the relief of cognitive dysfunction in an effort to improve memory, language, praxis, attention and orientation 3) to slow the rate of progression of the illness, in an effort to preserve quality of life and independence, and 4) to delay the time of onset of illness. The targets of treatment include: 1) decreasing amyloid beta production by affecting the processing of β APP 2) preventing or reducing amyloid beta aggregation and plaque maturation or improving clearance of amyloid beta through microglia or alphalipoprotein E or J 3) inhibiting neurotoxic effects of amyloid beta by restoring calcium homeostasis, reducing oxidative damage with antioxidants or decreasing inflammation with anti-inflammatory drugs, and 4) decreasing cellular response to injury.

Therapeutic agents used to treat behavioral symptoms include antipsychotics such as haloperidol, lithium and thioridazine, anticonvulsants, antidepressants, anti-anxiety meds such as buspirone, anti-parkinson drugs such as selegiline, beta adrenergic blocking agents and minor tranquilizers such as the benzodiazepines (diazepam, lorazepam, etc.)

Cholinesterase inhibitors such as tacrine and cholinergic receptor agents such as arecoline and pilocarpine are used in an effort to improve cognitive function. To restore the precursor compounds of acetylcholine, compounds such as choline and lecithin are sometimes prescribed.

Nerve growth factor is prescribed experimentally in an effort to enhance or stimulate neuronal sprouting. Animal studies suggest that NGF administration may promote neuronal survival even when damage is present. Anti-inflammatory agents are sometimes prescribed because of evidence that these drugs may prevent Alzheimer's disease.

To delay the onset of illness, treatment may target single components of the complex biological mechanism that leads to senile plaque formation. In particular, treatment may focus on preventing, removing, and decreasing aggregates of beta amyloid with the use of vaccines, cholinesterase inhibitors, secretase enzyme inhibitors, and drugs that affect APP secretion. Drugs that increase alpha secretase directly or indirectly, changing the pathway and reducing production of beta amyloid protein, are also promising.

However, patients may still need drugs that prevent the formation of tangles that disrupt nerve cells from within. Different therapies may also be used to reduce the associated free radical toxicity, inflammation and cell membrane damage. In addition, tranquilizers and antidepressants are often employed to reduce the anxiety and restlessness associated with Alzheimer's disease. Other therapies commonly employed include nutrient supplements to correct calcium, copper and zinc imbalances, antioxidant vitamins, non-steroidal inflammatory drugs, cholesterol-lowering drugs and estrogens.

Triune brain. Proposed by Paul MacLean in 1967, the triune brain is a model of brain development based on the theory that our brain developed by keeping areas found to be useful in our predecessors and adding new structures by chance mutations designed to aid in the survival of the fittest.

Trophic factors. Trophic factors are chemical signals that regulate cells away from their origin. Trophic factors found in neurotransmitters control axonal connections. Where axonal connections are made and how long they are sustained determines whether a given neuron lives or dies.

Ubiquinone *see* Coenzyme-Q-10

Ultrasonography. Ultrasonography is a non-invasive imaging technique based on the principle that body tissues have a property called acoustic impedance. Sound waves entering tissue can be either transmitted through the tissue or reflected. Changes in tissue density caused by changes in density result in different properties of acoustic impedance. Ultrasonography is helpful in measuring changes in brain density.

Valproic Acid (Valproate). The anticonvulsant medication valproic acid (Depakene, Depakote) is being evaluated in ADCS clinical trials for its ability to reduce agitation and psychosis in Alzheimer's disease patients in the later disease stages. The drug is also being evaluated for its neuroprotective effects. In trials, the drug is being studied to see if it can prevent clinical disease progression, including agitation and psychosis, in patients in the early stages of Alzheimer's disease.

Vascular dementia. Vascular dementia is a term used to describe a wide range of disorders characterized by marked loss of intellectual abilities resulting from some abnormality to blood flow in the brain. Next to Alzheimer's disease, vascular dementia is the second most common form of dementia in the elderly. Many patients with Alzheimer's disease have been found to have coexisting vascular dementia. High levels of low-density lipoproteins (LDL) are significantly associated with the development of both vascular dementia and stroke.

The two most common forms of vascular dementia are multi-infarct dementia and Binswanger's disease. Common risk factors are high blood pressure, heart disease, and diabetes. Because specific areas of the brain control specific functions and any part of the brain can be affected, patients with vascular dementia do not have a consistent pattern or symptoms.

CADASIL (Cerebral Autosomal Dominant Arteriopathy with Subcortical Infarcts and Leukoencephalopathy) is the first known genetic form of vascular dementia with an identified gene. Mutations of the Notch3 gene located on chromosome 19 are responsible for CADASIL. CADASIL is a hereditary cause of stroke, dementia, and migraine with aura and mood disorders. Symptoms of this disorder emerge from the mid-twenties to around 45 years of age. Affected individuals usually die by age 65. The most common symptom is stroke. Patients exhibit cerebral non-atherosclerotic, non-amyloid angiopathy (disease of the blood vessels feeding the brain). The small arteries that innervate the white matter of the brain are primarily affected. Individuals with CADASIL rarely have the usual risk factors for stroke such as hypertension. Migraine headaches with aura are one of the earliest symptoms and occur in about 1/3 of patients with this disorder.

The second most common feature is a slowly progressing form of dementia, which causes frontal-like symptoms and memory impairment. Dementia commonly occurs after a history of recurrent stroke. Other accompanying symptoms include gait disturbances, pyramidal signs, and sphincter incontinence. These symptoms are all related to vascular dementia. Patients may also exhibit mood disorders, including severe depression, often with alternating manic episodes. Melancholia may also be present.

MRI studies reveal diffuse white matter cerebral lesions. These lesions typically occur two decades before the onset of disease although patients may suffer migraines with aura. CADASIL should be considered in affected individuals who have migraine with aura in mid-adulthood, when aura is atypical or prolonged, and when there is a family history of stroke, dementia, or depression. The prevalence of this order is unknown but it's suspected that many previously reported cases of vascular dementia were caused by CADASIL.

Vascular dementia includes all dementia syndromes resulting from failure of the brain to receive adequate oxygen, causing ischemic, anoxic or hypoxic brain damage. Multi-infarct dementia is currently considered a type of vascular dementia. Other types of vascular dementia include that resulting from stroke, cerebrovascular disease and hypertension.

Vascular disorder can also cause cognitive dysfunction and psychiatric symptoms often associated with focal motor signs and seizures. An elevated erythrocyte sedimentation laboratory test often suggests that the disorder may have an autoimmune origin.

Ventricles of the brain. The brain's ventricles or cavities include the lateral ventricles, the third ventricle, and the fourth ventricle.

Veteran's Affairs. The Department of Veteran's Affairs provides healthcare benefits to military service veterans and their families.

Vinpocetine. Drug used in Europe and Japan to correct cognitive impairment inflicted by degenerative brain disease.

Vitamin B12 deficiency. Deficiencies of vitamin B12 (cobalamin) can cause a dementia that looks exactly like Alzheimer's disease. Other symptoms of B12 deficiency include memory loss, confusion, delusion, fatigue, loss of balance, decreased reflexes, numbing and tingling in the arms and legs, tinnitus and noise-induced hearing loss. Alzheimer's disease itself is characterized by brain deficiencies of both vitamin B12 and the methylating factor, S-adenosylmethionine (SAMe). Vitamin B12 deficiency in patients with Alzheimer's disease has been reported to cause two distinct personality changes—irritability and disturbed behavior.

In the body, vitamin B12 is methylated (combined with methyl groups) to form methylcobalamin. Methylcobalamin protects neurons from the damaging effects of glutamate, nitric oxide, low blood sugar and low oxygen. Glutamate and nitric oxide toxicity are features of both Alzheimer's and Parkinson's diseases. The proper synthesis of myelin is also dependent on adequate stores of vitamin B12. Vitamin B12 also plays an important role in reducing homocysteine levels in the body. High levels of homocysteine are associated with heart disease, cancer, DNA damage, and memory impairment.

Although the body's daily requirements for vitamin B12 are minimal (6 mcg), blood levels are diminished by H. Pylori infections, certain drugs, over-cooking meat, and other factors. However, many people older than age 60 cannot extract vitamin B12 from food because their stomachs no longer secrete adequate gastric acid, making supplements often necessary (Feinstein, Alice. *Prevention's Healing with Vitamins.* Emmous, PA: Rodale Press, 1996; Mitchell, Terri. "Vitamin B12:Surprising New Findings." *Life Extension*; Dec. 2000 6(12): 21–28).

Vitamin E therapy. A potent antioxidant, vitamin E, at doses as low as 100 nM, has been found to protect neurons in the brain against free radical damage associated with amyloid beta protein, hydrogen peroxide and the excitatory amino acid glutamate. Vitamin E prevents the oxidative damage induced by beta-amyloid in cell culture and delays memory deficits in animal models. Because of its antioxidant properties, vitamin E is reported to reduce the cell damage normally associated with aging.

Vitamin E also has been shown to induce the activation of the redox-sensitive transcription factor NF-kappa B, which is involved in control of nerve cell survival. In ADCS clinical trials, vitamin E therapy is being evaluated to see if it can help prevent progression to Alzheimer's disease in patients with mild cognitive impairment. A recent report showed that both high doses of vitamin E (2,000 I.U. daily) and the drug selegiline slowed mental deterioration by 7 months in patients ongoing clinical trials.

A placebo-controlled clinical trial of vitamin E in patients with moderately advanced Alzheimer's disease was conducted by the Alzheimer's Disease Cooperative Study. Subjects in the vitamin E group were treated with 2000 IU (1342 alpha-tocopherol equivalents) of vitamin E daily. The results indicated that vitamin E may slow functional deterioration leading to nursing home placement. A new clinical trial is planned that will examine whether vitamin E can delay or prevent a clinical diagnosis of Alzheimer's disease in elderly patients with mild cognitive impairment.

In a study of 341 Alzheimer's disease patients using 2000 IU of vitamin E in conjunction with 10 mg of selegeline, over a two-year period, progression of the disease was reduced in subjects using either of these compounds as compared to groups receiving placebos or both compounds. (Perlmutter, David. "Functional Therapeutics in Neurodegenerative Disease." Physicians Committee for Responsible Medicine website, http://www.pcrm.org/health/Preventive_Medicine/alzheimers.html)

Vitamins. Vitamins are nutrient substances essential for many metabolic functions. Deficiencies of B vitamins have long been associated with neurological disorders.

According to a number of researchers, a diet rich in antioxidant vitamins can help prevent the development of Alzheimer's disease. Studies conducted by researchers at the National Institute on Aging report that blueberries and other foods containing antioxidants may protect the body against damage from oxidative stress. Oxidative stress is one of the biological processes implicated in aging and the development of neurodegenerative diseases. Animals receiving blueberry and strawberry extracts scored the highest in tests of balance and coordination. The animals also showed signs of the presence of vitamin E, a key antioxidant in their brains.

Two large clinical trials involving 600 people over 4 years suggest that vitamins C and E may prevent the onset of Alzheimer's disease, improve cognitive skills in healthy individuals and decrease the symptoms of dementia. A total of 91 people developed Alzheimer's disease, but none of the subjects who took vitamins C and E supplements developed dementia.

Preliminary studies suggest that patients with Alzheimer's disease may have significantly lower levels of vitamin A, its precursor beta-carotene, folic acid and vitamin B12 than normal individuals. Further studies are needed to show if increasing these levels can affect symptoms of Alzheimer's disease. ("Alzheimer's Disease, Nutrition and Dietary Supplements." *Intellihealth*, http://www.intelihealth.com/IH/ihtIH/WSIHW000/8303/29429.html.)

Wandering. Wandering is a common symptom in Alzheimer's disease. Many patients set out on a mission, rushing from their homes in the middle of the night, although they are unable to say where they are going. Dressed inappropriately for the elements, these patients are at risk for injury. Most medical exerts agree that wandering, like other behaviors associated with Alzheimer's disease, has a purpose, such as expressing an emotion or need. According to researchers at the Mayo Clinic in Rochester, Minnesota, wandering may communicate feeling lost. Alternately, wandering may be express a feeling of being overwhelmed when there is too much stimulation, such as multiple conversations. Reasons for wandering include: side effects of medications, memory loss and disorientation, expressing emotions, expressing basic needs such as hunger or the need for exercise or rest, restlessness and boredom, and certain stimuli such as the presence of coats or boots.

While haloperidol has traditionally been used to treat wandering, haloperidol has very severe side effects that impair motor control and coordination. Newer atypical antipsychotic medications such as risperidone and olanzapine are generally used to treat symptoms of wandering and irritability. *See also* Safe Return Program.

Warning signs. The Alzheimer's Association has developed a list of warning signs, including several common symptoms of Alzheimer's disease. Individuals who exhibit several of these symptoms should see a physician for further evaluation.

1. Memory loss that affects job skills
2. Difficulty performing familiar tasks
3. Problems with language
4. Disorientation to time and place (getting lost)
5. Poor or decreased judgment
6. Problems with abstract thinking
7. Misplacing things
8. Changes in mood or behavior
9. Changes in personality
10. Loss of initiative

Wechsler Adult Intelligence Scale (WAIS). The Wechsler Adult Intelligence Scale is a test used to measure various parameters of intelligence in adults. In Alzheimer's patients, the WAIS test initially shows memory impairment, which persists over a plateau phase during which language and cognitive functions typically do not change for the first 9–35 months after diagnosis.

Wechsler Memory Scale. The Wechsler Memory Scale is an evaluation tool used to measure verbal and visual recent memory.

Wellness recommendations. Individuals with Alzheimer's disease benefit from wellness recommendations, including exercise, a nutrient rich diet, social activity, and maintaining a familiar routine and environment. Regular walking has been reported to improve cognitive function. Many of the risk factors for heart disease such as high cholesterol are also risk factors for Alzheimer's disease. Therefore, according to some researchers, reducing risk factors for heart disease may also reduce the risk of Alzheimer's disease. For instance, the anti-inflammatory drug aspirin, which also has anticoagulant properties, appears to lower the risk of both heart disease and Alzheimer's disease. (Stewart, W., et al." Risk of Alzheimer's disease and Duration of NSAID Use." *Neurology*, March, 1997; 48(3): 626–632)

Wernicke's aphasia. Individuals who sustain damage to Wenicke's area develop a condition known as Wernicke's aphasia, which is characterized by an inability to comprehend language. Language can be produced but not understood. Wernicke's aphasia is also known as fluent, sensory, or receptive aphasia.

Wernicke's area. Wernicke's area refers to the inferior parietal regions of the brain, specifically the posterior part of the superior temporal gyrus of the brain that controls the formulation of language. Damage to Wernicke's area causes a type of aphasia in which its victims have difficulty comprehending whether their own speech makes sense. Wernicke's aphasics can produce but not understand language because this area of the brain contains the mechanisms for the formulation of language. Wernicke's area, like Broca's area, is a region in which stimulation on the dominant side causes the patient to cease speaking make linguistic errors or be unable to find appropriate words.

Wernicke's encephalopathy. Wernicke's encephalopathy is a condition caused by inflammation of Wernicke's area of the brain causing aphasia.

White matter. The white matter of the central nervous system consists of nerve fibers and blood vessels embedded in neuroglia. In the spinal cord, white matter surrounds the gray matter, and its white color is associated with the high proportion of myelinated nerve fibers and axons. Subdivisions of white matter go by a variety of names including fasciculus, funiculus, lemniscus and peduncle. In the spinal cord, the white matter contains long descending tracts leading from the brainstem and cerebrum and long ascending tracts that lead to the brainstem, cerebellum, and cerebrum.

Wisconsin Card Sort Test. Psychological test used to measure attention and executive function.

Wise, Brad, M.D. Doctor Brad Wise is the Program Director of Fundamental Neuroscience for the Neuroscience and Neuropsychology of Aging Program of the National Institute on Aging in Bethesda, Maryland.

World Alzheimer's Day. World Alzheimer's day is celebrated worldwide on September 21 each year. This day is set aside to promote awareness of Alzheimer's disease.

Writing studies. Writing studies are part of the Nun Study, one of the first long-term studies of a well controlled population sponsored by the National Institute of Aging. In the writing studies, researchers reviewed the autobiographical writing of nuns written at an average age of 22. The autobiographies were examined for linguistic ability as a measure of cognitive function in early life. One component of linguistic ability, idea density, defined as the average number of ideas for each 10 written words, is associated with educational level, vocabulary, and general knowledge. A second measure, grammatical complexity, is linked with worked memory, test performance and writing skills. Approximately 58 years after these writings, the nuns were tested for cognitive ability.

Study results indicated that low idea density in early life was strongly linked with low cognitive test scores and later development of Alzheimer's disease. The nuns with low idea density scores were 30 times more likely to do poorly on a the MMSE exam, a standard measure of cognitive function when compared to those nuns with more complex writing ability. At autopsy, 90 percent of the nuns with low writing scores in early life were found to have neurofibrillary tangles in their brain tissue. ("Landmark Study Links Cognitive Ability of Youth With Alzheimer's Disease in Later Life." Press Release of U.S. Department of Health and Human Services, Feb 20, 1996.)

Xanomeline. Xanomeline, administered via a skin patch, is a selective M1 muscarinic receptor agonist. Xanomeline skin patch is currently being evaluated as a therapeutic agent for Alzheimer's disease.

Xenobiotics. Xenobiotics are environmental agents capable of causing biologic effects. Significant abnormalities in the metabolism of xenobiotics have been demonstrated in patients with Alzheimer's disease. Specifically, the detoxification process is impaired and involves decreased activity of phase II sulfation by the liver.

Zinc. Zinc is a trace mineral normally found in the body. Ashley Bush, a researcher at Harvard Medical School, first noticed that the addition of zinc to amyloid protein in vitro (in a test tube) caused strands of amyloid protein to clump together. Chelating, a process that removes minerals, has been found to reverse the process in studies of postmortem brain tissue. Subsequent studies show that zinc tends to accumulate in areas of the brain most prone to the damage typically seen in Alzheimer's disease. Zinc is suspected of aggregating beta amyloid deposits and also of pulling copper into the deposits. Together, the metals generate free radicals that are suspected of causing oxidative damage to nearby tissue. Current research is being done to develop chelating agents that can effectively remove zinc and copper deposits.

Several reports indicate that zinc levels that are abnormal, either too high or too low, seem to increase production of amyloid beta protein. It has also been reported that altered zinc metabolism and a subsequent imbalance in copper levels contribute to beta amyloid deposits. In the Nun Study, high levels of serum copper were found to correlate with the development of Alzheimer's disease.

Zyprexa *see* Olanzapine

Long Term and Day Care Treatment Centers

The following abbreviations are used in this section of the book:

HRF—Health-Related Facility
ICF—Intermediate Care Facility
ICF/MR—Intermediate Care Facility for Mentally Retarded
HIS—Integrated Health Services
MR—Mentally Retarded
RCF—Residential Care Facility
SCF—Skilled Care Facility
SNF—Skilled Nursing Facility

ALABAMA

Alexander City

Bill Nichols State Veterans Home
1784 Elkahatchee Rd., Alexander City, AL 35010, (256) 329-0868; Facility Type: Skilled care; Alzheimer's Beds: Skilled care 120; Alzheimers; Certified: Veterans Owner: Government/StateLocal License: Current state

Asheville

Healthcare Inc.
PO Box 130, Asheville, AL 35953, (205) 594-5148; Facility Type: Skilled care; ICF; ICF/MR; Alzheimer's; Beds: Skilled care 43; Certified: n/a; Owner: Private; License: Current state

Bessemer

Beverly Healthcare Center
820 Golf Course Rd., Bessemer, AL 35023 (205) 425-5241; Facility Type: Skilled care; ICF; ICF/MR; Alzheimer's; Beds: Skilled care 180; Certified: Medicaid; Medicare; Veterans; Owner: Beverly Enterprises Inc.; License: Current state

Birmingham

Estes Nursing Home—Northway
1424 N 25th St., Birmingham, AL 35234; Facility Type: Skilled care; Alzheimer's; Beds: Skilled care 113; Certified: Medicaid; Medicare; Owner: Northport Health Services Inc.; License: n/a

Fairview Nursing
Home 1028 Bessemer Rd., Birmingham, AL 35228, (205) 923-1777; Facility Type: Skilled care; ICF; Alzheimer's; Beds: Skilled care 165; Certified: Medicaid; Medicare; Veterans; Owner: Mariner Post Acute Network; License: Current state

Lakeview Nursing Home Inc.
8017 2nd Ave. S, Birmingham, AL 35206, (205)

836-4231; Facility Type: Skilled care; Alzheimer's; Beds: Skilled care 54; Certified: Medicare; Owner: Nonprofit corp.; License: Current state

Saint Martins in the Pines
4941 Montevallo Rd., Birmingham, AL 35210, (205) 956-1831; Facility Type: Skilled care; Alzheimer's; Beds: Skilled care 138; Alzheimer's 18; Dimiliary 106; Certified: Medicaid; Medicare; Owner: Nonprofit/Religious organization; License: Current state

Centre

Cherokee County Nursing Home
877 Cedar Bluff Rd., Centre, AL 35960, (256) 927-5778; Facility Type: Skilled care; ICF; ICF/MR; Alzheimer's; Beds: Skilled care 153; Certified: Medicaid; Medicare; Owner: Government/State/Local; License: Current state

Cullman

Cullman Health Care Center
1607 Main Ave. NE, Cullman, AL 35056, (256) 734-8745; Facility Type: Skilled care; Alzheimer's; Beds: Skilled care 95; Certified: Medicaid; Medicare; Owner: USA Healthcare; License: n/a

Daphne

Mercy Medical
PO Box 1090, Daphne, AL 36526, (334) 626-2694; Facility Type: Skilled care; Alzheimer's; Beds: Skilled care 20; Alzheimer's 16; Certified: Medicare; Veterans; Owner: Nonprofit/Religious Organization; License: Current state

Elmore

SunBridge Care & Rehabilitation for Elmore
Mt Hebron Rd., Box 7, Elmore, AL 36025, (334) 567-8484; Facility Type: Skilled care; ICF/MR; Alzheimer's; Beds: SNF/IC 124; Certified: Medicaid; Medicare; Veterans; Owner: Sun Healthcare Group, Inc.; License: Current state

Fairhope

Beverly Healthcare
108 S Church St., Fairhope, AL 36523, (334) 928-2153; Facility Type: Skilled care; Alzheimer's; Beds: Skilled care 131; Alzheimer's; Certified: Medicaid; Medicare; Veterans; Owner: Beverly Enterprises, Inc.; License: Current state

Florence

Florence Comprehensive Care
Center 2107 Cloyd Blvd., Florence, AL 35630, (256) 766-5771; Facility Type: Skilled care; Alzheimer's; Beds: Skilled care 147; Certified: Medicaid; Medicare; Owner: Beverly Enterprises Inc.; License: Current state

Guin

Sunset Manor
251 Sunset Pl., Guin, AL 35563, (205) 468-3331; Facility Type: Skilled care; ICF; Alzheimer's; Beds: Skilled care 61; Certified: Medicaid; Medicare; Owner: Private; License: Current state

Guntersville

Barfield Health Care
22444 Hwy 431, Guntersville, AL 35976, (256) 582-3112; Facility Type: Skilled care; ICF; Alzheimer's; Beds: Skilled care 91; Certified: Medicaid; Medicare; Owner: Private; License: Current state

Hartford

Hartford Healthcare
PO Box 190 217, Toro Rd., Hartford, AL 36344, (334) 588-3842; Facility Type: Skilled care; Alzheimer's; Beds: Skilled care 86; Certified: n/a; Owner: Diversicare Management Services Inc.; License: n/a

Huntsville

Big Springs Specialty Care Center
500 St Clair Ave. SW, Huntsville, AL 35801, (256) 539-5111; Facility Type: Skilled care; ICF; ICF/MR; Alzheimer's; Beds: Skilled care 145; Certified: Medicaid; Medicare; Owner: Vencor Inc.; License: Current state

Rehabilitation & Health Care Center
105 Teakwood Dr., Huntsville, AL 35811, (256) 852-5170; Facility Type: Skilled care; ICF; ICF/MR; Alzheimer's; Beds: Skilled Care 125; ICF; Certified: Medicaid; Medicare; Veterans; Owner: Vencor, Inc.; License: Current state

Windsor Home
4411 McAllister Dr., Huntsville, AL 35805, (256) 837-8585; Facility Type: Skilled care; ICF; Alzheimer's; Beds: Skilled care 117; ICF; ACLF; Certified: Medicaid; Medicare; Owner: Diversicare Management Services Inc.; License: Current state

Jasper

Ridgeview Health Care Center
907 11th St. NE, Jasper, AL 35501, (205) 221-9111; Facility Type: Skilled care; Alzheimer's; Beds: Skilled care 122; Alzheimers 26; Certified:

Medicaid; Medicare; Owner: Proprietary/Public corp.; License: Current state

Killen

El Reposo Nursing Facility Inc.
PO Box 999, Killen, AL 35645, (256) 757-2143; Facility Type: Skilled care; ICF; Alzheimer's; Beds: Skilled care 50; Certified: Medicaid; Medicare; Owner: Nonprofit corp; License: Current state

Luverne

Luverne Nursing Facility
142 W 3rd St., Luverne, AL 36049, (334) 335-6528; Facility Type: Skilled care; ICF; ICF/MR; Alzheimer's; Beds: Skilled care 151; Certified: Medicaid; Medicare; Owner: Northport Health Services Inc.; License: n/a

Marion

Perry County Nursing Home
PO Box 149., Marion, AL 36756, (334) 683-9696; Facility Type: Skilled care; ICF; ICF/MR; Alzheimer's; Beds: Skilled care 61; Certified: Medicaid; Medicare; Owner: Vaughan Healthcare; License: Current state

Mobile

Beverly Healthcare—Mobile
7020 Bruns Dr., Mobile, AL 36695, (334) 639-1588; Facility Type: Skilled care; Alzheimer's; Beds: Skilled care 120; Certified: Medicaid; Medicare; Veterans; Owner: Beverly Enterprises Inc.; License: Current state

Lynwood Nursing Home
4164 Halls Mill Rd., Mobile, AL 36693, (334) 661-5404; Facility Type: Skilled care; ICF; ICF/MR; Alzheimer's; Beds: Skilled care 127; Certified: Medicaid; Medicare; Owner: Diversicare Management Services; License: Current state

Rehabilitation & Healthcare Center of Mobile
1758 Springhill Ave., Mobile, AL 36607, (334) 479-0551; Facility Type: Skilled care; ICF; ICF/MR; Alzheimer's; Beds: Skilled care 28; ICF 114; Alzheimer's 28; Certified: Medicaid; Medicare; Veterans; Owner: Vencor, Inc.; License: Current state

Twin Oaks Nursing Home
857 Crawford Ln., Mobile, AL 36617, (334) 476-3420; Facility Type: Skilled care; ICF; ICF/MR; Alzheimer's; Beds: Skilled care 32; ICF 99; Certified: Medicaid; Medicare; Owner: Ball Healthcare; License: Current state

Montgomery

Capitol Hill Healthcare Center
520 S Hull St., Montgomery, AL 36104, (334) 834-2920; Facility Type: Skilled care; Alzheimer's; Beds: Skilled care 284; Certified: Medicaid; Medicare; Owner: Capitol Hill Healthcare & Rehabilitation Center; License: Current state

Crowne Health Care of Montgomery
1837 Upper Wetumpka Rd., Montgomery, AL 36107, (334) 264-8416; Facility Type: Skilled care; ICF; ICF/MR; Alzheimer's; Beds: Skilled care 185; Certified: Medicaid; Medicare; Veterans; Owner: Crowne Investments Inc.; License: n/a

Muscle Shoals

SunBridge Care & Rehabilitation for Muscle Shoals
200 Alabama Ave., Muscle Shoals, AL 35661, (256) 381-4330; Facility Type: Skilled care; ICF; Alzheimer's; Beds: SNF/ICF 90; Certified: Medicaid; Medicare; Owner: Sun Healthcare Group Inc.; License: Current state

Northport

Estes Glen Haven Rehabilitation Healthcare Center
2201 32nd St., Northport, AL 35476, (205) 339-5700; Facility Type: Skilled care; ICF; ICF/MR;Alzheimer's; Beds: Skilled care 182; Dimililiary care; Certified: Medicaid; Medicare; Owner: Northport Health Services Inc.; License: n/a

Estes Health Care Center—North
600 34th St., Northport, AL 35473, (205) 339-5900; Facility Type: Skilled care; ICF/MR; Alzheimer's; Beds: Skilled care 78; Certified: Medicaid; Medicare; Veterans; Owner: Northport Health Services Inc.; License: n/a

Opelika

Care Center of Opelika
1908 ? Pepperell Pkwy., Opelika, AL 36801, (334) 749-1471; Facility Type: Skilled care; ICF; Alzheimer's; Beds: Skilled care 224; Alzheimer's; SNF/ICF; Certified: Medicaid; Medicare; Owner: Proprietary/Public Corp.; License: Current state

Opp

Opp Nursing Facility
115 Paulk Ave., Box 730, Opp, AL 35467, (334) 493-4558; Facility Type: Akilled care; Alzheimer's; Beds: Skilled care 197; Certified: Medicaid; Medicare; Owner: Northport Health Services Inc.; License: Current state

Piedmont

Piedmont Health Care Center
612½ Calhoun St., Box 520, Piedmont, AL 36272, (256) 447-8258; Facility Type: Skilled care; ICF; ICF/MR; Alzheimer's; Beds: Skilled care 81; Certified: Medicaid; Medicare; Owner: Government/State/Local; License: Current state

Selma

Warren Manor Health & Rehabilitation Center
11 Bell Rd., Selma, AL 36701, (334) 874-7425; Facility Type: Skilled care; ICF; ICF/MR; Alzheimer's; Beds: Skilled care 176; Certified: Medicaid; Medicare; Owner: Mariner Post Acute Network; License: Current state

Tuskegee

Magnolia Haven Nursing Home
603 Wright St., Tuskegee, AL 36083, (334) 727-4960; Facility Type: Skilled care; ICF; ICF/MR; Alzheimer's; Beds: Skilled care 77; Certified: Medicaid; Medicare; Veterans; Owner: Ball Healthcare; License: Current state

ALASKA

Palmer

Palmer Pioneers' Home
250 E Fireweed, Palmer, AK 99645, (907) 745-4242; Facility Type: Skilled care; Alzheimer's; Beds: Skilled care 30; Alzheimer's 16; Certified: n/a; Owner: Government/State/Local; License: Current state

Petersburg

Petersburg Medical Center Long Term Care
PO Box 589, Petersburg, AK 99833, (907) 772-4291; Facility Type: Skilled care; ICF; Alzheimer's; Beds: Skilled care 15; Swing beds 5; Certified: Medicaid; Medicare; Veterans; Owner: Government/State/Local; License: Current state

ARKANSAS

Ash Flat

Ash Flat Convalescent Center
66 Ozborne St., Ash Flat, AR 72513, (870) 994-2341; Facility Type: Skilled care; Alzheimer's; Beds: Skilled care 105; Certified: Medicaid; Medicare; Veterans; Owner: Diversicare Management Services Inc.; License: Current state

Blytheville

Parkview Nursing Center—Blytheville
710 N Ruddle, Blytheville, AR 72315, (870) 763-3654; Facility Type: Skilled care; Alzheimer's; Beds: Skilled care 80; Certified: Medicaid; Owner: Proprietary/Public corp.; License: Current state

Camden

Valley Oaks Rehabilitation & Senior Living
1875 Owire Rd., Camden, AR 71701, (870) 836-6831; Facility Type: Skilled care; ICF; ICF/MR; Alzheimer's; Beds: Skilled care 70; ICF; Alzheimer's; Certified: Medicaid; Medicare; Veterans; Owner: Nonprofit Corp.; License: Current state

Danville

Mitchell's Nursing Home Inc.
501 W 10th St., Danville, AR 72833, (501) 495-2914; Facility Type: Skilled care; ICF; Alzheimer's; Beds: ICF 105; Certified: Medicaid; Owner: Private; License: Current state

England

England Manor Nursing Home Inc.
516 NE 4th, England, AR 72046, (501) 842-2771; Facility Type: Skilled care; ICF; Alzheimer's; Beds: SNF/ICF 63; Certified: Medicaid; Owner: Proprietary/Public corp.; License: Current state

Eureka Springs

Eureka Springs Nursing & Rehabilitation Center
235 Huntsville Rd., Eureka Springs, AR 72632, (501) 253-7038; Facility Type: Skilled care; Alz-

heimer's; Beds: Skilled care 100; Certified: Medicaid; Medicare; Owner: Diversicare Management Services Inc.; License: Current state

Fayetteville

Fayetteville Health & Rehabilitation
3100 Old Missouri Rd., Fayetteville, AR 72701, (501) 521-4353; Facility Type: Skilled care; ICF; Alzheimer's; Beds: Skilled care 108; ICF 16; Alzheimer's 16; Certified: Medicaid; Medicare; Owner: Private; License: Current state

Fordyce

Fordyce Healthcare Inc.
Smith & Baxter Sts., Fordyce, AR 71742, (870) 352-2104; Facility Type: Skilled care; Alzheimer's; Beds: Skilled care 105; Certified: Medicaid; Owner: Private; License: Current state

Heber Springs

Beverly Healthcare—Heber Springs
1040 Weddingford Rd., Heber Springs, AR 72543, (501) 362-8137; Facility Type: Skilled care; Alzheimer's; Beds: Skilled care 140; Certified: Medicaid; Medicare; Veterans; Owner: Beverly Enterprises Inc.; License: Current state

Jonesboro

Craighead Nursing Center
5101 Harrisburg Rd., Jonesboro, AR 72404, (870) 933-4535; Facility Type: Skilled care; ICF; Alzheimer's; Beds: Skilled care 110; Certified: Medicaid; Owner: Government/State/Local; License: Current state

Little Rock

Four Oaks Rehabilitation Center
2600 Barrow Rd., Little Rock, AR 72204, (501) 224-4173; Facility Type: Skilled care; ICF; Alzheimer's; Beds: Skilled care 139; SNF/ICF; Certified: Medicaid; Medicare; Owner: Private; License: Current state

Southwest Nursing Homes
2821 W Dixon Rd., Little Rock, AR 72206, (501) 888-4200; Facility Type: Skilled care; ICF; Alzheimer's; Beds: Skilled care 140; Certified: Medicaid; Owner: n/a; License: Current state

Malverne

Stillmeadow Nursing & Rehabilitation Center
105 Russelville Rd., Malvern, AR 72104, (501) 332-5251; Facility Type: Skilled care; ICF; Alzheimer's; Beds: Skilled care 104; Certified: Medicaid; Medicare; Veterans; Owner: Diversicare Management Services Inc.; License: Current state

Mountain Home

Auburn Hills Nursing & Rehabilitation Center
3545 Hwy 5 N, Mountain Home, AR 72653, (870) 425-6931; Facility Type: Skilled care; Alzheimer's; Beds: Skilled care 105; Certified: Medicaid; Owner: Proprietary/Public corp.; License: n/a

Pine Bluff

Arkansas Convalescent Center
6301 S Hazel, Pine Bluff, AR 71603, (870) 534-8153; Facility Type: Skilled care; Alzheimer's; Beds: Skilled care 91; Certified: Medicaid; Medicare; Owner: Proprietary/Public corp.; License: Current state

Prescott

Beverly Healthcare
700 Manor Dr., Prescott, AR 71857, (870) 887-6639; Facility Type: Skilled care; ICF; ICF/MR; Alzheimer's; Beds: Skilled care 17; ICF 42; Alzheimer's 15; Certified: Medicaid; Medicare; Veterans; Owner: Beverly Enterprises Inc.; License: Current state

Rogers

Kellmark Specialized Nursing Center
1603 W Walnut St., Rogers, AR 72756, (501) 636-9334; Facility Type: Skilled care; ICF; Alzheimer's; Beds: Skilled care 6; ICF 58; Alzheimer's 6; Certified: Medicaid; Medicare; Owner: Private; License: Current state

Stamps

Homestead Manor
826 North St., Stamps, AR 71860, (870) 533-4444; Facility Type: Skilled care; ICF; ICF/MR; Alzheimer's; Beds: Skilled care 116; Certified: Medicaid; Medicare; Owner: Rose Care Inc.; License: Current state

Wilmot

Beverly Healthcare—Wilmot
514 Lake St., Wilmot, AR 71676, (870) 473-2224; Facility Type: Skilled care; ICF; ICF/MR; Alzheimer's; Beds: Skilled care 10; ICF 90; Alz-

heimer's; Certified: Medicaid; Medicare; Owner: Beverly Enterprises Inc.; License: Current state

Yellville

Marion County Nursing Home
Hwy 14 N, Yellville, AR 72687, (870) 449-4201; Facility Type: Skilled care; Alzheimer's; Beds: Skilled care 105; Certified: Medicaid; Owner: Nonprofit/Religious organization; License: Current state

CALIFORNIA

Alameda

Bay View Nursing & Rehabilitation Center
516 Willow St., Alameda, CA 94501, (510) 521-5600; Facility Type: Skilled care; ICF; Alzheimer's; Beds: Skilled care 164; Certified: Medicaid; Medicare; Medi-Cal; Owner: Vencor Inc.; License: Current state

Alta Loma

Rancho Mesa Care Center
9333 La Mesa Dr., Alta Loma, CA 91701, (909) 987-2501; Facility Type: Skilled care; ICF/MR; Alzheimer's; Beds: Skilled care 59; Alzheimer's; Certified: Medicaid; Medical; Owner: Private; License: n/a

Anaheim

Leisure Court Nursing Center
1135 Leisure Ct., Anaheim, CA 92801, (714) 772-1353; Facility Type: Skilled care; Alzheimer's; Beds: Skilled care 99; Alzheimer's 44; Certified: Medicare; Medi-Cal; Owner: Proprietary/Public corp.; License: Current state

Bakersfield

Evergreen Health Care Center Inc.
6212 Tudor Way, Bakersfield, CA 93306, (661) 871-3133; Facility Type: Skilled care; Alzheimer's; Beds: Skilled care 99; Certified: Medicare; Medi-Cal; Owner: Evergreen Healthcare Management LLC; License: Current state

Hearthstone Alzheimer Residential Care
1932 Jessie St., Bakersfield, CA 93305, (661) 324-1024; Facility Type: Alzheimer's; Beds: Skilled care 87; Alzheimer's; Certified: n/a; Owner: Private; License: n/a

Valley Convalescent Hospital
1205 8th St., Bakersfield, CA 93304, (661) 334-2200; Facility Type: Skilled care; Alzheimer's; Beds: Skilled care 87; Certified: Medicare; Medi-Cal; Owner: Private; License: Current state

Berkeley

Ashby Care
Center 2270 Ashby Ave., Berkeley, CA 94705, (510) 841-9494; Facility Type: Skilled care; ICF; Alzheimer's; Beds: Skilled care 31; Certified: Medicare; Medi-Cal; Owner: Proprietary/Public corp.; License: Current state

Burbank

Beverly Manor Health Care Center
925 W Alameda Ave., Burbank, CA 91506, (818) 843-1771; Facility Type: Skilled care; Alzheimer's; Beds: Skilled care 89; Alzheimer's 89; Certified: Medicare; Medi-Cal; Veterans; Owner: Beverly Enterprises Inc.; License: Current state

Canoga Park

Canoga Care Center
22029 Saticoy St., Canoga Park, CA 91303, (818) 887-7050; Facility Type: Skilled care; Alzheimer's; Beds: Skilled care 200; Certified: Medicare; Medi-Cal; Owner: Private; License: Current state

Carmichael

Eskaton Village Care Center
3847 Walnut Ave., Carmichael, CA 95608, (916) 974-2060; Facility Type: Skilled care; Alzheimer's; Beds: Skilled care 30; Certified: Medicaid; Medicare; Medi-Cal; Owner: Eskaton; License: Current state

SunBridge Care & Rehabilitation for Carmichael
8336 Fair Oaks Blvd., Carmichael, CA 955608, (916) 944-3100; Facility Type: Skilled care; ICF; ICF/MR; Alzheimer's; Beds: Skilled care 126; ICF; Alzheimer's; Certified: Medicare; Medi-Cal; Veterans; Owner: Sun Healthcare Group Inc.; License: Current state

Claremont

Pilgrim Place Health Services Center
721 W Harrison Ave., Claremont, CA 91711,

(909) 399-5536; Facility Type: Skilled care; Alzheimer's; Beds: SNF/ICF 68; Certified: Medicaid; Medicare; Medi-Cal; Owner: Nonprofit corp.; License: Current state

Compton

San Migul Villa
1050 San Miguel Rd., Concord, CA 94518, (925) 825-4280; Facility Type: Skilled care; Alzheimer's; Beds: Skilled care 70; Certified: Medicare; Medi-Cal; Owner: Proprietary/Public corp.; License: Current state

Downey

Lakewood Park Health Center
12023 S Lakewood Blvd., Downey, CA 90242, (562) 869-0978; Facility Type: Skilled care; ICF; Alzheimer's; Beds: Skilled care 231; Certified: Medicaid; Medicare; Medi-Cal; Owner: Proprietary/Public corp.; License: Current state

El Cajon

Country Hills Health Center
1580 Broadway, El Cajon, CA 92021, (619) 441-8745; Facility Type: Skilled care; Alzheimer's; Beds: Skilled care 305; Certified: Medicare; Medi-Cal; Veterans; Owner: Proprietary/Public corp.; License: Current state

Parkside Special Care Centre
444 W Lexington Ave., El Cajon, CA 92020, (619) 442-7744; Facility Type: Skilled care; Alzheimer's; Beds: Skilled care 52; Alzheimer's 52; Certified: Medi-Cal; Owner: Kennon S Shea & Assoc; License: Current state

El Monte

Ramona Care Center
11900 Ramona Blvd., El Monte, CA 91732, (626) 442-5721; Facility Type: Skilled care; Alzheimer's; Beds: Skilled care 148; Alzheimer's; Certified: Medicare; Medi-Cal; Owner: Proprietary/Public corp.; License: Current state

Elk Grove

SunBridge Care & Rehabilitation for Elk Grove
9461 Batey Ave., Elk Grove, CA 95624, (916) 685-9525; Facility Type: Skilled care; ICF; Alzheimer's; Beds: Skilled care 136; Certified: Medicare; Medi-Cal; Veterans; Owner: Sun Healthcare Group Inc.; License: Current state

Escondido

Life Care Center of Escondido
1980 Felicita Rd., Escondido, CA 92025, (760) 741-6109; Facility Type: Skilled care; Alzheimer's; Beds: Skilled care 120; Certified: Medicare; Medi-Cal; Owner: Life Care Centers of America; License: Current state

Fresno

Horizon Health & Rehabilitation Center
3034 E Herndon, Fresno, CA 93705, (559) 237-0883; Facility Type: Skilled care; ICF; Alzheimer's; Beds: Alzheimer's; SNF/ICF; Certified: Medicaid; Medicare; Medi-Cal; Veterans; Owner: Proprietary/Public corp.; License: Current state

Gardena

Ayer-Lar Health Care Center
16530 S Broadway, Gardena, CA 90248, (310) 329-7581; Facility Type: Skilled care; Alzheimer's; Beds: Skilled care 50; Certified: Medicare; Medi-Cal; Owner: Private; License: Current state

Hawthorne

Windsor Gardens of Hawthorne
13922 Cerise Ave., Hawthorne, CA 90250, (310) 675-3304; Facility Type: Skilled care; Alzheimer's; Beds: Skilled care 99; Alzheimer's; Certified: Medicare; Medi-Cal; Owner: Proprietary/Public corp.; License: Current state

Hayward

Bethesda Home
22427 Montgomery St., Hayward, CA 94541, (510) 538-8300; Facility Type: Skilled care; Alzheimer's; Beds: Skilled care 40; Certified: Medicare; Medi-Cal; Owner: Proprietary/Public corp.; License: Current state

Saint Therese Convalescent Hospital Inc.
21863 Vallejo St., Hayward, CA 94541, (510) 538-3811; Facility Type: Skilled care; Alzheimer's; Beds: Skilled care 36; Certified: Medi-Cal; Owner: Private; License: Current state

La Mesa

Grossmont Gardens Health Care Center
5480 Marengo Ave., La Mesa, CA 91942, (619) 463-6445; Facility Type: Skilled care; ICF; Alzheimer's; Beds: Skilled care 39; Certified: Medicare; Owner: Private; License: Current state

Stanford Court Nursing Center of La Mesa
7800 Parkway Dr., La Mesa, CA 91942, (619) 460-2330; Facility Type: Skilled care; Alzheimer's; Beds: Skilled care 106; Certified: Medicare; Medi-Cal; Owner: Private; License: Current state

Long Beach

Candlewood Care Center
260 E Market St., Long Beach, CA 90805, (562) 428-4681; Facility Type: Skilled care; Alzheimer's; Beds: Skilled care 80; Alzheimer's 40; Certified: Medicaid; Medicare; Medi-Cal; Owner: Covenant Care Corporation; License: Current state

Colonial Care Center
1913 E 5th St., Long Beach, CA 90802, (562) 432-5751; Facility Type: Skilled care; Alzheimer's; Beds: Skilled care 120; Alzheimer's 73; Certified: Medicaid; Medicare; Medi-Cal; Owner: Private; License: Current state

Royal Care Skilled Nursing Center
2725 Pacific Ave., Long Beach, CA 90806, (562) 427-7493; Facility Type: Skilled care; Alzheimer's; Beds: Skilled care 60; Alzheimer's 33; Certified: Medicaid; Medicare; Medi-Cal; Owner: Covenant Care Corporation; License: Current state

Los Angeles

Alden Terrace Convalescent Hospital
1240 S Hoover St., Los Angeles, CA 90006, (213) 382-8461; Facility Type: Skilled care; Alzheimer's; Beds: Skilled care 110; Alzheimer's 100; Certified: Medicare; Medi-Cal;Veterans; Owner: Proprietary/Public corp.; License: Current state

Amberwood Convalescent Hospital
6071 York Blvd., Los Angeles, CA 90042, (323) 254-3407; Facility Type: Skilled care; ICF; Alzheimer's; Beds: Skilled care 50; ICF 27; Alzheimer's 30; Certified: Medicare; Medi-Cal; Owner: Proprietary/Public corp.; License: Current state

Country Villa Mar Vista Nursing Center
2966 Marcasel Ave., Los Angeles, CA 90066, (310) 397-2372; Facility Type: Skilled care; Alzheimer's; Beds: Skilled care 68; Alzheimer's 68; Certified: Medicare; Owner: Country Villa Healthcare Corporation; License: Current state

Kennedy Care Center
619 N Fairfax Ave., Los Angeles, CA 90036, (323) 651-0043; Facility Type: Skilled care; ICF; ICF/MR;Alzheimer's; Beds: Skilled care 40; ICF 15; ICF/MR 24; Alzheimer's 15; Certified: Medicare; Medi-Cal; Owner: Proprietary/Public corp.; License: Current state

Saint John of God Retirement & Care Center
2035 W Adams Blvd., Los Angeles, CA 90018, (323) 731-0641; Facility Type: Skilled care; ICF; Alzheimer's; Beds: Skilled care 131; Alzheimer's 22; Residential 75; Certified: Medicare; Medi-Cal; Owner: Nonprofit corp.; License: Current state

Sharon Care Center
8167 W 3rd St., Los Angeles, CA 90048, (323) 655-2023; Facility Type: Skilled care; Alzheimer's; Beds: Skilled care 60; Alzheimer's 28; Certified: Medicare; Medi-Cal; Owner: Fountain View Inc.; License: Current state

Windsor Gardens Convalescent Hospital
915 Crenshaw Blvd., Los Angeles, CA 90019, (323) 937-5466; Facility Type: Skilled care; Alzheimer's; Beds: Skilled care 40; ICF/MR 30; Alzheimer's 28; Certified: Medicare; Medi-Cal; Owner: Proprietary/Public corp.; License: Current state

Merced

Merced Living Care Center
510 W 26th St., Merced, CA 95340, (209) 723-2911; Facility Type: Skilled care; Alzheimer's; Beds: Skilled care 79; Alzheimer's; Certified: Medicaid; Medicare; Medi-Cal; Owner: Health Care Management; License: Current state

Modesto

Colony Park Nursing & Rehabilitation Center
159 E Orangeburg Ave., Modesto, CA 95350, (209) 526-2811; Facility Type: Skilled care; Alzheimer's; Beds: Skilled care 99; Certified: Medicaid; Medicare; Medi-Cal; Owner: Health Care Management; License: Current state

Monterey

SunBridge Care Center for Monterey
1575 Skyline Dr., Monterey, CA 93940, (831) 373-2731; Facility Type: Skilled care; ICF; Alzheimer's; Beds: Skilled care 76; Certified: Medicare; Medi-Cal; Owner: Sun Healthcare Group Inc.; License: Current state

North Hollywood

Valley Palms Care Center
13400 Sherman Way, North Hollywood, CA 91605, (818) 983-0103; Facility Type: Skilled care; ICF; Alzheimer's; Beds: Skilled care 33; ICF 33; Alzheimer's 33; Certified: Medicaid; Medicare; Medi-Cal; Owner: Proprietary/Public corp.; License: Current state

Oakland

Lakeshore Convalescent Hospital
1901 3rd Ave., Oakland, CA 94606, (510) 834-

9880; Facility Type: Skilled care; Alzheimer's; Beds: Skilled care 38; Certified: Medicare; Medi-Cal; Owner: Private; License: Current state

Mercy Retirement & Care Center
3431 Foothill Blvd., Oakland, CA 94601, (510) 534-8540; Facility Type: Skilled care; Alzheimer's; Beds: Skilled care 59; Residential 140; Certified: Medicare; Medi-Cal; Owner: Nonprofit corp.; License: Current state

Saint Paul's Tower
100 Bay Pl., Oakland CA 94610, (510) 835-4700; Facility Type: Skilled care; ICF; ICF/MR; Alzheimer's; Beds: Skilled care 43; SNF/ICF; Certified: Medicare; Owner: Nonprofit/Religious organization; License: Current state

Paramount

Paramount Convalescent Hospital
8558 E Rosecrans Ave., Paramount, CA 90723, (562) 634-6877; Facility Type: Skilled care; Alzheimer's; Beds: Skilled care 59; Certified: Medicaid; Medicare; Medi-Cal; Owner: Sun Mar Healthcare; License: Current state

Paramount Meadows
7039 Alondra Blvd., Paramount, CA 90723, (562) 531-0990; Facility Type: Skilled care; ICF; ICF/MR; Alzheimer's; Beds: Skilled care 25; ICF 25; ICF/MR 24; Alzheimer's 25; Certified: Medicaid; Medicare; Medi-Cal; Owner: Proprietary/Public corp.; License: Current state

Pasadena

Eisenhower Nursing & Convalescent Hospital
1470 N Fair Oaks Ave., Pasadena, CA 91103; (626) 798-9133; Facility Type: Skilled care; Alzheimer's; Beds: Skilled care 50; Alzheimer's 21; Certified: Medicaid; Medicare; Medi-Cal; Owner: Proprietary/Public corp.; License: Current state

Monte Vista Grove Homes
2889 San Pasqual Ave., Pasadena, CA 91107, (626) 796-6135; Facility Type: Skilled care; ICF; Alzheimer's; Beds: Skilled care 20; ICF 10; Alzheimer's 15; Assisted living 7; Certified: Medicare; Owner: Nonprofit corp.; License: Current state

Pomona

Pomona Vista Alzheimer's Center
651 N Main St., Pomona, CA 91768, (909) 623-2481; Facility Type: Skilled care; ICF; ICF/MR; Alzheimer's; Beds: Skilled care 59; Certified: Medicaid; Medicare; Medi-Cal; Owner: Proprietary/Public corp.; License: Current state

Reseda

Jewish Home for the Aging—Grancell Village
7150 Tampa Ave., Reseda, CA 91335, (818) 774-3307; Facility Type: Skilled care; ICF; Alzheimer's; Beds: Skilled care 837; ICF; Alzheimer's; Certified: Medicare; Medi-Cal; Owner: Jewish Home for the Aging; License: Current state

Los Angeles Jewish Home for the Aging—Eisenberg Village
18855 Victory Blvd., Reseda, CA 91335, (818) 774-3000; Facility Type: Skilled care; Alzheimer's; Beds: Skilled care 744; Alzheimer's RCF; Certified: Medicaid; Medicare; Medi-Cal; Owner: Jewish Home for the Aging; License: Current state

Sacramento

Asbury Park Nursing & Rehabilitation Center
2257 Fair Oaks Blvd., Sacramento, CA 95825, (916) 649-2000; Facility Type: Skilled care; Alzheimer's; Beds: Skilled care 110; Alzheimer's; Certified: Medicare; Medi-Cal; Owner: Private; License: Current state

Briarwood Health Care
5901 Lemon Hill Ave., Sacramento, CA 95824, (916) 383-2741; Facility Type: Skilled care; ICF; ICF/MR; Alzheimer's; Beds: Skilled care 49; ICF; Alzheimer's; Certified: Medicaid; Medicare; Medi-Cal; Veterans; Owner: Proprietary/Public corp.; License: Current state

Greenhaven Country Place
455 Florin Rd., Sacramento, CA 95831, (916) 393-2550; Facility Type: Skilled care; Alzheimer's; Beds: Skilled care 110; Certified: Medicaid; Medicare; Medi-Cal; Owner: Eskaton; License: Current state

Saylor Lane Health Care Center
3500 Folsom Blvd., Sacramento, CA 95816, (916) 457-6521; Facility Type: Skilled care; Alzheimer's; Beds: Skilled care 42; Alzheimer's; Certified: Medicare; Owner: Proprietary/Public corp.; License: Current state

San Bernardino

Hillcrest Care
4280 Cypress Dr., San Bernardino, CA 92403, (909) 882-2965; Facility Type: Skilled care; Alzheimer's; Beds: Skilled care 59; Certified: Medi-Cal; Owner: Proprietary/Public corp.; License: Current state

San Diego

Alvarado Convalescent & Rehabilitation Hospital
6599 Alvarado Rd., San Diego, CA 92120, (619) 286-7421; Facility Type: Skilled care; Alzheimer's; Beds: Skilled care; 241; Alzheimer's 28; Certified: Medicare; Medi-Cal; Owner: Proprietary/Public corp.; License: Current state

Care with Dignity Convalescent Hospital
8060 Frost St., San Diego, CA 92123, (858) 278-4750; Facility Type: Skilled care; Alzheimer's; Beds: Skilled care 99; Certified: Medicare; Owner: Proprietary/Public corp.; License: Current state

Pleasant Care
2828 Meadowlark Dr., San Diego, CA 92123, (858) 277-6460; Facility Type: Skilled care; Alzheimer's; Beds: Skilled care 305; Certified: Medicare; Medi-Cal; Veterans; Owner: Pleasant Care Corp.; License: Current state

SunBridge Care & Rehabilitation for Carmel Mountain
11895 Ave. of Industry San Diego, CA 92128, (858) 673-0101; Facility Type: Skilled care; Alzheimer's; Beds: Skilled care 120; Certified: Medicare; Medi-Cal; Veterans; Owner: Sun Healthcare Group Inc.; License: Current state

San Francisco

Golden Gate Care Center
2707 Pine St., San Francisco, CA 94115, (415) 563-7600; Facility Type: Skilled care; Alzheimer's; Beds: Alzheimer's 120; Certified: Medicare; Medi-Cal; Owner: Vencor Inc.; License: Current state

San Jacinto

The Bradley Gardens
980 W 7th St., San Jacinto, CA 92582, (909) 654-9347; Facility Type: Skilled care; ICF; Alzheimer's; Beds: Skilled care 102; ICF; Alzheimer's; Certified: Medicare; Medi-Cal; Owner: Private; License: Current state

Emanuel Convalescent Hospital
180 N Jackson Ave., San Jose, CA 95116, (408) 259-8700; Facility Type: Skilled care; Alzheimer's; Beds: Skilled care 181; ICF 17; Certified: Medicare; Medi-Cal; Owner: Nonprofit corp.; License: Current state

San Jose Care & Guidance Center
401 Ridge Vista Ave., San Jose, CA 95127, (408) 923-7232; Facility Type: Skilled care; Alzheimer's; Beds: Skilled care 108; Certified: Medi-Cal; Owner: Beverly Enterprises Inc.; License: Current state

San Leandro

Seaton Rehabilitation Hospital
1652 Mono Ave., San Leandro, CA 94578, (510) 357-5351; Facility Type: Skilled care; Alzheimer's; Beds: Skilled care 49; Vent program; Certified: Medicaid; Medicare; Medi-Cal; Veterans; Owner: Private; License: Current state

Santa Ana

Bartlett Care Center
600 E Washington Ave., Santa Ana, CA 92701, (714) 973-1656; Facility Type: Skilled care; Alzheimer's; Beds: Skilled care 134; Alzheimer's 22; Certified: Medicare; Medi-Cal; Owner: Sun Mar Healthcare; License: Current state

Country Villa Plaza
1209 Hemlock Way W, Santa Ana, CA 92707, (714) 546-1966; Facility Type: Skilled care; ICF; ICF/MR; Alzheimer's; Beds: Skilled care 141; Certified: Medicaid; Medicare; Medi-Cal; Owner: Country Villa Healthcare Corporation; License: Current state

Santa Monica

Santa Monica Convalescent Center II
2250 29th St., Santa Monica, CA 90405, (310) 450-7694; Facility Type: Skilled care; Alzheimer's; Beds: Skilled care 80; Certified: Medicare; Medi-Cal; Owner: Private; License: Current state

Spring Valley

Brighton Place—East
8625 La Mar St., Spring Valley, CA 91977, (619) 461-3222; Facility Type: Skilled care; Alzheimer's; Beds: Skilled care 50; Certified: Medicare; Medi-Cal; Owner: Proprietary/Public corp.; License: n/a

Mount Miguel Covenant Village Health Facility
325 Kempton St., Spring Valley, CA 91977, (619) 479-4790; Facility Type: Skilled care; Alzheimer's; Beds: Skilled care 59; Alzheimer's 40; Certified: Medicare; Medi-Cal; Owner: Covenant Retirement Communities Inc.; License: Current state

Sunland

High Valley Lodge
7912 Topley Ln., Sunland, CA 91040, (818) 352-

3158; Facility Type: Skilled care; ICF/MR; Alzheimer's; Beds: Skilled care 50; Certified: Medicaid; Medicare; Medi-Cal; Owner: Private; License: Current state

New Vista Nursing & Rehabilitation Center
8647 Fenwick St., Sunland, CA 91040, (818) 352-1421; Facility Type: Skilled care; Alzheimer's; Beds: Skilled care 121; Alzheimer's; SNF/ICF; Certified: Medicaid; Medicare; Medi-Cal; Veterans; Owner: Private; License: Current state

Sunnyvale

Hy-Lond Healthcare Center
797 E Fremont Ave., Sunnyvale, CA 9408, (408) 738-4880; Facility Type: Skilled care; ICF; Alzheimer's; Beds: Skilled care 99; ICF; Alzheimer's; Respiratory care; Certified: Medicaid; Medicare; Medi-Cal; Veterans; Owner: Beverly Enterprises Inc.; License: Current state

Torrance

Harbor Convalescent Hospital
21521 S Vermont Ave., Torrance, CA 90502, (310) 320-0961; Facility Type: Skilled care; ICF; ICF/MR; Alzheimer's; Beds: Skilled care 127; Certified: Medicare; Medi-Cal; Owner: Proprietary/Public corp.; License: Current state

Van Nuys

Balowen Care Center
16955 Vanowen St., Van Nuys, CA 91406, (818) 343-0700; Facility Type: Skilled care; Alzheimer's; Beds: Skilled care 50; Certified: Medicaid; Medicare; Medi-Cal; Veterans; Owner: Care Center Consultants Inc.; License: Current state

West Covina

Clara Baldwin Stocker Home
527 S Valinda Ave., West Covina, CA 91790, (626) 962-7151; Facility Type: Skilled care; Alzheimer's; Beds: Skilled care 48; Alzheimer's; SNF/ICF; Certified: n/a; Owner: Nonprofit corp.; License: Current state

COLORADO

Alamosa

Evergreen Nursing Home
1991 Carroll St., Alamosa, CO 81101, (719) 589-4951; Facility Type: Skilled care; Alzheimer's; Beds: Skilled care 42; Alzheimer's 18; Certified: Medicaid; Medicare; Owner: Private; License: Current state

Arvada

Arvada Health Center
6121 W 60th Ave., Arvada, CO 80003, (303) 420-4550; Facility Type: Skilled care; Alzheimer's; Beds: Skilled care 54; Certified: Medicaid; Medicare; Owner: Nonprofit corp.; License: Current state

Exempla/ Colorado Lutheran Home
7991 W 71 Ave., Arvada, CO 80004, (303) 403-3100; Facility Type: Skilled care; Alzheimer's; Beds: Skilled care 92; Alzheimer's 20; Certified: Medicaid; Medicare; Owner: Nonprofit corp.; License: Current state

Aurora

Aurora Care Center
10201 E 3rd Ave., Aurora, CO 80010, (303) 364-3364; Facility Type: Skilled care; ICF; Alzheimer's; Beds: Skilled care 80; ICF; Alzheimer's 19; Certified: Medicaid; Medicare; Veterans; Owner: Proprietary/Public corp.; License: Current state

Camelia Health Care Center
500 Geneva St., Aurora, CO 80010, (303) 364-9311; Facility Type: Skilled care; ICF; ICF/MR; Alzheimer's; Beds: Skilled care 130; Alzheimer's; SNF/ICF; Certified: n/a; Owner: Mariner Post Acute Network; License: Current state

Cherry Creek Nursing Center
14699 E Hampden Ave., Aurora, CO 80014, (303) 693-0111; Facility Type: Skilled care; ICF; Alzheimer's; Beds: Skilled care 220; ICF; Alzheimer's; SNF/ICF; Certified: Medicaid; Medicare; Veterans; Owner: Proprietary/Public corp.; License: Current state

Garden Terrace
1600 S Potomac St., Aurora, CO 80012, (303) 750-8418; Facility Type: Alzheimer's; Beds: Alzheimer's 120; Certified: Medicare; Owner: Proprietary/Public corp.; License: Current state

Boulder

Boulder Manor Progressive Care Center
4685 Baseline Rd., Boulder, CO 80303, (303) 494-0535; Facility Type: Skilled care; ICF; ICF/

MR; Alzheimer's; Beds: Skilled care 145; ICF 60; Certified: Medicaid; Medicare; Owner: Mariner Post Acute Network; License: Current state

Frasier Meadows Manor Health Care Center
4950 Thunderbird Dr., Boulder, CO 80303, (303) 499-8412; Facility Type: Skilled care; ICF; Alzheimer's; Beds: Skilled care 75; Alzheimer's 20; Retirement; Certified: Medicaid; Medicare; Owner: Nonprofit corp.; License: Current state

Brush

Eben Ezer Lutheran Care Center
122 Hospital Rd., Brush, CO 80723, (970) 842-2861; Facility Type: Skilled care; Alzheimer's; Beds: Skilled care 120; Certified: Medicaid; Medicare; Veterans; Owner: Nonprofit/Religious organization; License: Current state

Sunset Manor
2200 Edison St., Brush, CO 80723, (970) 842-2825; Facility Type: Skilled care; ICF; ICF/MR; Alzheimer's; Beds: Skilled care 44; ICF 41; Certified: Medicaid; Medicare; Owner: Mariner Post Acute Network; License: Current state

Canon City

Hilderbrand Care Center
1401 Phay Ave., Canon City, CO 81212, (719) 275-8656; Facility Type: Skilled care; Alzheimer's; Beds: Skilled care; Alzheimer's; Certified: Medicaid; Medicare; Veterans; Owner: Proprietary/Public corp.; License: Current state

Carbondale

Heritage Park Care Center
1200 Village Rd., Carbondale, CO 81623, (970) 963-1500; Facility Type: Skilled care; ICF; Alzheimer's; Beds: Skilled care 118; Certified: Medicaid; Medicare; Owner: Private; License: Current state

Castle Rock

Castle Rock Care Center
4001 Home St., Castle Rock, CO 80104, (303) 688-3174; Facility Type: Skilled care; Alzheimer's; Beds: Skilled care 80; Certified: Medicaid; Medicare; Owner: Nonprofit corp.; License: Current state

Colorado Springs

Cedarwood Health Care Center Inc.
924 W Kiowa St., Colorado Springs, CO 80905, (719) 636-5221; Facility Type: Skilled care; ICF; ICF/MR; Alzheimer's; Beds: SNF/ICF 85; Certified: Medicaid; Medicare; Owner: Mariner Post Acute Network; License: Current state

Colonial Columns Health Care Center
1340 E Fillmore St., Colorado Springs, CO 80907, (719) 473-1105; Facility Type: Skilled care; Alzheimer's; Beds: Skilled care 46; Alzheimer's 22; Hospice 11; Certified: Medicaid; Medicare; Owner: Mariner Post Acute Network; License: Current state

Garden of the Gods Care Center
104 Lois Ln., Colorado Springs, CO 80904, (719) 635-2569; Facility Type: Skilled care; Alzheimer's; Beds: Skilled care 50; Certified: Medicaid; Medicare; Owner: Nonprofit corp.; License: n/a

IHS at Pikes Peak
2719 N Union Blvd., Colorado Springs, CO 80909, (719) 636-1676; Facility Type: Skilled care; Alzheimer's; Beds: Skilled care 210; Certified: Medicaid; Medicare; Owner: Integrated Health Services Inc.; License: Current state

IHS at Prospect Lake
1420 E Fountain Blvd., Colorado Springs, CO 80910, (719) 632-7604; Facility Type: Skilled care; Alzheimer's; Beds: Skilled care 44; Certified: Medicaid; Medicare; Owner: Integrated Health Services Inc.; License: Current state

IHS at Springs Village
110 W Van Buren, Colorado Springs, CO 80907, (719) 475-8686; Facility Type: Skilled care; ICF; Alzheimer's; Beds: Skilled care 58; ICF 58; Wound care; Certified: Medicaid; Medicare; Owner: Integrated Health Services Inc.; License: Current state

Laurel Manor Care Center
920 S Chelton Rd., Colorado Springs, CO 80910, (719) 473-7780; Facility Type: Skilled care; ICF; Alzheimer's; Beds: Skilled care 98; Certified: Medicaid; Medicare; Veterans; Owner: Nonprofit/Religious organization; License: Current state

Mountain View Care Center
2612 W Cucharras St., Colorado Springs, CO 80904, (719) 632-7474; Facility Type: Skilled care; ICF/MR; Alzheimer's; Beds: Skilled care 57; Certified: Medicaid; Medicare; Owner: Nonprofit corp.; License: Current state

Namasté Alzheimer Center
Colorado Springs, CO, (719) 776-8398; http://www.centuraseniors.org; Facility Type: Alzheimer's; Beds: 64; Additional Information: Namasté Alzheimer Center is a long-term residential treatment center designed, staffed and operated specifically for people with Alzheimer's

Namasté Nursing Home, Colorado Springs, CO (courtesy Namasté Alzheimer Center).

disease and related disorders. Modeled after the pod system, patients are primarily housed in nursing units occupied by patients with similar levels of cognitive function. Located at the base of Cheyenne Mountain, Namasté is an attractive facility with a skilled nursing staff specifically trained to assist patients in maintaining their basic living skills. A member of the Centura-Health System, Namasté is affiliated with Penrose Hospital. As an innovative form of therapy, clinical massage students spend part of their internships at Namasté. Residents and adults in the day care program participate in art and music therapy and those who are able have access to exercise equipment. Although it is a secure facility, patients are allowed to spend time outside inclement weather. More information can be found on the Namasté web page, which is linked to the Skilled Nursing/Alzheimer's Facilities page of the Centura website.

Terrace Gardens Health Care Center
2438 Fountain Blvd., Colorado Springs, CO 80910, (719) 473-8000; Facility Type: Skilled care; ICF; ICF/MR; Alzheimer's; Beds: SNF/ICF 60; Certified: Medicaid; Medicare; Veterans; Owner: Mariner Post Acute Network; License: Current state

Commerce City

Rose Terrace Care Center
5230 E 66th Way, Commerce City, CO 80022, (303) 289-1848; Facility Type: Skilled care; Alzheimer's; Beds: Skilled care 116; Alzheimer's; Respite care; Certified: Medicaid; Medicare; Veterans; Owner: Nonprofit corp.; License: Current state

Cortez

Vista Grande Rehabilitation & Care Center
1221 N Mildred Rd., Cortez, CO 81321, (970) 564-2600; Facility Type: Skilled care; Alzheimer's; Beds: Skilled care 76; Certified: Medicaid; Medicare; Owner: Proprietary/Public corp.; License: Current state

Craig

Valley View Manor
943 W 8th Dr., Craig, CO 81625, (970) 824-

4432; Facility Type: Skilled care; ICF; Alzheimer's; Beds: Alzheimer's 18; SNF/ICF 40; Certified: Medicaid; Medicare; Owner: Mariner Post Acute Network; License: Current state

Denver

Briarwood Health Care Center
1440 Vine St., Denver, CO 80206, (303) 399-0350; Facility Type: Skilled care; Alzheimer's; Beds: Skilled care 201; Certified: Medicaid; Medicare; Owner: Life Care Centers of America; License: Current state

Brookshire House
4660 E Asbury Cir., Denver, CO 8022, (303) 756-1546; Facility Type: Skilled care; ICF; Alzheimer's; Beds: Skilled care 67; Certified: Medicaid; Medicare; Owner: Raintree Healthcare Corporation; License: Current state

Centura Senior Life Center
1601 Lowell Blvd., Denver, CO 80204, (303) 899-5088; Facility Type: ICF; Alzheimer's; Beds: ICF 38; Alzheimer's 26; Certified: Medicaid; Medicare; Owner: Catholic Health Initiatives; License: Current state

Iliff Care Center
6060 E Iliff Ave., Denver, CO 80222, (303) 759-4221; Facility Type: Skilled care; ICF; Alzheimer's; Beds: skilled care 180; Alzheimer's 21; Certified: Medicaid; Medicare; Owner: Vencor Inc.; License: Current state

ManorCare Nursing Center
290 S Monaco Pkwy., Denver, CO 80224, (303) 355-2525; Facility Type: Skilled care; ICF; Alzheimer's; Beds: Alzheimer's 26; SNF/ICF 100; Certified: Medicare; Owner: Proprietary/Public corp.; License: Current state

Porter Care Hospital—Transitional Care Unit
2525 S Downing St., Denver, CO 80210, (303) 778-5641; Facility Type: Skilled care; ICF; ICF/MR; Alzheimer's; Beds: Skilled care 35; Certified: Medicare; Owner: Nonprofit/Religious organization; License: n/a

Red Rocks HealthCare Center
4450 E Jewell Ave., Denver, CO 80222, (303) 757-7438; Facility Type: Skilled care; ICF; ICF/MR; Alzheimer's; Beds: Skilled care 106; Certified: Medicaid; Medicare; Owner: Mariner Post Acute Network; License: Current state

Rowan Community
4601 E Asbury Cir., Denver, CO 80222, (303) 757-1228; Facility Type: Skilled care; ICF; Alzheimer's; Beds: Skilled care 60; Certified: Medicaid; Medicare; Owner: Proprietary/Public corp.; License: Current state

Uptown Health Care Center Inc.
745 E 18th Ave., Denver, CO 80203, (303) 860-0500; Facility Type: Skilled care; ICF; Alzheimer's; Beds: Skilled care 30; ICF 50; Hospice; Certified: Medicaid; Medicare; Owner: Proprietary/Public corp.; License: Current state

Eckert

Horizons Health Care & Retirement Community
1141 Hwy 65, Eckert, CO 81418, (970) 835-3113; Facility Type: Skilled care; ICF; Alzheimer's; Beds: Skilled care 72; Certified: Medicaid; Medicare; Veterans; Owner: Volunteers of America National Services; License: Current state

Englewood

Julia Temple Center
3401 S Lafayette St., Englewood, CO 80110, (303) 761-0075; Facility Type: Skilled care; ICF; Alzheimer's; Beds: Alzheimer's 136; Residential care 48; Certified: Medicaid; Medicare; Owner: Nonprofit/Religious organization; License: Current state

Florence

Colorado State Veterans Nursing Home
903 Moore Dr., Florence, CO 81226, (719) 784-6331; Facility Type: Skilled care; Alzheimer's; Beds: Skilled care 67; Alzheimer's 53; Certified: Medicaid; Veterans; Owner: Nonprofit corp.; License: Current state

Fort Collins

Blue Grouse Health Care Center
1020 Patton St., Fort Collins, CO 80524, (970) 484-6133; Facility Type: Skilled care; Alzheimer's; Beds: Skilled care 60; Alzheimer's 22; Certified: Medicaid; Medicare; Veterans; Owner: Mariner Post Acute Network; License: Current state

SunBridge Care & Rehabilitation for Fort Collins
1005 E Elizabeth St., Fort Collins, CO 80524, (970) 482-2525; Facility Type: Skilled care; Alzheimer's; Beds: Skilled care 59; Alzheimer's; SNF/ICF; Certified: Medicaid; Medicare; Owner: Sun Healthcare Group Inc.; License: Current state

Fort Morgan

Valley View Villa
815 Fremont Ave., Fort Morgan, CO 80701, (970)

867-8261; Facility Type: Skilled care; Alzheimer's; Beds: Skilled care 80; Alzheimer's 20; Certified: Medicaid; Medicare; Owner: Life Care Centers of America; License: Current state

Fruita

Family Health West Nursing Home
228 N Cherry. Fruita, CO 81521, (970) 858-9871; Facility Type: Skilled care; Alzheimer's; Beds: Skilled care 150; Certified: Medicaid; Medicare; Owner: Nonprofit corp.; License: Current state

Grand Junction

Grand Junction Care Center
2425 Teller Ave., Grand Junction, CO 81501, (970) 243-3381; Facility Type: Skilled care; ICF; Alzheimer's; Beds: Skilled care 12; ICF 15; Alzheimer's 10; SNF/ICF 39; Behavioral 22; Certified: Medicaid; Medicare; Owner: Proprietary/Public corp.; License: Current state

IHS at LaVilla Grande
2501 Little Bookcliff Dr., Grand Junction, CO 81501, (970) 245-1211; Facility Type: Skilled care; Alzheimer's; Beds: Skilled care 90; Alzheimer's 17; Certified: Medicaid; Medicare; Veterans; Owner: Integrated Health Services Inc.; License: Current state

Greeley

Bonell Good Samaritan Center
708 22nd St., Greeley, CO 80631, (970) 352-6082; Facility Type: Skilled care; Alzheimer's; Beds: Skilled care 244; Alzheimer's; Personal care; Certified: Medicaid; Medicare; Veterans; Owner: Nonprofit corp.; License: Current state

Fairacres Manor Inc.
1700 18th Ave., Greeley, CO 80631, (970) 353-3370; Facility Type: Skilled care; Alzheimer's; Beds: Skilled care 58; Alzheimer's 18; Certified: Medicaid; Medicare; Owner: Private; License: Current state

Holly

Holly Nursing Care Center
320 N 8th St., Holly, CO 81047, (719) 537-6555; Facility Type: Skilled care; Alzheimer's; Beds: Alzheimer's 10; SNF/ICF 37; Certified: Medicaid; Medicare; Owner: Proprietary/Public corp.; License: Current state

Lakewood

Bethany Healthplex
5301 W 1st Ave., Lakewood, CO 80226, (303) 238-8333; Facility Type: Skilled care; ICF; Alzheimer's; Beds: Alzheimer's 60; SNF/ICF 100; Certified: Medicaid; Medicare; Owner: Private; License: Current state

Cambridge Care Center Inc.
1685 Eaton St., Lakewood, CO 80214, (303) 232-4405; Facility Type: Skilled care; ICF; Alzheimer's; Beds: Skilled care 100; Alzheimer's; Certified: Medicaid; Medicare; Owner: Private; License: Current state

Cornerstone Care Center
1432 Depew St., Lakewood, CO 80214, (303) 238-1375; Facility Type: Skilled care; ICF; Alzheimer's; Beds: Skilled care 105; ICF; Alzheimer's; Certified: Medicaid; Medicare; Owner: Proprietary/Public corp.; License: Current state

Evergreen Terrace Care Center
1625 Simms St., Lakewood, CO 80215, (303) 238-8161; Facility Type: Alzheimer's; Beds: ICF 57; Alzheimer's 57; Certified: Medicaid; Owner: Private; License: Current state

Glen Ayr Health Center
1655 Eaton St., Lakewood, CO 80214, (303) 238-5363; Facility Type: Skilled care; ICF; Alzheimer's; Beds: Skilled care 40; ICF 50; ICF/MR; Certified: Medicaid; Medicare; Owner: Private; License: Current state

Grand Oaks Care Center
1150 Oak St., Lakewood, CO 80215, (303) 238-7505; Facility Type: Skilled care; ICF; Alzheimer's; Beds: Skilled care 144; Certified: Medicaid; Medicare; Owner: Proprietary/Public corp.; License: Current state

Lakeridge Care Center—Ltd.
1655 Yarrow St., Lakewood, CO 80215, (303) 238-1275; Facility Type: Skilled care; ICF; Alzheimer's; Beds: Alzheimer's 24; SNF/ICF 97; Certified: Medicaid; Medicare; Owner: Solomon Health Services LLC; License: Current state

Las Animas

Bent County Memorial Nursing Home
Facility Type: Skilled care; ICF; Alzheimer's; Beds: Skilled care 30; Alzheimer's 30; Certified: Medicaid; Medicare; Veterans; Owner: Nonprofit corp.; License: Current state

Littleton

Christian Living Campus—Johnson Center
5000 E Arapahoe Rd., Littleton, CO 80122, (303) 779-5000; Facility Type: Skilled care; Alzheimer's; Beds: Skilled care 65; Alzheimer's 28; Certified: Medicaid; Medicare; Owner: Alzheimer's treatment; Alzheimer's secured unit; Re-

tirement facility; Life care community; License: Current state

Longmont

Life Care Center of Longmont
2451 Pratt St., Longmont, CO 80501, (303) 776-5000; Facility Type: Skilled care; Alzheimer's; Beds: Skilled care 187; Certified: Medicaid; Medicare; Owner: Life Care Centers of America; License: Current state

The Peaks Care Center
1440 Coffman St., Longmont, CO 80501, (303) 776-2814; Facility Type: Skilled care; ICF; Alzheimer's; Beds: Skilled care 8; ICF 75; Alzheimer's 16; SNF/ICF 75; Certified: Medicaid; Medicare; Owner: Private; License: Current state

Mancos

The Valley Inn
211 Third Ave., Mancos, CO 81328, (970) 533-9031; Facility Type: Skilled care; Alzheimer's; Beds: Skilled care 110; Alzheimer's; Certified: Medicaid; Medicare; Veterans; Owner: Private; License: Current state

Monte Vista

Mountain Meadows Nursing Center
2277 East Dr., Monte Vista, CO 81144, (719) 852-5138; Facility Type: Skilled care; ICF; Alzheimer's; Beds: Alzheimer's 16; SNF/ICF 44; Certified: Medicaid; Medicare; Owner: Proprietary/Public corp.; License: Current state

Montrose

San Juan Living Center
1043 Ridge St., Montrose, CO 81401, (970) 249-9638; Facility Type: Skilled care; Alzheimer's; Beds: Skilled care 104; Certified: Medicaid; Medicare; Owner: Mariner Post Acute Network; License: n/a

Morrison

SunBridge Bear Creek Care & Rehabilitation
150 Spring St., Morrison, CO 80465, (303) 697-8181; Facility Type: Skilled care; Alzheimer's; Beds: Skilled care 163; Alzheimer's; Medicare; Certified: Medicaid; Medicare; Veterans; Owner: Sun Healthcare Group Inc.; License: Current state

Palisade

Palisade Living Center
151 E 3rd St., Palisade, CO 81526, (970) 464-7500; Facility Type: Skilled care; Alzheimer's; Beds: Skilled care 24; Certified: Medicaid; Medicare; Veterans; Owner: Proprietary/Public corp.; License: Current state

Pueblo

Minnequa Midecenter Inc.
2701 California St., Pueblo, CO 81004, (719) 561-1300; Facility Type: Skilled care; Alzheimer's; Beds: Skilled care 15; Alzheimer's 20; Ins; Priv; Medicaid; Certified: Medicaid; Medicare; Veterans; Owner: Mariner Post Acute Network; License: Current state

University Park Care Center
945 Desert Flower Blvd., Pueblo, CO 81001, (719) 545-5321; Facility Type: Skilled care; Alzheimer's; Beds: Skilled care 173; Alzheimer's 21; Certified: Medicaid; Medicare; Owner: Proprietary/Public corp.; License: Current state

Westwind Special Care Center
1610 Scranton Ave., Pueblo, CO 81004, (719) 564-5161; Facility Type: Skilled care; Alzheimer's; Beds: Skilled care 49; Certified: Medicaid; Medicare; Owner: Private; License: Current state

Rocky Ford

Pioneer Health Care Center
900 S 12th St., Rocky Ford, CO 81067, (719) 254-3314; Facility Type: Skilled care; Alzheimer's; Beds: Skilled care 101; Certified: Medicaid; Medicare; Veterans; Owner: Nonprofit corp.; License: Current state

Salida

Columbine Manor Care Center
530 W 16th St., Salida, CO 81201, (719) 539-6112; Facility Type: Skilled care; Alzheimer's; Beds: Skilled care 100; Certified: Medicaid; Medicare; Owner: Life Care Centers of America; License: n/a

Springfield

Southeast Colorado Hospital & Long Term Care Center
373 E 10th Ave., Springfield, CO 81073, (719) 523-4501; Facility Type: ICF; Alzheimer's; Beds: ICF 40; Alzheimer's 16; Certified: Medicaid; Owner: Government/State/Local; License: Current state

Thornton

Elms Haven Care Center
12080 Bellaire Wy., Thornton, CO 80501, (303)

450-2700; Facility Type: Skilled care; Alzheimer's; Beds: Skilled care 242; Certified: Medicaid; Medicare; Owner: Peak Medical Corporation

Trinidad

Trinidad State Nursing Home
409 Benedicta Ave., Trinidad, CO 81082, (719) 846-9291; Facility Type: Skilled care; ICF; Alzheimer's; Beds: Skilled care 176; ICF; Certified: Medicaid; Owner: Government/State/Local; License: Current state

Walsenburg

Colorado State Veterans Nursing Home—Walsenburg
23500 US Hwy 160, Walsenburg, CO, 81089, (719) 738-5100; Facility Type: Skilled care; Alzheimer's; Beds: Skilled care 100; Alzheimer's 20; Certified: Medicaid; Veterans; Owner: Nonprofit corp.; License: Current state

Westminster

Creek Care Center
7481 Knox Pl., Westminster, CO 80030, (303) 427-7101; Facility Type: Skilled care; ICF; Alzheimer's; Beds: Skilled care 108; Certified: Medicaid; Medicare; Owner: Proprietary/Public corp.; License: Current state

Park Forest Care Center Inc.
7045 Stuart St., Westminster, CO 80030, (303) 427-7045; Facility Type: ICF; ICF/MR; Alzheimer's; Beds: ICF 103; Certified: Medicaid; Veterans; Owner: Proprietary/Public corp.; License: Current state

Wheat Ridge

Mountain Vista Health Center
4800 Tabor St., Wheat Ridge, CO 80033, (303) 421-4161; Facility Type: Skilled care; Alzheimer's; Beds: Skilled care 168; Certified: Medicaid; Medicare; Owner: Nonprofit corp.; License: Current state

Wheat Ridge Manor
2920 Fenton St., Wheat Ridge, CO 80214, (303) 238-0481; Facility Type: Skilled care; ICF; Alzheimer's; Beds: SNF/ICF 69; Certified: Medicaid; Medicare; Owner: Proprietary/Public corp.; License: Current state

Windsor

Windsor Health Care Center
710 3rd St., Windsor, CO 80550, (970) 686-7474; Facility Type: Skilled care; Alzheimer's; Beds: Skilled care 64; ICF; Alzheimer's 26; Mental health 26; Certified: Medicaid; Medicare; Veterans; Owner: Proprietary/Public corp.; License: Current state

CONNECTICUT

Avon

Avon Convalescent Home
652 W Avon Rd., Avon, CT 06001, (860) 673-2521; Facility Type: Skilled care; Alzheimer's; Beds: n/a; Certified: Medicaid; Medicare; Owner: Private; License: Current state

Bloomfield

Bloomfield Health Care Center
355 Park Ave., Bloomfield, CT 06002, (860) 242-8595; Facility Type: Skilled care; ICF; ICF/MR; Alzheimer's; Beds: Skilled care 120; Certified: Medicaid; Medicare; Veterans; Owner: Private; License: Current state

Mediplex of Greater Hartford
160 Coventry St., Bloomfield, CT 06002, (860) 243-2995; Facility Type: Skilled care; ICF; Alzheimer's; Beds: Skilled care 113; Certified: Medicaid; Medicare; Veterans; Owner: Sun Healthcare Group Inc.; License: Current state

Bridgeport

3030 Park Health Center
3030 Park Ave., Bridgeport, CT 06604, (203) 374-5611; Facility Type: Skilled care; ICF; Alzheimer's; Beds: Skilled care 58; ICF 42; Retirement 286; Certified: Medicaid; Medicare; Owner: Nonprofit/Religious organization

Bridgeport Health Care Center Inc.
600 Bond St., Bridgeport, CT 06610, (203) 384-6400; Facility Type: Skilled care; Alzheimer's; Beds: Skilled care 300; Specialty rehab; IVs; Certified: Medicaid; Medicare; Veterans; Owner: Private; License: Current state

Bristol

Nursing Care Center of Bristol
61 Bellevue Ave., Bristol, CT 06010, (860) 589-1682; Facility Type: Skilled care; ICF; Alzheimer's; Beds: Skilled care 132; Certified: Medicaid; Medicare; Owner: Eden Park Management Inc.; License: Current state

Sheriden Woods Health Care Center
321 Stonecrest Dr., Bristol, CT 06010, (860) 583-1827; Facility Type: Skilled care; Alzheimer's; Beds: Skilled care 116; SNF/ICF 30; Certified: Medicaid; Medicare; Veterans; Owner: Proprietary/Public corp.; License: Current state

Colchester

Harrington Court
59 Harrington Ct., Colchester, CT 06415, (860) 537-2339; Facility Type: Skilled care; ICF; ICF/MR; Alzheimer's; Beds: Skilled care 100; ICF 30; Certified: Medicaid; Medicare; Owner: Proprietary/Public corp.; License: Current state

Danbury

Filosa Convalescent Home Inc.
13 Hakim St., Danbury, CT 06810, (203) 744-3366; Facility Type: Skilled care; Alzheimer's; Beds: Skilled care 64; Short-term rehab; Certified: Medicaid; Medicare; Owner: Proprietary/Public corp.; License: Current state

Pope John Paul II Center for Health
Care 33 Lincoln Ave., Danbury, CT 06810, (203) 797-8300; Facility Type: Skilled care; ICF; Alzheimer's; Beds: Skilled care 98; ICF 32; Certified: Medicaid; Medicare; Owner: Nonprofit/Religious organization; License: Current state

Durham

Twin Maples Home
809R New Haven Rd., Durham, CT 06422, (860) 349-1041; Facility Type: ICF; Alzheimer's; Beds: ICF 44; Certified: Medicaid; Veterans; Owner: Proprietary/Public corp.; License: Current state

East Hartford
Riverside Health & Rehabilitation Center
745 Main St., East Hartford, CT 06108, (860) 289-2791; Facility Type: Skilled care; Alzheimer's; Beds: Skilled care 255; Alzheimer's 46; Certified: Medicaid; Medicare; Veterans; Owner: Proprietary/Public corp.; License: Current state

Greenwich

Greenwich Laurelton Nursing & Convalescent Home
PO Box 11029, Greenwich, CT 06831, (203) 531-8300; Facility Type: Skilled care; Alzheimer's; Beds: Skilled care 75; Certified: Medicaid; Medicare; Owner: Proprietary/Public corp.; License: Current state

Nathaniel Witherell
70 Parsonage Rd., Greenwich, CT 06836, (203) 869-4130; Facility Type: Skilled care; Alzheimer's; Beds: Skilled care 202; Certified: Medicaid; Medicare; Owner: Government/State/Local; License: Current state

Hamden

Hamden Health Care Center
1270 Sherman Ln., Hamden, CT 06514, (203) 281-7555; Facility Type: Skilled care; Alzheimer's; Beds: Skilled care 137; Certified: Medicaid; Medicare; Owner: Proprietary/Public corp.; License: Current state

Hartford

Ellis Manor
210 George St., Hartford, CT 06114, (860) 296-9166; Facility Type: Skilled care; ICF; ICF/MR; Alzheimer's; Beds: skilled care 105; Certified: Medicaid; Medicare; Owner: Affinity health Care Group; License: Current state

Middletown

Harbor Hill Care Center Inc.
111 Church St., Middletown, CT 06457, (860) 347-7286; Facility Type: Skilled care; Alzheimer's; Beds: Skilled care 90; Alzheimer's 30; SNF/ICF; Certified: Medicaid; Medicare; Owner: Private; License: Current state

Wadsworth Glen Health Care & Rehabilitation Center
30 Boston Rd., Middletown, CT 06457, (860) 346-9299; Facility Type: Skilled care; ICF; Alzheimer's; Beds: Skilled care 59; ICF 15; Certified: Medicaid; Medicare; Owner: Proprietary/Public corp.; License: n/a

Mystic Manor
475 High St., Mystic, CT 06355, (860) 536-6070; Facility Type: Skilled care; Alzheimer's; Beds: Skilled care 100; Certified: Medicaid; Medicare; Owner: Proprietary/Public corp.; License: Current state

Glendale Nursing & Rehabilitation
4 Hazel Ave., Naugatuck, CT 06770, (203) 723-

1456; Facility Type: Skilled care; ICF; Alzheimer's; Beds: Skilled care 120; Certified: Medicaid; Medicare; Owner: Genesis ElderCare; License: Current state

New Canaan

Jewish Home for the Aged Inc.
169 Davenport Ave., New Haven, CT 06519, (203) 789-0071; Facility Type: Skilled care; Alzheimer's; Beds: Skilled care 225; Certified: Medicaid; Medicare; Owner: Nonprofit corp.; License: Current state

West Rock Health Care Facility
34 Level St., New Haven, CT 06515 (203) 389-9744, Facility Type: ICF; ICF/MR; Alzheimer's; Beds: ICF 90; Certified: n/a; Owner: Proprietary/Public corp.; License: Current state

Norwich

Hamilton Rehabilitation & Healthcare Center
50 Palmer St., Norwich, CT 06360, (860) 889-8358; Facility Type: Skilled care; ICF; Alzheimer's; Beds: Alzheimer's 60; SNF/ICF 100; Certified: Medicaid; Medicare; Owner: Vencor Inc.; License: Current state

Old Saybrook

Saybrook Convalescent Hospital Inc.
1775 Boston Post Rd., Old Saybrook, CT 06475, (860) 399-6216; Facility Type: Skilled care; Alzheimer's; Beds: Skilled care 120; Certified: Medicaid; Medicare; Owner: Proprietary/Public corp.; License: Current state

Rocky Hill

Elm Hill Nursing Center
45 Elm St., Rocky Hill, CT 06067, (860) 529-8661; Facility Type: Skilled care; Alzheimer's; Beds: Skilled care 122; Certified: Medicaid; Medicare; Owner: Apple Health Care; License: Current state

West Hill Nursing Home
60 West St., Rocky Hill, CT 06067, (860) 529-2521; Facility Type: Skilled care; Alzheimer's; Beds: Skilled care 120; Alzheimer's; SNF/ICF; Certified: Medicaid; Medicare; Veterans; Owner: Private; License: Current state

Simsbury

Harborside Healthcare—Governor's House
36 Firetown Rd., Simsbury, CT 06070, (860) 658-1018; Facility Type: Skilled care; ICF; Alzheimer's; Beds: Skilled care 73; Certified: Medicaid; Medicare; Owner: Harborside Healthcare; License: Current state

South Windsor

Roncalli Health Center
1060 Main St., South Windsor, CT 06074, (860) 289-7771; Facility Type: Skilled care; Alzheimer's; Beds: Skilled care 120; Certified: Medicaid; Medicare; Owner: Nonprofit/Religious organization; License: Current state

Stamford

Courtland Gardens Health Center
53 Courtland Ave., Stamford, CT 06902, (203) 353-6118; Facility Type: Skilled care; ICF; Alzheimer's; Beds: Skilled care 180; Certified: Medicaid; Medicare; Owner: Vencor Inc.; License: Current state

Smith House Health Care Center
88 Rockrommon Rd., Stamford, CT 06903, (203) 322-3428; Facility Type: Skilled care; Alzheimer's; Beds: Skilled care 128; Alzheimer's; SNF/ICF; Certified: Medicaid; Medicare; Owner: Government/State/Local; License: Current state

Torrington

Wolcott Hall for Special Care
215 First St., Torrington, CT 06790, (860) 482-8554; Facility Type: Skilled care; ICF/MR; Alzheimer's; Beds: Skilled care 70; Rehab; Respite; Hosp 20; Certified: Medicaid; Medicare; Owner: Apple Health Care; License: Current state

Vernon

Vernon Manor Health Care Center
180 Regan Rd., Vernon, CT 06066, (860) 871-0385; Facility Type: Skilled care; Alzheimer's; Beds: Skilled care 120; Sub-acute; Hospice; Certified: Medicaid; Medicare; Owner: Proprietary/Public corp.; License: Current state

Wallingford

Regency House of Wallingford
181 E Main St., Wallingford, CT 06492, (203) 265-1661; Facility Type: Skilled care; Alzheimer's; Beds: Skilled care 86; Alzheimer's 44 Certified: Medicaid; Medicare; Owner: Proprietary/Public corp.; License: n/a

Waterbury

Cheshire House Health Care Facility & Rehabilitation Center

3396 E Main St., Waterbury, CT 06705, (203) 754-2161; Facility Type: Skilled care; Alzheimer's; Beds: Skilled care 60; Certified: Medicaid; Medicare; Owner: Private; License: Current state

Greenery Rehabilitation Center at Waterbury
177 Whitewood Rd., Waterbury, CT 06708, (203) 757-9491; Facility Type: Skilled care; ICF; Alzheimer's; Beds: Skilled care 180; Certified: Medicaid; Medicare; Veterans; Owner: Proprietary/Public corp.; License: Current state

West Hartford

Brookview Health Care Facility
130 Loomis Dr., West Hartford, CT 06107, (860) 521-8700; Facility Type: Skilled care; ICF; Alzheimer's; Beds: Skilled care 172; ICF 8; Certified: Medicaid; Medicare; Owner: Proprietary/Public corp.; License: n/a

Hebrew Home & Hospital Inc.
1 Abrahms Blvd., West Hartford, CT 06117, (860) 523-3800; Facility Type: Skilled care; Alzheimer's; Beds: Skilled care 334; Cardiac disease; Certified: Medicaid; Medicare; Owner: Nonprofit corp.; License: Current state

Wilton

Wilton Meadows Health Care Center
439 Danbury Rd., Rte. 7, Wilton, CT 06987, (203) 834-0199; Facility Type: Skilled care; ICF; Alzheimer's; Beds: Skilled care 112; ICF 2; Alzheimer's 34; Certified: Medicaid; Medicare; Owner: Private; License: Current state

Windsor

Windsor Rehabilitation & Healthcare Center
581 Poquonock Ave., Windsor, CT 06095, (860) 688-7211; Facility Type: Skilled care; Alzheimer's; Beds: Skilled care 120; Alzheimer's 30; Hospice; Certified: Medicaid; Medicare; Veterans; Owner: Vencor Inc.; License: Current state

DELAWARE

Dover

Capitol Healthcare Services
1225 Walker Rd., Dover, DE 19904 Facility Type: Skilled care; ICF; ICF/MR; Alzheimer's; Beds: Skilled care 30; ICF 60; Alzheimer's 30; Certified: Medicaid; Medicare; Veterans; Owner: Private; License: Current state

Courtland Manor Nursing & Convalescent Home
889 S Little Creek Rd., Dover, DE 19901, (302) 674-0566; Facility Type: Skilled care; ICF; Alzheimer's; Beds: SNF/ICF 100; Certified: Medicaid; Medicare; Veterans; Owner: Private; License: Current state

Westminster Village Health Care
1175 McKee Rd., Dover, DE 19904, (302) 674-8030; Facility Type: Skilled care; ICF; Alzheimer's; Beds: Alzheimer's; SNF/ICF 59; Certified: Medicaid; Medicare; Veterans; Owner: Nonprofit corp.; License: Current state

Georgetown

Harrison House of Georgetown
110 W North St., Georgetown, DE 19947, (302) 856-4574; Facility Type: Skilled care; ICF; ICF/MR; Alzheimer's; Beds: Alzheimer's; SNF/ICF 109; Certified: Medicaid; Medicare; Veterans; Owner: Proprietary/Public corp.; License: Current state

Hockessin

Saint Francis Care Center at Brackenville
100 S Claire Dr., Hockessin, DE 19707, (302) 234-5420; Facility Type: Skilled care; ICF; Alzheimer's; Beds: Skilled care 29; ICF 71; Alzheimer's; Secured unit 20; Certified: Medicaid; Medicare; Veterans; Owner: Catholic Health Initiatives; License: n/a

Milford

Milford Center—Genesis ElderCare Network
700 Marvel Rd., Milford, DE 19963, (302) 422-3303; Facility Type: Skilled care; ICF; Alzheimer's; Beds: Skilled care 50; ICF 54; Alzheimer's 32; Residential care; Certified: Medicaid; Medicare; Owner: Genesis ElderCare; License: Current state

Wilmington

Foulk Manor South
407 Foulk Rd., Wilmington, DE 19803, (302) 855-6249; Facility Type: ICF; Alzheimer's; Beds: ICF 57; Respite; Assisted 51; Certified: n/a; Owner: Marriott Senior Living Services; License: Current state license

Hillside Center
810 S Broom St., Wilmington, DE 19805, (302) 652-1181; Facility Type: Skilled care; ICF; Alzheimer's; Beds: Skilled care 34; ICF 72; Certified: Medicaid; Medicare; Veterans; Owner: Genesis ElderCare; License: Current state

Milton & Hattie Kutz Home
704 River Rd., Wilmington, DE 19809, (302) 764-7000; Facility Type: Skilled care; ICF; Alzheimer's; Beds: SNF/ICF 90; Certified: Medicaid; Medicare; Owner: Nonprofit corp.; License: Current state

Parkview Nursing & Rehab
2801 W 6th St., Wilmington, DE 19805, (302) 655-6135; Facility Type: Skilled care; ICF; Alzheimer's; Beds: Skilled care; ICF 56; Alzheimer's 34; SNF/ICF; Swing beds 50; Certified: Medicaid; Medicare; Veterans; Owner: Genesis Eldercare; License: Current state

DISTRICT OF COLUMBIA

Washington

Washington Center for Aging Services
2601 18th St., NE Washington, DC 20018 (202) 541-6200; Facility Type: Skilled care; ICF; Alzheimer's; Beds: Skilled care 31; ICF 209; Alzheimer's 23; Certified: Medicaid; Medicare; Owner: Government/State/Local; License: Current state

The Washington Home & Hospice of Washington
3720 Upton St., NW Washington, DC 20016, (202) 966-3720; Facility Type: Skilled care; Alzheimer's; Beds: Skilled care 117; Alzheimer's 39; Hospice; Respite 9; Certified: Medicaid; Medicare; Owner: Genesis ElderCare; License: Current state

FLORIDA

Altamonte Springs

Life Care Center of Altamonte Springs
989 Orienta Ave., Altamonte Springs, FL 32701, (407) 831-3446; Facility Type: Skilled care; ICF; Alzheimer's; Beds: Skilled care 240; Certified: Medicaid; Medicare; Veterans; Owner: Proprietary/Public corp.; License: Current state

Apalachicola

Apalachicola Health Care Center Inc.
150 10th St., Apalachicola, FL 32320, (850) 653-8844; Facility Type: Skilled care; ICF; Alzheimer's; Beds: Skilled care 60; Certified: Medicaid; Medicare; Veterans; Owner: Private; License: Current state

Atlantic Beach

Fleet Landing
1 Fleet Landing Blvd., Atlantic Beach, FL 32233, (904) 246-9900; Facility Type: Skilled care; ICF; Alzheimer's; Beds: Skilled care 60; Alzheimer's 20; CCRC; Certified: Medicare; Veterans; Owner: Nonprofit corp.; License: Current state

Avon Park

The Oaks at Avon
1010 US 27 N, Avon Park, FL 33825, (863) 453-5200; Facility Type: Skilled care; Alzheimer's; Beds: Skilled care 82; Alzheimer's 22; Certified: Medicaid; Medicare; Owner: Proprietary/Public corp.; License: Current state

Boca Raton

Avante at Boca Raton Inc.
1130 NW 15th St., Boca Raton, FL 33486, (561) 394-6282; Facility Type: Skilled care; ICF; Alzheimer's; Beds: Skilled care 120; ICF 75; Alzheimer's 15; Assisted living 75; Certified: Medicaid; Medicare; Owner: Avante Group; License: Current state

Heartland Health Care Center of Boca Raton
722 Boca Del Mar Dr., Boca Raton, FL 33433, (561) 362-9644; Facility Type: Skilled care; ICF; Alzheimer's; Beds: Skilled care 19; ICF 31; Alzheimer's 20; Certified: Medicare; Owner: HCR Manor Care; License: Current state

Boynton Beach

Heartland Health Care Center of Boynton

3600 Old Boynton Rd., Boynton Beach, FL 33436, (561) 736-9992; Facility Type: Skilled care; Alzheimer's; Beds: Alzheimer's 120; Certified: Medicaid; Medicare; Owner: HCR Manor Care; License: Current state

Bradenton

Casa Mora Rehabilitation & Extended Care
1902 59th St., W Bradenton, FL 34209, (941) 761-1000; Facility Type: Skilled care; ICF; Alzheimer's; Beds: Skilled care 240; ICF; Alzheimer's; SNF/ICF; Certified: Medicaid; Medicare; Owner: Proprietary/Public corp.; License: Current state

The Shores
1700 3rd Ave., W Bradenton, FL 34205, (941) 748-1700; Facility Type: Skilled care; Alzheimer's; Beds: Skilled care 21; Certified: n/a; Owner: Senior Life Style; License: Current state

Brooksville

Brooksville Healthcare Center
114 Chatman Blvd., Brooksville, FL 34601, (352) 796-67-1; Facility Type: Skilled care; ICF; Alzheimer's; Beds: Skilled care; SNF/ICF 180; Certified: Medicaid; Medicare; Veterans; Owner: Private; License: Current state

Clearwater

Westchester Gardens Rehabilitation & Care Center
3301 McMullen Booth Rd., Clearwater, FL 33761, (727) 785-8335; Facility Type: Skilled care; ICF; Alzheimer's; Beds: Skilled care 120; Certified: Medicaid; Medicare; Owner: Private; License: Current state

Dade City

Pasco Nursing
14433 N 5th St., Dade City, FL 33525, (352) 567-1978; Facility Type: Skilled care; ICF; Alzheimer's; Beds: Skilled care 40; Certified: Medicaid; Medicare; Owner: Proprietary/Public corp.; License: Current state

Daytona Beach

Halifax Convalescent Center Ltd.
820 N Clyde Morris Blvd., Daytona Beach, FL 32117, (904) 274-5020; Facility Type: Skilled care; ICF; Alzheimer's; Beds: Skilled care 120; Certified: Medicaid; Medicare; Owner: Private; License: Current state

Indigo Manor
595 Williamson Blvd., Daytona Beach, FL 32114, (904) 257-4400; Facility Type: Skilled care; ICF; Alzheimer's; Beds: Skilled care 166; ICF 60; ACLF; Certified: Medicaid; Medicare; Veterans; Owner: Private; License: Current state

Olds Hall Good Samaritan Center
325 S Segrave St., Daytona Beach, FL 32114, (904) 253-6791; Facility Type: Skilled care; ICF; Alzheimer's; Beds: Skilled care 60; ICF 30; Alzheimer's 30; Retire; Assisted; Certified: Medicaid; Medicare; Owner: Nonprofit/Religious org.; License: Current state

DeLand

Age Institute of Florida
545 W Euclid Ave., DeLand, FL 32720, (904) 734-9085; Facility Type: Skilled care; ICF; Alzheimer's; Beds: Skilled care 60; Certified: Medicaid; Medicare; Veterans; Owner: Genesis ElderCare; License: Current state

Mariner Health Care of DeLand
1200 N Stone St., DeLand, FL 32720, (904) 734-6200; Facility Type: Skilled care; Alzheimer's; Beds: Skilled care 130; Alzheimer's 50; Certified: Medicaid; Medicare; Owner: Private; License: Current state

Delray Beach

Harbour's Edge Health Center
401 E Linton Blvd., Delray Beach, FL 33483, (561) 272-7979; Facility Type: Skilled care; Alzheimer's; Beds: Skilled care 54; Certified: Medicare; Owner: Nonprofit corp.; License: Current state

Dunedin

Spanish Gardens Nursing & Rehabilitation Center
1061 Virginia St., Dunedin, FL 34698, (727) 733-4189; Facility Type: Skilled care; ICF; Alzheimer's; Beds: Skilled care 93; ICF; SNF/ICF; Retirement 16; Certified: Medicaid; Medicare; Veterans; Owner: Proprietary/Public corp.; License: Current state

Fort Lauderdale

Harbor Beach Convalescent Home
1615 S Miami Rd., Fort Lauderdale, FL 33316, (954) 523-5673; Facility Type: Skilled care; Alzheimer's; Beds: Skilled care 64; Certified: Medicaid; Medicare; Owner: Proprietary/Public corp.; License: Current state

National Health Care Center of Fort Lauderdale
2000 E Commercial Blvd., Fort Lauderdale, FL

33308, (954) 771-2300; Facility Type: Skilled care; ICF; Alzheimer's; Beds: Skilled care 169; Certified: Medicaid; Medicare; Owner: Proprietary/Public corp.; License: n/a

Fort Myers

Lee Convalescent Center
2826 Cleveland Ave., Fort Myers, FL 33901, (941) 334-1091; Facility Type: Skilled care; Alzheimer's; Beds: Skilled care 90; Alzheimer's 30; Certified: Medicaid; Medicare; Veterans; Owner: Beverly Enterprises Inc.; License: Current state

The Pavilion at Shell Point
15000 Shell Point Blvd., Fort Myers, FL 33908, (941) 415-5430; Facility Type: Skilled care; Alzheimer's; Beds: Skilled care 116; Alzheimer's 64; Assisted living; Certified: Medicare; Owner: Nonprofit/Religious org.; License: Current state

Shady Rest Care Pavilion Inc.
2310 N Airport Rd., Fort Myers, FL 33907, (941) 277-5000; Facility Type: Skilled care; Alzheimer's; Beds: Skilled care 180; Alzheimer's; Certified: Medicaid; Medicare; Owner: Nonprofit corp.; License: Current state

Fort Pierce

Beverly Healthcare & Rehabilitation Center
611 S 13th St., Fort Pierce, FL 34950, (561) 464-5262; Facility Type: Skilled care; ICF; Alzheimer's; Beds: n/a; Certified: Medicaid; Medicare; Veterans; Owner: Beverly Enterprises Inc.; License: Current state

Gainesville

Oaks Residential & Rehabilitation Center
3250 SW 41st Pl., Gainesville, FL 32608, (352) 378-1558; Facility Type: Skilled care; ICF; Alzheimer's; Beds: Skilled care 179; ICF; Alzheimer's; Certified: Medicaid; Medicare; Veterans; Owner: Proprietary/Public corp.; License: Current state

Inverness

Avante at Inverness Inc.
304 S Citrus Ave., Inverness, FL 34452, (352) 726-3141; Facility Type: Skilled care; Alzheimer's; Beds: Skilled care 104; Certified: Medicaid; Medicare; Owner: Proprietary/Public corp.; License: Current state

Mariner Health Care of Inverness
611 E Turner Camp Rd., Inverness, FL 34453, (352) 637-1130; Facility Type: Skilled care; ICF; Alzheimer's; Beds: Skilled care 116; Certified: Medicaid; Medicare; Owner: Mariner Post Acute Network; License: Current state

Jacksonville

Heartland of South Jacksonville
3648 University Blvd., S Jacksonville, FL 32216, (904) 733-7440; Facility Type: Skilled care; ICF; Alzheimer's; Beds: Skilled care 120; Certified: Medicaid; Medicare; Owner: HCR Manor Care; License: Current state

Lanier Manor
12740 Lanier Rd., Jacksonville, FL 32226, (904) 757-0600; Facility Type: Skilled care; ICF; Alzheimer's; Beds: Skilled care 120; Certified: Medicaid; Medicare; Veterans; Owner: Private; License: Current state

The Riverwood Center
2802 Parental Home Rd., Jacksonville, FL 32216, (904) 721-0088; Facility Type: Skilled care; ICF; Alzheimer's; Beds: Skilled care 240; Certified: Medicaid; Medicare; Veterans; Owner: Genesis ElderCare; License: Current state

Taylor Care Center
6535 Chester Ave., Jacksonville, FL 32217, (904) 731-8230; Facility Type: Skilled care; ICF; Alzheimer's; Beds: Skilled care 120; ICF; Alzheimer's; SNF/ICF; Certified: Medicaid; Medicare; Owner: Nonprofit corp.; License: Current state

Kissimmee

Oaks of Kissimmee
320 N Mitchell St., Kissimmee, FL 34741, (407) 847-7200; Facility Type: Skilled care; ICF; Alzheimer's; Beds: Skilled care 14; ICF 45; ICF/MR; Alzheimer's; SNF/ICF; Certified: Medicaid; Medicare; Owner: Proprietary/Public corp.; License: Current state

Lake City

NHC Health Care
920 McFarlane Ave., Lake City, FL 32025, (904) 758-4777; Facility Type: Skilled care; ICF; Alzheimer's; Beds: Skilled care; ICF; Alzheimer's 28; SNF/ICF 94; Certified: Medicaid; Medicare; Veterans; Owner: Proprietary/Public corp.; License: Current state

Lake Wales

Dove Healthcare at Lake Wales
730 N Scenic Hwy., Lake Wales, FL 33853, (863) 676-1512; Facility Type: Skilled care; ICF; Alzheimer's; Beds: Skilled care 50; ICF 25; Alzheimer's 25; Certified: Medicaid; Medicare; Veterans; Owner: Private; License: Current state

The Groves Center
512 S 11th St., Lake Wales, FL 33853, (863) 676-8502; Facility Type: Skilled care; ICF; Alzheimer's; Beds: Skilled care 22; ICF 98; Certified: Medicaid; Medicare; Veterans; Owner: Nonprofit/Religious org.; License: Current state

Lake Worth

Avante at Lake Worth
2501 North A St., Lake Worth, FL 33460, (561) 585-9301; Facility Type: Skilled care; ICF; ICF/MR; Alzheimer's; Beds: Skilled care 162; Certified: Medicaid; Medicare; Owner: Avante Group; License: Current state

Terraces of Lake Worth
1711 6th Ave., S Lake Worth, FL 33460, (561) 585-2997; Facility Type: Skilled care; ICF; Alzheimer's; Beds: Skilled care 99; Certified: Medicaid; Medicare; Owner: Proprietary/Public corp.; License: Current state

Lakeland

Highlands Lake Center
4240 Lakeland Highlands Rd., Lakeland, FL 33813, (863) 646-8699; Facility Type: Skilled care; ICF; Alzheimer's; Beds: Skilled care 179; Certified: Medicaid; Medicare; Owner: Private; License: Current state

Lakeland Hills Center
610 E Bella Vista Dr., Lakeland, FL 33805, (863) 688-8591; Facility Type: Skilled care; ICF; Alzheimer's; Beds: Skilled care 120; SNF/ICF; Certified: Medicaid; Medicare; Veterans; Owner: Genesis ElderCare; License: Current state

Tandem Health Care of Lakeland
5245 Socrum Loop Rd., N Lakeland, FL 33809, (863) 859-1446; Facility Type: Skilled care; ICF; Alzheimer's; Beds: Skilled care 120; Certified: Medicaid; Medicare; Veterans; Owner: Private; License: Current state

Largo

Sabal Palms Health Care Center
499 Alternate Keene Rd., Largo, FL 33771, (727) 586-4211; Facility Type: Skilled care; ICF; Alzheimer's; Beds: Skilled care 30; ICF 124; Alzheimer's 29; Pediatric OTC 29; Certified: Medicaid; Medicare; Owner: Private; License: Current state

Live Oak

Suwannee Health Care Center
1620 E Helvenston St., Live Oak, FL 32060, (904) 362-7860; Facility Type: Skilled care; ICF; ICF/MR; Alzheimer's; Beds: SNF/ICF 180; Certified: Medicaid; Medicare; Veterans; Owner: Beverly Enterprises Inc.; License: Current state

Melbourne

Carnegie Gardens Nursing Center
1415 S Hickory St., Melbourne, FL 32901, (321) 723-1321; Facility Type: Skilled care; ICF; Alzheimer's; Beds: Skilled care 137; Certified: Medicaid; Medicare; Owner: Proprietary/Public corp.; License: Current state

Miami

Coral Reef Nursing & Rehabilitation Center
9869 SW 152 St., Miami, FL 33157, (305) 255-3220; Facility Type: Skilled care; ICF; Alzheimer's; Beds: Skilled care 120; ICF; Alzheimer's; Certified: Medicaid; Medicare; Owner: n/a; License: Current state

Florida Club Care Center
220 Sierra Dr., Miami, FL 33179, (305) 653-8427; Facility Type: Skilled care; ICF; Alzheimer's; Beds: Skilled care 180; Certified: Medicaid; Medicare; Owner: Proprietary/Public corp.; License: Current state

Hialeah Shores
8785 NW 32nd Ave., Miami, FL 33147, (305) 691-5711; Facility Type: Skilled care; ICF; ICF/MR; Alzheimer's; Beds: Skilled care 120; Certified: Medicaid; Medicare; Owner: Private; License: Current state

Miami Jewish Home & Hospital for the Aged at Douglas Gardens
5200 NE 2nd Ave., Miami, FL 33137, (305) 751-8626; Facility Type: Skilled care; Alzheimer's; Beds: Skilled care 285; Alzheimer's 109; Rehabilitation 68; Certified: Medicaid; Medicare; Owner: Nonprofit/Religious org.; License: Current state

Monticello

Brynwood Center
Rte. 1 Box 21 Monticello, FL 32344, (850) 997-1800; Facility Type: Skilled care; ICF; Alzheimer's; Beds: Skilled care 97; ICF; Alzheimer's; Certified: Medicaid; Medicare; Owner: Nonprofit corp.; License: Current state

Naples

Harborside Healthcare—Naples
2900 12th St., N Naples, FL 34103, (941) 261-2554; Facility Type: Skilled care; ICF; ICF/MR; Alzheimer's; Beds: Skilled care 120; Certified: Medicaid; Medicare; Owner: Proprietary/Public corp.; License: Current state

New Port Richey Manor Rehabilitation & Specialty Care Center
6020 Indiana Ave., New Port Richey, FL 34653, (727) 849-7555; Facility Type: Skilled care; Alzheimer's; Beds: Skilled care 119; Certified: Medicaid; Medicare; Veterans; Owner: Proprietary/Public corp.; License: Current state

Premier Place at the Glenview
100 Glenview Pl., Naples, FL 34108, (941) 591-0011; Facility Type: Skilled care; ICF; Alzheimer's; Beds: Skilled care 35; Alzheimer's 10; SNFICF 25; Certified: Medicare; Owner: Nonprofit corp.; License: Current state

Southern Pines Nursing Center
6140 Congress St., New Port Richey, FL 34653, (727) 842-8402; Facility Type: Skilled care; Alzheimer's; Beds: Skilled care 70; Alzheimer's 50; Certified: Medicaid; Medicare; Owner: Proprietary/Public corp.; License: Current state

North Miami

Villa Marie Nursing Center
1050 NE 125th St., North Miami, FL 33161, (305) 891-8850; Facility Type: Skilled care; ICF; Alzheimer's; Beds: Skilled care 212; Certified: Medicaid; Medicare; Owner: Nonprofit corp.; License: Current state

North Miami Beach

Greynolds Park Manor Rehabilitation
17400 W Dixie Hwy., North Miami Beach, FL 33160, (305) 944-2361; Facility Type: Skilled care; Alzheimer's; Beds: Skilled care 324; Certified: Medicaid; Medicare; Veterans; Owner: Proprietary/Public corp.; License: Current state

Hampton Court Nursing & Rehabilitation
16100 NW Second Ave., North Miami Beach, FL 33169, (305) 354-8800; Facility Type: Skilled care; ICF; Alzheimer's; Beds: Skilled care 30; ICF 90; ICF/MR; Alzheimer's; SNF/ICF; Hospice; Certified: Medicaid; Medicare; Owner: Private; License: Current state

Ocala

Palm Garden of Ocala
3400 SW 27th Ave., Ocala, FL 34474, (352) 854-6262; Facility Type: Skilled care; Alzheimer's; Beds: Skilled care 180; Certified: Medicaid; Medicare; Owner: Private; License: Current state

Orlando

Guardian Care Convalescent Center
2500 W Church St., Orlando, FL 32805, (407) 295-5371; Facility Type: Skilled care; ICF; Alzheimer's; Beds: Skilled care 120; Certified: Medicaid; Medicare; Veterans; Owner: Nonprofit corp.; License: Current state

Westminster Towers
70 W Lucerne Cir., Orlando, FL 32801, (407) 841-1310; Facility Type: Skilled care; Alzheimer's; Beds: Skilled care 120; Certified: Medicaid; Medicare; Owner: Nonprofit/Religious org.; License: Current state

Panama City

GlenCove Nursing Pavilion
1027 E Business 98, Panama City, FL 32401, (850) 872-1438; Facility Type: Skilled care; ICF; Alzheimer's; Beds: Alzheimer's 54; SNFICF 61; Certified: Medicaid; Medicare; Owner: Proprietary/Public corp.; License: Current state

Wagner Rehabilitation & Nursing Center
3409 W 19th St., Panama City, FL 32405, (850) 785-0239; Facility Type: Skilled care; ICF; Alzheimer's; Beds: Skilled care 38; ICF 24; Alzheimer's; SNF/ICF; Certified: Medicaid; Medicare; Owner: Private; License: Current state

Pensacola

Cross Creek Health Care Center
10040 Hillview Rd., Pensacola, FL 32514, (850) 474-0570; Facility Type: Skilled care; ICF; Alzheimer's; Beds: Skilled care 120; Certified: Medicaid; Medicare; Owner: Private; License: Current state

Palm Garden of Pensacola
8475 University Pkwy Pensacola, FL 32514, (850) 474-1252; Facility Type: Skilled care; ICF; Alzheimer's; Beds: Skilled care 180; Certified: Medicaid; Medicare; Veterans; Owner: Proprietary/Public corp.; License: Current state

Rosewood Manor
3107 North H St., Pensacola, FL 32501, (850) 435-8400; Facility Type: Skilled care; Alzheimer's; Beds: Skilled care 33; Alzheimer's 59; SNF/ICF 63; Certified: Medicaid; Medicare; Owner: Private; License: Current state

Plantation

ManorCare Health Services
6931 W Sunrise Blvd., Plantation, FL 33313, (954) 583-6200; Facility Type: Skilled care; Alzheimer's; Beds: Skilled care 120; Certified: Medicaid; Medicare; Owner: HCR Manor Care; License: Current state

Pompano Beach

John Knox Village Health Center
661 SW 6th St., Pompano Beach, FL 33060, (954) 783-4001; Facility Type: Skilled care; ICF; Alzheimer's; Beds: Skilled care 177; ICF; Alzheimer's; Certified: Medicaid; Medicare; Owner: Nonprofit corp.; License: Current state

St. Petersburg

Bon Secours—Maria Manor Nursing & Rehabilitation Center
10300 4th St. N, St. Petersburg, FL 33716, (727) 576-1025; Facility Type: Skilled care; Alzheimer's; Beds: Skilled care 274; Alzheimer's 66; SNF/ICF; Certified: Medicaid; Medicare; Owner: Nonprofit/Religious org.; License: Current state

IHS of Saint Petersburg
811 Jackson St. N, St. Petersburg, FL 33705, (727) 896-3651; Facility Type: Skilled care; ICF; ICF/MR; Alzheimer's; Beds: Skilled care 88; Certified: Medicaid; Medicare; Veterans; Owner: Integrated Health Services Inc.; License: Current state

South Heritage Health & Rehabilitation Center
718 Lakeview Ave. S, St. Petersburg, FL 33705, (727) 894-5125; Facility Type: Skilled care; ICF; Alzheimer's; Beds: Skilled care 74; Certified: Medicaid; Medicare; Medi-Cal; Owner: ExtendiCare Health Services Inc.; License: Current state

Vencor—The Abbey
7101 9th St. N, St. Petersburg, FL 33702, (727) 527-7231; Facility Type: Skilled care; ICF; Alzheimer's; Beds: Skilled care 120; Certified: Medicaid; Medicare; Veterans; Owner: Proprietary/Public corp.; License: Current state

Sanford

Lakeview Nursing Center
919 E 2nd St., Sanford, FL 32771, (407) 322-6707; Facility Type: Skilled care; ICF; Alzheimer's; Beds: Skilled care 105; Alzheimer's; SNF/ICF; Certified: Veterans; Owner: Private; License: Current state

Sarasota

Sarasota Health Care Center
5157 Park Club Dr., Sarasota, FL 34235, (941) 377-0022; Facility Type: Skilled care; ICF; Alzheimer's; Beds: Skilled care 120; ICF; Alzheimer's; SNF/ICF; Certified: Medicaid; Medicare; Owner: Private; License: Current state

Sun City Center

Plaza West
912 American Eagle Blvd., Sun City Center, FL 33573, (813) 633-3066; Facility Type: Skilled care; ICF; Alzheimer's; Beds: Skilled care 42; Certified: Medicaid; Medicare; Owner: Private; License: Current state

Sun Terrace Health Care Center
105 Trinity Lakes Dr., Sun City Center, FL 33573, (813) 634-3324; Facility Type: Skilled care; ICF; Alzheimer's; Beds: Skilled care 120; SNF/ICF; Certified: Medicaid; Medicare; Veterans; Owner: Private; License: Current state

Tampa

Beverly Healthcare & Rehabilitative Services—Fletcher
518 W Fletcher Ave., Tampa, FL 33612, (813) 265-1600; Facility Type: Skilled care; Alzheimer's; Beds: Skilled care 120; ICF; Alzheimer's; Certified: Medicaid; Medicare; Owner: Proprietary/Public corp.; License: Current state

Palm Garden of Tampa
3612 138th Ave., Tampa, FL 33613, (813) 972-8775; Facility Type: Skilled care; ICF; Alzheimer's; Beds: Skilled care 31; ICF 95; ICF/MR 89; SNF/ICF; Certified: Medicaid; Medicare; Owner: Proprietary/Public corp.; License: Current state

University Village Nursing Center
12250 N 22nd St., Tampa, FL 33612, (813) 975-5001; Facility Type: Skilled care; ICF; Alzheimer's; Beds: Skilled care 120; Certified: Medicaid; Medicare; Veterans; Owner: Proprietary/Public corp.; License: Current state

Venice

Heritage Health Care Center—Venice
1026 Albee Farm Rd., Venice, FL 34292, (941) 484-0425; Facility Type: Skilled care; ICF; Alzheimer's; Beds: Skilled care 178; Certified: Medicaid; Medicare; Owner: Proprietary/Public corp.; License: Current state

West Palm Beach

The Joseph L Morse Geriatric Center Inc.
4847 Fred Gladstone Dr., West Palm Beach, FL 33417, (561) 471-5111; Facility Type: Skilled care; Alzheimer's; Beds: Skilled care 280; Certified: Medicaid; Medicare; Owner: Nonprofit corp.; License: Current state

Palm Garden of West Palm Beach
300 Executive Center Dr., West Palm Beach, FL

33401, (561) 471-5566; Facility Type: Skilled care; ICF; Alzheimer's; Beds: Skilled care 187; Certified: Medicaid; Medicare; Owner: Proprietary/ Public corp.; License: Current state

Winter Haven

Mariner Health Care of Winter Haven
1540 6th St. NW, Winter Haven, FL 33881, (863) 294-3055; Facility Type: Skilled care; ICF; Alzheimer's; Beds: Skilled care 120; Certified: Medicaid; Medicare; Medi-Cal; Owner: Private; License: Current state

Winter Haven Health
202 Ave. O NE, Winter Haven, FL 33881, (863) 293-3103; Facility Type: Skilled care; Alzheimer's; Beds: Skilled care 144; Certified: Medicaid; Medicare; Veterans; Owner: Proprietary/ Public corp.; License: Current state

Winter Park

Mary Lee DePugh Nursing Home
550 W Morse Blvd., Winter Park, FL 32789, (407) 644-6634; Facility Type: Skilled care; ICF; Alzheimer's; Beds: Skilled care 40; Certified: Medicaid; Medicare; Veterans; Owner: Nonprofit/Religious org.; License: Current state

Zephyrhills

Zephyr Haven Nursing Home
38250 Ave. A, Zephyrhills, FL 33541, (813) 782-5508; Facility Type: Skilled care; Alzheimer's; Beds: Skilled care 120; Alzheimer's; Certified: Medicaid; Medicare; Veterans; Owner: Nonprofit/Religious org.; License: Current state

GEORGIA

Albany

Albany Health Care Inc.
223 Third Ave., Albany, GA 31701, (912) 435-0741; Facility Type: Skilled care; ICF; Alzheimer's; Beds: Skilled care 252; Certified: Medicaid; Owner: Proprietary/public corp.; License: Current state

Alma

Twin Oaks Convalescent Center Inc.
301 S Baker St., Alma, GA 31510, (912) 632-7293; Facility Type: Skilled care; ICF; Alzheimer's; Beds: Skilled care 88; Certified: Medicaid; Medicare; Veterans; Owner: Nonprofit/Religious organization; License: Current state

Atlanta

A G Rhodes Home Inc.
350 Boulevard SE Atlanta, GA 30312, (404) 688-6731; Facility Type: Skilled care; ICF; Alzheimer's; Beds: Skilled care 138; Certified: Medicaid; Medicare; Owner: Nonprofit corp.; License: n/a

American Transitional Care—Northside
5470 Meridian Mark Rd., Atlanta, GA 30342, (404) 256-5131; Facility Type: Skilled care; ICF; Alzheimer's; Beds: Skilled care 302; Certified: Medicaid; Veterans; Owner: Beverly Enterprises Inc.; License: Current state

Budd Terrace Intermediate Care Home
1833 Clifton Rd., NE Atlanta, GA 30329, (404) 728-6500; Facility Type: ICF; Alzheimer's; Beds: ICF 250; Alzheimer's 75; Certified: n/a; Owner: Nonprofit corp.; License: Current state

Fountainview Center for Alzheimer's Disease
2631 N Druid Hills Rd., NE Atlanta, GA 30329, (404) 325-7994; Facility Type: ICF; Alzheimer's; Beds: n/a; Certified: n/a; Owner: Private; License: Current state

IHS of Atlanta at Buckhead
54 Peachtree Park Dr., Atlanta, GA 30309, (404) 351-6041; Facility Type: Skilled care; ICF; ICF/MR; Alzheimer's; Beds: Skilled care 28; ICF; Alzheimer's 31; SNF/ICF 149; Certified: Medicaid; Medicare; Owner: Private; License: Current state

Nurse Care of Buckhead
2920 Pharr Ct., S Atlanta, GA 30305, (404) 261-9043; Facility Type: Skilled care; ICF; ICF/MR: Alzheimer's; Beds: Skilled care 22; Alzheimer's 56; Certified: Medicaid; Medicare; Veterans; Owner: Private; License: Current state

Augusta

Georgia War Veterans Nursing Home
1101 15th St., Augusta, GA 30901, (706) 721-2531; Facility Type: Skilled care; ICF; Alzheimer's; Beds: Skilled care 185; Certified: n/a; Owner: Government/State/Local; License: Current state

Magnolia Hill
2122 Cumming Rd., Augusta, GA 30914, (706) 737-8258; Facility Type: Skilled care; ICF; ICF/MR; Alzheimer's; Beds: Skilled care 49; ICF; SNF/ICF; Certified: Medicaid; Medicare; Owner: Nonprofit corp.; License: Current state

Salem Nursing & Rehabilitation Center of Augusta
2021 Scott Rd., Augusta, GA 30906, (706) 793-1057; Facility Type: Skilled care; ICF; ICF/MR; Alzheimer's; Beds: Skilled Care 213; SNF/ICF; Certified: Medicaid; Medicare; Veterans; Owner: Proprietary/Public corp.; License: Current state

Byromville

Pinehill Nursing Center
712 Patterson St., Byromville, GA 31007, (912) 433-5711; Facility Type: Skilled care; ICF; Alzheimer's; Beds: Skilled care 102; Certified: Medicaid; Owner: Proprietary/Public corp.; License: Current state

Calhoun

Calhoun Health Care Center Inc.
1387 Hwy. 41 N, Calhoun, GA 30701, (706) 629-1289; Facility Type: Skilled care; ICF; ICF/MR; Alzheimer's; Beds: SNF/ICF 100; Certified: Medicaid; Medicare; Owner: Proprietary/Public corp.; License: Current state

Carrollton

Carrollton Nursing & Rehabilitation Center
2327 N Hwy. 27, Carrollton, GA 30117, (770) 834-4404; Facility Type: Skilled care; ICF; ICF/MR; Alzheimer's; Beds: Skilled care 152; Certified: Medicaid; Medicare; Owner: Integrated Health Services Inc.; License: n/a

Chatsworth

Chatsworth Health Care Center
102 Hospital Dr., Chatsworth, GA 30705, (706) 695-8313; Facility Type: Skilled care; ICF; Alzheimer's; Beds: Skilled care 20; Alzheimer's 16; Certified: Medicaid; Medicare; Veterans; Owner: n/a; License: n/a

Cleveland

Gateway Community Living Center
3201 Westmoreland Rd., Cleveland, GA 30528, (706) 865-5686; Facility Type: Skilled care; Alzheimer's; Beds: Skilled care 60; Alzheimer's; Certified: Medicaid; Medicare; Owner: Community Eldercare Services LLC; License: Current state

Columbus

Azalea Trace Nursing Center
910 Talbotton Rd., Columbus, GA 31995, (706) 323-9513; Facility Type: Skilled care; ICF; ICF/MR; Alzheimer's; Beds: Skilled care 22; ICF 88; Certified: Medicaid; Medicare; Owner: Nonprofit corp.; License: Current state

Fountain City Care & Rehabilitation
5131 Warm Springs Rd., Columbus, GA 31908, (706) 561-1371; Facility Type: Skilled care; ICF; Alzheimer's; Beds: Skilled care 28; SNF/ICF 182; Certified: Medicaid; Medicare; Owner: Sun Healthcare Group Inc.; License: Current state

Muscogee Manor & Rehabilitation Center
7150 Manor Rd., Columbus, GA 31907, (706) 561-3218; Facility Type: Skilled care; ICF; Alzheimer's; Beds: Skilled care 32; ICF 210; Certified: Medicaid; Medicare; Veterans; Owner: Government/State/Local; License: Current state

Pine Manor Nursing Home Inc.
2000 Warm Springs Rd., Columbus, GA 31908, (706) 324-2252; Facility Type: Skilled care; ICF; Alzheimer's; Beds: SNF/ICF 210; Certified: Medicaid; Medicare; Owner: Oak & Pine Manor Nursing Home Inc.; License: Current state

Commerce

Crystal Springs Nursing Home Inc.
800 Ridgeway Rd., Commerce, GA 30529, (706) 335-5118; Facility Type: Skilled care; ICF; ICF/MR; Alzheimer's; Beds: Skilled care 70; Certified: Medicaid; Owner: Proprietary/Public corp.; License: n/a

Dahlonega

Gold City Community Living Center
222 Moore's Dr., Dahlonega, GA 30533, (706) 864-3045; Facility Type: Skilled care; ICF; ICF/MR; Alzheimer's; Beds: Skilled care 102; Certified: Medicaid; Medicare; Owner: Community Eldercare Services LLC

Dalton

Ridgewood Manor
1110 Burleyson Rd., Dalton, GA 30720, (706) 226-1021; Facility Type: Skilled care; ICF; Alzheimer's; Beds: Skilled care 102; Certified: Medicaid; Medicare; Owner: Proprietary/Public corp.; License: n/a

Decatur

HCR Manor Care Health Services
2722 N Decatur Rd., Decatur, GA 30033, (404)

296-5440; Facility Type: Skilled care; Alzheimer's; Beds: Skilled care 70; Alzheimer's 21; SNF/ICF 44; Rehabilitation; Certified: Medicaid; Medicare; Medi-Cal; Owner: HCR Manor Care; License: Current state

East Point

Bonterra Nursing Center
2801 Felton Dr., East Point, GA 30344, (404) 767-7591; Facility Type: Skilled care; ICF; Alzheimer's; Beds: Skilled care 118; Certified: Medicaid; Medicare; Owner: Integrated Health Services Inc.; License: Current state

Eastman

Heart of Georgia Nursing Home
815 Legion Dr., Eastman, GA 31023, (912) 374-5571; Facility Type: Skilled care; ICF; ICF/MR; Alzheimer's; Beds: Skilled care 100; Certified: Medicaid; Medicare; Owner: Integrated Health Services Inc.; License: Current state

Elberton

Spring Valley Health Care Center Inc.
651 Rhodes Dr., Elberton, GA 30635, (706) 283-3880; Facility Type: Skilled care; ICF; Alzheimer's; Beds: Skilled care 60; Certified: Medicaid; Medicare; Owner: Private; License: Current state

Fairburn

Dogwood Health & Rehabilitation Center
7560 Butner Rd., Fairburn, GA 30213, (770) 306-7878; Facility Type: Skilled care; ICF; Alzheimer's; Beds: SNF/ICF 54; Hospice 82; Certified: Medicaid; Medicare; Veterans; Owner: Proprietary/Public corp.; License: Current state

Fairburn Health Care
178 W Campbellton St., Fairburn, GA 30213, (770) 964-1320; Facility Type: Skilled care; ICF; Alzheimer's; Beds: Skilled care 120; Certified: Medicaid; Medicare; Veterans; Owner: Proprietary/Public corp.; License: Current state

Fort Valley

Church Home for the Aged
2470 Hwy. 41 N, Fort Valley, GA 31030, (912) 987-1239; Facility Type: Skilled care; ICF; ICF/MR; Alzheimer's; Beds: Skilled care; SNF/ICF 49; Certified: Medicaid; Owner: Nonprofit/Religious organization; License: Current state

Franklin

Franklin Health Care Center
PO Box 460, Franklin, GA 30217, (706) 675-6674; Facility Type: Skilled care; ICF; ICF/MR; Alzheimer's; Beds: Skilled care 78; Certified: Medicaid; Owner: Proprietary/Public corp.; License: n/a

Gainesville

Lakeshore Heights Nursing Center
1293 Dawsonville Hwy., Gainesville, GA 30501, (770) 536-3391; Facility Type: Skilled care; Alzheimer's; Beds: Skilled care 104; Certified: Medicaid; Medicare; Veterans; Owner: UHS Pruitt Corporation; License: Current state

Greensboro

Boswell-Parker Nursing Center
1201 Siloam Rd., Greensboro, GA 30642, (706) 453-7331; Facility Type: Skilled care; ICF; ICF/MR; Alzheimer's; Beds: Skilled care 29; SNF/ICF; Certified: Medicaid; Medicare; Owner: Government/State/Local; License: Current state

Jasper

Mountainside Nursing Home
1350 E Church St., Jasper, GA 30143, (706) 692-2441; Facility Type: Skilled care; ICF; ICF/MR; Alzheimer's; Beds: Skilled care 60; Certified: Medicaid; Owner: Proprietary/Public corp.; License: Current state

Jesup

Beverly Healthcare & Rehabilitation Center—Jesup
1090 W Orange St., Jesup, GA 31545, (912) 427-6858; Facility Type: Skilled care; ICF; Alzheimer's; Beds: Skilled care 71; ICF; Alzheimer's; Certified: Medicaid; Medicare; Owner: Beverly Enterprises Inc.; License: Current state

Jonesboro

Centers for Long Term Care—Jonesboro
239 Arrowhead Blvd., Jonesboro, GA 30236, (770) 478-3013; Facility Type: Skilled care; ICF; Alzheimer's; Beds: Skilled care 103; ICF; SNF/ICF; Certified: Medicaid; Medicare; Owner: Proprietary/Public corp.; License: Current state

Keysville

Keysville Nursing & Rehabilitation Center
1005 Hwy. 88 N, Keysville, GA 30816, (706) 547-2591; Facility Type: Skilled care; ICF; Alzhei-

mer's; Beds: SNF/ICF 64; Certified: Medicaid; Medicare; Veterans; Owner: Proprietary/Public corp.; License: Current state

LaGrange

Florence Hand Home
200 Medical Dr., LaGrange, GA 30240, (706) 845-3256; Facility Type: Skilled care; ICF; ICF/MR; Alzheimer's; Beds: Skilled care 115; ICF; Certified: Medicaid; Medicare; Owner: n/a; License: Current state

Lithonia

Starcrest of Lithonia
2816 Evans Mill Rd., Lithonia, GA 30058, (770) 482-2961; Facility Type: Skilled care; ICF; Alzheimer's; Beds: Skilled care 150; Alzheimer's 32; Certified: Medicaid; Medicare; Veterans; Owner: Proprietary/Public corp.; License: Current state

Macon

Bel-Arbor Health Care
3468 Napier Ave., Macon, GA 31204, (912) 477-4464; Facility Type: Skilled care; ICF; Alzheimer's; Beds: Skilled care 104; Certified: Medicaid; Medicare; Owner: Proprietary/Public corp.; License: Current state

Bolingreen Nursing Center
529 Bolingreen Dr., Macon, GA 31210, Facility Type: ICF; ICF/MR; Alzheimer's; Beds: Skilled care 121; Certified: Medicaid; Medicare; Owner: Nonprofit/Religious organization; License: n/a

Marietta

A G Rhodes Home Inc.
900 Wylie Rd., Marietta, GA 30067, (770) 427-8727; Facility Type: Skilled care; ICF; Alzheimer's; Beds: Skilled care 130; Certified: Medicaid; Medicare; Veterans; Owner: Nonprofit corp.; License: Current state

Mancor Nursing & Rehabilitation Center
4360 Johnson Ferry Pl., Marietta, GA 30068, (770) 971-5870; Facility Type: Skilled care; ICF; Alzheimer's; Beds: Skilled care 117; Certified: Medicare; Veterans; Owner: HCR Manor Care; License: Current state

SunBridge Rehabilitation & Care Center for Marietta
50 Saine Dr., SW Marietta, GA 30060, (770) 429-8600; Facility Type: Skilled care; ICF; Alzheimer's; Beds: Skilled care 119; Certified: Medicaid; Medicare; Owner: Sun Healthcare Group Inc.; License: n/a

Monroe

Park Place Nursing Facility
1865 Bold Springs Rd., Monroe, GA 30656, (770) 267-8677; Facility Type: Skilled care; ICF; ICF/MR: Alzheimer's; Beds: Skilled care 107; Certified: Medicaid; Owner: n/a; License: n/a

Moultrie

Moultrie Nursing Center
422 5th Ave. SE, Moultrie, GA 31768, (912) 985-3637; Facility Type: Skilled care; ICF; ICF/MR: Alzheimer's; Beds: Skilled care 59; Certified: Medicaid; Owner: Health Management Resources Inc.; License: Current state

Nashville

Berrien Nursing Center
405 Laurel St., Nashville, GA 31639, (912) 686-7471; Facility Type: Skilled care; ICF; ICF/MR: Alzheimer's; Beds: Skilled care 108; Certified: Medicaid; Medicare; Owner: Proprietary/Public corp.; License: Current state

Ocilla

Palemon Gaskin Memorial Nursing Home
201 W Dismuke Ave., Ocilla, GA 31774, (912) 468-3890; Facility Type: Skilled care; ICF; Alzheimer's; Beds: Skilled care; ICF; SNF/ICF 30; Certified: Medicaid; Owner: Government/State/Local; License: Current state

Peachtree City

Southland Nursing Home
151 Wisdom Rd., Peachtree City, GA 30269, (770) 631-9000; Facility Type: Skilled care; Alzheimer's; Beds: Skilled care 152; Certified: Medicaid; Medicare; Owner: Proprietary/Public corp.; License: Current state

Pelham

Pelham Parkway Nursing Home
608 Dogwood Dr., NE Pelham, GA 31779, (912) 294-8602; Facility Type: Skilled care; Alzheimer's; Beds: Skilled care 108; Certified: Medicaid; Medicare; Owner: Nonprofit corp.; License: Current state

Powder Springs

Brian Center Nursing Care
3460 Powder Springs Rd., Powder Springs, GA 30127, (770) 439-9199; Facility Type: Skilled care; ICF; ICF/MR; Alzheimer's; Beds: Skilled care 174; Alzheimer's 34; SNF/ICF 174; Certified: Medicaid; Medicare; Veterans; Owner: Private; License: Current state

Pulaski

Pulaski Nursing Home
PO Box 118, Pulaski, GA 30451, (912) 685-5072; Facility Type: Skilled care; ICF; ICF/MR: Alzheimer's; Beds: Skilled care 88; SNF/ICF; Certified: Medicaid; Medicare; Veterans; Owner: Taylor & Bird Inc.; License: Current state

Richmond Hill

Bryan County Health & Rehabilitation Center
127 Carter St., Richmond Hill, GA, 31324; (912) 756-6131; Facility Type: Skilled care; ICF; Alzheimer's; Beds: Skilled care 64; ICF; Alzheimer's; ICF; Certified: Medicaid; Medicare; Owner: n/a; License: Current state

Rome

Fifth Avenue Health Care Center
505 N 5th Ave., Rome, GA 30165, (706) 291-0521; Facility Type: Skilled care; ICF; Alzheimer's; Beds: Skilled care 100; ICF; Alzheimer's; SNF/ICF; Certified: Medicaid; Medicare; Veterans; Owner: Proprietary/Public corp.; License: Current state

Savannah

Azalealand Nursing Home Inc.
2040 Colonial Dr., Savannah, GA 31406, (912) 354-2752; Facility Type: Skilled care; ICF; Alzheimer's; Beds: Skilled care 107; Certified: Medicare; Owner: n/a; License:

Savannah Square Health Care
1 Savannah Square Dr., Savannah, GA 31406, (912) 927-7550; Facility Type: Skilled care; ICF; ICF/MR; Alzheimer's; Beds: Skilled care 20; ICF 20; Certified: Medicare; Owner: Private; License: Current state

Snellville

Parkwood Nursing & Rehabilitation Center
3000 Lenora Church Rd., Snellville, GA 30078, (770) 972-2040; Facility Type: Skilled care; ICF; ICF/MR; Alzheimer's; Beds: Skilled care; ICF; ICF/MR; Alzheimer's; SNF/ICF 167; Certified: Medicaid; Veterans; Owner: Health Management Resources Inc.; License: Current state

Statesboro

Statesboro Nursing Home
405 S College St., Statesboro, GA 30458, (912) 764-6108; Facility Type: Skilled care; ICF; ICF/MR; Alzheimer's; Beds: Skilled care 43; ICF 46; Alzheimer's 10; Certified: Medicaid; Owner: Taylor & Bird Inc.; License: Current state

Stone Mountain

Rosemont at Stone Mountain
5160 Spring View Ave., Stone Mountain, GA 30083, (770) 498-4144; Facility Type: Skilled care; ICF; Alzheimer's; Beds: Skilled care 116; Alzheimer's 22; Certified: Medicaid; Medicare; Veterans; Owner: Private; License: Current state

Swainsboro

Swainsboro Nursing Home
PO Box 1758 Swainsboro, GA 30401, (912) 237-7022; Facility Type: Skilled care; ICF/MR; Alzheimer's; Beds: SNF/ICF 103; Certified: Medicaid; Medicare; Veterans; Owner: Taylor & Bird Inc.; License: Current state

Sylvester

Sylvester Health Care Inc.
PO Box 406 Sylvester, GA 31791, (912) 776-5541; Facility Type: Skilled care; ICF; Alzheimer's; Beds: Skilled care 117; ICF; Certified: Medicaid; Medicare; Owner: Proprietary/Public corp.; License: Current state

Thomasville

Glenn-Mor Nursing Home
10629 US Hwy. 19 S, Thomasville, GA 31792, (912) 226-8942; Facility Type: Skilled care; ICF; ICF/MR; Alzheimer's; Beds: Skilled care 85; SNF/ICF 64; Certified: Medicaid; Medicare; Veterans; Owner: Nonprofit corp.; License: Current state

Toomsboro

Toomsboro Nursing Center
210 Main St., Toomsboro, GA 31090, (912) 933-5395; Facility Type: Skilled care; ICF; ICF/MR; Alzheimer's; Beds: Skilled care 12; ICF 50; Certified: Medicaid; Medicare; Veterans; Owner: UHS Pruitt Corporation; License: n/a

Tucker

Meadowbrook Nursing Home Inc.
4608 Lawrenceville Hwy., Tucker, GA 30084, (770) 491-9444; Facility Type: Skilled care; ICF; Alzheimer's; Beds: Skilled care 144; Certified: Medicaid; Medicare; Owner: Private; License: Current state

Tybee Island

Oceanside Nursing Home
PO Box 2509, Tybee Island, GA 31328, (912) 786-4511; Facility Type: Skilled care; ICF; ICF/MR; Alzheimer's; Beds: Skilled care 79; SNF/ICF 6; Certified: Medicaid; Medicare; Owner: n/a; License: Current state

Union City

Christian City Convalescent Center
7300 Lester Rd., Union City, GA 30291, (770) 964-3301; Facility Type: Skilled care; ICF' Alzheimer's; Beds: SNF/ICF 196; Certified: Medicaid; Medicare; Veterans; Owner: Nonprofit corp; License: Current state

Valdosta

Holly Hill Nursing Home
413 Pendleton Pl., Valdosta, GA 31602, (912) 244-6968; Facility Type: Skilled care; ICF; Alzheimer's; Beds: SNF/ICF 100; Certified: Medicaid; Medicare; Owner: Proprietary/Public corp.; License: Current state

Warner Robins

Peachbelt Health & Rehabilitation Center
801 Elberta Rd., Warner Robins, GA 31093, (912) 923-3156; Facility Type: Skilled care; ICF; ICF/MR; Alzheimer's; Beds: Skilled care 106; SNF/ICF; Certified: Medicaid; Medicare; Veterans; Owner: Proprietary/Public corp; License: Current state

Waverly Hall

Oak View Home
119 Oak View St., Waverly Hall, GA 31831, (706) 582-2117; Facility Type: Skilled care; ICF; ICF/MR; Alzheimer's; Beds: Skilled care 100; Alzheimer's; Certified: Medicaid; Medicare; Owner: Golden Age Properties; License: Current state

Wrightsville

Wrightsville Manor Inc.
608 W Court St., Wrightsville, GA 31096, (912) 864-2286; Facility Type: Skilled care; ICF; Alzheimer's; Beds: Skilled care 94; Certified: Medicaid; Medicare; Veterans; Owner: Private; License: Current state

---

HAWAII

Hilo

Life Care Center of Hilo
944 W Kawailani St., Hilo, HI 96720, (808) 959-9151; Facility type: Skilled care, Alzheimer's; Beds: 250; Certified: Medicaid, Medicare; Owner: Private; License: state; Activities: Arts & Crafts; Dances; Pet therapy; Group exercise; Outings; Support Groups; Other: Alzheimer's secured unit.

Honolulu

Hale Nani Rehabilitation & Nursing Center
1677 Pensacola St., Honolulu, HI 96822, (808) 537-3371; Facility type: Skilled care, Alzheimer's; Beds: 290; Certified: Medicaid, Medicare; Owner: Proprietary/Public; License: state; Activities: Arts & Crafts; Dances; Pet therapy; Group exercise; Outings; Support Groups.

Island Nursing Home
1205 Alexander St., Honolulu, HI 96826, (808) 946-5027; Facility type: Skilled care, Alzheimer's; Beds: 50; Certified: Medicaid, Medicare; Owner: Private; License: state; Activities: Arts & Crafts; Dances; Pet therapy; Group exercise; Outings; Support Groups.

Kailua Kona

Keauhou Rehabilitation & Healthcare Center
78-6957 Kamehameha III Rd., Kailua Kona, HI 96740, (808) 322-2790; Facility type: Skilled care, Alzheimer's; Beds: 150; Certified: Medicaid, Medicare; Owner: Lenox Healthcare; License: state; Activities: Arts & Crafts; Dances; Pet therapy; Group exercise; Outings; Support Groups; Other: Alzheimer's secured unit.

Kaneohe

Aloha Nursing & Rehabilitation Center
45-545 Kamehameha Hwy., Kaneohe, HI 96744, (808) 247-2220; Facility type: Skilled care, Alzheimer's; Beds: 150; Certified: Medicaid, Medicare, Veterans; Owner: Private; License: state; Activities: Arts & Crafts; Dances; Pet therapy; Group exercise; Outings; Support Groups; Other: Adult day care.

Pohai Nani Good Samaritan Hauhale
45-090 Namoku St., Kaneohe, HI 96744, (808) 247-1670; Facility type: Skilled care, Alzheimer's; Beds: 50; Certified: Medicaid, Medicare, Veterans; Owner: Private; License: state; Activities: Arts & Crafts; Dances; Pet therapy; Group exercise; Outings; Support Groups; Other: Home health care.

Kapaau

Kohala Hospital
PO Box 10, Kapaau, HI 96775; Facility type: Skilled care, Alzheimer's; Beds: 30; Certified: Medicaid, Medicare, Veterans; Owner: State & Local Gov; License: state; Activities: Arts & Crafts; Dances; Pet therapy; Group exercise; Outings; Support Groups.

Kaunakakai

Molokai General Hospital
280 Puali St., Kaunakakai, HI 96748, (808) 553-331; Facility type: Skilled care, Alzheimer's; Beds: 30; Certified: Medicaid, Medicare, Veterans; Owner: Private; License: state; Activities: Arts & Crafts; Dances; Pet therapy; Group exercise; Outings; Support Groups; Other: Alzheimer's secured unit.

Lawai

Hale Omao
4297-C Omao Rd., Lawai, HI 96765, (808) 742-7591; Facility type: Skilled care, Alzheimer's; Beds: 80; Certified: Medicaid; Owner: Private; License: state; Activities: Arts & Crafts; Dances; Pet therapy; Group exercise; Outings; Support Groups; Other: Alzheimer's secured unit, Home health care.

IDAHO

Boise

Boise Samaritan Village Healthcare & Rehabilitation Center
3115 Sycamore Dr., Boise, ID 83703, (208) 343-7726; Facility type: Skilled care, Alzheimer's; Certified: Medicaid, Medicare, Veterans; Owner: The Evangelical Lutheran Good Samaritan Society; License: state; Activities: Arts & Crafts; Dances; Pet therapy; Group exercise; Outings.

Capitol Care Center
8211 Ustick Rd., Boise, ID 83704, (208) 375-3800; Facility type: Skilled care, Alzheimer's; Beds: 140; Certified: Medicaid, Medicare; Owner: Peak Medical Corporation; License: state; Activities: Arts & Crafts; Dances; Pet therapy; Group exercise; Outings; Support Groups; Other: Alzheimer's secured unit.

Idaho State Veteran's Home—Boise
320 Collins Rd., Boise, ID 83702, (208) 334-5000; Facility type: Skilled care, Alzheimer's; Beds: 140; Certified: Medicaid, Medicare; Owner: Peak Medical Corporation; License: state; Activities: Arts & Crafts; Dances; Pet therapy; Group exercise; Outings; Support Groups; Other: Alzheimer's secured unit.

Life Care Center of Boise
808 N Curtis, Boise, ID 83706, (208) 376-5274; Facility type: Skilled care, Alzheimer's; Beds: 160; Certified: Medicaid, Medicare, Veterans; Owner: Life Care Centers of America; License: state; Activities: Arts & Crafts; Dances; Pet therapy; Group exercise; Outings; Support Groups; Other: Alzheimer's secured unit.

Bonner's Ferry

Boundary County Nursing Home
6640 Kaniksu, Bonners Ferry, ID 83805, (208) 267-3141; Facility type: Skilled care, Alzheimer's; Beds: 100; Certified: Medicaid, Medicare; Owner: State & Local Gov; License: state; Activities: Arts & Crafts; Dances; Pet therapy; Group exercise; Outings; Support Groups; Other: Alzheimer's secured unit, Home health care.

Coeur D'Alene

LaCrosse Health & Rehabilitation Center
210 La Crosse St., Coeur D'Alene, ID 83814, (208) 664-2185; Facility type: Skilled care, Alzheimer's; Beds: 130; Certified: Medicaid, Medicare, Veterans; Owner: ExtendiCare Health Services; License: state; Activities: Arts & Crafts; Dances; Pet therapy; Group exercise; Outings;

Support Groups; Other: Alzheimer's secured unit.

Life Care Center of Coeur D'Alene
500 W Aqua Ave., Coeur D'Alene, ID 83815, (208) 762-1122; Facility type: Skilled care, Alzheimer's; Beds: 120; Certified: Medicaid, Medicare; Owner: Life Care Centers of America; License: state; Activities: Arts & Crafts; Dances; Pet therapy; Group exercise; Outings; Support Groups; Other: Alzheimer's secured unit.

Pinewood Care Center
2514 N 7th St., Coeur D'Alene, ID 83814, (208) 664-8128; Facility type: Skilled care, Alzheimer's; Beds: 110; Certified: Medicaid, Medicare; Owner: Centennial Healthcare; License: state; Activities: Arts & Crafts; Dances; Pet therapy; Group exercise; Outings; Support Groups; Other: Alzheimer's secured unit, Adult day care.

Emmett

Emmett Rehabilitation & Health Care
714 N Butte Ave., Emmett, ID 83617, (208) 365-4425; Facility type: Skilled care, Alzheimer's; Beds: 90; Certified: Medicaid, Medicare, Veterans; Owner: Vencor, Inc.; License: state; Activities: Arts & Crafts; Dances; Pet therapy; Group exercise; Outings; Support Groups; Other: Alzheimer's secured unit, Adult day care, Home health care.

Gooding

Gooding Rehabilitation & Care Center
1220 Montana St., Gooding, ID 83330, (208) 934-5601; Facility type: Skilled care, Alzheimer's; Beds: 90; Certified: Medicaid, Medicare, Veterans; Owner: Proprietary/Public; License: state; Activities: Arts & Crafts; Dances; Pet therapy; Group exercise; Outings; Support Groups; Other: Alzheimer's secured unit, Adult day care.

Idaho Falls

Idaho Falls Good Samaritan Center
840 E Elva St., Idaho Falls, ID 83401, (208) 523-4795; Facility type: Skilled care, Alzheimer's; Beds: 120; Certified: Medicaid, Medicare; Owner: Evangelical Lutheran Good Samaritan Society; License: state; Activities: Arts & Crafts; Dances; Pet therapy; Group exercise; Outings; Support Groups; Other: Alzheimer's secured unit, Adult day care, Home health care.

Life Care Center of Idaho Falls
2725 E 17th St., Idaho Falls, ID 83406, (208) 529-4567; Facility type: Skilled care, Alzheimer's; Beds: 110; Certified: Medicaid, Medicare; Owner: Life Care Centers of America; License: state; Activities: Arts & Crafts; Dances; Pet therapy; Group exercise; Outings; Support Groups; Other: Alzheimer's secured unit, Adult day care, Adult day care.

Kellogg

Mountain Valley Rehabilitation Center
601 W Cameron, Kellogg, ID 83837, (208) 784-1283; Facility type: Skilled care, Alzheimer's; Beds: 70; Certified: Medicaid, Medicare; Owner: Vencor, Inc.; License: state; Activities: Arts & Crafts; Dances; Pet therapy; Group exercise; Outings; Support Groups; Other: Adult day care.

Lewiston

The Orchards Rehabilitation & Care Center
1014 Burrell Ave., Lewiston, ID 83501, (208) 743-4558; Facility type: Skilled care, Alzheimer's; Beds: 100; Certified: Medicaid, Medicare, Veterans; Owner: Proprietary/Public; License: state; Activities: Arts & Crafts; Dances; Pet therapy; Group exercise; Outings; Support Groups; Other: Alzheimer's secured unit.

McCall

SunBridge Care & Rehabilitation for McCall
418 Floyd St., McCall, ID 83638, (208) 634-2112; Facility type: Skilled care, Alzheimer's; Beds: 70; Certified: Medicaid, Medicare, Veterans; Owner: Sun Healthcare; License: state; Activities: Arts & Crafts; Dances; Pet therapy; Group exercise; Outings; Support Groups.

Moscow

Good Samaritan Village
640 N Eisenhower St., Moscow, ID 83843, (208) 882-6560; Facility type: Skilled care, Alzheimer's; Beds: 80; Certified: Medicaid, Medicare, Veterans, Medi-Cal; Owner: Evangelical Lutheran Good Samaritan Society; License: state; Activities: Arts & Crafts; Dances; Pet therapy; Group exercise; Outings; Support Groups; Other: Alzheimer's secured unit, Home health care.

Latah Health Services Inc.
510 W Palouse River Dr., Moscow, ID 83843, (208) 882-7486; Facility type: Skilled care, Alzheimer's; Beds: 140; Certified: Medicaid, Medicare, Veterans; Owner: Nonprofit; License: state; Activities: Arts & Crafts; Dances; Pet therapy; Group exercise; Outings; Support Groups; Other: Home health care.

Nampa

Midland Care Center
436 N Midland Blvd., Nampa, ID 83651, (208) 466-7803; Facility type: Skilled care, Alzheimer's; Beds: 110; Certified: Medicaid, Medicare, Veterans; Owner: Private; License: state; Activities: Arts & Crafts; Dances; Pet therapy; Group exercise; Outings; Support Groups; Other: Alzheimer's secured unit, Adult day care.

Nampa Care Center
404 N Horton St., Nampa, ID 83651, (208) 466-9292; Facility type: Skilled care, Alzheimer's; Beds: 110; Certified: Medicaid, Medicare, Veterans; Owner: Private; License: state; Activities: Arts & Crafts; Dances; Pet therapy; Group exercise; Outings; Support Groups; Other: Alzheimer's secured unit, Adult day care.

Pocatello

Idaho State Veterans Home—Pocatello
1957 Alvin Ricken Dr., Pocatello, ID 83201, (208) 236-6340; Facility type: Skilled care, Alzheimer's; Beds: 70; Certified: Medicaid, Medicare, Veterans; Owner: State & Local Gov; License: state; Activities: Arts & Crafts; Dances; Pet therapy; Group exercise; Outings; Support Groups; Other: Alzheimer's secured unit.

Portneuf Valley Hospital Rehabilitation Center
2200 E Terry St., Pocatello, ID 83201, (208) 232-2570; Facility type: Skilled care, Alzheimer's; Beds: 70; Certified: Veterans; Owner: State & Local Gov; License: state; Activities: Arts & Crafts; Dances; Pet therapy; Group exercise; Outings; Support Groups; Other: Alzheimer's secured unit.

Saint Maries

Valley Vista Care Center
820 Elm St., Saint Maries, ID 83861, (208) 245-4576; Facility type: Skilled care, Alzheimer's; Beds: 90; Certified: Medicaid, Medicare, Veterans; Owner: Nonprofit; License: state; Activities: Arts & Crafts; Dances; Pet therapy; Group exercise; Outings; Support Groups; Other: Alzheimer's secured unit.

Silverton

Silver Wood Good Samaritan Center
7th St., Box 358, Silverton, ID 83867, (208) 556-1147; Facility type: Skilled care, Alzheimer's; Beds: 70; Certified: Medicaid, Medicare, Veterans; Owner: Evangelical Lutheran Good Samaritan Society; License: state; Activities: Arts & Crafts; Dances; Pet therapy; Group exercise; Outings; Support Groups; Other: Alzheimer's secured unit.

Twin Falls

SunBridge Care
640 Filer Ave. W, Twin Falls, ID 83301, (208) 734-8645; Facility type: Skilled care, Alzheimer's; Beds: 170; Certified: Medicaid, Medicare, Veterans; Owner: Sun Healthcare; License: state; Activities: Arts & Crafts; Dances; Pet therapy; Group exercise; Outings; Support Groups; Other: Alzheimer's secured unit, Adult day care.

ILLINOIS

Aledo

Lynncrest Manor
304 SW 12th St., Aledo, IL 61231, (309) 582-5376; Facility type: Skilled care, Alzheimer's; Beds: 100; Certified: Medicaid, Medicare, Veterans; Owner: Nonprofit; License: state; Activities: Arts & Crafts; Dances; Pet therapy; Group exercise; Outings; Support Groups; Other: Alzheimer's secured unit, Adult day care.

Arlington Heights

Lutheran Home for the Aged
800 W Oakton St., Arlington Heights, IL 60004, (847) 253-3710; Facility type: Skilled care, Alzheimer's; Beds: 400; Certified: Medicaid, Medicare; Owner: Private; License: state; Activities: Arts & Crafts; Dances; Pet therapy; Group exercise; Support Groups; Other: Alzheimer's secured unit, Adult day care.

Belvidere

Northwoods Health Care Center
2250 Pearl St., Belvidere, IL 61008, (815) 544-0358; Facility type: Skilled care, Alzheimer's; Beds: 140; Certified: Medicaid, Medicare; Owner: Private; License: state; Activities: Arts & Crafts; Dances; Pet therapy; Group exercise; Support Groups; Other: Alzheimer's secured unit.

Berwyn

Fairfax Nursing Home Inc.
3601 S Harlem Ave., Berwyn, IL 60402, (708) 749-4160; Facility type: Skilled care, Alzheimer's; Beds: 160; Certified: Medicaid, Medicare, Veterans; Owner: Private; License: state; Activities: Arts & Crafts; Dances; Pet therapy; Group exercise; Support Groups; Other: Alzheimer's secured unit.

Bloomingdale

Bloomingdale Pavilion
311 Edgewater Dr., Bloomingdale, IL 60108, (630) 894-7400; Facility Type: Skilled care; ICF; Alzheimer's; Beds: Skilled care 259; Alzheimer's 60; Certified: Medicaid, Medicare; Owner: Private; License: Current state

Bolingbrook

Meadowbrook Manor—Bolingbrook
431 W Remington Blvd., Bolingbrook, IL 60440, (630) 759-1112; Facility type: Skilled care, Alzheimer's; Beds: 290; Certified: Medicaid, Medicare, Veterans; Owner: Private; License: state; Activities: Arts & Crafts; Dances; Pet therapy; Group exercise; Support Groups; Other: Alzheimer's secured unit.

Buffalo Grove

Claremont Rehabilitation & Living Center
150 N Weiland Rd., Buffalo Grove, IL 60089, (847) 465-0200; Facility type: Skilled care, Alzheimer's; Beds: 200; Certified: Medicaid, Medicare; Owner: Private; License: state; Activities: Arts & Crafts; Dances; Pet therapy; Group exercise; Support Groups; Other: Alzheimer's secured unit.

Byron

The Neighbors
PO Box 585, Byron, IL 61010, (815) 235-2511; Facility type: Skilled care, Alzheimer's; Beds: 100; Certified: Medicaid, Medicare, Veterans; Owner: Proprietary/Public; License: state; Activities: Arts & Crafts; Dances; Pet therapy; Group exercise; Support Groups; Other: Alzheimer's secured unit, Adult day care.

Carlinville

CLC Centers for Long Term Care
1730 Rte. 4, Carlinville, IL 62626, (217) 854-4491; Facility type: Skilled care, Alzheimer's; Beds: 70; Certified: Medicaid, Medicare, Veterans; Owner: Proprietary/Public; License: state; Activities: Arts & Crafts; Dances; Pet therapy; Group exercise; Support Groups; Other: Alzheimer's secured unit, Adult day care.

Champaign

ManorCare at Champaign
309 E Springfield Ave., Champaign, IL 61820, (217) 352-5135; Facility type: Skilled care, Alzheimer's; Beds: 100; Certified: Medicaid, Medicare; Owner: HCR Manor Care; License: state; Activities: Arts & Crafts; Dances; Pet therapy; Group exercise; Support Groups; Other: Alzheimer's secured unit.

Chenoa

Meadows Mennonite Home
RR 1, Chenoa, IL 61726, (309) 747-2702; Facility type: Skilled care, Alzheimer's; Beds: 100; Certified: Medicaid; Owner: Nonprofit/Religious; License: state; Activities: Arts & Crafts; Dances; Pet therapy; Group exercise; Support Groups; Other: Alzheimer's secured unit.

Chicago

Alden Nursing Center—Lakeland
820 W Lawrence Ave., Chicago, IL 60640, (773) 769-2570; Facility type: Skilled care, Alzheimer's; Beds: 300; Certified: Medicaid, Medicare, Veterans; Owner: Nonprofit/Religious; License: state; Activities: Arts & Crafts; Dances; Pet therapy; Group exercise; Support Groups; Other: Alzheimer's secured unit.

Alden-Lincoln Park Rehabilitation & Health Care Center Inc.
504 W Wellington St., Chicago, IL 60657, (773) 281-6200; Facility type: Skilled care, Alzheimer's; Beds: 100; Certified: Medicaid, Medicare; Owner: Nonprofit/Religious; License: state; Activities: Arts & Crafts; Dances; Pet therapy; Group exercise; Support Groups; Other: Alzheimer's secured unit, Home health care.

Balmoral Home
2055 W Balmoral Ave., Chicago, IL 60625, (773) 561-8661; Facility type: Skilled care, Alzheimer's; Beds: 220; Certified: Medicaid, Medicare, Veterans; Owner: Proprietary/Public; License: state; Activities: Arts & Crafts; Dances; Pet therapy; Group exercise; Support Groups.

Birchwood Plaza Nursing Home
1426 W Birchwood Ave., Chicago, IL 60626, (773) 274-4405; Facility type: Skilled care, Alzheimer's; Beds: 200; Certified: Medicaid, Medicare, Veterans; Owner: Proprietary/Public;

License: state; Activities: Arts & Crafts; Dances; Pet therapy; Group exercise; Support Groups; Other: Adult day care.

Brightview Care Center Inc.
4538 N Beacon, Chicago, IL 60640, (773) 275-7200; Facility type: Skilled care, Alzheimer's; Beds: 200; Certified: Medicaid, Medicare; Owner: Proprietary/Public; License: state; Activities: Arts & Crafts; Dances; Pet therapy; Group exercise; Support Groups; Other: Alzheimer's secured unit.

Covenant Home of Chicago
2720 W Foster Ave., Chicago, IL 60625, (773) 506-6900; Facility type: Skilled care, Alzheimer's; Beds: 100; Certified: Medicaid, Medicare; Owner: Covenant Retirement Communities; License: state; Activities: Arts & Crafts; Dances; Pet therapy; Group exercise; Support Groups.

Glencrest Nursing Rehabilitation Center Ltd.
2451 W Touhy Ave., Chicago, IL 60645, (773) 338-6800; Facility type: Skilled care, Alzheimer's; Beds: 200; Certified: Medicaid, Medicare, Veterans; Owner: Health & Home Care Management; License: state; Activities: Arts & Crafts; Dances; Pet therapy; Group exercise; Support Groups; Other: Home health care.

Harmony Nursing & Rehabilitation Center
3919 W Foster Ave., Chicago, IL 60625, (773) 588-9500; Facility type: Skilled care, Alzheimer's; Beds: 80; Certified: Medicaid, Medicare, Veterans; Owner: Itex Corp; License: state; Activities: Arts & Crafts; Dances; Pet therapy; Group exercise; Support Groups; Other: Alzheimer's secured unit.

Heritage Nursing Home Inc.
5888 N Ridge Ave., Chicago, IL 60660, (773) 769-2626; Facility type: Skilled care, Alzheimer's; Beds: 120; Certified: Medicaid, Medicare; Owner: Health & Home Care Management; License: state; Activities: Arts & Crafts; Dances; Pet therapy; Group exercise; Support Groups; Other: Alzheimer's secured unit; Home health care.

IMMC Warren N Barr Pavilion
66 W Oak St., Chicago, IL 60610, (312) 337-5400; Facility type: Skilled care, Alzheimer's; Beds: 120; Certified: Medicaid, Medicare, Veterans; Owner: Health & Home Care Management; License: state; Activities: Arts & Crafts; Dances; Pet therapy; Group exercise; Support Groups; Other: Alzheimer's secured unit; Home health care, Adult day care.

Mid-America Convalescent Centers Inc.
4920 N Kenmore Ave., Chicago, IL 60640, (773) 769-2700; Facility type: Skilled care, Alzheimer's; Beds: 310; Certified: Medicaid, Medicare; Owner: Proprietary/Public License: state; Activities: Arts & Crafts; Dances; Pet therapy; Group exercise; Support Groups; Other: Alzheimer's secured unit; Adult day care.

Montgomery Place
5550 S Shore Dr., Chicago, IL 60637, (773) 753-4100; Facility type: Skilled care, Alzheimer's; Beds: 100; Certified: Medicaid, Medicare, Veterans; Owner: Nonprofit; License: state; Activities: Arts & Crafts; Dances; Pet therapy; Group exercise; Support Groups; Other: Alzheimer's secured unit; Home health care.

Northwest Home for the Aged
6300 N California Ave., Chicago, IL 60659, (773) 973-1900; Facility type: Skilled care, Alzheimer's; Beds: 160; Certified: Medicaid, Medicare; Owner: Nonprofit/Religious; License: state; Activities: Arts & Crafts; Dances; Pet therapy; Group exercise; Support Groups; Other: Alzheimer's secured unit.

Peterson Park Health Care Center
6141 N Pulaski Rd., Chicago, IL 60646, (773) 478-2000; Facility type: Skilled care, Alzheimer's; Beds: 180; Certified: Medicaid, Veterans; Owner: Nonprofit/Religious; License: state; Activities: Arts & Crafts; Dances; Pet therapy; Group exercise; Support Groups.

United Methodist Home & Care
1415 W Foster Ave., Chicago, IL 60640, (773) 769-5500; Facility type: Skilled care, Alzheimer's; Beds: 120; Certified: Medicaid, Medicare; Owner: Nonprofit/Religious; License: state; Activities: Arts & Crafts; Dances; Pet therapy; Group exercise; Support Groups; Alzheimer's secured unit.

Waterfront Terrace
7750 S Shore Dr., Chicago, IL 60649, (773) 731-4200; Facility type: Skilled care, Alzheimer's; Beds: 120; Certified: Medicaid, Veterans; Owner: Proprietary/Public License: state; Activities: Arts & Crafts; Dances; Pet therapy; Group exercise; Support Groups; Alzheimer's secured unit.

Whitestone Convalescent & Nursing Home
1901 N Lincoln Park W, Chicago, IL 60614, (312) 943-2846; Facility type: Skilled care, Alzheimer's; Beds: 90; Owner: Private; License: state; Activities: Arts & Crafts; Dances; Pet therapy; Group exercise; Support Groups; Alzheimer's secured unit.

Chicago Heights

Riviera Manor Inc.
490 W 16th Pl., Chicago Heights, IL 60411, (708) 481-4444; Facility type: Skilled care, Alz-

heimer's; Beds: 100; Certified: Medicaid, Medicare, Veterans; Owner: Nonprofit/Religious; License: state; Activities: Arts & Crafts; Dances; Pet therapy; Group exercise; Support Groups.

Chicago Ridge

Lexington of Chicago Ridge
10300 Southwest Hwy., Chicago Ridge, IL 60415, (708) 425-1100; Facility type: Skilled care, Alzheimer's; Beds: 220; Certified: Medicaid, Medicare; Owner: Nonprofit/Religious; License: state; Activities: Arts & Crafts; Dances; Pet therapy; Group exercise; Support Groups; Other: Alzheimer's secured unit, Home health care.

Danforth

Prairieview Lutheran Home
PO Box 4, Danforth, IL 60930, (815) 269-2970; Facility type: Skilled care, Alzheimer's; Beds: 90; Certified: Medicaid, Medicare; Owner: Nonprofit/Religious; License: state; Activities: Arts & Crafts; Dances; Pet therapy; Group exercise; Support Groups; Other: Alzheimer's secured unit.

De Kalb

Pine Acres Care Center
1212 S 2nd St., De Kalb, IL 60115, (815) 758-8151; Facility type: Skilled care, Alzheimer's; Beds: 120; Certified: Medicaid, Medicare; Owner: Nonprofit/Religious; License: state; Activities: Arts & Crafts; Dances; Pet therapy; Group exercise; Support Groups; Other: Alzheimer's secured unit, Adult day care.

Deerfield

The Whitehall North
300 Waukegan Rd., Deerfield, IL 60015, (847) 945-4600; Facility type: Skilled care, Alzheimer's; Beds: 120; Certified: Medicare; Owner: Nonprofit/Religious; License: state; Activities: Arts & Crafts; Dances; Pet therapy; Group exercise; Support Groups; Other: Alzheimer's secured unit.

Des Plaines

Ballard/THC PARC at 9300
9300 Ballard Rd., Des Plaines, IL 60016, (847) 294-2300; Facility type: Skilled care, Alzheimer's; Beds: 210; Certified: Medicaid, Medicare; Owner: Nonprofit/Religious; License: state; Activities: Arts & Crafts; Dances; Pet therapy; Group exercise; Support Groups; Other: Alzheimer's secured unit, Adult day care.

Lee Manor
1301 Lee St., Des Plaines, IL 60018, (847) 635-4000; Facility type: Skilled care, Alzheimer's; Beds: 280; Certified: Medicaid, Medicare; Owner: Private; License: state; Activities: Arts & Crafts; Dances; Pet therapy; Group exercise; Support Groups; Other: Alzheimer's secured unit.

Dixon

Dixon Health Care Center
141 North Ct, Dixon, IL 61021, (815) 288-1477; Facility type: Skilled care, Alzheimer's; Beds: 110; Certified: Medicaid, Medicare; Owner: Proprietary/Public; License: state; Activities: Arts & Crafts; Dances; Pet therapy; Group exercise; Support Groups; Other: Alzheimer's secured unit.

Downer's Grove

Fairview Baptist Home
250 Village Dr., Downers Grove, IL 60516, (630) 769-6200; Facility type: Skilled care, Alzheimer's; Beds: 250; Certified: Medicaid, Medicare; Owner: Nonprofit/Religious; License: state; Activities: Arts & Crafts; Dances; Pet therapy; Group exercise; Support Groups; Other: Alzheimer's secured unit, Home health care; Affiliations: Baptist Church.

Rest Haven West Christian Nursing Center
3450 Saratoga Ave., Downers Grove, IL 60515, (630) 969-2900; Facility type: Skilled care, Alzheimer's; Beds: 150; Certified: Medicaid, Medicare; Owner: Nonprofit/Religious; License: state; Activities: Arts & Crafts; Dances; Pet therapy; Group exercise; Support Groups; Other: Alzheimer's secured unit, Home health care.

East Moline

Forest Hill Health Rehabilitation
4747 11th St., East Moline, IL 61244, (309) 796-0922; Facility type: Skilled care, Alzheimer's; Beds: 140; Certified: Medicaid, Medicare; Owner: Proprietary/Public; License: state; Activities: Arts & Crafts; Dances; Pet therapy; Group exercise; Support Groups; Other: Alzheimer's secured unit, Home health care.

Edwardsville

Anna-Henry Nursing & Rehabilitation
637 Hillsboro Ave., Edwardsville, IL 62025 (618) 656-1136; Facility type: Skilled care, Alzheimer's; Beds: 40; Certified: Medicaid, Medicare, Veterans; Owner: Private; License: state; Activities: Arts & Crafts; Dances; Pet therapy; Group exercise; Support Groups; Other: Alzheimer's secured unit.

Effingham

Lakeland Healthcare Center
800 W Temple St., Effingham, IL 62401, (217) 342-2171; Facility type: Skilled care, Alzheimer's; Beds: 140; Certified: Medicaid, Medicare; Owner: Nonprofit/Religious; License: state; Activities: Arts & Crafts; Dances; Pet therapy; Group exercise; Support Groups; Other: Alzheimer's secured unit.

Eldorado

Eldorado Care Center Inc.
3rd & Railroad Sts, Eldorado, IL 62930, (618) 273-3318; Facility type: Skilled care, Alzheimer's; Beds: 70; Certified: Medicaid; Owner: Nonprofit/Religious; License: state; Activities: Arts & Crafts; Dances; Pet therapy; Group exercise; Support Groups; Other: Alzheimer's secured unit.

Elgin

ManorCare Health Services Elgin
180 S State St., Elgin, IL 60123, (847) 742-3310; Facility type: Skilled care, Alzheimer's; Beds: 80; Certified: Medicaid, Medicare; Owner: HCR Manor Care; License: state; Activities: Arts & Crafts; Dances; Pet therapy; Group exercise; Support Groups; Other: Alzheimer's secured unit, Adult day care.

Maplewood Care
50 N Jane Dr., Elgin, IL 60123, (847) 697-3750; Facility type: Skilled care, Alzheimer's; Beds: 200; Certified: Medicaid, Medicare; Owner: Proprietary/Public; License: state; Activities: Arts & Crafts; Dances; Pet therapy; Group exercise; Support Groups.

Elk Grove Village

ManorCare at Elk Grove Village
1920 Nerge Rd., Elk Grove Village, IL 60007, (847) 301-0550; Facility type: Skilled care, Alzheimer's; Beds: 190; Certified: Medicaid, Medicare; Owner: HCR Manor Care; License: state; Activities: Arts & Crafts; Dances; Pet therapy; Group exercise; Support Groups; Other: Alzheimer's secured unit, Adult day care.

Elmhurst

Elmhurst Extended Care Center Inc.
200 E Lake St., Elmhurst, IL 60126, (630) 834-4337; Facility type: Skilled care, Alzheimer's; Beds: 110; Certified: Medicaid, Medicare; Owner: Proprietary/Public; License: state; Activities: Arts & Crafts; Dances; Pet therapy; Group exercise; Support Groups; Other: Alzheimer's secured unit.

York Convalescent Center Ltd.
127 W Diversey Ave., Elmhurst, IL 60126, (630) 530-5225; Facility type: Skilled care, Alzheimer's; Beds: 130; Certified: Medicaid, Medicare, Veterans; Owner: Proprietary/Public; License: state; Activities: Arts & Crafts; Dances; Pet therapy; Group exercise; Support Groups.

Eureka

Apostolic Christian Home of Eureka
610 W Cruger Ave., Eureka, IL 61530, (309) 467-2311; Facility type: Skilled care, Alzheimer's; Beds: 120; Certified: Medicaid, Medicare, Veterans; Owner: Nonprofit/Religious; License: state; Activities: Arts & Crafts; Dances; Pet therapy; Group exercise; Support Groups, Alzheimer's secured unit, Home health care.

Evanston

Dobson Plaza
120 Dodge Ave., Evanston, IL 60202, (847) 869-7744; Facility type: Skilled care, Alzheimer's; Beds: 100; Certified: Medicaid, Medicare; Owner: Nonprofit/Religious; License: state; Activities: Arts & Crafts; Dances; Pet therapy; Group exercise; Support Groups, Alzheimer's secured unit, Adult day care.

Wagner Health Center
820 Foster St., Evanston, IL 60201, (847) 492-7700; Facility type: Skilled care, Alzheimer's; Beds: 190; Certified: Medicare; Owner: Proprietary/Public; License: state; Activities: Arts & Crafts; Dances; Pet therapy; Group exercise; Support Groups, Alzheimer's secured unit.

Franklin Park

Westlake Nursing & Rehabilitation Center
10500 Grand Ave., Franklin Park, IL 60131, (847) 451-1520; Facility type: Skilled care, Alzheimer's; Beds: 150; Certified: Medicaid, Medicare; Owner: Proprietary/Public; License: state; Activities: Arts & Crafts; Dances; Pet therapy; Group exercise; Support Groups, Alzheimer's secured unit.

Freeport

Stephenson Nursing Center
2946 S Walnut Rd., Freeport, IL 61032, (815) 235-6173; Facility type: Skilled care, Alzheimer's; Beds: 160; Certified: Medicaid, Medicare; Owner: State & Local Gov; License: state; Activities: Arts & Crafts; Dances; Pet therapy; Group exercise; Support Groups, Alzheimer's secured unit, Adult day care.

Geneva

Geneva Care Center
1101 E State St., Geneva, IL60134, (630) 232-7544; Facility type: Skilled care, Alzheimer's; Beds: 110; Certified: Medicaid; Owner: Proprietary/Public; License: state; Activities: Arts & Crafts; Dances; Pet therapy; Group exercise; Support Groups, Alzheimer's secured unit.

Girard

Pleasant Hill Village
1010 W North St., Girard, IL 62640, (217) 627-2181; Facility type: Skilled care, Alzheimer's; Beds: 100; Certified: Medicaid, Medicare; Owner: Nonprofit/Religious; License: state; Activities: Arts & Crafts; Dances; Pet therapy; Group exercise; Support Groups, Alzheimer's secured unit.

Glen Carbon

Eden Village Care Center
400 S Station Rd., Glen Carbon, IL 62034, (618) 288-5014; Facility type: Skilled care, Alzheimer's; Beds: 120; Certified: Medicaid, Medicare; Owner: Nonprofit/Religious; License: state; Activities: Arts & Crafts; Dances; Pet therapy; Group exercise; Support Groups, Alzheimer's secured unit.

Glenview

Abington of Glenview
3901 Glenview Rd., Glenview. IL 60025, (847) 729-0000; Facility type: Skilled care, Alzheimer's; Beds: 200; Certified: Medicare; Owner: Nonprofit/Religious; License: state; Activities: Arts & Crafts; Dances; Pet therapy; Group exercise; Support Groups, Alzheimer's secured unit.

Glenview Terrace Nursing Center
1511 Greenwood Rd., Glenview, IL 60025, (847) 729-9090; Facility type: Skilled care, Alzheimer's; Beds: 350; Certified: Medicaid, Medicare; Owner: Private; License: state; Activities: Arts & Crafts; Dances; Pet therapy; Group exercise; Support Groups, Alzheimer's secured unit.

Hinsdale

HCR Manor Care
600 W Ogden Ave., Hindsdale, IL 60521, (630) 325-9630; Facility type: Skilled care, Alzheimer's; Beds: 200; Certified: Medicaid, Medicare; Owner: Private; License: state; Activities: Arts & Crafts; Dances; Pet therapy; Group exercise; Support Groups, Alzheimer's secured unit, Adult day care, Home health care.

Itasca

The Arbor of Itasca
535 S Elm St., Itasca, IL 60143, (630) 773-9416; Facility type: Skilled care, Alzheimer's; Beds: 110; Certified: Medicaid, Medicare; Owner: Private; License: state; Activities: Arts & Crafts; Dances; Pet therapy; Group exercise; Support Groups, Alzheimer's secured unit.

Jacksonville

Modern Care Convalescent & Nursing Home
1500 W Walnut St., Jacksonville, IL 62650, (217) 245-4183; Facility type: Skilled care, Alzheimer's; Beds: 70; Certified: Medicaid, Medicare; Owner: Private; License: state; Activities: Arts & Crafts; Dances; Pet therapy; Group exercise; Support Groups, Alzheimer's secured unit, Adult day care.

NBA Barton W Stone Christian Home
873 Grove St., Jacksonville, IL 62650, (217) 479-3400; Facility type: Skilled care, Alzheimer's; Beds: 210; Certified: Medicaid, Medicare; Owner: Private; License: state; Activities: Arts & Crafts; Dances; Pet therapy; Group exercise; Support Groups, Alzheimer's secured unit.

Joliet

Deerbrook Care Centre
306 N Larkin Ave., Joliet, IL 60435, (815) 744-5560; Facility type: Skilled care, Alzheimer's; Beds: 220; Certified: Medicaid, Medicare; Owner: Private; License: state; Activities: Arts & Crafts; Dances; Pet therapy; Group exercise; Support Groups, Alzheimer's secured unit.

Provena Villa Franciscan
210 N Springfield Ave., Joliet, IL 60435, (815) 725-3400; Facility type: Skilled care, Alzheimer's; Beds: 210; Certified: Medicaid, Medicare; Owner: Nonprofit; License: state; Activities: Arts & Crafts; Dances; Pet therapy; Group exercise; Support Groups, Alzheimer's secured unit.

Salem Village
1314 Rowell Ave., Joliet, IL 60433, (815) 727-5451; Facility type: Skilled care, Alzheimer's; Beds: 250; Certified: Medicaid, Medicare; Owner: Nonprofit; License: state; Activities: Arts & Crafts; Dances; Pet therapy; Group exercise; Support Groups, Alzheimer's secured unit, Adult day care.

Kankakee

Koukakee Nursing & Rehabilitation Center
1050 W Jeffrey St., Kankakee, IL 60901, (815) 933-1660; Facility type: Skilled care, Alzheimer's; Beds: 200; Certified: Medicaid, Medicare, Veter-

ans; Owner: Proprietary/Public; License: state; Activities: Arts & Crafts; Dances; Pet therapy; Group exercise; Support Groups, Alzheimer's secured unit.

ManorCare at Kankakee
900 W River Pl., Kankakee, IL 60901, (815) 933-1711; Facility type: Skilled care, Alzheimer's; Beds: 100; Certified: Medicaid, Medicare, Veterans; Owner: HCR Manor Care; License: state; Activities: Arts & Crafts; Dances; Pet therapy; Group exercise; Support Groups, Alzheimer's secured unit.

LaGrange

SunBridge Care & Rehabilitation for La Grange
339 S 9th Ave., La Grange, IL 60525, (708) 354-4660; Facility type: Skilled care, Alzheimer's; Beds: 200; Certified: Medicaid, Medicare, Veterans; Owner: Sun Healthcare; License: state; Activities: Arts & Crafts; Dances; Pet therapy; Group exercise; Support Groups, Alzheimer's secured unit.

Lake Bluff

Pebble Brook Nursing & Rehabilitation Center
700 Jenkisson Ave., Lake Bluff, IL 60044, (847) 295-3900; Facility type: Skilled care, Alzheimer's; Beds: 200; Certified: Medicaid, Medicare, Veterans; Owner: Proprietary/Public; License: state; Activities: Arts & Crafts; Dances; Pet therapy; Group exercise; Support Groups, Alzheimer's secured unit.

Lawrenceville

The United Methodist Village
1616 Cedar St., Lawrenceville, IL 62439. (618) 943-3347; Facility type: Skilled care, Alzheimer's; Beds: 300; Certified: Medicaid, Medicare, Veterans; Owner: Proprietary/Public; License: state; Activities: Arts & Crafts; Dances; Pet therapy; Group exercise; Support Groups, Alzheimer's secured unit.

Lemont

Lemont Center
12450 Walker Rd., Lemont, IL 60439, (630) 243-0400; Facility type: Skilled care, Alzheimer's; Beds: 150; Certified: Medicaid, Medicare, Veterans; Owner: Genesis ElderCare; License: state; Activities: Arts & Crafts; Dances; Pet therapy; Group exercise; Support Groups, Alzheimer's secured unit.

Leroy

Leroy Manor
PO Box 149, Leroy, IL 61752, (309) 962-5000; Facility type: Skilled care, Alzheimer's; Beds: 100; Certified: Medicaid, Medicare, Veterans; Owner: Proprietary/Public; License: state; Activities: Arts & Crafts; Dances; Pet therapy; Group exercise; Support Groups, Alzheimer's secured unit.

Libertyville

Winchester House
1125 N Milwaukee Ave., Libertyville, IL 60048, (847) 362-4340; Facility type: Skilled care, Alzheimer's; Beds: 400; Certified: Medicaid, Medicare, Veterans; Owner: State & Local Gov; License: state; Activities: Arts & Crafts; Dances; Pet therapy; Group exercise; Support Groups, Alzheimer's secured unit.

Lincoln

Maple Ridge Care Centre
2202 N Kickapoo St., Lincoln, IL 62656, (217) 735-1538; Facility type: Skilled care, Alzheimer's; Beds: 120; Certified: Medicaid, Medicare, Veterans; Owner: Proprietary/Public; License: state; Activities: Arts & Crafts; Dances; Pet therapy; Group exercise; Support Groups, Alzheimer's secured unit.

Lindenhurst

Victory Lakes Continuing Care Center
1055 E Grand Ave., Lindenhurst, IL 60046, (847) 356-5900; Facility type: Skilled care, Alzheimer's; Beds: 100; Certified: Medicare, Veterans; Owner: Proprietary/Public; License: state; Activities: Arts & Crafts; Dances; Pet therapy; Group exercise; Support Groups, Alzheimer's secured unit.

Mattoon

Convalescent Care Center—Mattoon
1000 Palm Ave., Mattoon, IL 61938, (217) 234-7403; Facility type: Skilled care, Alzheimer's; Beds: 180; Certified: Medicare, Veterans; Owner: Proprietary/Public; License: state; Activities: Arts & Crafts; Dances; Pet therapy; Group exercise; Support Groups, Alzheimer's secured unit.

Odd Fellow & Rebekah Home
201 Lafayette Ave. E, Mattoon, IL 61938, (217) 235-5449; Facility type: Skilled care, Alzheimer's; Beds: 160; Certified: Medicaid, Veterans; Owner: Proprietary/Public; License: state; Activities: Arts & Crafts; Dances; Pet therapy;

Group exercise; Support Groups, Alzheimer's secured unit.

Maywood

Baptist Retirement Community
316 Randolph St., Maywood, IL 60153, (708) 344-1541; Facility type: Skilled care, Alzheimer's; Beds: 80; Certified: Medicaid, Veterans; Owner: Nonprofit/Religious; License: state; Activities: Arts & Crafts; Dances; Pet therapy; Group exercise; Support Groups, Alzheimer's secured unit, Home health care.

Moline

Heartland Health Care Center
833 16th Ave., Moline, IL 61265, (309) 764-6744; Facility type: Skilled care, Alzheimer's; Beds: 130; Certified: Medicaid, Medicare, Veterans; Owner: HCR Manor Care; License: state; Activities: Arts & Crafts; Dances; Pet therapy; Group exercise; Support Groups.

Morton Grove

Bethany Terrace Nursing Care
8425 N Waukegan Rd., Morton Grove, IL 60053, (847) 965-8100; Facility type: Skilled care, Alzheimer's; Beds: 350; Certified: Medicaid, Medicare; Owner: Nonprofit/Religious; License: state; Activities: Arts & Crafts; Dances; Pet therapy; Group exercise; Support Groups, Alzheimer's secured unit.

Mount Carmel

Oakview Heights
1320 W 9th St., Mount Carmel, IL 62863, (618) 263-4337; Facility type: Skilled care, Alzheimer's; Beds: 160; Certified: Medicaid, Medicare, Veterans; Owner: Nonprofit/Religious; License: state; Activities: Arts & Crafts; Dances; Pet therapy; Group exercise; Support Groups, Alzheimer's secured unit.

Murphysboro

Rehabilitation & Care Center of Jackson County
1441 N 14th St., Murphysboro, IL 62966; (618) 684-2136; Facility type: Skilled care, Alzheimer's; Beds: 260; Certified: Medicaid, Medicare, Veterans; Owner: State & Local Gov; License: state; Activities: Arts & Crafts; Dances; Pet therapy; Group exercise; Support Groups, Alzheimer's secured unit.

Nashville

Friendship Manor Nashville
485 S Friendship Dr., Nashville, IL 62263, (618) 327-3041; Facility type: Skilled care, Alzheimer's; Beds: 260; Certified: Medicaid, Medicare, Veterans; Owner: Proprietary/Public; License: state; Activities: Arts & Crafts; Dances; Pet therapy; Group exercise; Support Groups, Alzheimer's secured unit.

Oak Lawn

ManorCare at Oak Lawn—West
6300 W 95th St., Oak Lawn, IL 60453, (708) 599-8800; Facility type: Skilled care, Alzheimer's; Beds: 190; Certified: Medicaid, Medicare, Veterans; Owner: HCR Manor Care; License: state; Activities: Arts & Crafts; Dances; Pet therapy; Group exercise; Support Groups, Alzheimer's secured unit, Adult day care.

Olney

Burgin Nursing Manor
900-928 E Scott St., Olney, IL 62450, (618) 393-2914; Facility type: Skilled care, Alzheimer's; Beds: 120; Certified: Medicaid, Medicare, Veterans; Owner: HCR Manor Care; License: state; Activities: Arts & Crafts; Dances; Pet therapy; Group exercise; Support Groups, Alzheimer's secured unit, Adult day care.

Ottawa

Pleasant View Luther Home
505 College Ave., Ottawa, IL 61350, (815) 434-1130; Facility type: Skilled care, Alzheimer's; Beds: 210; Certified: Medicaid, Medicare; Owner: Nonprofit/Religious; License: state; Activities: Arts & Crafts; Dances; Pet therapy; Group exercise; Support Groups, Alzheimer's secured unit.

Palos Heights

ManorCare at Palos Heights
7850 W College Dr., Palos Heights, IL 60463, (708) 361-6990; Facility type: Skilled care, Alzheimer's; Beds: 180; Certified: Medicaid, Medicare; Owner: HCR Manor Care; License: state; Activities: Arts & Crafts; Dances; Pet therapy; Group exercise; Support Groups, Alzheimer's secured unit, Adult day care.

Park Ridge

Saint Matthew Lutheran Home
1601 N Western Ave., Park Ridge, IL 60068, (847) 825-5531; Facility type: Skilled care, Alz-

heimer's; Beds: 180; Certified: Medicaid, Medicare; Owner: Nonprofit/Religious; License: state; Activities: Arts & Crafts; Dances; Pet therapy; Group exercise; Support Groups, Alzheimer's secured unit.

Pekin

Pekin Manor
1520 El Camino Dr., Pekin, IL 61554, (309) 353-1099; Facility type: Skilled care, Alzheimer's; Beds: 180; Certified: Medicaid, Medicare; Owner: Nonprofit/Religious; License: state; Activities: Arts & Crafts; Dances; Pet therapy; Group exercise; Support Groups, Alzheimer's secured unit, Adult day care.

Peoria

Apostolic Peoria
7023 NE Skyline Dr., Peoria, IL 61614, (309) 691-2816; Facility type: Skilled care, Alzheimer's; Beds: 80; Certified: Medicaid; Owner: Nonprofit/Religious; License: state; Activities: Arts & Crafts; Dances; Pet therapy; Group exercise; Support Groups, Alzheimer's secured unit.

Rosewood Care Center Inc.—Peoria
1500 W Northmoor Rd., Peoria, IL 61614, (309) 691-2200; Facility type: Skilled care, Alzheimer's; Beds: 120; Certified: Medicaid, Medicare; Owner: Proprietary/Public; License: state; Activities: Arts & Crafts; Dances; Pet therapy; Group exercise; Support Groups.

Sharon Health Care Pines Inc.
3614 N Rochelle Ln., Peoria, IL 61604, (309) 688-0350; Facility type: Skilled care, Alzheimer's; Beds: 120; Certified: Medicaid, Medicare; Owner: Nonprofit/Religious; License: state; Activities: Arts & Crafts; Dances; Pet therapy; Group exercise; Support Groups, Alzheimer's secured unit.

Quincy

Brighton Pavilion Ltd.
720 Sycamore St., Quincy, IL 62301, (217) 222-1480; Facility type: Skilled care, Alzheimer's; Beds: 190; Certified: Medicaid, Medicare; Owner: Nonprofit/Religious; License: state; Activities: Arts & Crafts; Dances; Pet therapy; Group exercise; Support Groups, Alzheimer's secured unit.

Good Samaritan Home Inc.
2130 Harrison St., Quincy, IL 62301, (217) 223-8717; Facility type: Skilled care, Alzheimer's; Beds: 190; Certified: Medicaid, Medicare; Owner: Nonprofit/Religious; License: state; Activities: Arts & Crafts; Dances; Pet therapy; Group exercise; Support Groups, Alzheimer's secured unit.

Richton Park

Glenshire Nursing & Rehabilitation Center
22660 S Cicero Ave., Richton Park, IL 60471, (708) 747-6120; Facility type: Skilled care, Alzheimer's; Beds: 300; Certified: Medicaid, Medicare, Veterans; Owner: Nonprofit/Religious; License: state; Activities: Arts & Crafts; Dances; Pet therapy; Group exercise; Support Groups, Alzheimer's secured unit, Home health care.

Riverwoods

Brentwood North Nursing, Rehabilitation & Specialized Health Care Center
3705 Deerfield Rd., Riverwoods, IL 60015, (847) 459-1200; Facility type: Skilled care, Alzheimer's; Beds: 250; Certified: Medicare; Owner: Nonprofit/Religious; License: state; Activities: Arts & Crafts; Dances; Pet therapy; Group exercise; Support Groups, Alzheimer's secured unit, Home health care.

Rock Island

OSF St. Anthony's Continuing Care Center
767 30th St., Rock Island, IL 61201, (309) 788-7631; Facility type: Skilled care, Alzheimer's; Beds: 120; Certified: Medicaid, Medicare; Owner: Nonprofit/Religious; License: state; Activities: Arts & Crafts; Dances; Pet therapy; Group exercise; Support Groups.

Rockford

Highview Retirement Home Association
4149 Safford Rd., Rockford, IL 61101, (815) 964-3368; Facility type: Skilled care, Alzheimer's; Beds: 60; Owner: Nonprofit/Religious; License: state; Activities: Arts & Crafts; Dances; Pet therapy; Group exercise; Support Groups, Alzheimer's secured unit.

P A Peterson Center for Health
1311 Parkview Ave., Rockford, IL 61107; (815) 399-8832; Facility type: Skilled care, Alzheimer's; Beds: 150; Certified: Medicare; Owner: Nonprofit/Religious; License: state; Activities: Arts & Crafts; Dances; Pet therapy; Group exercise; Support Groups, Alzheimer's secured unit, Home health care.

Riverbluff Nursing Home
4401 N Main St., Rockford, IL 61103, (815) 877-8061; Facility type: Skilled care, Alzheimer's; Beds: 290; Certified: Medicaid, Medicare; Owner: State & Local Gov; License: state; Ac-

tivities: Arts & Crafts; Dances; Pet therapy; Group exercise; Support Groups, Alzheimer's secured unit, Home health care.

Willows Health Center
4054 Albright Ln., Rockford, IL 61103, (815) 654-2534; Facility type: Skilled care, Alzheimer's; Beds: 160; Certified: Medicaid; Owner: Nonprofit/Religious; License: state; Activities: Arts & Crafts; Dances; Pet therapy; Group exercise; Support Groups, Alzheimer's secured unit, Adult day care.

Rolling Meadows

ManorCare at Rolling Meadows
4225 Kirchoff Rd., Rolling Meadows, IL 60008, (847) 387-2400; Facility type: Skilled care, Alzheimer's; Beds: 160; Certified: Medicaid, Medicare; Owner: Nonprofit/Religious; License: state; Activities: Arts & Crafts; Dances; Pet therapy; Group exercise; Support Groups, Alzheimer's secured unit.

Saint Elmo

Friendship Manor of Saint Elmo
221 E Cumberland Rd., Saint Elmo, IL 62458, (618) 829-5581; Facility type: Skilled care, Alzheimer's; Beds: 130; Certified: Medicaid, Medicare; Owner: Proprietary/Public; License: state; Activities: Arts & Crafts; Dances; Pet therapy; Group exercise; Support Groups, Alzheimer's secured unit, Adult day care.

Savoy

The Carle Arbours
302 W Burwash, Savoy, IL 61874, (217) 383-3090; Facility type: Skilled care, Alzheimer's; Beds: 170; Certified: Medicaid, Medicare; Owner: Nonprofit/Religious; License: state; Activities: Arts & Crafts; Dances; Pet therapy; Group exercise; Support Groups, Alzheimer's secured unit, Adult day care.

Schaumburg

Friendship Village of Schaumburg
350 W Schaumburg Rd., Schaumburg, IL 60194, (847) 884-5000; Facility type: Skilled care, Alzheimer's; Beds: 120; Certified: Medicaid, Medicare; Owner: Nonprofit/Religious; License: state; Activities: Arts & Crafts; Dances; Pet therapy; Group exercise; Support Groups, Alzheimer's secured unit, Home health care.

Lexington of Schaumburg
675 S Roselle Rd., Schaumburg, IL 60193, (847) 352-5500; Facility type: Skilled care, Alzheimer's; Beds: 220; Certified: Medicaid, Medicare; Owner: Nonprofit/Religious; License: state; Activities: Arts & Crafts; Dances; Pet therapy; Group exercise; Support Groups, Alzheimer's secured unit, Home health care.

South Holland

HCR Manor Care Health Services
2145 E 170th St., South Holland, IL 60473, (708) 895-3255; Facility type: Skilled care, Alzheimer's; Beds: 190; Certified: Medicaid, Medicare; Owner: HCR Manor Care; License: state; Activities: Arts & Crafts; Dances; Pet therapy; Group exercise; Support Groups, Alzheimer's secured unit, Adult day care.

Rest Haven South Nursing Home
16300 Wausau Ave., South Holland, IL 60473, (708) 596-5500; Facility type: Skilled care, Alzheimer's; Beds: 170; Certified: Medicare; Owner: Nonprofit/Religious; License: state; Activities: Arts & Crafts; Dances; Pet therapy; Group exercise; Support Groups, Alzheimer's secured unit.

Springfield

Lewis Memorial Christian Village
3400 W Washington, Springfield, IL 62707, (217) 787-9600; Facility type: Skilled care, Alzheimer's; Beds: 160; Certified: Medicare; Owner: Nonprofit/Religious; License: state; Activities: Arts & Crafts; Dances; Pet therapy; Group exercise; Support Groups, Alzheimer's secured unit.

Springfield Terrace Ltd.
525 S Martin Luther Kind Dr., Springfield, IL 62803, (217) 789-1680; Facility type: Skilled care, Alzheimer's; Beds: 70; Certified: Medicaid; Owner: Proprietary/Public: state; Activities: Arts & Crafts; Dances; Pet therapy; Group exercise; Support Groups, Alzheimer's secured unit.

Swansea

Castlehaven Care Center
25 Castellano Dr., Swansea, IL 62226, 18) 235-1300; Facility type: Skilled care, Alzheimer's; Beds: 240;Certified: Medicaid, Medicare, Veterans/Public; Licensed: state; Activities: Arts & Crafts; Dances; Pet therapy; Group exercise; Support Groups; Other: Alzheimer's secured unit, Adult day care.

Urbana

Champaign County Nursing Home
701 E Main St., Urbana, IL 61801, 17) 384-3784; Facility type: Skilled care, Alzheimer's; Beds: 250; Certified: Medicaid, Medicare, Veterans/

Public: Owner: State & Local Gov; Licensed: state; Activities: Arts & Crafts; Dances; Pet therapy; Group exercise; Support Groups, Alzheimer's secured unit, Adult day care.

Clark-Lindsey Village
101 W Windsor Rd., Urbana, IL 61802, (217) 344-2144; Facility type: Skilled care, Alzheimer's; Beds: 100; Certified: Medicare, Veterans; Owner: State & Local Gov; Licensed: state; Activities: Arts & Crafts; Dances; Pet therapy; Group exercise; Support Groups, Alzheimer's secured unit, Home health care.

Waterloo

Monroe County Nursing Home
500 Illinois Ave., Waterloo, IL 62298 (618) 939-3488; Facility type: Skilled care, Alzheimer's; Beds: 210; Certified: Medicaid, Medicare, Veterans; Owner: State & Local Gov; Licensed: state; Activities: Arts & Crafts; Dances; Pet therapy; Group exercise; Support Groups, Alzheimer's secured unit, Adult day care.

Watseka

Watseka Health Care Center
715 E Raymond Watseka, IL 60970, (815) 432-5476; Facility type: Skilled care, Alzheimer's; Beds: 120; Certified: Medicaid, Medicare, Veterans; Owner: State & Local Gov; Licensed: state; Activities: Arts & Crafts; Dances; Pet therapy; Group exercise; Support Groups, Alzheimer's secured unit.

Wheaton

Du Page Convalescent Center
400 N County Farm Rd., Wheaton, IL 60187; (630) 665-6400; Facility type: Skilled care, Alzheimer's; Beds: 510; Certified: Medicaid, Medicare, Veterans; Owner: State & Local Gov; Licensed: state; Activities: Arts & Crafts; Dances; Pet therapy; Group exercise; Support Groups, Alzheimer's secured unit.

White Hall

White Hall Multicare Center
620 W Bridgeport, White Hall, IL 62092, (217) 374-2144; Facility type: Skilled care, Alzheimer's; Beds: 120; Certified: Medicaid, Medicare, Veterans; Owner: Crescent Health Services; Licensed: state; Activities: Arts & Crafts; Dances; Pet therapy; Group exercise; Support Groups.

Willowbrook

Chateau Center
7050 Madison St., Willowbrook, IL 60521, (630) 323-6380; Facility type: Skilled care, Alzheimer's; Beds: 150; Certified: Medicaid, Medicare, Veterans; Owner: Genesis Elder Care; Licensed: state; Activities: Arts & Crafts; Dances; Pet therapy; Group exercise; Support Groups, Alzheimer's secured unit.

Wilmette

ManorCare Health Services—Wilmette
432 Poplar Dr., Wilmette, IL 60091, (847) 256-5000; Facility type: Skilled care, Alzheimer's; Beds: 100; Certified: Medicaid, Medicare; Owner: HCR Manor Care; Licensed: state; Activities: Arts & Crafts; Dances; Pet therapy; Group exercise; Support Groups, Alzheimer's secured unit.

Wilmington

The Embassy Care Center
555 Kahler Rd., Wilmington, IL 60481, (815) 476-2200; Facility type: Skilled care, Alzheimer's; Beds: 150; Certified: Medicaid, Medicare, Veterans; Owner: Proprietary/Public; Licensed: state; Activities: Arts & Crafts; Dances; Pet therapy; Group exercise; Support Groups, Alzheimer's secured unit.

INDIANA

Alexandria

Alexandria Care Center
1912 S Park Ave., Alexandria, IN 46001; (765) 724-4478; Facility type: Skilled care, Alzheimer's; Beds: 70; Certified: Medicaid; Owner: Private; License: state; Activities: Arts & Crafts; Dances; Pet therapy; Group exercise; Outings; Support Groups; Other: Alzheimer's secured unit.

The Willows
1817 S Park Ave., Alexandria, IN 46001, (765) 724-4464; Facility type: Skilled care, Alzheimer's; Beds: 70; Certified: Medicaid, Medicare; Owner: Proprietary/Public; License: state; Ac-

tivities: Arts & Crafts; Dances; Pet therapy; Group exercise; Outings; Support Groups; Other: Alzheimer's secured unit.

Anderson

ManorCare Health Services
1345 N Madison Ave., Anderson, IN 46011, (765) 644-2888; Facility type: Skilled care, Alzheimer's; Beds: 220; Certified: Medicaid, Medicare; Owner: HCR Manor Care; License: state; Activities: Arts & Crafts; Dances; Pet therapy; Group exercise; Outings; Support Groups; Other: Alzheimer's secured unit.

Angola

Carlin Park Healthcare Center
516 N Williams St., Angola, IN 46703, (219) 665-9467; Facility type: Skilled care, Alzheimer's; Beds: 100; Certified: Medicaid, Medicare; Owner: Crescent Health Care Services; License: state; Activities: Arts & Crafts; Dances; Pet therapy; Group exercise; Outings; Support Groups; Other: Alzheimer's secured unit.

Avon

Avon Healthcare—Hendrichs County
75 S Rd. 400, Avon, IN 45123, (317) 745-5184; Facility type: Skilled care, Alzheimer's; Beds: 90; Certified: Medicaid, Medicare; Owner: Proprietary/Public; License: state; Activities: Arts & Crafts; Dances; Pet therapy; Group exercise; Outings; Support Groups; Other: Alzheimer's secured unit.

Berne

Swiss Village Inc.
1350 W Main St., Berne, IN 46711, (219) 589-3173; Facility type: Skilled care, Alzheimer's; Beds: 110; Certified: Medicaid; Owner: Nonprofit; License: state; Activities: Arts & Crafts; Dances; Pet therapy; Group exercise; Outings; Support Groups; Other: Alzheimer's secured unit.

Bloomington

Beverly Healthcare of Bloomington
3305 S Hwy. 37, Bloomington, IN 47401, (812) 332-4437; Facility type: Skilled care, Alzheimer's; Beds: 160; Certified: Medicaid, Medicare, Veterans; Owner: Beverly Enterprises; License: state; Activities: Arts & Crafts; Dances; Pet therapy; Group exercise; Outings; Support Groups; Other: Alzheimer's secured unit.

Hospitality House Care Center
1100 S Curry Pike, Bloomington, IN 47403, (812) 339-1657; Facility type: Skilled care, Alzheimer's; Beds: 100; Certified: Medicaid, Medicare, Veterans; Owner: Nonprofit; License: state; Activities: Arts & Crafts; Dances; Pet therapy; Group exercise; Outings; Support Groups; Other: Alzheimer's secured unit, Home health care.

Brazil

Holly Hill Health Care Facility
501 S Murphy Ave., Brazil, IN 47834, (812) 446-2636; Facility type: Skilled care, Alzheimer's; Beds: 100; Certified: Medicaid, Medicare; Owner: Nonprofit; License: state; Activities: Arts & Crafts; Dances; Pet therapy; Group exercise; Outings; Support Groups; Other: Alzheimer's secured unit.

Elsie Dreyer Nursing Home—Special Services Unit
273 Main St., Brookville, IN 47012, (765) 647-6231; Facility type: Skilled care, Alzheimer's; Beds: 40; Certified: Medicaid; Owner: Nonprofit; License: state; Activities: Arts & Crafts; Dances; Pet therapy; Group exercise; Outings; Support Groups; Other: Alzheimer's secured unit, Home health care.

Carmel

Carmel Care Center
118 Medical Dr., Carmel, IN 46032, (317) 844-4211; Facility type: Skilled care, Alzheimer's; Beds: 300; Certified: Medicaid, Medicare; Owner: Nonprofit; License: state; Activities: Arts & Crafts; Dances; Pet therapy; Group exercise; Outings; Support Groups; Other: Alzheimer's secured unit.

Lakeview Health Care Center
2907 E 136th St., Carmel, IN 46033, (317) 846-0265; Facility type: Skilled care, Alzheimer's; Beds: 40; Certified: Medicaid; Owner: Nonprofit; License: state; Activities: Arts & Crafts; Dances; Pet therapy; Group exercise; Outings; Support Groups; Other: Adult day care.

Chandler

Pine Lake Manor
6324 Gardner Rd., Chandler, IN 47610, (812) 925-3381; Facility type: Skilled care, Alzheimer's; Beds: 80; Certified: Medicaid, Medicare, Veterans; Owner: Private; License: state; Activities: Arts & Crafts; Dances; Pet therapy; Group exercise; Outings; Support Groups; Other: Alzheimer's secured unit.

Columbus

Columbus Convalescent Center
2100 Midway St., Columbus, IN 47201, (812) 372-8447; Facility type: Skilled care, Alzheimer's; Beds: 330; Certified: Medicaid, Medicare, Veterans; Owner: Private; License: state; Activities: Arts & Crafts; Dances; Pet therapy; Group exercise; Outings; Support Groups; Other: Alzheimer's secured unit, Adult day care, Home health care.

Crown Point

Saint Anthony Home Inc.
203 Franciscan Dr., Crown Point, IN 46307, (219) 757-6281; Facility type: Skilled care, Alzheimer's; Beds: 260; Certified: Medicaid, Medicare; Owner: Private; License: state; Activities: Arts & Crafts; Dances; Pet therapy; Group exercise; Outings; Support Groups; Other: Alzheimer's secured unit, Adult day care, Home health care.

Wittenberg Lutheran Village
1200 E Luther Dr., Crown Point, IN 46307, (219) 663-3860; Facility type: Skilled care, Alzheimer's; Beds: 50; Certified: Medicaid, Medicare; Owner: Private; License: state; Activities: Arts & Crafts; Dances; Pet therapy; Group exercise; Outings; Support Groups; Other: Alzheimer's secured unit.

Decatur

Woodcrest Nursing Center
1300 Mercer Ave., Decatur, IN 46733, (219) 724-3311; Facility type: Skilled care, Alzheimer's; Beds: 140; Certified: Medicaid, Medicare, Veterans; Owner: State & Local Gov; License: state; Activities: Arts & Crafts; Dances; Pet therapy; Group exercise; Outings; Support Groups; Other: Alzheimer's secured unit.

Demotte

Crestmark of Rose Lawn
10352 N 600 E, Demotte, IN 46310, (219) 345-5211; Facility type: Skilled care, Alzheimer's; Beds: 100; Certified: Medicaid, Medicare; Owner: Private; License: state; Activities: Arts & Crafts; Dances; Pet therapy; Group exercise; Outings; Support Groups; Other: Alzheimer's secured unit.

East Chicago

Rosewood Terrace
1001 W Hively Ave., Elkhart, IN 46517, (219) 294-7641; Facility type: Skilled care, Alzheimer's; Beds: 310; Certified: Medicaid, Medicare, Veterans; Owner: Private; License: state; Activities: Arts & Crafts; Dances; Pet therapy; Group exercise; Outings; Support Groups; Other: Alzheimer's secured unit.

Elkhart

SunBridge Care & Rehabilitation for Elkhart
343 S Nappanee St., Elkhart, IN 46514, (219) 295-0096; Facility type: Skilled care, Alzheimer's; Beds: 150; Certified: Medicaid, Medicare, Veterans; Owner: Private; License: state; Activities: Arts & Crafts; Dances; Pet therapy; Group exercise; Outings; Support Groups; Other: Alzheimer's secured unit, Adult day care.

Elwood

Community Parkview Care Center
2300 Parkview Ln., Elwood, IN 46036, (765) 552-9884; Facility type: Skilled care, Alzheimer's; Beds: 250; Certified: Medicaid, Medicare; Owner: Private; License: state; Activities: Arts & Crafts; Dances; Pet therapy; Group exercise; Outings; Support Groups; Other: Alzheimer's secured unit, Adult day care.

Evansville

Beverly Healthcare—Woodbridge
816 N 1st Ave., Evansville, IN 47710, (812) 426-2841; Facility type: Skilled care, Alzheimer's; Beds: 90; Certified: Medicaid, Medicare; Owner: Beverly Enterprises; License: state; Activities: Arts & Crafts; Dances; Pet therapy; Group exercise; Outings; Support Groups; Other: Alzheimer's secured unit, Adult day care.

Good Samaritan Home Inc.
601 N Boeke Rd., Evansville, IN 47728, (812) 476-4912; Facility type: Skilled care, Alzheimer's; Beds: 170; Certified: Medicaid; Owner: Nonprofit/Religious; License: state; Activities: Arts & Crafts; Dances; Pet therapy; Group exercise; Outings; Support Groups; Other: Alzheimer's secured unit, Adult day care.

Highland Pointe Health Care
6015 Kratzville Rd., Evansville, IN 47710, (812) 425-8182; Facility type: Skilled care, Alzheimer's; Beds: 70; Certified: Medicaid; Owner: Nonprofit/Religious; License: state; Activities: Arts & Crafts; Dances; Pet therapy; Group exercise; Outings; Support Groups; Other: Alzheimer's secured unit, Adult day care.

Fort Wayne

Arbors at Fort Wayne
2827 Northgate Blvd., Fort Wayne, IN 46835,

(219) 485-9691; Facility type: Skilled care, Alzheimer's; Beds: 140; Certified: Medicaid, Medicare; Owner: ExtendiCare; License: state; Activities: Arts & Crafts; Dances; Pet therapy; Group exercise; Outings; Support Groups; Other: Alzheimer's secured unit, Adult day care.

Beverly Health & Rehabilitation Center
2940 N Clinton St., Fort Wayne, IN 46805, (219) 484-0602; Facility type: Skilled care, Alzheimer's; Beds: 120; Certified: Medicaid, Medicare, Veterans; Owner: Beverly Enterprises; License: state; Activities: Arts & Crafts; Dances; Pet therapy; Group exercise; Outings; Support Groups; Other: Alzheimer's secured unit, Adult day care, Home health care.

Byron Health Center
12101 Lima Rd., Fort Wayne, IN 46818, (219) 637-3166; Facility type: Skilled care, Alzheimer's; Beds: 260; Certified: Medicaid, Medicare; Owner: Beverly Enterprises; License: state; Activities: Arts & Crafts; Dances; Pet therapy; Group exercise; Outings; Support Groups; Other: Alzheimer's secured unit.

Golden Years Homestead Inc.
8300 Maysville Rd., Fort Wayne, IN 46815, (219) 749-9655; Facility type: Skilled care, Alzheimer's; Beds: 110; Certified: Medicaid; Owner: Nonprofit/Religious; License: state; Activities: Arts & Crafts; Dances; Pet therapy; Group exercise; Outings; Support Groups; Other: Alzheimer's secured unit.

Heritage Park
2001 Hobson Rd., Fort Wayne, IN 46805, (219) 484-9557; Facility type: Skilled care, Alzheimer's; Beds: 120; Certified: Medicaid, Medicare, Veterans; Owner: Eagle Care; License: state; Activities: Arts & Crafts; Dances; Pet therapy; Group exercise; Outings; Support Groups; Other: Alzheimer's secured unit.

Regency Place of Fort Wayne
6006 Brandy Chase Cove, Fort Wayne, IN 46815 (219) 486-3001; Facility type: Skilled care, Alzheimer's; Beds: 160; Certified: Medicaid, Medicare, Veterans; Owner: Vencor; License: state; Activities: Arts & Crafts; Dances; Pet therapy; Group exercise; Outings; Support Groups; Other: Alzheimer's secured unit.

University Park Nursing Center
1400 Medical Park Dr., Fort Wayne, IN 46825, (219) 484-1558; Facility type: Skilled care, Alzheimer's; Beds: 110; Certified: Medicaid, Medicare; Owner: Covenant Care; License: state; Activities: Arts & Crafts; Dances; Pet therapy; Group exercise; Outings; Support Groups; Other: Alzheimer's secured unit.

The Franklin United Methodist Home
1070 W Jefferson St., Fort Wayne, IN 46131, (317) 736-7185; Facility type: Skilled care, Alzheimer's; Beds: 160; Owner: Covenant Care; License: state; Activities: Arts & Crafts; Dances; Pet therapy; Group exercise; Outings; Support Groups; Other: Alzheimer's secured unit.

Todd-Aikens Health Center
1125 W Jefferson St., Fort Wayne, IN 46131, (317) 736-3240; Facility type: Skilled care, Alzheimer's; Beds: 110; Certified: Medicaid, Medicare; Owner: Nonprofit; License: state; Activities: Arts & Crafts; Dances; Pet therapy; Group exercise; Outings; Support Groups; Other: Adult day care.

Goshen

Greencroft Gables Health
Care 1904 S 15th St., Goshen, IN 46527, (219) 537-4000; Facility type: Skilled care, Alzheimer's; Beds: 30; Certified: Medicare; Owner: Nonprofit; License: state; Activities: Arts & Crafts; Dances; Pet therapy; Group exercise; Outings; Support Groups; Other: Alzheimer's secured unit.

Greenfield

Regency Place of Greenfield
200 Green Meadows Dr., Greenfield, IN 46140, (317) 462-3311; Facility type: Skilled care, Alzheimer's; Beds: 220; Certified: Medicaid, Medicare, Veterans; Owner: Vencor; License: state; Activities: Arts & Crafts; Dances; Pet therapy; Group exercise; Outings; Support Groups; Other: Alzheimer's secured unit, Adult day care.

Greenwood

Greenwood—Regency Place
377 Westridge Blvd., Greenwood, IN 46142, (317) 888-4948; Facility type: Skilled care, Alzheimer's; Beds: 200; Certified: Medicaid, Medicare, Veterans; Owner: Vencor; License: state; Activities: Arts & Crafts; Dances; Pet therapy; Group exercise; Outings; Support Groups; Other: Alzheimer's secured unit, Home health care.

Hanover

Hanover Nursing Center
410 W La Grange Rd., Hanover, IN 47243, (812) 866-2625; Facility type: Skilled care, Alzheimer's; Beds: 200; Certified: Medicaid, Medicare; Owner: Nonprofit; License: state; Activities: Arts & Crafts; Dances; Pet therapy; Group exercise; Outings; Support Groups; Other: Alzheimer's secured unit, Adult day care.

Huntington

Miller's Merry Manor
1500 Grant St., Huntington, IN 46750, (219) 356-5713; Facility type: Skilled care, Alzheimer's; Beds: 150; Certified: Medicaid, Medicare; Owner: Private; License: state; Activities: Arts & Crafts; Dances; Pet therapy; Group exercise; Outings; Support Groups; Other: Alzheimer's secured unit, Adult day care.

Indianapolis

Community Nursing & Rehabilitation
5600 E 16th St., Indianapolis, IN 46218, (317) 356-0911; Facility type: Skilled care, Alzheimer's; Beds: 120; Certified: Medicaid, Medicare; Owner: Private; License: state; Activities: Arts & Crafts; Dances; Pet therapy; Group exercise; Outings; Support Groups.

Forest Creek Village
525 E Thompson Rd., Indianapolis, IN 46227, (317) 787-8253; Facility type: Skilled care, Alzheimer's; Beds: 160; Certified: Medicaid, Medicare; Owner: Nonprofit; License: state; Activities: Arts & Crafts; Dances; Pet therapy; Group exercise; Outings; Support Groups; Other: Alzheimer's secured unit.

Georgetown Manor Healthcare
46 Westfield Rd., Indianapolis, IN 46254, (317) 293-3006; Facility type: Skilled care, Alzheimer's; Beds: 50; Certified: Medicaid, Medicare; Owner: Nonprofit; License: state; Activities: Arts & Crafts; Dances; Pet therapy; Group exercise; Outings; Support Groups; Other: Alzheimer's secured unit, Adult day care.

Harrison Healthcare Group
2026 E 54th St., Indianapolis, IN 46220, (317) 253-6950; Facility type: Skilled care, Alzheimer's; Beds: 130; Certified: Medicaid, Medicare; Owner: Nonprofit; License: state; Activities: Arts & Crafts; Dances; Pet therapy; Group exercise; Outings; Support Groups; Other: Alzheimer's secured unit, Home health care, Hospice.

Hoover Nursing Home
7001 Hoover Rd., Indianapolis, IN 46260, (317) 251-2261; Facility type: Skilled care, Alzheimer's; Beds: 190; Certified: Medicaid, Medicare; Owner: Nonprofit; License: state; Activities: Arts & Crafts; Dances; Pet therapy; Group exercise; Outings; Support Groups; Other: Alzheimer's secured unit, Adult day care.

Lakeview Manor Inc.
45 Beachway Dr., Indianapolis, IN 46224, (317) 243-3721; Facility type: Skilled care, Alzheimer's; Beds: 190; Certified: Medicaid, Medicare; Owner: Nonprofit; License: state; Activities: Arts & Crafts; Dances; Pet therapy; Group exercise; Outings; Support Groups; Other: Alzheimer's secured unit, Adult day care.

ManorCare Health Services
8350 Naab Rd., Indianapolis, IN 46260, (317) 872-4051; Facility type: Skilled care, Alzheimer's; Beds: 200; Certified: Medicaid, Medicare, Veterans; Owner: Nonprofit; License: state; Activities: Arts & Crafts; Dances; Pet therapy; Group exercise; Outings; Support Groups; Other: Alzheimer's secured unit, Adult day care.

Marquette Manor
8140 Township Line Rd., Indianapolis, IN 46260, (317) 875-9700; Facility type: Skilled care, Alzheimer's; Beds: 200; Certified: Medicare; Owner: Nonprofit; License: state; Activities: Arts & Crafts; Dances; Pet therapy; Group exercise; Outings; Support Groups; Other: Home health care, Adult day care.

Springfield Healthcare Center Inc.
6130 N Michigan Rd., Indianapolis, IN 46228, (317) 253-3486; Facility type: Skilled care, Alzheimer's; Beds: 100; Certified: Medicaid; Owner: Nonprofit; License: state; Activities: Arts & Crafts; Dances; Pet therapy; Group exercise; Outings; Support Groups; Other: Alzheimer's secured unit, Adult day care.

Wellington Manor HealthCare Center
1924 Wellesley Blvd., Indianapolis, IN 46219, (317) 353-6270; Facility type: Skilled care, Alzheimer's; Beds: 140; Certified: Medicaid, Medicare; Owner: Proprietary/Public; License: state; Activities: Arts & Crafts; Dances; Pet therapy; Group exercise; Outings; Support Groups; Other: Alzheimer's secured unit.

Lafayette

Rosewalk Village Healthcare Center
1903 Union St., Lafayette, IN 47904, (765) 447-9431; Facility type: Skilled care, Alzheimer's; Beds: 200; Certified: Medicaid, Medicare, Veterans; Owner: Eagle Care; License: state; Activities: Arts & Crafts; Dances; Pet therapy; Group exercise; Outings; Support Groups; Other: Adult day care.

Saint Mary Health Care
2201 Cason St., Lafayette, IN 47904, (765) 47-4102; Facility type: Skilled care, Alzheimer's; Beds: 110; Certified: Medicaid, Medicare; Owner: Proprietary/Public; License: state; Activities: Arts & Crafts; Dances; Pet therapy; Group exercise; Outings; Support Groups.

Lebanon

Parkwood Health Care Center
1001 N Grant St., Lebanon, IN 46052, (765) 482-6400; Facility type: Skilled care, Alzheimer's; Beds: 140; Certified: Medicaid, Medicare; Owner: Vencor; License: state; Activities: Arts & Crafts; Dances; Pet therapy; Group exercise; Outings; Support Groups; Other: Alzheimer's secured unit.

Marion

Bradner Village Health Care Center
505 Bradner Ave., Marion, IN 46952, (765) 662-3981; Facility type: Skilled care, Alzheimer's; Beds: 250; Certified: Medicaid, Medicare, Veterans; Owner: Proprietary/Public; License: state; Activities: Arts & Crafts; Dances; Pet therapy; Group exercise; Outings; Support Groups; Other: Alzheimer's secured unit, Adult day care, Home health care, Assisted living.

Wesleyan Health Care Center
729 W 35th St., Marion, IN 46953, (765) 674-3371; Facility type: Skilled care, Alzheimer's; Beds: 160; Certified: Medicaid, Medicare, Medi-Cal; Owner: Proprietary/Public; License: state; Activities: Arts & Crafts; Dances; Pet therapy; Group exercise; Outings; Support Groups; Other: Alzheimer's secured unit.

Markle

Markle Health Care
170 N Tracy St., Markle, IN 46770, (219) 758-2131; Facility type: Skilled care, Alzheimer's; Beds: 100; Certified: Medicaid, Medicare; Owner: Proprietary/Public; License: state; Activities: Arts & Crafts; Dances; Pet therapy; Group exercise; Outings; Support Groups; Other: Alzheimer's secured unit, Adult day care.

Martinsville

Grandview Convalescent Center
1959 E Columbus St., Martinsville, IN 46151, (765) 342-7114; Facility type: Skilled care, Alzheimer's; Beds: 100; Certified: Medicaid, Medicare, Veterans; Owner: Private; License: state; Activities: Arts & Crafts; Dances; Pet therapy; Group exercise; Outings; Support Groups; Other: Alzheimer's secured unit, Adult day care, Home health care.

Michigan City

Michigan City Health Care Center
1101 E Coolspring Ave., Michigan City, IN 46360, (219) 874-5211; Facility type: Skilled care, Alzheimer's; Beds: 250; Certified: Medicaid, Medicare; Owner: Integrated Health Services; License: state; Activities: Arts & Crafts; Dances; Pet therapy; Group exercise; Outings; Support Groups; Other: Alzheimer's secured unit.

Middletown

Millers Merry Manor
981 Beechwood Rd., Middletown, IN 47356, (765) 354-2278; Facility type: Skilled care, Alzheimer's; Beds: 60; Certified: Medicaid, Medicare; Owner: Miller's Health Care Systems; License: state; Activities: Arts & Crafts; Dances; Pet therapy; Group exercise; Outings; Support Groups; Other: Alzheimer's secured unit.

Milan

Milan Health Care Center
301 W Carr St., Milan, IN 47031, (812) 654-2231; Facility type: Skilled care, Alzheimer's; Beds: 68; Certified: Medicaid; Owner: Proprietary/Public; License: state; Activities: Arts & Crafts; Dances; Pet therapy; Group exercise; Outings; Support Groups; Other: Alzheimer's secured unit.

Muncie

Community Care Center of Muncie
3400 W Community Dr., Muncie, IN 47304, (765) 289-2273; Facility type: Skilled care, Alzheimer's; Beds: 120; Certified: Medicaid, Medicare; Owner: Proprietary/Public; License: state; Activities: Arts & Crafts; Dances; Pet therapy; Group exercise; Outings; Support Groups.

Williamsburg Village
2701 Lyn-Mar Dr., Muncie, IN 47302, (765) 286-5979; Facility type: Skilled care, Alzheimer's; Beds: 150; Certified: Medicaid, Medicare; Owner: Proprietary/Public; License: state; Activities: Arts & Crafts; Dances; Pet therapy; Group exercise; Outings; Support Groups.

New Castle

New Castle Healthcare Center
990 N 16th St., New Castle, IN 47362, (765) 529-0230; Facility type: Skilled care, Alzheimer's; Beds: 170; Certified: Medicaid, Medicare; Owner: Mariner Post Acute Network; License: state; Activities: Arts & Crafts; Dances; Pet therapy; Group exercise; Outings; Support Groups; Other: Alzheimer's secured unit, Adult day care.

New Harmony

New Harmony Healthcare Center
251 Hwy., 66, New Harmony, IN 47631, (812) 682-4104; Facility type: Skilled care, Alzheimer's; Beds: 100; Certified: Medicaid, Medicare; Owner: Centennial Healthcare; License: state; Activities: Arts & Crafts; Dances; Pet therapy; Group exercise; Outings; Support Groups; Other: Alzheimer's secured unit, Adult day care.

Oakland City

Good Samaritan Home Inc.
210 N Givson St., Oakland City, IN 47660, (812) 749-4774; Facility type: Skilled care, Alzheimer's; Beds: 120; Certified: Medicaid, Veterans; Owner: Nonprofit/Religious; License: state; Activities: Arts & Crafts; Dances; Pet therapy; Group exercise; Outings; Support Groups; Other: Alzheimer's secured unit.

Osgood

Manderley Health Care Center
806 S Buckeye St., Osgood, IN 47037, (812) 689-4143; Facility type: Skilled care, Alzheimer's; Beds: 70; Certified: Medicaid, Medicare; Owner: Proprietary/Public; License: state; Activities: Arts & Crafts; Dances; Pet therapy; Group exercise; Outings; Support Groups; Other: Alzheimer's secured unit.

Petersburg

Petersburg Healthcare & Rehabilitation
309 W Pike Ave., Petersburg, IN 47567, (812) 354-8833; Facility type: Skilled care, Alzheimer's; Beds: 140; Certified: Medicaid, Medicare, Veterans; Owner: Centennial Healthcare; License: state; Activities: Arts & Crafts; Dances; Pet therapy; Group exercise; Outings; Support Groups; Other: Alzheimer's secured unit, Home health care.

Poseyville

Allison Healthcare Corp
181 S Locust St., Poseyville, IN 47633, (812) 874-2814; Facility type: Skilled care, Alzheimer's; Beds: 40; Certified: Medicaid; Owner: Proprietary/Public; License: state; Activities: Arts & Crafts; Dances; Pet therapy; Group exercise; Outings; Support Groups; Other: Alzheimer's secured unit, Home health care.

Rensselaer

Rensselaer Care Center
1309 E Grace St., Rensselaer, IN 47978, (219) 866-4181; Facility type: Skilled care, Alzheimer's; Beds: 180; Certified: Medicaid, Medicare; Owner: Life Care Centers of America; License: state; Activities: Arts & Crafts; Dances; Pet therapy; Group exercise; Outings; Support Groups; Other: Alzheimer's secured unit, Adult day care.

Richmond

Friends Fellowship Community Inc.
2030 Chester Blvd., Richmond, IN 47374, (765) 962-6546; Facility type: Skilled care, Alzheimer's; Beds: 120; Owner: Nonprofit; License: state; Activities: Arts & Crafts; Dances; Pet therapy; Group exercise; Outings; Support Groups; Other: Alzheimer's secured unit.

San Pierre

Our Lady of Holy Cross Care Center
7520 S US Hwy. 421, San Pierre, IN 46374, (219) 828-4111; Facility type: Skilled care, Alzheimer's; Beds: 200; Certified: Medicaid, Medicare; Owner: Nonprofit; License: state; Activities: Arts & Crafts; Dances; Pet therapy; Group exercise; Outings; Support Groups; Other: Alzheimer's secured unit.

Shelbyville

Heritage Manor Inc.
2311 S Miller St., Shelbyville, IN 46176, (317) 398-9777; Facility type: Skilled care, Alzheimer's; Beds: 100;Owner: Nonprofit; License: state; Activities: Arts & Crafts; Dances; Pet therapy; Group exercise; Outings; Support Groups; Other: Alzheimer's secured unit.

South Bend

Healthwin Specialized Care Facility
20531 Darden Rd., South Bend, IN 46637, (219) 272-0100; Facility type: Skilled care, Alzheimer's; Beds: 140; Certified: Medicaid, Medicare; Owner: Nonprofit; License: state; Activities: Arts & Crafts; Dances; Pet therapy; Group exercise; Outings; Support Groups; Other: Alzheimer's secured unit.

Ironwood Health & Rehabilitation Center
1950 E Ridgedale Rd., South Bend, IN 46614, (219) 291-6722; Facility type: Skilled care, Alzheimer's; Beds: 210; Certified: Medicaid, Medicare, Veterans; Owner: Nonprofit; License: state; Activities: Arts & Crafts; Dances; Pet therapy; Group exercise; Outings; Support Groups; Other: Alzheimer's secured unit.

Saint Joseph's Care Center
4600 W Washington Ave., South Bend, IN

46619, (219) 282-1294; Facility type: Skilled care, Alzheimer's; Beds: 180; Certified: Medicaid, Medicare; Owner: Nonprofit/ Religious; License: state; Activities: Arts & Crafts; Dances; Pet therapy; Group exercise; Outings; Support Groups; Other: Alzheimer's secured unit.

Spencer

Countryside Health Care Center
RR 2, Box 77, Spencer, IN 47460, (812) 879-4275; Facility type: Skilled care, Alzheimer's; Certified: Medicaid, Medicare; Owner: Nonprofit/Religious; License: state; Activities: Arts & Crafts; Dances; Pet therapy; Group exercise; Outings; Support Groups; Other: Alzheimer's secured unit.

Terre Haute

Royal Oaks Health Care & Rehabilitation Center
3500 Maple Ave., Terre Haute, IN 47804, (812) 238-1555; Facility type: Skilled care, Alzheimer's; Beds: 200; Certified: Medicaid, Medicare, Veterans; Owner: Nonprofit/ Religious; License: state; Activities: Arts & Crafts; Dances; Pet therapy; Group exercise; Outings; Support Groups; Other: Alzheimer's secured unit, Adult day care.

Westridge Health Care
120 W Margaret Dr., Terre Haute, IN 47802, (812) 232-3311; Facility type: Skilled care, Alzheimer's; Beds: 120; Certified: Medicaid, Medicare; Owner: Nonprofit/ Religious; License: state; Activities: Arts & Crafts; Dances; Pet therapy; Group exercise; Outings; Support Groups.

Valparaiso

Valparaiso Care & Rehabilitation Center
606 Wall St., Valparaiso, IN 46383, (219) 464-4976; Facility type: Skilled care, Alzheimer's; Beds: 170; Certified: Medicaid, Medicare, Veterans; Owner: Proprietary/Public; License: state; Activities: Arts & Crafts; Dances; Pet therapy; Group exercise; Outings; Support Groups; Other: Alzheimer's secured unit.

Wabash

Wabash Healthcare Center
600 Washington St., Wabash, IN 46992, (219) 563-8402; Facility type: Skilled care, Alzheimer's; Beds: 100; Certified: Medicaid, Medicare, Veterans; Owner: Mariner Post Acute Network; License: state; Activities: Arts & Crafts; Dances; Pet therapy; Group exercise; Outings; Support Groups; Other: Alzheimer's secured unit, Adult day care.

West Lafayette

Indiana Veterans Home
3851 N River Rd., West Lafayette, IN 47906, (765) 463-1502; Facility type: Skilled care, Alzheimer's; Beds: 560; Certified: Medicaid, Veterans; Owner: Nonprofit; License: state; Activities: Arts & Crafts; Dances; Pet therapy; Group exercise; Outings; Support Groups; Other: Alzheimer's secured unit.

Westfield

Westfield Village Healthcare
776 N Union St., Westfield, IN 46074, (317) 896-2515; Facility type: Skilled care, Alzheimer's; Beds: 80; Certified: Medicaid, Medicare, Veterans; Owner: Nonprofit; License: state; Activities: Arts & Crafts; Dances; Pet therapy; Group exercise; Outings; Support Groups; Other: Alzheimer's secured unit.

IOWA

Algona

Algona Good Samaritan Center
412 W Kennedy St., Algona, IA 50511, (515) 295-2414; Facility type: Skilled care, Alzheimer's; Beds: 140; Certified: Medicaid, Veterans; Owner: Evangelical Lutheran Good Samaritan Society; License: state; Activities: Arts & Crafts; Dances; Pet therapy; Group exercise; Outings; Support Groups; Other: Alzheimer's secured unit.

Altoona

Altoona Manor Care Center
200 7th Ave., SW, Altoona, IA 50009, (515) 967-4267; Facility type: Skilled care, Alzheimer's; Beds: 100; Certified: Medicaid, Medicare Veterans; Owner: Mariner Post Acute Network; License: state; Activities: Arts & Crafts; Dances; Pet therapy; Group exercise; Outings; Support Groups; Other: Alzheimer's secured unit.

Audubon

Friendship Home
714 N Division St., Audubon, IA 50025, (712) 563-2651; Facility type: Skilled care, Alzheimer's; Beds: 160; Certified: Medicaid, Medicare; Owner: Nonprofit/Religious; License: state; Activities: Arts & Crafts; Dances; Pet therapy; Group exercise; Outings; Support Groups.

Bloomfield

Bloomfield Care Center
800 N Davis St., Bloomfield, IA 52537, (515) 664-2699; Facility type: Skilled care, Alzheimer's; Beds: 100; Certified: Medicaid, Medicare; Owner: Private; License: state; Activities: Arts & Crafts; Dances; Pet therapy; Group exercise; Outings; Support Groups; Other: Adult day care.

Britt

Westview Care Center
445 8th Ave., SW, Britt, IA 50423, (515) 843-3835; Facility type: Skilled care, Alzheimer's; Beds: 70; Certified: Medicaid; Owner: Nonprofit; License: state; Activities: Arts & Crafts; Dances; Pet therapy; Group exercise; Outings; Support Groups; Other: Alzheimer's secured unit.

Cedar Falls

Heritage Nursing & Rehabilitation Center
200 Clive Dr., SW, Cedar Rapids, IA 52404, (319) 396-7171; Facility type: Skilled care, Alzheimer's; Beds: 180; Certified: Medicaid, Medicare; Owner: Care Initiatives; License: state; Activities: Arts & Crafts; Dances; Pet therapy; Group exercise; Outings; Support Groups; Other: Alzheimer's secured unit.

Clarinda

IHS at Clarinda
600 Manor Dr., Clarinda, IA 51632, (712) 542-5161; Facility type: Skilled care, Alzheimer's; Beds: 110; Certified: Medicaid, Medicare, Veterans; Owner: Nonprofit; License: state; Activities: Arts & Crafts; Dances; Pet therapy; Group exercise; Outings; Support Groups; Other: Alzheimer's secured unit.

Clarion

USA Health Care Clarion
110 13th Ave., SW, Clarion, IA 50525, (515) 532-2893; Facility type: Skilled care, Alzheimer's; Beds: 110; Certified: Medicaid, Medicare, Veterans; Owner: USA Healthcare; License: state; Activities: Arts & Crafts; Dances; Pet therapy; Group exercise; Outings; Support Groups; Other: Alzheimer's secured unit.

Council Bluffs

Bethany Lutheran Home
7 Elliott St., Council Bluffs, IA 51503, (712) 328-9500; Facility type: Skilled care, Alzheimer's; Beds: 130; Certified: Medicaid, Medicare, Veterans; Owner: Nonprofit/Religious; License: state; Activities: Arts & Crafts; Dances; Pet therapy; Group exercise; Outings; Support Groups; Other: Alzheimer's secured unit, Independent living.

Loess Hills Nursing & Rehabilitation
2452 N Broadway, Council Bluffs, IA 51503, (712) 323-7135; Facility type: Skilled care, Alzheimer's; Beds: 110; Certified: Medicaid, Medicare, Veterans; Owner: USA Healthcare; License: state; Activities: Arts & Crafts; Dances; Pet therapy; Group exercise; Outings; Support Groups.

Risen Son Christian Village
2452 N Broadway, Council Bluffs, IA 51503, (712) 323-7135; Facility type: Skilled care, Alzheimer's; Beds: 110; Certified: Medicaid; Owner: Christian Homes, Inc.; License: state; Activities: Arts & Crafts; Dances; Pet therapy; Group exercise; Outings; Support Groups; Other: Alzheimer's secured unit.

Cresco

Howard Residential Care Facility Patty Elwood Center
21668 80th St., Cresco, IA 52136, (319) 547-2398; Facility type: Skilled care, Alzheimer's; Beds: 80; Certified: Medicaid, Medicare, Veterans; Owner: Nonprofit; License: state; Activities: Arts & Crafts; Dances; Pet therapy; Group exercise; Outings; Support Groups; Other: Alzheimer's secured unit, Adult day care.

Davenport

Davenport Good Samaritan Center
700 Waverly Rd., Davenport, IA 52804, (319) 324-1651; Facility type: Skilled care, Alzheimer's; Beds: 210; Certified: Medicaid, Medicare; Owner: Evangelical Lutheran Good Samaritan Society; License: state; Activities: Arts & Crafts; Dances; Pet therapy; Group exercise; Outings; Support Groups; Other: Alzheimer's secured unit.

Davenport Lutheran Home
1130 W 53rd St., Davenport, IA 52806, (319) 391-5342; Facility type: Skilled care, Alzheimer's; Beds: 130; Certified: Medicaid; Owner: Lutheran Home for the Aged Society; License: state; Ac-

tivities: Arts & Crafts; Dances; Pet therapy; Group exercise; Outings; Support Groups; Other: Alzheimer's secured unit; Home health care.

Kahl Home for the Aged & Infirm
1101 W 9th St., Davenport, IA 52804, (319) 324-1621; Facility type: Skilled care, Alzheimer's; Beds: 130; Certified: Medicaid, Medicare; Owner: Carmelite Sisters for the Aged & Infirm; License: state; Activities: Arts & Crafts; Dances; Pet therapy; Group exercise; Outings; Support Groups.

ManorCare Health Services
815 E Locust St., Davenport, IA 52803, (319) 324-3276; Facility type: Skilled care, Alzheimer's; Beds: 120; Certified: Medicaid, Medicare, Veterans; Owner: HCR Manor Care; License: state; Activities: Arts & Crafts; Dances; Pet therapy; Group exercise; Outings; Support Groups; Other: Alzheimer's secured unit.

Des Moines

NBA Ramsey Home
1611 27th St., Des Moines, IA 50310, (515) 274-3612; Facility type: Skilled care, Alzheimer's; Beds: 120; Certified: Medicaid; Owner: Nonprofit; License: state; Activities: Arts & Crafts; Dances; Pet therapy; Group exercise; Outings.

Parkridge Nursing & Rehabilitation Center
4755 Parkridge Ave., Des Moines, IA 50317, (515) 265-5348; Facility type: Skilled care, Alzheimer's; Beds: 70; Certified: Medicaid; Owner: Care Initiatives; License: state; Activities: Arts & Crafts; Dances; Pet therapy; Group exercise; Outings; Support Groups.

University Nursing & Rehab
233 University Ave., Des Moines, IA 50314, (515) 284-1280; Facility type: Skilled care, Alzheimer's; Beds: 160; Certified: Medicaid, Medicare, Veterans; Owner: Proprietary/Public; License: state; Activities: Arts & Crafts; Dances; Pet therapy; Group exercise; Outings; Support Groups

Dubuque

Luther Manor
3131 Hillcrest Rd., Dubuque, IA 52001, (319) 588-1413; Facility type: Skilled care, Alzheimer's; Beds: 100; Certified: Medicaid; Owner: HCR Manor Care; License: state; Activities: Arts & Crafts; Dances; Pet therapy; Group exercise; Outings; Support Groups; Other: Adult day care.

Stonehill Care Center
3485 Windsor Ave., Dubuque, IA 52001, (319) 557-7180; Facility type: Skilled care, Alzheimer's; Beds: 160; Certified: Medicaid, Veterans; Owner: HCR Manor Care; License: state; Activities: Arts & Crafts; Dances; Pet therapy; Group exercise; Outings; Support Groups; Other: Alzheimer's secured unit, Adult day care.

Eldora

Eldora Nursing & Rehabilitation Center
1510 22nd St., Eldora, IA 50627, (515) 858-3491; Facility type: Skilled care, Alzheimer's; Beds: 70; Certified: Medicaid, Medicare; Owner: Care Initiatives; License: state; Activities: Arts & Crafts; Dances; Pet therapy; Group exercise; Outings; Support Groups; Other: Alzheimer's secured unit.

Emmetsburg

Lakeside Lutheran Home
301 N Lawler St., Emmetsburg, IA 50536, (712) 852-4060; Facility type: Skilled care, Alzheimer's; Beds: 60; Certified: Medicaid, Veterans; Owner: Nonprofit/Religious; License: state; Activities: Arts & Crafts; Dances; Pet therapy; Group exercise; Outings; Support Groups; Other: Alzheimer's secured unit.

Estherville

Estherville Good Samaritan Center
1646 5th Ave., N, Estherville, IA 51334, (712) 362-3522; Facility type: Skilled care, Alzheimer's; Beds: 130; Certified: Medicaid, Medicare, Veterans; Owner: Evangelical Lutheran Good Samaritan Society; License: state; Activities: Arts & Crafts; Dances; Pet therapy; Group exercise; Outings; Support Groups; Other: Alzheimer's secured unit.

Fort Dodge

Friendship Haven
420 S Kenon Rd., Fort Dodge, IA 50501, (515) 573-2121; Facility type: Skilled care, Alzheimer's; Beds: 130; Certified: Medicaid, Medicare, Veterans; Owner: Nonprofit/Religious; License: state; Activities: Arts & Crafts; Dances; Pet therapy; Group exercise; Outings; Support Groups; Other: Alzheimer's secured unit, Adult day care, Home health care.

Green Leaf Health Center Inc.
1305 N 22nd St., Fort Dodge, IA 50501, (515) 955-4145; Facility type: Skilled care, Alzheimer's; Beds: 100; Certified: Medicaid, Medicare, Veterans; Owner: Nonprofit; License: state; Activities: Arts & Crafts; Dances; Pet therapy; Group exercise; Outings; Support Groups; Other: Alzheimer's secured unit.

Grinnell

Mayflower Home
616 Broad St., Grinnell, IA 50112, (515) 236-6151; Facility type: Skilled care, Alzheimer's; Beds: 60; Certified: Medicaid; Owner: Nonprofit; License: state; Activities: Arts & Crafts; Dances; Pet therapy; Group exercise; Outings; Support Groups; Other: Alzheimer's secured unit.

Holstein

Holstein Good Samaritan Center
505 W 2nd St., Holstein, IA 51025, (712) 368-4304; Facility type: Skilled care, Alzheimer's; Beds: 60; Certified: Medicaid, Medicare, Veterans; Owner: Nonprofit; License: state; Activities: Arts & Crafts; Dances; Pet therapy; Group exercise; Outings; Support Groups; Other: Alzheimer's secured unit; Adult day care, Home health care.

Hubbard

Hubbard Care Center
403 S State St., Hubbard, IA 50122, (515) 864-3264; Facility type: Skilled care, Alzheimer's; Beds: 60; Certified: Medicaid, Medicare; Owner: Nonprofit; License: state; Activities: Arts & Crafts; Dances; Pet therapy; Group exercise; Outings; Support Groups; Other: Alzheimer's secured unit, Adult day care.

Indianola

Good Samaritan Center
708 S Jefferson St., Box 319, Indianola, IA 50125, (515) 961-2596; Facility type: Skilled care, Alzheimer's; Beds: 120; Certified: Medicaid, Medicare, Veterans; Owner: Evangelical Lutheran Good Samaritan Society; License: state; Activities: Arts & Crafts; Dances; Pet therapy; Group exercise; Outings; Support Groups; Other: Alzheimer's secured unit.

Iowa City

Iowa City Rehabilitation & Health Care Center
4635 Herbert Hoover Hwy. SE, Iowa City, IA 52240, (319) 351-7460; Facility type: Skilled care, Alzheimer's; Beds: 90; Certified: Medicaid; Owner: HCM Inc.; License: state; Activities: Arts & Crafts; Dances; Pet therapy; Group exercise; Outings; Support Groups; Other: Alzheimer's secured unit.

Oaknoll Retirement Residence
701 Oaknoll Dr., Iowa City, IA 52246, (319) 351-1720; Facility type: Skilled care, Alzheimer's; Beds: 60; Certified: Medicaid, Medicare; Owner: Nonprofit; License: state; Activities: Arts & Crafts; Dances; Pet therapy; Group exercise; Outings; Support Groups; Other: Alzheimer's secured unit.

Johnston

Bishop Drumm Care Center
5837 Winwood Dr., Johnston, IA 50131, (515) 270-1100; Facility type: Skilled care, Alzheimer's; Beds: 160; Certified: Medicaid, Medicare; Owner: Catholic Health Initiatives; License: state; Activities: Arts & Crafts; Dances; Pet therapy; Group exercise; Outings; Support Groups; Other: Alzheimer's secured unit.

Kalona

Pleasantview Home
PO Box 309, Kalona, IA 52247, (319) 656-2421; Facility type: Skilled care, Alzheimer's; Beds: 160; Certified: Medicaid; Owner: Nonprofit; License: state; Activities: Arts & Crafts; Dances; Pet therapy; Group exercise; Outings; Support Groups; Other: Alzheimer's secured unit.

Keosauqua

Van Buren Good Samaritan Center
RR 1 Box 48B, Keosqaua, IA 52565, (319) 293-3761; Facility type: Skilled care, Alzheimer's; Beds: 100; Certified: Medicaid, Medicare; Owner: Evangelical Lutheran Good Samaritan Society; License: state; Activities: Arts & Crafts; Dances; Pet therapy; Group exercise; Outings; Support Groups; Other: Alzheimer's secured unit, Home health care, Adult day care.

Madrid

Madrid Home for the Aging
613 W North St., Madrid, IA 50156, (515) 795-3007; Facility type: Skilled care, Alzheimer's; Beds: 170; Certified: Medicaid, Medicare, Veterans; Owner: Nonprofit/Religious; License: state; Activities: Arts & Crafts; Dances; Pet therapy; Group exercise; Outings; Support Groups; Other: Alzheimer's secured unit.

Marshalltown

Iowa Veterans Homes
1301 Summit St., Marshalltown, IA 50158, (515) 753-4325; Facility type: Skilled care, Alzheimer's; Beds: 700; Certified: Medicaid, Medicare, Veterans; Owner: State & Local Gov; License: state; Activities: Arts & Crafts; Dances; Pet therapy; Group exercise; Outings; Support Groups; Other: Alzheimer's secured unit.

Monticello

Senior Home
500 Pine Haven Dr., Monticello, IA 52310, (319) 465-5415; Facility type: Skilled care, Alzheimer's; Beds: 120; Certified: Medicaid; Owner: Proprietary/Public; License: state; Activities: Arts & Crafts; Dances; Pet therapy; Group exercise; Outings; Support Groups; Other: Alzheimer's secured unit.

Newton

USA Healthcare
200 S 8th Ave., E, Newton, IA 50208, (515) 792-7440; Facility type: Skilled care, Alzheimer's; Beds: 80; Certified: Medicaid; Owner: USA Healthcare; License: state; Activities: Arts & Crafts; Dances; Pet therapy; Group exercise; Outings; Support Groups; Other: Alzheimer's secured unit.

Oelwein

Grandview Healthcare Center
800 5th St., SE, Oelwein, IA 50662, (319) 283-1908; Facility type: Skilled care, Alzheimer's; Beds: 90; Certified: Medicaid; Owner: Nonprofit; License: state; Activities: Arts & Crafts; Dances; Pet therapy; Group exercise; Outings; Support Groups; Other: Alzheimer's secured unit, Adult day care.

Ottumwa

Ottumwa Good Samaritan Health & Rehabilitation Center
2035 Chester Ave., W, Ottumwa, IA 52501, (515) 682-8041; Facility type: Skilled care, Alzheimer's; Beds: 150; Certified: Medicaid, Medicare; Owner: Evangelical Lutheran Good Samaritan Society; License: state; Activities: Arts & Crafts; Dances; Pet therapy; Group exercise; Outings; Support Groups; Other: Alzheimer's secured unit, Home health care.

Pleasantville

Pleasant Care Living Center
909 N State St., Pleasantville, IA 50225; (515) 848-5718; Facility type: Skilled care, Alzheimer's; Beds: 80; Certified: Medicaid, Medicare, Veterans; Owner: Proprietary/Public; License: state; Activities: Arts & Crafts; Dances; Pet therapy; Group exercise; Outings; Support Groups; Other: Alzheimer's secured unit.

Postville

Postville Good Samaritan Center
400 Hardin Dr., Postville, IA 52162, (319) 864-7425; Facility type: Skilled care, Alzheimer's; Beds: 70; Certified: Medicaid, Medicare; Owner: Nonprofit; License: state; Activities: Arts & Crafts; Dances; Pet therapy; Group exercise; Outings; Support Groups; Other: Alzheimer's secured unit.

Red Oak

Red Oak Good Samaritan Center
201 Alix Ave., Red Oak, IA 51566, (712) 623-3170; Facility type: Skilled care, Alzheimer's; Beds: 90; Certified: Medicaid, Medicare; Owner: Evangelical Lutheran Good Samaritan Society; License: state; Activities: Arts & Crafts; Dances; Pet therapy; Group exercise; Support Groups; Other: Alzheimer's secured unit.

Remsen

Happy Siesta Nursing Home
423 Roosevelt St., Remsen, IA 51050, (712) 786-1117; Facility type: Skilled care, Alzheimer's; Beds: 90; Certified: Medicaid; Owner: Proprietary/Public; License: state; Activities: Arts & Crafts; Dances; Pet therapy; Group exercise; Outings; Support Groups; Other: Alzheimer's secured unit.

Story City

Bethany Manor
212 Lafayette St., Story City, IA 50248, (515) 733-4325; Facility type: Skilled care, Alzheimer's; Beds: 180; Certified: Medicaid; Owner: Proprietary/Public; License: state; Activities: Arts & Crafts; Dances; Pet therapy; Group exercise; Outings.

Stratford

Stratford Nursing & Rehabilitation Center
1200 Hwy., 175 E, Stratford, IA 50249, (515) 838-2795; Facility type: Skilled care, Alzheimer's; Beds: 70; Certified: Medicaid, Medicare; Owner: Care Initiatives; License: state; Activities: Arts & Crafts; Dances; Pet therapy; Group exercise; Outings; Support Groups; Other: Alzheimer's secured unit.

Strawberry Point

Lutheran Home
313 Elkader St., Strawberry Point, IA 52076, (319) 933-6037; Facility type: Skilled care, Alzheimer's; Beds: 100; Certified: Medicaid, Medicare, Veterans; Owner: Nonprofit/Religious; License: state; Activities: Arts & Crafts; Dances; Pet therapy; Group exercise; Outings; Support Groups; Other: Alzheimer's secured unit.

Urbandale

USA Healthcare—Urbandale
4614 84th St., Urbandale, IA 50322, (515) 270-6838; Facility type: Skilled care, Alzheimer's; Beds: 130; Certified: Medicaid, Medicare, Veterans; Owner: Proprietary/Public; License: state; Activities: Arts & Crafts; Dances; Pet therapy; Group exercise; Outings; Support Groups; Other: Alzheimer's secured unit, Home health care.

Villisca

Villisca Good Samaritan Center
202 Central Ave., Villisca, IA 50864, (712) 826-9592; Facility type: Skilled care, Alzheimer's; Beds: 70; Certified: Medicaid, Medicare, Veterans; Owner: The Evangelical Lutheran Good Samaritan Society; License: state; Activities: Arts & Crafts; Dances; Pet therapy; Group exercise; Outings; Support Groups; Other: Alzheimer's secured unit, Home health care.

Waterloo

Country View
1410 W Dunkerton Rd., Waterloo, IA 50703, (319) 291-2509; Facility type: Skilled care, Alzheimer's; Beds: 110; Certified: Medicaid, Medicare, Veterans; Owner: State & Local Gov; License: state; Activities: Arts & Crafts; Dances; Pet therapy; Group exercise; Outings; Support Groups; Other: Alzheimer's secured unit,

ManorCare Health Service
201 W Ridgeway Ave., Waterloo, IA 50701, (319) 234-7777; Facility type: Skilled care, Alzheimer's; Beds: 100; Certified: Medicaid, Medicare, Veterans; Owner: State & Local Gov; License: state; Activities: Arts & Crafts; Dances; Pet therapy; Group exercise; Outings; Support Groups; Other: Alzheimer's secured unit.

KANSAS

Abilene

Beverly Healthcare of Abilene
705 N Brady St., Abilene, KS 67410, (785) 263-1431; Facility Type: Skilled care; ICF; Alzheimer's; Beds: Skilled care 60; ICF; Certified: Medicare; Owner: Beverly Enterprises Inc.; License: Current state

Arkansas City

Medicoladge Post-Acute & Rehabilitation Center
2575 Greenway Rd., Arkansas City, KS 67005, (316) 442-1120; Facility Type: Skilled care; Alzheimer's; Beds: ICF 55; Certified: Medicaid; Owner: Medicalodges Inc.; License: n/a

Canton

Shiloh Manor of Canton
601 S Kansas, Box 67 Canton, KS 67428, (316) 628-4404; Facility Type: ICF; ICF/MR; Alzheimer's; Beds: ICF 54; Certified: Medicaid; Owner: Nonprofit/Religious organization; License: Current state

Heritage Health Care Center
1630 W 2nd St., Chanute, KS 66720, (316) 431-4151; Facility Type: Skilled care; ICF; Alzheimer's; Beds: Skilled care; ICF 53; SNF/ICF; Medicare; Certified: Medicaid; Medicare; Owner: Americare Systems Inc.; License: Current state

Cherryvale

Cherryvale Care Center
1001 W Main St., Cherryvale, KS 67335, (316) 336-2102; Facility Type: Skilled care; ICF; Alzheimer's; Beds: Skilled care; ICF 49; Alzheimer's; SNF/ICF; Certified: Medicaid; Medicare; Owner: Pioneer Health Care Services Inc.; License: Current state

Cottonwood Falls

Beverly Healthcare & Rehabilitation Center—Chase County
612 Walnut St. Cottonwood Falls, KS 66845, (316) 273-6369; Facility Type: Skilled care; ICF; ICF/MR; Alzheimer's; Beds: ICF 69; Certified: Medicaid; Medicare; Veterans; Owner: Beverly Enterprises Inc.; License: Current state

Council Grove

Twin Lakes Healthcare Center
400 Sunset Dr., Council Grove, KS 66846, (316) 767-5172; Facility Type: Skilled care; ICF; Alzheimer's; Beds: skilled care; SNF/ICF 88; Certified: Medicaid; Medicare; Owner: Lenox Healthcare Inc.; License: Current state

Dodge City

Dodge City Good Samaritan Center
501 W Beeson Rd., Dodge City, KS 67801, (316) 227-7512; Facility Type: Skilled care; ICF; Alzheimer's; Beds: Skilled care 65; Certified: Medicaid; Medicare; Owner: The Evangelical Lutheran Good Samaritan Society; License: Current state

Trinity Manor
510 W Frontview St., Dodge City, KS 67801, (316) 227-8551; Facility Type: Skilled care; ICF; Alzheimer's; Beds: Skilled care 83; Alzheimer's 23; Certified: Medicaid; Medicare; Owner: Nonprofit/Religious organization; License: Current state

Douglass

Medicalodge of Douglass
619 S Hwy., 77 Douglass, KS 67039, (316) 747-2157; Facility Type: Skilled care; ICF; Alzheimer's; Beds: Skilled care 6; ICF 29; Alzheimer's 23; Certified: Medicaid; Medicare; Owner: Medicalodges Inc.; License: Current state

El Dorado

Lakepoint Nursing & Rehabilitation Center of El Dorado
1313 S High St., El Dorado, KS 67042, (316) 321-4140; Facility Type: Skilled care; ICF; Alzheimer's; Beds: Skilled care 60; ICF 40; Alzheimer's 17; Certified: Medicaid; Medicare; Veterans; Owner: Proprietary/Public corp.; License: Current state

Emporia

Emporia Rehabilitation Center
221 W Logan Ave., Emporia, KS 66801, (316) 342-4212; Facility Type: Skilled care; ICF; Alzheimer's; Beds: Skilled care 79; Residential care; Certified: Medicaid; Medicare; Owner: Centennial HealthCare Corp.; License: Current state

Eudora

Eudora Nursing Center
1415 Maple Eudora, KS 66025, (785) 542-2176; Facility Type: ICF; Alzheimer's; Beds: ICF 86; Certified: Medicaid; Owner: Proprietary/Public corp.; License: Current state

Fort Scott

Fort Scott Manor
736 Heylman St., Fort Scott, KS 66701, (316) 223-3120; Facility Type: Skilled care; ICF; Alzheimer's; Beds: Skilled care 4; ICF 85; Alzheimer's 10; Certified: Medicaid; Medicare; Owner: Proprietary/Public corp.; License: Current state

Medicalodge of Fort Scott
915 S Horton Ave., Fort Scott, KS 66701, (316) 223-0210; Facility Type: Skilled care; ICF; Alzheimer's; Beds: Skilled care 101; ICF; Alzheimer's; Certified: Medicaid; Medicare; Owner: Medicalodges Inc.; License: Current state

Garden City

Garden Valley Retirement Village
1505 E Spruce St., Garden City, KS 67846, (316) 275-9651; Facility Type: Skilled care; ICF; Alzheimer's; Beds: Skilled care 100; ICF; Retirement; Certified: Medicaid; Medicare; Owner: Nonprofit corp.; License: Current state

Terrace Garden Care Center
2308 N 3rd Garden City, KS 67846, (316) 276-7643; Facility Type: Skilled care; ICF; Alzheimer's; Beds: Skilled care 60; ICF; Alzheimer's 14; Certified: Medicaid; Medicare; Owner: Vetter Health Services Inc.; License: Current state

Goodland

Sherman County Good Samaritan Center
208 W 2nd St., Goodland, KS 67735, (785) 899-7517; Facility Type: Skilled care; ICF; Alzheimer's; Beds: ICF 48; Alzheimer's 12; Certified: Medicaid; Medicare; Owner: Nonprofit/Religious organization; License: Current state

Great Bend

Cherry Village
1401 Cherry Ln., Great Bend, KS 67530, (316) 792-2165; Facility Type: ICF; Alzheimer's; Beds: Skilled care 72; ICF; Alzheimer's; Certified: Medicaid; Owner: Nonprofit corp.; License: Current state

Haysville

Prestige Rehabilitation & Nursing Center
215 N Lamar Ave., Haysville, KS 67060, (316) 524-3211; Facility Type: Skilled care; ICF; Alzheimer's; Beds: Skilled care 120; ICF; SNF/ICF; Certified: Medicaid; Medicare; Veterans; Owner: Proprietary/Public corp.; License: Current state

Horton

Tri-County Manor Living Center
1890 Euclid Ave., Horton, KS 66439, (785) 486-2697; Facility Type: ICF; Alzheimer's; Beds: ICF 60; Residential; Certified: Medicaid; Owner: Nonprofit corp.; License: Current state

Hugoton

Pioneer Manor
6th & Polk, Box 758, Hugoton, KS 67951, (316) 544-2023; Facility Type: ICF; Alzheimer's; Beds: ICF 36; Alzheimer's 24; Certified: Medicaid; Owner: Government/State/Local; License: Current state

Humboldt

Pinecrest Nursing Home
1020 Pine St., Humboldt, KS 66748, (316) 473-2393; Facility Type: Skilled care; ICF; Alzheimer's; Beds: Skilled care 38; Alzheimer's 14; Certified: Medicaid; Medicare; Owner: Nonprofit corp.; License: Current state

Hutchinson

Silver Oak Health Center
2813 S Broadacres Rd., Hutchinson, KS 67501, (316) 663-2829; Facility Type: Skilled care; ICF; Alzheimer's; Beds: ICF 55; Certified: Medicaid; Medicare; Owner: Proprietary/Public corp.; License: Current state

Wesley Towers
700 Monterey Pl., Hutchinson, KS 67502, (316) 663-9175; Facility Type: Skilled care; ICF; Alzheimer's; Beds: SNF/ICF 130; Certified: Medicaid; Medicare; Owner: Nonprofit/Religious organization; License: Current state

Independence

Glenwood Estate
621 S 2nd St., Independence, KS 67301, (316) 331-2260; Facility Type: ICF; Alzheimer's; Beds: ICF 43; Certified: Medicaid; Owner: Private; License: Current state

The Lodge
1000 Mulberry St., Independence, KS 67301, (316) 331-8420; Facility Type: Skilled care; ICF; Alzheimer's; Beds: Skilled care 55; Certified: Medicaid; Medicare; Owner: Lenox Healthcare Inc.; License: Current state

Junction City

Junction City Good Samaritan Center
416 W Spruce St., Junction City, KS 66441, (785) 238-1187; Facility Type: Skilled care; ICF; Alzheimer's; Beds: ICF 60; Certified: Medicaid; Owner: The Evangelical Lutheran Good Samaritan Society; License: Current state

Kansas City

The Alzheimer's Center of Kansas City
6501 Greeley Ave., Kansas City, KS 66104, (913) 334-5252; Facility Type: ICF; Alzheimer's; Beds: Skilled care 96; Certified: Medicaid; Owner: Medicalodges Inc.; License: Current state

Kansas City Presbyterian Manor
7850 Freeman Ave., Kansas City, KS 66112, (913) 334-3666; Facility Type: Skilled care; ICF; Alzheimer's; Beds: ICF; Alzheimer's 43; SNF/ICF 134; Personal care 36; Certified: Medicaid; Medicare; Owner: Nonprofit corp.; License: Current state

Kingman

The Wheatlands Health Care Center
750 W Washington St., Kingman, KS 67068, (316) 532-5801; Facility Type: ICF; Alzheimer's; Beds: ICF 36; Alzheimer's 18; Assisted living 20; Certified: Medicaid; Owner: Nonprofit corp.; License: Current state

Larned

Larned Healthcare Living Center
1114 W 11th St., Larned, KS 67550, (316) 285-6914; Facility Type: Skilled care; ICF; Alzheimer's; Beds: Skilled care 69; Certified: Medicaid; Medicare; Owner: Proprietary/Public corp.; License: Current state

Lawrence

Brandon Woods
1501 Inverness Dr., Lawrence, KS 66047, (785) 843-4571; Facility Type: Skilled care; Alzheimer's; Beds: Skilled care 60; ICF 60; Alzheimer's 40; Certified: Medicaid; Medicare; Owner: Proprietary/Public corp.; License: Current state

Liberal

Liberal Good Samaritan Center
2160 Zinnia Ln., Liberal, KS 67901, (316) 624-3832; Facility Type: Skilled care; ICF; Alzheimer's; Beds: Skilled care 65; ICF; Alzheimer's 16; Independent living; Certified: Medicaid; Medicare; Owner: The Evangelical Lutheran Good Samaritan Society; License: Current state

Lincoln

Mid-America Health Care
922 N 5th St., Lincoln, KS 67455, (785) 524-4428; Facility Type: ICF; Alzheimer's; Beds: ICF 53; Assisted living 13; Certified: Medicaid; Medicare; Owner: Proprietary/Public corp.; License: Current state

Logan

Logan Manor Community Health Services
108 S Adams Logan, KS 67646, (785) 689-4201; Facility Type: ICF; Alzheimer's; Beds: ICF 48; Alzheimer's; Certified: Medicaid; Owner: Nonprofit/Religious org.; License: Current state

Lyons

Lyons Good Samaritan Center
1311 S Douglass Ave., Lyons, KS 67554, (316) 257-5163; Facility Type: Skilled care; Alzheimer's; Beds: Alzheimer's 15; SNF/ICF 72; Certified: Medicaid; Medicare; Owner: The Evangelical Lutheran Good Samaritan Society

Madison

Madison Manor
PO Box 277 Madison, KS 66860, (316) 437-2470; Facility Type: ICF; Alzheimer's; Beds: ICF 49; Certified: Medicaid; Owner: Nonprofit corp.; License: Current state

Manhattan

Meadowlark Hills
2121 Meadowlark Rd., Manhattan, KS 66502, (785) 537-4610; Facility Type: Skilled care; Alzheimer's; Beds: Skilled care 60; Alzheimer's; Certified: Medicaid; Medicare; Owner: Nonprofit corp.; License: Current state

Wharton Manor
2101 Claflin Rd., Manhattan, KS 66502, (785) 776-0636; Facility Type: Skilled care; ICF; Alzheimer's; Beds: ICF 60; Certified: Medicaid; Medicare; Owner: Nonprofit/Religious org.; License: Current state

McPherson

The Cedars Inc.
1021 Cedars Dr., McPherson, KS 67460, (316) 241-0919; Facility Type: Skilled care; Alzheimer's; Beds: ICF; SNF/ICF 11; Certified: Medicaid; Owner: Nonprofit/Religious organization; License: Current state

Highland Manor
1601 N Main St., McPherson, KS 67460, (316) 241-5360; Facility Type: ICF; Alzheimer's; Beds: Skilled care 60; Certified: Medicaid; Owner: Proprietary/Public corp.; License: n/a

Medicine Lodge

Cedar Crest Manor
601 N Cedar St., Medicine Lodge, KS 67104, (316) 886-3781; Facility Type: Skilled care; ICF; Alzheimer's; Beds: Skilled care 42; Certified: Medicaid; Medicare; Owner: Proprietary/Public corp.; License: Current state

Merriam

Trinity Lutheran Manor
9700 W 62nd St., Merriam, KS 66203, (913) 384-0800; Facility Type: Skilled care; ICF; Alzheimer's; Beds: skilled Care 5; ICF 115; Certified: Medicaid; Medicare; Owner: Nonprofit/Religious org.; License: Current state

Minneapolis

Minneapolis Good Samaritan Center
815 N Rothsay Minneapolis, KS 67467, (785) 392-2162; Facility Type: Skilled care; ICF; Alzheimer's; Beds: ICF 93; Retirement; Certified: Medicaid; Medicare; Owner: The Evangelical Lutheran Good Samaritan Society; License: Current state

Newton

Newton Presbyterian Manor
1200 E 7th St., Newton, KS 67114, (316) 283-5400; Facility Type: Skilled care; ICF; Alzheimer's; Beds: Skilled care 167; ICF; Alzheimer's; Certified: Medicaid; Medicare; Veterans; Owner: Nonprofit corp.; License: Current state

Onaga

Golden Acres
500 Western St., Onaga, KS 66521, (785) 889-4227; Facility Type: Skilled care; ICF; Alzheimer's; Beds: Skilled care 50; ICF; Certified: Medicaid; Medicare; Owner: Beverly Enterprises Inc.; License: Current state

Osawatomie

Heritage Manor of Osawatomie
1615 Parker Ave., Osawatomie, KS 66064, (913) 755-4165; Facility Type: Skilled care; ICF; Alzheimer's; Beds: Skilled care 112; Certified: Medicaid; Medicare; Veterans; Owner: Life Care Centers of America; License: n/a

Oskaloosa

Hickory Pointe Care & Rehabilitation Center
700 Cherokee Oskaloosa, KS 66066, (785) 863-2108; Facility Type: Skilled care; ICF; Alzheimer's; Beds: Skilled care 70; Certified: Medicaid; Medicare; Owner: Proprietary/Public corp.; License: Current state

Oswego

Potomac Healthcare
1212 Ohio St., Oswego, KS 67356, (316) 795-4429; Facility Type: Skilled care; ICF; Alzheimer's; Beds: ICF; Covering all aspects 40; Certified: Medicaid; Medicare; Owner: Proprietary/Public corp.

Overland Park

Indian Meadows Nursing Center & Rehabilitation Center
6505 W 103rd St., Overland park, KS 66212, (913) 649-5110; Facility Type: Skilled care; Alzheimer's; Beds: Skilled care 79; Certified: Medicaid; Medicare; Owner: Integrated Health Services Inc.; License: Current state

Parsons

Parsons Good Samaritan Center
809 Leawood Ave., Parsons, KS 67357, (316) 421-1110; Facility Type: ICF; Alzheimer's; Beds: ICF 60; Certified: Medicaid; Medicare; Owner: The Evangelical Lutheran Good Samaritan Society; License: Current state

Peabody

Peabody Community Living Center Inc.
407 N Locust St., Peabody, KS 66866, (316) 983-2152; Facility Type: ICF; Alzheimer's; Beds: ICF 93; Alzheimer's; Residential; Indep.; Certified: Medicaid; Veterans; Owner: Nonprofit corp.; License: Current state

Richmond

Oak Haven Nursing Center
340 E South St., Richmond, KS 66080, (785) 835-6135; Facility Type: ICF; Alzheimer's; Beds: Skilled care 63; Certified: Medicaid; Owner: Government/State/Local; License: Current state

Russell

Wheatland Nursing & Rehabilitation Center
320 S Lincoln St., Box 913 Russell, KS 67665, (785) 483-536; Facility Type: Skilled care; ICF; Alzheimer's; Beds: Skilled care 55; Certified: Medicaid; Medicare; Veterans; Owner: Americare Systems Inc.; License: Current state

Salina

Salina Presbyterian Manor
2601 E Crawford St., Salina, KS 67401, (785) 825-1366; Facility Type: Skilled care; ICF; Alzheimer's; Beds: Skilled care 60; Certified: Medicaid; Medicare; Owner: Nonprofit/Religious org.; License: Current state

Smith Center

Infinia at Smith Center
117 W 1st St., Smith Center, KS 66967, (785) 282-6696; Facility Type: Skilled care; ICF; Alzheimer's; Beds: Skilled care 40; ICF 40; Alzheimer's 40; SNF/ICF 40; Boarding home care 10; Certified: Medicaid; Medicare; Medi-Cal; Veterans; Owner: Private; License: Current state

Spring Hill

Beverly Healthcare—Spring Hill
251 E Wilson St., Spring Hill, KS 66083, (913) 592-3100; Facility Type: Skilled care; ICF; Alzheimer's; Beds: Skilled care 6; ICF 50; Certified: Medicaid; Medicare; Owner: Proprietary/Public corp.; License: Current state

Topeka

Aldersgate Village Health Unit
3220 SW Albright Dr., Topeka, KS 66614, (785) 478-9440; Facility Type: Skilled care; Alzheimer's; Beds: Skilled care 134; Alzheimer's 20; Licensed child 95; Certified: Medicaid; Medicare; Owner: Nonprofit/Religious org.; License: Current state

Brewster Health Center
1001 SW 29th St., Topeka, KS 66611, (785) 267-1666; Facility Type: Skilled care; Alzheimer's; Beds: Skilled care 6; SNF/ICF 20; Certified: Medicaid; Medicare; Owner: Nonprofit/Religious org.; License: Current state

Fairlawn Heights Nursing Center
5400 SW 7th St., Topeka, KS 66606, (785) 272-6880; Facility Type: Skilled care; ICF; Alzheimer's; Beds: Skilled care; ICF 52; Residential care; Certified: Medicaid; Medicare; Veterans; Owner: Proprietary/Public corp.; License: Current state

IHS at Highland Park
1821 SE 21st St., Topeka, KS 66607, (785) 234-0018; Facility Type: Skilled care; ICF; Alzheimer's; Beds: Skilled care 52; Certified: Medicaid; Medicare; Owner: Integrated Health Services Inc.; License: Current state

McCrite Plaza Health Center
1610 SW 37th St., Topeka, KS 66611, (785) 267-2960; Facility Type: Skilled care; Alzheimer's; Beds: Skilled care 46; ICF 74; Certified: Medicaid; Medicare; Owner: Private; License: Current state

Rolling Hills Health Center
2400 SW Urish Rd., Topeka, KS 66614, (785) 273-5001; Facility Type: Skilled care; ICF; ICF/MR; Alzheimer's; Beds: Skilled care 60; ICF 60; Certified: Medicaid; Medicare; Veterans; Owner: Proprietary/Public corp.; License: Current state

Topeka Presbyterian Manor
4712 SW 6th Ave., Topeka, KS 66606, (785) 272-6510; Facility Type: Skilled care; ICF; Alzheimer's; Beds: Skilled care 210; ICF; Alzheimer's; Certified: Medicaid; Medicare; Owner: Nonprofit corp.; License: Current state

United Methodist Home
1135 SW College Ave., Topeka, KS 66604, (785) 234-0421; Facility Type: ICF; Alzheimer's; Beds: Skilled care 110; Certified: Medicaid; Owner: Nonprofit corp.; License: Current state

Uniontown

Marmaton Valley Nursing Home Hwy
54 & K3 Uniontown, KS 66779, (316) 756-4661; Facility Type: ICF; Alzheimer's; Beds: ICF 30; Alzheimer's 10; Post-surg; Respite; Certified: Medicaid; Owner: Private; License: Current state

Victoria

Saint John Rest Home
701 7th St., Victoria, KS 67671, (785) 735-2208; Facility Type: ICF; Alzheimer's; Beds: ICF 90; Certified: Medicaid; Owner: Nonprofit/Religious org.; License: Current state

Wellington

Cedar View Good Samaritan Center
1600 W 8th St., Wellington, KS 67152, (316) 326-2232; Facility Type: Skilled care; ICF; Alzheimer's; Beds: Skilled care 80; Certified: Medicaid; Medicare; Owner: Nonprofit corp.; License: Current state

Wichita

Catholic Care Center
6700 E 45th St., N Wichita, KS 677226, (316) 744-2020; Facility Type: Skilled care; ICF; Alzheimer's; Beds: Skilled care 178; ICF 178; Alzheimer's 16; Certified: Medicaid; Medicare; Veterans; Owner: Nonprofit corp.; License: Current state

Cherry Creek Health Care Center
8100 E Pawnee Wichita, KS 67207, (316) 684-1313; Facility Type: Skilled care; ICF; Alzheimer's; Beds: Skilled care 60; ICF 26; Certified: Medicaid; Medicare; Owner: Private; License: Current state

Life Care Center of Wichita
622 N Edgemoor St., Wichita, KS 67208, (316) 686-5100; Facility Type: Skilled care; ICF; Alzheimer's; Beds: ICF; Certified: Medicaid; Medicare; Owner: Life Care Centers of America; License: Current state

Terrace Gardens Nursing Center
1315 N West St., Wichita, KS 67203, (316) 943-1294; Facility Type: Skilled care; ICF; Alzheimer's; Beds: Alzheimer's 22; SNF/ICF 120; Certified: Medicaid; Owner: Private; License: Current state

Winfield

Winfield Good Samaritan Village
1320 Wheat Rd., Winfield, KS 67156, (316) 221-4660; Facility Type: Skilled care; Alzheimer's; Beds: Skilled care 80; Certified: Medicaid; Medicare; Owner: Nonprofit corp.; License: Current state

---

KENTUCKY

Ashland

King's Daughters Medical Center
2201 Lexington Ave., Ashland, KY 41101, (606) 327-4000; Facility Type: Skilled care; Alzheimer's; Beds: Skilled care 10; Certified: Medicaid; Medicare; Owner: Nonprofit corp.; License: Current state

Woodland Oaks Health Care Facility
1820 Oakview Rd., Ashland, KY 41105, (606) 325-5200; Facility Type: Skilled care; ICF; ICF/MR; Alzheimer's; Beds: SNF/ICF 110; Personal care 10; Certified: Medicaid; Medicare; Owner: n/a; License: Current state

Barbourville

Valley Park Convalescent Center
PO Box 1090 Barbourville, KY 40906, (606) 546-5136; Facility Type: Skilled care; ICF; Alzheimer's; Beds: Skilled care 119; Certified: Medicaid; Owner: Proprietary/Public corp.; License: Current state

Beattyville

Lee County Constant Care Inc.
249 E Main St., Beattyville, KY 41311, (606) 464-3611; Facility Type: Skilled care; ICF; Alzheimer's; Beds: Skilled care 35; Alzheimer's 89; Personal care 6; Certified: Medicaid; Medicare; Owner: Nonprofit corp; License: Current state

Bowling Green

Panorama Rest Care
980 Morgantown Rd., Bowling Green, KY 42101, (270) 782-7770; Facility Type: ICF/MR; Alzheimer's; Beds: ICF/MR 58; Certified: Medicaid; Medicare; Owner: Private; License: Current state

Wellington Parc of Bowling Green
1381 Campbell Ln., Bowling Green, KY 42104, (270) 843-0587; Facility Type: Skilled care; Alzheimer's; Beds: Skilled care 60; Certified: n/a; Owner: n/a; License: Current state

Columbia

Summit Manor
400 Bomar Heights Columbia, KY 42728, (270) 384-2153; Facility Type: Skilled care; ICF; ICF/MR; Alzheimer's; Beds: Skilled care 104; Certified: Medicaid; Medicare; Owner: EPI Corp.; License: Current state

Corbin

Hillcrest Nursing Home
1245 American Greeting Rd., Corbin, KY 40702; (606) 528-8917; Facility Type: Skilled care; ICF; Alzheimer's; Beds: Skilled care 43; ICF 77; Certified: Medicaid; Medicare; Owner: Proprietary/Public corp.; License: Current state

Dawson Springs

NHC Health Care Center
100 Ramsey St., Dawson Springs, KY 42408, (270) 797-8131; Facility Type: Skilled care; ICF; Alzheimer's; Beds: Skilled care 80; Certified: Medicaid; Medicare; Veterans; Owner: Proprietary/Public corp.; License: Current state

Florence

Florence Park Care Center
6975 Burlington Pike Florence, KY 41042, (606) 525-0007; Facility Type: Skilled care; ICF; Alzheimer's; Beds: Skilled care 34; ICF 66; Alzheimer's 50; Adult day care; Certified: Medicaid; Medicare; Owner: Proprietary/Public corp.; License: Current state

Greenville

Belle Meade Home
521 Greene Dr., Greenville, KY 42345, (270) 338-1523; Facility Type: Skilled care; ICF; Alzheimer's; Beds: ICF 62; Personal care 30; Certified: Medicaid; Owner: Private; License: n/a

Highland Heights

Lakeside Place
3510 Alexandria Pike Highland Heights, KY 41076, (606) 441-1100; Facility Type: Skilled care; ICF; Alzheimer's; Beds: Skilled care 116; ICF 170; Personal care 38; Certified: Medicaid; Medicare; Owner: Proprietary/Public corp.; License: Current state

Lexington

Darby Square Nursing Rehabilitation Center
2770 Palumbo Dr., Lexington, KY 40509, (606) 263-2410; Facility Type: Skilled care; ICF; Alzheimer's; Beds: Skilled care 120; Certified: Medicaid; Medicare; Owner: Nonprofit/Religious org.; License: Current state

IHS at Mayfair Manor
3300 Tates Creek Rd., Lexington, KY 40502, (606) 266-2126; Facility Type: Skilled care; ICF; Alzheimer's; Beds: Skilled care; ICF 50; Alzheimer's; SNF/ICF 30; Certified: Medicaid; Medicare; Owner: Proprietary/Public corp.; License: Current state

SunRise Care & Rehabilitation for Cambridge Drive
2020 Cambridge Dr., Lexington, KY 40504, (606) 252-6747; Facility Type: Skilled care; ICF; ICF/MR; Alzheimer's; Beds: Skilled care 104; ICF; Personal care; Certified: Medicaid; Medicare; Owner: Proprietary/Public corp.; License: Current state

Louisville

Baptist Home East
3001 Hurstbourne Pkwy Louisville, KY 40241, (502) 426-5531; Facility Type: Skilled care; ICF; ICF/MR; Alzheimer's; Beds: SNF/ICF 110; Certified: Medicaid; Medicare; Owner: Nonprofit/Religious organization; License: Current state

Hurstbourne Care Center at Stony Brook
2200 Stony Brook Dr., Louisville, KY 40220, (502) 495-6240; Facility Type: Skilled care; ICF; Alzheimer's; Beds: Skilled care 140; ICF; Alzheimer's; SNF/ICF; Certified: Medicaid; Medicare; Owner: Centennial HealthCare Corp.; License: Current state

Nazareth Home
2000 Newburg Rd., Louisville, KY 40205, (502) 459-9681; Facility Type: Skilled care; ICF; Alzheimer's; Beds: SNF/ICF 118; Personal care 50; Certified: Medicaid; Medicare; Owner: Nonprofit/Religious org.; License: Current state

Wesley Manor Nursing Center & Retirement Community
5012 E Manslick Rd., Louisville, KY 40219, (502) 969-3277; Facility Type: Skilled care; ICF; Alzheimer's Beds: ICF 160; Personal; Certified: Medicaid; Medicare; Owner: Nonprofit corp. License: n/a

Owensboro

Hillcrest Health Care Center
3740 Old Hartford Rd., Owensboro, KY 42303, (270) 684-7259; Facility Type: Skilled care; ICF; Alzheimer's; Beds: Skilled care 40; ICF 92; Alzheimer's 24; Certified: Medicaid; Medicare; Veterans; Owner: Vencor Inc.; License: Current state

Wellington Parc of Owensboro
2885 New Hartford Rd., Owensboro, KY 42303, (270) 685-2374; Facility Type: Skilled care; Alzheimer's; Beds: Skilled care 80; ICF; Alzheimer's; Certified: Medicaid; Medicare; Veterans; Owner: Private; License: Current state

South Shore

South Shore Nursing & Rehabilitation Center
PO Box 489 South Shore, KY 41175, (606) 932-3127; Facility Type: Skilled care; ICF; ICF/MR; Alzheimer's; Beds: Skilled care 60; Certified: Medicaid; Medicare; Owner: Proprietary/Public corp.; License: Current state

South Williamson

Williamson Appalachian Regional Hospital—Skilled Nursing Facility
260 Hospital Dr., South Williamson, KY 42503, (606) 237-1725; Facility Type: Skilled care; Alzheimer's; Beds: Skilled care 50; Converted 10; Certified: Medicaid; Medicare; Owner: Nonprofit corp.; License: Current state

Williamstown

Grant Manor Inc.
201 Kimberly Ln., Williamstown, KY 41097, (606) 824-7803; Facility Type: Skilled care; ICF; ICF/MR; Alzheimer's; Beds: Skilled care 25; ICF 70; Certified: Medicaid; Medicare; Owner: Proprietary/Public corp.; License: Current state

---

LOUISIANA

Baker

Community Care Center of Baker
3612 Baker Blvd., Baker, LA 70714, (225) 778-0573; Facility Type: Skilled care; ICF; Alzheimer's; Beds: Skilled care 12; ICF 92; Alzheimer's 16; Certified: Medicaid; Medicare; Veterans; Owner: Nonprofit corp.; License: Current state

Baton Rouge

Baton Rouge Health Care Center
5550 Thomas Rd., Baton Rouge, LA 70811, (225) 774-2141; Facility Type: Skilled care; ICF; Alzheimer's; Beds: Skilled care 12; ICF 126; Alzheimer's 24; Certified: Medicaid; Medicare; Veterans; Owner: Private; License: Current state

Guest House of Baton Rouge
10145 Florida Blvd., Baton Rouge, LA 70815, (225) 272-0111; Facility Type: Skilled care; ICF; Alzheimer's; Beds: Skilled care 144; SNF/ICF; Certified: Medicaid; Owner: Nonprofit corp.; License: Current state

Oasis Rehabilitation Hospital
4363 Convention St., Baton Rouge, LA 70806, (225) 383-6134; Facility Type: Skilled care; ICF; Alzheimer's; Beds: Skilled care 100; Certified: Medicaid; Medicare; Owner: Proprietary/Public corp.; License: Current state

Saint Clare Manor
7435 Bishop Ott Dr., Baton Rouge, LA 70806, (225) 216-3604; Facility Type: Skilled care; ICF; Alzheimer's; Beds: Alzheimer's 26; SNF/ICF 94; Certified: Medicaid; Owner: Nonprofit/Religious org.; License: Current state

Bernice

Pinecrest Health Care Center
101 Reeves St., Bernice, LA 71222, (318) 285-7600; Facility Type: Skilled care; ICF; Alzheimer's; Beds: ICF 50; Alzheimer's; Certified: Medicaid; Owner: Private; License: Current state

Bossier City

Garden Court Nursing Center
4405 Airline Dr., Bossier City, LA 71111, (318)

747-5440; Facility Type: Skilled care; ICF; Alzheimer's; Beds: Skilled care 12; ICF 52; Alzheimer's 13; Certified: Medicare; Owner: Proprietary/Public corp.; License: Current state

Columbia

Haven Nursing Center Inc.
7726 Hwy. 165 S, Columbia, LA 71418, (318) 649-9800; Facility Type: Skilled care; ICF; Alzheimer's; Beds: Skilled care 41; ICF 92; Alzheimer's; Independent living; Certified: Medicaid; Medicare; Owner: Private; License: Current state

DeRidder

Beauregard Rehabilitation & Retirement Center
1420 Blankenship Dr., DeRidder, LA 70634, (337) 463-9022; Facility Type: Skilled care; ICF; Alzheimer's; Beds: Alzheimer's 52; SNF/ICF 90; Certified: Medicaid; Medicare; Veterans; Owner: Proprietary/Public corp.; License: Current state

Denham Springs

Golden Age Nursing Home
26739 Hwy., 1032 Denham Springs, LA 70726, (225) 665-5544 Facility Type: Skilled care; ICF; Alzheimer's; Beds: ICF 174; Certified: Medicaid; Owner: Private; License: Current state

Donaldsonville

The DeVille House Nursing Home
401 Vatican House Donaldsonville, LA 70346, (225) 473-8614; Facility Type: Skilled care; ICF; Alzheimer's; Beds: Skilled care 136; SNF/ICF; Certified: Medicaid; Medicare; Veterans; Owner: Nonprofit corp.; License: Current state

Ferriday

Concordia Nursing Home and Camelot Leisure Living
6818 Hwy., 84 Ferriday, LA 71334, (318) 757-2181; Facility Type: Skilled care; ICF; Alzheimer's; Beds: Skilled care 91; ICF; Alzheimer's; SNF/ICF; Certified: Medicaid; Owner: Private; License: Current state

Hammond

Landmark Nursing Center—Hammond
1300 Derek Dr., Hammond, LA 70401, (504) 542-8570; Facility Type: Skilled care; ICF; Alzheimer's; Beds: Skilled care 10; ICF 112; Alzheimer's; Certified: Medicaid; Owner: Private; License: Current state

Harvey

Maison De Ville Nursing Home of Harvey
2233 8th St., Harvey, LA 70058, (504) 362-9522; Facility Type: Skilled care; ICF; Alzheimer's; Beds: ICF 101; Certified: Medicaid; Owner: Private; License: Current state

Houma

Maison De Ville of Houma
107 S Hollywood Dr., Houma, LA 70360, (504) 876-3250; Facility Type: ICF; Alzheimer's; Beds: ICF 105; Certified: Medicaid; Owner: Private; License: Current state

Jackson

Louisiana War Veterans Home
4739 Hwy. 10, Jackson, LA 70748, (225) 634-5265; Facility Type: ICF; Alzheimer's; Beds: ICF 190; Alzheimer's 50; Certified: Veterans; Owner: Government/State/Local; License: Current state

Jefferson

Jefferson Health Care Center
2200 Jefferson Hwy., Jefferson, LA 70121, (504) 837-3144; Facility Type: ICF; Alzheimer's; Beds: Skilled care; ICF 240; Alzheimer's; Certified: Medicaid; Medicare; Veterans; Owner: Proprietary/Public corp.; License: Current state

Kaplan

Vermilion Health Care Center
14008 Cheneau, Kaplan, LA 70548, (337) 643-1949; Facility Type: Skilled care; ICF; ICF/MR; Alzheimer's; Beds: ICF/MR 100; Alzheimer's 120; SNF/ICF 200; Certified: Medicaid; Owner: Private; License: Current state

Lacombe

Lacombe Nursing Centre
28119 Hwy. 190, Davis Ave., Lacombe, LA 70445, (504) 882-5417; Facility Type: Skilled care; ICF; Alzheimer's; Beds: Skilled care 16; ICF 82; Certified: Medicaid; Medicare; Owner: Private; License: Current state

Lafayette

Amelia Manor Nursing Home Inc.
903 Center St., Lafayette, LA 70501, (337) 234-7331; Facility Type: Skilled care; ICF; Alzheimer's; Beds: SNF/ICF 151; Certified: Medicaid; Medicare; Veterans; Owner: Proprietary/Public corp.; License: Current state

Lady of the Oaks Nursing Home
1005 Eraste Landry Rd., Lafayette, LA 70506, (337) 232-6370; Facility Type: ICF; Alzheimer's; Beds: ICF 136; SNF/ICF; Certified: Medicaid; Owner: Private; License: Current state

Oakwood Village Nurse Care Center
2500 E Simcoe St., Lafayette, LA 70501, (337) 233-7115; Facility Type: Skilled care; ICF; Alzheimer's; Beds: ICF 160; Certified: Medicaid; Owner: Proprietary/Public corp.; License: Current state

Lake Charles

SunBridge Care & Rehabilitation for Lake Charles
2717 1st Ave., Lake Charles, LA , 601, (337) 478-2920; Facility Type: Skilled care; ICF; ICF/MR; Alzheimer's; Beds: Skilled care 187; ICF; Alzheimer's; Certified: Medicaid; Medicare; Veterans; Owner: Nonprofit/Religious org.; License: Current state

Mandeville

Pontchartrain Health Care Centre
PO Box 338 Mandeville, LA 70470, (504) 626-8581; Facility Type: Skilled care; ICF; Alzheimer's; Beds: Skilled care; ICF 182; Alzheimer's 14; Certified: Medicaid; Medicare; Veterans; Owner: Private; License: Current state

Metairie

Saint Anthony Nursing Home Inc.
6001 Airline Dr., Metairie, LA 70003, (504) 733-8448; Facility Type: ICF; Alzheimer's; Beds: ICF 124; Certified: Medicaid; Owner: Proprietary/Public corp.; License: Current state

Monroe

Riverside Nursing Home
3001 S Grand St., Monroe, LA 71201, (318) 388-3200; Facility Type: Skilled care; ICF; Alzheimer's; Beds: Alzheimer's 57; SNF/ICF 110; Certified: Medicaid; Owner: Proprietary/Public corp.; License: n/a

Napoleonville

Heritage Manor of Napoleonville
252 Hwy., 402 Napoleonville, LA 70390, (504) 369-6011; Facility Type: Skilled care; ICF; ICF/MR; Alzheimer's; Beds: ICF 140; Alzheimer's; SNF/ICF; Certified: Medicaid; Veterans; Owner: Private; License: Current state

Natchitoches

Heritage Manor of Natchitoches Rehabilitation & Retirement
720 Keyser Ave., Natchitoches, LA 71457, (318) 352-8296; Facility Type: Skilled care; ICF; Alzheimer's; Beds: Skilled care 10; ICF 104; Alzheimer's 18; Certified: Medicaid; Medicare; Owner: Private; License: Current state

New Iberia

Consolata Home
2319 E Main St., New Iberia, LA 70560, (337) 365-8226; Facility Type: ICF; Alzheimer's; Beds: ICF 114; Certified: Medicaid; Owner: Nonprofit/Religious org. License: Current state

New Orleans

Covenant Nursing Home
5919 Magazine St., New Orleans, LA 70115, (504) 897-6216; Facility Type: ICF; Alzheimer's; Beds: ICF 96; Certified: Medicaid; Owner: Nonprofit/Religious org.; License: Current state

Fern Crest Manor Living Center
14500 Hayne Blvd., New Orleans, LA 70128, (504) 246-1426; Facility Type: Skilled care; ICF; Alzheimer's; Beds: skilled care 282; ICF; Alzheimer's; Certified: Medicaid; Medicare; Owner: Private; License: Current state

Lutheran Home of New Orleans
6400 Hayne Blvd., New Orleans, LA 70126, (504) 246-7900; Facility Type: Skilled care; ICF; Alzheimer's; Beds: Skilled care; ICF 200; SNF/ICF; Certified: Medicaid; Owner: Nonprofit corp.; License: Current state

Maison Orleans II Nursing Home
13500 Chef Menteur Hwy., New Orleans, LA 70129, (504) 254-9431; Facility Type: Skilled care; ICF; Alzheimer's; Beds: Alzheimer's 67; SNF/ICF 150; Certified: Medicaid; Owner: Proprietary/Public corp; License: Current state

Touro Shakespeare Nursing Home
2621 General Meyer Ave., New Orleans, LA, 70114, (504) 364-4030; Facility Type: ICF; Alzheimer's; Beds: Skilled care; ICF 109; SNF/ICF; Homeless 10; Certified: Medicaid; Veterans; Owner: Government/State/Local; License: Current state

New Roads

Pointe Coupee Parish Nursing Home
2202-A Hospital Rd., New Roads, LA 70760, (225) 638-4431; Facility Type: ICF; Alzheimer's; Beds: ICF 100; Alzheimer's 20; Certified: Med-

icaid; Owner: Government/State/Local; License: Current state

Oberlin

Saint Francis Nursing & Rehabilitation Center
417 Industrial Park Dr., Oberlin, LA 70655, (337) 639-2934; Facility Type: Skilled care; ICF; Alzheimer's; Beds: Skilled care; ICF 50; Alzheimer's 25; SNF/ICF; Rehabilitation 25; Certified: Medicaid; Veterans; Owner: Private; License: Current state

Opelousas

Maison De Ville Nursing Home of Opelousas
308 W Grolee St., Opelousas, LA 70570, (337) 942-7588; Facility Type: Skilled care; ICF; Alzheimer's; Beds: Skilled care 99; Certified: Medicaid; Medicare; Owner: Proprietary/Public corp.; License: Current state

Rayville

Colonial Manor Guest House
114 Whatley St., Rayville, LA 71269, (318) 728-3251; Facility Type: Skilled care; ICF; Alzheimer's; Beds: Skilled care; ICF 134; Alzheimer's; SNF/ICF; Certified: Medicaid; Medicare; Owner: Private; License: Current state

Ruston

Community Care Center of Ruston
1405 White St., Ruston, LA 71270, (318) 255-4400; Facility Type: Skilled care; ICF; Alzheimer's; Beds: Skilled care 116; Certified: Medicaid; Medicare; Veterans; Owner: Nonprofit corp.; License: Current state

Saint Bernard

Poydras Manor Nursing Facility
Rte. 1 Box 132 Saint Bernard, LA 70085, (504) 682-0012; Facility Type: Skilled care; ICF; ICF/MR; Alzheimer's; Beds: Skilled care 36; Certified: Medicaid; Owner: Private; License: Current state

Saint Martinville

Saint Martinville Rehabilitation & Nursing Center
203 Clair Dr., Saint Martinville, LA 70582, (337) 394-6044; Facility Type: Skilled care; ICF; Alzheimer's; Beds: Alzheimer's 47; SNF/ICF 130; Certified: Medicaid; Veterans; Owner: Proprietary/Public corp.; License: Current state

Shreveport

Garden Park Nursing Home
9111 Lynnwood, Shreveport, LA 71106, (318) 688-0961; Facility Type: Skilled care; ICF; ICF/MR; Alzheimer's; Beds: ICF/MR 35; Alzheimer's 40; SNF/ICF 65; Certified: Medicaid; Medicare; Veterans; Owner: Central Management Co.; License: Current state

Live Oak Retirement Center
600 E Flournoy Lucas Rd., Shreveport, LA 71115, (318) 797-1900; Facility Type: Skilled care; ICF; Alzheimer's; Beds: Alzheimer's 50; SNF/ICF 70; Certified: Medicaid; Owner: Nonprofit/Religious org.; License: Current state

Magnolia Manor Nursing Home Inc.
1411 Claiborne Ave., Shreveport, LA 71103, (318) 861-2526; Facility Type: Skilled care; ICF; Alzheimer's; Beds: SNF/ICF 98; Certified: Medicaid; Medicare; Owner: Central Management Co.; License: Current state

South Park Guest Care Center
3050 Baird Rd., Shreveport, LA 71118, (318) 688-1010; Facility Type: ICF; Alzheimer's; Beds: ICF 100; Alzheimer's 24; SNF/ICF 20; Certified: Medicaid; Medicare; Owner: Gamble Guest Care Corp.; License: Current state

Simmesport

Bayou Chateau Nursing Center
1632 Rte. 1 Simmesport, LA 71369, (318) 941-2294; Facility Type: Skilled care; ICF; ICF/MR; Alzheimer's; Beds: Skilled care 28; ICF 92; ICF/MR 8; Alzheimer's 24; SNF/ICF 44; Certified: Medicaid; Veterans; Owner: Proprietary/Public corp.; License: Current state

Wisner

Mary Anna Nursing Home Inc.
125 Turner ST Wisner, LA 71378, (318) 724-7244; Facility Type: Skilled care; ICF; Alzheimer's; Beds: Skilled care 6; ICF 75; Certified: Medicaid; Owner: Private; License: Current state

MAINE

Augusta

Maine Veterans Home
RFD 7 Box 901, Cony Rd., Augusta, ME 04330, (207) 622-2454; Facility Type: Skilled care; ICF; Alzheimer's; Beds: Skilled care 120; Certified: Medicaid; Medicare; Veterans; Owner: Nonprofit corp.; License: Current state

Bangor

Eastside Rehabilitation & Living Center
516 Mt Hope Ave., Bangor, ME 04401, (207) 947-6131; Facility Type: Skilled care; ICF; ICF/MR; Alzheimer's; Beds: Alzheimer's; SNF/ICF 67; Certified: Medicaid; Medicare; Owner: Vencor Inc.; License: n/a

Westgate Manor
750 Union St., Bangor, ME 04401, (207) 942-7336; Facility Type: Skilled care; ICF; Alzheimer's; Beds: Skilled care 100; Assisted living 35; Certified: Medicaid; Medicare; Veterans; Owner: Vencor Inc.; License: Current state

Belfast

Harbor Hill
33 Footbridge Rd., Belfast, ME 04915, (207) 338-3666; Facility Type: Skilled care; ICF; Alzheimer's; Beds: Alzheimer's 16; SNF/ICF 24; Certified: Medicaid; Medicare; Veterans; Owner: Private; License: Current state

Biddeford

The Renaissance
355 Pool St., Biddeford, ME 04005, (207) 283-3646; Facility Type: Skilled care; ICF; Alzheimer's; Beds: Skilled care 20; ICF 19; Alzheimer's 25; Certified: Medicaid; Medicare; Owner: First Atlantic Corp.; License: Current state

Saint Andre Health Care Facility
407 Pool St., Bideford, ME 04005, (207) 282-5171; Facility Type: Skilled care; ICF; Alzheimer's; Beds: Alzheimer's 32; SNF/ICF 64; Certified: Medicaid; Medicare; Owner: Nonprofit/Religious organization; License: Current state

Brewer

Brewer Rehabilitation & Living Center
74 Parkway S Brewer, ME 04412, (207) 989-7300; Facility Type: Skilled care; ICF; ICF/MR; Alzheimer's; Beds: Skilled care 36; ICF 60; Certified: Medicaid; Medicare; Owner: Vencor Inc.; License: Current state

Cape Elizabeth

Viking Nursing Facility Inc.—Crescent House
126 Scott Dyer Rd., Cape Elizabeth, ME 04107, (207) 767-3373; Facility Type: Skilled care; ICF; Alzheimer's; Beds: Skilled care 31; ICF 17; Alzheimer's 12; Assisted living; Certified: Medicaid; Medicare; Owner: Proprietary/Public corp.; License: Current state

Caribou

Caribou Nursing Home
10 Bernadette St., Caribou, ME 04736, (207) 498-3102; Facility Type: ICF; Alzheimer's; Beds: ICF 86; Alzheimer's 18; Certified: Medicaid; Medicare; Veterans; Owner: Private; License: Current state

Deer Isle

Island Nursing Home Inc.
RFD Box 124 Deer Isle, ME 04627, (207) 348-2351; Facility Type: Skilled care; ICF; Alzheimer's; Beds: Skilled care; ICF 38; Alzheimer's; Residential 32; Certified: Medicaid; Medicare; Veterans; Owner: Nonprofit corp.; License: Current state

Ellsworth

Courtland Rehabilitation & Living Center
42 Bucksport Rd., Ellsworth, ME 04605, (207) 667-9036; Facility Type: Skilled care; ICF; Alzheimer's; Beds: Skilled care 20; ICF 60; Certified: Medicaid; Medicare; Owner: North Country Associates; License: Current state

Falmouth

Sedgewood Commons
22 Northbrook Dr., Falmouth, ME 04105, (207) 781-5775; Facility Type: Skilled care; ICF; Alzheimer's; Beds: Skilled care; Alzheimer's; Certified: Medicaid; Medicare; Owner: Private; License: Current state

Freeport

Hawthorne House
6 Old County Rd., Freeport, ME 04032, (207) 865-4782; Facility Type: Skilled care; ICF; Alzheimer's; Beds: Skilled care 24; ICF 32; Alzheimer's 50; Gero-psychiatric 18; Certified: Medi-

caid; Medicare; Veterans; Owner: First Atlantic Corp.; License: Current state

Kennebunk

Kennebunk Nursing Home
158 Ross Rd., Kennebunk, ME 04043, (207) 985-7141; Facility Type: Skilled care; ICF; Alzheimer's; Beds: ICF 62; Medicare certified 18; Certified: Medicaid; Medicare; Owner: Vencor Inc.; License: Current state

Lewiston

Montello Manor
540 College St., Lewiston, ME 04240, (207) 783-2039; Facility Type: Skilled care; ICF; Alzheimer's; Beds: Skilled care 20; ICF 21; Alzheimer's; Certified: Medicaid; Medicare; Owner: Proprietary/Public corp.; License: Current state

Saint Marguerite d'Youville Pavilion
102 Campus Ave., Lewiston, ME 04240, (207) 777-4250; Facility Type: Skilled care; ICF; Alzheimer's; Beds: Skilled care 72; ICF 208; SNF/ICF 280; Certified: Medicaid; Medicare; Owner: Nonprofit/Religious org.; License: Current state

Portland

Barron Center
1145 Brighton Ave., Portland, ME 04102, (207) 774-2623; Facility Type: Skilled care; ICF; Alzheimer's; Beds: Skilled care 235; Certified: Medicaid; Medicare; Owner: Government/State/Local; License: Current state

Seaside Rehabilitation & Healthcare Center
850 Baxter Blvd., Portland, ME 04103, (207) 774-7878; Facility Type: Skilled care; ICF; Alzheimer's; Beds: Skilled care 38; ICF 46; Alzheimer's 35; Assisted living 28; Certified: Medicaid; Medicare; Owner: First Atlantic Corp.; License: Current state

Sanford

Maine Stay Nursing & Lodging Home
965 Main St., Sanford, ME 04073, (207) 324-7999; Facility Type: Skilled care; ICF; Alzheimer's; Beds: Skilled care 35; Certified: Medicaid; Medicare; Owner: Private; License: Current state

Skowhegan

Cedar Ridge Center for Health Care & Rehabilitation
Dr. Mann Rd., RR 1 Box 1283, Skowhegan, ME 04976, (207) 474-9686; Facility Type: Skilled care; ICF; Alzheimer's; Beds: Skilled care 20; ICF 55; Certified: Medicaid; Medicare; Veterans; Owner: Private; License: Current state

Van Buren

Borderview Manor Inc.
90 State St., Van Buren, ME 04785, (207) 868-5211; Facility Type: Skilled care; ICF; Alzheimer's; Beds: Skilled care 18; ICF 65; Boarding care 36; Certified: Medicaid; Owner: Proprietary/Public corp.; License: Current state

Waterville

Mount Saint Joseph Holistic Care Community
7 Highwood St., Waterville, ME 04901, (207) 873-0705; Facility Type: Skilled care; ICF; Alzheimer's; Beds: Skilled care; ICF 88; Alzheimer's 50; Hospice 5; Certified: Medicaid; Medicare; Owner: Nonprofit/Religious org.; License: Current state

Oak Grove Rehabilitation & Living Center
27 Cool St., Waterville, ME 04901, (207) 873-0721; Facility Type: Skilled care; ICF; Alzheimer's; Beds: Skilled care 16; ICF 66; Certified: Medicaid; Medicare; Veterans; Owner: Proprietary/Public corp.; License: Current state

Westbrook

Springbrook Center for Health Care & Rehabilitation
300 Spring St., Westbrook, ME 04092, (207) 856-1230; Facility Type: Skilled care; ICF; Alzheimer's; Beds: Skilled care 17; ICF 83; Alzheimer's; Dementia unit 23; Certified: Medicaid; Medicare; Owner: Private; License: Current state

Winthrop

Heritage Rehabilitation & Living Center
RR 3, Old Lewiston Rd., Winthrop, ME 04364, (207) 377-8453; Facility Type: Skilled care; ICF; ICF/MR; Alzheimer's; Beds: Skilled care 23; ICF 35; Residential; Certified: Medicaid; Medicare; Owner: Proprietary/Public corp.; License: Current state

Yarmouth

Brentwood Rehabilitation & Nursing Center
370 Portland St., Yarmouth, ME 04096, (207) 846-9021; Facility Type: Skilled care; ICF; Alzheimer's; Beds: Skilled care 30; ICF 48; Certified: Medicaid; Medicare; Owner: Proprietary/Public corp.; License: Current state

Coastal Manor
20 W Main St., Yarmouth, ME 04096, (207) 846-5013; Facility Type: Skilled care; ICF; Alzheimer's; Beds: Skilled care 4; ICF 40; Certified: Medicaid; Medicare; Owner: Private; License: Current state

York

Harbor Home
2 Norwood Farms Rd., York, ME 03911, (207) 363-2422; Facility Type: Skilled care; ICF; Alzheimer's; Beds: ICF; SNF/ICF 60; Residential 9; Certified: Medicaid; Medicare; Owner: Private; License: Current state

---

MARYLAND

Adelphi

Hartland Health Care Center—Adelphi
1801 Metzerott Rd., Adelphi, MD 20783, (301) 434-0500; Facility Type: Skilled care; ICF; Alzheimer's; Beds: Skilled care 203; Certified: Medicaid; Medicare; Veterans; Owner: HCR Manor Care; License: Current state

Baltimore

Alice Manor
2095 Rockrose Ave., Baltimore, MD 21211, (410) 889-9700; Facility Type: Skilled care; ICF; ICF/MR; Alzheimer's; Beds: Skilled care 40; ICF 55; Alzheimer's 40; Certified: Medicaid; Medicare; Owner: Proprietary/Public corp.; License: Current state

Caton Manor—Genesis ElderCare
3330 Wilkens Ave., Baltimore, MD 21229, (410) 525-1544; Facility Type: Skilled care; ICF; ICF/MR; Alzheimer's; Beds: Skilled care; Comprehensive care 160; Certified: Medicaid; Medicare; Veterans; Owner: Proprietary/Public corp.; License: Current state

Levindale Hebrew Geriatric Center & Hospital Inc.
2434 W Belvedere Ave., Baltimore, MD 21215, (410) 466-8700; Facility Type: Skilled care; ICF; Alzheimer's; Beds: Skilled care 196; Alzheimer's; Certified: Medicaid; Medicare; Owner: Nonprofit/Religious org.; License: Current state

Bel Air

Mariner Health of Bel Air
410 E MacPhail Rd., Bel Air, MD 21014, (410) 879-1120; Facility Type: Skilled care; ICF; Alzheimer's; Beds: Skilled care 44; ICF 111; Alzheimer's 20; Certified: Medicaid; Medicare; Veterans; Owner: Proprietary/Public corp.; License: Current state

Bethesda

Mariner Health & Rehabilitation Center—Bethesda
5721 Grosvenor Ln., Bethesda, MD 30814, (301) 530-1600; Facility Type: Skilled care; ICF; Alzheimer's; Beds: Skilled care 14; ICF 79; Alzheimer's 32; Certified: Medicaid; Medicare; Veterans; Owner: Proprietary/Public corp.; License: Current state

Brooklyn Park

Hammonds Lane Genesis Center
613 Hammonds Ln., Brooklyn Park, MD 21225, (410) 636-3400; Facility Type: Skilled care; ICF; Alzheimer's; Beds: Skilled care; ICF 129; Certified: Medicaid; Medicare; Owner: Proprietary/Public corp.; License: Current state

Cambridge

Chesapeake Woods Center—Genesis Eldercare
525 Glenburn Ave., Cambridge, MD 21613, (410) 221-1400; Facility Type: Skilled care; Alzheimer's; Beds: Skilled care 98; ICF; Alzheimer's; SNF/ICF; Certified: Medicaid; Medicare; Owner: Proprietary/Public corp.; License: Current state

Catonsville

Catonsville Commons
16 Fusting Ave., Catonsville, MD 21228, (410) 747-1800; Facility Type: Skilled care; ICF; ICF/MR; Alzheimer's; Beds: Skilled care 18; ICF 160; Alzheimer's 36; Certified: Medicaid; Medicare; Veterans; Owner: Genesis Eldercare; License: Current state

Chestertown

Magnolia Hall Rehabilitation & Nursing Center
200 Morgnec Rd., Chestertown, MD 21620, (410) 778-4554; Facility Type: Skilled care; ICF;

Alzheimer's; Beds: Skilled care 94; ICF; SNF/ICF; Certified: Medicaid; Medicare; Veterans; Owner: Nonprofit corp.; License: Current state

Clinton

Pineview Nursing & Rehabilitation Center
9106 Pineview Ln., Clinton, MD 20735, (301) 856-2930; Facility Type: Skilled care; ICF; Alzheimer's; Beds: Skilled care 192; Certified: Medicaid; Medicare; Owner: Proprietary/Public corp.; License: n/a

Cumberland

Allegany County Nursing Home
730 Furnace St., Cumberland, MD 21502, (301) 777-5941; Facility Type: Skilled care; ICF; Alzheimer's; Beds: Skilled care 24; ICF 129; Alzheimer's 51; Certified: Medicaid; Medicare; Owner: Government/State/Local; License: Current state

Frederick

Frederick Health Care Center
30 North Pl., Frederick, MD 21701, (301) 695-6618; Facility Type: Skilled care; ICF; ICF/MR; Alzheimer's Beds: Skilled care 120; Certified: Medicaid; Medicare; Veterans; Owner: Beverly Enterprises Inc. License: Current state

Hagerstown

Avalon Manor Inc.
14014 Mash Pike Hagerstown, MD 21742, (301) 739-9360; Facility Type: Skilled care; ICF; ICF/MR; Alzheimer's; Beds: Skilled care 221; Certified: Medicaid; Medicare; Veterans; Owner: Private; License: n/a

Hyattsville

Heartland Health Care Center of Hyattsville
6500 Riggs Rd., Hyattsville, MD 20783, (301) 559-0300; Facility Type: Skilled care; ICF; Alzheimer's; Beds: Skilled care 150; ICF; Certified: Medicaid; Medicare; Medi-Cal; Veterans; Owner: Proprietary/Public corp.; License: Current state

Kensington

Mariner Health at Circle Manor
10231 Carroll Pl., Kensington, MD 20895, (301) 949-0230; Facility Type: Skilled care; ICF; Alzheimer's; Beds: Skilled care; ICF 84; Certified: Medicaid; Medicare; Owner: Proprietary/Public corp.; License: Current state

Laurel

Cherry Lane Nursing Center
9001 Cherry Ln., Laurel, MD 20708, (410) 792-7436; Facility Type: Skilled care; ICF/MR; Alzheimer's; Beds: Skilled care 150; Alzheimer's 20; Certified: Medicaid; Medicare; Owner: Government/State/Local; License: Current state

Manchester

Long View Nursing Home Inc.
3332 Main St., Manchester, MD 21102, (410) 239-7139; Facility Type: Skilled care; Alzheimer's; Beds: Skilled care 109; Alzheimer's 24; Certified: Medicaid; Medicare; Owner: Private; License: Current state

Oakland

Cuppett & Weeks Nursing Home Inc.
706 E Alder St., Oakland, MD 21550, (301) 334-2319; Facility Type: Skilled care; ICF; Alzheimer's; Beds: Alzheimer's; SNF/ICF 112; Assisted living 16; Certified: Medicaid; Medicare; Veterans; Owner: Proprietary/Public corp.; License: Current state

Rockville

Collingswood Nursing & Rehabilitation Center
299 Hurley Ave., Rockville, MD 20850, (301) 762-8900; Facility Type: Skilled care; ICF; Alzheimer's; Beds: Skilled care 80; ICF 38; Alzheimer's 42; Certified: Medicaid; Medicare; Veterans; Owner: Private; License: Current state

Potomac Valley Nursing & Wellness Center
1235 Potomax Valley Rd., Rockville, MD 20850, (301) 762-0700; Facility Type: Skilled care; Alzheimer's; Beds: Skilled care 47; ICF 66; Alzheimer's; Certified: Medicaid; Medicare; Owner: Private; License: Current state

Salisbury

Salisbury Center Genesis Eldercare Network
200 Civic Ave., Salisbury, MD 21801, (410) 860-8750; Facility Type: Skilled care; ICF; ICF/MR; Alzheimer's; Beds: Skilled care 348; ICF; Domiciliary care; Certified: Medicaid; Medicare; Owner: Proprietary/Public corp. License: Current state

Silver Spring

Fairland Adventist Nursing & Rehabilitation Center
2101 Fairland Rd., Silver Spring, MD 20904,

(301) 384-6161; Facility Type: Skilled care; ICF; Alzheimer's; Beds: Skilled care; ICF; SNF/ICF 82; Certified: Medicaid; Medicare; Owner: Nonprofit/Religious org.; License: Current state

HCR Manor Care
2501 Musgrove Rd., Silver Spring, MD 20904, (301) 890-5552; Facility Type: Skilled care; ICF; ICF/MR; Alzheimer's; Beds: Skilled care 16; ICF 70; Alzheimer's 34; Certified: Medicaid; Medicare; Owner: Proprietary/Public corp.; License: Current state

Sykesville

Continuum Care at Sykesville
7309 2nd Ave., Sykesville, MD 21784, (410) 795-1100; Facility Type: Skilled care; ICF; Alzheimer's; Beds: Skilled care 19; SNF/ICF 130; Certified: Medicaid; Medicare; Veterans; Owner: Continuum Care Corporation; License: Current state

Fairhaven Nursing Home
7200 Third Ave., Sykesville, MD 21784, (410) 795-8800; Facility Type: Skilled care; ICF; Alzheimer's; Beds: Skilled care 72; SNF/ICF 35; Certified: Medicare; Owner: Nonprofit corp.; License: Current state

Towson

ManorCare Health Services
7001 Charles St., Towson, MD 21204; Facility Type: Skilled care; ICF; Alzheimer's; Beds: Skilled care 165; Certified: Medicaid; Medicare; Owner: Proprietary/Public corp.; License: Current state

Multi-Medical Center
7700 York Rd., Towson, MD 21204, (410) 821-5500; Facility Type: Skilled care; ICF; Alzheimer's; Beds: Skilled care 15; ICF 90; Certified: Medicaid; Medicare; Veterans; Owner: Proprietary/Public corp.; License: Current state

Wheaton

Randolph Hills Nursing Center
4011 Randolph Rd., Wheaton, MD 20902, (301) 933-2500; Facility Type: Skilled care; ICF; Alzheimer's; Beds: Skilled care; ICF; Alzheimer's; Comprehensive care 112; Certified: Medicaid; Medicare; Veterans; Owner: Private; License: Current state

Williamsport

Homewood at Williamsport Maryland Inc.
16505 Virginia Ave., Williamsport, MD 21795, (301) 582-1628; Facility Type: Skilled care; ICF; Alzheimer's; Beds: Skilled care; SNF/ICF 122; Assisted living 23; Certified: Medicaid; Medicare; Owner: Nonprofit/Religious org.; License: Current state

MASSACHUSETTS

Abington

Colony House Nursing & Rehabilitation Center
277 Washington St., Abington, MA 02351, (781) 871-0200; Facility Type: Skilled care; ICF; Alzheimer's; Beds: Skilled care 35; ICF 59; Certified: Medicaid; Medicare; Veterans; Owner: Vencor Inc.; License: Current state

Agawan

Heritage Hall South Nursing Home
65 Cooper St., Agawam, MA 01001, (413) 786-8000; Facility Type: Skilled care; ICF; ICF/MR; Alzheimer's; Beds: Skilled care 82; ICF 40; Certified: Medicaid; Medicare; Veterans; Owner: Genesis ElderCare; License: Current state

Amherst

Center for Extended Care at Amherst
150 University Dr., Amherst, MA 01002, (413) 256-8185; Facility Type: Skilled care; ICF; Alzheimer's; Beds: Skilled care 45; Alzheimer's 53; Certified: Medicaid; Medicare; Owner: Private; License: Current state

Andover

Academy Manor of Andover Nursing Home
89 Morton St., Andover, MA 01810, (978) 475-0944; Facility Type: Skilled care; ICF; Alzheimer's Beds: Skilled care 174; Certified: Medicaid; Medicare; Veterans; Owner: Genesis ElderCare; License: Current state

Athol

Quabbin Valley Health Care
821 Daniel Shays Hwy., Athol, MA 01331, (978)

249-3717; Facility Type: Skilled care; ICF; Alzheimer's; Beds: Skilled care 142; Certified: Medicaid; Medicare; Veterans; Owner: Proprietary/Public corp.; License: Current state

Bedford

Carleton-Willard Village Nursing Center
100 Old Billerica Rd., Bedford, MA 01730, (781) 275-8700; Facility Type: Skilled care; ICF; Alzheimer's; Beds: Skilled care 80; ICF 40; Alzheimer's 80; Certified: Medicaid; Medicare; Owner: Nonprofit corp.; License: Current state

Boston

Benjamin Health Care Center
120 Fisher Ave., Boston, MA 02120, (617) 738-1500; Facility Type: Skilled care; ICF; ICF/MR; Alzheimer's; Beds: Skilled care; ICF; ICF/MR; Alzheimer's' SNF/ICF 164; Certified: Medicaid; Medicare; Veterans; Owner: Nonprofit corp.; License: Current state

Hyde Park Convalescent Home
113 Central Ave., Boston, MA 02136, (617) 364-1135; Facility Type: Skilled care; ICF; Alzheimer's; Beds: Skilled care 53; Certified: Medicaid; Medicare; Veterans; Owner: Proprietary/Public corp.; License: Current state

Riverside Nursing Home
405 River St., Boston, MA 02126, (617) 296-5585; Facility Type: Skilled care; ICF; ICF/MR; Alzheimer's; Beds: Skilled care 85; Certified: Medicaid; Medicare; Owner: Proprietary/Public corp.; License: n/a

Village Manor Nursing Home Inc.
25 Alpine St., Boston, MA 02136, (617) 361-5400; Facility Type: Skilled care; ICF; Alzheimer's; Beds: Skilled care 41; ICF 41; Certified: Medicaid; Medicare; Veterans; Owner: Nonprofit corp.; License: Current state

Braintree

Elihu White Nursing & Rehabilitation Center
95 Commercial St., Braintree, MA 02184; Facility Type: Skilled care; ICF; Alzheimer's; Beds: Alzheimer's 64; SNF/ICF 140; Certified: Medicaid; Medicare; Veterans; Owner: Private; License: Current state

Hollingsworth House
1120 Washington St., Braintree, MA 02184, (781) 848-3100; Facility Type: Skilled care; ICF; Alzheimer's; Beds: Skilled care 120; Certified: Medicaid; Medicare; Veterans; Owner: Proprietary/Public corp.; License: Current state

Brockton

Guardian Center
888 N Main St., Brockton, MA 02301, (508) 587-6556; Facility Type: Skilled care; ICF; Alzheimer's Beds: Skilled care 123; Certified: Medicaid; Owner: Proprietary/Public corp.; License: Current state

Cambridge

Cambridge Nursing Home
1 Russell St., Cambridge, MA 02140, (617) 491-6110; Facility Type: Skilled care; ICF; Alzheimer's; Beds: Skilled care 39; ICF 80; Certified: Medicaid; Medicare; Veterans; Owner: Proprietary/Public corp.; License: Current state

Chelsea

Chelsea Jewish Nursing Home
17 Lafayette Ave., Chelsea, MA 02150, (617) 884-6766; Facility Type: Skilled care; ICF; Alzheimer's; Beds: Skilled care 82; ICF 41 Certified: Medicaid; Medicare; Owner: Nonprofit/Religious org.; License: Current state

Soldiers' Home in Massachusetts
91 Crest Ave., Chelsea, MA 02150, (617) 884-5660; Facility Type: Skilled care; Alzheimer's; Beds: Skilled care 122; Alzheimer's 12; Rehabilitation 10; Certified: Medicaid; Veterans; Owner: Government/State/Local; License: n/a

Danvers

Hunt Nursing & Retirement Center
90 Lindall St., Danvers, MA 01923, (978) 777-3740; Facility Type: Skilled care; ICF; Alzheimer's; Beds: Skilled care 80; ICF 40; Certified: Medicaid; Medicare; Owner: Nonprofit corp.; License: Current state

East Longmeadow

East Longmeadow Skilled Nursing Center
305 Maple St., East Longmeadow, MA 01028; Facility Type: Skilled care; ICF; Alzheimer's; Beds: Skilled care 17; Alzheimer's 41; SNF/ICF 41; Certified: Medicaid; Medicare; Owner: Nonprofit corp.; License: Current state

Everett

Woodlawn Manor Nursing & Rehabilitation Center
289 Elm St., Everett, MA 02149, (617) 387-6557; Facility Type: Skilled care; ICF; Alzheimer's; Beds: Skilled care 39; Alzheimer's 42; Young adults 30; Certified: Medicaid; Medicare; Veter-

ans; Owner: Nonprofit/Religious org.; License: Current state

Fall River

Catholic Memorial Home
2446 Highland Ave., Fall River, MA 02720, (508) 679-0011; Facility Type: Skilled care; Alzheimer's; Beds: Skilled care 206; Alzheimer's 94; Certified: Medicaid; Medicare; Owner: Nonprofit/Religious org.; License: Current state

Kimwell Rehabilitation & Nursing—A Centennial Health Care Facility
495 New Boston Rd., Fall River, MA 02720, (508) 679-0106; Facility Type: Skilled care; ICF; ICF/MR; Alzheimer's; Beds: Skilled care 82; ICF 42; Certified: Medicaid; Medicare; Veterans; Owner: Centennial HealthCare Corp.; License: Current state

Falmouth

Center for Optimum Care Falmouth
359 Jones Rd., Falmouth, MA 02540, (508) 457-9000; Facility Type: Skilled care; ICF; Alzheimer's; Beds: Skilled care; ICF 120; Alzheimer's; Certified: Medicaid; Medicare; Owner: Private; License: Current state

JML Care Center Inc.
184 Ter Heun Dr., Falmouth, MA 02540, (508) 457-4621; Facility Type: Skilled care; Alzheimer's; Beds: Skilled care 92; Certified: Medicaid; Medicare; Owner: Nonprofit corp. License: Current state

Royal Nursing & Alzheimer's Care Center
545 Main St., Falmouth, MA 02540, (508) 548-3800; Facility Type: Skilled care; ICF; Alzheimer's; Beds: Skilled care 81; ICF 40; Certified: Medicaid; Owner: Proprietary/Public corp.; License: n/a

Fitchburg

Health Alliance—The Highlands
335 Nichols Rd., Fitchburg, MA 01420, (978) 343-4411; Facility Type: Skilled care; ICF; Alzheimer's; Beds: Skilled care 84; Alzheimer's 46; Certified: Medicaid; Medicare; Owner: Nonprofit corp.; License: Current state

Framingham

Carlyle Nursing Home Inc.
342 Winter St., Framingham, MA 01702, (508) 879-6100; Facility Type: Skilled care; Alzheimer's; Beds: n/a; Certified: Medicaid; Medicare; Owner: Private; License: Current state

Kathleen Daniel Rehabilitation Nursing Center
485 Franklin St., Framingham, MA 01702, (617) 872-8802; Facility Type: Skilled care; ICF; Alzheimer's; Beds: SNF/ICF 124;Certified: Medicaid; Medicare; Veterans; Owner: Centennial HealthCare Corp.; License: Current state

Saint Patrick's Manor Inc.
863 Central St., Framingham, MA 01701, (508) 879-0000; Facility Type: Skilled care; ICF; Alzheimer's; Beds: Skilled care 292; ICF 41; Certified: Medicaid; Medicare; Owner: Nonprofit corp.; License: Current state

Great Barrington

Willowood of Great Barrington
151 Christian Rd., Great Barrington, MA 01230, (413) 528-4560; Facility Type: Skilled care; ICF; Alzheimer's; Beds: Alzheimer's 60; SNF/ICF 60; Certified: Medicaid; Medicare; Owner: Proprietary/Public corp.; License: Current state

Greenfield

Charlene Manor Extended Care Facility
130 Colrain Rd., Greenfield, MA 01301, (413) 774-3724; Facility Type: Skilled care; ICF; Alzheimer's; Beds: Skilled care 96; Certified: Medicaid; Medicare; Veterans; Owner: Nonprofit corp.; License: Current state

Harwich

Cranberry Pointe Rehabilitation & SCC
111 Headwaters Dr., Harwich, MA 02645, (508) 430-1717; Facility Type: Skilled care; Alzheimer's; Beds: Skilled care 53; Alzheimer's 41; Certified: Medicaid; Medicare; Veterans; Owner: Private; License: Current state

Haverhill

Baker Katz Nursing Home
194 Boardman St., Haverhill, MA 01830, (978) 373-5697; Facility Type: ICF; Alzheimer's; Beds: ICF 77; Certified: Medicaid; Owner: Proprietary/Public corp; License: Current state

The Oxford
689 Main St., Haverhill, MA 01830, (978) 373-1131; Facility Type: Skilled care; Alzheimer's; Beds: Skilled care 100; ICF; SNF/ICF 20; Certified: Medicaid; Medicare; Veterans; Owner: Proprietary/Public corp.; License: Current state

Holyoke

Mount Saint Vincent Nursing Home
35 Holy Family Rd., Holyoke, MA 01040, (413)

532-3246; Facility Type: Skilled care; ICF; Alzheimer's; Beds: Skilled care 125; Certified: Medicaid; Medicare; Owner: Nonprofit/Religious org.; License: Current state

Hopedale

Adin Manor Convalescent Home
34 Adin St., Hopedale, MA 01747, (508) 473-0171; Facility Type: Skilled care; ICF; Alzheimer's; Beds: Skilled care 28; ICF 28; Alzheimer's 28; Gero-psychiatric 28; Certified: Medicaid; Medicare; Owner: Private; License: Current state

Jamaica Plain

Pond View Nursing Facility
81 S Huntington Ave., Jamaica Plain, MA 02130, (617) 277-2633; Facility Type: Skilled care; ICF; ICF/MR; Alzheimer's; Beds: Skilled care 43; Certified: Medicaid; Medicare; Veterans; Owner: Proprietary/Public corp.; License: Current state

Lawrence

MI Nursing & Restorative Center
172 Lawrence St., Lawrence, MA 01841, (978) 685-6321; Facility Type: Skilled care; ICF; Alzheimer's; Beds: Skilled care 167; ICF 42; Alzheimer's 41; Congregate care; Certified: Medicaid; Medicare; Owner: Nonprofit/Religious org.; License: Current state

SunBridge Care & Rehabilitation for Wood Mill
800 Essex St., Lawrence, MA 01841, (978) 686-2994; Facility Type: Skilled care; ICF; Alzheimer's; Beds: Alzheimer's 30; SNF/ICF 64; Certified: Medicaid; Medicare; Veterans; Owner: Private; License: Current state

Lexington

Fairlawn Nursing Home Inc.
265 Lowell St., Lexington, MA 02420, (781) 862-7640; Facility Type: ICF; Alzheimer's; Beds: ICF 104; Certified: n/a; Owner: Proprietary/Public corp.; License: Current state

Lowell

D'Youville Senior Care Center
981 Varnum Ave., Lowell, MA 01854, (978) 454-5681; Facility Type: Skilled care; Alzheimer's Beds: Skilledcare 42; ICF 53; SNF/ICF 84; Adult day care 20; Certified: Medicaid; Medicare; Owner: Nonprofit/Religious org.; License: Current state

Wentworth Nursing & Rehabilitation Center
500 Wentworth Ave., Lowell, MA 01852, (978) 458-1271; Facility Type: Skilled care; ICF; Alzheimer's; Beds: Skilled care 103; Long-term care; Certified: Medicaid; Medicare; Owner: Proprietary/Public corp.; License: Current state

Lynn

Crestview Manor Nursing Home
72 Nahant St., Lynn, MA 02149, (781) 598-6363; Facility Type: ICF; ICF/MR; Alzheimer's; Beds: ICF 27; Certified: Medicaid; Medicaid; Owner: Private; License: Current state

Lawrence Manor Nursing Home
26 Henry Ave., Lynn, MA 01902, (781) 595-2941; Facility Type: Skilled care; ICF; Alzheimer's; Beds: Skilled care 17; ICF 21; Certified: Medicaid; Medicare; Owner: Private; License: Current state

Malden

Dexter House Nursing Facility
120 Main St., Malden, MA 02148, (781) 324-5600; Facility Type: Skilled care; ICF; ICF/MR; Alzheimer's; Beds: Skilled care 71; ICF 30; SNF/ICF 29; Certified: Medicaid; Medicare; Veterans; Owner: Beverly Enterprises Inc.; License: Current state

Glen Ridge Nursing Care Center
Hospital Rd., Malden, MA 02148, (781) 391-0800; Facility Type: Skilled care; Alzheimer's; Beds: Skilled care 123; Alzheimer's 41; Certified: Medicaid; Medicare; Owner: Proprietary/Public corp.; License: Current state

Marblehead

Devereux House Nursing Home
39 Lafayette St., Marblehead, MA 01945, (781) 631-6120; Facility Type: Skilled care; ICF; Alzheimer's; Beds: Skilled care 64; ICF; SNF/ICF; Certified: Medicaid; Medicare; Owner: Proprietary/Public corp.; License: Current state

Milford

Blaire House of Milford
20 Claflin St., Milford, MA 01757, (508) 473-1272; Facility Type: Skilled care; Alzheimer's Beds: Skilled care 73; Alzheimer's; Certified: Medicaid; Medicare; Veterans; Owner: Proprietary/Public corp.; License: Current state

Natick

Mary Ann Morse Nursing & Rehabilitation Center
45 Union St., Natick, MA 01760, (508) 650-

9003; Facility Type: Skilled care; Alzheimer's; Beds: Skilled care 82; ICF 41; Alzheimer's; Certified: Medicaid; Medicare; Owner: Nonprofit corp.; License: Current state

New Bedford

Blaire House Long Term Care of New Bedford
397 County St., New Bedford, MA 02740, (508) 990-3336; Facility Type: Skilled care; Alzheimer's; Beds: Skilled care 69; ICF 22; Alzheimer's 44; Certified: Medicaid; Medicare; Veterans; Owner: Private; License: Current state

Hathaway Manor Extended Care Facility
863 Hathaway Rd., New Bedford, MA 02743, (508) 996-6763; Facility Type: Skilled care; Alzheimer's; Beds: Skilled care 142; Certified: Medicaid; Medicare; Owner: Proprietary/Public corp.; License: Current state

Newton

Waban Health & Rehabilitation Inc.
20 Kinmonth Rd., Newton, MA 02168, (617) 332-8481; Facility Type: Skilled care; ICF; ICF/MR; Alzheimer's; Beds: Skilled care 18; ICF; ICF/MR; Alzheimer's' SNF/ICF; Certified: Medicaid; Medicare; Veterans; Owner: Private; License: Current state

North Andover

Prescott House Nursing Home
140 Prescott St., North Andover, MA 01845, (978) 685-8086; Facility Type: Skilled care; ICF; Alzheimer's; Beds: Skilled care 70; SNF/ICF; Certified: Medicaid; Medicare; Owner: Proprietary/Public corp.; License: Current state

Northampton

Northampton Nursing Home Inc.
737 Bridge Rd., Northampton, MA 01060, (413) 586-3300; Facility Type: Skilled care; ICF; Alzheimer's; Beds: Skilled care 123; Alzheimer's 41; Pediatric 41; Certified: Medicaid; Medicare; Veterans; Owner: Proprietary/Public corp.; License: Current state

Norwell

Norwell Knoll Nursing Home
329 Washington St., Norwell, MA 02061, (781) 659-4901; Facility Type: Skilled care; ICF; Alzheimer's; Beds: Skilled care 52; ICF 34; Certified: Medicaid; Medicare; Veterans; Owner: Proprietary/Public corp.; License: Current state

Norwood

Charlwell House Skilled Nursing Facility
305 Walpole St., Norwood, MA 02062, (781) 762-7700; Facility Type: Skilled care; ICF; Alzheimer's; Beds: Skilled care 41; ICF 83; Certified: Medicaid; Medicare; Veterans; Owner: Proprietary/Public corp.; License: Current state

Peabody

Peabody Glen Nursing Center
199 Andover St., Peabody, MA 01960, (978) 531-0772; Facility Type: Skilled care; ICF; Alzheimer's; Beds: Skilled care 90; ICF 60; Medicare certified; Certified: Medicaid; Medicare; Owner: Proprietary/Public corp.; License: Current state

Pittsfield

Willowood of Pittsfield
169 Valentine Rd., Pittsfield, M/a 01201, (413) 445-2300; Facility Type: Skilled care; Alzheimer's; Beds: Skilled care 265; Certified: Medicaid; Medicare; Veterans; Owner: Proprietary/Public corp.; License: Current state

Rockland

Coyne Healthcare Center
56 Webster St., Rockland, MA 02370, (781) 871-0555; Facility Type: Skilled care; Alzheimer's; Beds: Skilled care 64; ICF 46; Alzheimer's 110; Certified: Medicaid; Medicare; Veterans; Owner: Proprietary/Public corp.; License: Current state

Roslindale

Boston Center for Rehabilitative & Subacute Care
1245 Centre St., Roslindale, MA 02131, (617) 325-5400; Facility Type: Skilled care; Alzheimer's; Beds: Skilled care 77; Certified: Medicaid; Medicare; Owner: Private; License: Current state

Saugus

Harborside Healthcare—North Shore
266 Lincoln Ave., Saugus, MA 01906, (781) 233-6830; Facility Type: Skilled care; Alzheimer's; Beds: Skilled care 42; ICF 38; Certified: Medicaid; Medicare; Owner: Harborside Healthcare; License: Current state

South Dartmouth

Brandon Woods of Dartmouth
567 Dartmouth St., South Dartmouth, MA 02748, (508) 997-0797; Facility Type: Skilled

care; ICF; ICF/MR; Alzheimer's; Beds: Skilled care 108; Certified: Medicaid; Medicare; Veterans; Owner: Proprietary/Public corp.; License: Current state

South Dennis

Eagle Pond Rehabilitation & Living Center
1 Love Ln., South Dennis, MA 02660, (508) 385-6034; Facility Type: Skilled care; ICF; Alzheimer's; Beds: Skilled care 62; ICF 60; Alzheimer's 20; Certified: Medicare; Owner: Proprietary/Public corp.; License: Current state

Springfield

Olympus Specialty Hospital—Springfield
1400 State St., Springfield, MA 01109, (413) 787-6700; Facility Type: Skilled care; Alzheimer's; Beds: Skilled care 300; Alzheimer's 94; SNF/ICF; Certified: Medicaid; Medicare; Owner: Proprietary/Public corp.; License: Current state

Wakefield

The Center for Optimum Care
Bathol St., Wakefield, MA 01880, (781) 245-7600; Facility Type: Skilled care; ICF; Alzheimer's; Beds: Skilled care 139; Certified: Medicaid; Medicare; Owner: Proprietary/Public corp.; License: Current state

Waltham

Larchwood Lodge Nursing Home Inc.
221 Worcester Ln., Waltham, MA 02154, (781) 894-4720; Facility Type: Skilled care; ICF; ICF/MR; Alzheimer's; Beds: Skilled care 32; Certified: Medicaid; Medicare; Owner: Proprietary/Public corp.; License: Current state

Meadow Green Nursing & Rehabilitation Center
45 Woburn St., Waltham, MA 02452, (781) 899-8600; Facility Type: Skilled care; Alzheimer's; Beds: Skilled care 82; ICF 41; Certified: Medicaid; Medicare; Owner: Proprietary/Public corp.; License: Current state

Reservoir Nursing Home—ADS
1841 Trapelo Rd., Waltham, MA 02154, (781) 890-5000; Facility Type: Skilled care; ICF; ICF/MR; Alzheimer's; Beds: Skilled care 20; ICF 80; Certified: Medicaid; Medicare; Veterans; Owner: Proprietary/Public corp.; License: Current state

Wellesley

Newton & Wellesley Alzheimer Center
694 Worcester St., Wellesley, MA 02482, (781) 237-6400; Facility Type: Skilled care; ICF; Alzheimer's; Beds: Skilled care 50; ICF 40; Alzheimer's 20; Certified: Medicaid; Medicare; Owner: Proprietary/Public corp.; License: n/a

West Newton

Beverly Healthcare of West Newton
25 Armory St., West Newton, MA 02465, (617) 969-2300; Facility Type: Skilled care; ICF; Alzheimer's; Beds: Alzheimer's 30; SNF/ICF 100; Certified: Medicare; Owner: Nonprofit corp.; License: Current state

West Roxbury

Brook Farm Rehabilitation & Nursing Center
1190 VFW Pkwy West Roxbury, MA 02132, (617) 325-1688; Facility Type: Skilled care; ICF; Alzheimer's; Beds: Skilled care 71; ICF 49; Certified: Medicaid; Medicare; Veterans; Owner: Vencor Inc.; License: Current state

Deutsches Altenheim—German Center for Extended Care
2222 Centre St., West Roxbury, MA 02132, (617) 325-1230; Facility Type: Skilled care; Alzheimer's; Beds: Skilled care 133; Certified: Medicaid; Medicare; Owner: Nonprofit/Religious organization; License: Current state

Westborough

Beaumont Rehabilitation & Skilled Nursing Center
1 Lyman St., Westborough, MA 01581, (508) 366-9933; Facility Type: Skilled care; ICF; Alzheimer's; Beds: Skilled care 50; ICF 38; Alzheimer's 22; Certified: Medicaid; Medicare; Veterans; Owner: Private; License: Current state

Westford

Westford Nursing & Rehabilitation Center
3 Park Dr., Westford, MA 01886, (978) 392-1144; Facility Type: Skilled care; ICF; Alzheimer's; Beds: Skilled care 41; ICF 41; Certified: Medicaid; Medicare; Veterans; Owner: Private; License: Current state

Williamstown

Sweet Brook Care Centers Inc.
1561 Cold Spring Rd., Williamstown, MA 01267, (413) 458-8127; Facility Type: Skilled care; Alzheimer's; Beds: Skilled care 184; Alzheimer's; Certified: Medicaid; Medicare; Owner: Proprietary/Public corp.; License: Current state

Worcester

Blaire House Long Term Care of Worcester
116 Houghton St., Worcester, MA 01604, (508) 791-5543; Facility Type: Skilled care; ICF; Alzheimer's; Beds: Skilled care 75; SNF/ICF; Certified: Medicaid; Medicare; Veterans; Owner: Proprietary/Public corp.; License: Current state

Clark Manor Health Care Center
1350 Main St., Worcester, MA 01603, (508) 791-4200; Facility Type: Skilled care; ICF; Alzheimer's; Beds: Skilled care 96; ICF 66; Alzheimer's; Certified: Medicaid; Medicare; Owner: Proprietary/Public corp.; License: Current state

Knollwood Nursing Center
271 E Mountain St., Worcester, MA 01606, (508) 853-6910; Facility Type: Skilled care; ICF/MR; Alzheimer's; Beds: Skilled care 70; Certified: Medicaid; Medicare; Owner: Nonprofit corp.; License: Current state

Saint Mary Health Care
39 Queen St., Worcester, MA 02610, (508) 753-4791; Facility Type: Skilled care; ICF; Alzheimer's; Beds: Skilled care 125; ICF; Alzheimer's; SNF/ICF; Respite care; Certified: Medicaid; Medicare; Owner: Nonprofit/Religious org.; License: Current state

University Commons Nursing Center
378 Plantation St., Worcester, MA 01605, (508) 755-7300; Facility Type: Skilled care; ICF; Alzheimer's; Beds: Skilled care 41; ICF 90; Alzheimer's 33; Certified: Medicaid; Medicare; Owner: Private; License: Current state

MICHIGAN

Adrian

Adrian Health Care Center
130 Sand Creek Hwy., Adrian, MI 49221, (517) 265-6554; Facility Type: Skilled care; ICF; ICF/MR; Alzheimer's; Beds: Skilled care 60; ICF 60; Certified: Medicaid; Medicare; Veterans; Owner: Proprietary/Public corp.; License: Current state

Albion

Albion Manor Care Center
1000 W Erie St., Albion, MI 49224, (517) 629-5501; Facility Type: Skilled care; ICF/MR; Alzheimer's; Beds: Skilled care 80; Certified: Medicaid; Medicare; Owner: Beverly Enterprises Inc.; License: Current state

Alma

Michigan Masonic Home
1200 Wright Ave., Alma, MI 48801, (517) 463-3141; Facility Type: Skilled care; ICF; Alzheimer's; Beds: Skilled care 400; Certified: Medicaid; Medicare; Owner: Nonprofit corp.; License: Current state

Alpena

Tendercare Green View
1234 Golf Course Rd., Alpena, MI 49707, (517) 356-1030; Facility Type: Skilled care; ICF; ICF/MR; Alzheimer's; Beds: Skilled care 43; Certified: Medicaid; Owner: Proprietary/Public corp.; License: Current state

Ann Arbor

Glacier Hills Nursing Center
1200 Earhart Rd., Ann Arbor, MI 48105, (734) 769-6410; Facility Type: Skilled care; Alzheimer's; Beds: Skilled care 163; Certified: Medicaid; Medicare; Owner: Nonprofit corp.; License: n/a

Whitehall Healthcare Center of Ann Arbor
3370 Morgan Rd., Ann Arbor, MI 48108, (734) 971-3230; Facility Type: Skilled care; ICF; Alzheimer's; Beds: Skilled care 100; Certified: Medicaid; Medicare; Owner: Centennial HealthCare Corp.; License: Current state

Bad Axe

Huron County Medical Care Facility
1116 S Van Dyke Rd., Bad Axe, MI 48413, (517) 269-6425; Facility Type: Skilled care; ICF; Alzheimer's; Beds: Skilled care 112; Certified: Medicaid; Medicare; Veterans; Owner: Government/State/Local; License: Current state

Battle Creek

The Laurels of Bedford
270 N Bedford Rd., Battle Creek, MI 49017, (616) 968-2296; Facility Type: Skilled care; ICF; Alzheimer's; Beds: Skilled care; ICF 96; SNF/ICF 27; Certified: Medicaid; Medicare; Owner: Private; License: Current state

Tendercare Riverside Battle Creek
675 Wagner Dr., Battle Creek, MI 49017, (616) 969-6244; Facility Type: Skilled care; ICF; Alzheimer's; Beds: Skilled care 24; ICF 75; Alzheimer's 12; SNF/ICF 99; Certified: Medicaid; Medicare; Veterans; Owner: Tendercare Inc.; License: Current state

Berrien Center Cambridge Court
6786 Deans Hill Rd., Berrien Center, MI 49102, (616) 473-4911; Facility Type: ICF; Alzheimer's; Beds: ICF 46; Alzheimer's 16; Certified: Medicaid; Medicare; Owner: Private; License: Current state

Bloomfield Hills

Heartland Health Care Center—Georgian Bloomfield
2975 N Adams Rd., Bloomfield Hills, MI 48304, (248) 645-2900; Facility Type: Skilled care; ICF; ICF/MR; Alzheimer's; Beds: Skilled care 260; Certified: Medicare; License: n/a

Charlotte

Eaton County Medical Care Facility
530 W Beech St., Charlotte, MI 48813, (517) 643-2940; Facility Type: Skilled care; ICF; ICF/MR; Alzheimer's; Beds: SNF/ICF 100; Certified: Medicaid; Medicare; Owner: Government/State/Local; License: Current state

Cheboygan

Cheboygan Health Care Center
824 S Huron St., Cheboygan, MI 49721, (231) 627-4347; Facility Type: Skilled care; ICF; Alzheimer's; Beds: Alzheimer's 42; SNF/ICF 70; Certified: Medicaid; Medicare; Veterans; Owner: Nonprofit corp.; License: Current state

Chelsea

Chelsea Retirement Community
805 W Middle St., Chelsea, MI 48118, (734) 475-8633; Facility Type: Skilled care; ICF; Alzheimer's; Beds: Skilled care 110; Certified: Medicaid; Medicare; Owner: United Methodist Retirement Communities; License: Current state

Clawson

Cambridge North Health Care Center
535 N Main St., Clawson, MI 48017, (248) 435-5200; Facility Type: Skilled care; ICF; Alzheimer's; Beds: Alzheimer's 28; SNF/ICF 60; Certified: Medicaid; Medicare; Owner: Mariner Post Acute Network; License: Current state

Crystal Falls

Iron County Medical Care Facility
1523 W US 2, Crystal Falls, MI 49920, (906) 875-6671; Facility Type: Skilled care; ICF; Alzheimer's; Beds: Skilled care; ICF; Alzheimer's; SNF/ICF 129; Certified: Medicaid; Medicare; Veterans; Owner: Government/State/Local; License: Current state

Detroit

Americare Convalescent Center of Detroit
19211 Anglin Rd., Detroit, MI 48234, (313) 893-9745; Facility Type: Skilled care; ICF; ICF/MR; Alzheimer's; Beds: Skilled care 139; SNF/ICF 139; Certified: Medicaid; Medicare; Owner: Private; License: Current state

Barton Nursing Home
722 E Grand Blvd., Detroit, MI 48207, (313) 923-8080; Facility Type: ICF; Alzheimer's; Beds: Skilled care 50; Certified: Medicaid; Owner: Proprietary/Public corp.; License: Current state

Cadillac Nursing Home
1533 Cadillac Blvd., Detroit, MI 48214, (313) 823-0435; Facility Type: Skilled care; Alzheimer's; Beds: Skilled care 97; Certified: Medicaid; Medicare; Owner: Private; License: Current state

Fairlane Nursing Center
15750 Joy Rd., Detroit, MI 48228, (313) 273-6850; Facility Type: Skilled care; ICF; Alzheimer's; Beds: Skilled care 250; Certified: Medicaid; Medicare; Owner: Proprietary/Public corp.; License: Current state

LaSalle Nursing Home
2411 W Grand Blvd., Detroit, MI 48208, (313) 897-5144; Facility Type: ICF; Alzheimer's; Beds: ICF 75; Certified: Medicaid; Owner: Private; License: Current state

New Detroit Nursing Center
716 E Grand Blvd., Detroit, MI 48207, (313) 923-0300; Facility Type: ICF; Alzheimer's; Beds: ICF 50; Certified: Medicaid; Medicare; Owner: Private; License: Current state

Pembrook Nursing Center
9146 Woodward, Detroit, MI 48202, (313) 875-1263; Facility Type: Skilled care; ICF; ICF/MR; Alzheimer's; Beds: SNF/ICF 153; Certified: Medicaid; Medicare; Owner: Private; License: Current state

Redford Geriatric Village
22811 W Seven Mile Rd., Detroit, MI 48219, (313) 534-1440; Facility Type: Skilled care; ICF; ICF/MR; Alzheimer's; Beds: Skilled care 106; Certified: Medicaid; Medicare; Owner: Private; License: n/a

Westwood Nursing Center
16588 Schaefer Detroit, MI 48235, (313) 345-5000; Facility Type: Skilled care; Alzheimer's; Beds: Skilled care 136; Certified: Medicaid; Medicare; Owner: Proprietary/Public corp.; License: Current state

East Lansing

Burcham Hills Retirement Center II
2700 Burcham Dr., East Lansing, MI 48823, (517) 351-8377; Facility Type: Skilled care; ICF; ICF/MR; Alzheimer's; Beds: Skilled care 40; ICF 4; Alzheimer's 89; SNF/ICF; Basic care 94; Certified: Medicaid; Medicare; Owner: Nonprofit corp.; License: Current state

Escanaba

Christian Park Village
2525 7th Ave. S, Escanaba, MI 49829, (906) 786-0408; Facility Type: Skilled care; Alzheimer's; Beds: Skilled care 59; Certified: Medicaid; Medicare; Owner: Proprietary/Public corp.; License: Current state

Farmington Hills

Charter House of Farmington Hills
21017 Middlebelt Rd., Farmington Hills, MI 48336, (248) 476-8300; Facility Type: Skilled care; ICF; Alzheimer's; Beds: Skilled care 106; ICF; Alzheimer's; Certified: Medicaid; Medicare; Owner: Centennial HealthCare Corp.; License: Current state

Flint

Heartland Health Care Center at Briarwood
3011 N Center Rd., Flint, MI 48506, (810) 736-0600; Facility Type: Skilled care; Alzheimer's; Beds: Skilled care 97; ICF; Alzheimer's; SNF/ICF; Certified: Medicaid; Medicare; Owner: HCR Manor Care; License: Current state

Heritage Manor Healthcare Center
G-3201 Beecher Rd., Flint, MI 48532, (810) 732-9200; Facility Type: Skilled care; ICF/MR; Alzheimer's; Beds: Skilled care 42; ICF 180; Certified: Medicaid; Medicare; Owner: Mariner Post Acute Network; License: Current state

Frankfurt

Paul Oliver Memorial Hospital—Long Term Care Unit
224 Park Ave., Frankfurt, MI 49635, (231) 352-9621; Facility Type: Skilled care; Alzheimer's; Beds: Skilled care 40; Certified: Medicaid; Medicare; Owner: Nonprofit corp.; License: Current state

Fremont

Transitional Health Services of Fremont
4554 W 48th St., Fremont, MI 49412, (231) 924-3990; Facility Type: Skilled care; ICF; Alzheimer's; Beds: Skilled care 29; ICF 50; Alzheimer's 46; Certified: Medicaid; Medicare; Owner: Private; License: Current state

Grand Rapids

Heartland Health Care Center—Grand Rapids
2320 E Beltline SE, Grand Rapids, MI 49546, (616) 949-3000; Facility Type: Skilled care; ICF; ICF/MR; Alzheimer's; Beds: Skilled care 194; ICF; Alzheimer's; Certified: Medicaid; Medicare; Owner: HCR Manor Care; License: Current state

Holland Home—Fulton Manor
1450 E Fulton Ave., Grand Rapids, MI 49503, (616) 235-5001; Facility Type: Skilled care; Alzheimer's; Beds: Skilled care 79; Alzheimer's; SNF/ICF; Home for aged 290; Certified: Medicaid; Medicare; Owner: Nonprofit corp.; License: Current state

Porter Hills Presbyterian Village
3600 E Fulton St., Grand Rapids, MI 49546, (616) 949-4971; Facility Type: Skilled care; ICF; Alzheimer's; Beds: Skilled care 101; Independent living 109; Certified: Medicaid; Medicare; Owner: Nonprofit/Religious org.; License: Current state

Holland

Holland Health Care Center
493 W 32nd St., Holland, MI 49423, (616) 396-1438; Facility Type: Skilled care; ICF; ICF/MR; Alzheimer's; Beds: Skilled care 38; ICF 73; Alzheimer's 111; Certified: Medicaid; Medicare; Owner: HCR Manor Care; License: Current state

The Inn at Freedom Village
145 Columbia Ave., Holland, MI 49423, (616) 392-6800; Facility Type: Skilled care; ICF; Alzheimer's; Beds: Skilled care 15; ICF 74; Alzheimer's 29; Certified: Medicare; Owner: n/a License: Current state

Howell

Greenery Health Care Center at Howell
3003 W Grand River Ave., Howell, MI 48843, (517) 546-4210; Facility Type: Skilled care; ICF;

ICF/MR; Alzheimer's; Beds: Skilled care 100; Alzheimer's 76; Certified: Medicaid; Medicare; Owner: Integrated Health Services Inc.; License: Current state

Ishpeming

Marquette County Medical Care Facility
200 Saginaw, Ishpeming, MI 49849, (906) 485-1061; Facility Type: Skilled care; Alzheimer's; Beds: Skilled care 120; Certified: Medicaid; Medicare; Owner: Government/State/Local; License: Current state

Jackson

Faith Haven—A Mercy Living Center
6531 W Michigan Ave., Jackson, MI 49201, (517) 750-3822; Facility Type: Skilled care; ICF; ICF/MR; Alzheimer's; Beds: Skilled care; ICF 88; Home for aged 20; Certified: Medicaid; Medicare; Owner: Nonprofit/Religious org.; License: Current state

Kalamazoo

HCR—Kalamazoo
3625 W Michigan Ave., Kalamazoo, MI 49006, (616) 375-4550; Facility Type: Skilled care; ICF; ICF/MR; Alzheimer's; Beds: Skilled care 46; ICF 134; Alzheimer's 42; Certified: Medicaid; Medicare; Owner: HCR Manor Care; License: Current state

Metron of Kalamazoo
1430 Alamo Ave., Kalamazoo, MI 49006, (616) 349-2661; Facility Type: Skilled care; ICF; ICF/MR; Alzheimer's; Beds: Skilled care 82; Alzheimer's 57; Certified: Medicaid; Owner: Nonprofit/Religious org.; License: n/a

Lansing

Mary Avenue Care Center
1313 Mary Ave., Lansing, MI 48910, (517) 393-6130; Facility Type: Skilled care; ICF; ICF/MR; Alzheimer's; Beds: Skilled care 134; Certified: Medicaid; Medicare; Owner: Proprietary/Public corp.; License: Current state

Tendercare South
2100 E Provincial House Dr., Lansing, MI 48910, (517) 882-2458; Facility Type: Skilled care; ICF; ICF/MR; Alzheimer's; Beds: Skilled care 120; Certified: Medicaid; Medicare; Owner: Tendercare Inc.; License: Current state

Livonia

Camelot Hall Convalescent Center
35100 Ann Arbor Trl, Livonia, MI 48150, (734) 522-1444; Facility Type: Skilled care; Alzheimer's; Beds: Skilled care 166; Certified: Medicaid; Medicare; Veterans; Owner: Proprietary/Public corp.; License: Current state

Heartland Health Care Center—University
28550 Five Mile Rd., Livonia, MI 48154, (734) 427-8270; Facility Type: Skilled care; Alzheimer's; Beds: Skilled care 170; Alzheimer's; Certified: Medicaid; Medicare; Owner: HCR Manor Care; License: n/a

Middlebelt Health Care Centre
14900 Middlebelt Rd., Livonia, MI 48154, (734) 425-4200; Facility Type: Skilled care; ICF; Alzheimer's; Beds: Skilled care 27; ICF 135; Certified: Medicaid; Medicare; Owner: Proprietary/Public corp.; License: Current state

Marne

Birchwood Care Center
15140 16th Ave., Marne, MI 49435, (616) 677-1215; Facility Type: Skilled care; ICF; Alzheimer's; Beds: Skilled care 239; Certified: Medicaid; Medicare; Owner: Proprietary/Public corp.; License: Current state

Midland

Brittany Manor
3615 E Ashman St., Midland, MI 48642, (517) 631-0460; Facility Type: Skilled care; ICF; ICF/MR; Alzheimer's; Beds: Skilled care 58; ICF 95; Certified: Medicaid; Medicare; Veterans; Owner: Proprietary/Public corp.; License: Current state

Monroe

Lutheran Home—Monroe
1236 S Monroe St., Monroe, MI 48161, (734) 241-9533; Facility Type: Skilled care; ICF; Alzheimer's; Beds: SNF/ICF 102; HFA 20; Certified: Medicaid; Medicare; Owner: Nonprofit corp.; License: Current state

Mount Clemens

Lakepoint Villa
37700 Harper, Mount Clemens, MI 48046, (810) 468-0827; Facility Type: Skilled care; ICF; ICF/MR; Alzheimer's; Beds: Skilled care 210; ICF; Medicare; Certified: Medicaid; Medicare; Owner: Proprietary/Public corp.; License: Current state

Mount Pleasant

Isabella County Medical Care Facility
1222 North Dr., Mount Pleasant, MI 48858,

(517) 772-2957; Facility Type: Skilled care; ICF; ICF/MR; Alzheimer's; Beds: Skilled care 80; Certified: Medicaid; Medicare; Owner: Government/State/Local; License: Current state

The Laurels of Mt. Pleasant
400 S Crapo St., Mount Pleasant, MI 48858, (517) 773-5918; Facility Type: Skilled care; ICF; Alzheimer's; Beds: Skilled care 24; ICF 88; Certified: Medicaid; Medicare; Veterans; Owner: Proprietary/Public corp.; License: Current state

Muskegon

McAuley Place—A Mercy Living Center
1380 E Sherman Blvd., Muskegon, MI 49444, (231) 733-2578; Facility Type: Skilled care; ICF; ICF/MR; Alzheimer's; Beds: Skilled care 50; Alzheimer's 48; Certified: Medicaid; Medicare; Owner: Nonprofit/Religious org.; License: Current state

Pontiac

Orchard Hill—A Mercy Living Center
532 Orchard Lake Rd., Pontiac, MI 28341, (248) 338-7151; Facility Type: Skilled care; ICF; ICF/MR; Alzheimer's; Beds: Skilled care 244; Certified: Medicaid; Medicare; Owner: Trinity Continuing Care Services; License: n/a

Powers

Pinecrest Medical Care Facility N
15995 Main S, Box 603, Powers, MI 49874, (906) 497-5244; Facility Type: Skilled care; ICF; Alzheimer's; Beds: Skilled care 140; Alzheimer's 34; Certified: Medicaid; Medicare; Veterans; Owner: Government/State/Local; License: Current state

Riverview

Rivergate Terrace
14141 Pennsylvania Rd., Riverview, MI 48192, (734) 284-8000; Facility Type: Skilled care; ICF; Alzheimer's; Beds: SNF/ICF 247; Certified: Medicaid; Medicare; Owner: Life Care Centers of America; License: Current state

Saginaw

Heartland Health Car Center—Saginaw
2901 Galaxy Dr., Saginaw, MI 48601, (517) 777-5110; Facility Type: Skilled care; Alzheimer's; Beds: Skilled care 121; Certified: Medicaid; Medicare; Owner: HCR Manor Care; License: n/a

Saint Clair Shores

Saint Mary's Nursing Home
22601 E Nine Mile Rd., Saint Clair Shores, MI 48080, (810) 772-4300; Facility Type: Skilled care; ICF; Alzheimer's; Beds: SNF/ICF 107; Certified: Medicaid; Medicare; Owner: Private; License: n/a

Saint Johns

Hazel I. Findlay Country Manor
1101 S Scott Rd., Saint Johns, MI 48879, (517) 224-8936; Facility Type: ICF; Alzheimer's; Beds: ICF 157; Alzheimer's; Assisted living 22; Certified: Medicaid; Owner: Nonprofit corp.; License: Current state

Southfield

Bedford Villa Nursing Care Center
16240 W Twelve Mile Rd., Southfield, MI 4876, (248) 557-3333; Facility Type: Skilled care; Alzheimer's; Beds: Skilled care 61; Certified: Medicare; Owner: Proprietary/Public corp.; License: Current state

Tawas City

Iosco Medical Care Facility
1201 Harris Ave., Tawas City, MI 48763, (517) 362-4424; Facility Type: Skilled care; Alzheimer's; Beds: Skilled care 64; Alzheimer's; Certified: Medicaid; Medicare; Owner: Government/State/Local; License: Current state

Taylor

Pine Knoll Convalescent Center
23600 Northline Rd., Taylor, MI 48180, (734) 287-8580; Facility Type: Skilled care; Alzheimer's; Beds: Skilled care 142; Certified: Medicaid; Medicare; Owner: Private; License: Current state

Traverse City

Birchwood Nursing Center
2950 Lafranier Rd., Traverse City, MI 49684, (231) 947-0506; Facility Type: Skilled care; ICF; ICF/MR; Alzheimer's; Beds: Alzheimer's 24; ICF/MR; Alzheimer's; Certified: Medicaid; Medicare; Veterans; Owner: Tendercare Inc.; License: Current state

The Grand Traverse Pavilions
1000 Andrew Weiszer Dr., Traverse City, MI 49684, (231) 932-3000; Facility Type: Skilled care; Alzheimer's; Beds: Alzheimer's; SNF/ICF 201; Certified: Medicaid; Medicare; Owner: Government/State/Local; License: Current state

Warren

Nightingale Health Care Center
11535 E Ten Mile Rd., Warren, MI 48089, (810) 759-0700; Facility Type: Skilled care; ICF; ICF/MR; Alzheimer's; Beds: Skilled care 30; ICF 155; Certified: Medicaid; Medicare; Owner: Mariner Post Acute Network; License: Current state

Wayne

Transitional Health Services of Wayne
34330 Van Born Rd., Wayne, MI 48184, (734) 721-0740; Facility Type: Skilled care; ICF; Alzheimer's; Beds: SNF/ICF 108; Certified: Medicaid; Medicare; Owner: Proprietary/Public corp.; License: Current state

Wayne Living Center Nursing Care
4429 Venoy Rd., Wayne, MI 48184, (734) 326-6424; Facility Type: Skilled care; ICF; ICF/MR; Alzheimer's; Beds: ICF 99; Certified: Medicaid; Owner: Proprietary/Public corp.; License: Current state

Westland

Hope Health Care Center
38410 Cherry Hill Rd., Westland, MI 48184, (734) 326-1200; Facility Type: Skilled care; ICF; Alzheimer's; Beds: Skilled care 142; Certified: Medicaid; Medicare; Veterans; Owner: Mariner Post Acute Network; License: Current state

Woodhaven

Applewood Nursing Center
18500 Vanhorn Rd., Woodhaven, MI 48183, (734) 676-7575; Facility Type: Skilled care; ICF/MR; Alzheimer's; Beds: Skilled care 150; Certified: Medicaid; Medicare; Owner: Proprietary/Public corp.; License: Current state

Zeeland

Haven Park Christian Nursing Home
285 N State St., Zeeland, MI 49464, (616) 772-4641; Facility Type: Skilled care; Alzheimer's; Beds: Skilled care 123; Alzheimer's 30; Certified: Medicaid; Medicare; Owner: Nonprofit/Religious org.; License: Current state

MINNESOTA

Alexandria

Bethany Home Inc.
1020 Lark St., Alexandria, MN 56398, (320) 762-1567; Facility Type: Skilled care; Alzheimer's; Beds: Skilled care 160; Certified: Medicaid; Medicare; Veterans; Owner: Nonprofit corp.; License: Current state

Baudette

Lakewood Care Center
Rte. 1 Box 1180, Baudette, MN 5623, (218) 634-1588; Facility Type: Skilled care; ICF; Alzheimer's; Beds: Skilled care 52; ICF; Alzheimer's; Certified: Medicaid; Medicare; Owner: Nonprofit/Religious org.; License: Current state

Belle Plaine

The Lutheran Home & Belle Plaine
611 W Main St., Belle Plaine, MN 56011, (612) 873-2215; Facility Type: Skilled care; ICF; ICF/MR; Alzheimer's; Beds: Skilled care 126; ICF/MR 52; Certified: Medicaid; Medicare; Veterans; Owner: The Lutheran Home Association; License: Current state

Bloomington

Martin Luther Manor
1401 E 100th St., Bloomington, MN 55425, (812) 888-7751; Facility Type: Skilled care; Alzheimer's; Beds: Skilled care 218; SNF/ICF 20; Certified: Medicaid; Medicare; Owner: Nonprofit corp.; License: Current state

Canby

Sioux Valley Canby Campus
112 St. Olaf Ave. S, Canby, MN 56620, (507) 223-7277; Facility Type: Skilled care; Alzheimer's; Beds: Skilled care 75; Alzheimer's 16; Certified: Medicaid; Medicare; Veterans; Owner: Nonprofit corp.; License: Current state

Cannon Falls

Our Lady of the Angels Care Center
300 N Dow St., Cannon Falls, MN 55009, (507) 263-4658; Facility Type: Skilled care; ICF/MR; Alzheimer's; Beds: Skilled care 84; Certified: Medicaid; Medicare; Veterans; Owner: Nonprofit/Religious org.; License: Current state

Chaska

Auburn Village
501 Oak St., Chaska, MN 55318, (952) 361-0304; Facility Type: Skilled care; Alzheimer's; Beds: Skilled care 61; Alzheimer's 14; Assisted living; Certified: Medicaid; Medicare; Owner: Nonprofit/Religious org.; License: Current state

Crystal

Crystal Care Center
3245 Vera Cruz Ave. N, Crystal, MN 55422, (612) 535-6260; Facility Type: Skilled care; Alzheimer's; Beds: Skilled care 181; Certified: Medicaid; Medicare; Veterans; Owner: Nonprofit/Religious org.; License: Current state

Detroit Lakes

Emmanuel Nursing Home
1415 Madison Ave., Detroit Lakes, MN 56501, (218) 847-4488; Facility Type: Skilled care; Alzheimer's; Beds: Skilled care 144; Certified: Medicaid; Medicare; Veterans; Owner: Nonprofit corp.; License: Current state

Duluth

Nopeming Nursing Home
2650 Nopeming Rd., Duluth, MN 55810, (218) 628-2381; Facility Type: Skilled care; ICF; Alzheimer's; Beds: Skilled care 101; Alzheimer's 58; Certified: Medicaid; Medicare; Owner: Government/State/Local; License: Current state

The Waters of Park Point
1601 St., Louis Ave., Duluth, MN 55802, (218) 727-8651; Facility Type: Skilled care; Alzheimer's; Beds: Skilled care 215; Certified: Medicaid; Medicare; Owner: Proprietary/Public corp.; License: Current state

Faribault

Saint Lucas Care Center
500 SE 1st St., Faribault, MN 55021, (507) 332-5100; Facility Type: Skilled care; Alzheimer's; Beds: Skilled care 109; Certified: Medicaid; Medicare; Owner: Nonprofit corp.; License: Current state

Fergus Falls

Pioneer Home Apartments
1006 S Sheridan St., Fergus Falls, MN 56537, (218) 739-3361; Facility Type: Skilled care; Alzheimer's; Beds: Skilled care 110; Retirement; Certified: Medicaid; Medicare; Owner: Nonprofit corp.; License: Current state

Frazee

Frazee Care Center
311 W Maple Ave., Frazee, MN 56544, (218) 334-4501; Facility Type: Skilled care; Alzheimer's; Beds: Skilled care 102; Certified: Medicaid; Medicare; Veterans; Owner: Proprietary/Public corp.; License: Current state

Golden Valley

Trevilla of Golden Valley
7505 Country Club Dr., Golden Valley, MN 55427, (612) 545-0416; Facility Type: Skilled care; ICF; Alzheimer's; Beds: Skilled care 225; Certified: Medicaid; Medicare; Owner: Extendi-Care Health Services Inc.; License: n/a

Grand Rapids

Itasca Nursing Home
923 County Home Rd., Grand Rapids, MN 5744, (218) 326-0543; Facility Type: Skilled care; Alzheimer's; Beds: Skilled care 118; Certified: Medicaid; Medicare; Owner: Government/State/Local; License: Current state

Hopkins

Hopkins Care Center
725 2nd Ave., S Hopkins, MN 55343, (612) 935-3338; Facility Type: Skilled care; Alzheimer's; Beds: Skilled care 140; Certified: Medicaid; Medicare; Owner: Proprietary/Public corp.; License: n/a

Janesville

Janesville Nursing Home
102 E North St., Janesville, MN 56048, (507) 231-5113; Facility Type: Skilled care; Alzheimer's; Beds: Skilled care 45; Certified: Medicaid; Medicare; Owner: Government/State/Local; License: Current state

Le Sueur

Minnesota Valley Health Center
621 S 4th St., Le Sueur, MN 56058, (507) 665-3375; Facility Type: Skilled care; Alzheimer's; Beds: Skilled care 55; Alzheimer's 30; Certified:

Medicaid; Medicare; Owner: Nonprofit corp.; License: Current state

Long Lake

Long Lake Health Care Center
345 N Brown Rd., Long Lake, MN 55356, (612) 473-2527; Facility Type: Skilled care; Alzheimer's; Beds: Skilled care 107; Alzheimer's 22; Rehabilitation 6; Certified: Medicaid; Medicare; Veterans; Owner: Nonprofit/Religious org.; License: Current state

McIntosh

McIntosh Nursing Home Inc.
700 NE Riverside Ave., McIntosh, MN 56556, (218) 563-2715; Facility Type: Skilled care; Alzheimer's; Beds: Skilled care 89; Certified: Medicaid; Medicare; Veterans; Owner: Proprietary/Public corp.; License: Current state

Melrose

Melrose Pine Villa
11 N 5th Ave. W, Melrose, MN 56352, (320) 256-4231; Facility Type: Skilled care; Alzheimer's; Beds: Skilled care 28; Certified: Medicaid; Medicare; Owner: Nonprofit corp.; License: Current state

Minneapolis

Augustana Home of Minneapolis
1007 E 14th St., Minneapolis, MN 55404, (612) 333-1551; Facility Type: Skilled care; Alzheimer's; Beds: Skilled care 230; Alzheimer's 70; Geriatric behavioral; Certified: Medicaid; Medicare; Owner: Nonprofit/Religious org.; License: Current state

Careview Home Inc.
5517 Lyndale Ave. S, Minneapolis, MN 55419, (612) 827-5677; Facility Type: Skilled care; Alzheimer's; Beds: Skilled care 137; Alzheimer's 16; Certified: Medicaid; Medicare; Owner: Nonprofit corp.; License: Current state

City of Lakes Transitional Care Center
110 E 18th St., Minneapolis, MN 55403, (612) 879-2800; Facility Type: Skilled care; Alzheimer's; Beds: Skilled care 65; Certified: Medicaid; Medicare; Owner: Nonprofit/Religious org.; License: Current state

Minnesota Veterans Home
5101 Minnehaha Ave. S, Minneapolis, MN 55417, (612) 721-0600; Facility Type: Skilled care; ICF; Alzheimer's; Beds: Skilled care 346; ICF 194; Alzheimer's 50; Certified: Veterans; Owner: Government/State/Local; License: Current state

Regina Terrace
4544 4th Ave. S, Minneapolis, MN 55409, (612) 827-3526; Facility Type: Skilled care; Alzheimer's; Beds: Skilled care 72; Certified: Medicaid; Medicare; Veterans; Owner: Proprietary/Public corp.; License: Current state

University Good Samaritan Center
22 27th Ave. SE, Minneapolis, MN 55414, (612) 332-4262; Facility Type: Skilled care; Alzheimer's; Beds: Skilled care 90; Alzheimer's; CD; Certified: Medicaid; Medicare; Veterans; Owner: The Evangelical Lutheran Good Samaritan Society; License: Current state

Walker Southview
6130 Lyndale Ave. S, Minneapolis, MN 55419, (612) 866-3095; Facility Type: Skilled care; Alzheimer's; Beds: Skilled care 134; Certified: Medicaid; Medicare; Owner: Nonprofit/Religious org.; License: Current state

Moorhead

Eventide Lutheran Home
1405 7th St. S, Moorhead, MN 56560, (218) 233-7508; Facility Type: Skilled care; Alzheimer's; Beds: Skilled care; Alzheimer's 195; Certified: Medicaid; Medicare; Owner: Nonprofit corp.; License: Current state

New Hope

Minnesota Masonic North Ridge
5430 Boone Ave. N, New Hope, MN 55428, (612) 536-7000; Facility Type: Skilled care; Alzheimer's; Beds: Skilled care 559; Certified: Medicaid; Medicare; Owner: Proprietary/Public corp.; License: n/a

Onamia

Mille Lacs Health System
200 N Elm St., Onamia, MN 56359, (320) 532-3154; Facility Type: Skilled care; ICF; Alzheimer's; Beds: Skilled care 108; Certified: Medicaid; Medicare; Veterans; Owner: Nonprofit corp.; License: Current state

Plymouth

Mission Nursing Home
3401 E Medicine Lake Blvd., Plymouth, MN 55441, (612) 559-3123; Facility Type: Skilled care; ICF; Alzheimer's; Beds: Skilled care 104; Certified: Medicaid; Medicare; Owner: Nonprofit corp.; License: Current state

Red Wing

Red Wing Health Center
1412 W 4th St., Red Wing, MN 55066, (651) 388-2843; Facility Type: Skilled care; Alzheimer's; Beds: Skilled care 168; Certified: Medicaid; Medicare; Veterans; Owner: Private; License: Current state

Richfield

Richfield Health Center
7727 Portland Ave. S, Richfield, MN 55423, (612) 861-1691; Facility Type: Skilled care; Alzheimer's; Beds: Skilled care 119; Certified: Medicaid; Medicare; Owner: ExtendiCare Health Services Inc.; License: Current state

Roseville

Lake Ridge Rehabilitation Specialty Care Center
2727 N Victoria, Roseville, MN 55113, (651) 483-5431; Facility Type: Skilled care; Alzheimer's; Beds: Skilled care 160; Alzheimer's 16; Certified: Medicare; Owner: Private; License: Current state

Saint Cloud

Talahi Care Center
1717 Michigan Ave. SE, Saint Cloud, MN 56304, (320) 251-9120; Facility Type: Skilled care; Alzheimer's; Beds: Skilled care 81; Alzheimer's; Board & lodge; Certified: Medicaid; Medicare; Veterans; Owner: Proprietary/Public corp.; License: Current state

Saint Louis Park

Saint Louis Park Plaza Healthcare Center
3201 Virginia Ave. S, Saint Louis Park, MN 55426, (952) 935-0333; Facility Type: Skilled care; Alzheimer's; Beds: Skilled care 262; Alzheimer's; Certified: Medicaid; Medicare; Owner: Proprietary/Pubic corp.; License: Current state

Saint Paul

Good Shepard Care Center
324 Johnson Pkwy, Saint Paul, MN 55106, (651) 774-9737; Facility Type: Skilled care; ICF; Alzheimer's; Beds: Skilled care 180; Alzheimer's; Certified: Medicaid; Medicare; Veterans; Owner: Nonprofit/Religious org.; License: Current state

Health East Care Center on Humboldt
512 Humboldt Ave., Saint Paul, MN 55107, (651) 227-8091; Facility Type: Skilled care; Alzheimer's; Beds: Skilled care 86; Alzheimer's 41; Certified: Medicaid; Medicare; Owner: Nonprofit corp.; License: Current state

Saint Anthony Park Home
2237 Commonwealth Ave., Saint Paul, MN 55108, (651) 646-7486; Facility Type: Skilled care; Alzheimer's; Beds: Skilled care 93; Certified: Medicaid; Medicare; Owner: Proprietary/Public corp.; License: Current state

Sholom Home East Inc.
1554 Midway Pkwy, Saint Paul, MN 55108, (651) 646-6311; Facility Type: Skilled care; Alzheimer's; Beds: Skilled care 74; Certified: Medicaid; Medicare; Owner: Nonprofit/Religious org.; License: Current state

Saint Peter

Saint Peter Community Hospital & Health Care Center
618 W Broadway, Saint Peter, MN 56082, (507) 931-2200; Facility Type: Skilled care; Alzheimer's; Beds: Skilled care 85; Alzheimer's; Certified: Medicaid; Medicare; Owner: Government/State/Local; License: Current state

Slayton

Slayton Manor
2957 Redwood Ave. S, Slayton, MN 56172, (507) 836-6135; Facility Type: Skilled care; Alzheimer's; Beds: Skilled care 64; Certified: Medicaid; Medicare; Owner: Beverly Enterprises Inc.; License: Current state

Wabasha

Saint Elizabeth's Hospital
1200 5th Grant Blvd. W, Wabasha, MN 44981, (651) 565-4531; Facility Type: Skilled care; Alzheimer's; Beds: Skilled care 51; Certified: Medicaid; Medicare; Veterans; Owner: Nonprofit/Religious org.; License: Current state

Wayzata

Hillcrest Rehabilitation & Health Care Center
15409 Wayzata Blvd., Wayzata,, MN 55391, (952) 473-5466; Facility Type: Skilled care; ICF; Alzheimer's; Beds: Skilled care 208; Certified: Medicare; Owner: Beverly Enterprises Inc.; License: Current state

Winnebago

Parker Oaks
211 6th St., NW Winnebago, MN 56098, (507) 893-3171; Facility Type: Skilled care; Alzheimer's; Beds: Skilled care 61; Alzheimer's; Assisted living 27; Certified: Medicaid; Medicare; Owner: American Baptist Homes of the Midwest; License: Current state

MISSISSIPPI

Ackerman

Choctow County Nursing Home
148 W Cherry St., Ackerman, MS 39735, (662) 285-6235; Facility Type: ICF; ICF/MR; Alzheimer's; Beds: Skilled care 68; Certified: Medicaid; Owner: Government/State/Local; License: Current state

Clarksdale

Delta Manor ICF/MR
701 US Hwy. 322 W, Clarksdale, MS 38614, (662) 627-2212; Facility Type: Skilled care; ICF; ICF/MR; Alzheimer's; Beds: Skilled care 50; Certified: Medicaid; Owner: Proprietary/Public corp.; License: Current state

Columbia

The Grove
11 Pecan Dr., Columbia, MS 39429, (601) 736-4747; Facility Type: Skilled care; ICF/MR; Alzheimer's; Beds: Skilled care 78; Certified: Medicaid; Medicare; Owner: Proprietary/Public corp.; License: Current state

De Kalb

Mississippi Care Center of Dekalb LLC
PO Box 577, De Kalb, MS 39328, (601) 743-5888; Facility Type: Skilled care; ICF; ICF/MR; Alzheimer's; Beds: Skilled care 6; ICF 54; Certified: Medicaid; Medicare; Owner: Proprietary/Pubic corp.; License: Current state

Fulton

Daniel Health Care Complex
804 S Adams, Fulton, MS 38843, (662) 862-2165; Facility Type: Skilled care; Alzheimer's; Beds: Skilled care 87; Alzheimer's 18; Certified: Medicaid; Medicare; Owner: Private; License: Current state

Gulfport

Driftwood Nursing Center
1500 Broad Ave., Gulfport, MS 39501, (228) 868-1314; Facility Type: Skilled care; ICF; Alzheimer's; Beds: Skilled care 151; Certified: Medicaid; Veterans; Owner: Proprietary/Public corp.; License: Current state

Hattiesburg

Hattiesburg Convalescent Center
514 Bay St., Hattiesburg, MS 39401, (601) 544-4230; Facility Type: Skilled care; Alzheimer's; Beds: Skilled care 184; Certified: Medicaid; Owner: Proprietary/Public corp.; License: Current state

Jackson

Compere's Nursing Home
865 North St., Jackson, MS 39202, (601) 948-6531; Facility Type: Skilled care; ICF; Alzheimer's; Beds: Skilled care; ICF 52; SNF/ICF 8; Certified: Medicaid; Medicare; Owner: Private; License: Current state

Lakeland Health Care Center
3680 Lakeland Ln., Jackson, MS 39216, (601) 982-5505; Facility Type: Skilled care; ICF; Alzheimer's; Beds: Skilled care 69; ICF 36; Certified: Medicaid; Medicare; Veterans; Owner: Beverly Enterprises Inc.; License: Current state

Natchez

Adams County Nursing Center
John R Junkin Dr., Natchez, MS 39120, (601) 446-8426; Facility Type: Skilled care; ICF; ICF/MR; Alzheimer's; Beds: Skilled care 12; ICF/MR 86; Alzheimer's 22; SNF/ICF; Certified: Medicaid; Medicare; Veterans; Owner: Private; License: Current state

Quitman

Lakeside Living Center
191 Hwy. 511 E, Quitman, MS 39355, (601) 776-2141; Facility Type: Skilled care; ICF; Alzheimer's; Beds: Skilled care 120; Certified: Medicaid; Owner: Proprietary/Public corp.; License: n/a

Ruleville

Ruleville Health Care Center
800 Stansel Dr., Ruleville, MS 38771, (662) 756-4361; Facility Type: Skilled care; ICF; ICF/MR; Alzheimer's; Beds: Skilled care 99; Certified: Medicaid; Medicare; Owner: Beverly Enterprises Inc.; License: Current state

Southaven

Beverly Healthcare—Southaven
1730 Dorchester Dr., Southaven, MS 38671, (662) 393-0050; Facility Type: Skilled care; ICF; ICF/MR; Alzheimer's; Beds: Skilled care 120; Certified: Medicaid; Medicare; Veterans; Owner: Beverly Enterprises Inc.; License: Current state

West Point

Dugan Memorial Home
804 E Main St., West Point, MS 39773, (662) 494-2640; Facility Type: Skilled care; Alzheimer's; Beds: Skilled care 60; Certified: n/a; Owner: Nonprofit/Religious org.; License: Current state

Wiggins

Conner Enterprises Nursing Home
530 Hall St., Wiggins, MS 39577, (601) 928-5231; Facility Type: Skilled care; ICF; Alzheimer's; Beds: Skilled care 149; ICF; Certified: Medicaid; Veterans; Owner: Private; License: Current state

---

MISSOURI

Ash Grove

AshGrove Healthcare Facility
400 Meadowview, Box 427, Ash Grove, MO 65604, (417) 751-2575; Facility Type: Skilled care; ICF; ICF/MR; Alzheimer's; Beds: Skilled care 62; ICF; Medicare; Certified: Medicaid; Medicare; Owner: Proprietary/Public corp.; License: Current state

Belleview

Belleview Valley Nursing Home
HCR 63, Box 1620, Belleview, MO 63623, (573) 697-5311; Facility Type: Skilled care; ICF; ICF/MR; Alzheimer's; Beds: Skilled care 122; Certified: Medicaid; Medicare; Owner: Proprietary/Public corp.; License: Current state

Bethany

Crestview Home Inc.
1313 S 25th St., Bethany, MO 64424, (660) 425-3128; Facility Type: Skilled care; Alzheimer's; Beds: Skilled care 130; Alzheimer's; RCF 24; Certified: Medicaid; Owner: Nonprofit corp.; License: Current state

Birch Tree

Birch View Nursing Center
Hwy. 60 W, Birch Tree, MO 65438, (573) 292-3212; Facility Type: Skilled care; Alzheimer's; Beds: Skilled care 74; Alzheimer's 16; Certified: Medicaid; Medicare; Owner: Americare Systems Inc.; License: Current state

Boonville

Riverdell Health Care Center
1121 11th St., Boonville, MO 65233, (660) 882-7600; Facility Type: Skilled care; ICF; ICF/MR; Alzheimer's Beds: Skilled care 58; Alzheimer's; Certified: Medicaid; Medicare; Owner: Nonprofit corp.; License: Current state

Butler

Medicalodge of Butler
103 E Nursery, Butler, MO 64730, (660) 679-3179; Facility Type: ICF; Alzheimer's; Beds: Skilled care 120; Certified: Medicaid; Medicare; Owner: Medicalodges Inc.; License: Current state

Cameron

Quail Run Health Center
1405 W Grand Ave., Cameron, MO 64429, (816) 632-2151; Facility Type: Skilled care; ICF; ICF/MR; Alzheimer's; Beds: Skilled care 76; Certified: Medicaid; Medicare; Veterans; Owner: Proprietary/Public corp.; License: Current state

Cape Girardeau

Heartland Care & Rehabilitation
2525 Boutin Dr., Cape Girardeau, MO 63701, (573) 334-5225; Facility Type: Skilled care; ICF; Alzheimer's; Beds: Skilled care 102; ICF; Residential care; Certified: Medicaid; Medicare; Owner: Health Facilities Management Corp.; License: Current state

Cassville

Red Rose Inn of Cassville
812 Old Exeter Rd., Cassville, MO 65625, (417) 847-2184; Facility Type: Skilled care; ICF; Alzheimer's; Beds: Skilled care 90; Alzheimer's; Certified: Medicaid; Medicare; Owner: Rose Care Inc.; License: Current state

Charleston

Charleston Manor Skilled Nursing Facility
1220 E Marshall Charleston, MO 63834, (573) 683-3721; Facility Type: Skilled care; ICF; Alzheimer's; Beds: Skilled care 120; Certified: Medicaid; Medicare; Veterans; Owner: Americare Systems Inc.; License: Current state

Chesterfield

Brooking Park
307 S Woods Mill Rd., Chesterfield, MO 63017, (314) 576-5545; Facility Type: Skilled care; Alzheimer's; Beds: Skilled care 90; Assisted living 90; Certified: n/a; Owner: Nonprofit/Religious org.; License: Current state

Columbia

Lenoir Health Care Center
3300 New Haven Rd., Columbia, MO 65201, (673) 876-5800; Facility Type: Skilled care; Alzheimer's; Beds: Skilled care 92; Certified: Medicaid; Medicare; Owner: Nonprofit/Religious org.; License: Current state

Crane

Ozark Mountain Regional Healthcare Center
127 Northwest Blvd., Crane, MO 65633, (417) 723-5281; Facility Type: Skilled care; Alzheimer's; Beds: Skilled care 120; Certified: Medicaid; Medicare; Owner: Lenox Healthcare Inc.; License: Current state

De Soto

Baisch Nursing Center
3260 Baisch Dr., De Soto, MO 63020, (636) 586-2291; Facility Type: Skilled care; ICF; Alzheimer's; Beds: Skilled care 79; Certified: n/a; Owner: Proprietary/Public corp.; License: Current state

Dexter

Crowley Ridge Care Center
1204 N Outer Rd., Dexter, MO 63841, (573) 624-5557; Facility Type: Skilled care; ICF; Alzheimer's; Beds: Skilled care 90; Certified: Medicaid; Veterans; Owner: Proprietary/Public corp.; License: Current state

El Dorado Springs

Community Nursing Home
400 E Hospital Rd., El Dorado, MO 64744, (417) 676-2531; Facility Type: Skilled care; Alzheimer's; Beds: Skilled care 120; Certified: Medicaid; Medicare; Owner: Proprietary/Public corp.; License: Current state

Eureka

Marymount Manor SNF
313 Augustine Rd., Eureka, MO 63025, (636) 938-6770; Facility Type: Skilled care; Alzheimer's; Beds: Skilled care 176; Residential care 100; Certified: Medicaid; Medicare; Veterans; Owner: Private; License: Current state

Farmington

Easter's Care Center
401 S Henry, Farmington, MO 63640, (573) 756-4559; Facility Type: ICF; Alzheimer's; Beds: ICF 19; RCF II 23; Certified: Veterans; Owner: Proprietary/Public corp.; License: Current state

Fenton

Cori Manor Skilled & Residential Center
560 Corisande Hill Rd., Fenton, MO 63026, (636) 343-2282; Facility Type: Skilled care; ICF; ICF/MR; Alzheimer's; Beds: Skilled care 124; ICF; ICF/MR; Alzheimer's; SNF/ICF; Residential care 22; Certified: Medicaid; Medicare; Owner: Healthcare Corp.; License: Current state

Festus

Arbor Place
12827 State Rd. TT, Festus, MO 63028, (636) 937-3150; Facility Type: Skilled care; Alzheimer's; Beds: Skilled care 81; Certified: Medicaid; Veterans; Owner: Private; License: Current state

Florissant

Florissant Nursing Center
615 Rancho Dr., Florissant, MO 63031, (314) 839-2150; Facility Type: Skilled care; ICF; Alzheimer's; Beds: Skilled care 120; Certified: Medicaid; Medicare; Owner: Proprietary/Pubic corp.; License: n/a

Gerald

Gerald Caring Center
PO Box 180, Gerald, MO 63037, (573) 764-2135; Facility Type: Skilled care; Alzheimer's; Beds: Skilled care 60; Certified: Medicaid; Medicare; Owner: Proprietary/Public corp.; License: Current state

Grandview

Grandview Manor Care Center
5301 Harry Truman Dr., Grandview, MO 64030, (816) 763-2855; Facility Type: Skilled care; ICF; ICF/MR; Alzheimer's; Beds: Skilled care; ICF 100; SNF/ICF; Certified: Medicaid; Medicare; Veterans; Owner: Proprietary/Public corp.; License: Current state

Hannibal

Beth Haven Nursing Home
2500 Pleasant St., Hannibal, MO 3401, (573) 221-6000; Facility Type: Skilled care; Alzheimer's; Beds: Skilled care 96; Alzheimer's 20; Certified: Medicaid; Medicare; Owner: Nonprofit corp.; License: n/a

Hermann

Frene Valley Geriatric & Rehabilitation Center
18th & Jefferson St., Hermann, MO 65041, (573) 486-3193; Facility Type: Skilled care; ICF; ICF/MR; Alzheimer's; Beds: Skilled care 60; Certified: Medicaid; Medicare; Owner: Proprietary/Public corp.; License: Current state

Jefferson City

Oak View Living Center
1221 Southgate Ln., Jefferson City, MO 65109, (573) 635-3131; Facility Type: Skilled care; Alzheimer's; Beds: Skilled care 22; Alzheimer's 24; SNF/ICF 74; Certified: Medicaid; Medicare; Owner: Private; License: Current state

Joplin

Joplin Health & Rehabilitation Center
2218 W 32nd St., Joplin, MO 64804, (417) 623-5264; Facility Type: Skilled care; Alzheimer's; Beds: Skilled care 120; Certified: Medicaid; Medicare; Owner: Proprietary/Public corp.; License: Current state

National Health Care Center of Joplin
2700 E 34th Joplin, MO 64803, (417) 781-1737; Facility Type: Skilled care; ICF; Alzheimer's; Beds: Skilled care 119; Certified: Medicaid; Medicare; Veterans; Owner: National Healthcare Company; License: Current state

Kansas City

Ballantree Health & Rehab
7801 Holmes Rd., Kansas City, MO 64131, (816) 333-7800; Facility Type: Skilled care; Alzheimer's; Beds: Skilled care 145; Alzheimer's 49; Certified: Medicaid; Medicare; Owner: Nonprofit corp.; License: Current state

Blue Ridge Nursing Home
7505 E 87th St., Kansas City, MO 64138, (816) 761-6838; Facility Type: ICF; Alzheimer's; Beds: ICF 35; Certified: Veterans; Owner: Proprietary/Public corp.; License: Current state

South Park Care Center
904 R 68th St., Kansas City, MO 64131, (816) 333-5485; Facility Type: Skilled care; Alzheimer's; Beds: Skilled care 174; Alzheimer's 36; HIV/AIDS 15; Certified: Medicaid; Medicare; Veterans; Owner: Proprietary/Public corp.; License: Current state

Kimberling City

Tablerock Retirement Village
276 Fountain Ln., Kimberling City, MO 65686, (417) 739-2481; Facility Type: Skilled care; ICF; Alzheimer's; Beds: Skilled care 106; Medicare certified; Certified: Medicaid; Medicare; Owner: Lenox Healthcare Inc.; License: Current state

La Belle

La Belle Manor Care Center
Hwy. 6 W, La Belle, MO 63447, (660) 462-3234; Facility Type: Skilled care; Alzheimer's; Beds: Skilled care 94; RCF 8; Certified: Veterans; Owner: Proprietary/Public corp.; License: Current state

Lamar

Lakeview Healthcare & Rehabilitation
206 W 1st, Lamar, MO 64759, (417) 682-3315; Facility Type: Skilled care; Alzheimer's; Beds: Skilled care 123; Alzheimer's 26; SNF/ICF 77; Certified: Medicaid; Medicare; Owner: Private; License: Current state

Lexington

Santa Fe Trail Healthcare Center
PO Box 4559, Lexington, MO 64067, (660) 259-4697; Facility Type: Skilled care; Alzheimer's; Beds: Skilled care 160; Alzheimer's 22; Certified: Medicaid; Medicare; Veterans; Owner: Proprietary/Public corp.; License: Current state

Liberty

Ashton Court Care/Rehabilitation Center
1200 W College, Liberty, MO 64068, (816) 781-3020; Facility Type: Skilled care; Alzheimer's; Beds: Skilled care 140; Alzheimer's 34; Certified: Medicaid; Medicare; Owner: Centennial Health-Care Corp.; License: Current state

Linn

Green Meadows Skilled Care Center
1 Green Meadows Ln., Re 2, Box 251 Linn, MO 65051, (573) 897-2218; Facility Type: Skilled care; Alzheimer's; Beds: Skilled care 132; Certi-

fied: Medicaid; Medicare; Veterans; Owner: Private; License: Current state

Marble Hill

Eldercare of Marble Hill
Rte. 1 Box 3070, Marble Hill, MO 63764, (573) 238-2614; Facility Type: Skilled care; ICF; ICF/MR; Alzheimer's; Beds: Skilled care 120; Certified: Medicaid; Medicare; Owner: Private; License: Current state

Maryland Heights

NHC Health Care—Maryland Heights
2920 Fee Fee Rd., Maryland Heights, MO 63043, (314) 291-0121; Facility Type: Skilled care; Alzheimer's; Beds: Skilled care 220; Certified: Medicaid; Medicare; Owner: Proprietary/Public corp.; License: Current state

Maryville

Beverly Healthcare of Maryville
524 N Laura, Maryville, MO 64468, (660) 582-7447; Facility Type: Skilled care; Alzheimer's; Beds: Skilled care 108; Alzheimer's 24; Certified: Medicaid; Medicare; Veterans; Owner: Proprietary/Public corp.; License: Current state

Memphis

Scotland County Care Center
Rte. 1 Box 52, Sigler Ave., Memphis, MO 63555, (660) 65-7221; Facility Type: Skilled care; Alzheimer's; Beds: Skilled care 120; Certified: Medicaid; Owner: Government/State/Local; License: Current state

Moberly

Moberly Nursing & Rehabilitation
700 E Urbandale, Moberly, MO 65270, (660) 263-9060; Facility Type: Skilled care; Alzheimer's; Beds: Skilled care 120; Alzheimer's 12; Certified: Medicaid; Medicare; Owner: Private; License: Current state

Mountain Grove

Autumn Oaks Caring Center
1310 Hovis St., Mountain Grove, MO 65711, (417) 926-5128; Facility Type: Skilled care; Alzheimer's; Beds: Skilled care 120; Certified: Medicaid; Medicare; Owner: Proprietary/Public corp.; License: Current state

Nevada

Nevada City Nursing Home
901 S Adams, Nevada, MO 64772, (417) 448-2841; Facility Type: Skilled care; ICF; Alzheimer's; Beds: Skilled care 12; SNF/ICF 100; Certified: Medicaid; Medicare; Owner: Government/State/Local; License: Current state

Ozark

Ozark Nursing & Care Center
1486 N Riverside Rd., Ozark, MO 65721, (417) 581-7126; Facility Type: Skilled care; Alzheimer's; Beds: Skilled care 62; Certified: Medicaid; Owner: Proprietary/Public corp.; License: Current state

Pacific

Pacific Care Center Inc.
105 S 6th St., Pacific, MO 63069, (636) 271-4222; Facility Type: Skilled care; ICF; ICF/MR; Alzheimer's; Beds: Skilled care 74; Alzheimer's 26; Certified: Medicaid; Medicare; Owner: Proprietary/Public corp.; License: Current state

Perryville

Perry Oaks Nursing & Rehab
430 N West St., Perryville, MO 63775, (573) 547-1011; Facility Type: Skilled care; ICF; Alzheimer's; Beds: Skilled care 156; Certified: Medicaid; Medicare; Owner: Nonprofit corp.; License: Current state

Poplar Bluff

Oakdale Care Center
2702 Debbie Ln., Poplar Bluff, MO 63902, (573) 686-5242; Facility Type: Skilled care; ICF; ICF/MR; Alzheimer's; Beds: Skilled care 2, ICF 22; ICF/MR 22; Certified: Medicaid; Medicare; Owner: Proprietary/Public corp.; License: Current state

Puxico

Puxico Nursing & Rehabilitation Center
540 N Hwy. 51, Puxico, MO 63960, (573) 222-3125; Facility Type: Skilled care; ICF; Alzheimer's; Beds: Skilled care 60; Certified: Medicaid; Medicare; Veterans; Owner: Proprietary/Public corp.; License: Current state

Saint James

Saint James Nursing Center
415 Sidney St., Saint James, MO 65559, (573) 265-8921; Facility Type: Skilled care; Alzhei-

mer's; Beds: Skilled care 90; Certified: Medicaid; Medicare; Owner: Proprietary/Public corp.; License: Current state

Saint Joseph

Carriage Square Health Care Center Inc.
4009 Gene Field Rd., Saint Joseph, MO 64506, (816) 364-1526; Facility Type: Skilled care; Alzheimer's; Beds: Skilled care 120; Certified: Medicaid; Medicare; Owner: Proprietary/Public corp.; License: Current state

Saint Louis

Alexian Brothers Lansdowne Village
4624 Lansdowne Ave., Saint Louis, MO 63116, (314) 351-6888; Facility Type: Skilled care; ICF; Alzheimer's; Beds: Skilled care 161; Certified: Medicaid; Medicare; Owner: Nonprofit corp.; License: Current state

Bethesda Dilworth Memorial Home
9645 Big Bend Blvd., Saint Louis, MO 63122, (314) 968-5460; Facility Type: Skilled care; ICF; Alzheimer's; Beds: Skilled care 430; Alzheimer's 60; Certified: Medicaid; Owner: Nonprofit corp.; License: Current state

Friendship Village of South County
12509 Village Circle Dr., Saint Louis, MO 63127, (314) 842-6840; Facility Type: Skilled care; Alzheimer's; Beds: Skilled care 118; Certified: Medicaid; Owner: Nonprofit corp.; License: Current state

IHS of Saint Louis at Gravois
10954 Kennedy Rd., Saint Louis, MO 63128, (314) 843-4242; Facility Type: Skilled care; Alzheimer's; Beds: Skilled care 165; Certified: Medicaid; Medicare; Owner: Proprietary/Public corp.; License: Current state

South Gate Care Center
5943 Telegraph Rd., Saint Louis, MO 63129, (314) 846-2000; Facility Type: Skilled care; Alzheimer's; Beds: Skilled care 180; Alzheimer's; Certified: Medicaid; Medicare; Owner: Proprietary/Public corp.; License: Current state

Salisbury

Chariton Park Nursing Facility
902 Manor Dr., Salisbury, MO 65281, (660) 388-6486; Facility Type: Skilled care; ICF; ICF/MR; Alzheimer's; Beds: Skilled care 74; Alzheimer's 14; Residential care 12; Certified: Medicaid; Medicare; Owner: Proprietary/Public corp.; License: Current state

Sikeston

Hunter Acres Care Center
628 N West St., Sikeston, MO 63801, (573) 471-7130; Facility Type: Skilled care; ICF; ICF/MR; Alzheimer's; Beds: Skilled care 76; ICF; Alzheimer's; Certified: Medicaid; Medicare; Owner: Nonprofit corp.; License: Current state

Springfield

Balanced Care
3403 W Mt Vernon, Springfield, MO 65802, (417) 864-5600; Facility Type: Skilled care; Alzheimer's; Beds: Skilled care 150; Alzheimer's 30; SNF/ICF; Certified: Medicaid; Medicare; Owner: Proprietary/Public corp.; License: Current state

Greene County Nursing Care Center Inc.
910 S West Ave., Springfield, MO 65802, (417) 865-8741, Facility Type: Skilled care; Alzheimer's; Beds: Skilled care 16; Alzheimer's 16; SNF/ICF 120; Certified: Medicaid; Medicare; Owner: Nonprofit corp.; License: Current state

ManorCare Health Services
2915 S Fremont, Springfield, MO 65804, (417) 883-4022; Facility Type: Skilled care; Alzheimer's; Beds: Skilled care 194; Alzheimer's 53; Assisted living 40; Certified: Medicaid; Medicare; Owner: Proprietary/Public corp.; License: Current state

Woodland Manor
1347 E Valley Water Mill Rd., Springfield, MO 65803, (417) 833-1220; Facility Type: Skilled care; Alzheimer's; Beds: Skilled care 110; Certified: Medicaid; Medicare; Owner: Proprietary/Public corp.; License: Current state

Town & Country

Clayton House
13995 Clayton Rd., Town & Country, MO 63017, (636) 227-5070; Facility Type: Skilled care; Alzheimer's; Beds: Skilled care 282; Alzheimer's; SNF/ICF; Certified: Medicaid; Medicare; Owner: Proprietary/Public corp.; License: Current state

Union

Sunset Health Care Center
400 W Park Ave., Union, MO 63084, (636) 583-2252; Facility Type: Skilled care; ICF; Alzheimer's; Beds: Skilled care 120; Certified: Medicaid; Medicare; Veterans; Owner: Proprietary/Public corp.; License: Current state

Vandalia

Tri-County Care Center
601 N Galloway Rd., Vandalia, MO 63382, (573) 594-6467; Facility Type: Skilled care; Alzheimer's; Beds: Skilled care 70; Alzheimer's 20; Certified: Medicaid; Medicare; Owner: Government/State/Local; License: Current state

Warrensburg

Johnson County Care Center
122 E Market St., Warrensburg, MO 64093, (660) 747-8181; Facility Type: ICF; Alzheimer's; Beds: ICF 87; Certified: Medicaid; Owner: Leisure Care Corp.; License: Current state

Ridge Crest Nursing Center
706 S Mitchell, Warrensburg, MO 64093, (660) 429-2177; Facility Type: Skilled care; Alzheimer's; Beds: Skilled care 120; Certified: Medicaid; Medicare; Veterans; Owner: Proprietary/Public corp.; License: Current state

Washington

Cedarcrest Manor
324 W 5th St., Washington, MO 63090, (636) 239-7848; Facility Type: Skilled care; ICF; ICF/MR; Alzheimer's; Beds: Skilled care 184; Certified: Medicaid; Medicare; Owner: Private; License: Current state

Webb City

Webb City Health & Rehabilitation Center
2077 W Carl Junction Rd., Webb City, MO 64870, (417) 673-1933; Facility Type: Skilled care; ICF; ICF/MR; Alzheimer's; Beds: Skilled care; ICF; ICF/MR; Alzheimer's; Certified: Medicaid; Medicare; Owner: Private; License: Current state

Willow Springs

Willow Care Nursing Inc.
PO Box 309, Willow Springs, MO 65793, (417) 469-3152; Facility Type: Skilled care; Alzheimer's; Beds: Skilled care 120; Certified: Medicaid; Medicare; Owner: Nonprofit corp.; License: Current state

---

MONTANA

Big Sandy

Prairie Vista Manor
PO Box 70, Big Sandy, MT 59520, (406) 378-2402; Facility Type: Skilled care; ICF; ICF/MR; Alzheimer's; Beds: Skilled care 29; ICF; Certified: Medicaid; Medicare; Owner: Proprietary/Public corp.; License: Current state

Billings

Eagle Cliff Manor
1415 Yellowstone River Rd., Billings, MT 59105, (406) 245-9330; Facility Type: Skilled care; ICF; Alzheimer's; Beds: Skilled care 24; ICF 79; Alzheimer's 26; SNF/ICF; Assisted living 18; Certified: Medicaid; Medicare; Owner: Proprietary/Public corp.; License: Current state

Saint John's Lutheran Home
3940 Rimrock Rd., Billings, MT 59102, (406) 655-5600; Facility Type: Skilled care; ICF; Alzheimer's; Beds: Skilled care; ICF 59; Alzheimer's 32; SNF/ICF 94; Certified: Medicaid; Medicare; Owner: Nonprofit/Religious org.; License: Current state

Bozeman

Evergreen Bozeman Health & Rehabilitation Center
321 N 5th Ave., Bozeman, MT 59715, (406) 587-4404; Facility Type: Skilled care; Alzheimer's; Beds: Skilled care 48; ICF 46; Certified: Medicaid; Medicare; Veterans; Owner: Private; License: Current state

Choteau

Teton Nursing Home
24 Main Ave., Choteau, MT 59422, (406) 466-5338; Facility Type: Skilled care; ICF; Alzheimer's; Beds: Skilled care 40; Certified: Medicaid; Medicare; Owner: Government/State/Local; License: Current state

Columbus

Beartooth Manor
350 W Pike Ave., Columbus, MT 59019, (406) 322-5342; Facility Type: Skilled care; Alzheimer's; Beds: Skilled care 82; Alzheimer's 12; Home health; Certified: Medicaid; Medicare; Veterans; Owner: Nonprofit corp.; License: Current state

Ennis

Madison Valley Manor
211 N Main St., Ennis, MT 59729, (406) 682-7271; Facility Type: Skilled care; ICF; Alzheimer's; Beds: Skilled care 20; ICF 20; Certified: Medicaid; Medicare; Veterans; Owner: Government/State/Local; License: Current state

Fort Benton

Missouri River Medical Center—Nursing Home
1501 St., Charles St., Fort Benton, MT 59442, (406) 622-3331; Facility Type: Skilled care; ICF; ICF/MR; Alzheimer's; Beds: Skilled care 37; Personal care 6; Certified: Medicaid; Medicare; Owner: Government/State/Local; License: Current state

Helena

Big Sky Care Center
2475 Winne Ave., Helena, MT 59601, (406) 442-1350; Facility Type: Skilled care; ICF; Alzheimer's; Beds: Skilled care 108; CFP 10; Certified: Medicaid; Medicare; Veterans; Owner: Proprietary/Public corp.; License: Current state

Rocky Mountain Care Center
30 S Rodney, Helena, MT 59601, (406) 443-5880; Facility Type: Skilled care; ICF; ICF/MR; Alzheimer's; Beds: Skilled care 64; ICF 31; Certified: Medicaid; Medicare; Veterans; Owner: Private; License: Current state

Lewistown

Valle Vista Manor
402 Summitt Ave., Lewistown, MT 59457, (406) 538-8775; Facility Type: Skilled care; ICF; Alzheimer's; Beds: Skilled care 8; ICF 75; Assisted living 18; Certified: Medicaid; Medicare; Veterans; Owner: Private; License: Current state

Miles City

Friendship Villa Care Center
2300 Wilson, Miles City, MT 59301, (406) 232-2687; Facility Type: Skilled care; ICF; Alzheimer's; Beds: Skilled care 8; ICF 99; Certified: Medicaid; Medicare; Veterans; Owner: Proprietary/Public corp.; License: Current state

Holy Rosary Extended Care Unit
2600 Wilson, Miles City, MT 59301, (406) 233-4082; Facility Type: Skilled care; ICF; Alzheimer's; Beds: Skilled care 107; Certified: Medicaid; Medicare; Veterans; Owner: Nonprofit corp.; License: Current state

Missoula

Evergreen Missoula Health & Rehabilitation Center
3018 Rattlesnake Dr., Missoula, MT 59802, (406) 549-0988; Facility Type: Skilled care; ICF; ICF/MR; Alzheimer's Beds: Skilled care 53; ICF; Assisted living 22; Certified: Medicaid; Medicare; Veterans; Owner: Proprietary/Pubic corp.; License: Current state

The Village Health Care Center
2651 South Ave. W, Missoula, MT 59804, (406) 728-9162; Facility Type: Skilled care; Alzheimer's; Beds: Skilled care 46; ICF 61; Alzheimer's 57; Certified: Medicaid; Medicare; Veterans; Owner: Private; License: Current state

Red Lodge

Cedar Wood Villa
1 S Oaks, Red Lodge, MT 59068, (406) 446-2525; Facility Type: Skilled care; ICF; ICF/MR; Alzheimer's; Beds: Skilled care 64; Certified: Medicaid; Medicare; Veterans; Owner: Private; License: Current state

Sheridan

Tobacco Root Mountains Care Center
PO Box 308, Sheridan, MT 59749, (406) 842-5600; Facility Type: Skilled care; ICF; Alzheimer's; Beds: ICF 39; Certified: Medicaid; Owner: Government/State/Local; License: Current state

---

NEBRASKA

Alliance

Alliance Good Samaritan Village
1016 E 6th St., Alliance, NE 69301, (308) 762-5675; Facility Type: Skilled care; ICF; Alzheimer's; Beds: Skilled care 85; ICF; Certified: Medicaid; Owner: The Evangelical Lutheran Good Samaritan Society; License: Current state

Ashland

IHS at Ashland
1700 Furnas St., Ashland, NE 68003, (402) 944-7031; Facility Type: Skilled care; ICF; Alzheimer's; Beds: ICF 101; Certified: Medicaid; Medicare; Owner: Proprietary/Public corp.; License: Current state

Auburn

Nehema County Good Samaritan Center
Rte. 1 Box 4, Auburn, NE 68305, (402) 274-4954; Facility Type: Skilled care; ICF; ICF/MR; Alzheimer's; Beds: ICF 110; Alzheimer's; SNF/ICF; Certified: Medicaid; Medicare; Veterans; Owner: The Evangelical Lutheran Good Samaritan Society; License: Current state

Beatrice

Beatrice Good Samaritan Center
1306 S 9th St., Beatrice, NE 68310, (402) 228-3304; Facility Type: Skilled care; Alzheimer's; Beds: ICF 93; Alzheimer's; Certified: Medicaid; Medicare; Veterans; Owner: The Evangelical Lutheran Good Samaritan Society; License: Current state

Callaway

Callaway Good Samaritan Center
PO Box 250, Callaway, NE 68825, (308) 836-2267; Facility Type: Skilled care; ICF; ICF/MR; Alzheimer's; Beds: Skilled care 43; ICF; Certified: Medicaid; Medicare; Owner: Nonprofit/Religious org.; License: Current state

Crete

Crete Manor
830 E 1st St., Crete, NE 68333, (402) 826-4325; Facility Type: Skilled care; ICF; ICF/MR; Alzheimer's; Beds: Skilled care 8; ICF; Alzheimer's 14; SNF/ICF 108; Certified: Medicaid; Medicare; Owner: Mariner Post Acute Network; License: Current state

David City

David Place
260 S 10th St., David City, NE 68632, (402) 367-3144; Facility Type: Skilled care; ICF; ICF/MR; Alzheimer's; Beds: Skilled care 96; Certified: Medicaid; Medicare; Veterans; Owner: Vetter Health Services Inc.; License: Current state

Edgar

IHS at Edgar
106 5th St., Edgar, NE 68935, (402) 224-5015; Facility Type: Skilled care; ICF; ICF/MR; Alzheimer's; Beds: ICF 36; Certified: Medicaid; Medicare; Veterans; Owner: Integrated Health Services Inc.; License: Current state

Gering

Heritage Health Care Center
2025 21st St., Gering, NE 69341, (308) 436-5007; Facility Type: Skilled care; ICF; Alzheimer's; Beds: Skilled care 59; Alzheimer's 25; Certified: Medicaid; Medicare; Veterans; Owner: Private; License: Current state

Gothenburg

Hilltop Estates
2520 Ave. M, Gothenburg, NE 69138, (308) 537-7138; Facility Type: Skilled care; ICF; Alzheimer's; Beds: Skilled care 64; Certified: Medicaid; Medicare; Veterans; Owner: Private; License: Current state

Hastings

Good Samaritan Village of Hastings
926 East E St., Hastings, NE 68902, (402) 463-3181; Facility Type: Skilled care; ICF; Alzheimer's; Beds: Skilled care 296; ICF; Alzheimer's 21; SNF/ICF 296; Certified: Medicaid; Medicare; Owner: Nonprofit/Religious org.; License: Current state

Hebron

Blue Valley Lutheran Homes Society Inc.
220 Park, Hebron, NE 68470, (402) 768-6045; Facility Type: Skilled care; ICF; Alzheimer's; Beds: ICF 100; Certified: Medicaid; Owner: Nonprofit corp.; License: Current state

Kearney

Mount Carmel Home—Keens Memorial
412 W 18th St., Kearney, NE 68847, (308) 237-2287; Facility Type: Skilled care; Alzheimer's; Beds: Skilled care 75; Alzheimer's 16; Certified: Medicaid; Medicare; Owner: Nonprofit/Religious org.; License: Current state

Lexington

Plum Creek Care Center
1505 N Adams St., Lexington, NE 68850, (308) 324-5531; Facility Type: Skilled care; Alzhei-

mer's; Beds: Skilled care 90; Alzheimer's 16; Certified: Medicaid; Medicare; Owner: Proprietary/Public corp.; License: Current state

Lincoln

Holmes Lake Manor
6101 Normal Blvd., Lincoln, NE 68506, (402) 489-7175; Facility Type: Skilled care; ICF; Alzheimer's; Beds: Skilled care 120; SNF/ICF; Certified: Medicaid; Medicare; Owner: Private; License: Current state

Lancaster Manor
1001 South St., Lincoln, NE 68502, (402) 441-7101; Facility Type: Skilled care; ICF; Alzheimer's; Beds: Skilled care 60; ICF 240; Certified: Medicaid; Owner: Government/State/Local; License: Current state

Tabitha Nursing Home
4720 Randolph St., Lincoln, NE 68510, (402) 483-7671; Facility Type: Skilled care; ICF; Alzheimer's; Beds: Skilled care 195; Certified: Medicaid; Medicare; Owner: Nonprofit corp.; License: Current state

Nelson

Nelson Good Samaritan Center
150 W 8th St., Nelson, NE 68961, (402) 225-2411; Facility Type: Skilled care; ICF; Alzheimer's; Beds: Skilled care 48; Certified: Medicaid; Medicare; Owner: The Evangelical Good Samaritan Society; License: Current state

Ogallala

Indian Hills Manor
1720 N Spruce, Ogallala, NE 69153, (308) 284-4068; Facility Type: Skilled care; ICF; ICF/MR; Alzheimer's; Beds: Skilled care 10; Alzheimer's 10; SNF/ICF 62; Certified: Medicaid; Medicare; Veterans; Owner: Proprietary/Public corp.; License: Current state

Omaha

Beverly Healthcare at Oak Grove
4809 Redman Ave., Omaha, NE 68104, (402) 455-5025; Facility Type: Skilled care; ICF; ICF/MR; Alzheimer's; Beds: Skilled care 97; Certified: Medicaid; Medicare; Owner: Beverly Enterprises Inc.; License: Current state

Immanuel-Fontenelle Home
6901 N 72nd St., Omaha, NE 68122, (402) 572-2970; Facility Type: Skilled care; ICF; Alzheimer's; Beds: Skilled care 197; ICF; Alzheimer's; Certified: Medicaid; Veterans; Owner: Nonprofit/Religious org.; License: Current state

Mercy Care Center
1870 S 75th St., Omaha, NE 68124, (402) 343-8500; Facility Type: Skilled care; ICF; Alzheimer's; Beds: Skilled care 236; Certified: Medicaid; Medicare; Owner: Nonprofit corp.; License: Current state

Nebraska Skilled Nursing & Rehabilitation
7410 Mercy Rd., Omaha, NE 68124, (402) 397-1220; Facility Type: Skilled care; Alzheimer's; Beds: Skilled care 174; Certified: Medicaid; Medicare; Veterans; Owner: Proprietary/Public corp.; License: Current state

Papillion

Huntington Park Care Center
1507 Gold Coast Rd., Papillion, NE 68128, (402) 339-6010; Facility Type: ICF; Alzheimer's; Beds: ICF 63; Alzheimer's 26; Certified: Medicaid; Owner: Proprietary/Public corp.; License: Current state

Pierce

Pierce Manor
515 E Main St., Pierce, NE 68767, (402) 329-6228; Facility Type: Skilled care; ICF; Alzheimer's; Beds: Skilled care 70; Certified: Medicaid; Owner: Mariner Post Acute Network; License: Current state

Plattsmouth

Beverly Healthcare—Plattsmouth
602 S 18th St., Plattsmouth, NE 68048, (402) 296-2800; Facility Type: Skilled care; Alzheimer's; Beds: Skilled care 22; Alzheimer's 24; SNF/ICF 60 ; Adult day care 4; Certified: Medicaid; Medicare; Veterans; Owner: Proprietary/Public corp.; License: Current state

Stanton

Stanton Health Center
301 17th St., Stanton, NE 68779, (402) 439-2111; Facility Type: Skilled care; ICF; Alzheimer's; Beds: Skilled care 76; ICF 76; Alzheimer's 16; SNF/ICF 76; Adult day care 98; Certified: Medicaid; Medicare; Owner: Government/State/Local; License: Current state

Tilden

Beverly Healthcare—Tilden
401 Park St., Tilden, NE 68781, (402) 368-5335; Facility Type: Skilled care; Alzheimer's; Beds: Skilled care 49; Alzheimer's 6; Certified: Medicaid; Medicare; Veterans; Owner: Proprietary/Public corp.; License: Current state

Valentine

Pine View Good Samaritan Center
601 W 4th St., Valentine, NE 69201, (402) 376-1260; Facility Type: Skilled care; ICF; Alzheimer's; Beds: Skilled care 69; Certified: Medicaid; Medicare; Veterans; Owner: The Evangelical Lutheran Good Samaritan Society; License: Current state

Verdigree

Alpine Village Retirement Center
706 James St., Verdigree, NE 68783, (402) 668-2209; Facility Type: Skilled care; ICF; ICF/MR; Alzheimer's; Beds: Skilled care 79; ICF; Certified: Medicaid; Medicare; Veterans; Owner: Nonprofit corp.; License: Current state

Wauneta

Heritage of Wauneta
427 Legion St., Wauneta, NE 69045, (308) 394-5738; Facility Type: Skilled care; Alzheimer's; Beds: Skilled care 36; Certified: Medicaid; Owner: Proprietary/Public corp.; License: Current state

York

The Hearthstone
2319 Lincoln Ave., York, NE 68467, (402) 362-4333; Facility Type: Skilled care; Alzheimer's; Beds: Skilled care 127; SNF/ICF 8; Certified: Medicaid; Medicare; Veterans; Owner: Nonprofit corp.; License: Current state

NEVADA

Carson City

Sietta Convalescent Center Skilled Nursing Facility & Rehabilitation
201 Koontz Ln., Carson City, NV 89701, (775) 883-3622; Facility Type: Skilled care; Alzheimer's; Beds: Skilled care 100; Alzheimer's 44; Certified: Medicaid; Medicare; Veterans; Owner: Integrated Health Services Inc.; License: Current state

Henderson

Delmar Gardens of Green Valley
100 Delmar Gardens Dr., Henderson, NV 89014, (702) 361-6111; Facility Type: Skilled care; Alzheimer's; Beds: Skilled care 100; Alzheimer's 84; Certified: n/a; Owner: Private; License: Current state

North Las Vegas

North Las Vegas Care Center
3215 E Cheyenne Ave., North Las Vegas, NV 89030, (702) 649-7800; Facility Type: Skilled care; ICF; Alzheimer's; Beds: Skilled care 100; ICF 40; Alzheimer's 42; Certified: Medicaid; Medicare; Veterans; Owner: Integrated Health Care Services Inc.; License: Current state

Reno

ManorCare Health Services
3101 Plumas, Reno, NV 89509, (775) 829-7220; Facility Type: Skilled care; ICF; Alzheimer's; Beds: Skilled care 180; Certified: Medicaid; Medicare; Owner: HCR Manor Care; License: Current state

Sparks

Washoe Care Center Nursing Home
1375 Baring Blvd., Sparks, NV 89434, (775) 356-2707; Facility Type: Skilled care; Alzheimer's; Beds: Skilled care 80; Alzheimer's 42; Certified: Medicaid; Medicare; Veterans; Owner: Proprietary/Public corp.; License: Current state

Washoe Progressive Care Center Long Term Care/Skilled Nursing Facility
1835 Oddie Blvd., Sparks, NV 89431, (775) 982-5140; Facility Type: Skilled care; ICF; Alzheimer's; Beds: Skilled care 25; Certified: Medicaid; Medicare; Owner: Proprietary/Public corp.; License: Current state

Winnemucca

Humboldt General Hospital Harmony Manor
118 E Haskell St., Winnemucca, NV 89445, (775) 623-5222; Facility Type: Skilled care; Alzheimer's; Beds: Skilled care 30; Alzheimer's 15; Certified: Medicaid; Medicare; Owner: Government/State/Local; License: Current state

NEW HAMPSHIRE

Bedford

Harborside Healthcare—Northwood
30 Colby Ct., Bedford, NH 03110, (603) 625-6462; Facility Type: Skilled care; Alzheimer's; Beds: ICF 147; Certified: Medicaid; Owner: Private; License: Current state

Ridgewood Center Genesis ElderCare
25 Ridgewood Rd., Bedford, NH 03110, (603) 623-8805; Facility Type: Skilled care; ICF; Alzheimer's; Beds: Skilled care 150; Certified: Medicaid; Medicare; Veterans; Owner: Genesis ElderCare; License: Current state

Concord

Havenwood
33 Christian Ave., Concord, NH 03301, (603) 224-5363; Facility Type: Skilled care; ICF; Alzheimer's; Beds: Skilled care 10; ICF 25;Alzheimer's 22; SNF/ICF 63; Residential care 60; Certified: Medicaid; Medicare; Owner: Nonprofit/Religious org.; License: Current state

Dover

Dover Rehabilitation & Living Center
307 Plaza Dr., Dover, NH 03820, (603) 742-2676; Facility Type: Skilled care; ICF; Alzheimer's; Beds: Skilled care 110; Certified: Medicaid; Medicare; Veterans; Owner: Vencor Inc.; License: Current state

Saint Ann Home
195 Dover Point Rd., Dover, NH 03820, (603) 742-2612; Facility Type: Skilled care; ICF; Alzheimer's; Beds: Skilled care 54; Certified: Medicaid; Medicare; Owner: Nonprofit/Religious org.; License: Current state

Exeter

Riverwoods at Exeter
7 Riverwoods Dr., Exeter, NH 03833, (603) 772-4700; Facility Type: Skilled care; ICF; Alzheimer's; Beds: Skilled care 39; Certified: Medicare; Owner: Nonprofit corp.; License: Current state

Goffstown

Hillsborough County Nursing Home
400 Mast Rd., Goffstown, NH 03045, (603) 627-5540; Facility Type: Skilled care; ICF; Alzheimer's; Beds: Skilled care 300; Certified: Medicaid; Medicare; Owner: Government/State/Local; License: Current state

Hanover

Hanover Terrace Healthcare
53 Lyme Rd., Hanover, NH 03755, (603) 643-2854; Facility Type: Skilled care; ICF; Alzheimer's; Beds: Skilled care 26; Alzheimer's 38; SNF/ICF 36; Independent living; Certified: Medicaid; Medicare; Veterans; Owner: Proprietary/Public corp.; License: Current state

Laconia

Laconia Center Genesis ElderCare Network
175 Blueberry Ln., Laconia, NH 03246, (603) 524-3340; Facility Type: Skilled care; ICF; Alzheimer's; Beds: Skilled care 108; Certified: Medicaid; Medicare; Veterans; Owner: Private; License: Current state

Manchester

Hanover Hill Health Care Center
700 Hanover St., Manchester, NH 03104, (603) 627-3826; Facility Type: Skilled care; ICF; Alzheimer's; Beds: Skilled care 24; ICF 100; Alzheimer's 24; SNF/ICF; Certified: Medicaid; Medicare; Veterans; Owner: Private; License: Current state

IHS of Manchester
191 Hackett Hill Rd., Manchester, NH 03102, (603) 668-8161; Facility Type: Skilled care; ICF; Alzheimer's; Beds: Skilled care 10; ICF 14; SNF/ICF 30; Certified: Medicaid; Medicare; Veterans; Owner: Proprietary/Public corp.; License: Current state

Villa Crest Nursing & Retirement Community
1276 Hanover St., Manchester, NH 03104, (603) 622-3262; Facility Type: Skilled care; ICF; Alzheimer's; Beds: Skilled care 20; ICF 54; Alzheimer's 20; SRC 29; Certified: Medicaid; Medicare; Owner: Proprietary/Public corp.; License: Current state

North Conway SunBridge Care & Rehabilitation for North Conway
1251 White Mountain Hwy., North Conway, NH 03860, (603) 356-7194; Facility Type: Skilled care; ICF; Alzheimer's; Beds: ICF 80; Alzheimer's 16; Certified: Medicaid; Veterans; Owner: Private; License: Current state

North Haverhill

Grafton County Home
RR 1 Box 71 North Haverhill, NH 03774, (603) 787-6871; Facility Type: Skilled care; ICF; Alzheimer's; Beds: Skilled care 130; ICF; Alzhei-

mer's; Certified: Medicaid; Medicare; Owner: Government/State/Local; License: Current state

Ossipee

Mountain View Nursing Home
10 County Farm Rd., Ossipee, NH 03864, (603) 539-7511; Facility Type: ICF; Alzheimer's; Beds: ICF 53; Alzheimer's 50; SNF/ICF; Certified: Medicaid; Medicare; Owner: Government/State/Local; License: Current state

Peterborough

Harborside Healthcare—Pheasant Wood
50 Pheasant Rd., Peterborough, NH 03458, (603) 924-7267; Facility Type: Skilled care; ICF; ICF/MR; Alzheimer's; Beds: Skilled care 8; ICF 91; Alzheimer's; Certified: Medicaid; Medicare; Veterans; Owner: Harborside Healthcare; License: Current state

West Stewartstown

Coos County Nursing Hospital
PO Box 10, West Stewartstown, NH 03597, (603) 246-3321; Facility Type: ICF; Alzheimer's; Beds: ICF 97; Certified: Medicaid; Owner: Government/State/Local; License: Current state

NEW JERSEY

Atlantic City

Eastern Pines Convalescent Center
29 & 33 N Vermont Ave., Atlantic City, NJ 08401, (609) 344-8911; Facility Type: Skilled care; Alzheimer's; Beds: Skilled care 208; Certified: Medicaid; Medicare; Owner: Private; License: Current state

Seashore Gardens
3850 Atlantic Ave., Atlantic City, NJ 08401, (609) 345-5941; Facility Type: Skilled care; ICF; Alzheimer's; Beds: Skilled care 151; Residential health; Certified: Medicaid; Medicare; Owner: Nonprofit/Religious org.; License: Current state

Belleville

Clara Maass Continuing Care Center
1 Franklin Ave., Belleville, NJ 07109, (973) 450-2900; Facility Type: Skilled care; Alzheimer's; Beds: Skilled care 120; Certified: Medicaid; Medicare; Owner: Nonprofit corp.; License: Current state

Bloomfield

Job Haines Home for the Aged
250 Bloomfield Ave., Bloomfield, NJ 07003, (973) 743-0792; Facility Type: Skilled care; Alzheimer's; Beds: Skilled care 30; Assisted living 63; Certified: Medicaid; Medicare; Owner: Nonprofit corp.; License: Current state

Brick

Laurelton Village
475 Jack Martin Blvd., Brick, NJ 08724, (732) 458-6600; Facility Type: Skilled care; ICF; Alzheimer's; Beds: Skilled care 180; Certified: Medicaid; Medicare; Owner: Proprietary/Public corp.; License: Current state

Bridgewater

Harborside Healthcare—Woods Edge
875 Rte. 202-206 N, Bridgewater, NJ 08875, (908) 526-8600; Facility Type: Skilled care; ICF; Alzheimer's; Beds: Skilled care 176; Certified: Medicaid; Medicare; Owner: Private; License: Current state

Camden

SunBridge Care & Rehabilitation for Southern New Jersey
2 Cooper Plaza, Camden, NJ 08103, (856) 342-7600; Facility Type: Skilled care; Alzheimer's; Beds: Skilled care 120; Certified: Medicaid; Medicare; Veterans; Owner: Sun Healthcare Group Inc. License: Current state

Cape May Court House

Cape May Care Center
502 Rte. 9 N, Cape May Court House, NJ 08210, (609) 465-7633; Facility Type: Skilled care; ICF; Alzheimer's; Beds: Skilled care 62; Alzheimer's 24; Certified: Medicaid; Medicare; Veterans; Owner: Private; License: Current state

Cedar Grove

Arbor Glen Care & Rehabilitation Center
25 Pompton Ave. & E Lindsley Rd., Cedar Grove, NJ 07009, (973) 256-7220; Facility Type: Skilled care; Alzheimer's; Beds: Skilled care 122;

Certified: Medicaid; Medicare; Owner: Genesis ElderCare; License: Current state

Waterview Center
536 Ridge Rd., Cedar Grove, NJ 07009, (973) 239-9300; Facility Type: Skilled care; Alzheimer's; Beds: Skilled care 5; Alzheimer's; SNF/ICF 138; Certified: Medicaid; Medicare; Owner: Genesis ElderCare; License: Current state

Cherry Hill

Silver Care Center
1417 Brace Rd., Cherry Hill, NJ 08034, (856) 795-3131; Facility Type: Skilled care; ICF; Alzheimer's; Beds: Alzheimer's 40; SNF/ICF 144; Dialysis 18; Certified: Medicaid; Medicare; Owner: Private; License: Current state

Eatontown

Gateway Care Center
139 Grant Ave., Eatontown, NJ 07724, (732) 542-4700; Facility Type: Skilled care; ICF; Alzheimer's; Beds: Skilled care 170; Certified: Medicaid; Medicare; Owner: Proprietary/Public corp.; License: Current state

Edison

JFK Hartwyck at Edison Estates
465 Plainfield Ave., Edison, NJ 08817, (732) 985-1500; Facility Type: Skilled care; Alzheimer's; Beds: Skilled care 896; Alzheimer's' Certified: Medicaid; Medicare; Owner: Nonprofit corp.; License: Current state

Elizabeth

New Jersey Geriatric Center of Workmens Circle
225 W Jersey St., Elizabeth, NJ 07202, (908) 353-1220; Facility Type: Skilled care; ICF; ICF/MR; Alzheimer's; Beds: Skilled care 180; Certified: Medicaid; Medicare; Owner: Nonprofit/Religious org.; License: Current state

Hackensack

Regent Care Center
50 Polifly Rd., Hackensack, NJ 07601, (201) 646-1166; Facility Type: Skilled care; Alzheimer's; Beds: Skilled care 134; Certified: Medicaid; Medicare; Owner: Proprietary/Public corp.; License: Current state

Hammonton

Greenbriar Health Care Center of Hammonton
43 N White Horse Pike, Hammonton, NJ 08037, (609) 567-3100; Facility Type: Skilled care; Alzheimer's; Beds: Skilled care 240; Alzheimer's; Certified: Medicaid; Medicare; Owner: Proprietary/Public corp.; License: Current state

Jersey City

Franciscan Home & Rehabilitation Center
198 Stevens Ave., Jersey City, NJ 07305, (201) 451-9000; Facility Type: Skilled care; ICF; Alzheimer's; Beds: Skilled care 132; Alzheimer's 51; Certified: Medicaid; Medicare; Owner: Nonprofit/Religious org.; License: Current state

Saint Ann's Home for the Aged
198 Old Bergen Rd., Jersey City, NJ 07305, (201) 433-0950; Facility Type: Skilled care; ICF/MR; Alzheimer's; Beds: Skilled care 116; Certified: Medicaid; Owner: Nonprofit corp.; License: Current state

Lakewood

Lakeview Center—Genesis Healthcare
963 Ocean Ave., Lakewood, NJ 08701, (732) 367-7444; Facility Type: Skilled care; ICF; ICF/MR; Alzheimer's; Beds: Skilled care 120; Certified: Medicaid; Medicare; Owner: Proprietary/Public corp.; License: Current state

Leisure Park Health Center
1400 Rte. 70 Lakewood, NJ 08701, (732) 370-0444; Facility Type: Skilled care; ICF; Alzheimer's; Beds: Skilled care 4; ICF 56; Certified: Medicare; Owner: Proprietary/Public corp.; License: Current state

Linwood

Linwood Care Center
New Rd. & Central Ave., Linwood, NJ 08221, (609) 927-6131; Facility Type: Skilled care; Alzheimer's; Beds: Skilled care 74; Ventilator 16; Certified: Medicaid; Medicare; Owner: Proprietary/Pubic corp.; License: Current state

Manahawkin

Southern Ocean Center
1361 Rte. 72, Manahawkin, NJ 08050, (609) 978-0600; Facility Type: Skilled care; ICF; Alzheimer's; Beds: Skilled care 130; Certified: Medicaid; Medicare; Owner: Proprietary/Pubic corp.; License: Current state

Mendham

Holly Manor Center
84 Cold Hill Rd., Mendham, NJ 07945, (973) 543-2500; Facility Type: Skilled care; Alzhei-

mer's; Beds: Skilled care; Long-term care 124; Certified: Medicaid; Medicare; Owner: Genesis ElderCare; License: Current state

Monroe Township

Cranbury Genesis ElderCare
292 Applegarth Rd., Monroe Township, NJ 08831, (609) 860-2500; Facility Type: Skilled care; ICF; Alzheimer's; Beds: Skilled care 150; ICF; Alzheimer's; SNF/ICF; Certified: Medicaid; Medicare; Owner: Proprietary/Pubic corp.; License: Current state

Morristown

Morris Hills Center
77 Madison Ave., Morristown, NJ 07960, (973) 540-9800; Facility Type: Skilled care; ICF; Alzheimer's; Beds: Skilled care 304; Alzheimer's; SNF/ICF; Certified: Medicaid; Medicare; Veterans; Owner: Proprietary/Public corp.; License: Current state

Neptune

King Manor Care Center
2303 W Bangs Ave., Neptune, NJ 07753, (732) 774-3500; Facility Type: Skilled care; Alzheimer's; Beds: Skilled care 120; Certified: Medicaid; Medicare; Owner: Proprietary/Public corp.; License: Current state

New Brunswick

Rose Mountain Care Center
US Rtes 1 & 18, New Brunswick, NJ 08901, (732) 828-2400; Facility Type: Skilled care; Alzheimer's; Beds: Skilled care 112; Certified: Medicaid; Owner: Private; License: Current state

New Providence

Glenside Nursing Center
144 Gales Dr., New Providence, NJ 07974, (908) 464-8600; Facility Type: Skilled care; ICF; Alzheimer's; Beds: Skilled care 106; Certified: Medicaid; Medicare; Owner: HCR Manor Care; License: Current state

Newton

Barn Hill Care Center
249 High St., Newton NJ 07860, (973) 383-5600; Facility Type: Skilled care; Alzheimer's; Beds: Skilled care 135; Certified: Medicaid; Medicare; Owner: Private; License: Current state

North Bergen

Fritz Reuter Altenheim
3161 Kennedy Blvd., North Bergen, NJ 07047, (201) 867-3585; Facility Type: Skilled care; ICF; Alzheimer's; Beds: Skilled care 156; Certified: n/a; Owner: Nonprofit corp.; License: Current state

Hudson View Health Care Center LLC
9020 Wall St., North Bergen, NJ 07047, (201) 861-4040; Facility Type: Skilled care; Alzheimer's; Beds: Skilled care 273; Certified: Medicaid; Medicare; Owner: Proprietary/Public corp.; License: Current state

Ocean Grove

Manor by the Sea
160 Main St., Ocean Grove, NJ 07756, (732) 775-0554; Facility Type: Skilled care; Alzheimer's; Beds: Skilled care 120; Long-term care; Certified: Medicaid; Medicare; Owner: Nonprofit/Religious org.; License: Current state

Passaic

Hamilton Plaza Nursing & Rehabilitation Center
56 Hamilton Ave., Passaic, NJ 07055, (973) 773-7070; Facility Type: Skilled care; ICF; ICF/MR; Alzheimer's; Beds: Skilled care 120; ICF; Certified: Medicaid; Medicare; Owner: Proprietary/Public corp.; License: Current state

Paterson

Preakness Health Center
40 Valley View Rd., Paterson, NJ 07470, (973) 904-5000; Facility Type: Skilled care; Alzheimer's; Beds: Skilled care 400; Alzheimer's; SNF/ICF; Certified: Medicaid; Medicare; Owner: Government/State/Local; License: Current state

Philipsburg

Brakeley Park Center
290 Red School Ln., Phillipsburg, NJ 08865, (908) 859-2800; Facility Type: Skilled care; ICF; Alzheimer's; Beds: Skilled care 120; Certified: Medicaid; Medicare; Owner: Proprietary/Public corp.; License: Current state

Pleasantville

Our Lady's Residence Health Care Center
1100 Clematis Ave., Pleasantville, NJ 08232, (609) 646-2450; Facility Type: Skilled care; Alzheimer's; Beds: Skilled care 214; Certified: Med-

icaid; Medicare; Owner: Nonprofit/Religious org.; License: Current state

Red Bank

Avante at Red Bank
100 Chapin Ave., Red Bank, NJ 07701, (732) 741-8811; Facility Type: Skilled care; ICF; ICF/MR; Alzheimer's; Beds: Skilled care 180; Certified: Medicaid; Medicare; Owner: Private; License: Current state

Navesink House
40 Riverside Ave., Red Bank, NJ 07701, (732) 842-3400; Facility Type: Skilled care; Alzheimer's; Beds: Skilled care 43; RHCU 19; Certified: n/a; Owner: Nonprofit/Religious org.; License: Current state

Scotch Plains

Ashbrook Nursing Home
1610 Raritan Rd., Scotch Plains, NJ 07076, (908) 889-5500; Facility Type: Skilled care; ICF; Alzheimer's; Beds: SNF/ICF 120; Certified: Medicaid; Medicare; Owner: Nonprofit/Religious org.; License: Current state

Sewell

Health Care Center at Washington
535 Egg Harbor Rd., Sewell, NJ 08080, (856) 582-3170; Facility Type: Skilled care; ICF; Alzheimer's; Beds: Skilled care 65; ICF 65; Certified: Medicaid; Medicare; Owner: Nonprofit corp.; License: Current state

Somerset

Margaret McLaughlin McCarrick Care
15 Dellwood Ln., Somerset, NJ 08873, (732) 545-4200; Facility Type: Skilled care; Alzheimer's; Beds: Skilled care 120; Certified: Medicaid; Medicare; Owner: Nonprofit corp.; License: Current state

Toms River

Arbors Care Center
1750 Rte. 37W Toms River, NJ 08757, (732) 914-0090; Facility Type: Skilled care; ICF; ICF/MR; Alzheimer's; Beds: Skilled care 120; Certified: Medicaid; Medicare; Owner: Private; License: Current state

Green Acres Manor
1931 Lakewood Rd., Toms River, NJ 08755, (732) 286-2323; Facility Type: Skilled care; ICF; ICF/MR; Alzheimer's; Beds: Skilled care 200; Certified: Medicaid; Medicare; Owner: Proprietary/Public corp.; License: Current state

Trenton

The Millhouse
325 Jersey St., Trenton, NJ 08611, (609) 394-3400; Facility Type: Skilled care; ICF; Alzheimer's; Beds: Skilled care 61; ICF 121; Alzheimer's 28; Certified: Medicaid; Medicare; Veterans; Owner: Private; License: Current state

Water's Edge Convention Center
512 Union St., Trenton, NJ 08611, (609) 393-8622; Facility Type: Skilled care; Alzheimer's; Beds: Skilled care 60; ICF 220; Certified: Medicaid; Medicare; Owner: Proprietary/Public corp.; License: n/a

Vorhees

Kresson View Center
2601 Evesham Rd., Voorhees, NJ 08043, (856) 596-1113; Facility Type: Skilled care; ICF; ICF/MR; Alzheimer's; Beds: Skilled care; ICF; Long-term care 240; Certified: Medicaid; Medicare; Veterans; Owner: Genesis ElderCare; License: Current state

Watchung

McAuley Hall
1633 Hwy., 22 Watchung, NJ 07069, (908) 754-3663; Facility Type: Skilled care; ICF; Alzheimer's; Beds: Skilled care 67; Certified: Medicaid; Medicare; Owner: Nonprofit/Religious org.; License: Current state

Wayne

The Atrium at Wayne
1120 Alps Rd., Wayne, NJ 07478, (973) 694-2100; Facility Type: Skilled care; ICF; ICF/MR; Alzheimer's; Beds: Skilled care 140; Certified: Medicaid; Owner: Proprietary/Public corp.; License: n/a

West Orange

Daughters of Israel
1155 Pleasant Valley Way West Orange, NJ 07052, (973) 731-5100; Facility Type: Skilled care; Alzheimer's; Beds: Skilled care 252; Alzheimer's 49; Certified: Medicaid; Medicare; Owner: Nonprofit/Religious org.; License: Current state

Northfield Manor
787 Northfield Ave., West Orange, NJ 07052, (973) 731-4500; Facility Type: Skilled care; Alzheimer's; Beds: Skilled care 131; Certified: Medicare; Owner: Proprietary/Public corp.; License: Current state

Summit Ridge Center
20 Summit St., West Orange, NJ 07052, (973) 736-2000; Facility Type: Skilled care; ICF; Alzheimer's; Beds: ICF 79; Alzheimer's 24; Certified: Medicaid; Medicare; Owner: Proprietary/Public corp.; License: Current state

Whiting

Whiting Health Care Center
3000 Hilltop Rd., Whiting, NJ 08759, (732) 849-4400; Facility Type: Skilled care; Alzheimer's; Beds: SNF/ICF 170; Certified: Medicaid; Medicare; Owner: Proprietary/Public corp.; License: Current state

Woodstown

Friends Home at Woodstown
Friends Dr., Box 457 Woodstown, NJ 08098, (856) 769-1500; Facility Type: Skilled care; ICF; Alzheimer's; Beds: Skilled care 120; Certified: Medicaid; Medicare; Owner: Nonprofit/Religious org.; License: Current state

Wyckoff

Christian Health Care Center
301 Sicomac Ave., Wyckoff, NJ 07481, (201) 848-5200; Facility Type: Skilled care; Alzheimer's; Beds: Skilled care 190; Alzheimer's 60; Behavior management 32; Certified: Medicaid; Owner: Nonprofit/Religious org.; License: Current state

NEW MEXICO

Alamogordo

Betty Dare Good Samaritan Center
3101 N Florida Ave., Alamogordo, NM 88310, (505) 434-0033; Facility Type: Skilled care; ICF; Alzheimer's; Beds: Skilled care 12; ICF 78; Certified: Medicaid; Medicare; Owner: Nonprofit/Religious org.; License: Current state

Albuquerque

Albuquerque Manor Nursing Center
500 Louisiana Blvd. NE, Albuquerque, NM 87108, (505) 255-1717; Facility Type: Skilled care; ICF; Alzheimer's; Beds: Skilled care 36; ICF 323; Alzheimer's 120; Certified: Medicaid; Medicare; Veterans; Owner: Private; License: Current state

ManorCare Health Services—Juan
5123 Juan Tabo Blvd. NE, Albuquerque, NM 87111, (505) 292-3333; Facility Type: Skilled care; ICF; Alzheimer's; Beds: Skilled care 12; ICF 140; Alzheimer's 28; Certified: Medicaid; Medicare; Veterans; Owner: Proprietary/Public corp.; License: Current state

Montebello on Academy Healthcare Center
10500 Academy Rd. NE, Albuquerque, NM 87111, (505) 294-9944; Facility Type: Skilled care; ICF; Alzheimer's; Beds: Skilled care 4; ICF 56; Assisted living 35; Certified: Medicare; Owner: Proprietary/Public corp.; License: Current state
Valle Norte Caring Center
8820 Horizon Blvd. NE, Albuquerque, NM 87113, (505) 823-1885; Facility Type: Skilled care; ICF; ICF/MR; Alzheimer's; Beds: Skilled care 18; ICF 29; Alzheimer's 66; Certified: Medicaid; Medicare; Veterans; Owner: Proprietary/Public corp.; License: Current state

Carlsbad

Lakeview Christian Home of the Southwest Inc.
1300 N Canal St., Carlsbad, NM 88220, (505) 887-0551; Facility Type: ICF; Alzheimer's; Beds: ICF 103; Alzheimer's 17; Assisted living; Certified: Medicaid; Medicare; Veterans; Owner: Nonprofit corp.; License: Current state

Northgate Unit of Lakeview Christian Home of the Southwest
1905 W Pierce, Carlsbad, NM 88220, (505) 885-3161; Facility Type: Skilled care; ICF; Alzheimer's; Beds: Skilled care 8; ICF 104; Assisted living 30; Certified: Medicaid; Medicare; Veterans; Owner: Nonprofit corp.; License: Current state

Fort Bayard

Fort Bayard Medical Center
100 Calle EL, Fort Bayard, NM 88036, (505) 537-3302; Facility Type: Skilled care; ICF; Alzheimer's; Beds: SNF/ICF 250; Certified: Medicaid; Medicare; Veterans; Owner: Government/State/Local; License: Current state

Hobbs

Hobbs Health Care Center
5715 Lovington Hwy., Hobbs, NM 88240, (505) 392-6845; Facility Type: Skilled care; ICF; ICF/MR; Alzheimer's; Beds: Skilled care 14; ICF 76; Alzheimer's 28; Certified: Medicaid; Medicare; Veterans; Owner: Proprietary/Public corp.; License: Current state

Las Cruces

Casa De Oro Care Center
1005 Hill Rd., Las Cruces, NM 88005, (505) 523-4573; Facility Type: Skilled care; ICF; ICF/MR; Alzheimer's; Beds: Skilled care 20; ICF 115; Certified: Medicaid; Medicare; Owner: Proprietary/Public corp.; License: Current state

Rio Rancho

Rio Rancho Nursing & Rehabilitation Center
4210 Sabana Grande SE, Rio Rancho, NM 87124, (505) 892-6603; Facility Type: Skilled care; ICF; ICF/MR; Alzheimer's; Beds: Skilled care 14; ICF 106; Certified: Medicaid; Medicare; Veterans; Owner: Integrated Health Services Inc.; License: Current state

Roswell

Roswell Nursing Center
3200 Mission Arch Dr., Roswell, NM 88201, (505) 624-2583; Facility Type: Skilled care; ICF; Alzheimer's; Beds: Skilled care 24; ICF 96; Certified: Medicaid; Medicare; Veterans; Owner: Proprietary/Public corp.; License: Current state

Sante Fe

Casa Real Health Care Center
1650 Galisteo St., Santa Fe, NM 87505, (505) 984-8313; Facility Type: Skilled care; ICF; Alzheimer's; Beds: Skilled care 16; ICF 80; Alzheimer's 22; Certified: Medicaid; Medicare; Owner: Integrated Health Services Inc.; License: Current state

La Residencia Nursing Center
820 Paseo de Peralta, Santa Fe, NM 87501, (505) 983-2273; Facility Type: Skilled care; ICF; Alzheimer's; Beds: Skilled care 126; Certified: Medicaid; Medicare; Owner: Nonprofit/Religious org.; License: Current state

Santa Fe Care Center
635 Harkle Rd., Santa Fe, NM 87505, (505) 982-2574; Facility Type: Skilled care; ICF; Alzheimer's; Beds: Skilled care 120; Certified: Medicaid; Medicare; Veterans; Owner: Integrated Health Services Inc.; License: Current state

---

NEW YORK

Albany

Ann Lee Home
820 Albany-Shaker Rd., Albany, NY 12211, (518) 869-1221; Facility Type: Skilled care; ICF; ICF/MR; Alzheimer's; Beds: Skilled care 175; Certified: Medicaid; Medicare; Veterans; Owner: Government/State/Local; License: Current state

Teresian House Nursing Home Co Inc.
200 Washington Ave., Ext Albany, NY 12203, (518) 456-2000; Facility Type: Skilled care; Alzheimer's; Beds: Skilled care 250; Alzheimer's 50; Respite care 2; Certified: Medicaid; Medicare; Owner: Nonprofit/Religious org.; License: Current state

Amityville

Broadlawn Manor Nursing & Rehabilitation Center
399 County Line Rd., Amityville, NY 11701, (516) 264-0222; Facility Type: Skilled care; ICF; Alzheimer's; Beds: Skilled care 320; Alzheimer's; Assisted living; Certified: Medicaid; Medicare; Owner: Nonprofit corp.; License: Current state

Arverne

Horizon Care Center
64-11 Beach Channel Dr., Arverne, NY 11692, (718) 945-0700; Facility Type: Skilled care; Alzheimer's; Beds: Skilled care 280; Certified: Medicaid; Medicare; Owner: Proprietary/Public corp.; License: Current state

Lawrence Nursing Care Center
350 Beach 54th St., Arverne, NY 11692, (718) 945-0400; Facility Type: Skilled care; Alzheimer's; Beds: Skilled care 200; Certified: Medicaid; Medicare; Owner: Proprietary/Public corp.; License: Current state

Batavia

Genese County Nursing Home
278 Bank St., Batavia, NJ 14020, (716) 344-0584; Facility Type: Skilled care; ICF; Alzheimer's; Beds: Skilled care 240; Certified: Medicaid; Medicare; Owner: Government/State/Local; License: Current state

Bronx

Beth Abraham Health Services
612 Allerton Ave., Bronx, NY 10467, (718) 881-3000; Facility Type: Skilled care; Alzheimer's; Beds: Skilled care 520; Short-term rehab 120; Certified: Medicaid; Medicare; Owner: Nonprofit/Religious org.; License: Current state

Daughters of Jacob Nursing Home Co Inc.
1160 Teller Ave., Bronx, NY 10456, (718) 293-1500; Facility Type: Skilled care; ICF; Alzheimer's; Beds: Skilled care 515; Certified: Medicaid; Medicare; Owner: Nonprofit corp.; License: Current state

Hebrew Home for the Aged at Riverdale—Fairfield Division
3220 Henry Hudson Pkwy Bronx, NY 10463, (718) 549-9400; Facility Type: Skilled care; Alzheimer's; Beds: Skilled care 167; Alzheimer's; Certified: Medicaid; Medicare; Owner: Nonprofit corp.; License: Current state

Kings Harbor Care Center
2000 E Gun Hill Rd., Bronx, NY 10469, (212) 320-0400; Facility Type: Skilled care; Alzheimer's; Beds: Skilled care; Alzheimer's; Certified: Medicaid; Medicare; Owner: Proprietary/Public corp.; License: Current state

Riverdale Nursing Home
641 W 230th St., Bronx, NY 10463, (718) 796-4800; Facility Type: Skilled care; Alzheimer's; Beds: Skilled care 146; Certified: Medicaid; Medicare; Owner: Proprietary/Public corp.; License: n/a

Brooklyn

Center for Nursing & Rehabilitation Inc.
520 Prospect Pl., Brooklyn, NY 11238, (718) 636-1000; Facility Type: Skilled care; Alzheimer's; Beds: Skilled care 200; Alzheimer's 40; Certified: Medicaid; Medicare; Owner: Nonprofit corp.; License: Current state

Haym Salomon Home for the Aged
2300 Cropsey Ave., Brooklyn, NY 11214, (718) 373-1700; Facility Type: Skilled care; ICF; Alzheimer's; Beds: Alzheimer's 80; SNF/ICF 140; Certified: Medicaid; Medicare; Veterans; Owner: Private; License: Current state

MJG Nursing Home Co Inc.
4915 10th Ave., Brooklyn, NY 11219, (718) 851-3700; Facility Type: Skilled care; Alzheimer's; Beds: Skilled care; Alzheimer's; Certified: Medicaid; Medicare; Owner: Nonprofit corp.; License: Current state

Parkshore Health Care Center
1555 Rockaway Pkwy Brooklyn, NY 11236, (718) 498-6400; Facility Type: Skilled care; Alzheimer's; Beds: Skilled care 270; SNF/ICF; Certified: Medicaid; Medicare; Owner: Private; License: Current state

Prospect Park Nursing Home Inc.
1455 Coney Island Ave., Brooklyn, NY 11230, (718) 252-9800; Facility Type: Skilled care; Alzheimer's; Beds: Skilled care 215; Certified: Medicaid; Medicare; Owner: Nonprofit corp.; License: Current state

Buffalo

Episcopal Residential Health Care Facility Inc.
24 Rhode Island St., Buffalo, NY 14213, (716) 884-6500; Facility Type: Skilled care; Alzheimer's; Beds: Skilled care 66; Alzheimer's 88; Certified: Medicaid; Medicare; Veterans; Owner: Nonprofit/Religious organization; License: Current state

Ridge View Manor Nursing Home
300 Dorrance Ave., Buffalo, NY 14220, (716) 825-4984; Facility Type: Skilled care; ICF; Alzheimer's; Beds: Skilled care 120; Certified: Medicaid; Medicare; Veterans; Owner: Private; License: Current state

Canandaigua

F F Thompson Continuing Care Center Inc.
350 Parrish St., Canandaigua, NY 14424, (716) 396-6044; Facility Type: Skilled care; Alzheimer's; Beds: Skilled care 130; Skilled care 40; Certified: Medicaid; Medicare; Owner: Nonprofit corp.; License: Current state

Cortlandt Manor

Cortlandt Nursing Care Center Inc.
110 Oregon Rd., Cortlandt Manor, NY 10567, (914) 739-9150; Facility Type: Skilled care; ICF; Alzheimer's; Beds: Skilled care 40; ICF 80; Certified: Medicaid; Medicare; Veterans; Owner: Proprietary/Public corp.; License: Current state

Endicott

Ideal Senior Living Center
508 High Ave., Endicott, NY 13760, (607) 786-

7300; Facility Type: Skilled care; Alzheimer's; Beds: Skilled care 150; Certified: Medicaid; Medicare; Owner: Nonprofit corp.; License: Current state

Far Rockaway

Bezalel Nursing Home
29-38 Far Rockaway Blvd., Far Rockaway, NY 11691, (718) 471-2600; Facility Type: Skilled care; ICF; Alzheimer's; Beds: Skilled care 120; Certified: Medicaid; Medicare; Owner: Nonprofit corp.; License: Current state

Peninsula Center for Extended Care & Rehabilitation
50-15 Beach Channel Dr., Far Rockaway, NY 11691, (718) 734-2000; Facility Type: Skilled care; Alzheimer's; Beds: Skilled care 200; Certified: Medicaid; Medicare; Owner: Nonprofit corp.; License: Current state

Flushing

Flushing Manor Care
139-66 35th Ave., Flushing, NY 11354, (718) 961-5300; Facility Type: Skilled care; Alzheimer's; Beds: Skilled care 278; Certified: Medicaid; Medicare; Veterans; Owner: Proprietary/Public corp.; License: Current state

Jamaica

Highland Care Center
91-31 175th St., Jamaica, NY 11432, (718) 657-6363; Facility Type: Skilled care; ICF; Alzheimer's; Beds: Alzheimer's 100; SNF/ICF 200; Certified: Medicaid; Medicare; Owner: Proprietary/Public corp.; License: Current state

Margaret Tietz for Nursing Care Inc.
164-11 Chapin Pkwy Jamaica, NY 11432, (718) 523-6400; Facility Type: Skilled care; ICF; Alzheimer's; Beds: SNF/ICF 150; Certified: Medicaid; Medicare; Owner: Nonprofit corp.; License: Current state

Johnson City

Susquehanna Nursing Home & Health Related Facility
282 Riverside Dr., Johnson City, NY 13790, (607) 729-9206; Facility Type: Skilled care; ICF; Alzheimer's; Beds: Skilled care 160; Certified: Medicaid; Medicare; Owner: Private; License: Current state

Long Beach

Komanoff Center for Geriatric & Rehabilitative Medicine of Long Beach
375 E Bay Dr., Long Beach, NY 11561, (516) 897-1000; Facility Type: Skilled care; Alzheimer's; Beds: Skilled care 200; Certified: Medicaid; Medicare; Owner: Nonprofit corp.; License: Current state

Massapequa

Park View Nursing Home Inc.
5353 Merrick Rd., Massapequa, NY 11758, (516) 798-1800; Facility Type: Skilled care; Alzheimer's; Beds: Skilled care 169; Certified: Medicaid; Medicare; Owner: Proprietary/Public corp.; License: Current state

Middle Island

Oak Hollow Nursing Center & Rehabilitation Center
PO Box 488, Middle Island, NY 11953, (631) 924-8820; Facility Type: Skilled care; Alzheimer's; Beds: Skilled care 144; Certified: Medicaid; Medicare; Veterans; Owner: Proprietary/Public corp.; License: Current state

Mount Vernon

Waltemade Health Care Center of Wartburg
Wartburg Pl., Mount Vernon, NY 10552, (914) 699-0800; Facility Type: Skilled care; Alzheimer's; Beds: Skilled care 160; Certified: Medicaid; Medicare; Owner: Nonprofit/Religious org.; License: Current state

New Rochelle

Bayberry Nursing Home
40 Keogh Ln., New Rochelle, NY 10805, (914) 636-3947; Facility Type: Skilled care; Alzheimer's; Beds: Skilled care 60; Certified: Medicaid; Medicare; Veterans; Owner: Private; License: Current state

New York

Isabella Geriatric Center
525 Audubon Ave., New York NY 10040, (212) 342-9200; Facility Type: Skilled care; ICF; Alzheimer's; Beds: Skilled care 665; Alzheimer's 40; Certified: Medicaid; Medicare; Owner: Nonprofit corp.; License: Current state

Newark

DE & MAY Living Center
100 Sunset Dr., Newark, NY 14513, (315) 332-2700; Facility Type: Skilled care; Alzheimer's; Beds: Skilled care 176; Certified: Medicaid; Medicare; Owner: Nonprofit corp.; License: Current state

Niagara Falls

Niagara Falls Memorial Nursing Home Co. Inc.
621 10th St., Niagara Falls, NY 14302, (716) 278-4578; Facility Type: Skilled care; ICF; ICF/MR; Alzheimer's; Beds: Skilled care 120; Certified: Medicaid; Medicare; Owner: Nonprofit corp.; License: Current state

North Tonawanda

North Gate Manor
7264 Nash Rd., North Tonawanda, NY 14120, (716) 694-7700; Facility Type: Skilled care; Alzheimer's; Beds: Skilled care 200; Certified: Medicaid; Medicare; Veterans; Owner: Private; License: Current state

Ossining

Chandler Care Center
31 Overton Rd., Ossining, NY 10562, (914) 941-4047; Facility Type: Skilled care; Alzheimer's; Beds: Skilled care 86; Respite care; Certified: Medicaid; Medicare; Veterans; Owner: Proprietary/Public corp.; License: Current state

Rochester

Blossom Health Care Center
989 Blossom Rd., Rochester, NY 14610, (716) 482-3500; Facility Type: Skilled care; Alzheimer's; Beds: Skilled care 80; Certified: Medicaid; Medicare; Veterans; Owner: Private; License: Current state

Church Home of the Protestant Episcopal
505 Mt. Hope Ave., Rochester, NY 14620, (716) 546-8400; Facility Type: Skilled care; Alzheimer's; Beds: Skilled care 180; Certified: Medicaid; Medicare; Owner: Nonprofit corp.; License: Current state

Jewish Home of Rochester Inc.
2021 Winton Rd. S, Rochester, NY 14618, (716) 427-7760; Facility Type: Skilled care; ICF; Alzheimer's; Beds: Skilled care 362; ICF; Certified: Medicaid; Medicare; Owner: Nonprofit corp.; License: Current state

Monroe Community Hospital
435 E Henrietta Rd., Rochester, NY 14620, (716) 760-6500; Facility Type: Skilled care; ICF; Alzheimer's; Beds: Skilled care 566; Certified: Medicaid; Medicare; Owner: Government/State/Local; License: Current state

Saint Ann's Nursing Home Co Inc.
1500 Portland Ave., Rochester, NY 14621, (716) 342-1700; Facility Type: Skilled care; Alzheimer's; Beds: Skilled care 355; Certified: Medicaid; Medicare; Owner: Nonprofit corp.; License: Current state

Wesley Gardens Inc.
8 N Goodman St., Rochester, NY 14607, (716) 241-2100; Facility Type: Skilled care; Alzheimer's; Beds: Skilled care 200; Certified: Medicaid; Medicare; Owner: Nonprofit corp.; License: Current state

Rome

Betsy Ross Health Related Facility
1 Elsie St., Rome, NY 13440, (315) 339-2220; Facility Type: Skilled care; ICF; Alzheimer's; Beds: Skilled care 120; ICF; Certified: Medicaid; Medicare; Owner: Private; License: Current state

Scarsdale

Sprain Brook Manor Nursing Home
77 Jackson Ave., Scarsdale, NY 10583, (914) 472-3200; Facility Type: Skilled care; Alzheimer's; Beds: Skilled care 121; Short-term rehab.; Certified: Medicaid; Medicare; Owner: Private; License: Current state

Staten Island

Lily Pond Nursing Home
150 Lily Pond Ave., Staten Island, NY 10305, (718) 981-5300; Facility Type: Skilled care; ICF/MR; Alzheimer's; Beds: Skilled care 35; Certified: Medicaid; Medicare; Owner: Private; License: Current state

Verrazano Nursing Home
100 Castleton Ave., Staten Island, NY 10301, (718) 273-1300; Facility Type: Skilled care; ICF/MR; Alzheimer's; Beds: Skilled care 120; Certified: Medicaid; Medicare; Owner: Private; License: Current state

Syracuse

James Square Health & Rehabilitation Center
918 James St., Syracuse, NY 13203, (315) 474-1561; Facility Type: Skilled care; Alzheimer's; Beds: Skilled care 455; Alzheimer's; Certified: Medicaid; Medicare; Veterans; Owner: Private; License: Current state

Plaza Nursing Home Co. Inc.
614 S Crouse Ave., Syracuse, NY 13210, (315) 474-4431; Facility Type: Skilled care; Alzheimer's; Beds: Skilled care 184; Alzheimer's 46; Wellness unit 12; Certified: Medicaid; Medicare; Veterans; Owner: Nonprofit corp.; License: Current state

Utica

Eden Park Nursing Home
1800 Butterfield Ave., Utica, NY 13501, (315) 797-3570; Facility Type: Skilled care; Alzheimer's; Beds: Skilled care 117; ICF; Respite care 1; Certified: Medicaid; Medicare; Owner: Private; License: Current state

Warsaw

Wyoming County Nursing Home
400 N Main St., Warsaw, NY 14569, (716) 786-2233; Facility Type: Skilled care; Alzheimer's; Beds: Skilled care 160; Certified: Medicaid; Medicare; Owner: Government/State/Local; License: Current state

Watertown

Genesis Health Care of New York
218 Stone St., Watertown, NY 13601, (315) 782-7400; Facility Type: Skilled care; Alzheimer's; Beds: Skilled care 300; Alzheimer's 30; Certified: Medicaid; Medicare; Owner: Nonprofit corp.; License: Current state

West Islip

Our Lady of Consolation
111 Beach Dr., West Islip, NY 11795, (516) 587-1600; Facility Type: Skilled care; Alzheimer's; Beds: Skilled care 330; Alzheimer's 40; Long-term care 75; Certified: Medicaid; Medicare; Owner: Nonprofit/Religious org.; License: Current state

Yonkers

The Guild Home for Aged Blind
75 Stratton St. S, Yonkers, NY 10701, (914) 963-4861; Facility Type: Skilled care; Alzheimer's; Beds: Skilled care 177; Alzheimer's 20; HIV/AIDS 20; Certified: Medicaid; Medicare; Owner: Nonprofit/Religious org.; License: Current state

Saint Joseph's Hospital
127 S Broadway Yonkers, NY 10701, (914) 378-7210; Facility Type: Skilled care; Alzheimer's; Beds: Skilled care 200; Certified: Medicaid; Medicare; Owner: Nonprofit corp.; License: Current state

NORTH CAROLINA

Albemarle

Britthaven of Piedmont
33426 Old Salisbury Rd., Albemarle, NC 28001, (704) 983-1195; Facility Type: Skilled care; ICF; Alzheimer's; Beds: Skilled care 190; Certified: Medicaid; Medicare; Owner: License: Current state

Stanley Manor
625 Bethany Rd., Albemarle, NC 28002, (704) 982-0770; Facility Type: Skilled care; ICF; Alzheimer's; Beds: Skilled care 100; Certified: Medicaid; Medicare; Owner: License: Current state

Asheville

Aston Park Health Care Center Inc.
380 Brevard Rd., Asheville, NC 28806, (828) 253-4437; Facility Type: Skilled care; ICF; Alzheimer's; Beds: Alzheimer's; SNF/ICF; Rest home 122; Certified: Medicaid; Medicare; Veterans; Owner: Nonprofit corp.; License: Current state

Deerfield Episcopal Retirement Community Inc.
1617 Hendersonville Rd., Asheville, NC 28803, (828) 274-1531; Facility Type: Skilled care; ICF; Alzheimer's; Beds: Skilled care 40; ICF; Assisted living 40; Certified: n/a; Owner: Nonprofit/Religious org.; License: Current state

Rickman Nursing Care Center
213 Richmond Hill Dr., Asheville, NC 28806, (828) 254-9675; Facility Type: Skilled care; ICF; Alzheimer's; Beds: Skilled care 100; Assisted living; Certified: Medicaid; Medicare; Owner: Nonprofit/Religious org.; License: Current state

Black Mountain

Black Mountain Center—Alzheimer's Unit
1280 Old US 70 W Black Mountain, NC 28771, (828) 669-3100; Facility Type: Skilled care; ICF; ICF/MR; Alzheimer's; Beds: n/a; Certified: Medicaid; Owner: Government/State/Local; License: Current state

Burlington

White Oak Manor
323 Baldwin Dr., Burlington, NC 27215, (336) 229-5571; Facility Type: Skilled care; ICF; Alzheimer's; Beds: Skilled care 100; ICF 60; Certified: Medicaid; Medicare; Veterans; Owner: White Oak Manor Inc.; License: Current state

Candler

Pisgah Manor Health Care Center
95 Holcombe Cove Rd., Candler, NC 28715, (828) 667-9851; Facility Type: Skilled care; ICF; Alzheimer's; Beds: SNF/ICF 118; Certified: Medicaid; Medicare; Owner: Nonprofit/Religious org.; License: Current state

Charlotte

Brian Center Health & Retirement
5939 Reddman Rd., Charlotte, NC 28212, (704) 563-6862; Facility Type: Skilled care; ICF; Alzheimer's; Beds: Skilled care 90; ICF 30; Lodge assisted care; Certified: Medicaid; Medicare; Veterans; Owner: Private; License: Current state

Hunter Woods
620 Tom Hunter Rd., Charlotte, NC 28213, (704) 598-5136; Facility Type: Skilled care; ICF; ICF/MR; Alzheimer's; Beds: Skilled care 130; Certified: Medicaid; Medicare; Owner: Centennial HealthCare Corp.; License: Current state

Presbyterian Wesley Care Center
3700 Shamrock Dr., Charlotte, NC 28215, (704) 384-8300; Facility Type: Skilled care; Alzheimer's; Beds: Skilled care 289; Certified: Medicaid; Medicare; Owner: Nonprofit corp.; License: Current state

Concord

Five Oaks Nursing Center
413 Winecoff School Rd., Concord, NC 28027, (704) 788-2131; Facility Type: Skilled care; ICF; Alzheimer's; Beds: Skilled care 184; Certified: Medicaid; Medicare; Veterans; Owner: Private; License: Current state

Durham

Meadowbrook Manor—Durham
5935 Mt Sinai Rd., Durham, NC 27705, (919) 489-2361; Facility Type: Skilled care; ICF; Alzheimer's; Beds: Skilled care 140; Alzheimer's; Certified: Medicaid; Medicare; Owner: Proprietary/Public corp.; License: Current state

Rose Manor Healthcare Center
4230 N Roxboro Rd., Durham, NC 27704, (919) 477-9805; Facility Type: Skilled care; ICF; Alzheimer's; Beds: Skilled care 123; Certified: Medicaid; Medicare; Owner: Vencor Inc.; License: Current state

Elizabethtown

SunBridge Care & Rehabilitation for Elizabethtown
8045 Popular St., Elizabethtown, NC 28337, (910) 862-8100; Facility Type: Skilled care; ICF; Alzheimer's; Beds: SNFICF 90; Rest home 30; Certified: Medicaid; Medicare; Veterans; Owner: Sun Healthcare Group Inc.; License: Current state

Fayetteville

Highland House of Fayetteville Inc.
1700 Pamallee Fayetteville, NC 28303, (910) 488-2295; Facility Type: Skilled care; ICF; Alzheimer's; Beds: Skilled care 159; Certified: Medicaid; Medicare; Veterans; Owner: Private; License: Current state

Whispering Pines Nursing Home
523 Country Club Dr., Fayetteville, NC 28301, (910) 488-0711; Facility Type: Skilled care; ICF; Alzheimer's; Beds: Skilled care; ICF 88; Home for aged; Certified: Medicaid; Medicare; Owner: Private; License: Current state

Hendersonville

Brian Center Health & Rehabilitation—Hendersonville
1870 Pisgah Dr., Hendersonville, NC 28739, (828) 693-9796; Facility Type: Skilled care; ICF; Alzheimer's; Beds: Skilled care 60; ICF 30; Alzheimer's 30; Rest home 18; Certified: Medicaid; Medicare; Veterans; Owner: Proprietary/Public corp.; License: Current state

Hickory

Lutheran Nursing Homes Inc.—Hickory Unit
1265 21st NE Hickory, NC 28601, (828) 328-2006; Facility Type: Skilled care; ICF; Alzheimer's; Beds: Skilled care 74; Certified: Medicaid; Medicare; Owner: Nonprofit corp.; License: Current state

Lumberton

Wesley Pines—Methodist Retirement Community
1000 Wesley Pines Rd., Lumberton, NC 28358, (910) 738-9691; Facility Type: Skilled care; ICF; Alzheimer's; Beds: Skilled care 117; Certified: Medicaid; Medicare; Veterans; Owner: Nonprofit/Religious org.; License: Current state

Woodhaven Nursing & Alzheimer Care Center
1150 Pine Run Dr., Lumberton, NC 28358, (910) 671-5703; Facility Type: Skilled care; ICF; Alzheimer's; Beds: Skilled care 115; Certified: Medicaid; Medicare; Owner: Nonprofit corp.; License: Current state

Monroe

Guardian Care of Monroe
1212 E Sunset Dr., Monroe, NC 28112, (704) 283-8548; Facility Type: Skilled care; ICF; Alzheimer's; Beds: Skilled care 174; Certified: Medicaid; Medicare; Owner: Vencor Inc.; License: Current state

New Bern

Britthaven of New Bern
2600 Old Cherry Point Rd., New Bern, NC 28563, (252) 637-4730; Facility Type: Skilled care; ICF; Alzheimer's; Beds: Skilled care 123; ICF; Alzheimer's; Certified: Medicaid; Medicare; Veterans; Owner: Britthaven Inc.; License: Current state

Raleigh

Dan E & Mary Louise Steward Health Center of Springmoor
1500 Sawmill Rd., Raleigh, NC 27615, (919) 848-7000; Facility Type: Skilled care; Alzheimer's; Beds: Skilled care 141; Home for aged 18; Certified: n/a; Owner: Nonprofit corp.; License: Current state

Sunnybrook Alzheimer & Healthcare
25 Sunnybrook Rd., Raleigh, NC 27610, (919) 231-6150; Facility Type: Skilled care; ICF; Alzheimer's; Beds: Skilled care 43; ICF 55; Alzheimer's; Certified: Medicaid; Medicare; Veterans; Owner: Vencor Inc.; License: Current state

Southern Pines

Penick Village
PO Box 2001, Southern Pines, NC 28388, (910) 692-0300; Facility Type: Skilled care; ICF; Alzheimer's; Beds: Skilled care 37; ICF 13; home for aged 29; Certified: Medicaid; Medicare; Owner: Nonprofit corp.; License: Current state

Stokesdale

Countryside Manor
7700 US 158 E, Stokesdale, NC 27357, (336) 643-6301; Facility Type: Skilled care; ICF; Alzheimer's; Beds: Skilled care 30; ICF 30; Alzheimer's 10; Assisted living 6; Certified: Medicaid; Medicare; Veterans; Owner: Proprietary/Public corp.; License: Current state

Thomasville

Piedmont Center
100 Hedrick Dr., Thomasville, NC 27360, (336) 472-2017; Facility Type: Skilled care; ICF; Alzheimer's; Beds: Skilled care 100; Certified: Medicaid; Medicare; Veterans; Owner: Nonprofit/Religious org.; License: Current state

Wake Forest

Hillside Nursing Center of Wake Forest
968 E Wait Ave., Wake Forest, NC 27587, (919) 556-4082; Facility Type: Skilled care; ICF; Alzheimer's; Beds: Skilled care 150; Certified: Medicaid; Medicare; Owner: Proprietary/Public corp.; License: Current state

Williamston

IHS of Williamston
119 Gatlin St., Williamston, NC 27842, (252) 792-1616; Facility Type: Skilled care; ICF; Alzheimer's; Beds: Skilled care 36; ICF 88; Certified: Medicaid; Medicare; Owner: Proprietary/Public corp.; License: Current state

Wilmington

Liberty Commons Nursing & Rehabilitation Center
121 Racine Dr., Wilmington, NC 28403, (910) 452-4070; Facility Type: Skilled care; ICF; Alzheimer's; Beds: Skilled care 32; ICF 40; Alzheimer's 20; Certified: Medicaid; Medicare; Owner: Private; License: Current state

Wilson

Avante at Wilson
1804 Forest Hills Rd. W, Wilson, NC 27895, (252) 237-8161; Facility Type: Skilled care; ICF; Alzheimer's; Beds: Skilled care 60; ICF 50; Certified: Medicaid; Medicare; Veterans; Owner: Avante Group; License: n/a

Triangle East Nursing Care Center
1705 S Tarboro St., Wilson, NC 27893, (252) 399-8998; Facility Type: Skilled care; ICF; Alzheimer's; Beds: Skilled care 90; ICF; Certified: Medicaid; Medicare; Owner: Nonprofit corp.; License: Current state

Winston-Salem

Salemtowne Retirement Community
1000 Salemtown Rd., Winston-Salem, NC 27106, (336) 767-8130; Facility Type: Skilled care; ICF; Alzheimer's; Beds: Skilled care 80; Certified: n/a; Owner: Nonprofit/Religious org.; License: Current state

Yadkinville

Willowbrook Health Care Center
333 E Lee St., Yadkinville, NC 27055, (336) 679-8028; Facility Type: Skilled care; ICF; Alzheimer's; Beds: Skilled care 80; Certified: Medicaid; Medicare; Veterans; Owner: Centennial Health-Care Corp.; License: Current state

Yanceyville

Brian Center Nursing Care—Yanceyville
1086 Main St., N Yanceyville, NC 27379, (336) 694-5916; Facility Type: Skilled care; ICF; Alzheimer's; Beds: Skilled care 137; Certified: Medicaid; Medicare; Owner: Proprietary/Public corp.; License: Current state

---

NORTH DAKOTA

Aneta

Aneta Parkview Health Center
PO Box 287, Aneta, ND 58212, (701) 326-4234; Facility Type: Skilled care; ICF; Alzheimer's; Beds: Skilled care 47; Certified: Medicaid; Medicare; Owner: Nonprofit corp.; License: Current state

Bismarck

Baptist Home Inc.
1100 E Boulevard Ave., Bismarck, ND 58501, (701) 223-3040; Facility Type: Skilled care; Alzheimer's; Beds: Skilled care 141; Certified: Medicaid; Medicare; Owner: Nonprofit corp.; License: Current state

Saint Vincent's Care Center
1021 N 26th St., Bismarck, ND 58501, (701) 223-6888; Facility Type: Skilled care; Alzheimer's; Beds: Skilled care 81; Alzheimer's 20; Certified: Medicaid; Medicare; Owner: Nonprofit/Religious org.; License: Current state

Dickinson

Saint Benedict's Health Center
851 4th Ave. E, Dickinson, ND 58601, (701) 225-5138; Facility Type: Skilled care; Alzheimer's; Beds: Skilled care 180; Certified: Medicaid; Medicare; Owner: Benedictine Health System; License: Current state

Ellendale

Prince of Peace Care Center
201 8th St. N, Ellendale, ND 58436, (701) 349-3312; Facility Type: Skilled care; Alzheimer's; Beds: Skilled care 74; Respite care; Certified: Medicaid; Medicare; Veterans; Owner: Nonprofit/Religious org.; License: Current state

Fargo

Bethany Home
201 S University Dr., Fargo, ND 58103, (701) 239-3000; Facility Type: Skilled care; Alzheimer's; Beds: Skilled care 144; Alzheimer's 48; Retirement; Assisted 151; Certified: Medicaid; Medicare; Owner: Nonprofit corp.; License: Current state

Villa Maria
3102 S University Dr., Fargo, ND 58103, (701) 293-7750; Facility Type: Skilled care; ICF; ICF/MR; Alzheimer's; Beds: Skilled care 138; Certified: Medicaid; Medicare; Owner: Nonprofit corp.; License: Current state

Garrison

Benedictine Living Center
609 4th Ave. NE, Garrison, ND 58540, (701) 463-2226; Facility Type: Skilled care; Alzheimer's; Beds: Skilled care 71; Certified: Medicaid; Medicare; Veterans; Owner: Nonprofit/Religious org.; License: Current state

Minot

Trinity Nursing Home
8th Ave. NE, Minot, ND 58701, (701) 857-5000; Facility Type: Skilled care; Alzheimer's; Beds: Skilled care 294; Alzheimer's 22; Certified: Medicaid; Medicare; Veterans; Owner: Nonprofit corp.; License: Current state

Mohall

North Central Good Samaritan Center
602 E Main St., Mohall, ND 58761, (701) 756-6831; Facility Type: Skilled care; Alzheimer's; Beds: Skilled care 59; Certified: Medicaid; Owner: The Evangelical Lutheran Good Samaritan Society; License: Current state

Parshall

Rock View Good Samaritan Center
Hwy., 37 #37 Parshall, ND 58770, (701) 862-3138; Facility Type: Skilled care; ICF/MR; Alzheimer's; Beds: Skilled care 49; Certified: Medicaid; Medicare; Owner: Nonprofit org.; License: Current state

Wahpeton

Saint Catherine's Living Center
1307 N 7th St., Wahpeton, ND 58075, (701) 642-2691; Facility Type: Skilled care; Alzheimer's; Beds: Skilled care 180; Certified: Medicaid; Medicare; Veterans; Owner: Benedictine Health System; License: Current state

Williston

Bethel Lutheran Home Inc.
1512 2nd Ave., W Williston, ND 58802, (701) 572-6766; Facility Type: Skilled care; Alzheimer's; Beds: Skilled care 155; Alzheimer's 24; Basic care 19; Certified: Medicaid; Medicare; Owner: Nonprofit corp.; License: Current state

Wishek

Wishek Nursing Home
PO Box 187 Wishek, ND 58495, (701) 452-2333; Facility Type: Skilled care; Alzheimer's; Beds: Skilled care 98; Certified: Medicaid; Medicare; Owner: Nonprofit corp.; License: Current state

---

OHIO

Akron

Bath Manor Special Care Center
2330 Smith Road, Akron, OH 44333, (330) 836-1006; Facility type: Skilled care, Alzheimer's, Intermediate care; Beds: 150; Certified: Medicaid, Medicare, Veterans; License: Current state; Other: Home Health Care.

Bridgepark Center for Rehabilitation & Nursing Services
145 Olive Street, Akron, OH 44310, (330) 762-0901; Facility Type: Skilled care; Alzheimer's, intermediate care, special nursing units, home health care; Beds: 180; Certified: Medicaid; Medicare; Veterans; Owner: Vencor Inc. (Proprietary/Public); License: Current state.

Healthaven Nursing Home
615 Latham Lane, Akron, OH 44319, (330) 644-3914; Facility Type: Skilled care; Alzheimer's, Intermediate care; Beds: 56; Certified: Medicaid; Medicare; Veterans; Owner: Health Network of Ohio (Nonprofit); License: Current state; Activities: Arts & Crafts; Cards; Games; Reading groups; Religious activities; Other: Affiliated with United Methodist Association.

Lorantffy Care Center Incorporated
2631 Copley Road, Akron, Ohio 44321 (330) 666-1313 http://www.lorantfy.com Facility Type: Skilled care, Alzheimer's; Beds: 130; Certified: Medicaid; Medicare; intermediate care; special nursing unit; retirement and life care community; Payer mix—Medicaid—65%, Medicare—13%; Owner: Nonprofit/Religious; License: Current state; Activities: Arts & Crafts; Other: Affiliated with Ohio Health Care; languages spoken: Hungarian, German and Romanian.

ManorCare Health Services
1211 W. Market Street, Akron, OH 44313 (330) 867-8530 http://www.hcr-manorcare.com; Facility Type: Skilled care, Alzheimer's, Intermediate care; Beds: 120; Certified: Medicaid, Medicare; Payer mix: 40% Medicare; Owner: HCR Manor Care; License: Current state; Activities: Arts & Crafts; Pet therapy; Library.

Ridgewood Place
3558 Ridgewood Road, Akron, OH 44313 (330) 273-4055; Facility Type: Skilled care, Alzheimer's; Beds: Skilled care—180; Certified: Medicaid, Medicare; Veterans; Veterans—1%; Owner: Proprietary/Public; License: Current state; Activities: Arts & Crafts; Pet therapy; Other: Alzheimer's Secured Unit; Speech therapists; Podiatrists, Audiologists, Dentists; Languages spoken: Greek and Hungarian.

Sumner on Merriman
209 Merriman Road Akron, Ohio 44303 (330) 762-9341; Facility Type: Skilled care, Alzheimer's; Beds: 130; Certified: Medicaid; Medicare; Payer mix: Medicaid—29%, Private Pay—71%; Owner: Nonprofit corporation; License: Current state; Activities: Arts & Crafts; Cards; Games; Pet therapy; Outings/Sightseeing; Group exercise; Group dining; Support groups, Library, Patios

Alliance

Canterbury Villa of Alliance
1785 Freshley Road, Alliance, OH 44601, (330) 821-4000; http://www.his-inc.com; Facility Type: Skilled care; Alzheimer's, Intermediate care; Beds: 100; Certified: Medicaid, Medicare; Owner: Integrated Health Services, Inc. (Proprietary/Public); License: Current state; Activities: Arts & Crafts; Pet therapy.

McCrea Manor Nursing & Rehabilitation Center

2040 McCrea Street, Alliance, OH 44601, (330) 823-9005; Facility Type: Skilled care; Alzheimer's, Assisted Living; Beds: 150; Certified: Medicaid; Medicare; Veterans; Owner: Proprietary/Public; License: Current state; Activities: Arts & Crafts; Cards; Games; Reading groups; Religious activities; Movies; Shopping trips; Dances/Social/Cultural; Outings; Pet therapy.

Amherst

Golden Acres Lorain County Nursing Home
459999 N. Ridge Rd., Amherst, OH 44001, (440) 988-2322; Facility Type: Skilled care, Alzheimer's; Beds: 82; Certified: Medicaid; Medicare; Payer mix: Medicaid—60%, Private pay—38%, other—2%; Owner: Government/State and Local; License: Current state; Activities: Arts & Crafts; Pet therapy; Outings; Exercise; Support groups; Other: Alzheimer's Secured Unit.

Andover

Miller Memorial Health Care Center
486 S. Main St., Rte. 7, Andover, OH 44003; (440) 293-5416; Facility Type: Skilled care, Alzheimer's; Beds: 200; Certified: Medicaid; Medicare; Payer mix: Medicare—80%, Medicare—5%, Private Pay—10%, Other—5%; Owner: Ohio Health Ventures; License: Current state; Activities: Arts & Crafts; Cards; Games; Reading groups; Religious activities; Movies; Pet therapy.

Ashland

Brethren Care Incorporated
2000 Center St., Ashland, OH 44805, (419) 289-1585 Facility Type: Skilled care, Alzheimer's; Beds: 91; Certified: Medicaid; Payer mix: Medicaid—68%, Private pay—32%; Owner: Nonprofit corporation; License: Current state; Activities: Crafts; Movies; Shopping; Pet therapy; Outings; Support groups; Other: Affiliated with the Church of the Brethren, the Ohio Philanthropic Homes for the Aging.

Kingston of Ashland
20 Amberwood Pkwy, Ashland, OH 44805, (419) 289-3859; Facility Type: Skilled care, Alzheimer's, Intermediate care; Beds: 100; Certified: Medicaid; Medicare; Payer mix: Medicaid—30%, Medicare—20%, Private pay—50%; Owner: Proprietary/Public; License: Current state; Activities: Arts & Crafts; Pet therapy; Support groups; Other: Audiologists, Podiatrists, Speech therapists.

Ashtabula

Carrington Park Nursing Home
2217 West Ave., Ashtabula, OH 44004, (440) 964-8446; Facility Type: Skilled care; Alzheimer's; Beds: 207; Certified: Medicaid; Medicare; Veterans; Payer mix: Medicaid—10%, Medicare—85%, Private pay—4%, Veterans—1%; Owner: Strategic Nursing; License: Current state; Activities: Arts & Crafts; Cards; Pet therapy; Other: Outdoor patio/yard; Languages spoken—Spanish.

Country Club Center
925 E 26th St., Ashtabula, OH 44004, (440) 992-0022, Facility Type: Skilled care, Alzheimer's, Intermediate care; Beds: 100; Certified: Medicaid, Medicare; Payer mix: Private pay—40%, Other—60%; Owner: Proprietary/Public; License: Current state; Activities: Arts & Crafts; Cards; Games; Reading; Pet therapy; Outings; Group exercise; Group dining; Support groups; enclosed patio yard, chapel.

Park Haven Home
4533 Park Ave., Ashtabula, OH 44004, (440) 992-9441; Facility Type: Skilled care, Alzheimer's; Beds: 50; Certified: Medicaid, Medicare; Payer mix: Private pay—12%, Other—76%; Owner: Private; License: Current state; Activities: Arts & Crafts; Dances/Social/Cultural gatherings; Intergenerational programs; Pet therapy; Outings; Support groups; Other: Alzheimer's secured unit; Languages spoken—Latvian.

Aurora

Ann Maria of Aurora Incorporated
889 N. Aurora Rd., Aurora, OH 44202, (330) 562-6171; Facility Type: Skilled care, Alzheimer's; Beds: 40; Certified: Medicaid, Medicare; Owner: Proprietary; License: state; Activities: Arts & Crafts; Cards; Games; Reading groups; Religious activities; Movies; Shopping trips; Dances/Social/Cultural gatherings; Pet therapy; Support groups; Other: Alzheimer's secured unit.

Aurora Manor Special Care Centre
101 Bissell Rd., Aurora, OH 44202, (330) 562-5000; Facility Type: Skilled care, Alzheimer's, Intermediate care; Beds: 100; Certified: Medicaid; Medicare; Veterans; Payer mix: Medicaid—0%, Medicare—18%, Private pay—30%, Other—2%; License: Current state; Activities: Arts & Crafts; Cards; Games; Reading groups; Religious activities; Movies; Pet therapy; Outings; Group exercise.

Avon

Avon Oaks Nursing Facility
37800 French Creek Rd., Avon, OH 44011, (440) 934-5204, Facility Type: Skilled care, Alzheimer's; Beds: 105; Certified: Medicaid; Medicare;

Payer mix: Medicaid—64%, Medicare—7%, Private pay—23%; Owner: Private: License: Current state; Activities: Arts & Crafts; Outings; Other: Alzheimer's secured unit; hospice; Languages spoken: Hungarian and Spanish; Greenhouse/Garden

Good Samaritan Nursing Home
32900 Detroit Rd., Avon, OH 44011, (888) 467-6708; Facility Type: Skilled care, Alzheimer's; Beds: 220; Certified: Medicaid, Medicare; Payer mix: Medicaid—60%, Private pay—30%; Owner: Proprietary; License: state; Activities: Arts & Crafts; Pet therapy; Greenhouse/Garden; Other: Languages spoken- Spanish; Affiliated with Avon Lake & Westlake Chambers of Commerce.

Baltic

Baltic Country Manor
130 Buena Vista St., Baltic, OH 43804, (330) 897-4311; Facility Type: Skilled care, Alzheimer's, Intermediate Care; Beds: 100; Certified: Medicaid; Medicare, Veterans; Payer mix: Medicaid—76%,Private pay—14%, Veterans—5%; Owner: Integrated Health Services; License: state; Activities: Arts & Crafts; Outings; Other: Alzheimer's secured unit; Languages spoken—Pennsylvania Dutch.

Baltimore

Gaulden Manor Incorporated
225 Hansberger Ave., Baltimore, OH 43105; (740) 862-8093, Facility Type: Skilled care; Alzheimer's, Intermediate care; Beds: 50; Certified: Medicaid, Medicare; Payer mix: Medicaid—50%, Private pay—50%; Owner: Alpha Homes; License: Current state; Activities: Arts & Crafts; Cards; Pet therapy; Outings; Group exercise; Support groups Other: Alzheimer's secured unit.

Barberton

ManorCare Health Services
85 3rd St. SE, Barberton, OH 44203, (330) 753-5005; Facility Type: Skilled care, Alzheimer's; Beds: 120; Certified: Medicaid; Medicare; Veterans; Owner: HCR Manor Care; License: Current state; Activities: Arts & Crafts; Cards; Games; Pet therapy; Outings/Sightseeing; Group exercise; Group dining; Support groups, Library; Other: Ophthalmologists, Audiologists, Podiatrists, Speech therapists.

Batavia

Batavia Nursing & Convalescent Inn
4000 Golden Age Dr., Batavia, OH 45103, (513) 732-6500; Facility Type: Skilled care; Alzheimer's, Special Nursing Unit, Intermediate Care; Beds: 215; Certified: Medicaid, Medicare; Payer mix: Medicaid- 80%, Private Pay- 16%; Owner: Carrington Health Systems; License: state; Activities: Arts & Crafts; Cards; Games; Pet therapy; Outings/Sightseeing; Group exercise; Group dining; Support groups

Bay Village

Bradley Bay Health Center
605 Bradley Rd., Bay Village, OH 44140, (440) 871-3474; Facility Type: Skilled care, Alzheimer's; Beds: 125; Certified: Medicaid; Medicare; Payer mix: Medicare—10%, Private pay—90%; Owner: Private; License: state; Activities: Arts & Crafts; Pet therapy; Outings/Sightseeing; Group exercise; Greenhouse/Garden; Other: Alzheimer's secured unit; Languages spoken—Spanish.

Beachwood

Beachwood Nursing & Health Care Center
23900 Chagrin Blvd., Beachwood, OH 44122 (216) 464-1000; Facility Type: Skilled care, Alzheimer's, Beds: 210; Certified: Medicaid, Medicare; Veterans; Payer mix: Medicaid—80%, Medicare—10%, Private pay—6%, Veterans—2%, other—2%; Owner: Proprietary; License: state; Activities: Arts & Crafts; Cards; Games; Movies; Shopping; Dances; Pet therapy; Outings; Library; Other: Alzheimer's secured unit; Languages spoken: Polish, Russian, Hungarian and German.

Harborside Healthcare—Beachwood
3800 Park E, Beachwood, OH 44122, (216) 831-4303; http://www.hbrside.com; Facility Type: Skilled care, Alzheimer's; Beds: 260; Certified: Medicaid; Medicare; Veterans; Owner: Harborside Healthcare; License: state; Activities: Arts & Crafts; Cards; Games; Reading groups; Religious activities; Movies; Pet therapy; Outings; Group exercise; Support groups; Other: Alzheimer's secured unit.

Menorah Park Center for the Aging
27100 Cedar Rd., Beachwood, OH 44122; (216) 831-6500; Facility Type: Skilled care, Alzheimer's; Beds: 110; Certified: Medicaid; Medicare; Payer mix: Private pay—35%, Other—65%; Owner: Nonprofit/Religious; License: Current state; Activities: Arts & Crafts; Cards; Games; Pet therapy; Outings; Support groups; Other: Alzheimer's secured unit; Adult day care.

Villa Santa Anna Nursing Home for the Aged
25000 Chagrin Blvd., Beachwood, OH 44122-5665, (216) 464-9250; Facility Type: Skilled care, Alzheimer's; Beds: 70; Certified: Medicaid; Med-

icare; Payer mix: Medicaid—85%, Private pay—15%; Owner: Santa Anna Home for the Aged; License: state; Activities: Arts & Crafts; Cards; Pet therapy; Outings; Other: Languages: Slavic, Italian, Hungarian, Polish, and Bohemian.

Bellevue

Bellevue Care Center
1 Audrich Gardner Rd., Bellevue, OH 44811, (419) 483-6225; Facility Type: Skilled care; Alzheimer's; Beds: 75; Certified: Medicaid; Owner: Proprietary/Public; License: Current state; Activities: Arts & Crafts; Cards; Games; Reading groups; Religious activities; Movies; Shopping trips; Dances; Pet therapy; Outings/Sightseeing; Group exercise; Group dining; Support groups.

Belmont

Bell Nursing Home
42350 National Rd., Belmont, OH 43718, (740) 782-1561; Facility Type: Skilled care, Alzheimer's, Intermediate care; Beds: 105; Certified: Medicaid, Medicare; Payer mix: Medicaid—73%, Private pay—27%; Owner: Proprietary/Public; License: Current state; Activities: Arts & Crafts; Cards; Games; Reading groups; Religious activities; Movies; Shopping; Pet therapy; Outings/Sightseeing; Group exercise; Group dining; Support groups; Other: Language spoken: Greek.

Berea

Aristocrat Berea
255 Front St., Berea, OH 44017, (440) 243-4000; Facility Type: Skilled care, Alzheimer's, Intermediate care; Beds: 210; Certified: Medicaid; Medicare; Payer mix: Medicaid—65%, Medicare—15%, Private pay—20%; Owner: CommuniCare Health Services; License: Current state; Activities: Arts & Crafts; Cards; Games; Reading groups; Religious activities; Movies; Shopping; Other: Alzheimer's secured unit; Languages spoken: Spanish, Outdoor patio/yard; Affiliated with OHCA.

Bidwell

Scenic Hills Nursing Center
311 Buckridge Rd., Bidwell, OH 45614, (740) 446-7150; Facility Type: Skilled care, Alzheimer's; Beds: 100, Certified: Medicaid; Medicare; Owner: Integrated Health Services; License: Current state; Activities: Arts & Crafts; Cards; Games; Reading groups; Pet therapy; Other: Alzheimer's secured unit.

Bloomville

Ruffin Care Center of Bloomville
22 Clinton St., Bloomville, OH 44818, (419) 983-2021; Facility Type: Skilled care, Alzheimer's; Beds: 30; Certified: Medicaid; Medicare; Veterans; Owner: St. Catherine's Health Care Management; License: Current state; Activities: Arts & Crafts; Cards; Games; Pet therapy; Outings; Exercise.

Bluffton

Mennonite Memorial Home
410 W. Elm St., Bluffton, OH 45817, (419) 358-1015; Facility Type: Skilled care; Alzheimer's, Intermediate Care; Beds: 135; Certified: Medicaid; Owner: Nonprofit; License: Current state; Activities: Arts & Crafts; Cards; Games; Reading groups; Movies; Shopping; Dances; Pet therapy; Outings/Sightseeing; Group exercise; Support groups; Other: Affiliated with the Mennonite religion.

Bowling Green

Bowling Green Manor
1021 W. Poe Rd., Bowling Green, OH 43402, (419) 352-4694; Facility Type: Skilled care, Alzheimer's; Beds: 100; Certified: Medicaid; Medicare; Owner: Private; License: Current state; Activities: Arts & Crafts; Cards; Games.

Broadview Heights

Harborside Healthcare, Broadview Heights
2801 E. Royalton Rd., Broadview Heights, OH 44147, (440) 526-4770; Facility Type: Skilled care; Alzheimer's; Beds: 160; Certified: Medicaid; Medicare; Payer mix: Medicaid—65%; Medicare—5%; Private pay—30%; Owner: Harborside Healthcare; License: Current state; Activities: Arts & Crafts; Movies; Shopping; Pet therapy; Outings/Sightseeing; Group exercise; Group dining; Support groups, Library, Outdoor patio; Other: Languages spoken: Polish, Italian.

Bryan

Williams County Hillside Country Living
09-876 County Rd., 16, Bryan, OH 43506; (419) 636-4508, Facility Type: Skilled care; Alzheimer's; Beds: 71; Certified: Medicaid, Medicare; Owner: Government/ state and local; License: Current state; Activities: Arts & Crafts; Cards; Games; Reading; Movies; Shopping; Other: Languages spoken: Spanish.

Bucyrus

Altercare of Bucyrus
1929 Whetstone St., Bucyrus, OH 44820, (419) 562-7644, Facility Type: Skilled care; Alzheimer's; Beds:130; Certified: Medicaid, Medicare; Owner: Altercare; License: Current state; Activities: Arts & Crafts; Cards; Games; Reading.

Carlisle House
1721 Whetstone St., Bucyrus, OH 44820, (419) 562-4927; Facility Type: Skilled care, Alzheimer's; Beds: 45; Certified: Medicaid, Medicare, Veterans; Owner: Private; License: Current state; Activities: Arts & Crafts; Cards; Games, Pet therapy.

Caldwell

Summit Acres Nursing Home
44565 Township Rd., 497, Caldwell, OH 43724, (740) 732-5488, Facility Type: Skilled care, Alzheimer's' Beds: 150; Certified: Medicaid, Medicare, Veterans; Owner: Proprietary/Public; License: Current state; Activities: Arts & Crafts; Cards; Games; Movies; Shopping trips; Dances; Pet therapy; Outings/Sightseeing; Group exercise; Support groups, Greenhouse/Garden, Outdoor patio/yard.

Cambridge

Cambridge Health & Rehabilitation Center
1471 Wills Creek Valley Dr., Cambridge, OH 43725, Facility Type: Skilled care; Alzheimer's, Intermediate, Special Nursing care; Beds: 159 Payer mix: Medicaid—75%, Medicare—15%, Private pay—10%; Certified: Medicaid, Medicare, Veterans; Owner: Vencor; License: Current state; Activities: Arts & Crafts; Cards; Games; Reading; Pet therapy; Outings; Other: Alzheimer's secured unit.

Canal Fulton

Chapel Hill Community
12200 Strausser St., NW, Canal Fulton, OH 44614, (330) 854-4177; Facility Type: Skilled care, Alzheimer's, Assisted living; Beds: 165; Certified: Medicaid, Medicare, Veterans; Owner: United Church Homes; License: Current state; Activities: Religious activities; Movies; Pet therapy; Alzheimer's secured unit; Assisted living facility; Retirement facility; Affiliated with the United Church of Christ;

Canton

Bethany Nursing Home
626 34th St., NW, Canton, OH 44709, (330) 492-7171; Facility Type: Skilled care, Alzheimer's, Intermediate care; Beds: 40; Certified: Medicaid, Medicare; Owner: Proprietary/Public; License: Current state; Activities: Arts & Crafts; Cards; Games; Reading groups; Religious activities; Movies; Pet therapy; Outings/Sightseeing; Group exercise; Group dining; Support groups.

Canton Health Care Center
1223 Market Ave., N, Canton, OH 44714, (330) 454-2152; Facility Type: Skilled care, Alzheimer's; Intermediate care; Beds: 200; Certified: Medicaid; Medicare; Payer mix: Medicaid—92%, Medicare—4%, Private pay—2%; Owner: Essex Healthcare Corporation; License: Current state; Activities: Arts & Crafts; Cards; Games; Reading groups; Religious activities; Movies; Shopping; Dances; Pet therapy.

Manor Care
5005 Higbee Ave., NW, Canton, OH 44718, (330) 492-7835, http://www.hcr-manorcare.com, Facility Type: Skilled care, Alzheimer's; Beds: 180; Certified: Medicaid, Medicare; Owner: HCR Manor Care; License: Current state; Activities: Arts & Crafts; Cards; Games; Reading groups; Shopping trips; Dances/ Social/Cultural gatherings; Pet therapy; Other: Alzheimer's secured unit.

McKinley Health Care
800 Market Ave., N, Canton, OH 44702, (330) 456-1014; Facility Type: Skilled care, Alzheimer's, Adult Day care; Beds: 170; Certified: Medicaid, Medicare; Owner: Proprietary/Public; License: Current state; Activities: Arts & Crafts; Cards; Games; Religious activities; Movies; Shopping; Pet therapy; Outings; Other: Alzheimer's secured unit; Adult day care.

Carey

Eaglewood Care Center
821 E Findlay St., Carey, OH 43316, (419) 396-6344; Facility Type: Skilled care, Alzheimer's; Beds: 50; Certified: Medicaid; Medicare; Veterans; Owner: Private; License: Current state; Activities: Arts & Crafts; Cards; Games; Movies; Dances; Pet therapy; Outings/Sightseeing; Group exercise; Group dining; Support groups; Other: Alzheimer's secured unit; Adult day care

Carlisle

Carlisle Manor Health Care
730 Hillcrest Dr., Carlisle, OH 45005, (513) 746-2662; Facility Type: Skilled care, Alzheimer's, Beds: 50; Certified: Medicaid; Medicare; Veterans; Owner: Proprietary/Public; License: Current state; Activities: Arts & Crafts; Movies;

Shopping trips; Dances; Pet therapy; Other: Alzheimer's secured unit.

Carrollton

Carroll Health Care Center
648 Longhorn St., Carrollton, OH 44615-9471, (330) 627-5501, Facility Type: Skilled care, Alzheimer's; Beds: 100; Certified: Medicaid, Medicare; Owner: Private; License: Current state; Activities: Arts & Crafts; Games; Reading groups; Movies; Shopping; Pet therapy; Outings/Sightseeing; Group exercise; Group dining; Support groups; Other: Alzheimer's secured unit.

Centerburg

Canterbury Villa of Centerburg
80 Miller St., Centerburg, OH 43011, (740) 625-6873; Facility Type: Skilled care, Alzheimer's; Beds: 50; Certified: Medicaid, Medicare; Veterans; License: Current state; Activities: Arts & Crafts; Cards; Games; Movies; Shopping trips; Dances; Group exercise; Other: Alzheimer's secured unit

Morning View Care Center of Centerburg
4531 Columbus Rd., Centerburg, OH 43011, (740) 625-5401, Facility Type: Skilled care, Alzheimer's; Beds: 40; Certified: Medicaid; Owner: Proprietary/Public; License: Current state; Activities: Arts & Crafts; Cards; Games; Reading groups; Religious activities; Movies; Shopping; Pet therapy.

Centerville

The Franciscan at Saint Leonard Center
1203 Clyo Rd., Centerville, OH 45458, (513) 433-0480; Facility Type: Skilled care, Alzheimer's, Adult day care; Beds: 320; Certified: Medicaid; Medicare; Owner: Nonprofit/Religious; License: Current state; Activities: Arts & Crafts; Cards; Games; Other: Adult day care; Home Health Care.

Chardon

Heather Hill Inc.
12340 Bass Lake Rd., Chardon, OH 44024,(440) 285-4040; Facility Type: Skilled care, Alzheimer's, Adult day care; Beds: 250; Certified: Medicaid, Medicare; Owner: Nonprofit; License: Current state; Activities: Arts & Crafts; Cards; Games; Reading Pet therapy; Outings/Sightseeing; Group exercise; Group dining; Support groups; Other: Alzheimer's secured unit; Adult day care; Home health care

Chesterville

Morrow Manor State
Rtes 95 & 314, Chesterville, OH 43317, (419) 768-2401; Facility Type: Skilled care, Alzheimer's; Beds: 50; Certified: Medicaid, Medicare, Veterans; License: Current state; Activities: Arts & Crafts; Cards; Games; Reading groups; Religious activities; Movies; Shopping trips; Other: Alzheimer's secured unit.

Chillicothe

Westmoreland Place
230 Cherry St., Chillicothe, OH 45601, (740) 773-6470; Facility Type: Skilled care, Alzheimer's; Beds: 150; Certified: Medicaid; Medicare; Veterans; Owner: Proprietary/Public; License: Current state; Activities: Arts & Crafts; Cards; Games; Pet therapy; Greenhouse/Garden; Other: Alzheimer's secured unit.

Cincinnati

The Alois Alzheimer Center
70 Damon Rd., Cincinnati, OH 45218, (513) 825-2255; Facility Type: Alzheimer's; Beds: 102; Certified: Medicaid; Payer mix: 100% Private pay; Owner: Private, Affiliated with the University of Cincinnati; License: Current state; Activities: Arts & Crafts; Cards; Games;; Movies; Pet therapy; Group exercise; Group dining; Greenhouse/Garden; Other: Alzheimer's secured unit; Adult day care.

The Anderson
8139 Beechmont Ave., Cincinnati, OH 45255, (513) 474-6200; Facility Type: Skilled care, Alzheimer's; Beds: 218 (100 Alzheimer's); Certified: Medicaid, Medicare; License: state; Activities: Arts & Crafts; Cards; Games; Pet therapy; Other: Languages spoken: German, Spanish, American Sign Language, Hebrew and Russian.

Bayley Place
990 Bayley Place Dr., Cincinnati, OH 45233, (513) 347-5500, http://www.bayleyplace.org, Facility Type: Skilled care, Alzheimer's; Beds: 125; Certified: Medicaid, Medicare; Veterans; Owner: Catholic Church; License: Current state; Activities: Arts & Crafts; Cards; Games; Reading Pet therapy; Outings/Sightseeing

Beechknoll Convalescent Center
6550 Hamilton Ave., Cincinnati, OH 45224, (513) 522-5516; Facility Type: Skilled care, Alzheimer's; Beds: 200; Certified: Medicaid; Medicare; Payer mix: Medicaid—25%, Private pay—75%; Owner: Integrated Health Services; License: Current state; Activities: Arts & Crafts;

Cards; Games; Reading groups; Religious activities; Movies; Shopping trips; social programs; Pet therapy

Columbia Healthcare Center
21 W. Columbia Ave., Cincinnati, OH 4525, (513) 563-3600; Facility Type: Skilled care, Alzheimer's; Beds: 60; Independent Living—262; Certified: Medicaid; Medicare; Veterans; Owner: Nonprofit; License: Current state; Activities: Arts & Crafts; Games; Pet therapy; Group exercise; Group dining; Support groups, Greenhouse/ Garden; Other: Alzheimer's secured unit; Home health care

Hilltop Rehabilitation & Nursing Center
2586 LaFeuille Ave., Cincinnati, OH 45211, (513) 662-2444; Facility Type: Skilled care, Alzheimer's; Beds: 190; Certified: Medicaid, Medicare, Veterans; Owner: CommuniCare Health Services; License: Current state; Activities: Arts & Crafts; Games; Pet therapy; Other: Alzheimer's secured unit.

Kenwood Terrace Nursing Center
8440 Montgomery Rd., Cincinnati, OH 45236, (513) 793-2255; Facility Type: Skilled care; Alzheimer's; Beds: 110; Certified: Medicaid, Medicare, Veterans; Owner: Private; License: Current state; Activities: Arts & Crafts; Movies; Pet therapy; Support groups; Other: Languages spoken: German

Ridge Pavilion
5500 Verulam St., Cincinnati, OH 45213, (513) 631-0003; Facility Type: Skilled care; Alzheimer's; Beds: 121; Certified: Medicaid; Medicare; Veterans; Owner: Private; License: Current state; Activities: Arts & Crafts; Cards; Games; Reading groups; Pet therapy; Support groups; Other: Alzheimer's treatment

Circleville

Pickway Manor Care Center
391 Clark Dr., Circleville, OH 43113,(740) 474-6036; Facility Type: Skilled care, Alzheimer's; Beds: 112; Certified: Medicaid, Medicare, Veterans; License: Current state; Activities: Arts & Crafts; Cards; Games; Pet therapy; Support groups; Other: Alzheimer's secured unit; Retirement facility; Home health care.

Cleveland

Aristocrat West Nursing Home
4387 W 150th St., Cleveland, OH 44135, (216) 252-7730; Facility Type: Skilled care, Alzheimer's; Beds: 150; Certified: Medicaid, Medicare; Veterans; Owner: Private; License: Current state; Activities: Arts & Crafts; Cards; Games; Pet therapy; Outings/Sightseeing; Group exercise; Group dining; Support groups; Other: Alzheimer's secured unit; Languages spoken: Spanish and Slavic

Franklin Plaza Extended Care
3600 Franklin Blvd., Cleveland, OH 44113, (216) 651-1600; Facility Type: Skilled care, Alzheimer's; Beds: 220; Certified: Medicaid; Medicare; Payer mix: Medicaid—91%, Medicare—8%, Private pay—1%; Owner: DMD Management Incorporated; Activities: Arts & Crafts; Cards; Games; Pet therapy; Other: Languages spoken: Hungarian, Romanian, and Spanish.

Kethley House at Benjamin Rose Place
11900 Fairhill Rd., Cleveland, OH 44120, (216) 795-5450; Facility Type: Skilled care; Alzheimer's; Beds: 50; Certified:; Medicaid, Medicare; Owner: Nonprofit; License: Current state; Activities: Arts & Crafts; Cards; Games; Movies; Shopping trips; Dances/ Other: Alzheimer's secured unit.

ManorCare Health Services—Cleveland
16101 Lake Shore Blvd., Cleveland, OH 44110, (216) 486-2300, Facility Type: Skilled care, Alzheimer's, Beds: 200; Certified: Medicaid; Medicare; Owner: HCR Manor Care; License: Current state; Activities: Arts & Crafts; Cards; Games; Reading groups; Religious activities; Movies; Support groups; Other: Languages spoken: Slavic, Croatian, Italian, German, and Lithuanian; Affiliated with the Euclid Chamber of Commerce.

Sunset Nursing Home
1802 Crawford Rd., Cleveland, OH 44106, (216) 795-5710; Facility Type: Skilled care, Alzheimer's; Beds: 75; Certified: Medicaid, Medicare; License: Current state; Activities: Arts & Crafts; Cards; Games; Reading groups; Religious activities; Movies; Shopping; Support groups; Other: Alzheimer's secured unit.

University Manor Health & Rehabilitation Center
2186 Ambleside Rd., Cleveland OH 44106, (216) 721-1400; Facility Type: Skilled care, Alzheimer's; Beds: 20; Certified: Medicaid; Medicare; Veterans; Payer mix: Medicaid—93%, Medicare—5%, Private Pay—1%, Veterans—1%; Owner: Proprietary/Public; License: Current state; Activities: Arts & Crafts; Cards; Games; Reading groups; Religious activities; Movies;

Westpark Health Care Center
4401 W 150th St., Cleveland, OH 44135, (216) 252-7555; Facility Type: Skilled care; Alzheimer's; Beds: 100; Certified: Medicaid; Medicare; Owner: Private; License: Current state; Activities: Arts & Crafts; Cards; Games; Reading

groups; Religious activities; Movies; Shopping trips; Dances; Pet therapy.

Cleves

Miami Haven Nursing Home
5485 State Rte. 128, Cleves, OH 45002, (513) 353-2900; Facility Type: Skilled care, Alzheimer's; Beds: 30; Certified: Medicaid, Medicare; Owner: Private; License: Current state; Activities: Arts & Crafts; Cards; Game; Pet therapy; Support groups; Other: Alzheimer's secured unit; Life care community

Cloverdale

Paradise Oaks Quality Care Nursing & Rehabilitation Center
152 Main St., Cloverdale, OH 45827, (419) 488-3911; Facility Type: Skilled care, Alzheimer's; Beds: 82; Certified: Medicaid; Medicare, Veterans; Owner: Genesis Elder Care; License: Current state; Activities: Arts & Crafts; Cards; Games; Pet therapy; Support groups; Other: Alzheimer's secured unit; Adult day care; Languages spoken: Spanish.

Coldwater

Briarwood Manor
830 W Main St., Coldwater, OH 45828. (419) 678-2311; Facility Type: Skilled care; Alzheimer's; Beds: 110; Certified: Medicaid; Medicare; Veterans; Owner: Private; License: Current state; Activities: Arts & Crafts; Cards; Games; Reading groups; Religious activities; Movies; Shopping trips; Dances; Pet therapy.

Columbiana

Saint Mary's Alzheimer's Center
1899 Garfield Rd., Columbiana, OH 44408, (330) 549-9259, Facility Type: Skilled care, Alzheimer's; Beds: 300; Certified: Medicaid, Medicare; Owner: Windsor House Incorporated; License: Current state; Activities: Arts & Crafts; Dances; Pet therapy; Other: Alzheimer's secured unit; Affiliated with the Catholic and Protestant Churches.

Columbus

Beverly Healthcare & Rehabilitation Center—Columbus
1425 Yorkland Rd., Columbus, OH 43232, (614) 861-6666; Facility Type: Skilled care, Alzheimer's; Beds: 200; Certified: Medicaid, Medicare; Owner: Beverly Enterprises Incorporated; License: Current state; Activities: Arts & Crafts; Cards; Games; Pet therapy; Outings.

Broadview Health Center
5151 N Hamilton Rd., Columbus, OH, (614) 337-1066; Facility Type: Skilled care, Alzheimer's; Beds: 150; Certified: Medicaid, Medicare, Veterans; Owner: Private; License: Current state; Activities: Arts & Crafts; Cards; Games; Pet therapy; Other: Alzheimer's secured unit; Adult day care.

Columbus Alzheimer Care Center
700 Jasonway Ave., Columbus, OH 43214, (614) 459-7050; Facility Type: Skilled care, Alzheimer's; Beds: 100; Certified: Medicaid; Owner: Proprietary/Public; License: Current state; Activities: Arts & Crafts; Cards; Games; Reading groups; Movies; Pet therapy; Support groups.

First Community Village Healthcare Center
1801 Riverside Dr., Columbus, OH 43212, (614) 487-3999; Facility Type: Skilled care; Alzheimer's; Beds: 210; Certified: Medicaid; Medicare; Owner: Nonprofit; License: Current state; Activities: Arts & Crafts; Pet therapy; Other: Alzheimer's secured unit; Home health care; Affiliated with First Community Church and the Riverside/Grant Hospice.

Health Center at Wesley Glen
5155 N High St., Columbus, OH 43214, (614) 888-7492; Facility Type: Skilled care, Alzheimer's, Beds: 170; Certified: Medicaid, Medicare, Veterans; Activities: Arts & Crafts; Movies; Other: Alzheimer's treatment; Alzheimer's secured unit; Affiliated with the Methodist Church, AAHA, and AOPHA.

Isabelle Ridgeway Nursing Center
1520 Hawthorne Ave., Columbus, OH 43202, (614) 252-4931, Email: ridgewayisabel@compuserv.com; Facility Type: Skilled care; Alzheimer's, Adult day care, Home health care; Beds: 100' Certified: Medicaid, Medicare; Owner: Nonprofit; License: Current state; Activities: Arts & Crafts; Cards; Games; Movies; Pet therapy; Outings/Sightseeing; Group exercise; Greenhouse/Garden, Chapel, Crafts room; Other: Alzheimer's secured unit; Adult day care; Home health care.

Lutheran Village of Columbus Care Center
935 N Cassady Ave., Columbus, OH 43219, (614) 252-4987, Facility Type: Skilled care, Alzheimer's; Beds: 250; Certified: Medicaid, Medicare; Veterans; Owner: Nonprofit/Religious; License: Current state; Activities: Arts & Crafts; Pet therapy; Other: Alzheimer's secured unit; Retirement facility; Life care community; Affiliated with Lutheran Social Services.

Regency Manor Rehabilitation & Subacute Center
2000 Regency Manor Cir, Columbus, OH 43207,

(614) 445-8261;Facility Type: Skilled care; Alzheimer's; Beds: 270; Certified: Medicaid, Medicare; Owner: CommuniCare Health Services; License: Current state; Activities: Arts & Crafts; Pet therapy; Other: Alzheimer's secured unit; Languages spoken: Spanish, Greek, Vietnamese and Sign Language

Saint Raphael Home for the Aged
1550 Roxbury Rd., Columbus, OH 43212, (614) 486-0436; Facility Type: Skilled care, Alzheimer's; Beds: 100; Certified: Medicaid, Medicare; Owner: Carmelite Sisters for the Aged & Infirm; License: Current state; Other: Affiliated with the Catholic Church; Languages spoken: Italian and Spanish.

Cortland

Cortland Healthcare Center
369 N High St., Cortland, OH 44410, (330) 638-4015; Facility Type: Skilled care; Alzheimer's, Adult Day Care; Beds: 50; Certified: Medicaid; Owner: Genesis Elder Care; License: Current state; Activities: Arts & Crafts; Cards; Games; Reading groups; Pet therapy; Other: Adult day care.

Cuyahoga Falls

Cuyahoga Falls Country Place
2728 Bailey Rd., Cuyahoga Falls, OH 44221, (330) 929-4231, Facility Type: Skilled care; Alzheimer's, Beds: 110, Certified: Medicaid, Medicare, Veterans; Activities: Arts & Crafts; Cards; Games; Reading groups; Religious activities; Movies; Pet therapy; Group dining; Support groups, Library.

Dayton

Bethany Lutheran Village
6451 Far Hills Ave., Dayton, OH 45459, (937) 433-2110, Facility Type: Skilled care, Alzheimer's, Beds: 270, Certified: Medicaid, Medicare, Owner: Nonprofit/Religious; License: Current state; Activities: Arts & Crafts; Cards; Games; Movies; Shopping trips; Pet therapy; Other: Alzheimer's secured facility; Affiliated with the Lutheran Church.

Carriage Inn of Dayton
5040 Philadelphia Dr., Dayton, OH 45415, (937) 278-0404; http://www.his-inc.com, Facility Type: Skilled care, Alzheimer's; Beds: 90; Certified: Medicaid; Medicare; Owner: Integrated Health Services Incorporated; License: Current state; Activities: Arts & Crafts; Cards; Games; Reading groups; Religious activities; Movies; Shopping; Pet therapy; Other: Alzheimer's secured unit.

The Fountainview
250 Park Dr., Dayton, OH 45410, (937) 224-7906; Facility Type: Skilled care, Alzheimer's; Beds: 50; Certified: Medicaid, Medicare; Owner: Private; Activities: Arts & Crafts; Cards; Games; Movies; Shopping trips; Pet therapy.

Franciscan at Saint Leonard
8100 Clyo Rd., Dayton, OH 4458, (937) 439-7187; Facility Type: Skilled care; Alzheimer's, Adult day care, Retirement facility; Beds: 120; Certified: Medicaid; Medicare; Veterans; Owner: Nonprofit/Religious; License: Current state; Activities: Arts & Crafts; Cards; Movies; Shopping trips; Dances; Pet therapy; Other: Alzheimer's secured unit; Adult day care; Affiliated with the Catholic Church.

The Maria-Joseph Center
4830 Salem Ave., Dayton, OH 45416, (937) 278-2692; Facility Type: Skilled care, Alzheimer's, Beds: 300; Certified: Medicaid, Medicare; Payer mix: Medicaid—55%, Private pay—43%; Owner: Catholic Health Initiatives; License: state; Activities: Arts & Crafts; Pet therapy; Other: Alzheimer's secured unit; Affiliated with the Catholic Church; Languages spoken: Spanish.

Mercy Siena Woods
235 Orchard Springs Dr., Dayton, OH 45415, (937) 278-8211; http://www.health-partners.org; Facility Type: Skilled care, Alzheimer's; Beds: 100; Certified: Medicaid; Medicare; Owner: Catholic Healthcare Partners; License: Current state; Activities: Arts & Crafts; Games; Pet therapy; Group exercise; Group dining; Support groups; Other: Alzheimer's secured unit; Affiliated with the Catholic Church.

Sanctuary at Whispering Meadows
437 Blackwood Ave., Dayton, OH 45403, (937) 253-8944, Facility Type: Skilled care; Alzheimer's, Adult day care; Beds: 40; Certified: Medicaid; Medicare; Veterans; Owner: Medicap Inc.; License: Current state; Activities: Arts & Crafts; Cards; Games; Pet therapy; Outings; Other: Adult day care.

Wood Glen Alzheimer's Community
3800 Summit Glen Dr., Dayton, OH 45449, (937) 436-2273, Facility Type: Skilled care, Alzheimer's, Beds: 150; Certified: Medicaid; Medicare; Owner: AdCare Health Systems Incorporated; License: Current state; Activities: Arts & Crafts; Cards; Games; Reading groups; Religious activities; Movies; Shopping trips; Dances; Outings; Support groups; Other: Alzheimer's secured unit.

Defiance

Leisure Oaks Convalescent Center
214 Harding St., Defiance, OH 43512, (419) 784-1014; Facility Type: Skilled care, Alzheimer's, Adult day care; Beds: 80; Certified: Medicaid, Medicare, Veterans; Owner: Proprietary; License: state; Activities: Arts & Crafts; Cards; Games; Reading groups; Movies; Shopping Pet therapy; Other: Alzheimer's secured unit; Adult day care; Languages spoken: Spanish.

Dover

Country Club Center
860 Iron Ave., Dover, OH 44622, (330) 343-5568; Facility Type: Skilled care; Alzheimer's; Beds: 100; Certified: Medicaid; Medicare; Owner: Proprietary/Public; License: Current state; Activities: Arts & Crafts; Cards; Games; Movies; Shopping trips; Dances/ Social/Cultural gatherings; Pet therapy; Outings/Sightseeing; Group exercise; Group dining; Support groups.

Hennis Care Center
1720 Cross St., Dover, OH 44622, (330) 364-8849, Facility Type: Skilled care, Alzheimer's; Beds: 170; Certified: Medicaid, Medicare; Owner: Private; License: state; Activities: Crafts; Greenhouse/Garden; Other: Alzheimer's secured unit.

East Liverpool

East Liverpool Convalescent Center
701 Armstrong Ln., East Liverpool, OH 43920, (330) 385-3600; Facility Type: Skilled care; Alzheimer's; Beds: 110; Certified: Medicaid, Medicare, Veterans; Owner: Private; License: Current state; Activities: Arts & Crafts; Cards; Games; Reading groups; Pet therapy; Support groups.

Nentwick Convalescent Home Incorporated
500 Selfridge St., East Liverpool, OH, 43920, (330) 385-5001; Facility Type: Skilled care, Alzheimer's; Beds: 100; Certified: Medicaid; Medicare, Veterans; License: state; Activities: Arts & Crafts; Pet therapy.

Eaton

Greenbriar Nursing Center
501 W Lexington Rd., Eaton, OH 45320, (937) 456-9535; Facility Type: Skilled care, Alzheimer's; Beds: 120; Certified: Medicaid, Medicare; Owner: Public; License: state; Activities: Arts & Crafts; Cards; Games; Movies; Pet therapy; Outings; Dances; Other: Alzheimer's secured unit

Elyria

Elyria United Methodist Village
807 West Ave., Elyria, OH 44035, (440) 284-9000; Facility Type: Skilled care; Alzheimer's, Adult day care; Beds: 210; Certified: Medicaid; Medicare; Veterans; Owner: Religious; Activities: Arts & Crafts; Cards; Games; Pet therapy; Other: Alzheimer's secured unit; Adult day care; Affiliated with the United Methodist Church of East Ohio.

Euclid

BracView Manor Health Care Facility
20611 Euclid Ave., Euclid, OH 44117, (216) 486-9300; Facility Type: Skilled care; Alzheimer's; Beds: 110; Certified: Medicaid; Medicare; Veterans; Owner: Public; License: Current state; Activities: Arts & Crafts; Cards; Reading groups; Religious activities; Movies; Shopping trips; Dance; Pet therapy.

Fairfield

Lillian Houston Geriatric Center Incorporated
6200 Pleasant Ave., Fairfield, OH 45018, (513) 829-5349, Facility Type: Skilled care, Alzheimer's; Beds: 60; Certified: Medicaid, Medicare; Owner: Proprietary; License: state; Activities: Arts & Crafts; Cards; Games; Reading groups; Religious activities; Movies; Pet therapy; Outings/Sightseeing.

Tri-County Extended Care Center
5200 Camelot Dr., Fairfield, OH 45014, (513) 829-8100; Facility Type: Skilled care, Alzheimer's; Beds: 280; Certified: Medicaid; Medicare, Veterans; Owner: Private; License: Current state; Activities: Arts & Crafts; Cards; Movies; Shopping; Pet therapy; Other: Alzheimer's secured unit.

Fairlawn

Arbors at Fairlawn
575 S Cleveland-Massilon Rd., Fairlawn, OH 44333, (330) 666-5866; Facility Type: Skilled care; Alzheimer's, Assisted living; Beds: 100; Certified: Medicaid, Medicare; Owner: Extendi-Care Health Services; License: Current state.

Saint Edward Home
3131 Smith Rd., Fairlawn, OH 44313, (330) 666-1183, Facility Type: Skilled care; Alzheimer's, Beds: 122, Certified: Medicaid; Owner: Proprietary; License: Current state; Activities: Arts & Crafts; Cards; Games; Reading groups; Religious activities; Support groups; Other: Affiliated with the Catholic Church.

Findlay

Saint Catherine's Care Center of Findlay
8455 CR 140, Findlay, OH 45840, (419) 422-3978; Facility Type: Skilled care; Alzheimer's; Beds: 100; Certified: Medicaid, Medicare, Veterans; Owner: St. Catherine's Health Care; License: Current state; Activities: Arts & Crafts; Cards; Games; Reading groups; Religious activities; Movies; Shopping; Pet therapy; Support groups; Other: Languages: Spanish.

Winebrenner Village
415 College St., Findlay, OH 45840, (419) 424-3000; Facility Type: Skilled care, Alzheimer's; Beds: 174; Certified: Medicaid; Owner: Proprietary/Public; License: Current state; Activities: Arts & Crafts; Cards; Games; Reading groups; Religious activities; Movies; Shopping trips; Pet therapy; Outings; Group exercise; Group dining; Support groups; Other: Affiliated with the Church of God.

Fostoria

Good Shepherd Home
725 Columbus Ave., Fostoria, OH 44830, (419) 435-1801; Facility Type: Skilled care; Alzheimer's, assisted Living; Beds: 150; Certified: Medicaid, Medicare, Veterans; Owner: Religious; License: Current state; Activities: Arts & Crafts; Pet therapy; Outings/Sightseeing; Group exercise; Group dining; Support groups; Other: Alzheimer's secured unit; Affiliated with: Church of the Brethren; Languages: Spanish.

Saint Catherine's Center of Fostoria
25 Christopher Dr., Fostoria, OH 44830, (419) 435-8112; Facility Type: Skilled care; Alzheimer's; Beds: 100; Certified: Medicaid, Medicare; Owner: Saint Catherine's Health Care; License: state; Activities: Arts & Crafts; Movies; Pet therapy; Outings/Sightseeing; Group exercise; Support groups.

Fowler

Meadowbrook Manor—Hartford
3090 Five Point-Hartford Rd., Fowler, OH 44418; (330) 772-5253; Facility Type: Skilled care, Alzheimer's; Beds: 70; Certified: Medicaid, Medicare; Owner: Private; License: Current state; Activities: Arts & Crafts; Cards; Games; Reading groups; Pet therapy; Outings; Other: Alzheimer's secured unit.

Frankfort

Valley View Alzheimer's Care Center
3363 Ragged Ridge Rd., Frankfort, OH 45628, (740) 998-2948; Facility Type: Skilled care, Alzheimer's; Beds: 100; Certified: Medicaid; Medicare; Veterans: Payer mix: Medicaid—60% Private pay—30%, Veterans—9%, Other—1%; Owner: AdCare Health Systems; License: state; Activities: Arts & Crafts; Cards; Games; Reading Groups; Pet therapy; Other: Alzheimer's secured unit.

Franklin

Franklin Ridge
421 Mission Ln., Franklin, OH 45005, (513) 746-3943; Facility Type: Skilled care, Alzheimer's; Beds: 100; Certified: Medicaid, Medicare, Veterans; Owner: Proprietary; License: state; Activities: Arts & Crafts; Cards; Games; Reading groups.

Fredericktown

Hillcrest Nursing Center
1765 Painter Rd., RD 3, Fredericktown, OH 43019, (419) 886-3931; Facility Type: Skilled care; Alzheimer's; Beds: 50; Certified: Medicaid, Medicare; Owner: Proprietary; License: Current state; Activities: Arts & Crafts; Cards; Games.

Fremont

Bethesda Care Center
600 N Brush St., Fremont, OH 43420, (419) 334-9521; Facility Type: Skilled care, Alzheimer's; Beds: 110; Certified: Medicaid; Medicare; Veterans; Owner: Volunteers of America National Services; License: Current state; Activities: Arts & Crafts; Cards; Games; Pet therapy; Dances; Other: Languages spoken: Spanish.

Fremont Center Genesis Eldercare
825 June St., Fremont, OH 43420, (419) 332-0357; Facility Type: Skilled care, Alzheimer's, Adult day care; Beds: 300; Certified: Medicaid, Medicare; Owner: Genesis ElderCare; License: state; Activities: Arts & Crafts; Cards; Games; Pet therapy; Alzheimer's secured unit, Adult day care; Languages: Spanish.

Garfield Heights

Jennings Hall
10204 Granger Rd., Garfield Heights, OH 44125, (216) 581-2900; Facility Type: Skilled care, Alzheimer's; Beds: 130; Certified: Medicaid, Medicare; Owner: Religious; License: state; Activities: Pet therapy; Support groups; Other: Alzheimer's secured unit; Languages: Polish and Spanish; Affiliated with Sisters of the Holy Spirit.

Geneva

Esther Marie Nursing Center
60 West St., Geneva, OH 44041,(440) 466-1181; Facility Type: Skilled care, Alzheimer's; Beds: 100; Certified: Medicaid; Medicare; Payer mix: Medicaid—68%, Medicare—12%, Private pay—13%; Owner: Proprietary/Public; License: Current state; Activities: Arts & Crafts; Cards; Games; Reading groups; Movies; Pet therapy; Outings; Support groups; Other: Alzheimer's secured unit.

Green Springs

Elmwood
430 Broadway St., Green Springs, OH 44836, (419) 639-2581; Facility Type: Skilled care, Alzheimer's, Assisted Living; Beds: 50' Certified: Medicaid, Medicare, Veterans; Owner: Elmwood Centers; License: state; Other: Alzheimer's secured unit.

Greenfield

Long Term Care of Greenfield
850 Nellie St., Greenfield, OH 45123, (937) 981-2165; Facility Type: Skilled care, Alzheimer's; Beds: 65 Certified: Medicaid, Medicare, Veterans; Owner: McQuen Management; License: state; Other: Languages: Filipino.

Holgate

Holgate Quality Care Nursing & Rehabilitation Center
600 Joe E Brown Ave., Holgate, OH 43527, (419) 264-2921; Facility Type: Skilled care; Alzheimer's, Adult day care; Beds: 50; Certified: Medicaid; Medicare; Owner: Genesis ElderCare; License: Current state; Activities: Arts & Crafts; Cards; Games; Reading groups; Religious activities; Movies; Pet therapy; Other: Adult day care: Languages: Spanish.

Kent

Kent Center
1290 Fairchild Ave., Kent, OH 44240, (330) 678-4912; Facility Type: Skilled care, Alzheimer's; Beds: 100; Certified: Medicaid; Medicare; Owner: Genesis ElderCare; License: Current state; Activities: Arts & Crafts; Cards; Games; Reading groups; Religious activities; Movies; Shopping trips; Dances/ Social/Cultural gatherings; Intergenerational programs; Pet therapy; Greenhouse/ Garden.

Kenton

Baldwin Manor Incorporated
117 Jacob Parrott Blvd., Kenton, OH 43326, (419) 674-4197; Facility Type: Skilled care; Alzheimer's; Beds: 120; Certified: Medicaid, Medicare; Owner: Proprietary/Public; License: Current state; Activities: Arts & Crafts; Cards; Games; Movies; Pet therapy; Other: Alzheimer's secured unit.

Rarier Wood Care Center
911 W Pattison Ave., Kenton, OH 43326, (419) 673-1160; Facility Type: Skilled care; Alzheimer's; Beds: 50;Certified: Medicaid; Owner: Proprietary/Public; License: Current state; Activities: Arts & Crafts; Cards.

Kettering

Kettering Convalescent Center
1150 W Dorothy Ln., Kettering, OH 4409, (937) 293-1152; Facility Type: Skilled care, Alzheimer's; Beds: 100; Certified: Medicaid, Medicare, Veterans; Owner: Aegis Consulting Services, Private; License: Current state; Activities: Arts & Crafts; Cards; Other: Alzheimer's secured unit; Languages: Polish.

Lincoln Park Manor
694 Isaac Prugh Way, Kettering, OH 45429, (937) 297-4300; Facility Type: Skilled care, Alzheimer's, Assisted Living; Beds: 94; Certified: Medicaid, Medicare, Veterans; Owner: Proprietary/Public, Osborne Management; License: Current state; Activities: Arts & Crafts; Cards; Games; Reading groups; Movies; Pet therapy.

Walnut Creek Nursing Center
5070 Lamme Rd., Kettering, OH 45439, (937) 293-7703; Facility Type: Skilled care; Alzheimer's, Special Nursing Facility, Assisted Living; Beds: 180; Certified: Medicaid; Medicare; Owner: Proprietary/Public, the Mariner Management Company; License: Current state; Activities: Arts & Crafts; Cards; Games; Reading groups; Outings; Pet therapy; Support groups; Other: Alzheimer's secured unit.

Kingsville

Ashtabula County Nursing Home
5740 Dibble Rd., Kingsville, OH 44048, (440) 224-2161; Facility Type: Skilled care; Alzheimer's, Adult day care; Beds: 200; Certified: Medicaid; Medicare; Veterans; Owner: State and Local Gov; License: Current state; Activities: Movies; Shopping; Pet therapy; Outings/Sightseeing; Group exercise; Support groups; Other: Alzheimer's secured unit; Adult day care; Languages: Spanish.

Kirkersville

Pine Kirk Nursing Home
205 E Main St., Kirkersville, OH 43033, (740) 927-3209; Facility Type: Skilled care; Alzheimer's; Beds: 40; Certified: Medicaid; Medicare; Veterans; Owner: Proprietary/Public; License: Current state; Activities: Arts & Crafts; Cards; Games; Reading groups; Religious activities; Movies; Shopping trips; Pet therapy; Outings; Group exercise; Group dining; Support groups; Other: Alzheimer's secured unit.

Lancaster

SunBridge Care & Rehabilitation for Homestead
1900 E Main St., Lancaster, OH 43130, (740) 653-8630; Facility Type: Skilled care, Alzheimer's; Beds: 100; Certified: Medicaid; Medicare; Owner: Sun Healthcare Group; License: state; Activities: Arts & Crafts; Cards; Games; Reading groups; Religious activities; Movies; Shopping trips; Dances; Pet therapy; Outings/Sightseeing; Support groups; Other: Languages: Hungarian.

Lebanon

Cedars of Lebanon
102 E Silver St., Lebanon, OH 45036, (513) 932-0300; Facility Type: Skilled care, Alzheimer's; Beds: 50; Certified: Medicaid; Owner: Health Care Opportunities; License: Current state; Activities: Arts & Crafts; Cards; Games; Reading groups; Dances; Pet therapy; Outings; Support groups; Greenhouse/Garden.

Otterbein-Lebanon Retirement Community
585 N State Rte. 741, Lebanon, OH 45036, (513) 932-2020; Facility Type: Skilled care; Alzheimer's, Adult day care; Beds: 300; Certified: Medicaid; Medicare; Owner: Otterbein Homes; License: Current state; Activities: Pet therapy; Other: Alzheimer's secured unit; Adult day care, Home health care; Life care community; Affiliated with the United Methodist Church.

Lima

Columbia Care Center
651 Columbia Dr., Lima, OH 45805, (419) 227-2441; Facility Type: Skilled care, Alzheimer's; Beds: 50; Certified: Medicaid; Medicare; Owner: Beverly Enterprises; License: Current state; Activities: Arts & Crafts; Cards; Games; Reading groups; Pet therapy; Outings/Sightseeing; Group exercise; Group dining; Support groups; Greenhouse/Garden; Other: Alzheimer's secured unit.

Lima Convalescent Home
1650 Allentown Rd., Lima, OH 45805, (419) 224-9741; http://www.limaconvalescenthome.com; Facility Type: Skilled care, Alzheimer's; Beds: 132; Certified: Medicaid; Payer mix: Private pay—100%; Owner: Nonprofit; License: Current state; Activities: Arts & Crafts; Cards; Games; Reading groups; Pet therapy; Support groups; Other: Alzheimer's secured unit; Life care community.

Lorain

Anchor Lodge Nursing Home
3756 W Erie Ave., Lorain, OH 44053, (440) 244-2019; Facility Type: Skilled care, Alzheimer's; Beds: 102; Certified: Medicaid, Medicare; Owner: Proprietary/Public; License: Current state; Activities: Arts & Crafts; Movies; Pet therapy; Outings; Support groups; Other: Languages: Hungarian, Italian and Spanish.

Ohio Extended Care Center
3364 Kolbe Rd., Lorain, OH 44053, (440) 282-2244; Facility Type: Skilled care, Alzheimer's; Beds: 180; Certified: Medicaid, Medicare; Owner: CommuniCare Health Services; License: state; Activities: Arts & Crafts; Cards; Games; Pet therapy; Outings/Sightseeing; Group exercise; Group dining; Support groups; Other: Alzheimer's secured unit; Languages: Lithuanian and Spanish.

Louisville

Joseph T Nist Health Care Center
7770 Columbus Rd. NE, Louisville, OH 44641, (330) 875-1456; Facility Type: Skilled care; Alzheimer's; Beds: 200; Certified: Medicaid; Medicare; Veterans; Owner: Government/ State and Local; License: state; Activities: Arts & Crafts; Movies; Shopping trips; Pet therapy; Support groups; Other: Languages: Italian, Polish, Romanian, Spanish and Sign Language.

Loveland

Loveland Health Care Center
501 N 2nd St., Rte. 48, Loveland, OH 45140, (513) 683-0010; Facility Type: Skilled care, Alzheimer's; Beds: 110; Certified: Medicaid, Medicare; Owner: Private; License: Current state; Activities: Arts & Crafts; Cards; Games; Reading groups; Religious activities; Movies; Shopping trips; Dances/ Social/Cultural gatherings; Intergenerational programs; Pet therapy; Outings/ Sightseeing; Group exercise; Group dining; Support groups; Other: Languages: German and Spanish.

Madeira

ManorCare Nursing Center—Woodside
5970 Kenwood Rd., Madeira, OH 45243, (513) 561-4111; Facility Type: Skilled care, Alzheimer's; Beds: 145; Certified: Medicaid, Medicare; Veterans; Owner: HCR Manor Care; License: state; Activities: Arts & Crafts; Cards; Games; Pet therapy; Outings/Sightseeing; Other: Alzheimer's secured unit.

Mansfield

Crystal Care Center of Mansfield
1159 Wyandotte Ave., Mansfield, OH 44906, (419) 747-2666; Facility Type: Skilled care; Alzheimer's; Beds: 50; Certified: Medicaid, Medicare; Owner: Private; License: Current state; Activities: Arts & Crafts; Pet therapy.

Mansfield Memorial Homes
50 Blymyer Ave., Mansfield, OH 44901, (419) 774-5100; Facility Type: Skilled care, Alzheimer's, Adult day care; Beds: 100; Certified: Medicaid, Medicare; Owner: Nonprofit; License: Current state; Activities: Arts & Crafts; Cards; Games; Reading groups; Religious activities; Movies; Pet; Support groups; Other: Alzheimer's secured unit; Adult day care; Home health care; Life care community.

Maple Heights SunRise Care & Rehabilitation
19900 Clare Ave., Maple Heights, OH 44137, (216) 662-3343; Facility Type: Skilled care, Alzheimer's; Beds: 116; Certified: Medicaid, Medicare, Veterans; Owner: Private, Alliance Systems; License: Current state; Activities: Arts & Crafts; Cards; Games; Reading groups; Religious activities; Movies.

Marietta

Harmar Place Rehabilitation & Extended Care
401 Harmar St., Marietta, OH 45750, (740) 376-5600; Facility Type: Skilled care, Alzheimer's; Beds: 70; Certified: Medicaid, Medicare, Veterans; Owner: Extendicare; License: Current state; Activities: Arts & Crafts; Cards; Games; Exercise; Pet therapy; Other: Affiliated: O'Neill Senior Center.

Marietta Center for Health & Rehabilitation
117 Bartlett St., Marietta, OH 45750, (740) 373-1867; Facility Type: Skilled care, Alzheimer's; Beds: 70; Certified: Medicaid, Medicare, Veterans; Owner: Vencor Health Services; License: Current state; Activities: Arts & Crafts; Cards; Games; Reading groups; Pet therapy; Outings/Sightseeing; Group exercise; Group dining; Support groups; Other: Alzheimer's secured unit.

Marion

Community Healthcare Center
175 Community Dr., Marion, OH 43302, (740) 387-7537; Facility Type: Skilled care, Alzheimer's; Beds: 88; Certified: Medicaid, Medicare; Owner: Vencor; License: state; Activities: Arts & Crafts; Cards; Games; Reading groups; Movies; Pet therapy; Outings; Support groups; Other: Alzheimer's secured unit.

Medina

Evergreen Rehabilitation & Specialty Care Center
555 Springbrook Dr., Medina, OH 44256, (330) 725-3393; Facility Type: Skilled care, Alzheimer's; Beds: 120; Certified: Medicaid, Medicare, Veterans; Owner: Home Health Care; License: state; Activities.

Life Care Center of Medina
2400 Columbia Rd., Medina, OH 44256, (888) 483-3131; Facility Type: Skilled care, Alzheimer's, Assisted living; Beds: 50; Certified: Medicaid, Medicare, Veterans; Owner: Life Care Centers of America; License: state; Activities: Arts & Crafts; Cards; Pet therapy; Other: Alzheimer's secured unit; Home health care

Middleburg Heights

Century Oak Care Center
7250 Old Oak Blvd., Middleburg Heights, OH 44130, (440) 243-7888; Facility Type: Skilled care, Alzheimer's; Beds: 116; Certified: Medicaid, Medicare; Owner: Proprietary/Public; License: state; Activities: Arts & Crafts; Cards; Games; Reading groups; Religious activities; Alzheimer's secured unit.

Royal Oak Nursing & Rehabilitation
6973 Pearl Rd., Middleburg Heights, OH 44130, (440) 884-9191; Facility Type: Skilled care, Alzheimer's; Beds: 100;Certified: Medicaid, Medicare; Owner: Private; License: Current state; Activities: Arts & Crafts; Cards; Games; Reading groups; Religious activities; Movies; Shopping trips; Pet therapy; Other: Languages spoken: German, Italian, Latin, Romanian, Slovenian and Yiddish.

Middletown

Residence at Kensington
751 Kensington St., Middletown, OH 45044, (513) 621-3874; Facility Type: Skilled care, Alz-

heimer's; Beds: 110; Certified: Medicaid, Medicare; Owner: Envision Group; License: Current state; Activities: Arts & Crafts; Cards; Games; Pet therapy; Outings/Sightseeing; Support groups; Other: Alzheimer's secured unit.

Willow Knoll Retirement Community
4400 Vannest Ave., Middletown, OH 45042, (513) 422-5600; Facility Type: Skilled care, Alzheimer's; Beds: 100; Certified: Medicaid, Medicare; Owner: Nonprofit; License: Current state; Activities: Arts & Crafts; Cards; Games; Reading groups; Religious activities; Movies; Pet therapy; Outings; Support groups; Greenhouse/garden; Other: Alzheimer's secured unit; Affiliated with the Southeastern Ecumenical Ministry

Millersburg

Majora Lane Care Center
105 Majora Ln., Millersburg, OH 44654, (330) 674-4444; Facility Type: Skilled care, Alzheimer's; Beds: 100; Certified: Medicaid, Medicare; Owner: Proprietary/Public; License: Current state; Activities: Arts & Crafts; Cards; Pet therapy; Support groups; Other: Affiliated: Holmes County Chamber of Commerce.

Scenic View Nursing Home
434 N Washington St., Millersburg, OH 44654, (330) 674-0015; Facility Type: Skilled care, Alzheimer's; Beds: 165; Certified: Medicaid, Medicare, Veterans; Owner: Castle Nursing Homes; License: Current state; Activities: Arts & Crafts; Cards; Games; Reading groups; Religious activities; Movies; Pet therapy; Support groups; Other: Alzheimer's secured unit

Minerva

Minerva Elder Care
1035 E. Lincoln Way, Minerva, OH 44657, (330) 868-4147; Facility Type: Skilled care, Alzheimer's; Beds: Certified: Medicaid, Medicare, Veterans; License: state; Activities: Arts & Crafts; Pet therapy; Other: Alzheimer's secured unit.

Monroe

Mount Pleasant Retirement Village
225 Britton Ln., Monroe, OH 45050, (513) 539-7760; Facility Type: Skilled care, Alzheimer's, Adult day care; Beds: 100; Certified: Medicaid, Medicare; Owner: Presbyterian Retirement Services; License: Current state; Activities: Arts & Crafts; Cards; Games; Support groups; Pet therapy. Other: Alzheimer's secured unit; Adult day care, Affiliated with the Presbyterian Church.

Montgomery

Meadowbrook Care Center
8211 Weller Rd., Montgomery, OH 45242, (513) 489-2444; Facility Type: Skilled care, Alzheimer's; Beds: 135; Certified: Medicaid; Medicare; Owner: Trinity Management Association; License: state; Activities: Arts & Crafts; Games; Reading groups; Pet therapy; Support groups; Greenhouse/Garden; Other: Alzheimer's secured unit; Affiliated with Trinity Foundation International.

Mount Saint Joseph

Mother Margaret Hall Nursing Home
5900 Delhi Rd., Mount Saint Joseph, OH 45051, (513) 347-5400; Facility Type: Skilled care, Alzheimer's; Beds: 97; Certified: Medicaid; Owner: Nonprofit; License: Current state; Activities: Arts & Crafts; Cards; Games; Reading groups; Religious activities; Movies; Shopping trips; Pet therapy; Other: Alzheimer's secured unit; Affiliated with the Catholic Church; Female Admissions only.

Mount Vernon

Country Club Retirement Center II
1350 Yauger Rd., Mount Vernon, OH 43050, (740) 397-2350; Facility Type: Skilled care, Alzheimer's; Adult day care; Beds: 80; Certified: Medicaid; Owner: Proprietary/Public; License: Current state; Activities: Arts & Crafts; Cards; Games; Pet therapy; Outings; Group exercise; Group dining; Support groups; Other: Adult day care; Affiliated: Ohio Academy of Nursing Homes.

Navarre

Altercare of Navarre
517 Park St., Navarre, OH 44662, (330) 879-2765; Facility Type: Skilled care, Alzheimer's; Beds: 115; Certified: Medicaid, Medicare; Owner: Altercare; License: Current state; Activities: Arts & Crafts; Cards; Games; Pet therapy; Support groups; Other: Ophthalmologist, Podiatrist, Speech therapist.

Country Lawn Nursing Home
10608 Navarre Rd., SW, Navarre, OH 44662, (330) 767-3455; Facility Type: Skilled care, Alzheimer's; Beds: 110; Certified: Medicaid, Medicare; Owner: Consolidated Healthcare Related; Altercare; License: Current state; Activities: Arts & Crafts; Pet therapy; Outings/Sightseeing; Group exercise; Group dining; Support groups; Other: Alzheimer's secured unit; Affiliated: OHCA.

New Carlisle

Belle Manor Nursing Home
197 N Pike St., New Carlisle, OH 45344, (937) 845-3561; Facility Type: Skilled care, Alzheimer's, Beds: 75, Certified: Medicaid; Medicare; Owner: Proprietary/Public; License: Current state; Activities: Arts & Crafts; Cards; Games; Reading groups; Movies; Pet therapy; Outings; Support groups; Other: Alzheimer's secured unit; Affiliated with the Ohio Academy of Nursing Homes.

New Concord

Becket House at New Concord
1280 Friendship Dr., New Concord, OH 43762, (740) 826-7640; http://www.zandex.com Facility Type: Skilled care, Alzheimer's; Beds: 100; Certified: Medicaid; Owner: Zandex Health Care; License: Current state; Support groups.

New Lexington

SunBridge Care & Rehabilitation for New Lexington
920 S Main St., New Lexington, OH 43764, (740) 342-5161; Facility Type: Skilled care, Alzheimer's; Beds: 100; Certified: Medicaid, Medicare; Owner: Sun Healthcare Group; License: Current state; Activities: Movies; Shopping trips; Support groups; Other: Alzheimer's secured unit.

New London

IHS of New London at Firelands
204 W Main St., New London, OH 44851, (419) 929-1563; Facility Type: Skilled care, Alzheimer's, Home Health care; Beds: 50; Certified: Medicaid, Medicare; Owner: Integrated Health Services; License: state; Activities: Movies; Pet therapy; Outings; Group exercise; Group dining; Support groups.

Newark

Flint Ridge Nursing & Rehabilitation Center
1450 W Main St., Newark, OH 43055, (740) 344-9465; Facility Type: Skilled care, Alzheimer's; Beds: 100; Certified: Medicaid, Medicare, Veterans; Owner: Proprietary/Public; License: state; Activities: Arts & Crafts; Shopping trips; Exercise; Intergenerational programs; Pet therapy; Outings; Support groups; Other: Alzheimer's secured unit.

Newark Healthcare Center
75 McMillen Dr., Newark, OH 43055, (740) 344-0357; Facility Type: Skilled care, Alzheimer's; Beds: 100; Certified: Medicaid, Medicare, Veterans; Owner: Public; License: state; Activities: Arts & Crafts; Pet therapy; Exercise; Group dining; Support groups; Other: Alzheimer's secured unit; Home health care.

North Baltimore

Blakely Care Center
600 Sterling Dr., North Baltimore, OH 45872, (419) 257-2421; Facility Type: Skilled care, Alzheimer's; Beds: 75; Certified: Medicaid, Medicare; Veterans; Owner: Proprietary/Public; License: state; Activities: Arts & Crafts; Cards; Games; Reading groups; Pet therapy; Group exercise; Support groups.

North Canton

Saint Luke Lutheran Home for the Aging
220 Applegrove St., NE, North Canton, OH 44720, (330) 499-8341; Facility Type: Skilled care, Alzheimer's; Beds: 80; Certified: Medicaid, Medicare; Owner: Lutheran Church; License: state; Activities: Arts & Crafts; Cards; Pet therapy; Outings/Sightseeing; Group exercise; Support groups.

North Lima

The Assumption Village
9800 Market St., North Lima, OH 44452, (330) 549-0740; Facility Type: Skilled care; Alzheimer's, Assisted living; Beds: 200; Certified: Medicaid, Medicare, Veterans; Owner: Catholic Church; License: Current state; Activities: Crafts; Pet therapy; Support groups; Other: Alzheimer's secured unit; Languages: Spanish.

Rolling Acres Care Center
9625 Market St., North Lima, OH 44452, (330) 549-3939; Facility Type: Skilled care, Alzheimer's; Beds: 90; Certified: Medicaid; Medicare; Veterans; Owner: Government/ State and Local; License: Current state; Activities: Pet therapy; Other: Gero-psychiatric unit; Alzheimer's secured unit; Affiliated with the Catholic, Methodist, Protestant and Lutheran Churches; Languages: Italian and Spanish.

North Olmsted

Manor Care Health Services
23225 Lorain Rd., North Olmsted, OH 44070. (440) 779-6900; Facility Type: Skilled care, Alzheimer's; Beds: 145; Certified: Medicaid, Medicare; Owner: HCR Manor Care; License: state; Activities: Pet therapy; Support groups; Other: Alzheimer's secured unit.

Olmsted Manor Skilled Nursing Center
27500 Mill Rd., North Olmsted, OH 44070, (440) 777-8444; Facility Type: Skilled care, Alzheimer's; Beds: 100; Certified: Medicaid, Medicare; Owner: Private; License: Current state; Activities: Arts & Crafts; Cards; Movies; Pet therapy; Support groups; Other: Alzheimer's secured unit; Audiologists; Dentists; Ophthalmologists; Languages: Hungarian, Italian and Spanish.

Norwalk

Gaymont Nursing Center
66 Norwood Ave., Norwalk, OH 44857, (419) 668-8258; Facility type: Skilled care, Alzheimer's; Beds: 112; Certified: Medicaid, Medicare, Veterans; Owner: Public; License: state; Activities: Arts& Crafts; Dances; Support groups; Pet therapy; Group exercise; Outings; Other: Alzheimer's secured unit; Adult day care.

Oak Harbor

Ottawa County Riverview Nursing Home
8180 W State Rte. 163, Oak Harbor, OH 43449; (419) 898-2851; Facility type: Skilled care, Alzheimer's; Beds: 180; Certified: Medicaid, Medicare, Veterans; Owner: Private; License: state; Activities: Arts& Crafts; Dances; Support groups; Pet therapy; Other: Alzheimer's secured unit; Adult day care.

Oberlin

Kendal at Oberlin
600 Kendal Dr., Oberlin, OH 44074, (440) 775-1211; Facility type: Skilled care, Alzheimer's; Beds: 112; Certified: Medicaid, Medicare; Owner: Public; License: state; Activities: Arts & Crafts; Dances; Support groups; Pet therapy; Group exercise; Outings; Other: Alzheimer's secured unit; Home health care.

Ottawa

Putnam Acres Care Center
10170 Rd5-H, RR1, Ottawa, OH 45875; (419) 523-4092; Facility type: Skilled care, Alzheimer's; Beds: 100; Certified: Medicaid, Medicare, Veterans; Owner: State and Local Gov; License: state; Activities: Arts & Crafts; Dances; Support groups; Pet therapy; Group exercise; Outings; Other: Alzheimer's secured unit; Adult day care.

Port Clinton

Edgewood Manor Nursing Center
1330 S Fulton St., Port Clinton, OH 43452, (419) 734-5506; Facility type: Skilled care, Alzheimer's; Beds: 100; Certified: Medicaid, Medicare; Owner: Covenant Care; License: state; Activities: Arts & Crafts; Dances; Support groups; Pet therapy; Group exercise; Outings; Other: Home health care.

Ravenna

Altercare of Ravenna
245 New Milford Rd., Ravenna, OH 44266, (330) 296-6415; Facility type: Skilled care, Alzheimer's; Beds: 99; Certified: Medicaid, Medicare; Owner: State & Local Gov; License: state; Activities: Arts & Crafts; Dances; Pet therapy; Group exercise; Outings; Other: Languages: German.

Sandusky

Lutheran Memorial Home
795 Bardshar Rd., Sandusky, OH 44870, (419) 625-4046; Facility type: Skilled care, Alzheimer's; Beds: 100; Certified: Medicaid; Owner: Religious; License: state; Activities: Arts& Crafts; Dances; Other: Languages: Spanish.

Springfield

IOOF Home of Ohio
404 E McCreight Ave., Springfield, OH 45503, (937) 399-8311; Facility type: Skilled care, Alzheimer's; Beds: 180; Certified: Medicaid, Medicare; Owner: Nonprofit; License: state; Activities: Arts& Crafts; Dances; Support groups; Pet therapy; Group exercise; Outings; Other: Alzheimer's secured unit.

Mercy St. John's Center
100 W McCreight Ave., Springfield, OH 45504, (937) 399-9910; Facility type: Skilled care, Alzheimer's; Beds: 220; Certified: Medicaid, Medicare, Veterans; Owner: Catholic Healthcare Partners; License: state; Activities: Arts & Crafts; Dances; Support groups; Pet therapy; Other: Alzheimer's secured unit; Adult day care.

Stow

The Briarwood
3700 Englewood Dr., Stow, OH 44224, (330) 688-1828; Facility type: Skilled care, Alzheimer's, Assisted Living; Beds: 130; Certified: Medicaid, Medicare; Owner: Proprietary; License: state; Activities: Arts& Crafts; Dances; Pet therapy.

Maison Aine
2910 L'Ermitage Pl., Stow, OH 44224, (330) 668-1188; Facility type: Skilled care, Alzheimer's; Beds: 150; Certified: Medicaid, Medicare; Owner:

ExtendiCare Health Services; License: state; Activities: Art & Crafts; Dances; Support groups; Pet therapy; Group exercise; Outings; Other: Alzheimer's secured unit.

Sylvania

Goerlic Center
5320 Harroun Rd., Sylvania, OH 43560 (419) 824-1250; Facility type: Skilled care, Alzheimer's; Beds: 50; Certified: Medicaid, Medicare; Owner: Nonprofit; License: state; Activities: Arts & Crafts; Dances; Other: Alzheimer's secured unit.

Toledo

Briarfield at Glanzman
3121 Glanzman Rd., Toledo, OH 43614, (419) 385-6616; Facility type: Skilled care, Alzheimer's; Beds: 95; Certified: Medicaid, Medicare; Owner: Horizon Healthcare; License: state; Activities: Arts & Crafts; Dances; Support groups; Pet therapy; Other: Alzheimer's secured unit; Affiliated: OHCA, NWOHCA.

Fairview Manor Nursing Center
4420 South Ave., Toledo, OH 43615, (419) 531-3607; Facility type: Skilled care, Alzheimer's; Beds: 130; Certified: Medicaid, Medicare; Owner: Covenant Care; License: state; Activities: Arts& Crafts; Dances; Support groups; Pet therapy; Group exercise; Outings; Other: Languages: Spanish.

Foundation Park Dementia Care Center
1621 S Byrne Rd. Toledo, OH 43614, (419) 385-3958; Facility type: Skilled care, Alzheimer's; Beds: 118; Certified: Medicaid, Medicare; Payer mix: Medicaid—80%; Owner: Nursing Care Mgt; License: state; Activities: Arts & Crafts; Outings; Pet therapy; Other: Alzheimer's secured unit.

Upper Sandusky

Fairhaven Retirement & Health Care Community
850 Marseilles Ave., Upper Sandusky, OH 43351, (419) 294-4973; Facility type: Skilled care, Alzheimer's; Beds: 150; Certified: Medicaid, Medicare, Veterans; Owner: Nonprofit; License: state; Activities: Arts & Crafts; Dances; Support groups; Pet therapy; Group exercise; Outings; Other: Alzheimer's secured unit.

Urbana

Heartland of Urbana
741 E Water St., Urbana, OH 43078, (937) 652-1381; Facility type: Skilled care, Alzheimer's; Beds: 100; Certified: Medicaid, Medicare, Veterans; Owner: HCR Manor Care; License: state; Activities: Arts & Crafts; Dances; Support groups; Pet therapy; Group exercise; Outings; Other: Alzheimer's secured unit.

McAuley Center
906 Scioto St., Urbana, OH 43078, (937) 653-5432; Facility type: Skilled care, Alzheimer's; Beds: 130; Certified: Medicaid, Medicare, Veterans; Owner: Catholic Healthcare Partners; License: Current state; Activities: Arts& Crafts; Dances; Support groups; Pet therapy; Group exercise; Outings; Other: Alzheimer's secured unit.

Wadsworth

Altercare of Wadsworth
147 Garfield St., Wadsworth, OH 44281, (330) 335-2555; Facility type: Skilled care, Alzheimer's; Beds: 130; Certified: Medicaid, Medicare; Owner: Altercare; License: state; Activities: Arts & Crafts; Dances; Support groups; Pet therapy; Group exercise; Outings; Other: Alzheimer's secured unit; Adult day care.

Warren

Community Skilled Nursing Centre of Warren
1320 Mahoning Ave., NW, Warren, OH 44483, (330) 373-1160; Facility type: Skilled care, Alzheimer's; Beds: 160; Certified: Medicaid, Medicare; Owner: Nonprofit; License: state; Activities: Arts & Crafts; Dances; Support groups; Pet therapy; Group exercise; Outings; Other: Alzheimer's secured unit.

Gillette Nursing Home
3310 Elm Rd., NE, Warren, OH 44483, (330) 898-4033; Facility type: Skilled care, Alzheimer's; Beds: 110 Certified: Medicaid, Medicare, Medi-Cal, Veterans: Owner: Private; Activities: Crafts; Dances; Support groups; Pet therapy.

Ridge Crest Care Center
1926 Ridge Rd., SE, Warren, OH 44484, (330) 369-4672; Facility type: Skilled care, Alzheimer's; Beds: 100; Certified: Medicaid, Medicare, Medi-Cal, Veterans; Owner: Integrated Health Services; License: state; Activities: Arts & Crafts; Dances; Support groups; Pet therapy; Outings; Other: Alzheimer's secured unit.

Washington Court House

Court House Manor
250 Glenn Ave., Washington Court House, OH 43160, (740) 335-9290, Facility type: Skilled care, Alzheimer's; Beds: 100; Certified: Medicaid,

Medicare, Veterans; Owner: Proprietary/Public; License: state; Activities: Arts & Crafts; Dances; Support groups; Pet therapy; Group exercise; Outings.

Saint Catherine's Care Center
1771 Palmer Rd., Washington Court House, OH 43169, (740) 335-6391, Facility type: Skilled care, Alzheimer's; Beds: 110; Certified: Medicaid, Medicare, Veterans; Owner: Carington Health Systems; Proprietary/Public; License: state; Activities: Arts & Crafts; Dances; Support groups; Pet therapy; Group exercise; Outings; Other: Alzheimer's secured unit.

Xenia

Greene Oaks
164 Office Park Dr., Xenia, OH 45385, (937) 376-8217; Facility type: Skilled care, Alzheimer's; Beds: 75; Certified: Medicaid, Medicare; Owner: Med Health System; Proprietary/Public; License: state; Activities: Arts & Crafts; Dances; Support groups; Pet therapy; Group exercise; Outings; Other: Alzheimer's secured unit.

Youngstown

Boardman Community Care Center
5665 South Ave., Youngstown, OH 45512, (330) 782-1173; Facility type: Skilled care, Alzheimer's; Beds: 210; Certified: Medicaid, Medicare; Owner: Integrated Health Services; License: state; Activities: Crafts; Pet therapy; Group exercise; Outings; Other: Alzheimer's secured unit; Home health care.

Dandridge Burgundi Manor
31 Maranatha Dr., Youngstown, OH 44507, (330) 746-2508; Facility type: Skilled care, Alzheimer's; Beds: 65; Certified: Medicaid, Medicare; Owner: Proprietary/Public; License: state; Activities: Arts & Crafts; Dances; Support groups; Pet therapy; Group exercise; Outings; Other: Alzheimer's secured unit.

Zanesville

Adams Lane Care Center
1856 Adams Ln., Zanesville, OH 43701, (740) 454-9769, Facility type: Skilled care, Alzheimer's; Beds: 100; Certified: Medicaid, Medicare; Owner: Zandex; License: state; Activities: Arts & Crafts; Dances; Support groups; Pet therapy; Group exercise; Other: Alzheimer's secured unit; Affiliated: Catholic Church.

OKLAHOMA

Alva

Share Medical Center
730 Share Dr., Alva, OK 73717, (580) 327-2800; Facility type: Skilled care, Alzheimer's; Beds: 80; Certified: Medicaid; Owner: Nonprofit, Quarum; License: Current state; Activities: Arts & Crafts; Dances; Support groups; Pet therapy; Group exercise; Outings; Other: Alzheimer's secured unit, Home health care.

Ardmore

Ardmore Care Center
111 13th NW, Ardmore, OK 73401, (580) 223-4803; Facility type: Skilled care, Alzheimer's; Beds: 80; Certified: Medicaid, Medicare; Owner: Private; License: state; Activities: Arts & Crafts; Dances; Support groups; Pet therapy; Group exercise; Outings; Greenhouse/Garden; Other: Alzheimer's secured unit.

Woodview Home
1630 3rd NE, Ardmore, OK 73401, (580) 226-5454; Facility type: Skilled care, Alzheimer's; Beds: 70; Certified: Medicaid, Medicare, Veterans; Owner: Private; License: state; Activities: Arts & Crafts; Dances; Support groups; Pet therapy.

Arkoma

Medi-Home Inc. of Arkoma
1008 Arkansas St., Arkoma, OK 74901, (918) 875-3107; Facility type: Skilled care, Alzheimer's; Beds: 60; Certified: Medicaid, Medicare, Veterans; Owner: Proprietary/Public; License: state; Activities: Arts & Crafts; Dances; Support groups; Pet therapy; Group exercise; Outings; Other: Alzheimer's secured unit.

Bixby

Bixby Manor Nursing Home
76 W Rachel St., Bixby, OK 74008, (918) 366-4491; Facility type: Skilled care, Alzheimer's; Beds: 100; Certified: Medicaid, Medicare; Owner: Private; License: state; Activities: Arts & Crafts; Dances; Support groups; Pet therapy; Group exercise; Outings; Other: Languages: Spanish.

Boise City

Cimarron Nursing Home
100 S Ellis, Boise City, OK 73933, (580) 544-2501; Facility type: Skilled care, Alzheimer's; Beds: 100; Certified: Medicaid; Owner: State & Local Gov; License: Current state; Activities: Arts & Crafts; Dances; Support groups; Pet therapy; Group exercise; Outings; Other: Alzheimer's secured unit; Languages: Spanish.

Chandler

Pioneer Estate Nursing Facility
206 W 2nd, Chandler, OK 74834, (405) 258-1375; Facility type: Skilled care, Alzheimer's; Beds: 50; Certified: Medicaid, Medicare, Veterans; Owner: Proprietary/Public; License: state; Activities: Arts & Crafts; Dances; Support groups; Pet therapy; Group exercise; Outings.

Checotah

Cedar Manor
1001 W Gentry, Checotah, OK 74426, (918) 473-2247; Facility type: Skilled care, Alzheimer's; Beds: 80; Certified: Medicaid; Owner: Proprietary/Public; License: state; Activities: Arts & Crafts; Dances; Support groups; Pet therapy; Group exercise; Outings; Other: Alzheimer's secured unit, Adult day care.

Claremore

Wood Manor
630 N Dorothy, Claremore, OK 74017, (918) 341-4365; Facility type: Skilled care, Alzheimer's; Beds: 130; Certified: Medicaid, Medicare, Veterans; Owner: Private; License: state; Activities: Arts & Crafts; Dances; Support groups; Pet therapy; Group exercise; Outings; Other: Alzheimer's secured unit; Adult day care.

Clinton

Prairie View Healthcare Center
3200 Hayes W, Clinton, OK 73601, (580) 323-0990; Facility type: Skilled care, Alzheimer's; Beds: 70; Certified: Medicaid, Medicare; Owner: Private; License: state; Activities: Arts & Crafts; Dances; Support groups; Pet therapy; Group exercise; Outings; Other: Alzheimer's secured unit, Adult day care.

United Methodist Health Care Center
2316 Modelle, Clinton, OK 73601, (580) 323-0912; Facility type: Skilled care, Alzheimer's; Beds: 101; Certified: Medicaid; Owner: Nonprofit; License: state; Activities: Arts & Crafts; Dances; Support groups; Pet therapy; Group exercise; Outings; Other: Affiliation: Methodist.

Cushing

Cushing Regional Hospital
1027 E Cherry St., Cushing, OK 74023; Facility type: Skilled care, Alzheimer's; Beds: 45; Certified: Medicaid, Medicare; Owner: Nonprofit, Quorum; License: state; Activities: Arts & Crafts; Dances; Support groups; Pet therapy; Group exercise; Outings; Other: Alzheimer's secured unit, Home health care.

Linwood Village Nursing
5303 Linwood, Cushing, OK 74023, (918) 225-2220; Facility type: Skilled care, Alzheimer's; Beds: 70; Certified: Medicaid, Medicare, Veterans; Owner: Proprietary/Public; License: state; Activities: Arts & Crafts; Dances; Support groups; Pet therapy; Group exercise; Outings.

Duncan

Duncan Care Center
700 Palms St., Duncan, OK 73533, (580) 255-9000, Facility type: Skilled care, Alzheimer's; Beds: 150; Certified: Medicaid, Medicare; Owner: Private; License: state; Activities: Arts & Crafts; Dances; Support groups; Pet therapy; Group exercise; Outings; Other: Alzheimer's secured unit, Adult day care.

Wilkins Nursing Center
1205 S 4th, Duncan, OK 73533, (580) 252-3955; Facility type: Skilled care, Alzheimer's; Beds: 108; Certified: Medicaid; Owner: Proprietary/Public; License: state; Activities: Arts & Crafts; Dances; Support groups; Pet therapy.

Edmond

Heartland Health Care of Edmond
39 SE 33rd St., Edmond, OK 73013, (405) 341-5555; Facility type: Skilled care, Alzheimer's; Beds: 50; Certified: Medicaid, Medicare; Owner: Proprietary/Public; License: state; Activities: Arts & Crafts; Dances; Support groups; Pet therapy; Other: Alzheimer's secured unit; Languages: Korean and Spanish.

Elk City

Elk City Nursing Center
301 N Garrett, Elk City, OK 73644, (580) 225-2811; Facility type: Skilled care, Alzheimer's; Beds: 90; Certified: Medicaid, Medicare; Owner: Proprietary/Public; License: state; Activities: Arts & Crafts; Dances; Support groups; Pet therapy; Group exercise; Outings; Other: Alzheimer's secured unit; Sign Language.

Enid

The United Methodist Home of Enid
301 S Oakwood Rd., Enid, OK 73703, (580) 237-6164; Facility type: Skilled care, Alzheimer's; Beds: 130; Certified: Medicaid; Owner: Nonprofit; License: state; Activities: Arts & Crafts; Dances; Support groups; Pet therapy; Group exercise; Outings; Other: Alzheimer's secured unit.

Fairview

Fairview Fellowship Home for Senior Citizens
605 E State Rd., Fairview, OK 73737, (580) 227-3783; Facility type: Skilled care, Alzheimer's; Beds: 140; Certified: Medicaid; Owner: Nonprofit; License: state; Activities: Support groups; Pet therapy; Exercise; Other: Alzheimer's secured unit; Affiliated: Mennonite Brethren Church.

Grove

Betty Ann Nursing Center
1400 S Main St., Grove, OK 74345, (918) 786-2275; Facility type: Skilled care, Alzheimer's; Beds: 60; Certified: Medicaid; Owner: Private; License: state; Activities: Arts & Crafts; Pet therapy; Group exercise; Outings; Other: Alzheimer's secured unit; Languages: Cherokee; Affiliated: Greater OK Long-term Care Association.

Guymon

Dr. WF & Mada Dunaway Manor Nursing Home of Guymon
1401 N Leila, Guymon, OK 73942, (580) 338-3186; Facility type: Skilled care, Alzheimer's; Beds: 70; Certified: Medicaid; Owner: Proprietary/Public; License: state; Activities: Arts & Crafts; Dances; Support groups; Pet therapy; Outings; Other: Languages: Spanish; Affiliation: Methodist.

Hobart

B & K Nursing Center
101 S Main, Hobart, OK 73651; (580) 726-3394; Facility type: Skilled care, Alzheimer's; Beds: 50; Certified: Medicaid, Medicare; Owner: Proprietary/Public; License: state; Activities: Arts & Crafts; Dances; Support groups; Pet therapy; Group exercise; Outings; Other: Adult day care.

Hollis

Colonial Manor II
120 W Versa, Hollis, OK 73550, (580) 688-9431; Facility type: Skilled care, Alzheimer's; Beds: 95; Certified: Medicaid, Medicare, Veterans; Owner: State & Local Gov; License: state; Activities: Arts & Crafts; Dances; Support groups; Pet therapy; Group exercise; Outings; Other: Alzheimer's secured unit.

Hugo

Hugo Health & Rehabilitation Center
601 N Broadway, Hugo, OK 74743, (580) 326-6278; Facility type: Skilled care, Alzheimer's; Beds: 80; Certified: Medicaid, Medicare; Owner: Private; License: state; Activities: Arts & Crafts; Dances; Support groups; Pet therapy; Outings; Other: Alzheimer's secured unit; Adult day care.

Jay

Monroe Manor
226 E Monroe St., Jay, OK 74346, (918) 253-4500; Facility type: Skilled care, Alzheimer's; Beds: 100; Certified: Medicaid; Owner: State & Local Gov; License: state; Activities: Arts & Crafts; Support groups; Pet therapy; Other: Language: Cherokee.

Lawton

Crestview Life Center
1301 Andrews, Lawton, OK 73507, (580) 355-5720; Facility type: Skilled care, Alzheimer's; Beds: 95; Certified: Medicaid, Medicare; Owner: Proprietary/Public; License: state; Activities: Arts & Crafts; Dances; Support groups; Pet therapy; Group exercise; Outings; Other: Alzheimer's secured unit.

McMahon-Tomlinson Nursing Center
3126 NW Arlington, Lawton, OK 73505, (580) 357-3240; Facility type: Skilled care, Alzheimer's; Beds: 120; Certified: Medicaid; Owner: Proprietary/Public; License: state; Activities: Arts & Crafts; Dances; Support groups; Pet therapy; Other: Alzheimer's secured unit; Languages: Spanish.

Western Hills Health Care Center
5396 NW Cache Rd., Lawton, OK 73505, (580) 353-3653; Facility type: Skilled care, Alzheimer's; Beds: 150; Certified: Medicaid; Owner: Proprietary/Public; License: state; Activities: Arts & Crafts; Dances; Outings; Exercise; Pet therapy; Other: Alzheimer's secured unit: Languages: Spanish and Germ an.

McAlester

Blevins Retirement & Care Center
1220 E Gene Stipe Blvd., McAlester, OK 74501, (918) 423-9095; Facility type: Skilled care, Alz-

heimer's, Independent living; Beds: 40; Certified: Medicaid, Medicare; Owner: Private; License: state; Activities: Arts & Crafts; Dances; Support groups; Pet therapy; Group exercise; Outings.

Heartland Care Center
615 E Morris St., McAlester, OK 74501, (918) 426-0850; Facility type: Skilled care, Alzheimer's; Beds: 63; Payer mix: Medicaid- 90%; Certified: Medicaid, Medicare; Owner: Heartland Care Group; License: state; Activities: Arts & Crafts; Dances; Pet therapy; Outings; Other: Alzheimer's secured unit, Adult day care.

Heritage Hills Nursing Center
411 N West St., McAlester, OK 74502. (918) 423-2290; Facility type: Skilled care, Alzheimer's; Beds: 80; Certified: Medicaid, Medicare, Veterans; Owner: Private; License: state; Activities: Arts & Crafts; Pet therapy; Outings.

Mitchell Manor Convalescent Home
315 W Gene Stipe Blvd., McAlester, OK (918) 423-4661; Facility type: Skilled care, Alzheimer's; Beds: 100; Certified: Medicaid, Veterans; Owner: Proprietary/Public; License: state; Activities: Arts & Crafts; Support groups; Pet therapy.

Mountain View

Mountain View Healthcare
320 N 7th St., Mountain View, OK 73062, (580) 347-2120; Facility type: Skilled care, Alzheimer's; Beds: 40; Certified: Medicaid; Owner: Mountain View Health Care; License: state; Activities: Pet therapy; Outings; Other: Adult day care.

Muskogee

Eastgate Village Retirement Center
3500 Haskell Blvd., Muskogee, OK 74403; (918) 682-3191; Facility type: Skilled care, Alzheimer's; Beds: 100; Certified: Medicaid, Medicare, Veterans; Owner: Dale Scott Mgt; License: state; Activities: Arts & Crafts; Dances; Support groups; Pet therapy; Group exercise; Greenhouse/Garden.

Park Boulevard Care Center
841 N 38th St., Muskogee, OK 74401, (918) 683-3070; Facility type: Skilled care, Alzheimer's; Beds: 100; Certified: Medicaid, Medicare; Owner: Private; License: state; Activities: Arts & Crafts; Dances; Support groups; Pet therapy; Group exercise; Outings; Other: Alzheimer's secured unit.

Mustang

Mustang Nursing Home
400 N Clear Springs Rd., Mustang, OK 73064, (405) 376-3020; Facility type: Skilled care, Alzheimer's; Beds: 100; Certified: Medicaid; Owner: Private; License: state; Activities: Arts & Crafts; Dances; Support groups; Pet therapy; Group exercise; Outings; Other: Alzheimer's secured unit, Adult day care; Languages: Spanish.

Newkirk

Newkirk Nursing Center
1351 W Peckham Rd., Newkirk, OK 74647, (580) 362-3277; Facility type: Skilled care, Alzheimer's; Beds: 50; Certified: Medicaid; Owner: Proprietary/Public; License: state; Activities: Arts & Crafts; Support groups; Pet therapy.

Norman

Rosewood Manor
501 E Robinson, Norman, OK 73071, (405) 321-6666; Facility type: Skilled care, Alzheimer's; Beds: 150; Certified: Medicaid, Medicare; Owner: Private; License: state; Activities: Crafts; Outings; Pet therapy; Other: Alzheimer's secured unit.

Okeene

Okeene Nursing Center
119 N 6th, Okeene, OK 73763, (580) 822-4441; Facility type: Skilled care, Alzheimer's; Beds: 100; Certified: Medicaid, Medicare, Veterans; Owner: Private; License: state; Activities: Arts & Crafts; Dances; Support groups; Pet therapy.

Oklahoma City

Alvira Heights Manor
1215 NE 34th St., Oklahoma City, OK 73111, (405) 424-4000; Facility type: Skilled care, Alzheimer's; Beds: 70; Certified: Medicaid, Medicare; Owner: Private; License: state; Activities: Arts & Crafts; Group exercise; Support groups; Pet therapy; Outings; Other: Languages: Spanish.

Amberwood Nursing Center
5900 N Robinson, Oklahoma City, OK 73118, (405) 843-5900; Facility type: Skilled care, Alzheimer's; Beds: 120; Certified: Medicaid, Medicare; Owner: Private; License: state; Activities: Arts & Crafts; Dances; Support groups; Pet therapy; Group exercise; Outings; Other: Alzheimer's secured unit; Languages: Spanish.

Central Oklahoma Christian Home
6312 N Portland, Oklahoma City, OK 73112, (405) 946-6932; Facility type: Skilled care, Alzheimer's; Beds: 150; Certified: Medicaid; Owner: Church of Christ; License: state; Activities: Arts & Crafts; Dances; Support groups; Pet therapy; Group exercise; Outings; Other: Adult day care.

HCR Manor Care—Warr Acres
6501 N MacArthur Blvd., Oklahoma City, OK 73132, (405) 721-5444; Facility type: Skilled care, Alzheimer's; Beds: 100; Certified: Medicaid, Medicare; Owner: HCR Manor Care; License: state; Activities: Arts & Crafts; Dances; Support groups; Pet therapy; Group exercise; Outings; Other: Alzheimer's secured unit.

Skyview Nursing Center
2200 N Coltrane Rd., Oklahoma City, OK 73121, (405) 427-1322; Facility type: Skilled care, Alzheimer's; Beds: 60; Certified: Medicaid, Veterans; Owner: Private: state; Activities: Arts & Crafts; Dances; Support groups; Pet therapy; Group exercise; Outings; Other: Adult day care.

Southern Oaks Manor
301 SW 74th, Oklahoma City, OK 73139, (405) 634-0573; Facility type: Skilled care, Alzheimer's; Beds: 115; Certified: Medicaid, Medicare; Owner: Southwest Health Care; License: state; Activities: Arts & Crafts; Dances; Support groups; Pet therapy; Group exercise; Outings; Other: Home health care.

Owasso

Evergreen Care Center
12600 E 73rd St., N, Owasso, OK 74055 (918) 272-8007; Facility type: Skilled care, Alzheimer's; Beds: 120; Certified: Medicaid; Owner: Baptist Church; License: state; Activities: Arts & Crafts; Dances; Support groups; Pet therapy; Group exercise; Outings; Other: Alzheimer's secured unit, Home health care.

Ponca City

Ponca City Nursing & Rehabilitation Center
1400 N Waverly, Ponca City, OK 74601, (580) 762-6668; Facility type: Skilled care, Alzheimer's; Beds: 160; Certified: Medicaid, Medicare; Owner: Private; License: state; Activities: Crafts; Support groups; Pet therapy.

Tenderheart Health Care
1401 W Highland, Ponca City, OK 74601, (580) 765-4454; Facility type: Skilled care, Alzheimer's; Beds: 100; Certified: Medicaid, Medicare, Veterans; Owner: Crescent Health Services; License: state; Activities: Arts & Crafts; Dances; Support groups; Pet therapy; Outings; Other: Alzheimer's secured unit.

Poteau

The Oaks Healthcare Center
1501 Clayton St., Poteau, OK 74953, (918) 647-8236; Facility type: Skilled care, Alzheimer's; Beds: 160; Certified: Medicaid, Medicare, Veterans; Owner: Private; License: state; Activities: Arts & Crafts; Dances; Support groups; Pet therapy; Group exercise; Outings; Other: Alzheimer's secured unit.

Ringling

Ringling Nursing Home
2nd & H Sts., Ringling, OK 73456, (580) 662-2344; Facility type: Skilled care, Alzheimer's; Beds: 50; Certified: Medicaid; Owner: Proprietary/Public; License: state; Activities: Arts & Crafts; Dances; Support groups; Pet therapy; Group exercise; Outings; Other: Alzheimer's secured unit, Adult day care.

Shawnee

Golden Rule Home
38801 Hardesty Rd., Shawnee, OK 74802; (405) 273-7106; Facility type: Skilled care, Alzheimer's; Beds: 60; Certified: Medicaid; Owner: Church of God; License: state; Activities: Arts & Crafts; Dances; Support groups; Pet therapy; Group exercise; Outings; Other: Alzheimer's secured unit.

Shawnee Colonial Estates Nursing Home
535 W Federal, Shawnee, OK 74801, (405) 273-1826; Facility type: Skilled care, Alzheimer's; Beds: 170; Certified: Medicaid, Medicare; Owner: Proprietary/Public; License: state; Activities: Arts & Crafts; Dances; Support groups; Pet therapy; Group exercise; Outings; Other: Alzheimer's secured unit.

Stroud

Stroud Oakview Care Center
721 W Olive, Stroud, OK 74049, (918) 968-2075; Facility type: Skilled care, Alzheimer's; Beds: 60; Certified: Medicaid; Owner: Private; License: state; Activities: Arts & Crafts; Dances; Support groups; Pet therapy.

Sulphur

Callaway Nursing Home
1300 W Lindsay, Sulphur, OK 73086, (580) 622-2416; Facility type: Skilled care, Alzheimer's; Beds: 100; Certified: Medicaid, Veterans; Owner: Private; License: state; Activities: Arts & Crafts; Dances; Support groups; Pet therapy; Group exercise; Outings; Other: Alzheimer's secured unit.

Tahlequah

Go Ye Village Medical Center
1201 W 4th, Tahlequah, OK 744464, (918) 456-4542; Facility type: Skilled care, Alzheimer's;

Beds: 50; Payer mix: 100% Private pay; Owner: Golden Year Advisor; License: state; Activities: Arts & Crafts; Dances; Support groups; Pet therapy; Group exercise; Outings; Other: Home health care.

Tulsa

Ambassador Manor Nursing Center LLC
1340 E 61st St., Tulsa, OK 74136, (918) 743-8978; Facility type: Skilled care, Alzheimer's; Beds: 170; Certified: Medicaid, Medicare, Veterans; Owner: Proprietary/Public; License: state; Activities: Arts & Crafts; Dances; Support groups; Pet therapy; Group exercise; Outings; Other: Alzheimer's secured unit.

The Mayfair
7707 S Memorial, Tulsa, OK 74133, (918) 250-8571; Facility type: Skilled care, Alzheimer's; Beds: 100; Certified: Medicaid, Medicare; Owner: Peak Medical; License: state; Activities: Arts & Crafts; Pet therapy; Other: Languages: Spanish.

Saint John Medical Center Restorative Care Unit
1923 S Utica, Tulsa, OK 74012, (918) 744-2432; Facility type: Skilled care, Alzheimer's; Beds: 100; Certified: Medicaid, Medicare, Veterans; Owner: Nonprofit; License: state; Activities: Arts & Crafts; Dances; Support groups; Pet therapy; Group exercise; Outings; Other: Home health care.

Saint Simeon's Episcopal Home
3701 N Cincinnati, Tulsa, OK 74106, (918) 425-3583; Facility type: Skilled care, Alzheimer's; Beds: 170; Certified: Medicaid, Medicare, Veterans; Owner: Episcopal Diocese of OK; License: state; Activities: Arts & Crafts; Dances; Support groups; Pet therapy; Other: Alzheimer's secured unit, Assisted living.

Tulsa Christian Care Center
6201 E 36th St., Tulsa, OK 74125, (918) 622-3430; Facility type: Skilled care, Alzheimer's; Beds: 120; Certified: Medicaid; Owner: Church of Christ; License: state; Activities: Arts & Crafts; Dances; Support groups; Pet therapy.

Vinita

Rosewood Terrace
1200 W Canadian, Vinita, OK 74301, (918) 256-8768; Facility type: Skilled care, Alzheimer's; Beds: 100; Certified: Medicaid; Owner: Nonprofit; License: state; Activities: Arts & Crafts; Pet therapy; Other: Alzheimer's secured unit.

Wagoner

Wagoner Care Center
205 N Lincoln, Wagoner, OK 74467, (918) 485-2203; Facility type: Skilled care, Alzheimer's; Beds: 150; Certified: Medicaid; Owner: Nonprofit; License: state; Activities: Crafts; Pet therapy; Group exercise; Outings; Other: Alzheimer's secured unit.

Wilson

Wilson Nursing Center
406 E Main St., Wilson OK 73463, (580) 668-2337; Facility type: Skilled care, Alzheimer's; Beds: 70; Certified: Medicaid; Owner: Proprietary/Public; License: state; Activities: Arts & Crafts; Dances; Support groups; Pet therapy; Group exercise; Outings; Other: Alzheimer's secured unit; Adult day care.

OREGON

Baker City

Saint Elizabeth Care Center
3325 Pocahontas Rd., Baker City, OR 97814, (541) 523-4452; Facility type: Skilled care, Alzheimer's; Beds: 128; Certified: Medicaid, Medicare; Owner: Catholic Health Initiatives; License: state; Activities: Arts & Crafts; Dances; Support groups; Pet therapy; Outings; Other: Affiliations: Catholic Church.

Beaverton

Maryville Nursing Home
14645 SW Farmington Rd., Beaverton, OR 97007, (503) 643-8626; Facility type: Skilled care, Alzheimer's; Beds: 155; Certified: Medicaid, Medicare, Veterans; Owner: Nonprofit/Religious; License: state; Activities: Arts & Crafts; Dances; Support groups; Pet therapy; Other: Alzheimer's secured unit; Languages: Spanish.

Bend

Cascade View Nursing & Alzheimer's Care Center
119 SE Wilson Rd., Bend, OR 97702, (541) 382-

7161; Facility type: Skilled care, Alzheimer's; Beds: 90; Certified: Medicaid, Veterans; Owner: Sun River Living Centers; License: state; Activities: Arts & Crafts; Pet therapy; Exercise; Outings; Other: Alzheimer's secured unit, Adult day care.

Coos Bay

Hearthside Care Center
2625 Koosbay Blvd., Coos Bay, OR 97420, (541) 267-2161; Facility type: Skilled care, Alzheimer's; Beds: 95; Certified: Medicaid, Medicare, Veterans; Owner: Genesis Healthcare ; License: state; Activities: Arts & Crafts; Dances; Support groups; Pet therapy; Group exercise; Outings; Other: Home health care.

Corvallis

Corvallis Manor
160 NE Conifer Blvd., Corvallis, OR 97330, (541) 757-1651; Facility type: Skilled care, Alzheimer's; Beds:110; Certified: Medicaid, Medicare, Veterans; Owner: Private; License: state; Activities: Arts & Crafts; Dances; Support groups; Pet therapy; Other: Alzheimer's secured unit; Languages: Arabic, German, Spanish.

Heart of the Valley Center
2750 NW Harrison Blvd., Corvallis, OR 97330, (541) 757-1763; Facility type: Skilled care, Alzheimer's; Beds: 150; Certified: Medicaid, Medicare; Owner: Private; License: state; Activities: Arts & Crafts; Dances; Support groups; Pet therapy; Group exercise; Outings; Other: Alzheimer's secured unit; Home health care.

Dallas

Dallas Retirement Village Health Care Center
348 W Ellendale, Dallas, OR 97339, (503) 623-5581; Facility type: Skilled care, Alzheimer's; Beds:160; Certified: Medicaid, Medicare, Veterans; Owner: Retirement Management Co; License: state; Activities: Arts & Crafts; Dances; Support groups; Pet therapy; Group exercise; Outings; Other: Alzheimer's secured unit; Languages: German, Spanish; Affiliations: Mennonite.

Eugene

Eugene Rehabilitation & Specialty Care
2360 Chambers St., Eugene, OR 97405, (541) 687-1310; Facility type: Skilled care, Alzheimer's; Beds: 95; Certified: Medicaid, Medicare, Veterans; Owner: Private; License: state; Activities: Arts & Crafts; Dances; Support groups; Pet therapy; Group exercise; Outings; Other: Alzheimer's secured unit; Affiliations: Seventh Day Adventist.

South Hills Health Care Center
1166 E 28th Ave., Eugene, OR 97403, (541) 345-0534; Facility type: Skilled care, Alzheimer's; Beds: 110; Certified: Medicaid, Medicare; Owner: Private; License: state; Activities: Arts & Crafts; Dances; Support groups; Pet therapy; Group exercise; Outings; Other: Alzheimer's secured unit; Adult day care.

Valley West Health Care Center
2300 Warren St., Eugene, OR 97405, (541) 686-2828; Facility type: Skilled care, Alzheimer's; Beds: 90; Certified: Medicaid, Medicare; Owner: Life Care Centers of America; License: state; Activities: Arts & Crafts; Dances; Support groups; Pet therapy; Group exercise; Outings; Other: Alzheimer's secured unit.

Florence

Siuslaw Care Center
1951 21st St., Florence, OR 97439, (541) 997-8436; Facility type: Skilled care, Alzheimer's; Beds: 70; Certified: Medicaid, Medicare, Veterans; Owner: Cascade Health Care; License: state; Activities: Pet therapy; Other: Languages: Spanish.

Forest Grove

Lou-Del Health Care Center
2122 Oak St., Forest Grove, OR 97116 (502) 357-9780; Facility type: Skilled care, Alzheimer's; Beds: 50; Certified: Medicaid, Veterans; Owner: Private; License: state; Activities: Arts & Crafts; Dances; Support groups; Pet therapy; Group exercise; Outings; Other: Alzheimer's secured unit; Languages: Spanish, Swedish.

Gladstone

Gladstone Rehabilitation & Living Center
18000 SE Webster Rd., Gladstone, OR 97027, (503) 656-1644; Facility type: Skilled care, Alzheimer's; Beds:100; Certified: Medicaid, Medicare, Veterans; Owner: Genesis ElderCare; License: state; Activities: Arts & Crafts; Dances; Support groups; Pet therapy; Group exercise; Outings.

Grants Pass

Highland House Nursing & Rehabilitation Center
2201 NW Highland, Grants Pass, OR 97526, (541) 474-1901; Facility type: Skilled care, Alzheimer's; Beds:100; Certified: Medicaid, Medi-

care, Medi-Cal, Veterans; Owner: State & Local Gov; License: state; Activities: Arts & Crafts; Dances; Support groups; Pet therapy; Group exercise; Outings; Other: Alzheimer's secured unit; Languages: German, Spanish.

Royale Gardens Health & Rehabilitation Center
2075 NW Highland Ave., Grants Pass, OR 97526, (541) 476-8891; Facility type: Skilled care, Alzheimer's; Beds: 170; Certified: Medicaid, Medicare; Owner: Private; License: state; Activities: Arts & Crafts; Dances; Support groups; Pet therapy; Outings; Other: Languages: German, Spanish.

Gresham

Village Health Care
3955 SE 182nd Ave., Gresham, OR 97030, (503) 665-0183; Facility type: Skilled care, Alzheimer's; Beds: 105; Certified: Medicaid, Medicare, Veterans; Owner: Private; License: state; Activities: Arts & Crafts; Dances; Support groups; Pet therapy; Group exercise; Outings; Other: Home health care.

Hillsboro

Evergreen Hillsboro Health & Rehabilitation Center
1778 NE Cornell Rd., Hillsboro, OR 97124, (503) 648-6621, http://www.evergreenhealthcare.com Facility type: Skilled care, Alzheimer's; Beds:100; Certified: Medicaid, Medicare; Owner: Evergreen Healthcare Management; License: state; Activities: Arts & Crafts; Support groups; Pet therapy; Group exercise; Outings; Other: Alzheimer's secured unit; Languages: Spanish.

Keizer

Keizer Retirement & Health Care Village
5210 River Rd., N, Keizer, OR 97303, (503) 393-3624; Facility type: Skilled care, Alzheimer's; Beds: 70; Certified: Medicaid, Medicare; Owner: Private; License: state; Activities: Crafts; Support groups; Pet therapy; Greenhouse/Garden; Other: Alzheimer's secured unit: Languages: German, Spanish.

Sherwood Park Care Center
4062 Arleta Ave., NE, Keizer, OR 97303, (503) 390-2271; Facility type: Skilled care, Alzheimer's; Beds: 45; Certified: Medicaid, Medicare; Owner: Perception Health Care; License: state; Activities: Arts & Crafts; Dances; Support groups; Pet therapy; Group exercise; Outings; Other: Alzheimer's secured unit.

Klamath Falls

Plum Ridge Care Center
1401 Bryant Williams Dr., Klamath Falls, OR 97601, (541) 882-6691; Facility type: Skilled care, Alzheimer's; Beds: 100; Certified: Medicaid, Medicare, Medi-Cal, Veterans; Owner: Proprietary/Public; License: state; Activities: Arts & Crafts; Dances; Support groups; Pet therapy; Group exercise; Outings; Other: Alzheimer's secured unit; Languages: Spanish, Sign Language.

La Grande

Evergreen Vista Health Center
103 Adams Ave., La Grande, OR 97850, (541) 963-4184; Facility type: Skilled care, Alzheimer's; Beds: 80; Certified: Medicaid, Medicare, Veterans; Owner: Evergreen Health Care; License: state; Activities: Arts & Crafts; Dances; Support groups; Pet therapy; Group exercise; Outings; Other: Adult day care.

Lebanon

Villa Cascade Care Center
350 S 8th, Lebanon, OR 97355, (541) 259-1221; Facility type: Skilled care, Alzheimer's; Beds: 120; Certified: Medicaid, Medicare; Owner: Marquis Quality Healthcare; License: state; Activities: Arts & Crafts; Greenhouse/Garden; Dances; Support groups; Pet therapy; Group exercise; Outings; Other: Adult day care; Languages: German, Spanish.

McMinnville

Hillside Community
900 N Hill Rd., McMinnville, OR 97128, (503) 472-9534; Facility type: Skilled care, Alzheimer's; Beds: 40; Certified: Medicaid, Medicare, Veterans; Payer mix: 100% Private pay; Owner: Nonprofit/Religious; License: state; Activities: Arts & Crafts; Dances; Support groups; Pet therapy; Group exercise; Outings; Other: Alzheimer's secured unit; Adult day care.

Medford

Hearthstone Manor
2901 E Barnett Rd., Medford, OR 97504, (541) 779-4221; Facility type: Skilled care, Alzheimer's; Beds:160; Certified: Medicaid, Medicare; Owner: Nonprofit; License: state; Activities: Crafts; Dances; Pet therapy; Group exercise; Other: Alzheimer's secured unit; Adult day care; Languages: Norwegian, Spanish.

Rogue Valley Manor
1200 Mira Mar Ave., Medford, OR 97504, (541)

857-7777; Facility type: Skilled care, Alzheimer's; Beds: 100; Certified: Medicare; Payer mix: 100% Private pay; Owner: Nonprofit; License: state; Activities: Arts & Crafts; Dances; Support groups; Pet therapy; Outings; Greenhouse/Garden; Other: Home health care.

Three Fountains Nursing & Rehabilitation
835 Crater Lake Ave., Medford, OR 97504, (541) 773-7717; Facility type: Skilled care, Alzheimer's; Beds: 150; Certified: Medicaid, Medicare, Veterans; Owner: Proprietary/Public; License: state; Activities: Arts & Crafts; Dances; Support groups; Pet therapy; Group exercise; Outings; Other: Languages: German, Italian, Spanish, Tagalog.

Milton Freewater

Evergreen Milton Freewater Health & Rehabilitation Center
120 Elzora St., Milton Freewater, OR 97862, (541) 938-3318; Facility type: Skilled care, Alzheimer's, Assisted Living; Beds: 150; Certified: Medicaid, Medicare, Veterans; Owner: Evergreen Healthcare; License: state; Activities: Arts & Crafts; Dances; Support groups; Pet therapy; Group exercise; Outings; Other: Adult day care; Languages: Spanish.

North Bend

Saint Catherine's Residence
3959 Sheridan Ave., North Bend, OR 97459, (541) 756-4151; Facility type: Skilled care, Alzheimer's; Beds: 100; Certified: Medicaid, Medicare; Owner: Catholic Health Initiatives; License: state; Activities: Arts & Crafts; Dances; Support groups; Pet therapy; Group exercise; Outings; Other: Adult day care.

Ontario

Presbyterian Community Care Center
1085 N Oregon, Ontario, OR 97914 (541) 889-9133; Facility type: Skilled care, Alzheimer's; Beds: 110; Certified: Medicaid, Medicare; Owner: Nonprofit; License: state; Activities: Arts & Crafts; Dances; Support groups; Pet therapy; Group exercise; Outings; Other: Alzheimer's secured unit: Languages: Spanish.

Oregon City

Marquis Care at Oregon City
1680 Molalia Ave., Oregon City, OR 97045, (503) 655-2588; Facility type: Skilled care, Alzheimer's; Beds: 110; Certified: Medicaid, Medicare; Owner: Marquis Quality Healthcare; License: state; Activities: Arts & Crafts; Dances; Support groups; Pet therapy; Group exercise; Outings; Other: Alzheimer's secured unit.

Portland

Cherry Wood Rehabilitation at Mount Tabor
6040 SE Belmont, Portland, OR 97215, (503) 231-7166, Facility type: Skilled care, Alzheimer's; Beds: 165; Certified: Medicaid, Medicare, Veterans; Owner: Nonprofit/Religious; License: state; Activities: Arts & Crafts; Dances; Support groups; Pet therapy; Group exercise; Outings; Other: Languages: Chinese, Spanish, Russian, Vietnamese; Affiliations: Seventh Day Adventist Church.

Glisan Care Center
9750 NE Glisan St., Portland, OR 97220, (503) 256-3920; Facility type: Skilled care, Alzheimer's; Beds: 100; Certified: Medicaid, Medicare, Veterans; Owner: Prestige Care; License: state; Activities: Arts & Crafts; Dances; Support groups; Pet therapy; Group exercise; Other: Alzheimer's secured unit; Languages: Japanese.

Gracelen Terrace
10948 SE Boise St., Portland, OR 97266, (503) 760-1727, http://www.gracelenterrace.com; Facility type: Skilled care, Alzheimer's; Beds: 80; Certified: Medicaid; Owner: Private; License: state; Activities: Arts & Crafts; Dances; Support groups; Pet therapy; Group exercise; Outings; Other: Alzheimer's secured unit.

Holladay Park Plaza
1300 NE 16th Ave., Portland, OR 97232, (503) 288-6671; Facility type: Skilled care, Alzheimer's; Beds: 55; Payer mix: 97% Private pay; Owner: Nonprofit; License: state; Activities: Arts & Crafts; Support groups; Pet therapy; Group exercise; Other: Alzheimer's secured unit; Affiliations: Presbytery of the Cascades.

Mount Saint Joseph
3060 SE Stark St., Portland, OR 97214, (503) 232-6193; Facility type: Skilled care, Alzheimer's; Beds: 200; Certified: Medicaid, Medicare; Owner: Catholic Health Initiatives; License: state; Activities: Arts & Crafts; Dances; Pet therapy; Other: Alzheimer's secured unit; Languages: Spanish, Romanian, Russian.

Redwood Extended Care Center
3540 SE Francis St., Portland, OR 97202, (503) 232-5767; Facility type: Skilled care, Alzheimer's; Beds: 60; Certified: Medicaid, Medicare; Owner: Proprietary/Public; License: state; Activities: Arts & Crafts; Dances; Support groups; Pet therapy; Group exercise; Outings; Other: Alzheimer's secured unit.

Robinson Home
6125 SW Boundary St., Portland, OR 97221, (503) 535-4300; Facility type: Skilled care, Alzheimer's; Beds: 90; Certified: Medicaid, Medicare; Owner: Nonprofit; License: state; Activities: Crafts; Pet therapy; Outings; Other: Alzheimer's secured unit; Languages: Yiddish, Hebrew, Spanish, Russian; Affiliations: Jewish.

Rose City Nursing Home
34 NE 20th Ave., Portland, OR 97232, (503) 231-0276; Facility type: Skilled care, Alzheimer's; Beds: 30; Certified: Medicaid; Owner: Private; License: state; Activities: Arts & Crafts; Dances; Support groups; Pet therapy; Group exercise; Outings; Other: Alzheimer's secured unit, Adult day care.

Saint Jude Care Center
6003 SE 136th Ave., Portland, OR 97236, (503) 761-1155; Facility type: Skilled care, Alzheimer's; Beds: 140; Certified: Medicaid, Veterans; Owner: Proprietary/Public; License: state; Activities: Arts & Crafts; Dances; Support groups; Pet therapy; Group exercise; Outings; Other: Alzheimer's secured unit; Languages: German, Spanish; Affiliations: Order of Charity.

Prineville

Ochoco Care Center
950 N Elm St., Prineville, OR (541) 447-7667; Facility type: Skilled care, Alzheimer's; Beds: 70; Certified: Medicaid, Medicare, Veterans; Owner: Sun River Living Centers; License: state; Activities: Arts & Crafts; Dances; Support groups; Pet therapy; Group exercise; Outings; Other: Languages: Spanish.

Roseburg

Grandview Care Center
1199 NE Grandview Dr., Roseburg, OR 97470, (541) 672-1638; Facility type: Skilled care, Alzheimer's; Beds:100; Certified: Medicaid, Medicare, Veterans; Owner: Life Care Centers of America; License: state; Activities: Arts & Crafts; Dances; Support groups; Pet therapy; Group exercise; Outings; Other: Adult day care.

Mercy Care Rehabilitation Center
525 W Umpqua; Roseburg, OR 97470, (541) 677-2199; Facility type: Skilled care, Alzheimer's; Beds:100; Certified: Medicaid, Medicare, Veterans; Owner: Catholic Health Initiatives; License: state; Activities: Arts & Crafts; Dances; Support groups; Pet therapy; Outings; Other: Alzheimer's secured unit.

Salem

Oak Crest Rehabilitation & Health Services Center
2933 Center St. NE, Salem OR 97301, (503) 585-5850; Facility type: Skilled care, Alzheimer's; Beds: 80; Certified: Medicaid, Medicare, Veterans; Owner: Lenox Healthcare; License: state; Activities: Arts & Crafts; Dances; Support groups; Pet therapy; Group exercise; Outings; Other: Alzheimer's secured unit; Languages: German, Spanish.

Scappoose

Columbia Care Center
33910 E Columbia Ave., Scappoose, OR 97056, (503) 543-7131; Facility type: Skilled care, Alzheimer's; Beds:100; Certified: Medicaid; Owner: Nonprofit; License: state; Activities: Arts & Crafts; Dances; Support groups; Pet therapy; Group exercise; Outings; Other: Alzheimer's secured unit, Adult day care.

Sheridan

Sheridan Care Center
411 SE Sheridan Rd., Sheridan, OR 97378, (503) 843-2204; Facility type: Skilled care, Alzheimer's; Beds: 60; Certified: Medicaid; Owner: Private; License: state; Activities: Arts & Crafts; Dances; Support groups; Pet therapy; Group exercise; Outings; Other: Adult day care, Hospice.

Sublimity

Marian Estates
390 Church St., Sublimity, OR 97385, (503) 769-3499, http://www.marianestatesinc.com; Facility type: Skilled care, Alzheimer's; Beds: 100; Certified: Medicaid, Medicare; Owner: Proprietary/Public; License: state; Activities: Arts & Crafts; Dances; Support groups; Pet therapy; Group exercise; Outings; Other: Alzheimer's secured unit.

Troutdale

Village Manor
2060 NE 238th Dr., Troutdale, OR 97060, (503) 491-0553; Facility type: Skilled care, Alzheimer's; Beds: 60; Certified: Medicaid, Veterans; Owner: Proprietary/Public; License: state; Activities: Arts & Crafts; Dances; Support groups; Pet therapy; Group exercise; Outings; Other: Alzheimer's secured unit.

West Linn

Rose Linn Care Center
2330 DeBok Rd., West Linn, OR 97068, (503) 655-6331; Facility type: Skilled care, Alzheimer's; Beds: 60; Certified: Medicaid; Owner: Proprietary/Public; License: state; Activities: Arts & Crafts; Dances; Support groups; Pet therapy; Group exercise; Outings; Other: Alzheimer's secured unit: Languages: Spanish

---

PENNSYLVANIA

Allentown

Cedarbrook Nursing Home
350 S Cedarbrook Rd., Allentown, PA 18104, (610) 395-3727; Facility type: Skilled care, Alzheimer's; Beds: 600; Certified: Medicaid, Medicare; Owner: State & Local Gov; License: state; Activities: Arts & Crafts; Dances; Support groups; Pet therapy; Group exercise; Outings; Other: Languages: Arabic, French, German, Filipino, Hungarian, Italian, PA Dutch, Korean.

Luther Crest Nursing Facility
800 Hausman Rd., Allentown, PA 18104, (610) 398-8011; Facility type: Skilled care, Alzheimer's; Beds: 90; Certified: Medicaid, Medicare; Owner: Lutheran Services Northeast; License: state; Activities: Arts & Crafts; Dances; Support groups; Pet therapy; Group exercise; Outings; Other: Languages: Spanish.

Phoebe Home
1925 Turner St., Allentown, PA 18104, (610) 435-9037; Facility type: Skilled care, Alzheimer's; Beds: 400; Certified: Medicaid, Medicare; Owner: Nonprofit; License: state; Activities: Arts & Crafts; Dances; Support groups; Pet therapy; Group exercise; Outings; Other: Alzheimer's secured unit.

Allison Park

Rebecca Residence for Protestant Ladies
3746 Cedar Ridge Rd., Allison Park, PA 15101, (724) 444-0600; Facility type: Skilled care, Alzheimer's; Beds: 40; Certified: Medicaid; Payer mix: 100% Private pay; Owner: Proprietary/Public; License: state; Activities: Crafts; Pet therapy; Group exercise; Outings; Other: Alzheimer's secured unit.

Altoona

Beverly Healthcare—Hillview
700 S Cayuga Ave., Altoona, PA 16602, (814) 946-0471; Facility type: Skilled care, Alzheimer's; Beds: 135; Certified: Medicaid, Medicare, Veterans; Owner: Beverly Enterprises; License: state; Activities: Arts & Crafts; Dances; Support groups; Pet therapy; Group exercise; Outings; Other: Alzheimer's secured unit.

Ambler

Ambler Rest Center
3 S Bethlehem Pk, Ambler, PA, (215) 646-7050; Facility type: Skilled care, Alzheimer's; Beds: 100; Certified: Medicaid; Owner: Proprietary/Public; License: state; Activities: Arts & Crafts; Dances; Support groups; Pet therapy.

Artman Community
250 N Bethlehem Pk, Ambler, PA 19002, (21) 643-6333; http://www.artmanhome.com; Facility type: Skilled care, Alzheimer's; Beds: 100; Certified: Medicaid, Medicare; Owner: Nonprofit; License: state; Activities: Arts & Crafts; Support groups; Pet therapy; Other: Affiliations: Lutheran Evangelic Church.

Annville

United Christian Church Home
520 N Rte. 934, Annville, PA 17003; (717) 867-4636; Facility type: Skilled care, Alzheimer's; Beds: 35; Certified: Medicaid, Medicare; Owner: Nonprofit; License: state; Activities: Arts & Crafts; Dances; Support groups; Pet therapy.

Beaver Falls

Blair Nursing & Personal Care
1031 Mercer Rd., Beaver Falls, PA 15010, (724) 843-2209; Facility type: Skilled care, Alzheimer's; Beds: 200; Certified: Medicaid, Medicare; Owner: State & Local Gov; License: state; Activities: Arts & Crafts; Dances; Support groups; Pet therapy; Group exercise; Other: Alzheimer's secured unit, Adult day care.

Bellefonte

Centre Crest
502 E Howard St., Bellefonte, PA 16823, (814) 355-6777; Facility type: Skilled care, Alzheimer's; Beds: 220; Certified: Medicaid, Medicare; Owner: State & Local Gov; License: state; Activities: Arts & Crafts; Dances; Support groups;

Pet therapy; Group exercise; Outings; Other: Alzheimer's secured unit, Adult day care.

Bethel Park

Manor Care Health Services
60 Highland Rd., Bethel Park, PA 15102, (412) 831-6050; Facility type: Skilled care, Alzheimer's; Beds: 160; Certified: Medicaid, Medicare; Owner: HCR Manor Care; License: state; Activities: Arts & Crafts; Dances; Support groups; Pet therapy; Exercise; Outings; Other: Alzheimer's secured unit, Adult day care.

Meadowcrest Nursing Center
1200 Braun Rd., Bethel Park, PA 15102, (412) 854-5500; Facility type: Skilled care, Alzheimer's; Beds: 40; Certified: Medicaid, Medicare, Veterans; Owner: Extendicare Health Services; License: state; Activities: Arts & Crafts; Dances; Support groups; Pet therapy; Group exercise; Other: Alzheimer's secured unit.

Bethlehem

Blough Health Care Center
316 E Market St., Bethlehem, PA 18018, (610) 886-4982; Facility type: Skilled care, Alzheimer's; Beds: 100; Certified: Medicaid, Medicare; Owner: Proprietary/Public; License: state; Activities: Arts & Crafts; Dances; Support groups; Pet therapy; Group exercise; Outings; Other: Languages: Spanish.

Cedarbrook Fountain Hill Nursing Home
724 Delaware Ave., Bethlehem, PA 18015, (610) 691-6700; Facility type: Skilled care, Alzheimer's; Beds: 200; Certified: Medicaid, Medicare; Owner: State & Local Gov; License: state; Activities: Arts & Crafts; Dances; Support groups; Pet therapy; Group exercise; Outings; Other: Alzheimer's secured unit.

Bradford

Bradford Nursing Pavilion
200 Pleasant St., Bradford, PA, 16701, (814) 362-8293; http://www.bfdmed.org; Facility type: Skilled care, Alzheimer's; Beds: 100; Certified: Medicaid, Medicare; Owner: Proprietary/Public; License: state; Activities: Arts & Crafts; Dances; Support groups; Pet therapy; Group exercise; Other: Alzheimer's secured unit.

Bristol

Silver Lake Nursing & Rehabilitation Center
905 Tower Rd., Bristol, PA 19007, (215) 785-3201; Facility type: Skilled care, Alzheimer's; Beds: 175; Certified: Medicaid, Medicare, Veterans; Owner: Genesis ElderCare; License: state; Activities: Arts & Crafts; Dances; Support groups; Pet therapy; Group exercise; Other: Alzheimer's secured unit.

Broomall

Broomall Presbyterian Village
146 Maple Rd., Broomall, PA 19008, (610) 358-0100; Facility type: Skilled care, Alzheimer's; Beds: 150; Certified: Medicaid, Medicare; Owner: Nonprofit; License: state; Activities: Arts & Crafts; Dances; Support groups; Pet therapy; Group exercise; Outings; Other: Alzheimer's secured unit.

Bryn Mawr

Beaumont at Bryn Mawr
601 N Ithan Ave., Bryn Mawr, PA 19010, (610) 526-7000; Facility type: Skilled care, Alzheimer's; Beds: 50; Certified: Medicaid, Medicare; Owner: Proprietary/Public; License: state; Activities: Arts & Crafts; Support groups; Pet therapy.

Bryn Mawr Terrace Convalescent Center
Haverford & Rugby Rds, Bryn Mawr, PA 19010, (610) 525-8300; Facility type: Skilled care, Alzheimer's; Beds: 150; Certified: Medicare; Owner: Proprietary/Public; License: state; Activities: Arts & Crafts; Dances; Support groups; Pet therapy; Group exercise; Outings; Other: Alzheimer's secured unit.

Carlisle

Chapel Pointe at Carlisle
770 S Hanover St., Carlisle, PA 17013, (717) 249-1363; Facility type: Skilled care, Alzheimer's; Beds: 60; Certified: Medicaid, Medicare; Owner: Nonprofit: state; Activities: Arts & Crafts; Dances; Support groups; Pet therapy; Group exercise; Outings; Other: Affiliations: Christian & Missionary Alliance.

Claremont Nursing & Rehabilitation Center
375 Claremont Dr., Carlisle, PA 17013, (717) 243-2031; Facility type: Skilled care, Alzheimer's; Beds: 150; Certified: Medicaid, Medicare, Veterans; Owner: State & Local Gov; License: state; Activities: Arts & Crafts; Dances; Support groups; Pet therapy; Group exercise; Outings; Other: Alzheimer's secured unit; Languages: Spanish, Korean, Tagalog.

Forest Park Health Center
700 Walnut Bottom Rd., Carlisle, PA 17013, (717) 243-1032; Facility type: Skilled care, Alzheimer's; Beds: 100; Certified: Medicaid, Medi-

care; Owner: Presbyterian Homes, Inc.; License: state; Activities: Arts & Crafts; Dances; Support groups; Pet therapy; Group exercise; Outings; Other: Alzheimer's secured unit.

Chambersburg

Falling Spring Nursing & Rehabilitation Center
201 Franklin Farm Ln., Chambersburg, PA 17201, (717) 264-2715; Facility type: Skilled care, Alzheimer's; Beds: 300; Certified: Medicaid, Medicare; Owner: State & Local Gov; License: state; Activities: Arts & Crafts; Support groups; Pet therapy; Other: Alzheimer's secured unit.

Manor Care Health Services
1070 Stouffer Ave., Chambersburg, PA 17201, (717) 263-0436; Facility type: Skilled care, Alzheimer's; Beds: 200; Certified: Medicaid, Medicare; Owner: HCR Manor Care; License: state; Activities: Arts & Crafts; Dances; Support groups; Pet therapy; Group exercise; Outings; Other: Alzheimer's secured unit.

Menno Haven
2075 Scotland Ave., Chambersburg, PA 17201, (717) 263-8545; Facility type: Skilled care, Alzheimer's; Beds: 100; Certified: Medicaid, Medicare; Owner: Mennonite Church; License: state; Activities: Arts & Crafts; Dances; Support groups; Pet therapy; Group exercise; Outings; Other: Alzheimer's secured unit, Adult day care.

Shook Home
55 S 2nd Ave., Chambersburg, PA 17201, (717) 264-6815; Facility type: Skilled care, Alzheimer's; Beds: 40; Certified: Medicaid, Medicare; Owner: Nonprofit; License: state; Activities: Arts & Crafts; Dances; Support groups; Pet therapy; Group exercise; Outings; Other: Languages: Spanish.

Chester

Chester Care Center
15th St. & Shaw Terr, Chester, PA 19013, (610) 499-8800; Facility type: Skilled care, Alzheimer's; Beds: 260; Certified: Medicaid, Medicare; Owner: Keystone Care; License: state; Activities: Arts & Crafts; Dances; Support groups; Pet therapy; Other: Alzheimer's secured unit; Languages: Arabic, Spanish.

Coudersport

Sweden Valley Manor
1028 E 2nd St., Coudersport, PA 16915, (814) 274-7610; Facility type: Skilled care, Alzheimer's; Beds: 120; Certified: Medicaid, Medicare; Owner: Proprietary/Public; License: state; Activities: Arts & Crafts; Support groups; Pet therapy; Group exercise; Outings; Other: Alzheimer's secured unit; Affiliation: Catholic Church.

Danville

Gold Star Nursing Home
303 Schoolhouse Rd., Danville, PA 17821, (570) 275-4946; Facility type: Skilled care, Alzheimer's; Beds: 100; Certified: Medicaid, Medicare; Owner: Grand View Health Homes; License: state; Activities: Arts & Crafts; Dances; Support groups; Pet therapy; Group exercise; Outings.

Darby

Saint Francis Country House
1412 Landsdowne Ave., Darby, PA 19023, (610) 461-6510; Facility type: Skilled care, Alzheimer's; Beds: 100; Certified: Medicaid, Medicare; Owner: Nonprofit; License: state; Activities: Arts & Crafts; Dances; Support groups; Pet therapy; Outings; Other: Alzheimer's secured unit; Affiliations: Catholic Church.

Doylestown

Briarleaf Nursing & Convalescent Center
252 Belmont, Doylestown, PA 18901; (215) 348-2983; Facility type: Skilled care, Alzheimer's; Beds: 120; Certified: Medicare; Owner: Accord Health Services; License: state; Activities: Arts & Crafts; Dances; Support groups; Pet therapy; Other: Alzheimer's secured unit: Languages: French.

Pine Run Health Center
777 Ferry Rd., Doylestown, PA 18901, (215) 348-7700; Facility type: Skilled care, Alzheimer's; Beds: 200; Certified: Medicaid, Medicare; Owner: Constellation Senior Services; License: state; Activities: Arts & Crafts; Dances; Support groups; Pet therapy; Group exercise; Outings; Other: Alzheimer's secured unit, Adult day care, Home health care.

Easton

Easton Home
1022 Northampton St., Easton, PA 18042, (610) 258-7773; Facility type: Skilled care, Alzheimer's; Beds: 50; Private pay-99%; Owner: Presbyterian Homes Inc.; License: state; Activities: Arts & Crafts; Dances; Support groups; Pet therapy; Group exercise; Outings; Other: Alzheimer's secured unit, Adult day care.

Easton Nursing Center
498 Washington St., Easton, PA 18042, (610)

258-2985; http://www.pennmed.com; Facility type: Skilled care, Alzheimer's; Beds: 180; Certified: Medicaid, Medicare, Veterans; Owner: Penn Med Consultants; License: state; Activities: Arts & Crafts; Dances; Support groups; Pet therapy; Group exercise; Outings; Other: Alzheimer's secured unit; Languages: Spanish.

Praxis Alzheimer's Facility
500 Washington St., Easton, PA 18041, (610) 253-3573; Facility type: Skilled care, Alzheimer's; Beds: 110; Certified: Medicaid, Medicare; Owner: Penn Med Consultants; License: state; Activities: Arts & Crafts; Dances; Support groups; Pet therapy; Group exercise; Outings; Other: Alzheimer's secured unit; Languages: Chinese, Polish, Spanish.

Elizabethtown

Manor Care Health Services
320 S Market St., Elizabethtown, PA 17022, (717) 367-1377; Facility type: Skilled care, Alzheimer's, Assisted Living; Beds: 60; Certified: Medicaid, Medicare; Owner: HCR Manor Care; License: state; Activities: Arts & Crafts; Dances; Support groups; Pet therapy; Group exercise; Outings.

Masonic Homes
One Masonic Dr., Elizabethtown, PA 17022, (717) 367-1121; Facility type: Skilled care, Alzheimer's; Beds: 120; Certified: Medicaid, Medicare; Owner: Nonprofit; License: state; Activities: Arts & Crafts; Dances; Support groups; Pet therapy; Other: Alzheimer's secured unit, Adult day Care; Affiliations: Pennsylvania Freemasons.

Erie

Ball Pavilion
5416 E Lake Rd., Erie, PA 16511, (814) 899-8600; Facility type: Skilled care, Alzheimer's; Beds: 80; Certified: Medicaid, Medicare; Owner: Nonprofit; License: state; Activities: Arts & Crafts; Dances; Support groups; Pet therapy; Group exercise; Outings; Other: Alzheimer's secured unit; Affiliations: Episcopalian Church.

Beverly Healthcare
2686 Peach St., Erie, PA 16508 (814) 453-6641; Facility type: Skilled care, Alzheimer's; Beds: 100; Certified: Medicaid, Medicare, Veterans; Owner: Beverly Enterprises; License: state; Activities: Arts & Crafts; Support groups; Pet therapy; Group exercise; Outings; Other: Alzheimer's secured unit, Home health care.

Pennsylvania Soldiers' & Sailors' Home
560 E 3rd St., Erie, PA 16512, (814) 871-4531; Facility type: Skilled care, Alzheimer's; Beds: 180; Certified: Medicaid, Medicare; Owner: State & Local Gov; License: state; Activities: Arts & Crafts; Dances; Support groups; Pet therapy; Group exercise; Outings.

Saint Mary's Home of Erie
607 E 26th St., Erie, PA 16504, (814) 459-0621; Facility type: Skilled care, Alzheimer's; Beds: 220; Certified: Medicaid, Medicare; Owner: Nonprofit; License: state; Activities: Arts & Crafts; Dances; Support groups; Pet therapy; Group exercise; Outings; Other: Alzheimer's secured unit; Affiliations: Catholic Church.

Sarah A Reed Retirement Center
227 W 22 St., Erie, PA 16502, (814) 878-2600; Facility type: Skilled care, Alzheimer's; Beds: 150; Certified: Medicaid, Medicare; Owner: Nonprofit; License: state; Activities: Arts & Crafts; Dances; Support groups; Pet therapy; Group exercise; Outings; Other: Alzheimer's secured unit.

Gettysburg

Beverly Healthcare & Rehabilitation Center
741 Chambersburg Rd., Gettysburg, PA 17325, (717) 334-6764; Facility type: Skilled care, Alzheimer's; Beds: 100; Certified: Medicaid, Medicare, Veterans; Owner: Beverly Enterprises; License: state; Activities: Arts & Crafts; Dances; Pet therapy; Group exercise; Outings; Other: Adult day care.

Shepherd's Choice
867 York Rd., Gettysburg, PA 17325, (717) 337-3238; Facility type: Skilled care, Alzheimer's; Beds: 120; Certified: Medicaid, Medicare, Veterans; Owner: Affinity Health Services; License: state; Activities: Arts & Crafts; Dances; Support groups; Pet therapy; Group exercise; Outings; Other: Alzheimer's secured unit.

Glenside

Edgehill Nursing & Rehabilitation Center
146 Edgehill Rd., Glenside, PA 19038, (215) 886-1043; Facility type: Skilled care, Alzheimer's; Beds: 60; Certified: Medicaid, Medicare; Owner: AmCare; License: state; Activities: Crafts; Outings; Pet therapy.

Greensburg

Saint Anne Home
685 Angela Dr., Greensburg, PA 15601, (724) 837-6070; Facility type: Skilled care, Alzheimer's; Beds: 160; Certified: Medicaid, Medicare, Veterans; Owner: Nonprofit; License: state; Activities: Arts & Crafts; Pet therapy; Group exercise; Other: Languages: Italian, Polish; Affiliations: Catholic Church, Felician Sisters.

Westmoreland Manor
2480 S Grande Blvd., Greensburg, PA 15601, (724) 830-4000; Facility type: Skilled care, Alzheimer's; Beds: 200; Certified: Medicaid, Medicare; Owner: State & Local Gov, Complete Care Services; License: state; Activities: Arts & Crafts; Dances; Support groups; Pet therapy; Outings; Other: Alzheimer's secured unit.

Grove City

Buchannan Commons
400 Hillcrest Ave., Grove City, PA 16127, (724) 458-9501; Facility type: Skilled care, Alzheimer's; Beds: 120; Certified: Medicaid, Medicare, Veterans; Owner: Genesis ElderCare; License: state; Activities: Arts & Crafts; Dances; Support groups; Pet therapy; Group exercise; Outings; Other: Alzheimer's secured unit.

Grove Manor
435 N Broad St., Grove City, PA 16127, (724) 458-7800; Facility type: Skilled care, Alzheimer's; Beds: 100; Certified: Medicare; Payer mix: 98% Private pay; Owner: ExtendiCare; License: state; Activities: Arts & Crafts; Dances; Support groups; Pet therapy; Group exercise; Outings; Other: Alzheimer's secured unit, Adult day care.

Hanover

Hanover Hall
267 Frederick St., Hanover, PA 17331, (717) 637-8937; Facility type: Skilled care, Alzheimer's; Beds: 150; Certified: Medicaid, Medicare, Veterans; Owner: Proprietary/Public; License: state; Activities: Arts & Crafts; Dances; Support groups; Pet therapy; Group exercise; Outings; Other: Alzheimer's secured unit.

Homewood at Hanover PA
425 Westminister Ave., Hanover, PA 17331, (717) 637-4166; Facility type: Skilled care, Alzheimer's; Beds: 180; Certified: Medicaid, Medicare; Owner: Nonprofit; License: state; Activities: Arts & Crafts; Dances; Support groups; Pet therapy; Group exercise; Outings; Other: Alzheimer's secured unit.

Harrisburg

Blue Ridge East
3625 N Progress Ave., Harrisburg, PA 17110, (717) 652-2345; Facility type: Skilled care, Alzheimer's; Beds: 100; Certified: Medicaid, Medicare, Veterans; Owner: Beverly Enterprises; License: state; Activities: Arts & Crafts; Dances; Support groups; Pet therapy; Group exercise; Outings; Other: Languages: Spanish.

Dauphin Manor
1205 S 28th St., Harrisburg, PA 17111, (717) 558-1000; Facility type: Skilled care, Alzheimer's; Beds: 400; Certified: Medicaid, Medicare, Veterans; Owner: State & Local Gov; License: state; Activities: Arts & Crafts; Dances; Support groups; Pet therapy; Group exercise; Outings; Other: Alzheimer's secured unit, Adult day care; Languages: Polish, Russian, Spanish, Ukrainian, Vietnamese.

Homeland Center
1901 N 5th St., Harrisburg, PA 17102, (717) 221-7900; Facility type: Skilled care, Alzheimer's; Beds: 100; Certified: Medicaid, Medicare, Veterans; Owner: Nonprofit; License: state; Activities: Arts & Crafts; Dances; Support groups; Pet therapy; Group exercise; Outings; Other: Alzheimer's secured unit.

Jewish Home of Greater Harrisburg
4000 Linglestown Rd., Harrisburg, PA 17112, (717) 657-0700; Facility type: Skilled care, Alzheimer's; Beds: 140; Certified: Medicaid, Medicare; Owner: Nonprofit/Religious; License: state; Activities: Arts & Crafts; Dances; Pet therapy; Group exercise; Outings; Other: Affiliations: Jewish.

Susquehanna Center for Nursing & Rehabilitation
1909 N Front St., Harrisburg, PA 17102, (717) 234-4600; Facility type: Skilled care, Alzheimer's; Beds: 180; Certified: Medicaid, Medicare, Veterans; Owner: Genesis ElderCare; License: state; Activities: Arts & Crafts; Dances; Support groups; Pet therapy; Other: Alzheimer's secured unit.

Hazleton

Mountain City Nursing & Geriatric Center
1000 W 27th St., Hazleton, PA 18201, (570) 454-8888; Facility type: Skilled care, Alzheimer's; Beds: 180; Certified: Medicaid, Medicare; Owner: Proprietary/Public; License: state; Activities: Arts & Crafts; Dances; Support groups; Pet therapy; Group exercise; Outings; Other: Alzheimer's secured unit.

Saint Luke Pavilion
1000 Stacie Dr., Hazleton, PA 18201, (570) 453-5100; Facility type: Skilled care, Alzheimer's; Beds: 120; Certified: Medicaid, Medicare, Veterans; Owner: Nonprofit; License: state; Activities: Arts & Crafts; Dances; Support groups; Pet therapy; Group exercise; Outings; Affiliations: Lutheran.

Hershey

IHS of Hershey at Woodlands
820 Rhue Haus Ln., Hershey, PA 17033, (717) 533-3351; Facility type: Skilled care, Alzheimer's, Assisted Living; Beds: 200; Certified: Medicaid, Medicare, Veterans; Owner: Integrated Health Services; License: state; Activities: Arts & Crafts; Dances; Support groups; Pet therapy; Group exercise; Outings.

Hollidaysburg

Hollidaysburg Veterans Home
PO Box 319, Hollidaysburg, PA 16648, (814) 696-5201; Facility type: Skilled care, Alzheimer's; Beds: 260; Certified: Medicaid, Medicare, Veterans; Owner: State & Local Gov; License: state; Activities: Arts & Crafts; Dances; Support groups; Pet therapy; Group exercise; Outings.

Honey Brook

Tel Hai Nursing Center
1100 Tel Hai Cir., Honey Brook PA 19344, (610) 273-9333; Facility type: Skilled care, Alzheimer's; Beds: 140; Certified: Medicaid, Medicare; Owner: Nonprofit; License: state; Activities: Arts & Crafts; Dances; Support groups; Pet therapy; Group exercise; Outings; Other: Alzheimer's secured unit, Adult day care.

Indiana

Beacon Manor
1515 Wayne Ave., Indiana, PA 15701, (724) 349-5300; Facility type: Skilled care, Alzheimer's; Beds: 130; Certified: Medicaid, Medicare; Owner: Proprietary/Public; License: state; Activities: Arts & Crafts; Dances; Support groups; Pet therapy; Group exercise; Greenhouse/Garden.

Saint Andrew's Village
1155 Indian Springs Rd., Indiana, PA 15701, (724) 349-4870; Facility type: Skilled care, Alzheimer's; Beds: 200; Certified: Medicaid, Medicare; Owner: Presbyterian Homes, Inc.; License: state; Activities: Arts & Crafts; Dances; Support groups; Pet therapy; Other: Alzheimer's secured unit, Adult day care.

Johnstown

Laurel Wood Care Center
100 Woodmont Rd., Johnstown, PA 15905, (814) 255-1488; Facility type: Skilled care, Alzheimer's; Beds: 200; Certified: Medicaid, Medicare, Veterans; Owner: Grane Healthcare; License: state; Activities: Arts & Crafts; Dances; Support groups; Pet therapy; Group exercise; Outings; Greenhouse/Garden.

Kittanning

Armstrong County Health Center
265 S McKean St., Kittanning, PA 16201, (724) 548-2222; Facility type: Skilled care, Alzheimer's; Beds: 180; Certified: Medicaid, Medicare; Owner: State & Local Gov; License: state; Activities: Arts & Crafts; Dances; Support groups; Pet therapy; Group exercise; Outings; Other: Alzheimer's secured unit.

Kittanning Care Center
Rd., 1 Rte. 422 E, Kittanning, PA 16201, (724) 545-2273; Facility type: Skilled care, Alzheimer's; Beds: 120; Certified: Medicaid, Medicare; Owner: State & Local Gov; License: state; Activities: Arts & Crafts; Dances; Support groups; Pet therapy; Group exercise; Outings; Other: Alzheimer's secured unit.

Lancaster

Calvary Fellowship Homes
502 Elizabeth Dr., Lancaster, PA 17601, (717) 393-0711; Facility type: Skilled care, Alzheimer's; Beds: 50; Certified: Medicaid, Medicare; Owner: Nonprofit; License: state; Activities: Arts & Crafts; Dances; Support groups; Pet therapy; Group exercise; Outings; Other: Affiliations: Overseas Missionary Fellowship.

Conestoga View
900 E King St., Lancaster, PA 17602, (717) 299-7853; Facility type: Skilled care, Alzheimer's; Beds: 400; Certified: Medicaid, Medicare, Veterans; Owner: State & Local Gov; License: state; Activities: Arts & Crafts; Dances; Support groups; Pet therapy; Group exercise; Outings; Other: Alzheimer's secured unit.

Village Vista Skilled Nursing Facility
1941 Benmar Dr., Lancaster, PA 17603, (717) 397-5583; Facility type: Skilled care, Alzheimer's; Beds: 50; Certified: Medicaid, Medicare, Veterans; Owner: Proprietary/Public; License: state; Activities: Arts & Crafts; Dances; Support groups; Pet therapy; Group exercise; Outings; Other: Alzheimer's secured unit; Languages: Italian, Spanish.

Langhorne

Attleboro Nursing & Rehabilitation Center
300 E Winchester Ave., Langhorne, PA 19046, (215) 757-3739; Facility type: Skilled care, Alzheimer's; Beds: 160; Certified: Medicaid, Medicare; Owner: Private; License: state; Activities:

Arts & Crafts; Dances; Support groups; Pet therapy; Group exercise; Outings; Other: Alzheimer's secured unit.

Lansdale

Brittany Pointe Estates
1001 Valley Forge Rd., Lansdale, PA 19446, (215) 855-9700; Facility type: Skilled care, Alzheimer's; Beds: 90; Certified: Medicaid, Medicare; Owner: Acts Retirement Life Communities; License: state; Activities: Arts & Crafts; Dances; Support groups; Pet therapy; Group exercise; Outings; Other: Alzheimer's secured unit.

Lititz

Moravian Manor
300 W Lemon St. Lititz, PA 17543, (717) 626-0214; Facility type: Skilled care, Alzheimer's; Beds: 120; Certified: Medicaid, Medicare, Veterans; Owner: Moravian Church; License: state; Activities: Arts & Crafts; Dances; Support groups; Pet therapy; Group exercise; Outings; Other: Alzheimer's secured unit, Hospice.

Mechanicsburg

Messiah Village
100 T Allen Dr., Mechanicsburg, PA 17055, (717) 697-4666; Facility type: Skilled care, Alzheimer's; Beds: 190; Certified: Medicaid, Medicare; Owner: Brethren in Christ Church; License: state; Activities: Arts & Crafts; Dances; Support groups; Pet therapy; Group exercise; Outings; Other: Alzheimer's secured unit.

New Castle

Haven Convalescent Home
725 Paul St., New Castle, PA 16101, (724) 654-8833; Facility type: Skilled care, Alzheimer's; Beds: 90; Certified: Medicaid; Owner: Proprietary/Public; License: state; Activities: Arts & Crafts; Dances; Support groups; Pet therapy; Group exercise; Outings; Other: Languages: Italian.

Silver Oaks Nursing Center
715 Harbor St., New Castle, PA 16101, (724) 652-3863; Facility type: Skilled care, Alzheimer's; Beds: 70; Certified: Medicaid, Medicare, Veterans; Owner: Penn Med Consultants; License: state; Activities: Arts & Crafts; Dances; Support groups; Pet therapy; Outings; Other: Alzheimer's secured unit.

Newtown

Chandler Hall
99 Barclay St., Newtown, PA 18940, (215) 860-4000; Facility type: Skilled care, Alzheimer's; Beds: 120; Certified: Medicaid, Medicare, Veterans; Owner: Nonprofit; License: state; Activities: Arts & Crafts; Dances; Support groups; Pet therapy; Group exercise; Outings; Other: Adult day care; Languages: German, Spanish.

Pennswood Village
1382 Newtown Langhorne Rd., Newtown, PA 18940, (215) 968-9110, http://www.pennswood.org; Facility type: Skilled care, Alzheimer's; Beds: 100; Certified: Medicare; Owner: Nonprofit; License: state; Activities: Arts & Crafts; Dances; Support groups; Pet therapy; Group exercise; Outings; Other: Alzheimer's secured unit; Affiliations: Society of Friends

Newtown Square

Dunwoody Village
3500 W Chester Pike, Newtown Square, PA 19073, (610) 359-4400; Facility type: Skilled care, Alzheimer's; Beds: 110; Certified: Medicare; Payer mix: 100% Private pay; Owner: Nonprofit; License: state; Activities: Arts & Crafts; Dances; Support groups; Pet therapy; Group exercise; Outings; Other: Alzheimer's secured unit.

Oil City

Beverly Healthcare
1293 Grandview Rd., Oil City, PA 16301, (814) 676-8208; Facility type: Skilled care, Alzheimer's; Beds: 100; Certified: Medicaid, Medicare, Veterans; Owner: Beverly Enterprises; License: state; Activities: Arts & Crafts; Dances; Support groups; Pet therapy; Group exercise; Outings; Other: Alzheimer's secured unit.

Olyphant

Lackawanna County Health Care Center
Sturges Rd., Olyphant, PA 18447, (570) 489-8611; Facility type: Skilled care, Alzheimer's; Beds: 280; Certified: Medicaid, Medicare, Veterans; Owner: State & Local Gov; License: state; Activities: Crafts; Support groups; Pet therapy; Other: Alzheimer's secured unit; Languages: Italian, Polish, Russian.

Philadelphia

Ashton Hall Nursing & Rehabilitation Center
2109 Red Lion Rd., Philadelphia, PA 19115, (215) 673-7000; Facility type: Skilled care, Alzhei-

mer's; Beds: 140; Certified: Medicaid, Medicare, Veterans; Owner: Private; License: state; Activities: Arts & Crafts; Dances; Support groups; Pet therapy; Group exercise; Other: Alzheimer's secured unit.

Baptist Home of Philadelphia
8301 Roosevelt Blvd., Philadelphia, PA 19152, (215) 624-7575; Facility type: Skilled care, Alzheimer's; Beds: 350; Certified: Medicaid, Medicare, Veterans; Owner: Baptist Church; License: state; Activities: Arts & Crafts; Dances; Pet therapy; Group exercise; Outings; Other: Alzheimer's secured unit.

Care Pavilion of Walnut Park
6212 Walnut St., Philadelphia, PA 19139, (215) 476-6264; Facility type: Skilled care, Alzheimer's; Beds: 400; Certified: Medicaid, Medicare, Veterans; Owner: Genesis Elder Care; License: state; Activities: Arts & Crafts; Dances; Pet therapy; Group exercise; Outings; Reading Groups; Shopping trips.

Cheltenham Nursing & Rehabilitation Center
600 W Cheltenham Ave., Philadelphia, PA 19126, (215) 927-7300; Facility type: Skilled care, Alzheimer's; Beds: 350; Certified: Medicaid, Medicare, Veterans; Owner: Nonprofit; License: state; Activities: Arts & Crafts; Pet therapy; Outings; Other: Alzheimer's secured unit; Languages: Spanish.

Gemantown Home
6950 Germantown Ave., Philadelphia, PA 19119, (215) 951-7602: Facility type: Skilled care, Alzheimer's; Beds: 180; Certified: Medicaid, Medicare; Owner: Genesis Elder Care; License: state; Activities: Arts & Crafts; Dances; Pet therapy; Group exercise; Outings; Other: Adult day care; Languages: French, German, Italian, Spanish; Affiliations: Lutheran.

Mercy Douglass Human Services Center
4508 38 Chestnut St., Philadelphia, PA 19139, (215) 382-9490; Facility type: Skilled care, Alzheimer's; Beds: 180; Certified: Medicaid, Medicare, Veterans; Owner: Mercy Douglass Company; License: state; Activities: Arts & Crafts; Dances; Pet therapy; Group exercise; Outings; Other: Home health care.

Northwood Nursing & Convalescent Center
4621 Castor Ave., Philadelphia, PA 19124; Facility type: Skilled care, Alzheimer's; Beds: 150; Certified: Medicaid, Medicare, Veterans; Owner: Complete Care Services; License: state; Activities: Arts & Crafts; Dances; Pet therapy; Group exercise; Outings; Other: Alzheimer's secured unit.

Temple Continuing Care Center
5301 Old York Rd., Philadelphia, PA 19141, (215) 456-2900; Facility type: Skilled care, Alzheimer's; Beds: 150; Certified: Medicaid, Medicare; Owner: Nonprofit; License: state; Activities: Arts & Crafts; Dances; Pet therapy; Group exercise; Outings; Other: Alzheimer's secured unit; Adult day care; Languages: Russian; Affiliations: Jewish.

Pittsburgh

Asbury Health Center
700 Bower Hill Rd., Pittsburgh, PA 15243 (412) 341-1030; Facility type: Skilled care, Alzheimer's; Beds: 150; Certified: Medicaid, Medicare; Owner: United Methodist Church; License: state; Activities: Arts & Crafts; Dances; Pet therapy; Group exercise; Outings; Other: Alzheimer's secured unit, Adult day care.

Baptist Homes Nursing Center
489 Castle Shannon Blvd., Pittsburgh, PA 15234, (412) 563-6550; Facility type: Skilled care, Alzheimer's; Beds: 130; Certified: Medicaid, Medicare; Owner: Baptist Church; License: state; Activities: Arts & Crafts; Dances; Pet therapy; Group exercise; Outings; Other: Alzheimer's secured unit.

Beverly Healthcare-Mount Lebanon
350 Old Gilkeson Rd., Pittsburgh, PA 15228, (412) 254-4444; Facility type: Skilled care, Alzheimer's; Beds: 120; Certified: Medicaid, Medicare, Veterans; Owner: Beverly Enterprises; License: state; Activities: Arts & Crafts; Dances; Pet therapy; Group exercise; Outings; Other: Alzheimer's secured unit; Affiliations: St., Thomas More Catholic Church.

Canterbury Place
310 Fisk St., Pittsburgh, PA 15201, (412) 622-9000; Facility type: Skilled care, Alzheimer's; Beds: 70; Certified: Medicaid, Medicare; Owner: Nonprofit, Religious; License: state; Activities: Arts & Crafts; Dances; Pet therapy; Group exercise; Outings; Other: Alzheimer's secured unit.

Forbes Nursing Center
6655 Frankstown Ave., Pittsburgh, PA 15206; (412) 665-3232; Facility type: Skilled care, Alzheimer's; Beds: 150; Certified: Medicaid, Medicare; Owner: Nonprofit; License: state; Activities: Arts & Crafts; Dances; Pet therapy; Group exercise; Outings; Other: Alzheimer's secured unit, Home health care.

Heartland Health Care Center
550 S Negley Ave., Pittsburgh, PA 15232, (412) 665-2400; Facility type: Skilled care, Alzheimer's; Beds: 230; Certified: Medicaid, Medicare;

Owner: HCR Manor Care; License: state; Activities: Arts & Crafts; Dances; Pet therapy; Group exercise Other: Alzheimer's secured unit; Affiliations: Alzheimer Research org.

Marian Manor Corp
2695 Winchester Dr., Pittsburgh, PA 15220, (412) 563-6866; http://www.marianmanor.com; Facility type: Skilled care, Alzheimer's; Beds: 150; Certified: Medicaid, Medicare; Owner: Nonprofit, Religious; License: state; Activities: Arts & Crafts; Dances; Pet therapy; Group exercise; Outings; Other: Alzheimer's secured unit; Affiliations: Catholic Long Term Care Network.

Rolling Hills Manor
600 Newport Dr., Pittsburgh, PA 15234, (412) 561-5557; Facility type: Skilled care, Alzheimer's; Beds: 170; Certified: Medicaid, Medicare; Owner: Proprietary/Public; License: state; Activities: Arts & Crafts; Dances; Pet therapy; Group exercise; Outings; Other: Alzheimer's secured unit; Admissions: Males only.

Vincentian Home
111 Perrymont Rd., Pittsburgh, PA 15237, (412) 366-5600; Facility type: Skilled care, Alzheimer's; Beds: 170; Certified: Medicaid, Medicare; Owner: Nonprofit; License: state; Activities: Arts & Crafts; Dances; Pet therapy; Group exercise; Outings; Other: Alzheimer's secured unit; Affiliations: Catholic Church.

Pottstown

Manor Care Health Services
724 N charlotte St., Pottstown, PA 19464, (610) 323-1837; Facility type: Skilled care, Alzheimer's; Beds: 170; Certified: Medicaid, Medicare; Owner: HCR Manor Care; License: state; Activities: Arts & Crafts; Dances; Pet therapy.

Pottsville

Schuylkill Center
1000 Schuylkill Manor Rd., Pottsville, PA, (570) 622-9666; Facility type: Skilled care, Alzheimer's; Beds: 190; Certified: Medicaid, Medicare; Owner: Genesis ElderCare; License: state; Activities: Arts & Crafts; Dances; Pet therapy; Group exercise; Outings; Other: Alzheimer's secured unit.

Reading

Transitional Level of Care Center
145 N 6th St., Reading, PA 19603, (610) 378-2000; Facility type: Skilled care, Alzheimer's; Beds: 170; Certified: Medicare; Owner: St., Joseph Medical Center; License: state; Activities: Arts & Crafts; Dances; Pet therapy; Group exercise; Outings; Other: Alzheimer's secured unit; Languages: Spanish.

Saxonburg

Saxony Health Center
223 Pittsburg St., Saxonburg, PA 16056, (724) 352-9445; Facility type: Skilled care, Alzheimer's; Beds: 160; Certified: Medicaid, Medicare; Owner: Nonprofit/Religious; License: state; Activities: Arts & Crafts; Dances; Outings; Greenhouse/Garden; Pet therapy; Group exercise; Other: Alzheimer's secured unit.

Schuylkill Haven

Schuylkill County Home—Rest Haven
401 University Dr., Schuylkill Haven, PA 17972; (570) 385-0331; Facility type: Skilled care, Alzheimer's; Beds: 140; Certified: Medicaid, Medicare, Veterans; Owner: State & Local Gov; License: state; Activities: Arts & Crafts; Dances; Pet therapy; Group exercise; Outings; Other: Alzheimer's secured unit.

Scranton

Allied Services Skilled Nursing Center
303 Smallacombe Dr., Scranton, PA 18501, (570) 348-1424; Facility type: Skilled care, Alzheimer's; Beds: 350; Certified: Medicaid, Medicare, Veterans; Owner: Nonprofit; License: state; Activities: Arts & Crafts; Dances; Pet therapy; Group exercise; Outings; Support Groups; Other: Alzheimer's secured unit.

Mountain Rest Nursing Home
100 Linwood Ave., Scranton, PA 18505, (570) 346-7381; Facility type: Skilled care, Alzheimer's; Beds: 110; Certified: Medicaid, Medicare, Veterans; Owner: AmCare Management; License: state; Activities: Arts & Crafts; Dances; Pet therapy; Group exercise; Outings; Support Groups.

Tremont

Tremont Health & Rehabilitation Center
44 Donaldson Rd., Tremont, PA 17981, (570) 695-3141; Facility type: Skilled care, Alzheimer's; Beds: 150; Certified: Medicaid, Medicare, Veterans; Owner: ExtendiCare Health Services; License: state; Activities: Arts & Crafts; Dances; Pet therapy; Group exercise; Outings; Support Groups.

Upper Saint Clair

Friendship Village of South Hills
1290 Boyce Rd., Upper Saint Clair, PA 15241,

(724) 941-3100; Facility type: Skilled care, Alzheimer's; Beds: 110; Certified: Medicaid, Medicare, Veterans; Owner: Life Care Services; License: state; Activities: Arts & Crafts; Dances; Pet therapy; Group exercise; Support Groups; Other: Alzheimer's secured unit.

Verona

Saint Margaret Seneca Place
5360 Saltsburg Rd., Verona, PA 15147, (412) 798-8000, Facility type: Skilled care, Alzheimer's; Beds: 120; Certified: Medicaid, Medicare; Owner: St., Margaret Health Systems; License: state; Activities: Arts & Crafts; Dances; Pet therapy; Group exercise; Outings; Support Groups; Other: Alzheimer's secured unit.

Warrington

Neshaminy Manor Home
1660 Easton Rd., Warrington, PA 18976, (215) 345-3205; Facility type: Skilled care, Alzheimer's; Beds: 350; Certified: Medicaid, Medicare; Owner: Genesis ElderCare; License: state; Activities: Arts & Crafts; Dances; Pet therapy; Group exercise; Outings; Support Groups; Other: Alzheimer's secured unit.

Washington

Kade Nursing Home
1198 W Wylie Ave., Washington, PA 15301, (724) 222-2148; Facility type: Skilled care, Alzheimer's; Beds: 80; Certified: Medicaid, Medicare, Veterans; Owner: Penn Med Consultants; License: state; Activities: Arts & Crafts; Dances; Pet therapy; Group exercise; Outings; Support Groups.

Washington County Health Center
36 Old Hickory Ridge Rd., Washington, PA 15301, (724) 228-5010; Facility type: Skilled care, Alzheimer's; Beds: 300; Certified: Medicaid, Medicare; Owner: State & Local Gov; License: state; Activities: Arts & Crafts; Dances; Pet therapy; Group exercise; Outings; Other: Alzheimer's secured unit, Adult day care.

Waynesburg

Beverly Healthcare
300 Center Ave., Waynesburg, PA 15370, (724) 852-2020; Facility type: Skilled care, Alzheimer's; Beds: 120; Certified: Medicaid, Medicare, Veterans; Owner: Beverly Enterprises; License: state; Activities: Arts & Crafts; Dances; Pet therapy; Group exercise; Outings; Support Groups; Other: Alzheimer's secured unit.

West Chester

Barclay Friends
700 N Franklin St., West Chester, PA 19380, (610) 696-5211; Facility type: Skilled care, Alzheimer's, Assisted Living; Beds: 150; Certified: Medicaid, Medicare, Veterans; Owner: Kendal Corp; License: state; Activities: Arts & Crafts; Dances; Pet therapy; Group exercise; Outings; Support Groups; Other: Languages: Spanish; Affiliations: Society of Friends.

Pembrooke Health & Rehabilitation Residence
1130 Chester Pike, West Chester, PA 19382, (610) 692-3636; Facility type: Skilled care, Alzheimer's; Beds: 240; Certified: Medicaid, Medicare; Owner: Sunrise Assisted Living, Brandywine Senior Care; License: state; Activities: Arts & Crafts; Dances; Pet therapy; Group exercise; Outings; Support Groups; Other: Alzheimer's secured unit; Languages: Russian, Spanish.

Pocopson Home
1695 Lenape Rd., West Chester, PA 19382, (610) 793-1212; Facility type: Skilled care, Alzheimer's; Beds: 30; Certified: Medicaid, Medicare, Veterans; Owner: State & Local Gov; License: state; Activities: Arts & Crafts; Dances; Pet therapy; Group exercise; Outings; Support Groups; Other: Alzheimer's secured unit.

West Reading

HCR Manor Care
425 Buttonwood St., West Reading, PA 19611, (610) 375-5166; Facility type: Skilled care, Alzheimer's; Beds: 180; Certified: Medicaid, Medicare; Owner: HCR Manor Care; License: state; Activities: Arts & Crafts; Dances; Pet therapy; Group exercise; Support Groups; Other: Alzheimer's secured unit; Languages: Spanish.

Wilkes-Barre

Little Flower Manor & St., Therese Residence of the Diocese of Scranton
200 S Meade St., Wilkes-Barre, PA 18702, (570) 823-6131; Facility type: Skilled care, Alzheimer's; Beds: 200; Certified: Medicaid, Medicare; Owner: Nonprofit; License: state; Activities: Arts & Crafts; Dances; Pet therapy; Group exercise; Outings; Support Groups; Other: Alzheimer's secured unit; Affiliations: Roman Catholic Church.

Williamsport

HCR Manor Care—North
300 Leader Dr., Williamsport, PA 17701, (570) 323-8267; Facility type: Skilled care, Alzhei-

mer's; Beds: 150; Certified: Medicaid, Medicare, Veterans; Owner: HCR Manor Care; License: state; Activities: Arts & Crafts; Dances; Pet therapy; Outings; Support Groups; Other: Alzheimer's secured unit, Adult day care.

Manor Care Health Services—Williamsport South
101 Leader Dr., Williamsport, PA 17701, (570) 323-3758; Facility type: Skilled care, Alzheimer's; Beds: 350; Certified: Medicaid, Medicare; Owner: HCR Manor Care; License: state; Activities: Arts & Crafts; Dances; Pet therapy; Group exercise; Support Groups; Other: Alzheimer's secured unit.

Worthington

Sugar Creek Rest & Meadow Lake Manor
RD 2 Box 80, Worthington, PA 16262, (724) 445-3146; Facility type: Skilled care, Alzheimer's; Beds: 130; Certified: Medicaid, Medicare, Veterans; Owner: Private; License: state; Activities: Arts & Crafts; Dances; Pet therapy; Group exercise; Outings; Support Groups; Other: Alzheimer's secured unit, Adult day care; Languages: Spanish.

York

Manor Care Health Services—Kingston Court
2400 Kingston Ct, York, PA 17402, (717) 755-8811; Facility type: Skilled care, Alzheimer's; Beds: 140; Certified: Medicaid, Medicare; Owner: HCR Manor Care; License: state; Activities: Arts & Crafts; Dances; Pet therapy; Group exercise; Outings; Support Groups; Other: Alzheimer's secured unit.

Manor Care Health Services—North
1770 Barley Rd., York, PA 17404, (717) 767-6530; Facility type: Skilled care, Alzheimer's; Beds: 150; Certified: Medicaid, Medicare; Owner: HCR Manor Care; License: state; Activities: Arts & Crafts; Dances; Pet therapy; Group exercise; Support Groups; Other: Alzheimer's secured unit, Adult day care.

York County Nursing Home
118 Pleasant Acres Rd., York, PA 17402, (717) 840-7100; Facility type: Skilled care, Alzheimer's; Beds: 480; Certified: Medicaid, Medicare; Owner: State & Local Gov; License: state; Activities: Arts & Crafts; Dances; Pet therapy; Group exercise; Outings; Support Groups; Other: Alzheimer's secured unit.

Youngsville

Rouse-Warren County Home
701 Rouse Ave., Youngsville, PA 16371, (814) 563-7565; Facility type: Skilled care, Alzheimer's; Beds: 190; Certified: Medicaid, Medicare, Veterans; Owner: State & Local Gov; License: state; Activities: Arts & Crafts; Dances; Pet therapy; Group exercise; Outings; Support Groups; Other: Alzheimer's secured unit.

RHODE ISLAND

Bristol

Metacom Manor Health Center
1 Dawn Hill, Bristol, RI 08209, (401) 253-2300; Facility type: Skilled care, Alzheimer's; Beds: 170; Certified: Medicaid, Medicare; Owner: Nonprofit; License: state; Activities: Arts & Crafts; Pet therapy; Group exercise; Support Groups; Other: Alzheimer's secured unit; Languages: French, Portuguese.

Silver Creek Manor
7 Creek Ln., Bristol, RI 02809, (401) 253-3000; Facility type: Skilled care, Alzheimer's; Beds: 120; Certified: Medicaid, Medicare, Veterans; Owner: Private; License: state; Activities: Arts & Crafts; Dances; Pet therapy; Group exercise; Outings; Support Groups; Other: Languages: French, Portuguese.

Central Falls

Harris Health Care Center North
60 Eben Brown Ln., Central Falls, RI 02863, (401) 722-6000; Facility type: Skilled care, Alzheimer's; Beds: 70; Certified: Medicaid, Medicare, Veterans; Owner: Private; License: state; Activities: Arts & Crafts; Dances; Pet therapy; Group exercise; Outings; Support Groups; Greenhouse/Garden; Other: Languages: French, German, Irish, Italian, Polish, Portuguese, Spanish.

Rose Cottage Health Care Center
151 Hunt St., Central Falls, RI 02863, (401) 722-4610; Facility type: Skilled care, Alzheimer's; Beds: 120; Certified: Medicaid, Medicare; Owner: Private; License: state; Activities: Arts & Crafts; Dances; Pet therapy; Group exercise; Outings; Support Groups; Other: Languages: Creole, Spanish.

Coventry

Coventry Health Center
10 Woodland Dr., Coventry, RI 02816, (401) 826-2000; Facility type: Skilled care, Alzheimer's; Beds: 140; Certified: Medicaid, Medicare, Veterans; Owner: HealthCare Mgt; License: state; Activities: Arts & Crafts; Dances; Pet therapy; Group exercise; Outings; Support Groups; Other: Alzheimer's secured unit.

Healthcare Community
546 Main St., Coventry, RI 02816, (401) 821-6837; Facility type: Skilled care, Alzheimer's; Beds: 120; Certified: Medicaid, Medicare; Owner: Health Concepts, LTD; License: state; Activities: Arts & Crafts; Dances; Pet therapy; Group exercise; Support Groups; Other: Alzheimer's secured unit; Languages: French.

Cumberland

Diamond Hill Nursing Center
3579 Diamond Hill Rd., Cumberland, RI 02864, (401) 333-50550; Facility type: Skilled care, Alzheimer's; Beds: 50; Certified: Medicaid, Medicare; Owner: Private; License: state; Activities: Arts & Crafts; Dances; Pet therapy; Group exercise; Outings; Support Groups; Other: Languages: French, Portuguese.

East Providence

Harris Health Center
833 Broadway, East Providence, RI 02914, (401) 434-7404; Facility type: Skilled care, Alzheimer's; Beds: 130; Certified: Medicaid, Medicare; Owner: Private; License: state; Activities: Arts & Crafts; Dances; Pet therapy; Group exercise; Outings; Support Groups; Other: Alzheimer's secured unit: Languages, French, Portuguese, Spanish.

Health Haven Nursing & Rehabilitation Center
100 Wampanoag Tri, East Providence, RI 02915, (401) 438-275; Facility type: Skilled care, Alzheimer's; Beds: 60; Certified: Medicaid, Medicare; Payer mix: 55% Private pay; Owner: Nonprofit; License: state; Activities: Arts & Crafts; Dances; Pet therapy; Group exercise; Outings; Support Groups; Other: Alzheimer's secured unit; Languages: French, Italian, Portuguese, Spanish.

Orchard View Manor
135 Tripps Ln., East Providence, RI 02915, (401) 438-2250; Facility type: Skilled care, Alzheimer's; Beds: 350; Certified: Medicaid, Medicare, Veterans; Owner: Private; License: state; Activities: Arts & Crafts; Dances; Pet therapy.

Waterview Villa
1275 S Broadway, East Providence, RI 02914 (401) 438-7020; Facility type: Skilled care, Alzheimer's; Beds: 130; Certified: Medicaid, Medicare; Owner: Proprietary/Public; License: state; Activities: Arts & Crafts; Dances; Pet therapy; Group exercise; Outings; Support Groups; Other: Alzheimer's secured unit; Languages: Italian, Portuguese; Affiliations: American College of Healthcare.

Johnston

Briarcliffe Manor
49 Old Pocasset Rd., Johnston, RI 02919, (401) 944-2450; Facility type: Skilled care, Alzheimer's; Beds: 90; Certified: Medicaid, Medicare; Owner: Medical Homes of RI, Inc.; License: state; Activities: Arts & Crafts; Dances; Pet therapy; Group exercise; Outings; Support Groups; Other: Alzheimer's secured unit.

Manville

The Holiday Retirement Home
30 Sayles Hill Rd., Manville, RI 02838, (401) 765-1440; Facility type: Skilled care, Alzheimer's; Beds: 180; Certified: Medicaid, Medicare, Veterans; Owner: Proprietary/Public; License: state; Activities: Arts & Crafts; Dances; Pet therapy; Group exercise; Outings; Support Groups; Other: Alzheimer's secured unit; Languages: French, Polish, Portuguese.

Newport

Village House Nursing & Rehabilitation Center
70 Harrison Ave., Newport, RI 02840, (401) 849-5222; Facility type: Skilled care, Alzheimer's; Beds: 140; Certified: Medicaid, Medicare; Owner: Health Concepts LTD; License: state; Activities: Arts & Crafts; Dances; Pet therapy; Outings; Support Groups; Other: Alzheimer's secured unit; Languages: Portuguese.

North Kingstown

Roberts Health Center
990 Ten Rod Rd., North Kingstown, RI 02852, (401) 884-6661; Facility type: Skilled care, Alzheimer's; Beds: 60; Certified: Medicaid, Medicare, Veterans; Owner: Private; License: state; Activities: Arts & Crafts; Dances; Pet therapy; Group exercise; Outings; Support Groups; Other: Alzheimer's secured unit, Adult day care; Affiliations: Chamber of Commerce, AAHA.

Scalabrini Villa
860 N Quidnesset Rd., North Kingstown, RI

02852, (401) 884-1802; Facility type: Nonprofit, Alzheimer's; Beds: 350; Certified: Medicaid, Medicare; Owner: Nonprofit; License: state; Activities: Arts & Crafts; Dances; Pet therapy; Group exercise; Outings; Support Groups; Other: Alzheimer's secured unit; Languages: Italian; Affiliations: Roman Catholic Church.

North Providence

Golden Crest Nursing Center
100 Smithfield Rd., North Providence, RI 02904, (401) 353-1710; Facility type: Skilled care, Alzheimer's; Beds: 150; Certified: Medicaid, Medicare; Owner: Private; License: state; Activities: Arts & Crafts; Dances; Pet therapy; Outings; Support Groups; Other: Alzheimer's secured unit; Languages: Italian, Spanish.

Hopkins Manor
610 Smithfield Rd., North Providence, RI 02904, (401) 353-6300; Facility type: Skilled care, Alzheimer's; Beds: 210; Certified: Medicaid, Medicare; Owner: Health Mgt Systems; License: state; Activities: Arts & Crafts; Dances; Pet therapy; Group exercise; Outings; Support Groups; Other: Alzheimer's secured unit.

North Smithfield

Saint Antoine Residence
400 Mendon Rd., North Smithfield, RI 02896, (401) 767-3500; Facility type: Skilled care, Alzheimer's. Assisted Living; Beds: 330; Certified: Medicaid, Medicare; Owner: Nonprofit; License: state; Activities: Arts & Crafts; Dances; Pet therapy; Group exercise; Outings; Support Groups; Other: Alzheimer's secured unit; Languages: French, Italian; Affiliations: Roman Catholic Church.

Providence

Bannister Nursing Care Center
135 Dodge St., Providence, RI 02907, (401) 521-9600; Facility type: Skilled care, Alzheimer's; Beds: 140; Certified: Medicaid, Medicare, Veterans; Owner: The QAC Healthcare Group; License: state; Activities: Arts & Crafts; Dances; Pet therapy; Group exercise; Outings; Support Groups; Other: Alzheimer's secured unit; Languages: Spanish, French, Portuguese.

Charlesgate Nursing Center
100 Randall St., Providence, RI 02904, (401) 861-5858; Facility type: Skilled care, Alzheimer's; Beds: 160; Certified: Medicaid, Medicare; Owner: Davenport Assoc; License: state; Activities: Arts & Crafts; Dances; Pet therapy; Group exercise; Outings; Support Groups; Other: Alzheimer's secured unit; Languages: Italian, Portuguese, Spanish.

Hillside Health Center
99 Hillside Ave., Providence, RI 02906, (401) 351-4750; Facility type: Skilled care, Alzheimer's; Beds: 250; Certified: Medicaid, Medicare; Owner: Sterling HealthCare; License: state; Activities: Arts & Crafts; Dances; Pet therapy; Group 109 exercise; Support Groups; Other: Languages: Spanish, Portuguese, Russian, Yiddish.

Saint Elizabeth Home
Melrose St., Providence, RI 02907, (401) 941-0200; Facility type: Skilled care, Alzheimer's; Beds: 110; Certified: Medicaid, Medicare; Owner: Nonprofit; License: state; Activities: Arts & Crafts; Dances; Pet therapy; Group exercise; Outings; Support Groups; Other: Alzheimer's secured unit.

Steere House Nursing & Rehabilitation Center
100 Borden St., Providence, RI 02903, (401) 454-7070; Facility type: Skilled care, Alzheimer's; Beds: 90; Certified: Medicaid, Medicare; Owner: Nonprofit; License: state; Activities: Arts & Crafts; Dances; Pet therapy; Group exercise; Outings; Support Groups; Other: Alzheimer's secured unit; Languages: French, Spanish, Swahili.

Tocwotton Home
75 East St., Providence, RI 02903, (401) 272-5280; Facility type: Skilled care, Alzheimer's; Beds: 50; Certified: Medicaid, Medicare; Owner: Nonprofit; License: state; Activities: Arts & Crafts; Greenhouse/Garden; Dances; Pet therapy; Group exercise; Outings; Support Groups; Other: Alzheimer's secured unit; Languages: Portuguese; Affiliations: Alliance for Better Long Term Care.

Scituate

Harris Manor at Chopmist Hill
1057 Chopmist Hill Rd., Scituate, RI 02857, (401) 647-7425; http://www.harrishealth.com; Facility type: Skilled care, Alzheimer's; Beds: 50; Certified: Medicaid, Medicare; Owner: Private; License: state; Activities: Arts & Crafts; Dances; Pet therapy; Group exercise; Outings; Support Groups; Other: Alzheimer's secured unit; Languages: French, German, Spanish.

Warren

Grace Barker Nursing Center
54 Barker Ave., Warren, RI 02885, (401) 245-9100; Facility type: Skilled care, Alzheimer's; Beds: 90; Certified: Medicaid, Medicare, Veterans; Payer mix: Medicaid—84%, Medicare—5%,

Private pay—10%, Veterans—1%; Owner: Private; License: state; Activities: Arts & Crafts; Dances; Pet therapy; Group exercise; Outings; Support Groups; Other: Adult day care; Languages: Portuguese.

Warwick

Kent Nursing & Rehabilitation Center
660 Commonwealth Ave., Warwick, RI 02886, (401) 739-4241; Facility type: Skilled care, Alzheimer's; Beds: 120; Certified: Medicaid, Medicare; Owner: Genesis ElderCare; License: state; Activities: Arts & Crafts; Dances; Pet therapy; Group exercise; Outings; Support Groups.

Westerly

Westerly Nursing Home
79 Beach St., Westerly, RI 02891, (401) 596-4925; Facility type: Skilled care, Alzheimer's; Beds: 60; Certified: Medicaid, Medicare, Veterans; Owner: Private; License: state; Activities: Arts & Crafts; Dances; Pet therapy; Outings; Support Groups; Other: Affiliations: Alliance for Better Nursing Home Care; Eden.

Woonsocket

Mount Saint Francis Health Center
4 St., Joseph St., Woonsocket, RI 02895, (401) 765-5844; Facility type: Skilled care, Alzheimer's; Beds: 180; Certified: Medicaid, Medicare; Owner: Sterling Healthcare; License: state; Activities: Arts & Crafts; Dances; Pet therapy; Group exercise; Outings; Support Groups; Other: Languages: French; Affiliations: Roman Catholic Church.

Woonsocket Health Center
262 Polar St., Woonsocket, RI 02895, (401) 765-2100; Facility type: Skilled care, Alzheimer's; Beds: 300; Certified: Medicaid, Medicare, Veterans; Owner: Private; License: state; Activities: Arts & Crafts; Dances; Pet therapy; Group exercise; Outings; Support Groups; Other: Alzheimer's secured unit; Languages: French, Spanish.

SOUTH CAROLINA

Abbeville

Abbeville Nursing Home
Thompson Cir., Abbeville, SC 29620, (864) 459-5122; Facility type: Skilled care, Alzheimer's; Beds: 90; Certified: Medicaid, Medicare, Veterans; Owner: Proprietary/Public; License: state; Activities: Arts & Crafts; Dances; Pet therapy.

Aiken

Beverly Healthcare & Rehabilitation Center
123 DuPont Dr., Aiken, SC 29801, (803) 648-0434; Facility type: Skilled care, Alzheimer's; Beds: 80; Certified: Medicaid, Medicare, Veterans; Owner: Beverly Enterprises; License: state; Activities: Arts & Crafts; Dances; Pet therapy; Group exercise; Outings; Support Groups; Other: Alzheimer's secured unit; Affiliations: Chamber of Commerce, Advinet.

Mattie C. Hall Health Care Center
830 Laurens St., Aiken, SC 29801, (803) 649-6264; Facility type: Skilled care, Alzheimer's; Beds: 90; Certified: Medicaid, Medicare; Owner: State & Local Gov; License: state; Activities: Arts & Crafts; Dances; Pet therapy; Group exercise; Outings; Support Groups; Other: Alzheimer's secured unit.

Pepper Hill Nursing Center
3525 Augustus Rd., Aiken, SC 29802, (803) 642-8376; Facility type: Skilled care, Alzheimer's; Beds: 132; Certified: Medicaid, Medicare, Veterans; Owner: Private; License: state; Activities: Arts & Crafts; Dances; Pet therapy; Group exercise; Outings; Support Groups; Other: Alzheimer's secured unit.

Bamberg

Bamberg County Memorial Nursing Center
North & McGee, Bamberg, SC 29003, (803) 2-4321; Facility type: Skilled care, Alzheimer's; Beds: 350; Certified: Medicaid, Medicare, Veterans; Owner: State & Local Gov; License: state; Activities: Arts & Crafts; Dances; Pet therapy; Group exercise; Outings; Support Groups.

Charleston

Bishop Gadsen Episcopal Health Care Center
1 Gadsen Way, Charleston, SC 29412, (843) 762-3300; Facility type: Skilled care, Alzheimer's; Beds: 120; Certified: Medicaid, Medicare, Veterans; Owner: Nonprofit; License: state; Activities: Arts & Crafts; Dances; Pet therapy; Group exercise; Support Groups; Other: Affiliations: Episcopal Church.

HCR Manor Care Health Services
1137 Sam Rittenburg Blvd., Charleston, SC

29407, (843) 763-0233; Facility type: Skilled care, Alzheimer's; Beds: 110; Certified: Medicaid, Medicare, Veterans; Owner: HCR Manor Care; License: state; Activities: Arts & Crafts; Dances; Pet therapy; Group exercise; Outings; Support Groups; Other: Alzheimer's secured unit; Languages: Spanish.

Columbia

Central Carolina Health & Rehabilitation Center
2451 Forest Dr., Columbia, SC 29204; (803) 254-5960; Facility type: Skilled care, Alzheimer's; Beds: 300; Certified: Medicaid, Medicare, Veterans; Owner: Mariner Post Acute Network; License: state; Activities: Arts & Crafts; Dances; Pet therapy; Group exercise; Outings; Support Groups; Other: Alzheimer's secured unit; Languages: Korean, Spanish.

Life Care Center of Columbia
2514 Faraway Dr., Columbia, SC 29223, (803) 865-1999; Facility type: Skilled care, Alzheimer's, Assisted living; Beds: 180; Certified: Medicaid, Medicare, Veterans; Owner: Life Care Centers of America; License: state; Activities: Arts & Crafts; Dances; Pet therapy; Group exercise; Outings; Support Groups; Other: Alzheimer's secured unit.

Dillon

The Pines Nursing & Convalescent Home
413 Lakeside Ct., Dillon, SC 29536, (843) 774-2741; Facility type: Skilled care, Alzheimer's; Beds: 90; Certified: Medicaid, Medicare, Veterans; Owner: Beverly Enterprises; License: state; Activities: Arts & Crafts; Dances; Pet therapy; Group exercise; Outings; Support Groups.

Fountain Inn

Fountain Inn Nursing Home
501 Gulliver St., Fountain Inn, SC 29644, (864) 862-2554; Facility type: Skilled care, Alzheimer's; Beds: 50; Certified: Medicaid, Medicare; Owner: Cooke Mgt; License: state; Activities: Arts & Crafts; Dances; Pet therapy; Group exercise; Outings; Support Groups.

Greenville

Oakmont West Nursing Center
600 Sulphur Springs Rd., Greenville, SC 29617, (864) 246-2721; Facility type: Skilled care, Alzheimer's; Beds: 120; Certified: Medicaid, Medicare, Veterans; Owner: HCR Manor Care; License: state; Activities: Arts & Crafts; Dances; Pet therapy; Outings; Support Groups; Other: Alzheimer's secured unit.

Rolling Green Village—Mildred L. Smith Health Center
1 Hoke Smith Blvd., Greenville, SC 29615, (864) 987-9800; Facility type: Skilled care, Alzheimer's, Assisted Living; Beds: 110; Certified: Medicare; Payer mix: 100% Private pay; Owner: Life Care Services; License: state; Activities: Arts & Crafts; Dances; Pet therapy; Group exercise; Outings; Support Groups; Other: Alzheimer's secured unit; Affiliations: Greenville Baptist Association.

Westside Nursing Center
8 N Texas Ave., Greenville, SC 29611, (864) 295-1331; Facility type: Skilled care, Alzheimer's; Beds: 130; Certified: Medicaid, Medicare; Owner: Health Mgt Resources; License: state; Activities: Arts & Crafts; Pet therapy.

Greer

Piedmont Nursing & Rehabilitation Center
401 Chandler Rd., Greer, SC 29651, (864) 879-1370; Facility type: Skilled care, Alzheimer's; Beds: 130; Certified: Medicaid, Medicare; Owner: Health Mgt Resources; License: state; Activities: Arts & Crafts; Dances; Pet therapy; Group exercise; Outings; Support Groups; Other: Alzheimer's secured unit; Affiliations: Lutheran Church.

Roger Huntington Nursing Center
313 Memorial Dr., Greer, SC 29650, (864) 848-8200; Facility type: Skilled care, Alzheimer's; Beds: 90; Certified: Medicaid, Medicare; Owner: Nonprofit; License: state; Activities: Arts & Crafts; Dances; Pet therapy; Group exercise; Outings; Support Groups.

Hilton Head Island

Life Care Center of Hilton Head
120 Lamotte Dr., Hilton Head Island, SC 29926, (843) 681-6006; Facility type: Skilled care, Alzheimer's; Beds: 90; Certified: Medicaid, Medicare, Veterans; Owner: Life Care Centers of America; License: state; Activities: Arts & Crafts; Dances; Pet therapy; Group exercise; Outings; Support Groups.

The SeaBrook of Hilton Head
300 Woodhaven Dr., Hilton Head Island, SC 29928, 9843) 842-3747; Facility type: Skilled care, Alzheimer's; Beds: 50; Certified: Medicare; Payer mix: 91% Private pay. Owner: Nonprofit; License: state; Activities: Arts & Crafts; Dances; Pet therapy; Group exercise; Outings; Support Groups.

Lancaster

White Oak Manor
253 Craig Manor Rd., Lancaster, SC 29720,

(803) 286-2464; Facility type: Skilled care, Alzheimer's; Beds: 130; Certified: Medicaid, Medicare, Veterans; Owner: White Oak Manor, Inc.; License: state; Activities: Arts & Crafts; Dances; Pet therapy; Group exercise; Outings; Support Groups.

Laurens

Martha Franks Baptist Retirement Center
1 Martha Franks Dr., Laurens, SC 29360, (864) 984-4541: Facility type: Skilled care, Alzheimer's; Beds: 130; Certified: Medicare; Payer mix: 91% Private pay; Owner: Baptist Church; License: state; Activities: Arts & Crafts; Dances; Pet therapy; Group exercise; Outings; Support Groups; Other: Alzheimer's secured unit.

NHC Health Care
301 Pinehaven St., Laurens, SC 29360, (864) 984-6584; Facility type: Skilled care, Alzheimer's; Beds: 180; Certified: Medicaid, Medicare, Veterans; Owner: National Healthcare Company; License: state; Activities: Arts & Crafts; Dances; Pet therapy; Group exercise; Outings; Support Groups; Other: Alzheimer's secured unit.

Mount Pleasant

Charleston Nursing Center
921 Bowman Rd., Mount Pleasant, SC 29464, (843) 884-8903; Facility type: Skilled care, Alzheimer's; Beds: 350; Certified: Medicaid, Medicare, Veterans; Owner: Proprietary/Public; License: state; Activities: Arts & Crafts; Dances; Pet therapy; Group exercise; Outings; Support Groups; Other: Alzheimer's secured unit.

Sandpiper Convalescent Center
1049 Knapp Blvd., Mount Pleasant, SC 29464, (843) 881-3210; Facility type: Skilled care, Alzheimer's; Beds: 180; Certified: Medicaid; Owner: Proprietary/Public; License: state; Activities: Arts & Crafts; Dances; Pet therapy.

Myrtle Beach

Myrtle Beach Manor
9547 Hwy. 17 N, Myrtle Beach, SC 29572, (843) 449-5283: Facility type: Skilled care, Alzheimer's; Beds: 110; Certified: Medicaid, Medicare; Owner: Marriott Senior Living Services; License: state; Activities: Arts & Crafts; Dances; Pet therapy; Group exercise; Outings; Support Groups; Other: Alzheimer's secured unit.

Newberry

J. F. Hawkins Nursing Home
1330 Kinard St., Newberry, SC 29108, (803) 276-2601; Facility type: Skilled care, Alzheimer's; Beds: 120; Certified: Medicaid, Medicare, Veterans; Owner: State & Local Gov; License: state; Activities: Arts & Crafts; Dances; Pet therapy; Group exercise; Outings; Support Groups; Other: Alzheimer's secured unit.

North Charleston

Life Care Center of Charleston
2600 Elms Plantation Blvd., North Charleston, SC 29418, (8430 764-3500; Facility type: Skilled care, Alzheimer's; Beds: 170; Certified: Medicaid, Medicare, Veterans; Owner: Private; License: state; Activities: Arts & Crafts; Dances; Pet therapy; Group exercise; Outings; Support Groups; Other: Alzheimer's secured unit.

Rock Hill

White Oak Manor
1915 Ebenezer Rd., Rock Hill, SC 29732, (803) 366-8155; Facility type: Skilled care, Alzheimer's; Beds: 140; Certified: Medicaid, Medicare, Veterans; Owner: White Oak Manor, Inc.; License: state; Activities: Arts & Crafts; Dances; Pet therapy; Group exercise; Outings; Support Groups.

Saluda

Saluda Nursing Center
Hwy. 121 N, Saluda, SC 19138, (864) 445-2146; Facility type: Skilled care, Alzheimer's; Beds: 170; Certified: Medicaid, Medicare; Owner: State & Local Gov; License: state; Activities: Arts & Crafts; Dances; Pet therapy; Group exercise; Outings; Support Groups.

Seneca

Mariner Health Care of Seneca
140 Tokeena Rd., Seneca, SC 29678, (864) 882-1642; Facility type: Skilled care, Alzheimer's; Beds: 130; Certified: Medicaid, Medicare, Veterans; Owner: Proprietary/Public; License: state; Activities: Arts & Crafts; Dances; Pet therapy; Group exercise; Outings; Support Groups; Other: Languages: French, Slavic, Spanish; Affiliations: SC Health Care Association.

Spartanburg

Skylyn Place Health Center
1705 Skylyn Dr., Spartanburg, SC 29307, (864) 582-6838; Facility type: Skilled care, Alzheimer's; Beds: 50; Payer mix: 100% Private pay; Owner: Emeritus Corp; License: state; Activities: Arts & Crafts; Dances; Pet therapy; Group exercise; Outings; Support Groups; Other: Alzheimer's secured unit.

Sumter

Hopewell Healthcare Center
1761 Pinewood Rd., Sumter, SC 29151, (803) 481-8591; Facility type: Skilled care, Alzheimer's; Beds: 100; Certified: Medicaid, Medicare; Owner: Proprietary/Public; License: state; Activities: Arts & Crafts; Dances; Pet therapy; Group exercise; Outings; Support Groups.

National Health Care Center of Sumter
1018 N Guignard Dr., Sumter, SC 29151, (803) 773-5567; Facility type: Skilled care, Alzheimer's; Beds: 110; Certified: Medicaid, Medicare, Veterans; Owner: National Healthcare Co; License: state; Activities: Arts & Crafts; Dances; Pet therapy; Group exercise; Outings; Support Groups.

White Rock

Lowman Home Nursing Home
201 Fortress Dr., White Rock, SC 29177, (803) 732-3000; Facility type: Skilled care, Alzheimer's; Beds: 200; Certified: Medicaid, Medicare, Veterans; Owner: Nonprofit/ Religious; License: state; Activities: Arts & Crafts; Dances; Pet therapy; Group exercise; Outings; Support Groups; Other: Alzheimer's secured unit; Affiliations: Lutheran Church.

Woodruff

Woodruff Health Care
1114 E Georgia Rd., Woodruff, SC 29388, (864) 476-7092; Facility type: Skilled care, Alzheimer's; Beds: 90; Certified: Medicaid, Medicare; Owner: Integrated Health Services; License: state; Activities: Arts & Crafts; Dances; Pet therapy; Group exercise; Outings; Support Groups; Other: Alzheimer's secured unit.

SOUTH DAKOTA

Aberdeen

Aberdeen Living Center
1700 N Hwy. 281, Aberdeen, SD 57401, (605) 225-7315; http://www.bhshealth.org; Facility type: Skilled care, Alzheimer's; Beds: 170; Certified: Medicaid, Medicare, Veterans; Owner: Benedictine Health System; License: state; Activities: Arts & Crafts; Dances; Pet therapy; Group exercise; Outings; Support Groups; Other: Affiliations: Catholic Church.

Manor Care Health Services
400 8th Ave., NW, Aberdeen, SD 57401, (605) 225-2550; Facility type: Skilled care, Alzheimer's; Beds: 90; Certified: Medicaid, Medicare; Owner: HCR Manor Care; License: state; Activities: Arts & Crafts; Dances; Pet therapy; Group exercise; Outings; Support Groups; Other: Alzheimer's secured unit.

Alcester

Morningside Manor
101 Church St., Alcester, SD 57001, (605) 943-2011; Facility type: Skilled care, Alzheimer's; Beds: 95; Certified: Medicaid, Medicare, Veterans; Owner: Nonprofit; License: state; Activities: Arts & Crafts; Dances; Pet therapy; Group exercise; Outings; Support Groups; Other: Alzheimer's secured unit; Languages: Spanish.

Bristol

Sun Dial Manor
410 2nd St., Bristol, SD 57219, (605) 492-3615; Facility type: Skilled care, Alzheimer's; Beds: 60; Certified: Medicaid, Medicare; Owner: SunDial Manor; License: state; Activities: Arts & Crafts; Dances; Pet therapy; Group exercise; Outings; Support Groups; Other: Alzheimer's secured unit, Adult Day Care.

Britton

Wheatcrest Hills
W Hwy. 10, Britton, SD 57430, (605) 448-2251; Facility type: Skilled care, Alzheimer's; Beds: 80; Certified: Medicaid, Medicare; Owner: Private; License: state; Activities: Arts & Crafts; Dances; Pet therapy; Group exercise; Outings; Support Groups; Other: Alzheimer's secured unit, Adult day care.

Canton

Canton Good Samaritan Center
1022 N Dakota Ave., Canton, SD 57013, (605) 987-2696; http://www.good-sam.com; Facility type: Skilled care, Alzheimer's; Beds: 90; Certified: Medicaid, Medicare; Owner: Evangelic

Lutheran Good Samaritan Society; License: state; Activities: Arts & Crafts; Dances; Pet therapy; Group exercise; Outings; Support Groups; Other: Adult day care; Languages: German, Norwegian.

DeSmet

DeSmet Good Samaritan Center
411 Calumet Ave. NW, DeSmet, SD 57231, (605) 854-3327; Facility type: Skilled care, Alzheimer's, Assisted Living; Beds: 80; Certified: Medicaid, Medicare, Veterans; Owner: Evangelical Lutheran Good Samaritan Society; License: state; Activities: Arts & Crafts; Dances; Pet therapy; Group exercise; Outings.

Eureka

Eureka Health Care Center
202 J Ave., Eureka, SD 57437, (605) 284-2145; Facility type: Skilled care, Alzheimer's; Beds: 70; Certified: Medicaid, Medicare; Owner: Banner Health System; License: state; Activities: Arts & Crafts; Dances; Pet therapy; Group exercise; Outings; Support Groups; Other: Languages: German.

Gettysburg

Oahe Manor-Gettysburg Medical Center
700 E Garfield Ave., Gettysburg, SD 57442, (605) 765-2461; Facility type: Skilled care, Alzheimer's; Beds: 60; Certified: Medicaid; Owner: Catholic Health Initiatives; License: state; Activities: Arts & Crafts; Dances; Pet therapy; Group exercise; Outings; Support Groups; Greenhouse/Garden; Other: Alzheimer's secured unit, Home health care.

Gregory

Rosebud Country Care Center
300 Park St., Gregory, SD 57533, (605) 835-8296; Facility type: Skilled care, Alzheimer's; Beds: 60; Certified: Medicaid, Medicare; Owner: Nonprofit; License: state; Activities: Arts & Crafts; Dances; Pet therapy; Group exercise; Outings; Support Groups; Other: Adult day care, Home health care.

Highmore

Highmore Healthcare Center
8th & Maple St., Highmore, SD 57345, (605) 852-2255; http://www.tealwoodcc.com; Facility type: Skilled care, Alzheimer's; Beds: 50; Certified: Medicaid; Owner: Tealwood Care Centers; License: state; Activities: Arts & Crafts; Dances; Pet therapy; Group exercise; Outings; Support Groups.

Irene

Sunset Manor
129 E Clay St., Irene, SD 57037, (605) 263-3318; Facility type: Skilled care, Alzheimer's; Beds: 80; Certified: Medicaid; Owner: Proprietary/Public; License: state; Activities: Arts & Crafts; Dances; Pet therapy; Group exercise; Support Groups.

Lake Norden

Lake Norden Care Center
803 Park St., Lake Norden, SD 57248, (605) 785-3654; Facility type: Skilled care, Alzheimer's; Beds: 60; Certified: Medicaid, Medicare, Veterans; Owner: Beverly Enterprises; License: state; Activities: Arts & Crafts; Dances; Pet therapy; Group exercise; Outings; Support Groups; Other: Alzheimer's secured unit, Adult day care.

Madison

Bethel Lutheran Home
1001 S Egan Ave., Madison, SD 57042, (605) 256-4539; Facility type: Skilled care, Alzheimer's; Beds: 350; Certified: Medicaid, Medicare; Owner: Nonprofit; License: state; Activities: Arts & Crafts; Dances; Pet therapy; Group exercise; Support Groups; Other: Adult day care, Home health care; Affiliations: Lutheran.

Mobridge

Mobridge Care Center
100 4th Ave. E, Mobridge, SD 57601, (605) 845-7201; Facility type: Skilled care, Alzheimer's; Beds: 110; Certified: Medicaid, Medicare, Veterans; Owner: Beverly Enterprises; License: state; Activities: Arts & Crafts; Dances; Pet therapy; Group exercise; Outings; Support Groups; Other: Alzheimer's secured unit; Adult day care; Languages: German.

Pierre

Missouri Valley Nursing Center
950 E Park St., Pierre, SD 57501, (605) 224-8628; Facility type: Skilled care, Alzheimer's; Beds: 80; Certified: Medicaid, Medicare, Veterans; Owner: Beverly Enterprises; License: state; Activities: Arts & Crafts; Dances; Pet therapy; Group exercise; Outings; Support Groups.

Rapid City

Beverly Healthcare—Bella Vista
302 St., Cloud St., Rapid City, SD 57701, (605)

343-4738; Facility type: Skilled care, Alzheimer's; Beds: 70; Certified: Medicaid, Medicare, Veterans; Owner: Beverly Enterprises; License: state; Activities: Arts & Crafts; Dances; Pet therapy; Group exercise; Outings; Support Groups; Other: Alzheimer's secured unit.

Meadowbrook Manor
2500 Arrowhead Dr., Rapid City, SD 57702, (605) 348-0285; Facility type: Skilled care, Alzheimer's; Beds: 70; Certified: Medicaid, Medicare, Veterans; Owner: Beverly Enterprises; License: state; Activities: Arts & Crafts; Dances; Pet therapy; Group exercise; Outings; Support Groups.

Wesleyan Health Care Center
2000 Wesleyan Blvd., Rapid City, SD 57702, (605) 343-3555; Facility type: Skilled care, Alzheimer's; Beds: 90; Certified: Medicaid, Medicare, Veterans; Owner: Private; License: state; Activities: Arts & Crafts; Dances; Pet therapy; Group exercise; Outings; Support Groups.

Redfield

Beverly Healthcare—Redfield
1015 3rd St. E, Redfield, SD 57469, (605) 472-2288; Facility type: Skilled care, Alzheimer's; Beds: 80; Certified: Medicaid, Medicare, Veterans; Owner: Beverly Enterprises; License: state; Activities: Arts & Crafts; Dances; Pet therapy; Group exercise; Outings; Support Groups; Other: Alzheimer's secured unit, Adult day care.

Salem

Beverly Healthcare—Salem
500 Colonial Dr., Salem SD 57058, (605) 425-2203; Facility type: Skilled care, Alzheimer's; Beds: 60; Certified: Medicaid, Medicare, Veterans; Owner: Beverly Enterprises; License: state; Activities: Arts & Crafts; Dances; Pet therapy; Group exercise; Outings; Support Groups.

Sioux Falls

Bethany Lutheran Home
1901 S Holly Ave., Sioux Falls, SD 57105, (605) 338-2351; Facility type: Skilled care, Alzheimer's; Beds: 110; Certified: Medicaid, Medicare, Veterans; Owner: Nonprofit; License: state; Activities: Arts & Crafts; Dances; Pet therapy; Group exercise; Outings; Support Groups; Other: Affiliations: Lutheran.

Good Samaritan Luther Manor
2900 S Lake Ave., Sioux Falls, SD 57105, (605) 336-1997; Facility type: Skilled care, Alzheimer's; Beds: 120; Certified: Medicaid, Medicare; Owner: Evangelic Lutheran Good Samaritan Society; License: state; Activities: Arts & Crafts; Dances; Pet therapy; Group exercise; Outings; Support Groups; Other: Alzheimer's secured unit.

Prince of Peace Retirement Community
4500 Prince of Peace Pl., Sioux Falls, SD 57103, (605) 371-0700; Facility type: Skilled care, Alzheimer's; Beds: 350; Certified: Medicaid, Medicare; Owner: Nonprofit; License: state; Activities: Arts & Crafts; Dances; Pet therapy; Group exercise; Outings; Support Groups; Greenhouse/Garden; Other: Alzheimer's secured unit; Affiliations: Roman Catholic.

Sioux Falls Good Samaritan Village
3901 S Marion Rd., Sioux Falls, SD 57106, (605) 361-3311; Facility type: Skilled care, Alzheimer's; Beds: 220; Certified: Medicaid, Medicare, Veterans; Evangelical Lutheran Good Samaritan society: Nonprofit; License: state; Activities: Arts & Crafts; Dances; Pet therapy; Chapel; Group exercise; Outings; Support Groups; Other: Alzheimer's secured unit; Affiliations: Lutheran Church.

Vermillion

Sioux Valley Vermillion Care Center
20 S Plum, Vermillion, SD 57069, (605) 624-2611; Facility type: Skilled care, Alzheimer's; Beds: 70; Certified: Medicaid; Owner: Sioux Valley Services; License: state; Activities: Arts & Crafts; Dances; Pet therapy; Group exercise; Outings; Support Groups; Other: Alzheimer's secured unit, Home health care.

Viborg

Pioneer Memorial Nursing Home
315 N Washington, Viborg, SD 57070, (605) 326-5161; Facility type: Skilled care, Alzheimer's; Beds: 50; Certified: Medicaid, Medicare, Veterans; Owner: Nonprofit; License: state; Activities: Arts & Crafts; Dances; Pet therapy; Group exercise; Outings; Support Groups; Other: Adult day care, Home health care.

Winner

Winner Regional Healthcare Center
805 E 8th St., Winner, SD 57580, (605) 842-7200; Facility type: Skilled care, Alzheimer's; Beds: 80; Certified: Medicaid, Medicare, Veterans; Owner: Nonprofit; License: state; Activities: Arts & Crafts; Dances; Pet therapy; Group exercise; Outings; Support Groups; Other: Alzheimer's secured unit; Languages: Lakota.

TENNESSEE

Algood

Masters Healthcare Center
278 Dry Valley Rd., Algood, TN (931) 537-6524; Facility type: Skilled care, Alzheimer's; Beds: 170; Certified: Medicaid, Medicare; Owner: Vencor, Inc.; License: state; Activities: Arts & Crafts; Dances; Pet therapy; Group exercise; Outings; Support Groups; Other: Alzheimer's secured unit.

Ardmore

SunBridge Care & Rehabilitation
25385 Main St., Ardmore, TN 38449, (931) 427-2143; Facility type: Skilled care, Alzheimer's; Beds: 80; Certified: Medicaid, Medicare; Owner: Sun Healthcare; License: state; Activities: Arts & Crafts; Dances; Pet therapy; Group exercise; Outings; Support Groups.

Bruceton

Life Care Center of Bruceton—Hollow Rock
105 Rowland Ave., Bruceton, TN 38317, (901) 586-2061; Facility type: Skilled care, Alzheimer's; Beds: 130; Certified: Medicaid; Owner: Life Care Centers of America; License: state; Activities: Arts & Crafts; Dances; Pet therapy; Group exercise; Outings; Support Groups.

Chattanooga

Life Care Center of East Ridge
1500 Fincher Ave., Chattanooga, TN 37412, (423) 894-1254; Facility type: Skilled care, Alzheimer's; Beds: 160; Certified: Medicaid, Medicare; Owner: Nonprofit; License: state; Activities: Arts & Crafts; Dances; Pet therapy.

NHC Health Care—Chattanooga
2700 Parkwood Ave., Chattanooga, TN 37404, (423) 624-1533; Facility type: Skilled care, Alzheimer's; Beds: 200; Certified: Medicaid, Medicare; Owner: National Healthcare Co; License: state; Activities: Arts & Crafts; Dances; Pet therapy; Group exercise; Outings; Support Groups; Other: Alzheimer's secured unit; Home health care; Languages: Spanish.

Clarksville

General Care Convalescent Center
111 Ussery Rd., Clarksville, TN 37043, (931) 647-0269; Facility type: Skilled care, Alzheimer's; Beds: 130; Certified: Medicaid, Medicare; Owner: Tennessee Health Mgt; License: state; Activities: Arts & Crafts; Dances; Pet therapy; Group exercise; Outings; Support Groups.

Cleveland

Bradley Healthcare & Rehabilitation Center
2910 Peerless Rd. NW, Cleveland, TN 37312, (423) 472-7116; Facility type: Skilled care, Alzheimer's; Beds: 240; Certified: Medicaid, Medicare; Owner: Nonprofit; License: state; Activities: Arts & Crafts; Dances; Pet therapy; Group exercise; Outings; Support Groups; Other: Alzheimer's secured unit.

Royal Care of Cleveland
2750 Executive Park Pl., NW, Cleveland, TN, (423) 476-4444; Facility type: Skilled care, Alzheimer's; Beds: 350; Certified: Medicaid, Medicare, Veterans; Owner: Nonprofit; License: state; Activities: Arts & Crafts; Dances; Pet therapy; Group exercise; Outings; Support Groups; Other: Languages: Spanish.

Columbia

Life Care Center of Columbia
105 N Campbell Blvd., Columbia, TN 38401, (931) 388-5035; Facility type: Skilled care, Alzheimer's; Beds: 120; Certified: Medicaid, Medicare; Owner: Life Care Centers of America; License: state; Activities: Arts & Crafts; Dances; Pet therapy; Group exercise; Outings; Support Groups; Other: Alzheimer's secured unit.

NHC—Hillview Health Care Center
2710 Trotwood Ave., Columbia, TN 38401, (931) 388-7182; Facility type: Skilled care, Alzheimer's; Beds: 90; Certified: Medicaid, Medicare; Owner: National Healthcare Co; License: state; Activities: Arts & Crafts; Dances; Pet therapy; Group exercise; Outings; Support Groups.

Cordova

Cordova Rehabilitation & Nursing Center
955 Germantown Rd., Cordova, TN 38018, (901) 754-1393; Facility type: Skilled care, Alzheimer's; Beds: 220; Certified: Medicaid, Medicare, Veterans; Owner: Vencor, Inc.; License: state; Activities: Arts & Crafts; Dances; Pet therapy; Group exercise; Outings; Support Groups.

Memphis Jewish Home
36 Bazeberry Rd., Cordova, TN 38018, (901) 758-0036; Facility type: Skilled care, Alzheimer's; Beds: 140; Certified: Medicaid, Medicare, Veterans; Owner: Nonprofit; License: state; Activities: Arts & Crafts; Dances; Pet therapy; Group exercise; Outings; Support Groups; Other: Alzheimer's secured unit, Adult day Care; Languages: German, Hebrew, Yiddish, Russian; Affiliations: Jewish.

Crossville

Country Place Health Care Center
80 Justice St., Crossville, TN 38555, (931) 484-4782; Facility type: Skilled care, Alzheimer's; Beds: 350; Certified: Medicaid, Medicare, Veterans; Owner: Private; License: state; Activities: Arts & Crafts; Dances; Pet therapy; Group exercise; Outings; Support Groups; Other: Alzheimer's secured unit.

Elizabethton

Pine Ridge Care Center
1200 Spruce Ln., Elizabethton, TN 37643, (423) 543-3202; Facility type: Skilled care, Alzheimer's; Beds: 90; Certified: Medicaid, Medicare; Owner: Nonprofit; License: state; Activities: Arts & Crafts; Dances; Pet therapy; Group exercise; Outings; Support Groups; Other: Affiliations: Tennessee Health Care Association.

Etowah

Etowah Health Care Center
409 Grady Rd., Etowah, TN 37331, (423) 263-1138; Facility type: Skilled care, Alzheimer's; Beds: 120; Certified: Medicaid, Veterans; Owner: Nonprofit; License: state; Activities: Arts & Crafts; Dances; Pet therapy; Group exercise; Outings; Support Groups.

Fayetteville

Donalson Assisted Living
1681 Winchester Hwy., Fayetteville, TN 37334, (931) 433-7156; Facility type: Skilled care, Alzheimer's; Beds: 350; Certified: Medicaid, Medicare; Owner: State & Local Gov, Lincoln Care Center; License: state; Activities: Arts & Crafts; Dances; Pet therapy; Group exercise; Outings; Support Groups.

Lincoln Care Center
501 Amana Ave., Fayetteville, TN 37334, (931) 433-6146; Facility type: Skilled care, Alzheimer's; Beds: 120; Certified: Medicaid, Medicare; Owner: State & Local Gov; License: state; Activities: Arts & Crafts; Dances; Pet therapy; Group exercise; Outings; Support Groups.

Franklin

Claiborne & Hughes Health Center
200 Strahl St., Franklin, TN 37064, (615) 791-1103; Facility type: Skilled care, Alzheimer's; Beds: 350; Certified: Medicaid, Medicare; Owner: Nonprofit; License: state; Activities: Arts & Crafts; Dances; Pet therapy; Group exercise; Outings; Support Groups; Other: Alzheimer's secured unit, Home health care.

Hermitage

McKendree Village
4347 Lebanon Rd., Hermitage, TN 37076, (615) 871-8232; Facility type: Skilled care, Alzheimer's; Beds: 300; Certified: Medicaid, Medicare; Owner: Nonprofit; License: state; Activities: Arts & Crafts; Dances; Pet therapy; Group exercise; Outings; Support Groups; Other: Alzheimer's secured unit, Home health care; Languages: German, Spanish; Affiliations: United Methodist Church.

Humboldt

Tennessee State Veterans Home
2865 Main St., Humboldt, TN 38343, (901) 784-8405; Facility type: Skilled care, Alzheimer's; Beds: 120; Certified: Medicaid, Medicare, Veterans; Owner: State & Local Gov; License: state; Activities: Arts & Crafts; Dances; Pet therapy; Group exercise; Outings; Support Groups; Other: Alzheimer's secured unit.

Jackson

SunBridge Care & Community Center
131 Cloverdale St., Jackson, TN 38301, (901) 423-8750; Facility type: Skilled care, Alzheimer's; Beds: 110; Certified: Medicaid; Owner: Sun Healthcare Group; License: state; Activities: Arts & Crafts; Dances; Pet therapy; Group exercise; Outings; Support Groups.

Jellico

Beech Tree Manor
240 Hospital Ln., Jellico, TN 37762, (423) 784-6626; Facility type: Skilled care, Alzheimer's; Beds: 100; Certified: Medicaid, Medicare; Owner: Generations Health Assoc; License: state; Activities: Arts & Crafts; Dances; Pet therapy.

Knoxville

Farragut Health Care Center
12823 Kingston Pike, Knoxville, TN 37922, (865) 866-0600; Facility type: Skilled care, Alzheimer's; Beds: 130; Certified: Medicaid, Medicare, Veterans; Owner: Private; License: state; Activities: Arts & Crafts; Dances; Pet therapy; Group exercise; Outings; Support Groups; Other: Alzheimer's secured unit.

Little Creek Sanitarium
1810 Little Creek Ln., Knoxville, TN 37922, (423) 690-6727; Facility type: Skilled care, Alz-

heimer's; Beds: 40; Payer mix: 99% Private pay; Owner: Nonprofit; License: state; Activities: Arts & Crafts; Dances; Pet therapy; Group exercise; Outings; Support Groups; Other: Affiliations: Seventh Day Adventist Church.

La Follette

La Follette Community Nursing Home
200 Tory Rd., La Follette, TN 37766, (423) 566-1161; Facility type: Skilled care, Alzheimer's; Beds: 100; Certified: Medicaid, Medicare, Medi-Cal, Veterans; Owner: State & Local Gov; Managed by: Baptist Health System; License: state; Activities: Arts & Crafts; Dances; Pet therapy; Group exercise; Outings; Support Groups; Other: Home health care.

Lebanon

Quality Care Health Center
932 Baddour Pkwy, Lebanon, TN 37087, (615) 444-1836; Facility type: Skilled care, Alzheimer's; Beds: 250; Certified: Medicaid; Owner: Private; License: state; Activities: Arts & Crafts; Dances; Pet therapy; Group exercise; Outings; Support Groups; Other: Alzheimer's secured unit.

Lexington

Briarwood Community Living Center
PO Box 1067, Lexington, TN 38351, (901) 968-6629; Facility type: Skilled care, Alzheimer's; Beds: 60; Certified: Medicaid, Medicare; Owner: Eldercare Services; License: state; Activities: Arts & Crafts; Dances; Pet therapy; Group exercise; Outings; Support Groups.

Martin

Van Ayer Manor Nursing Center
640 Hannings Ln., Martin, TN 38237, (901) 587-3193; Facility type: Skilled care, Alzheimer's; Beds: 130; Certified: Medicaid; Owner: American Health Foundation; License: state; Activities: Arts & Crafts; Dances; Pet therapy; Group exercise; Outings; Support Groups; Other: Alzheimer's secured unit.

Maryville

Maryville Healthcare & Rehabilitation
1012 Jamestown Way, Maryville, TN 37803. (865) 984-7400; Facility type: Skilled care, Alzheimer's; Beds: 190; Certified: Medicaid, Medicare; Owner: Vencor, Inc.; License: state; Activities: Arts & Crafts; Dances; Pet therapy; Group exercise; Outings; Support Groups.

McMinnville

NHC—McMinnville Health Care Center
928 Old Smithyville Rd., McMinnville, TN 37110, (931) 473-8431; Facility type: Skilled care, Alzheimer's; Beds: 150; Certified: Medicaid, Medicare, Veterans; Owner: National Healthcare Co; License: state; Activities: Arts & Crafts; Dances; Pet therapy; Group exercise; Outings; Support Groups; Other: Alzheimer's secured unit.

Raintree Manor
415 Pace St., McMinnville, TN 37110, (931) 668-2011; Facility type: Skilled care, Alzheimer's; Beds: 140; Certified: Medicaid, Medicare; Owner: Proprietary/Public; License: state; Activities: Arts & Crafts; Dances; Pet therapy; Group exercise; Outings; Support Groups; Other: Alzheimer's secured unit.

Memphis

Allenbrooke Health Care Center
3933 Allenbrooke Cove, Memphis, TN 38118, (901) 795-2444; Facility type: Skilled care, Alzheimer's; Beds: 180; Certified: Medicaid, Medicare, Veterans; Owner: Beverly Enterprises; License: state; Activities: Arts & Crafts; Dances; Pet therapy; Group exercise; Outings; Support Groups; Other: Alzheimer's secured unit.

Bright Glade Convalescent Center
5070 Sanderlin Ave., Memphis, TN 38117, (901) 682-5677; Facility type: Skilled care, Alzheimer's; Beds: 85; Payer mix: 100% Private pay; Owner: Proprietary; License: state; Activities: Arts & Crafts; Dances; Pet therapy; Group exercise; Outings; Support Groups; Other: Alzheimer's secured unit.

Court Manor Nursing Center
1414 Court St., Memphis, TN 38104, (901) 272-2494; Facility type: Skilled care, Alzheimer's; Beds: 98; Certified: Medicaid; Owner: Proprietary/Public; License: state; Activities: Arts & Crafts; Dances; Pet therapy; Group exercise; Support Groups; Other: Alzheimer's secured unit; Languages: Spanish.

Kirby Pines Manor
3535 Kirby Rd., Memphis, TN 38115, (901) 365-0772; Facility type: Skilled care, Alzheimer's; Beds: 120; Certified: Medicare; Payer mix: 91% Private pay; 9% Medicare; Owner: Retirement Communities of America; License: state; Activities: Arts & Crafts; Dances; Pet therapy; Group exercise; Outings; Support Groups; Other: Alzheimer's secured unit, Adult day care.

Saint Peter Villa Rehabilitation & Nursing Center
141 N McLean, Memphis, TN 38104, (901) 276-2021; Facility type: Skilled care, Alzheimer's; Beds: 150; Certified: Medicaid, Medicare; Owner: Nonprofit; License: state; Activities: Arts & Crafts; Pet therapy; Group exercise; Outings; Support Groups; Other: Affiliations: Catholic Church.

Senior Services Healthcare Services
2380 James Rd., Memphis, TN 38127, (901) 358-1707; Facility type: Skilled care, Alzheimer's; Beds: 150; Certified: Medicaid; Owner: Nonprofit; License: state; Activities: Arts & Crafts; Dances; Pet therapy; Group exercise; Outings; Support Groups; Other: Affiliations: Church of Christ.

Nashville

Belcourt Terrace Nursing Home
1710 Belcourt Ave., Nashville, TN 37212, (615) 383-3570; Facility type: Skilled care, Alzheimer's; Beds: 50; Certified: Medicare; Owner: Nonprofit; License: state; Activities: Arts & Crafts; Dances; Pet therapy; Group exercise; Outings; Support Groups; Other: Alzheimer's secured unit.

Health Care Center at Richland Place
504 Elmington Ave., Nashville, TN 37205, (615) 292-4900; Facility type: Skilled care, Alzheimer's; Beds: 90; Certified: Medicare; Payer Mix: 10% Medicare; 90% Private pay; Owner: National Health Care Corp; License: state; Activities: Arts & Crafts; Dances; Pet therapy; Group exercise; Outings; Support Groups.

Mariner Health Care of Nashville
3939 Hillsboro Cir., Nashville, TN 37215, (615) 297-2100; Facility type: Skilled care, Alzheimer's; Beds: 50; Certified: Medicare; Payer mix: Medicare—40%, Private pay—60%; Owner: Mariner Post Acute Network; License: state; Activities: Arts & Crafts; Dances; Pet therapy; Group exercise; Outings; Support Groups; Other: Alzheimer's secured unit.

The Meadows
8044 Coley Davis Rd., Nashville, TN 37221, 9615) 646-4466; Facility type: Skilled care, Alzheimer's; Beds: 130; Payer mix: 100% Private pay; Owner: Nonprofit; License: state; Activities: Arts & Crafts; Pet therapy; Group exercise; Outings; Support Groups; Other: Alzheimer's secured unit; Affiliations: Church of Christ.

Trevecca Health Care Center
329 Murfreesboro Rd., Nashville, TN 37210, (615) 244-6900; Facility type: Skilled care, Alzheimer's; Beds: 240; Certified: Medicaid, Medicare; Owner: Private; License: state; Activities: Arts & Crafts; Dances; Pet therapy; Group exercise; Outings; Support Groups; Other: Alzheimer's secured unit; Affiliations: Nazarene Church.

Wedgewood
832 Wedgewood Ave., Nashville, TN 37202, (615) 383-4006; Facility type: Skilled care, Alzheimer's; Beds: 180; Payer mix: 100% Private; Owner: Nonprofit; License: state; Activities: Arts & Crafts; Dances; Pet therapy; Group exercise; Outings; Support Groups; Affiliations: Church of Christ.

Pulaski

Meadowbrook Nursing Home
1245 E College St., Pulaski, TN 38478, (931) 363-7548; Facility type: Skilled care, Alzheimer's; Beds: 80; Certified: Medicaid; Owner: Nonprofit; License: state; Activities: Arts & Crafts; Dances; Pet therapy; Group exercise; Outings; Support Groups; Other: Alzheimer's secured unit.

NHC Health Care
993 E College, Pulaski, TN 38478, (931) 363-3572; Facility type: Skilled care, Alzheimer's; Beds: 100; Certified: Medicaid, Medicare, Veterans; Owner: National Healthcare Co; License: state; Activities: Arts & Crafts; Dances; Pet therapy; Group exercise; Outings; Support Groups; Other: Home health care; Languages: Spanish.

Sneedville

Hancock Manor Nursing Home
E Main St., Sneedville, TN 37869, (423) 733-4783; Facility type: Skilled care, Alzheimer's; Beds: 50; Certified: Medicaid; Owner: Nonprofit; License: state; Activities: Arts & Crafts; Dances; Pet therapy; Group exercise; Outings; Support Groups; Other: Affiliations: Tennessee Health Care Association.

Tiptonville

SunBridge Care & Rehabilitation for Reelfoot
1034 Reelfoot Dr., Tiptonville, TN 38079, (901) 253-6681; Facility type: Skilled care, Alzheimer's; Beds: 130; Certified: Medicaid, Medicare; Owner: Nonprofit; License: state; Activities: Arts & Crafts; Dances; Pet therapy; Group exercise; Outings; Support Groups; Other: Alzheimer's secured unit.

Westmoreland

Royal Care of Westmoreland
1559 New Hwy., 52, Westmoreland, TN 37186, (615) 644-5111; Facility type: Skilled care, Alzheimer's; Beds: 100; Certified: Medicaid, Medicare; Owner: Royal Care Inc.; License: state; Activities: Arts & Crafts; Dances; Pet therapy; Group exercise; Outings; Support Groups.

Winchester

Beverly Healthcare
1360 Bypass Rd., Winchester, TN 37398, (931) 967-7082; Facility type: Skilled care, Alzheimer's; Beds: 120; Certified: Medicaid, Medicare, Veterans; Owner: Beverly Enterprises; License: state; Activities: Arts & Crafts; Dances; Pet therapy; Group exercise; Outings; Support Groups.

SunBridge Care & Rehabilitation Center
32 Memorial Dr., Winchester, TN 37398, (931) 967-0200; Facility type: Skilled care, Alzheimer's; Beds: 80; Certified: Medicaid; Owner: Sun Healthcare; License: state; Activities: Arts & Crafts; Dances; Pet therapy; Group exercise; Outings; Support Groups.

TEXAS

Abilene

Abilene Convalescent Center
2630 Old Anson Rd., Abilene, TX 79603, (915) 673-5101; Facility type: Skilled care, Alzheimer's; Beds: 105; Certified: Medicaid, Medicare; Owner: Pyramid Healthcare; License: state; Activities: Arts & Crafts; Dances; Pet therapy; Group exercise; Outings; Support Groups; Other: Languages: Spanish.

Coronado Nursing Center
1751 N 15th St., Abilene, TX 79603, (915) 673-3531; Facility type: Skilled care, Alzheimer's; Beds: 200; Certified: Medicaid, Medicare, Veterans; Owner: Fountain View, Inc.; License: state; Activities: Arts & Crafts; Dances; Pet therapy; Outings; Support Groups; Other: Alzheimer's secured unit; Languages: Spanish.

Wind Crest Alzheimer's Care Center
6050 Hospital Dr., Abilene, TX 79606, (915) 692-1533; Facility type: Skilled care, Alzheimer's; Beds: 100; Certified: Medicaid, Medicare, Veterans; Owner: Sears Methodist Retirement System; License: state; Activities: Pet therapy; Group exercise; Outings; Other: Alzheimer's secured unit.

Alvarado

Alvarado Nursing Home
101 N Parkway, Alvarado, TX 76009, (817) 790-3304; Facility type: Skilled care, Alzheimer's; Beds: 120; Certified: Medicaid, Medicare, Veterans; Owner: Nonprofit; License: state; Activities: Arts & Crafts; Dances; Pet therapy; Group exercise; Outings; Support Groups; Other: Alzheimer's secured unit.

Amarillo

Amarillo Nursing Center
4033 W 51st Ave., Amarillo, TX 79109, (806) 355-4488; Facility type: Skilled care, Alzheimer's; Beds: 150; Certified: Medicaid, Medicare, Veterans; Owner: Private; License: state; Activities: Arts & Crafts; Dances; Pet therapy; Outings; Support Groups; Other: Alzheimer's secured unit; Languages: Spanish.

Heritage Convalescent Center
1009 Clyde St., Amarillo, TX 79106, (806) 352-5295; Facility type: Skilled care, Alzheimer's; Beds: 120; Certified: Medicaid, Medicare, Veterans; Owner: Proprietary/Public. License: state; Activities: Arts & Crafts; Dances; Pet therapy; Group exercise; Outings; Support Groups.

HIS of Amarillo
5601 Plum Creek Dr., Amarillo, TX79124, (806) 351-1000; Facility type: Skilled care, Alzheimer's; Beds: 50; Certified: Medicaid, Medicare, Veterans; Owner: Private; License: state; Activities: Arts & Crafts; Dances; Pet therapy; Group exercise; Support Groups; Other: Alzheimer's secured unit; Languages: Spanish.

Palo Duro Care Center
1931 Medipark Dr., Amarillo, TX 79106, (806) 352-5600; Facility type: Skilled care, Alzheimer's; Beds: 120; Certified: Medicaid, Medicare, Veterans; Owner: Private; License: state; Activities: Arts & Crafts; Dances; Pet therapy; Group exercise; Outings; Support Groups; Other: Alzheimer's secured unit.

Arsansas Pass

Aransas Pass Nursing & Convalescent Center
1661 W Yoakum St., Aransas Pass, TX 78336, (361) 758-7686; Facility type: Skilled care, Alz-

heimer's; Beds: 170; Certified: Medicaid, Medicare; Owner: Nonprofit; License: state; Activities: Arts & Crafts; Dances; Pet therapy; Group exercise; Outings; Support Groups; Other: Alzheimer's secured unit.

Arlington

Mariner Health Care of Arlington
2645 W Randol Mill Rd., Arlington, TX 76012, (817) 277-6789; Facility type: Skilled care, Alzheimer's; Beds: 150; Certified: Medicaid, Medicare; Owner: Proprietary/Public; License: state; Activities: Arts & Crafts; Dances; Pet therapy; Group exercise; Outings; Support Groups; Other: Alzheimer's secured unit, Adult day care.

Austin

Buckner Villas
1110 Tom Adams Dr., Austin, TX 78753, (512) 836-1515; http://www.bucknervillas.citysearch.com; Facility type: Skilled care, Alzheimer's; Beds: 110; Certified: Medicaid, Medicare, Veterans; Owner: Nonprofit; License: state; Activities: Arts & Crafts; Pet therapy; Group exercise; Outings; Support Groups; Other: Alzheimer's secured unit, Adult day care; Affiliations: Baptist; Languages: Spanish.

Gracy Woods II Living Center
12042 Bittern Hollow, Austin, TX 78758, (512) 836-4241; Facility type: Skilled care, Alzheimer's; Beds: 110; Certified: Medicaid; Owner: Nonprofit; License: state; Activities: Arts & Crafts; Dances; Pet therapy; Group exercise.

Gracy Woods Nursing Center
12021 Metric Blvd., Austin, TX 78758, (512) 339-7687; Facility type: Skilled care, Alzheimer's; Beds: 120; Certified: Medicaid; Owner: Nonprofit; License: state; Activities: Arts & Crafts; Dances; Pet therapy; Group exercise; Outings; Support Groups; Other: Languages: Spanish.

Spring Season of Austin
3101 Govalle Ave., Austin, TX 78702, (512) 926-7871; Facility type: Skilled care, Alzheimer's; Beds: 80; Certified: Medicaid, Medicare; Owner: Care Centers Mgt; License: state; Activities: Arts & Crafts; Dances; Pet therapy; Group exercise; Support Groups; Other: Alzheimer's secured unit; Languages: Spanish.

Ballinger

Reynolds Nursing A Rehabilitation Center
1800 N Broadway Bronte Hwy., Ballinger, TX 76821; Facility type: Skilled care, Alzheimer's; Beds: 150; Certified: Medicaid, Medicare; Owner: Proprietary; License: state; Activities: Arts & Crafts; Dances; Pet therapy; Group exercise; Outings; Support Groups; Other: Alzheimer's secured unit.

Beaumont

Canterbury Villa of Beaumont
1020 S 23rd St., Beaumont, TX 77707, (409) 842-9700; Facility type: Skilled care, Alzheimer's; Beds: 150; Certified: Medicaid, Medicare; Owner: Nonprofit; License: state; Activities: Arts & Crafts; Dances; Pet therapy; Group exercise; Outings; Support Groups.

Big Spring

Comanche Trail Nursing Center
3200 Parkway Dr., Big Spring, TX 79720, (915) 263-4041; Facility type: Skilled care, Alzheimer's; Beds: 350; Certified: Medicaid, Medicare, Veterans; Owner: Fountain View, Inc.; License: state; Activities: Arts & Crafts; Dances; Pet therapy; Group exercise; Outings; Support Groups; Other: Alzheimer's secured unit; Languages: Spanish.

Brownsville

Ebony Lake Healthcare Center
1001 Central Blvd., Brownsville, TX 78520, (956) 541-0917; Facility type: Skilled care, Alzheimer's; Beds: 110; Certified: Medicaid, Medicare; Owner: Nonprofit; License: state; Activities: Arts & Crafts; Dances; Pet therapy; Group exercise; Outings; Support Groups; Other: Languages: Spanish.

Valley Grande Manor
901 Wild Rose Ln., Brownsville, TX 78520, (956) 546-4568; Facility type: Skilled care, Alzheimer's; Beds: 160; Certified: Medicaid, Medicare; Owner: Nonprofit; License: state; Activities: Arts & Crafts; Dances; Pet therapy; Support Groups; Other: Affiliations: Seventh Day Adventist Church; Languages: Spanish.

Columbus

River Oaks Convalescent Center
300 North St., Columbus, TX 78934, (979) 732-2347; Facility type: Skilled care, Alzheimer's; Beds: 150; Certified: Medicaid; Owner: Private; License: state; Activities: Arts & Crafts; Dances; Pet therapy; Group exercise; Outings; Support Groups; Other: Alzheimer's secured unit.

Corpus Christi

Alameda Oaks Nursing Center
1101 S Alameda St., Corpus Christi, TX 78404, (361) 882-2711; Facility type: Skilled care, Alzheimer's; Beds: 150; Certified: Medicaid, Medicare; Owner: Life Care Centers of America; License: state; Activities: Arts & Crafts; Dances; Pet therapy; Group exercise; Outings; Support Groups.

Harbor View Care Center
1310 3rd St., Corpus Christi, TX 78404, (361) 888-5511; Facility type: Skilled care, Alzheimer's; Beds: 80; Certified: Medicaid, Medicare; Owner: Nonprofit; License: state; Activities: Arts & Crafts; Dances; Pet therapy; Group exercise.

South Park Rehabilitation & Nursing Center
3115 McArdle, Corpus Christi, TX 78415, (361) 853-2577; Facility type: Skilled care, Alzheimer's; Beds: 190; Certified: Medicaid, Medicare; Owner: Proprietary/Public; License: state; Activities: Arts & Crafts; Dances; Pet therapy; Group exercise; Outings; Other: Alzheimer's secured unit.

Sunnybrook Health Care Center
3050 Sunnybrook Dr., Corpus Christi, TX 78415, (361) 853-9981; Facility type: Skilled care, Alzheimer's; Beds: 180; Certified: Medicaid; Owner: Proprietary/Public; License: state; Activities: Arts & Crafts; Dances; Pet therapy; Group exercise; Outings; Support Groups; Other: Alzheimer's secured unit.

Westwood Manor
801 Cantwell Ln., Corpus Christi, TX 78408, (361) 882-4284; Facility type: Skilled care, Alzheimer's; Beds: 70; Certified: Medicaid, Medicare; Owner: Proprietary/Public; License: state; Activities: Arts & Crafts; Dances; Pet therapy; Group exercise; Outings; Support Groups; Other: Alzheimer's secured unit.

Dallas

C.C. Young Memorial Home—Young Health Center
4829 Lawther Dr., Dallas, TX 75214, (214) 841-8080; http://www.ccyoung.org; Facility type: Skilled care, Alzheimer's; Beds: 95; Certified: Medicaid, Medicare, Veterans; Owner: Nonprofit; License: state; Activities: Arts & Crafts; Outings; Pet therapy; Other: Alzheimer's secured unit, Adult day care, Home health care; Affiliations: Methodist Church.

Dallas Home for Jewish Aged
2525 Centerville Rd., Dallas, TX 75228, (214) 327-4503; Facility type: Skilled care, Alzheimer's; Beds: 300; Certified: Medicaid, Medicare, Veterans; Owner: Nonprofit; License: state; Activities: Arts & Crafts; Dances; Pet therapy; Group exercise; Outings; Support Groups; Other: Alzheimer's secured unit; Languages: Yiddish, Spanish, Russian; Affiliations: Jewish.

Dallas Nursing & Rehabilitation Center
11301 Dennis Rd., Dallas, TX 75229, (972) 247-4866; Facility type: Skilled care, Alzheimer's; Beds: 180; Certified: Medicaid, Medicare, Veterans; Owner: New Care Health Corp; License: state; Activities: Arts & Crafts; Dances; Pet therapy; Group exercise; Outings; Support Groups; Other: Alzheimer's secured unit; Languages: Spanish, Korean.

IHS at Doctor's Healthcare Center
9009 White Rock Tr., Dallas, TX 75238, (214) 355-3300; Facility type: Skilled care, Alzheimer's; Beds: 300; Certified: Medicaid, Medicare; Owner: Proprietary/Public; License: state; Activities: Arts & Crafts; Dances; Pet therapy; Group exercise; Outings; Support Groups; Other: Alzheimer's secured unit.

Manor Care Health Services
3326 Burgoyne St., Dallas, TX 75233, (214) 330-9391; Facility type: Skilled care, Alzheimer's; Beds: 210; Certified: Medicaid, Medicare, Veterans; Owner: HCR Manor Care; License: state; Activities: Arts & Crafts; Dances; Pet therapy; Group exercise; Outings; Support Groups; Other: Alzheimer's secured unit, Adult day care.

Presbyterian Village North
8600 Skyline Dr., Dallas, TX 75243, 9214) 345-9000; Facility type: Skilled care, Alzheimer's; Beds: 330; Payer mix: 100% Private pay; Owner: Nonprofit; License: state; Activities: Arts & Crafts; Dances; Pet therapy; Group exercise; Outings; Support Groups; Other: Alzheimer's secured unit, Adult day care.

Walnut Place
5515 Glen Lakes Dr., Dallas, TX 75231, (214) 361-8923; Facility type: Skilled care, Alzheimer's; Beds: 310; Payer mix: 99% Private pay; Owner: Nonprofit; License: state; Activities: Arts & Crafts; Dances; Pet therapy; Group exercise; Outings; Support Groups; Other: Alzheimer's secured unit; Home health care.

Denton

Denton Rehabilitation & Nursing Center
2229 N Carroll Blvd., Denton, TX 76201, (940) 387-8505; Facility type: Skilled care, Alzheimer's; Beds: 210; Certified: Medicaid, Medicare, Veterans; Owner: Proprietary/Public; License: state; Activities: Arts & Crafts; Dances; Pet

therapy; Group exercise; Outings; Support Groups.

El Paso

Health Center at the Montevista at Coronado
1575 Belvidere St., El Paso, TX 79912, (915) 833-3864; Facility type: Skilled care, Alzheimer's; Beds: 130; Certified: Medicaid, Medicare; Owner: Marriott Senior Living Services; License: state; Activities: Arts & Crafts; Dances; Pet therapy; Group exercise; Outings; Support Groups; Other: Alzheimer's secured unit Languages: Spanish.

Sunset Haven Nursing Center
9001 N Loop Rd., El Paso, TX 79907, (915) 859-1650; Facility type: Skilled care, Alzheimer's; Beds: 50; Certified: Medicaid, Medicare, Veterans; Owner: Healthco, Inc.; License: state; Activities: Arts & Crafts; Dances; Pet therapy; Group exercise; Outings; Support Groups; Other: Languages: Spanish.

White Acres Good Samaritan Retirement Village & Nursing Center
7304 Good Samaritan Ct., El Paso, TX 79912, (915) 581-4683; Facility type: Skilled care, Alzheimer's; Beds: 60; Certified: Medicaid, Medicare; Owner: Nonprofit; License: state; Activities: Arts & Crafts; Dances; Pet therapy; Group exercise; Outings; Support Groups.

Ennis

Ennis Care Center
1200 S Hall St., Ennis, TX 75119, (972) 875-9051; Facility type: Skilled care, Alzheimer's; Beds: 150; Certified: Medicaid, Medicare, Veterans; Owner: Integrated Health Services; License: state; Activities: Arts & Crafts; Dances; Pet therapy; Group exercise; Support Groups; Other: Alzheimer's secured unit, Adult day care.

Odd Fellow & Rebekah Nursing Home
2300 Oak Grove Rd., Ennis, TX 75119, (972) 875-8643; Facility type: Skilled care, Alzheimer's; Beds: 120; Certified: Medicaid, Medicare; Owner: Nonprofit; License: state; Activities: Arts & Crafts; Dances; Pet therapy; Group exercise; Outings; Support Groups; Other: Alzheimer's secured unit.

Farwell

Farwell Convalescent Center
305 5th St., Farwell, TX 79325, (806) 481-9027; Facility type: Skilled care, Alzheimer's; Beds: 130; Certified: Medicaid, Medicare; Owner: Evangelic Lutheran Good Samaritan Society; License: state; Activities: Arts & Crafts; Dances; Pet therapy; Group exercise; Outings; Support Groups; Other: Alzheimer's secured unit: Languages: Spanish.

Fort Worth

Alta Mesa Nursing Center
5300 Alta Mesa Blvd., Fort Worth, TX 76133, (817) 346-1800; Facility type: Skilled care, Alzheimer's; Beds: 120; Certified: Medicaid; Owner: Proprietary/Public; License: state; Activities: Arts & Crafts; Dances; Pet therapy.

Haltom Convalescent Center
2936 Markum Dr., Fort Worth, TX 76117, (817) 831-0545; Facility type: Skilled care, Alzheimer's; Beds: 50; Certified: Medicaid, Medicare; Owner: State & Local Gov; License: state; Activities: Arts & Crafts; Dances; Pet therapy.

Heritage Western Hills
8001 Western Hills Blvd., Fort Worth, TX 76108, (817) 246-4953; Facility type: Skilled care, Alzheimer's; Beds: 70; Certified: Medicaid, Medicare, Veterans; Owner: Integrated Health Services; License: state; Activities: Arts & Crafts; Dances; Pet therapy; Group exercise; Outings; Other: Alzheimer's secured unit.

Lake Lodge Care Center
3899 Marina Dr., Fort Worth, TX 76135, (817) 237-7231; Facility type: Skilled care, Alzheimer's; Beds: 90; Certified: Medicaid, Medicare; Owner: Proprietary/Public; License: state; Activities: Arts & Crafts; Dances; Pet therapy; Group exercise; Outings; Support Groups; Other: Adult day care.

Renaissance Park Multi-Care Center
4252 Bryant Irvin Rd., Fort Worth, TX 76109, (817) 738-2975; Facility type: Skilled care, Alzheimer's; Beds: 120; Certified: Medicare; Payer mix: 83% Private pay, 17% Medicare; Owner: Life Care Centers of America; License: state; Activities: Arts & Crafts; Dances; Pet therapy; Group exercise; Outings; Support Groups; Other: Alzheimer's secured unit, Adult day care.

Friona

Prairie Acres
201 E 15th St., Friona, TX 79035, (806) 250-3922; Facility type: Skilled care, Alzheimer's; Beds: 150; Certified: Medicaid, Medicare, Veterans; Owner: State & Local Gov; License: state; Activities: Arts & Crafts; Dances; Pet therapy; Group exercise; Support Groups; Other: Alzheimer's secured unit; Languages: Spanish.

Garland

Castle Manor
1922 Castle Dr., Garland, TX 75040, (972) 494-1471; Facility type: Skilled care, Alzheimer's; Beds: 90; Certified: Medicaid, Medicare; Owner: Mariner Post Acute Network; License: state; Activities: Arts & Crafts; Dances; Pet therapy; Group exercise; Outings; Support Groups; Other: Alzheimer's secured unit.

Georgetown

Wesleyan Nursing Home
2001 Scenic Dr., Georgetown, TX 78626, (512) 863-9511; Facility type: Skilled care, Alzheimer's; Beds: 220; Certified: Medicaid, Medicare; Owner: Nonprofit; License: state; Activities: Arts & Crafts; Dances; Pet therapy; Group exercise; Outings; Support Groups; Other: Alzheimer's secured unit; Affiliations: Methodist Church; Languages: Spanish.

Giddings

Country Care Plex
1181 N Williamson, Giddings, TX 78942, (409) 542-3611; Facility type: Skilled care, Alzheimer's; Beds: 90; Certified: Medicaid; Owner: Nonprofit; License: state; Activities: Arts & Crafts; Dances; Pet therapy; Group exercise; Outings; Support Groups; Other: Alzheimer's secured unit; Languages: German.

Oakland Manor Nursing Center
1400 N Main St., Giddings, TX 78942, (409) 542-1755; Facility type: Skilled care, Alzheimer's; Beds: 120; Certified: Medicaid, Medicare, Veterans; Owner: Fountain View, Inc.; License: state; Activities: Arts & Crafts; Dances; Pet therapy; Group exercise; Outings; Support Groups; Other: Alzheimer's secured unit.

Goldthwaite

Goldthwaite Senior Health Center
1207 Reynolds St., Goldthwaite, TX 76844, 9915) 648-2258; Facility type: Skilled care, Alzheimer's; Beds: 50; Certified: Medicaid, Veterans; Owner: Proprietary/Public; License: state; Activities: Arts & Crafts; Dances; Pet therapy; Group exercise; Outings; Support Groups.

Hillview Manor
1110 Rice St., Goldthwaite, TX 76844, (915) 648-2247, Facility type: Skilled care, Alzheimer's; Beds: 350; Certified: Medicaid, Medicare, Veterans; Owner: Mariner Post Acute Network; License: state; Activities: Arts & Crafts; Dances; Pet therapy; Group exercise; Outings; Support Groups; Other: Alzheimer's secured unit.

Hamilton

Forest Ridge Care Center
199 Hwy. 22 E, Hamilton, TX 76531, (254) 386-3171; Facility type: Skilled care, Alzheimer's; Beds: 80; Certified: Medicaid, Medicare, Veterans; Owner: Nonprofit; License: state; Activities: Arts & Crafts; Dances; Pet therapy; Group exercise; Outings; Support Groups; Other: Adult day care.

Harlingen

Harlingen Nursing Center
3810 Hale St., Harlingen, TX 78550, (956) 412-8660; Facility type: Skilled care, Alzheimer's; Beds: 150; Certified: Medicaid, Medicare; Owner: Regency Nursing Centers; License: state; Activities: Arts & Crafts; Dances; Pet therapy; Group exercise; Outings; Support Groups; Other: Alzheimer's secured unit.

Houston

Beechnut Manor
12777 Beechnut St., Houston, TX 77072, (281) 879-8040; Facility type: Skilled care, Alzheimer's; Beds: 150; Certified: Medicaid, Medicare, Veterans; Owner: Living Centers of America; License: state; Activities: Arts & Crafts; Dances; Pet therapy; Group exercise; Outings; Support Groups; Other: Adult day care.

Clarewood House Extended Care Center
7400 Clarewood Dr., Houston, TX 77036, (713) 774-5821; Facility type: Skilled care, Alzheimer's; Beds: 60; Payer mix: 99% Private pay; Owner: Nonprofit; License: state; Activities: Arts & Crafts; Dances; Pet therapy; Group exercise; Outings; Support Groups; Other: Alzheimer's secured unit; Home health care; Affiliations: Methodist Church.

Heart of Texas Health Care & Rehabilitation Center—All Seasons
6150 S Loop E, Houston, TX 77087, (713) 643-2628; Facility type: Skilled care, Alzheimer's; Beds: 120; Certified: Medicaid, Medicare; Owner: Heart of TX Healthcare; License: state; Activities: Arts & Crafts; Dances; Pet therapy; Group exercise; Outings; Support Groups; Other: Alzheimer's secured unit; Languages: Spanish.

Manor Care of Sharpview
7505 Bellerive, Houston, TX 77036, (713) 774-9611; Facility type: Skilled care, Alzheimer's; Beds: 130; Certified: Medicare; Payer mix: 95% Private pay, 5% Medicare; Owner: HCR Manor Care; License: state; Activities: Arts & Crafts; Dances; Pet therapy; Group exercise; Outings;

Support Groups; Other: Alzheimer's secured unit, Adult day care; Languages: Spanish.

Parkway Place
1321 Park Bayou Dr., Houston, TX 77077, (281) 759-6270; Facility type: Skilled care, Alzheimer's; Beds: 150; Certified: Medicaid; Owner: Religious, Capital Senior Management; License: state; Activities: Arts & Crafts; Dances; Pet therapy; Group exercise; Outings; Support Groups; Other: Alzheimer's secured unit, Adult day care; Affiliations: Baptist Church.

Saint Dominic Nursing Home
2409 E Holcombe Blvd., Houston, TX 77021, (713) 741-8701; Facility type: Skilled care, Alzheimer's; Beds: 150; Certified: Medicaid; Owner: Nonprofit; License: state; Activities: Arts & Crafts; Dances; Pet therapy; Group exercise; Outings; Support Groups; Other: Alzheimer's secured unit; Affiliations: Catholic diocese of Galveston-Houston.

Irving

Ashford Hall
2021 Shoaf Dr., Irving, TX 75061, (972) 579-1919; Facility type: Skilled care, Alzheimer's; Beds: 250; Certified: Medicaid, Medicare, Veterans; Owner: Lion Health Centers; License: state; Activities: Arts & Crafts; Dances; Pet therapy; Group exercise; Outings; Support Groups; Other: Alzheimer's secured unit, Home health care.

Kerrville

Edgewater Care Center
1213 Water St., Kerrville, TX 78028, (830) 896-2411; Facility type: Skilled care, Alzheimer's; Beds: 180; Certified: Medicaid, Medicare, Veterans; Owner: Mariner Post Acute Network; License: state; Activities: Arts & Crafts; Dances; Pet therapy; Group exercise; Outings; Support Groups; Other: Alzheimer's secured unit.

Levelland

Levelland Nursing Home
210 W Ave., Levelland, TX 79336, (806) 894-7011; Facility type: Skilled care, Alzheimer's; Beds: 100; Certified: Medicaid, Medicare, Veterans; Owner: Mariner Post Acute Network; License: state; Activities: Arts & Crafts; Dances; Pet therapy; Group exercise; Outings; Support Groups; Other: Alzheimer's secured unit.

Lynwood Manor
803 S Alamo, Levelland, TX 79336, (806) 894-2806; Facility type: Skilled care, Alzheimer's; Beds: 370; Certified: Medicaid, Medicare, Veterans; Owner: Nonprofit; License: state; Activities: Arts & Crafts; Dances; Pet therapy; Group exercise; Outings; Support Groups; Other: Alzheimer's secured unit.

Lockhart

Chisolm Trail Living & Rehabilitation Center
107 N Medina, Lockhart, TX 78644, (512) 398-5213; Facility type: Skilled care, Alzheimer's; Beds: 100; Certified: Medicaid, Medicare; Owner: Diversicare Management Services; License: state; Activities: Arts & Crafts; Dances; Pet therapy; Group exercise; Other: Alzheimer's secured unit.

Longview

The Clairmont Longview
3201 N 4th St., Longview, TX 75605, (903) 263-4291; Facility type: Skilled care, Alzheimer's; Beds: 180; Certified: Medicaid, Medicare; Owner: Nonprofit; License: state; Activities: Arts & Crafts; Dances; Pet therapy; Group exercise; Outings; Support Groups; Other: Alzheimer's secured unit.

Lynn Lodge Nursing Center
111 Ruthlynn Dr., Longview, TX 75601, (903) 757-2557; Facility type: Skilled care, Alzheimer's; Beds: 110; Certified: Medicaid, Medicare; Owner: Mariner Post Acute Network; License: state; Activities: Arts & Crafts; Dances; Pet therapy; Group exercise; Outings; Other: Alzheimer's secured unit, adult day care.

Lubbock

Lubbock Hospitality House
4710 Slide Rd., Lubbock, TX 79414, (806) 797-3481; Facility type: Skilled care, Alzheimer's; Beds: 110; Certified: Medicaid, Medicare; Owner: Fountain View, Inc.; License: state; Activities: Arts & Crafts; Dances; Pet therapy; Group exercise; Outings; Support Groups.

Lutheran Home of West Texas
5502 W 4th St., Lubbock, TX 79416, (806) 793-1111; Facility type: Skilled care, Alzheimer's; Beds: 150; Certified: Medicaid, Medicare, Veterans; Owner: Nonprofit; License: state; Activities: Arts & Crafts; Dances; Pet therapy; Group exercise; Outings; Support Groups; Other: Alzheimer's secured unit.

Lufkin

Pine Haven Nursing Home
1712 N. Timberland, Lufkin, TX 75901, (409)

632-3347; Facility type: Skilled care, Alzheimer's; Beds: 80; Certified: Medicaid, Medicare; Owner: Medcare Cantex Healthcare; License: state; Activities: Arts & Crafts; Dances; Pet therapy; Group exercise; Outings; Support Groups; Other: Alzheimer's secured unit.

Pinecrest Retirement Community
1302 Tom Temple Dr., Lufkin, TX 75904, (409) 634-1054; Facility type: Skilled care, Alzheimer's; Beds: 50; Payer mix: 100% Private pay; Owner: Nonprofit; License: state; Activities: Arts & Crafts; Dances; Pet therapy; Group exercise; Outings; Support Groups; Other: Alzheimer's secured unit.

Luling

Cartwheel Lodge of Luling
105 N. Magnolia, Luling, TX 78648, (830) 875-5606; Facility type: Skilled care, Alzheimer's; Beds: 120; Certified: Medicaid; Owner: Private; License: state; Activities: Arts & Crafts; Dances; Pet therapy; Group exercise; Outings; Support Groups; Other: Alzheimer's secured unit, Adult day care.

Midland

Manor Park
2208 N Loop 250 W, Midland, TX 79707, (915) 689-9898; Facility type: Skilled care, Alzheimer's; Beds: 180; Certified: Medicaid; Owner: Nonprofit; License: state; Activities: Arts & Crafts; Dances; Pet therapy; Group exercise; Outings; Support Groups; Other: Alzheimer's secured unit.

Rockwood Manor
2000 N Main, Midland, TX 79705, (915) 686-1898; Facility type: Skilled care, Alzheimer's; Beds: 110; Certified: Medicaid, Medicare, Veterans; Owner: Nonprofit; License: state; Activities: Arts & Crafts; Dances; Pet therapy; Group exercise; Outings; Support Groups; Other: Alzheimer's secured unit.

Mount Pleasant

SunRise Care & Rehabilitation for Mount Pleasant
1606 Memorial St., Mount Pleasant, TX 75455, (903) 572-3618; Facility type: Skilled care, Alzheimer's; Beds: 130; Certified: Medicaid, Medicare, Veterans; Owner: Sun Healthcare; License: state; Activities: Arts & Crafts; Dances; Pet therapy; Group exercise; Outings; Support Groups; Other: Alzheimer's secured unit.

New Braunfels

Colonial Manor Nursing & Rehabilitation Center
821 Business 35 W, New Braunfels, TX 78130, (830) 625-7526; Facility type: Skilled care, Alzheimer's; Beds: 150; Certified: Medicaid, Medicare, Veterans; Owner: Fountain View, Inc.; License: state; Activities: Arts & Crafts; Dances; Pet therapy; Group exercise; Outings; Support Groups; Other: Alzheimer's secured unit, Adult day care.

Eden Home
631 Lakeview Blvd., New Braunfels, TX 78130, (830) 625-6291; Facility type: Skilled care, Alzheimer's, Assisted Living; Beds: 260; Certified: Medicaid, Medicare; Owner: Nonprofit; License: state; Activities: Arts & Crafts; Dances; Pet therapy; Group exercise; Outings; Support Groups; Other: Alzheimer's secured unit; Languages: Czechoslovakian, German, Polish, Spanish.

Odessa

Avalon Place
3800 Englewood Ln., Odessa, TX 79762, (915) 362-2583; Facility type: Skilled care, Alzheimer's; Beds: 110; Certified: Medicaid, Medicare, Veterans; Owner: Nonprofit; License: state; Activities: Arts & Crafts; Dances; Pet therapy; Group exercise; Outings; Support Groups; Other: Languages: Arabic, French, German, Spanish.

New Horizon Nursing Center
2510 W 8th St., Odessa, TX 79763, (915) 333-4511; Facility type: Skilled care, Alzheimer's; Beds: 80; Certified: Medicaid, Medicare; Owner: Nonprofit; License: state; Activities: Arts & Crafts; Dances; Pet therapy; Group exercise.

Pecos

Pecos Nursing Home
1819 Memorial Dr., Pecos, TX 79772, (915) 447-2183; Facility type: Skilled care, Alzheimer's; Beds: 90; Certified: Medicaid; Owner: Private; License: state; Activities: Arts & Crafts; Dances; Pet therapy; Group exercise; Outings; Support Groups; Other: Alzheimer's secured unit; Languages: Spanish.

Plano

Heritage Manor
1621 Coit Rd., Plano, TX 75075, (972) 596-7930; Facility type: Skilled care, Alzheimer's; Beds: 190; Certified: Medicaid, Medicare; Owner: Integrated Health Services; License: state; Activities: Arts & Crafts; Dances; Pet therapy; Group exer-

cise; Outings; Support Groups; Other: Alzheimer's secured unit.

San Antonio

Alta Vista Nursing Center
616 W Russell, San Antonio, TX 78212, (210) 735-9233; Facility type: Skilled care, Alzheimer's; Beds: 110; Certified: Medicaid, Medicare, Veterans; Owner: Nonprofit; License: state; Activities: Arts & Crafts; Dances; Pet therapy; Group exercise; Outings; Support Groups.

The Grand Court II
5100 Newcome Dr., San Antonio, TX 78229, (210) 6802280; Facility type: Skilled care, Alzheimer's; Beds: 50; Certified: Medicare; Owner: Nonprofit; License: state; Activities: Arts & Crafts; Dances; Pet therapy; Group exercise; Outings; Support Groups; Other: Alzheimer's secured unit.

IHS Medical Center Nursing Facility
7302 Oak Manor Dr., San Antonio, TX 78229, (210) 344-8537; Facility type: Skilled care, Alzheimer's; Beds: 150; Certified: Medicaid, Medicare, Veterans; Owner: Integrated Health Services; License: state; Activities: Arts & Crafts; Dances; Pet therapy; Group exercise; Outings; Support Groups; Other: Alzheimer's secured unit.

Manor Care Health Services
8300 Wurzbach Rd., San Antonio, TX 78229, (210) 614-1040; Facility type: Skilled care, Alzheimer's; Beds: 150; Certified: Medicaid, Medicare, Veterans; Owner: HCR Manor Care; License: state; Activities: Arts & Crafts; Dances; Pet therapy; Group exercise; Outings; Support Groups; Other: Alzheimer's secured unit, Adult day care.

Mission Oaks Manor
3030 Roosevelt Ave., San Antonio 78214, (210) 924-8151; Facility type: Skilled care, Alzheimer's; Beds: 150; Certified: Medicaid, Medicare, Veterans; Owner: Proprietary/Public; License: state; Activities: Arts & Crafts; Dances; Pet therapy; Group exercise; Outings; Support Groups; Other: Alzheimer's secured unit.

Morningside Manor
602 Babcock Rd., San Antonio, TX 78201, (210) 731-1010; Facility type: Skilled care, Alzheimer's; Beds: 300; Certified: Medicaid, Medicare; Owner: Nonprofit/Religious; License: state; Activities: Arts & Crafts; Dances; Pet therapy; Group exercise; Outings; Support Groups; Other: Alzheimer's secured unit.

Normandy Terrace
8607 Village Dr., San Antonio, TX 78217, (210) 656-6733; Facility type: Skilled care, Alzheimer's; Beds: 300; Certified: Medicaid, Medicare, Veterans; Owner: Vencor; License: state; Activities: Arts & Crafts; Dances; Pet therapy; Group exercise; Outings; Support Groups; Other: Alzheimer's secured unit, Adult day care; Affiliations: Case Management Society.

Tobius Hills Assisted Living
225 W Laurel, San Antonio, TX 78212, (210) 227-0267; Facility type: Skilled care, Alzheimer's; Beds: 50; Certified: Medicaid, Medicare; Owner: Private; License: state; Activities: Arts & Crafts; Dances; Pet therapy; Group exercise; Outings; Support Groups; Other: Alzheimer's secured unit.

San Marcos

The Arboretum of San Marcos
1600 N IH 35, San Marcos, TX 78666, (512) 353-5026; Facility type: Skilled care, Alzheimer's; Beds: 120; Certified: Medicaid, Medicare, Veterans; Owner: Proprietary/Public; License: state; Activities: Arts & Crafts; Dances; Pet therapy; Group exercise; Outings; Support Groups; Garden/Greenhouse; Other: Alzheimer's secured unit, Adult day care; Languages: Spanish.

Stephenville

Mulberry Manor
1670 Lingleville Rd., Stephenville, TX 76401, (254) 968-2158; Facility type: Skilled care, Alzheimer's; Beds: 120; Certified: Medicaid, Medicare, Veterans; Owner: Mariner Post Acute Network; License: state; Activities: Arts & Crafts; Dances; Pet therapy; Group exercise; Outings; Support Groups; Other: Alzheimer's secured unit.

Tahoka

Tahoka Care Center
1829 S 7th St., Tahoka, TX 79373, (806) 998-5018; Facility type: Skilled care, Alzheimer's; Beds: 50; Certified: Medicaid; Owner: MSC Assoc; License: state; Activities: Arts & Crafts; Dances; Pet therapy; Group exercise; Outings; Support Groups; Other: Alzheimer's secured unit.

Temple

Manor Care Health Services
1511 Marland Wood Rd., Temple, TX 765502, (254) 778-6616; Facility type: Skilled care, Alzheimer's; Beds: 120; Certified: Medicaid; Owner: HCR Manor Care; License: state; Activities: Arts

& Crafts; Dances; Pet therapy; Group exercise; Support Groups; Other: Alzheimer's secured unit; Languages: Spanish.

Regency Manor Healthcare & Rehabilitation Center
3011 W Adams Ave., Temple, TX 76504, (254) 773-1626; Facility type: Skilled care, Alzheimer's; Beds: 140; Certified: Medicaid, Medicare, Veterans; Owner: Complete Care Services; License: state; Activities: Arts & Crafts; Dances; Pet therapy; Group exercise; Outings; Support Groups; Other: Alzheimer's secured unit; Languages: Spanish, Sign Language.

Texarkana

Pine Haven Care Center
4808 Elizabeth St., Texarkana, TX 75503, (903) 794-3826; Facility type: Skilled care, Alzheimer's; Beds: 90; Certified: Medicaid, Medicare; Owner: Proprietary/Public; License: state; Activities: Arts & Crafts; Dances; Pet therapy; Group exercise; Outings; Support Groups.

Tyler

Atria Briarcliff Village Health Center
3403 S Vine St., Tyler, TX 75701, (903) 581-5714; Facility type: Skilled care, Alzheimer's; Beds: 150; Certified: Medicaid, Medicare; Owner: Briarcliff Mgt; License: state; Activities: Arts & Crafts; Dances; Pet therapy; Group exercise; Outings; Support Groups; Other: Alzheimer's secured unit.

Park Place
2450 E 5th St., Tyler, TX 592-6745; Facility type: Skilled care, Alzheimer's; Beds: 120; Certified: Medicare; Owner: Nonprofit/Religious; License: state; Activities: Arts & Crafts; Dances; Pet therapy; Group exercise; Outings; Support Groups.

Waco

Crestview Manor Retirement & Convalescent Center
1400 Lakeshore Dr., Waco, TX 76708, (254) 753-0291; Facility type: Skilled care, Alzheimer's; Beds: 200; Certified: Medicaid, Medicare; Owner: Private; License: state; Activities: Arts & Crafts; Dances; Pet therapy; Group exercise; Outings; Support Groups; Other: Alzheimer's secured unit; Languages: Czechoslovakian, Spanish.

Saint Catherine Center
1700 Providence Dr., Waco, TX 76707, (254) 755-4800; Facility type: Skilled care, Alzheimer's; Beds: 200; Certified: Medicaid, Medicare, Veterans; Owner: Nonprofit/Religious; License: state; Activities: Arts & Crafts; Dances; Pet therapy; Group exercise; Outings; Support Groups.

Saint Elizabeth Center
400 Austin, Waco, TX 76703, (254) 756-5441; Facility type: Skilled care, Alzheimer's; Beds: 120; Certified: Medicaid, Medicare, Veterans; Owner: Nonprofit/Religious; License: state; Activities: Arts & Crafts; Dances; Pet therapy; Group exercise; Support Groups; Other: Home health care; Affiliations: Catholic Church.

Weatherford

Peach Tree Place
315 Anderson St., W, Weatherford, TX 76086, (817) 599-4181; Facility type: Alzheimer's; Beds: 60; Certified: Medicaid; Owner: Living Centers of Texas; License: state; Activities: Arts & Crafts; Dances; Pet therapy; Group exercise; Outings; Support Groups; Other: Alzheimer's secured unit; Languages: Spanish.

Weatherford Healthcare Center
521 W 7th St., Weatherford, TX 76086, (817) 594-8713; Facility type: Skilled care, Alzheimer's; Beds: 120; Certified: Medicaid, Medicare, Veterans; Owner: Mariner Post Acute Network; License: state; Activities: Arts & Crafts; Dances; Pet therapy; Group exercise; Outings; Support Groups.

Webster

Manor Care Health Services
750 W Texas Ave., Webster, TX 77598, (281) 332-3496; Facility type: Skilled care, Alzheimer's; Beds: 120; Certified: Medicaid, Medicare; Owner: HCR Manor Care; License: state; Activities: Arts & Crafts; Dances; Pet therapy; Group exercise; Support Groups; Other: Alzheimer's secured unit, Adult day care.

Weimar

Parkview Manor
206 N Smith St., Weimar, TX 78962, (409) 725-8564; Facility type: Skilled care, Alzheimer's; Beds: 70; Certified: Medicaid; Owner: Nonprofit/Religious; License: state; Activities: Arts & Crafts; Dances; Pet therapy; Group exercise; Outings; Support Groups; Other: Alzheimer's secured unit Affiliations: Community Hospital Owned; Languages: Czechoslovakian, German, Spanish.

Wichita Falls

Southwest Parkway Nursing Center
2400 Southwest Pkwy, Wichita Falls, TX 76308,

(940) 691-5301; Facility type: Skilled care, Alzheimer's; Beds: 90; Certified: Medicaid; Owner: Nonprofit/Religious; License: state; Activities: Arts & Crafts; Dances; Pet therapy; Group exercise; Outings; Support Groups.

Texhoma Christian Care Center
300 Loop 11, Wichita Falls, TX 76305, (940) 723-8420, Facility type: Skilled care, Alzheimer's; Beds: 250; Certified: Medicaid, Medicare; Owner: Nonprofit/Religious; License: state; Activities: Arts & Crafts; Dances; Pet therapy; Group exercise; Outings; Support Groups; Other: Affiliations: Church of Christ.

Winnsboro

Winnsboro Nursing Home
402 S Chestnut St., Winnsboro, TX 75494, (903) 342-6156; Facility type: Skilled care, Alzheimer's; Beds: 60; Certified: Medicaid; Owner: Private, Charapata Development; License: state; Activities: Arts & Crafts; Dances; Pet therapy; Group exercise; Outings; Support Groups; Other: Alzheimer's secured unit.

Woodville

Holiday Pines Manor
1201 Cardinal Dr., Woodville, TX 75979, (409) 283-3397; Facility type: Skilled care, Alzheimer's; Beds: 110; Certified: Medicaid, Medicare; Owner: Nonprofit/Religious; License: state; Activities: Arts & Crafts; Dances; Pet therapy; Group exercise; Support Groups; Other: Alzheimer's secured unit, Adult day care.

Yoakum

Stevens Nursing Home
204 Walter St., Yoakum, TX 77955, (361) 293-3544; Facility type: Skilled care, Alzheimer's; Beds: 110; Certified: Medicaid, Medicare; Owner: New Covenant Care of TX; License: state; Activities: Arts & Crafts; Dances; Pet therapy; Group exercise; Outings; Support Groups.

UTAH

American Fork

Heritage Care Center
350 E 300 N, American Fork, UT 84003, (801) 756-5293; Facility type: Skilled care, Alzheimer's; Beds: 40; Certified: Medicaid, Medicare; Owner: Heritage Mgt Co; License: state; Activities: Arts & Crafts; Dances; Pet therapy; Group exercise; Outings; Support Groups; Other: Adult day care.

Bountiful

Heritage Management Bountiful Healthcare & Rehabilitation
523 N Main St., Bountiful, UT 84010, (801) 298-2234; Facility type: Skilled care, Alzheimer's; Beds: 100; Certified: Medicaid, Medicare, Veterans; Owner: Private; License: state; Activities: Arts & Crafts; Dances; Pet therapy; Group exercise; Outings; Support Groups; Other: Alzheimer's secured unit, Adult day care; Affiliations: Religious.

Rocky Mountain Care—Bountiful
350 S 400 E, Bountiful, UT 84010, (801) 397-4700; Facility type: Skilled care, Alzheimer's; Beds: 50; Certified: Medicaid, Medicare, Veterans; Owner: Rocky Mt Healthcare Services; License: state; Activities: Arts & Crafts; Dances; Pet therapy; Group exercise; Outings; Support Groups; Other: Alzheimer's secured unit, Home health care.

Brigham City

Brigham City Nursing & Rehabilitation Center
77 N 200 E, Brigham City, UT, 84302, (801) 723-7777; Facility type: Skilled care, Alzheimer's; Beds: 80; Certified: Medicaid, Medicare; Owner: Peak Medical Corp; License: state; Activities: Arts & Crafts; Dances; Pet therapy; Group exercise; Outings; Support Groups; Other: Adult day care; Languages: Japanese, Spanish.

Ferron

Emery County Care & Rehabilitation Center
455 W Mill Rd., Ferron, UT 84523, (435) 384-2301; Facility type: Skilled care, Alzheimer's; Beds: 60; Certified: Medicaid, Medicare; Owner: State & Local Gov; License: state; Activities: Arts & Crafts; Dances; Pet therapy; Group exercise; Outings; Support Groups; Other: Adult day care.

Heber City

Rocky Mountain Care Center
160 W 500 N, Heber City, UT, 84032, (435) 654-

5500; Facility type: Skilled care, Alzheimer's; Beds: 90; Certified: Medicaid, Medicare; Owner: Rocky Mt Healthcare Services; License: state; Activities: Arts & Crafts; Dances; Pet therapy; Group exercise; Outings; Support Groups; Other: Home health care.

Logan

Logan Nursing & Rehabilitation Center
1480 N 400 E, Logan, UT 84341, (435) 750-5501; Facility type: Skilled care, Alzheimer's; Beds: 120; Certified: Medicaid, Medicare; Owner: Private; License: state; Activities: Arts & Crafts; Dances; Pet therapy; Group exercise; Outings; Support Groups; Other: Alzheimer's secured unit, Home health care; Languages: German, Spanish; Affiliations: Church of Latter Day Saints.

Sunshine Terrace Foundation
225 N 200 W, Logan, UT 84321, (435) 725-0411; Facility type: Skilled care, Alzheimer's; Beds: 180; Certified: Medicaid, Medicare, Veterans; Owner: Nonprofit/Religious; License: state; Activities: Arts & Crafts; Dances; Pet therapy; Group exercise; Outings; Support Groups; Other: Alzheimer's secured unit.

Milford

Milford Valley Memorial Long Term Care Center
451 N Main St., Milford, UT 84751, (435) 387-2411; Facility type: Skilled care, Alzheimer's; Beds: 50; Certified: Medicaid, Medicare, Veterans; Owner: State & Local Gov; License: state; Activities: Arts & Crafts; Dances; Pet therapy; Group exercise; Outings; Support Groups; Other: Adult day care, Home health care.

Ogden

Aspen Care Center
2325 Madison Ave., Ogden, UT 84401, (801) 399-5846; Facility type: Skilled care, Alzheimer's; Beds: 70; Certified: Medicaid, Medicare; Owner: Nonprofit/Religious; License: state; Activities: Arts & Crafts; Dances; Pet therapy; Group exercise; Support Groups; Other: Alzheimer's secured unit, Adult day care.

Infinia Healthcare of Ogden
524 E 800 N, Ogden UT 84404, (801) 782-3740; Facility type: Skilled care, Alzheimer's; Beds: 100; Certified: Medicaid, Medicare; Owner: Private; License: state; Activities: Arts & Crafts; Dances; Pet therapy; Group exercise; Outings; Support Groups; Other: Alzheimer's secured unit.

South Ogden Rehabilitation Center
5865 S Wasatch Dr., Ogden, UT 84403, (801) 479-8480; Facility type: Skilled care, Alzheimer's; Beds: 100; Certified: Medicaid, Medicare; Owner: Private; License: state; Activities: Arts & Crafts; Dances; Pet therapy; Group exercise; Outings; Support Groups; Other: Adult day care; Languages: Spanish.

Orem

Orem Nursing & Rehabilitation Center
575 E 1400 St., Orem, UT 84058, (801) 225-4741; Facility type: Skilled care, Alzheimer's; Beds: 50; Certified: Medicaid, Medicare, Veterans; Owner: Utah Senior Services; License: state; Activities: Arts & Crafts; Dances; Pet therapy; Group exercise; Outings; Support Groups; Other: Alzheimer's secured unit, Adult day care, Home health care.

Price

Castle County Care Center
1340 E 300 N, Price, UT 845-1, (435) 637-9213; Facility type: Skilled care, Alzheimer's; Beds: 100; Certified: Medicaid, Medicare, Veterans; Owner: Quality Healthcare; License: state; Activities: Arts & Crafts; Dances; Pet therapy; Group exercise; Outings; Support Groups; Other: Alzheimer's secured unit, Adult day care, Home health care.

Provo

East Lake Care Center
1001 N 500 W, Provo, UT 84601, (801) 377-9661; Facility type: Skilled care, Alzheimer's; Beds: 210; Certified: Medicaid, Medicare; Owner: Quality Healthcare; License: state; Activities: Arts & Crafts; Dances; Pet therapy; Group exercise; Outings; Support Groups.

Richfield

Richfield Rehabilitation & Care Center
83 E 1100 N, Richfield, UT 84701. (435) 896-8211; Facility type: Skilled care, Alzheimer's; Beds: 120; Certified: Medicaid, Medicare, Veterans; Owner: Nonprofit/Religious; License: state; Activities: Arts & Crafts; Dances; Pet therapy; Group exercise; Outings; Support Groups; Other: Alzheimer's secured unit, Adult day care.

Salt Lake City

Christus St. Joseph Villa
451 Bishop Federal Ln., Salt Lake City, UT 84115, (801) 487-7557; Facility type: Skilled care,

Alzheimer's; Beds: 220; Certified: Medicaid, Medicare; Owner: Nonprofit/Religious; License: state; Activities: Arts & Crafts; Dances; Pet therapy; Group exercise; Outings; Support Groups; Other: Alzheimer's secured unit, Adult day care; Affiliations: Catholic Church.

Fairview Care Center East
455 S 900 E, Salt Lake City, UT 84102, (801) 366-6891; Facility type: Skilled care, Alzheimer's; Beds: 50; Certified: Medicaid; Owner: Private; License: state; Activities: Arts & Crafts; Dances; Pet therapy; Group exercise; Outings; Support Groups; Other: Alzheimer's secured unit, Adult day care.

Heritage Eastridge Rehabilitation Center
2730 E 3300 S, Salt Lake City, UT 84123, (801) 969-1420; Facility type: Skilled care, Alzheimer's; Beds: 100; Certified: Medicaid, Medicare, Veterans; Owner: Health Care Consulting; License: state; Activities: Arts & Crafts; Dances; Pet therapy; Group exercise; Outings; Other: Alzheimer's secured unit, Adult day care; Languages: French, Italian, Russian, Serbo-Croatian, Spanish, Swedish.

Highland Care Center
4285 Highland Dr., Salt Lake City, UT 84124, (801) 278-2839; Facility type: Skilled care, Alzheimer's; Beds: 110; Certified: Medicare; Payer mix: 60% Private pay, 40% Medicare; Owner: Nonprofit/Religious; License: state; Activities: Arts & Crafts; Pet therapy; Outings; Support Groups; Other: Alzheimer's secured unit.

Millcreek Health Center
3520 S Highland Dr., Salt Lake City, UT 84106, (801) 484-7638; Facility type: Skilled care, Alzheimer's; Beds: 60; Certified: Medicaid, Medicare; Owner: Private; License: state; Activities: Arts & Crafts; Dances; Pet therapy; Group exercise; Outings; Support Groups; Other: Alzheimer's secured unit.

Sandy

Sandy Regional Health Center
50 E 9000 S, Sandy, UT 84070, (801) 561-9839; Facility type: Skilled care, Alzheimer's; Beds: 150; Certified: Medicaid, Medicare; Owner: Horizon West, Inc.; License: state; Activities: Arts & Crafts; Dances; Pet therapy; Group exercise; Outings; Support Groups; Other: Alzheimer's secured unit, Affiliations: Church of Latter Day Saints.

Tooele

Tooele Valley Nursing Home
140 E 200 S, Tooele, UT 84074, (435) 882-6130; Facility type: Skilled care, Alzheimer's; Beds: 80; Certified: Medicaid, Medicare; Owner: State & Local Gov; License: state; Activities: Arts & Crafts; Dances; Pet therapy; Group exercise; Outings; Support Groups; Other: Alzheimer's secured unit, Home health care: Affiliations: Utah Gerontological Association.

Vernal

Uintah Care Center
510 S 500 W, Vernal, UT 84078, (435) 789-8851; Facility type: Skilled care, Alzheimer's; Beds: 50; Certified: Medicaid, Medicare, Veterans; Owner: State & Local Gov; License: state; Activities: Arts & Crafts; Dances; Pet therapy; Group exercise; Outings; Support Groups; Other: Alzheimer's secured unit, Adult day care.

West Jordan

South Valley Health Center
3706 W 9000 S, West Jordan, UT 84088, (801) 280-2273; Facility type: Skilled care, Alzheimer's; Beds: 120; Certified: Medicaid, Medicare, Veterans; Owner: Proprietary/Public; License: state; Activities: Arts & Crafts; Dances; Pet therapy; Group exercise; Outings; Support Groups; Other: Alzheimer's secured unit.

West Valley City

Hazen Nursing Home
2520 S Redwood Rd., West Valley City, UT 84119, (801) 972-1050; Facility type: Skilled care, Alzheimer's; Beds: 30; Certified: Veterans; Payer mix: 100% Private pay; Owner: Proprietary/Public; License: state; Activities: Arts & Crafts; Dances; Pet therapy; Group exercise; Outings; Support Groups; Other: Adult day care.

VERMONT

Barre

Berlin Health & Rehabilitation Center
98 Hospitality Dr., Barre, VT 05641, (802) 229-0308; Facility type: Skilled care, Alzheimer's; Beds: 150; Certified: Medicaid, Medicare, Veterans; Owner: Subacute Mgt Corp of America; License: state; Activities: Arts & Crafts; Dances; Pet therapy; Group exercise; Outings; Support Groups.

Barton

Maple Lane Nursing Home
2260 Maple Hill Rd., Barton, VT 05822, (802) 754-2112; Facility type: Skilled care, Alzheimer's; Beds: 100; Certified: Medicaid, Medicare; Owner: Private; License: state; Activities: Arts & Crafts; Dances; Pet therapy; Group exercise; Outings; Support Groups; Other: Alzheimer's secured unit, Adult day care.

Bennington

Bennington Health & Rehabilitation Center
2 Blackberry Ln., Bennington, VT 05201, (802) 442-8525; Facility type: Skilled care, Alzheimer's; Beds: 100; Certified: Medicaid, Medicare; Owner: Proprietary/Public; License: state; Activities: Arts & Crafts; Dances; Pet therapy; Group exercise; Outings; Support Groups.

Crescent Manor Nursing Home
312 Crescent Blvd., Bennington, VT 05201, (802) 447-1501; Facility type: Skilled care, Alzheimer's; Beds: 90; Certified: Medicaid, Medicare; Owner: Private; License: state; Activities: Arts & Crafts; Dances; Pet therapy; Group exercise; Outings; Support Groups; Other: Alzheimer's secured unit.

Vermont Veterans' Home
325 North St., Bennington, VT 05201, (802) 442-6353; Facility type: Skilled care, Alzheimer's; Beds: 2000; Certified: Medicaid, Medicare, Veterans; Owner: State & Local Gov; License: state; Activities: Arts & Crafts; Dances; Pet therapy; Group exercise; Outings; Support Groups; Other: Alzheimer's secured unit.

Burlington

Burlington Health & Rehabilitation Center
300 Pearl St., Burlington, VT 05401, (802) 658-4200; Facility type: Skilled care, Alzheimer's; Beds: 280; Certified: Medicaid, Medicare, Veterans; Owner: Vermont Subacute Corp; License: state; Activities: Arts & Crafts; Dances; Pet therapy; Group exercise; Outings; Support Groups.

Glover

Union House Nursing Home
3086 Glover St., Glover, VT 05839, (802) 525-6600; Facility type: Skilled care, Alzheimer's; Beds: 50; Certified: Medicaid, Medicare; Owner: Private; License: state; Activities: Arts & Crafts; Dances; Pet therapy; Group exercise; Outings; Support Groups; Other: Alzheimer's secured unit.

Northfield

Mayo Healthcare Inc.
71 Richardson Ave., Northfield, VT 05663, (802) 485-3161; Facility type: Skilled care, Alzheimer's; Beds: 50; Certified: Medicaid, Medicare, Veterans; Owner: Nonprofit/Religious; License: state; Activities: Arts & Crafts; Dances; Pet therapy; Group exercise; Outings; Support Groups; Other: Alzheimer's secured unit, Adult day care; Languages: French, Spanish.

Rutland

Mountain View Center
9 Haywood Ave., Rutland, VT 05702, (802) 775-0007; Facility type: Skilled care, Alzheimer's; Beds: 16; Certified: Medicaid, Medicare, Veterans; Owner: Genesis ElderCare; Activities: Arts & Crafts; Dances; Pet therapy; Group exercise; Outings; Support Groups; Other: Languages: French, Italian, German, Spanish, Portuguese.

Pleasant Manor Nursing Home
48 Nichols St., Rutland, VT 05701, (802) 775-2941; Facility type: Skilled care, Alzheimer's; Beds: 170; Certified: Medi-Cal, Medicare; Owner: Private; License: state; Activities: Arts & Crafts; Dances; Pet therapy; Group exercise; Outings; Support Groups; Other: Alzheimer's secured unit.

Saint Albans

Redstone Villa
7 Forest Hill Dr., Saint Albans, VT 05478, (802) 524-3489; Facility type: Skilled care, Alzheimer's; Beds: 50; Certified: Medicaid, Medicare; Owner: Nonprofit/Religious; License: state; Activities: Arts & Crafts; Dances; Pet therapy; Group exercise; Outings; Support Groups; Other: Languages: French.

Shelburne

The Arbors & The Pillars
687 Harbor Rd., Shelburne, VT 05482, (802)

985-8600; Facility type: Skilled care, Alzheimer's; Beds: 6; Payer mix: 90% Private pay; Owner: Nonprofit/Religious; License: state; Activities: Arts & Crafts; Dances; Pet therapy; Group exercise; Outings; Support Groups; Other: Alzheimer's secured unit.

Townshend

Stratton House Nursing Home
PO Box 216, Townshend, VT 05353, (802) 365-7344; Facility type: Skilled care, Alzheimer's; Beds: 40; Certified: Medicaid, Medicare; Owner: Nonprofit/Religious; License: state; Activities: Arts & Crafts; Dances; Pet therapy; Group exercise; Outings; Support Groups; Other: Adult day care.

Vernon

Vernon Green Nursing Home
61 Greenway Dr., Vernon, VT 05354, (802) 254-6041; Facility type: Skilled care, Alzheimer's; Beds: 60; Certified: Medicaid, Medicare; Owner: Nonprofit/Religious; License: state; Activities: Arts & Crafts; Dances; Pet therapy; Group exercise; Outings; Support Groups; Other: Alzheimer's secured unit, Affiliations: Advent Christian Church.

Windsor

Cedar Hill Continuing Care Community
49 Cedar Hill Dr., Windsor, VT 05089, (802) 674-6609; Facility type: Skilled care, Alzheimer's; Beds: 90; Certified: Medicaid, Medicare, Veterans; Owner: Proprietary/Public; License: state; Activities: Arts & Crafts; therapy; Group exercise; Outings; Support Groups; Other: Alzheimer's secured unit.

VIRGINIA

Alexandria

Hermitage in Northern Virginia
500 Fairbanks Ave., Alexandria, VA 22311, (703) 820-2434; Facility type: Skilled care, Alzheimer's; Beds: 120; Payer mix: 100% Private pay; Owner: United Methodist Homes; License: state; Activities: Arts & Crafts; Dances; Pet therapy; Group exercise; Outings; Support Groups.

Mount Vernon Nursing Center
8111 Tiswell Dr., Alexandria, VA 22306, (703) 360-4000; Facility type: Skilled care, Alzheimer's; Beds: 130; Certified: Medicaid, Medicare; Owner: Nonprofit/Religious; License: state; Activities: Arts & Crafts; Dances; Pet therapy; Group exercise; Outings; Support Groups.

Woodbine Rehabilitation & Healthcare Center
2729 King St., Alexandria, VA, 22302, (703) 836-8838; Facility type: Skilled care, Alzheimer's; Beds: 250; Certified: Medicaid, Medicare, Veterans; Owner: Proprietary/Public; License: state; Activities: Arts & Crafts; Dances; Pet therapy; Group exercise; Outings; Support Groups.

Annandale

Leewood Health Care Center
7120 Braddock Rd., Annandale, VA 22003, (703) 256-9779; Facility type: Skilled care, Alzheimer's; Beds: 130; Certified: Medicaid; Owner: Private; License: state; Activities: Arts & Crafts; Dances; Pet therapy; Group exercise; Outings; Support Groups; Other: Alzheimer's secured unit, Adult day care.

Arlington

Cherrydale Health & Rehabilitation Center
3719 Lee Hwy., Arlington, VA 22207, (703) 243-7640; Facility type: Skilled care, Alzheimer's; Beds: 250; Certified: Medicaid, Medicare, Veterans; Owner: Medical Facilities of America; License: state; Activities: Arts & Crafts; Dances; Pet therapy; Group exercise; Outings; Support Groups; Other: Languages: Spanish, Vietnamese, Korean, African.

Manor Care Health Services
550 S Carlin Springs Rd., Arlington, VA 22204, (703) 379-7200; Facility type: Skilled care, Alzheimer's; Beds: 200; Certified: Medicaid, Medicare, Veterans; Owner: HCR Manor Care; License: state; Activities: Arts & Crafts; Dances; Pet therapy; Group exercise; Outings; Support Groups; Other: Alzheimer's secured unit.

Potomac Center Genesis ElderCare Network
1785 S Hayes St., Arlington, VA 22202, (703) 920-5700; Facility type: Skilled care, Alzheimer's; Beds: 120; Certified: Medicaid, Medicare, Veterans; Owner: Genesis Elder Care; License: state; Activities: Arts & Crafts; Dances; Pet ther-

apy; Group exercise; Outings; Support Groups; Other: Alzheimer's secured unit; Languages: Tagalog, Swahili, German, Japanese, Korean, Italian, Thai.

Blacksburg

Heritage Hall
3610 S Main St., Blacksburg, VA 24060, (540) 951-7000; Facility type: Skilled care, Alzheimer's; Beds: 190; Certified: Medicaid, Veterans; Owner: Nonprofit/Religious; License: state; Activities: Arts & Crafts; Dances; Pet therapy; Group exercise; Outings; Support Groups; Other: Alzheimer's secured unit.

Blackstone

Heritage Hall
900 S Main St., Blackstone, VA 23824, (804) 292-5301; Facility type: Skilled care, Alzheimer's; Beds: 170; Certified: Medicaid, Veterans; Owner: Nonprofit/Religious; License: state; Activities: Arts & Crafts; Dances; Pet therapy; Group exercise; Outings; Support Groups; Other: Alzheimer's secured unit.

Burkeville Piedmont Geriatric Hospital
Hwy. 360, Burkeville, VA 23922, (804) 767-4401; Facility type: Skilled care, Alzheimer's; Beds: 200; Certified: Medicaid, Medicare; Owner: State & Local Gov; License: state; Activities: Arts & Crafts; Dances; Pet therapy; Group exercise; Outings; Support Groups; Other: Alzheimer's secured unit.

Charlottesville

Heritage Hall
505 W Rio Rd., Charlottesville, VA 22901, (804) 978-7015; Facility type: Skilled care, Alzheimer's; Beds: 140; Certified: Medicaid, Medicare, Veterans; Owner: Nonprofit/Religious; License: state; Activities: Arts & Crafts; Dances; Pet therapy; Group exercise; Outings; Support Groups; Other: Alzheimer's secured unit.

Our Lady of Peace
751 Hillsdale Dr., Charlottesville, VA 22901, (804) 973-1155; Facility type: Skilled care, Alzheimer's; Beds: 130; Certified: Medicaid; Owner: Nonprofit/Religious; License: state; Activities: Arts & Crafts; Dances; Pet therapy; Group exercise; Outings; Support Groups; Other: Alzheimer's secured unit.

Chesapeake

Sentara Village
778 Oak Grove Rd., Chesapeake, VA 23320, (757) 547-5666; Facility type: Skilled care, Alzheimer's, Assisted Living; Beds: 100; Certified: Medicaid, Medicare, Veterans; Owner: Sentara Life Care License: state; Activities: Arts & Crafts; Dances; Pet therapy; Group exercise; Outings; Support Groups.

Chesterfield

Chesterfield County Health Center Commission
6800 Lucy Corr Blvd., Chesterfield, VA 23832, (804) 748-1511; Facility type: Skilled care, Alzheimer's; Beds: 190; Certified: Medicaid, Medicare; Owner: Nonprofit; License: state; Activities: Arts & Crafts; Dances; Pet therapy; Group exercise; Outings; Support Groups; Other: Alzheimer's secured unit, Adult day care.

Culpeper

Culpeper Healthcare Center
602 Madison Rd., Culpeper, VA 22701, (540) 825-2884; Facility type: Skilled care, Alzheimer's; Beds: 180; Certified: Medicaid, Medicare, Veterans; Owner: Medical Facilities of America; License: state; Activities: Arts & Crafts; Dances; Pet therapy; Group exercise; Outings; Support Groups; Other: Alzheimer's secured unit.

Fairfax

Fairfax Nursing Center
10701 Main St., Fairfax, VA 22030, (703) 273-7705; Facility type: Skilled care, Alzheimer's; Beds: 200; Certified: Medicaid, Medicare, Veterans; Owner: Genesis Elder Care; License: state; Activities: Arts & Crafts; Dances; Pet therapy; Group exercise; Outings; Support Groups; Other: Alzheimer's secured unit, Adult day care.

Inova Commonwealth Care Center
4315 Chain Bridge Rd., Fairfax, VA 22030, (703) 934-5001; Facility type: Skilled care, Alzheimer's; Beds: 230; Certified: Medicaid, Medicare; Owner: Nonprofit/Religious; License: state; Activities: Arts & Crafts; Dances; Pet therapy; Group exercise; Outings; Support Groups; Other: Alzheimer's secured unit.

The Virginian Health Care Unit
9229 Arlington Blvd., Fairfax, VA 22031, (703) 385-0555; Facility type: Skilled care, Alzheimer's; Beds: 10; Certified: Medicare; Owner: Nonprofit/Religious; License: state; Activities: Arts & Crafts; Dances; Pet therapy; Group exercise; Support Groups; Other: Alzheimer's secured unit, Adult day care.

Falls Church

Goodwin House West Nursing Care Unit
3440 S Jefferson St., Falls Church, VA 22041, (703) 820-1488; Facility type: Skilled care, Alzheimer's; Beds: 70;Certified: Medicaid, Medicare; Owner: Nonprofit/Religious; License: state; Activities: Arts & Crafts; Dances; Pet therapy; Group exercise; Outings; Support Groups; Other: Alzheimer's secured unit, Home health; Affiliations: Episcopal Church.

Fredericksburg

Fredericksburg Nursing Home
3900 Plank Rd., Fredericksburg, VA 22407, (540) 786-8351; Facility type: Skilled care, Alzheimer's; Beds: 170; Certified: Medicaid, Medicare, Veterans; Owner: Beverly Enterprises; License: state; Activities: Arts & Crafts; Dances; Pet therapy; Group exercise; Outings; Support Groups; Other: Alzheimer's secured unit.

Front Royal

Warren Memorial Hospital—Lynn Care Center
1000 Shenandoah Ave., Front Royal, VA 22630, (540) 636-0242; Facility type: Skilled care, Alzheimer's; Beds: 120; Certified: Medicaid, Medicare; Owner: Nonprofit/Religious; License: state; Activities: Arts & Crafts; Dances; Pet therapy; Group exercise; Outings; Support Groups; Other: Alzheimer's secured unit, Home health care.

Harrisonburg

Oak Lea Nursing Home
1475 Virginia Ave., Harrisonburg, VA 22802, (540) 564-3500; Facility type: Skilled care, Alzheimer's; Beds: 130; Certified: Medicaid; Owner: Virginia Mennonite Retirement Community; License: state; Activities: Arts & Crafts; Dances; Pet therapy; Group exercise; Outings; Support Groups; Other: Alzheimer's secured unit, Affiliations: Mennonite.

Sunnyside Presbyterian Retirement Community
100 Sunnyside Dr., Harrisonburg, VA 22801, (540) 568-8200; Facility type: Skilled care, Alzheimer's; Beds: 96; Certified: Medicaid; Owner: Nonprofit/Religious; License: state; Activities: Arts & Crafts; Dances; Pet therapy; Group exercise; Outings; Support Groups; Other: Alzheimer's secured unit.

Lawrenceville

Brian Center Health & Rehabilitation
1722 Lawrenceville Plank Rd., Lawrenceville, VA 23868, (804) 848-4766; Facility type: Skilled care, Alzheimer's; Beds: 90; Certified: Medicaid, Medicare; Owner: Mariner Post Acute Network; License: state; Activities: Arts & Crafts; Dances; Pet therapy; Group exercise; Outings; Support Groups.

Leesburg

Heritage Hall Nursing & Rehabilitation Center
122 Morven Park Rd., NW, Leesburg, VA 20176, (703) 777-8700; Facility type: Skilled care, Alzheimer's; Beds: 190; Certified: Medicaid, Medicare, Veterans; Owner: HCMF Corp; License: state; Activities: Arts & Crafts; Dances; Pet therapy; Group exercise; Outings; Support Groups; Other: Alzheimer's secured unit.

Sunrise Assisted Living
246 W Market St., Leesburg, VA 20176, (703) 777-1971; Facility type: Skilled care, Alzheimer's; Beds: 50; Owner: Sunrise Terrace; License: state; Activities: Arts & Crafts; Dances; Pet therapy; Group exercise; Outings; Support Groups; Other: Adult day care.

Lynchburg

Medical Care Center
2200 Landover Pl., Lynchburg, VA 24501, (804) 846-4626; Facility type: Skilled care, Alzheimer's; Beds: 110; Certified: Medicaid, Medicare; Owner: HCR Manor Care; License: state; Activities: Arts & Crafts; Dances; Pet therapy; Group exercise; Outings; Support Groups.

Saint John's Nursing Home
3500 Powhatan St., Lynchburg, VA 24501, (804) 845-6045; Facility type: Skilled care, Alzheimer's; Beds: 50; Payer mix: 91% Private pay; Owner: Agape Healthcare; License: state; Activities: Arts & Crafts; Dances; Pet therapy; Group exercise; Outings; Support Groups; Other: Alzheimer's secured unit.

Manassas

Birmingham Green Nursing Facility
8605 Centreville Rd., Manassas, VA 20110, (703) 25700935; Facility type: Skilled care, Alzheimer's; Beds: 180; Certified: Medicaid; Owner: Nonprofit/Religious; License: state; Activities: Arts & Crafts; Dances; Pet therapy; Group exercise; Outings; Support Groups; Other: Alzheimer's secured unit.

Marion

Southwestern Virginia Mental Health Institute—Geriatric Services

340 Bagley Cir, Marion, VA 24354, (540) 783-1200; Facility type: Skilled care, Alzheimer's; Beds: 120; Certified: Medicaid; Owner: State & Local Gov; License: state; Activities: Arts & Crafts; Dances; Pet therapy; Group exercise; Support Groups; Other: Alzheimer's secured unit.

Martinsville

Beverly Healthcare
1607 Spruce St., Martinsville, VA 24112, (540) 632-7146; Facility type: Skilled care, Alzheimer's; Beds: 130; Certified: Medicaid, Medicare, Veterans; Owner: Beverly Enterprises; License: state; Activities: Arts & Crafts; Dances; Pet therapy; Group exercise; Outings; Support Groups; Other: Alzheimer's secured unit.

McLean

Arleigh Burke Pavilion
1739 Kirby Rd., McLean VA 22101, (703) 506-6900; Facility type: Skilled care, Alzheimer's; Beds: 50; Certified: Medicare; Owner: Nonprofit/Religious; License: state; Activities: Arts & Crafts; Dances; Pet therapy; Group exercise; Outings; Support Groups; Other: Alzheimer's secured unit.

Mechanicsville

Meadowbridge Transitional Care Unit
826 Atlee, Mechanicsville, VA 23116, (757) 764-6421; Facility type: Skilled care, Alzheimer's; Beds: 40; Certified: Medicaid, Medicare; Owner: Health Corp of VA; License: state; Activities: Arts & Crafts; Dances; Pet therapy; Group exercise; Outings; Support Groups; Other: Alzheimer's secured unit, Home health care.

Montvale

Woodhaven Nursing Home
13055 W Lynchburg-Salem Tpke., Montvale, VA 24122; (540) 947-2207; Facility type: Skilled care, Alzheimer's; Beds: 50; Payer mix: 100% Private pay; Owner: Proprietary/Public; License: state; Activities: Arts & Crafts; Dances; Pet therapy; Group exercise; Outings; Support Groups; Other: Alzheimer's secured unit.

Nassawadox

Heritage Hall
9468 Hospital Rd., Nassawadox, VA 23413, (757) 442-5600; Facility type: Skilled care, Alzheimer's; Beds: 150; Certified: Medicaid, Medicare, Veterans; Owner: HCMF Corp; License: state; Activities: Arts & Crafts; Dances; Pet therapy; Group exercise; Outings; Support Groups; Other: Alzheimer's secured unit.

Newport News

James Pointe Care Center
5015 Huntington Ave., Newport News, VA 23607, (757) 244-1734; Facility type: Skilled care, Alzheimer's; Beds: 90; Certified: Medicaid, Medicare, Veterans; Owner: Private; License: state; Activities: Arts & Crafts; Dances; Pet therapy; Group exercise; Outings; Support Groups; Other: Alzheimer's secured unit.

The Newport
11121 Warwick Blvd., Newport News, VA 23601, (757) 595-3733; Facility type: Skilled care, Alzheimer's; Beds: 50; Owner: Proprietary/Public; License: state; Activities: Arts & Crafts; Dances; Pet therapy; Group exercise; Outings; Support Groups; Other: Alzheimer's secured unit.

Riverside Regional Convalescent Center
1000 Old Denbigh Blvd., Newport News, VA 23602, (757) 875-2000; Facility type: Skilled care, Alzheimer's; Beds: 300; Certified: Medicaid, Medicare; Owner: Riverside Health System; License: state; Activities: Arts & Crafts; Dances; Pet therapy; Group exercise; Outings; Support Groups; Other: Alzheimer's secured unit, Adult day care.

Norfolk

Autumn Care of Norfolk
1401 Halstead Ave., Norfolk, VA 23502, (757) 857-0481; Facility type: Skilled care, Alzheimer's; Beds: 120; Certified: Medicaid, Medicare, Veterans; Owner: Autumn Corp; License: state; Activities: Arts & Crafts; Dances; Pet therapy; Group exercise; Outings; Support Groups; Other: Languages: Spanish.

Harbor Point
1005 Hampton Blvd., Norfolk, VA 23507, (757) 623-5602; Facility type: Skilled care, Alzheimer's; Beds: 120; Certified: Medicaid, Medicare; Owner: Vencor, Inc.; License: state; Activities: Arts & Crafts; Dances; Pet therapy; Group exercise; Outings; Support Groups; Other: Alzheimer's secured unit.

Sentara Nursing Center
249 S Newton Rd., Norfolk, VA 23502, (757) 892-5500; Facility type: Skilled care, Alzheimer's; Beds: 220; Certified: Medicaid, Medicare, Veterans; Owner: Sentara Life Care; License: state; Activities: Arts & Crafts; Dances; Pet therapy; Group exercise; Outings; Support Groups.

Thornton Hall Nursing & Rehabilitation Center
827 Norview Ave., Norfolk, VA 23509, (757)

853-6281; Facility type: Skilled care, Alzheimer's; Beds: 100; Certified: Medicaid, Medicare; Owner: Genesis ElderCare; License: state; Activities: Arts & Crafts; Dances; Pet therapy; Group exercise; Support Groups; Other: Alzheimer's secured unit.

Richmond

Beth Sholom Home of Central Virginia
1600 John Rolf Pkwy, Richmond, VA 23233, (804) 750-2183; Facility type: Skilled care, Alzheimer's; Beds: 120; Certified: Medicaid, Medicare; Owner: Nonprofit/Religious; License: state; Activities: Arts & Crafts; Dances; Pet therapy; Group exercise; Outings; Support Groups; Other: Alzheimer's secured unit, Affiliations: Jewish; Languages: Yiddish, Hebrew, Russian.

Libbie Convalescent Center
1901 Libbie Ave., Richmond, VA 23226, (804) 282-9767; Facility type: Skilled care, Alzheimer's; Beds: 190; Certified: Medicaid, Medicare, Veterans; Owner: Capitol Care Mgt Co; License: state; Activities: Arts & Crafts; Dances; Pet therapy; Group exercise; Outings; Support Groups.

Manor Care Health Services
2125 Hilliard Rd., Richmond, VA 23228, (804) 266-9666; Facility type: Skilled care, Alzheimer's; Beds: 140; Certified: Medicaid, Medicare; Owner: HCR Manor Care; License: state; Activities: Arts & Crafts; Dances; Pet therapy; Group exercise; Outings; Support Groups; Other: Alzheimer's secured unit.

Roxton Health & Rehabilitation Center
4403 Forest Hill Ave., Richmond, VA 23225, (804) 231-0231; Facility type: Skilled care, Alzheimer's; Beds: 180; Certified: Medicaid, Medicare, Veterans; Owner: Convalescent Care Inc.; License: state; Activities: Arts & Crafts; Dances; Pet therapy; Group exercise; Outings; Support Groups; Other: Alzheimer's secured unit.

Roanoke

Friendship Healthcare
327 Hershberger Rd., NW, Roanoke, VA 24012, (540) 265-2111; Facility type: Skilled care, Alzheimer's; Beds: 90; Certified: Medicaid, Medicare; Owner: Nonprofit/Religious; License: state; Activities: Arts & Crafts; Dances; Pet therapy; Group exercise; Outings; Support Groups; Other: Alzheimer's secured unit.

Staunton

Oak Hill Health Care Center
512 Houston St., Staunton, VA 24401, (540) 886-2335; Facility type: Skilled care, Alzheimer's; Beds: 160; Certified: Medicaid, Medicare, Veterans; Owner: Nonprofit/Religious; License: state; Activities: Arts & Crafts; Dances; Pet therapy; Group exercise; Outings; Support Group; Other: Alzheimer's secured unit.

Suffolk

Bon Secours-Maryview Nursing Care Center
4775 Bridge Rd., Suffok, VA 23435, (757) 686-0488; Facility type: Skilled care, Alzheimer's; Beds: 120; Certified: Medicaid, Veterans; Owner: Nonprofit/Religious; License: state; Activities: Arts & Crafts; Dances; Pet therapy; Group exercise; Outings; Support Groups; Other: Alzheimer's secured unit, Home health care.

Virginia Beach

Beth Sholom Home of Eastern Virginia
6401 Auburn Dr., Virginia Beach, VA 23464, (757) 420-2512; Facility type: Skilled care, Alzheimer's; Beds: 120; Certified: Medicaid, Medicare; Owner: Nonprofit/Religious; License: state; Activities: Arts & Crafts; Dances; Pet therapy; Group exercise; Outings; Support Groups; Other: Alzheimer's secured unit; Languages: Yiddish, Spanish, Russian, Hebrew; Affiliations: Greater Jewish Communities of Hampton Roads.

SNC Windermere
1604 Old Donation Pkwy, Virginia Beach, VA 23454, (757) 496-3939; Facility type: Skilled care, Alzheimer's; Beds: 60; Certified: Medicaid; Owner: Nonprofit/Religious; License: state; Activities: Arts & Crafts; Dances; Pet therapy; Group exercise; Outings; Support Groups.

SunBridge Care & Rehabilitation for Virginia Beach
340 Lynn Shores Dr., Virginia Beach, VA 23452, (757) 340-6611; Facility type: Skilled care, Alzheimer's; Beds: 190; Certified: Medicaid, Medicare, Veterans; Owner: Nonprofit/Religious; License: state; Activities: Arts & Crafts; Dances; Pet therapy; Group exercise; Outings; Support Groups.

Warrenton

Oak Springs of Warrenton
614 Hastings Ln., Warrenton, VA 20186, (800) 582-0312; Facility type: Skilled care, Alzheimer's; Beds: 130; Certified: Medicaid, Medicare; Owner: Private; License: state; Activities: Arts & Crafts; Dances; Pet therapy; Group exercise; Outings; Support Groups; Other: Alzheimer's secured unit.

Williamsburg

Williamsburg Landing
5700 Williamsburg Landing Dr., Williamsburg, VA 23185, (757) 253-0303; Facility type: Skilled care, Alzheimer's; Beds: 70; Certified: Medicare; Payer mix: 80% Private pay, 20% Medicare; Owner: Williamsburg Landing Inc.; License: state; Activities: Arts & Crafts; Dances; Pet therapy; Group exercise; Outings; Support Groups; Other: Alzheimer's secured unit.

Yorktown

Regency Healthcare Center
112 N Constitution Dr., Yorktown, VA 23692, (757) 890-0675; Facility type: Skilled care, Alzheimer's; Beds: 60; Certified: Medicaid, Medicare, Veterans; Owner: Medical Facilities of America; License: state; Activities: Arts & Crafts; Dances; Pet therapy; Group exercise; Outings; Support Groups; Other: Home health care.

York Convalescent Center
113 Battle Rd., Yorktown, VA 23692, (757) 898-1491; Facility type: Skilled care, Alzheimer's; Beds: 60; Certified: Medicaid; Owner: Nonprofit/Religious; License: state; Activities: Arts & Crafts; Dances; Pet therapy; Group exercise; Outings; Support Groups; Other: Alzheimer's secured unit.

WASHINGTON

Anacortes

Alliance Living Community of Anacortes
1105 27th St., Anacortes, WA 98221, (360) 293-3174; Facility type: Skilled care, Alzheimer's; Beds: 50; Certified: Medicaid, Medicare; Owner: HMH Management; License: state; Activities: Arts & Crafts; Dances; Pet therapy; Group exercise; Outings; Support Groups; Other: Alzheimer's secured unit, Adult day care.

Arlington

Regency Care Center
620 S Hazel St., Arlington, WA 98223, (360) 435-5521; Facility type: Skilled care, Alzheimer's; Beds: 100; Certified: Medicaid, Medicare; Owner: Regency Northwest; License: state; Activities: Arts & Crafts; Dances; Pet therapy; Group exercise; Outings; Support Groups; Other: Alzheimer's secured unit.

Bainbridge Island

Messenger House Care Center
10861 Manitou Park Blvd., NE, Bainbridge Island, WA 98110, (206) 842-2654; Facility type: Skilled care, Alzheimer's; Beds: 100; Certified: Medicaid, Medicare; Owner: Proprietary/Public; License: state; Activities: Arts & Crafts; Dances; Pet therapy; Group exercise; Outings; Support Groups; Other: Alzheimer's secured unit.

Bellevue

Care Center at Kelsey Creek
2210 132nd Ave., Se, Bellevue, WA 98005, (425) 957-2400; Facility type: Skilled care, Alzheimer's; Beds: 100; Certified: Medicaid, Medicare; Owner: Nonprofit/Religious; License: state; Activities: Arts & Crafts; Dances; Pet therapy; Group exercise; Outings; Support Groups; Other: Alzheimer's secured unit.

Bellingham

Sehome Park Care Center
700 32nd St., Bellingham, WA 98225, (360) 734-9330; Facility type: Skilled care, Alzheimer's; Beds: 110; Certified: Medicaid, Medicare; Owner: Sunrise Healthcare Corp; License: state; Activities: Arts & Crafts; Dances; Pet therapy; Group exercise; Outings; Support Groups; Other: Alzheimer's secured unit.

Bothell

Franciscan Health Care Center at Bothell
10909 NE 185th St., Bothell, WA 98011, (425) 486-7174; Facility type: Skilled care, Alzheimer's; Beds: 110; Certified: Medicaid, Medicare, Veterans; Owner: Nonprofit/Religious; License: state; Activities: Arts & Crafts; Dances; Pet therapy; Group exercise; Outings; Support Groups; Other: Affiliations: Catholic Church; Home health care.

Burlington

SunRise Care & Rehabilitation
1036 Victoria Ave., Burlington, WA 98233, (360) 755-0711; Facility type: Skilled care, Alzheimer's; Beds: 50; Certified: Medicaid, Medicare; Owner: Proprietary/Public; License: state; Activities: Arts & Crafts; Dances; Pet therapy; Group exercise; Outings; Support Groups; Other: Alzheimer's secured unit.

Cathlamet

SunRise Care & Rehabilitation Center
155 Adler, Cathlamet, WA 98612, (360) 795-3140; Facility type: Skilled care, Alzheimer's; Beds: 70; Certified: Medicaid, Medicare, Veterans; Owner: Sun Healthcare Group; License: state; Activities: Arts & Crafts; Dances; Pet therapy; Group exercise; Support Groups; Other: Alzheimer's secured unit.

Centralia

Liberty Country Place
917 S Scheuber Rd., Centralia, WA 98531, (360) 736-9384; Facility type: Skilled care, Alzheimer's; Beds: 130; Certified: Medicaid, Medicare; Owner: Nonprofit/Religious; License: state; Activities: Arts & Crafts; Dances; Pet therapy; Group exercise; Outings; Support Groups; Other: Alzheimer's secured unit.

Riverside Nursing & Rehabilitation Center
1305 Alexander Rd., Centralia, WA 98531, (360) 736-2823; Facility type: Skilled care, Alzheimer's; Beds: 80; Certified: Medicaid, Medicare, Veterans; Owner: ExtendiCare Health Services; License: state; Activities: Arts & Crafts; Dances; Pet therapy; Group exercise; Outings; Support Groups; Other: Alzheimer's secured unit.

Sharon Care Center
1509 Harrison Ave., Centralia, WA 98531, (360) 736-0112; Facility type: Skilled care, Alzheimer's, Assisted Living; Beds: 110; Certified: Medicaid, Medicare; Owner: Proprietary/Public; License: state; Activities: Arts & Crafts; Dances; Pet therapy; Group exercise; Outings; Support Groups; Other: Alzheimer's secured unit, Adult day care.

Chelan

Regency Manor
726 N Markeson, Chelan, WA 98816, (509) 682-2551; Facility type: Skilled care, Alzheimer's; Beds: 80; Certified: Medicaid, Medicare, Veterans; Owner: Regency Pacific; License: state; Activities: Arts & Crafts; Dances; Pet therapy; Group exercise; Support Groups; Other: Alzheimer's secured unit; Languages: Spanish.

Colville

Pinewood Terrace
1000 E Elep St., Colville WA 99114, (509) 684-2573; Facility type: Skilled care, Alzheimer's; Beds: 130; Certified: Medicaid, Medicare, Veterans; Owner: Beverly Enterprises; License: state; Activities: Arts & Crafts; Dances; Pet therapy; Group exercise; Outings; Support Groups; Other: Alzheimer's secured unit.

Everett

Bethany at Silver Lake
2235 Lake Heights Dr., Everett, WA 98208, (425) 338-3000; Facility type: Skilled care, Alzheimer's; Beds: 120; Certified: Medicaid, Medicare; Owner: Evangelical Lutheran Church; License: state; Activities: Arts & Crafts; Dances; Pet therapy; Group exercise; Outings; Support Groups; Other: Alzheimer's secured unit.

SunRise View Convalescent Center
2520 Madison St., Everett, WA 98203, (425) 353-4040; Facility type: Skilled care, Alzheimer's; Beds: 60; Certified: Medicaid, Medicare; Owner: Private; License: state; Activities: Arts & Crafts; Dances; Pet therapy; Group exercise; Outings; Support Groups.

Grand Coulee

Coulee Community Hospital
411 Fortuyn Rd., Grand Coulee, WA 99133, (509) 633-1753; Facility type: Skilled care, Alzheimer's; Beds: 30; Certified: Medicaid; Owner: Brim Healthcare; License: state; Activities: Arts & Crafts; Dances; Pet therapy; Group exercise; Outings; Support Groups; Other: Alzheimer's secured unit.

Grandview

Grandview Healthcare Center
912 Hillcrest Ave., Grandview WA 98930, (509) 882-1200; Facility type: Skilled care, Alzheimer's; Beds: 60; Certified: Medicaid, Medicare, Veterans; Owner: Nonprofit/Religious; License: state; Activities: Arts & Crafts; Dances; Pet therapy; Group exercise; Outings; Support Groups; Other: Alzheimer's secured unit.

Walnut Grove Boarding Home
5305 N Hicks Rd., Grandview, WA 98930, (509) 882-2400; Facility type: Skilled care, Alzheimer's; Beds: 70; Certified: Medicaid, Medicare, Veterans; Owner: Nonprofit/Religious; License: state; Activities: Arts & Crafts; Dances; Pet therapy; Group exercise; Outings; Support Groups; Other: Adult day care.

Issaquah

Issaquah Care Center
805 Front St. S, Issaquah, WA 98027, (425) 392-1271; Facility type: Skilled care, Alzheimer's; Beds: 110; Certified: Medicaid, Medicare, Veterans; Owner: Vencor; License: state; Activities: Arts & Crafts; Dances; Pet therapy; Group exercise; Outings; Support Groups; Other: Alzheimer's secured unit, Home health care.

Providence Marianwood
3725 Providence Point Dr., SE, Issaquah, WA 98029, (425) 391-2800; Facility type: Skilled care, Alzheimer's; Beds: 120; Certified: Medicaid, Medicare; Owner: Nonprofit/Religious; License: state; Activities: Arts & Crafts; Dances; Pet therapy; Group exercise; Outings; Support Groups; Other: Alzheimer's secured unit, Home health care.

Kent

Benson Heights Rehabilitation Center
22410 Benson Rd., SE, Kent, WA 98031, (253) 852-7755; Facility type: Skilled care, Alzheimer's; Beds: 90; Certified: Medicaid, Medicare, Veterans; Owner: Beverly Enterprises; License: state; Activities: Arts & Crafts; Dances; Pet therapy; Group exercise; Outings; Support Groups.

Long Beach

Ocean View Convalescent Center
211 W Pioneer Rd., Long Beach, WA 98631, (360) 642-3123; Facility type: Skilled care, Alzheimer's; Beds: 60; Certified: Medicaid, Medicare, Veterans; Owner: Life Care Centers of America; License: state; Activities: Arts & Crafts; Dances; Pet therapy; Group exercise; Outings; Support Groups; Other: Alzheimer's secured unit, Adult day care.

Lynden

Christian Health Care Center
205 S BC Ave., Lynden, WA 98264, (360) 354-4434; Facility type: Skilled care, Alzheimer's; Beds: 120; Certified: Medicaid, Medicare, Veterans; Owner: Christian Home for the Aged & Infirm, Inc.; License: state; Activities: Arts & Crafts; Dances; Pet therapy; Group exercise; Outings; Support Groups; Other: Alzheimer's secured unit; Languages: Spanish, Dutch, Russian, Flemish, German.

Lynnwood

Manor Care Health Services
3701 188th St., SW, Lynnwood, WA 98036, (425) 775-9222; Facility type: Skilled care, Alzheimer's; Beds: 130; Certified: Medicare; Owner: HCR Manor Health Care; License: state; Activities: Arts & Crafts; Dances; Pet therapy; Group exercise; Outings; Support Groups; Other: Alzheimer's secured unit.

Monroe

Regency Care Center
1355 W Main St., Monroe, WA 98272, (360) 794-4011; Facility type: Skilled care, Alzheimer's; Beds: 00; Certified: Medicaid, Medicare, Veterans; Owner: Regency Pacific; License: state; Activities: Arts & Crafts; Dances; Pet therapy; Group exercise; Outings; Support Groups; Other: Alzheimer's secured unit.

Moses Lake

SunBridge Special Care Center
817 E Plum St., Moses Lake, WA 98837, (509) 765-7835; Facility type: Skilled care, Alzheimer's; Beds: 150; Certified: Medicaid, Medicare, Veterans; Owner: Sun Healthcare Group; License: state; Activities: Arts & Crafts; Dances; Pet therapy; Group exercise; Outings; Support Groups; Other: Alzheimer's secured unit Languages: Spanish.

Olympia

Providence Mother Joseph Care Center
3333 Ensign Rd., NE, Olympia, WA 98506, (360) 493-4900; Facility type: Skilled care, Alzheimer's; Beds: 150; Certified: Medicaid, Medicare; Owner: Nonprofit/Religious; License: state; Activities: Arts & Crafts; Dances; Pet therapy; Group exercise; Outings; Support Groups; Other: Alzheimer's secured unit.

Port Orchard

Port Orchard Care Center
2031 Pottery Ave., Port Orchard, WA 98366, (360) 876-8035; Facility type: Skilled care, Alzheimer's; Beds: 110; Certified: Medicaid, Medicare, Veterans; Owner: Life Care Centers of America; License: state; Activities: Arts & Crafts; Dances; Pet therapy; Outings; Support Groups; Other: Alzheimer's secured unit.

Puyallup

Linden Grove
400 29th St. NE, Puyallup, WA 98372, (253) 84-4400; Facility type: Skilled care, Alzheimer's; Beds: 50; Certified: Medicaid, Medicare; Owner: Genesis ElderCare; License: state; Activities: Arts & Crafts; Dances; Pet therapy; Group exercise; Outings; Support Groups; Other: Alzheimer's secured unit.

Rainier Vista Care Center
920 12th Ave. SE, Puyallup, WA 98372, (253) 841-3422; Facility type: Skilled care, Alzheimer's; Beds: 70; Certified: Medicaid, Medicare, Veterans; Owner: Vencor, Inc.; License: state; Activities: Arts & Crafts; Dances; Pet therapy; Group exercise; Outings; Support Groups; Other: Alzheimer's secured unit.

Seattle

Bayview Manor
11 W Aloha St., Seattle, WA 98119, (206) 284-7330; Facility type: Skilled care, Alzheimer's; Beds: 230; Certified: Medicaid, Medicare; Owner: Nonprofit/Religious; License: state; Activities: Arts & Crafts; Dances; Pet therapy; Group exercise; Outings; Support Groups; Other: Home health care; Affiliations: First Methodist Church of Seattle, Pacific NW United Methodist Conference.

Bessie Burton Sullivan
1020 E Jefferson, Seattle, WA 98122, (206) 323-1028; Facility type: Skilled care, Alzheimer's; Beds: 140; Certified: Medicaid, Medicare; Owner: Nonprofit/Religious; License: state; Activities: Arts & Crafts; Dances; Pet therapy; Group exercise; Outings; Support Groups; Other: Alzheimer's secured unit, Adult day care; Affiliations: Catholic Church.

Branch Villa Health Care Center
2611 S Dearborn, Seattle, WA 98144, (206) 325-6700; Facility type: Skilled care, Alzheimer's; Beds: 230; Certified: Medicaid, Medicare, Veterans; Owner: Nonprofit/Religious; License: state; Activities: Arts & Crafts; Dances; Pet therapy; Group exercise; Outings; Support Groups; Other: Alzheimer's secured unit, Adult day care.

Caroline K. Galland Home
7500 Seward Park Ave. S, Seattle, WA 98118; Facility type: Skilled care, Alzheimer's; Beds: 120; Certified: Medicaid, Medicare; Owner: Nonprofit/Religious; License: state; Activities: Arts & Crafts; Dances; Pet therapy; Group exercise; Outings; Support Groups; Other: Alzheimer's secured unit, Adult day care; Affiliations: Jewish; Languages: Spanish, Hebrew, Russian.

Columbia Lutheran Home
4700 Phinney Ave. N, Seattle, WA 98103, (206) 632-7400; Facility type: Skilled care, Alzheimer's; Beds: 120; Certified: Medicaid, Medicare, Veterans; Owner: Nonprofit/Religious; License: state; Activities: Arts & Crafts; Dances; Pet therapy; Group exercise; Outings; Support Groups; Other: Alzheimer's secured unit; Affiliations: Evangelical Lutheran Church; Languages: Czech, Polish, Thai, Chinese, French, Spanish, Tagalog.

Crista Senior Community
19303 Fremont Ave. N, Seattle, WA 98133, (206) 546-7400; Facility type: Skilled care, Alzheimer's; Beds: 180; Certified: Medicaid, Medicare; Owner: Nonprofit/Religious; License: state; Activities: Arts & Crafts; Dances; Pet therapy; Group exercise; Outings; Support Groups; Other: Alzheimer's secured unit, Affiliations: Christian.

Greenwood Park Care Center
13333 Greenwood Ave. N, Seattle, WA 98133, (206) 362-0303; Facility type: Skilled care, Alzheimer's; Beds: 150; Certified: Medicaid, Medicare, Veterans; Owner: Evergreen Healthcare Mgt; License: state; Activities: Arts & Crafts; Dances; Pet therapy; Group exercise; Outings; Support Groups; Other: Alzheimer's secured unit.

Horizon House
900 University St., Seattle, WA 98101, (206) 624-3700; Facility type: Skilled care, Alzheimer's; Beds: 60; Certified: Medicare; Payer mix: 86% Private pay; Owner: Nonprofit/Religious; License: state; Activities: Arts & Crafts; Dances; Pet therapy; Group exercise; Outings; Support Groups; Other: Alzheimer's secured unit.

Jacobsen House
1810 11th Ave., Seattle, WA 98122, (206) 323-5321; Facility type: Skilled care, Alzheimer's; Beds: 40; Owner: Nonprofit/Religious; License: state; Activities: Arts & Crafts; Dances; Pet therapy; Group exercise; Outings; Support Groups; Other: Alzheimer's secured unit.

Magnolia Health Care Center
4646 36th Ave. W, Seattle. WA 98199, (206) 283-9322; Facility type: Skilled care, Alzheimer's; Beds: 70; Certified: Medicaid, Medicare, Veterans; Owner: Private; License: state; Activities: Arts & Crafts; Dances; Pet therapy; Group exercise; Outings; Support Groups; Other: Alzheimer's secured unit.

Seattle Keiro
1601 E Yesler Way, Seattle, WA 98122, (206) 323-7100; Facility type: Skilled care, Alzheimer's; Beds: 150; Certified: Medicaid, Medicare; Owner: Nonprofit/Religious; License: state; Activities: Arts & Crafts; Dances; Pet therapy; Group exercise; Outings; Support Groups; Other: Alzheimer's secured unit, Adult day care; Languages: Japanese Filipino, Vietnamese, Korean.

Washington Center for Comprehensive Rehabilitation
3831 S Walden St., Seattle, WA 98144, (206) 725-2800; Facility type: Skilled care, Alzheimer's; Beds: 10; Certified: Medicaid, Medicare, Veterans; Owner: Nonprofit/Religious; License: state; Activities: Arts & Crafts; Dances; Pet therapy; Group exercise; Outings; Support Groups; Other: Alzheimer's secured unit, Adult day care; Affiliations: University of Washington.

Wedgewood Rehabilitation Center
9132 Ravenna Ave. NE, Seattle, WA 98115, (206) 524-6535; Facility type: Skilled care, Alzheimer's; Beds: 70; Certified: Medicaid, Medicare; Owner: Sunrise Healthcare; License: state; Ac-

tivities: Arts & Crafts; Dances; Pet therapy; Group exercise; Outings; Support Groups; Other: Alzheimer's secured unit.

Shoreline

Park Ridge Care Center
1250 NE 145th, Shoreline, WA 98155, (206) 363-5856; Facility type: Skilled care, Alzheimer's; Beds: 110; Certified: Medicaid, Medicare; Owner: All Season Living Centers; License: state; Activities: Arts & Crafts; Dances; Pet therapy; Group exercise; Outings; Support Groups; Other: Alzheimer's secured unit.

Richmond Beach Medical & Rehabilitation
19235 15th Ave. W, Shoreline, WA 98177, (206) 546-2666; Facility type: Skilled care, Alzheimer's; Beds: 10; Certified: Medicaid, Medicare, Veterans; Owner: Sun Healthcare; License: state; Activities: Arts & Crafts; Dances; Pet therapy; Group exercise; Outings; Support Groups; Other: Alzheimer's secured unit.

Snohomish

Mercy Haven Health Care Center
800 10th St., Snohomish, WA 98291, (206) 568-3161; Facility type: Skilled care, Alzheimer's; Beds: 90; Certified: Medicaid, Medicare; Owner: Nonprofit/Religious; License: state; Activities: Arts & Crafts; Dances; Pet therapy; Group exercise; Outings; Support Groups; Other: Alzheimer's secured unit.

Spokane

Garden Terrace Manor W
424 7th Ave., Spokane, WA 99204, (509) 838-8223; Facility type: Skilled care, Alzheimer's; Beds: 60; Certified: Medicaid, Medicare, Veterans; Owner: Nonprofit/Religious; License: state; Activities: Arts & Crafts; Dances; Pet therapy; Group exercise; Outings; Support Groups; Other: Alzheimer's secured unit.

The Gardens
414 University Rd., Spokane, WA 99206, (509) 924-4650; Facility type: Skilled care, Alzheimer's; Beds: 90; Certified: Medicaid, Medicare, Veterans; Owner: ExtendiCare; License: state; Activities: Arts & Crafts; Dances; Pet therapy; Group exercise; Outings; Support Groups; Other: Alzheimer's secured unit.

Loganhurst Health Care
1515 E Illinois Ave., Spokane, WA 99207, (509) 484-3132; Facility type: Skilled care, Alzheimer's; Beds: 50; Certified: Medicaid, Medicare; Owner: Proprietary/Public; License: state; Activities: Arts & Crafts; Dances; Pet therapy; Group exercise; Outings; Support Groups.

Royal Park Care Center
7411 N Nevada, Spokane, WA 99208, (509) 489-2273; Facility type: Skilled care, Alzheimer's; Beds: 160; Certified: Medicaid, Medicare; Owner: Private; License: state; Activities: Arts & Crafts; Dances; Pet therapy; Group exercise; Outings; Support Groups; Other: Alzheimer's secured unit.

Sunshine Gardens
10410 E 9th Ave., Spokane, WA 99206, (509) 926-3547; Facility type: Skilled care, Alzheimer's; Beds: 80; Certified: Medicaid, Medicare, Veterans; Owner: Nonprofit/Religious; License: state; Activities: Arts & Crafts; Dances; Pet therapy; Group exercise; Outings; Support Groups; Other: Alzheimer's secured unit.

Tacoma

Franke Tobey Jones Retirement Estates
5340 N Bristol, Tacoma, WA 98407; Facility type: Skilled care, Alzheimer's; Beds: 50; Payer mix: 100% Private pay; Owner: Nonprofit/Religious; License: state; Activities: Arts & Crafts; Dances; Pet therapy; Group exercise; Outings; Support Groups; Other: Alzheimer's secured unit.

Georgian House
8407 Steilacoom Blvd., SW, Tacoma, WA 98498, (253) 588-2146; Facility type: Skilled care, Alzheimer's; Beds: 70; Certified: Medicaid, Medicare; Owner: Genesis ElderCare; License: state; Activities: Arts & Crafts; Dances; Pet therapy; Group exercise; Outings; Support Groups; Other: Alzheimer's secured unit, Adult day care.

The Highlands Healthcare Center
5954 N 26th St., Tacoma, WA 98407, (253) 752-7713; Facility type: Skilled care, Alzheimer's; Beds: 90; Certified: Medicaid, Medicare, Veterans; Owner: Genesis ElderCare; License: state; Activities: Arts & Crafts; Dances; Pet therapy; Group exercise; Outings; Support Groups; Other: Alzheimer's secured unit.

Orchard Park Health Care
4755 S 48th St., Tacoma, WA 98409, (253) 475-5611; Facility type: Skilled care, Alzheimer's; Beds: 10; Certified: Medicaid, Medicare, Veterans; Owner: Genesis ElderCare; License: state; Activities: Arts & Crafts; Dances; Pet therapy; Group exercise; Outings; Support Groups; Other.

Tukwila

Highline Community Hospital
12844 Military Rd., S, Tukwila, WA 98168, (206)

248-420; Facility type: Skilled care, Alzheimer's; Certified: Medicaid, Medicare; Owner: Nonprofit/Religious; License: state; Activities: Arts & Crafts; Dances; Pet therapy; Group exercise; Outings; Support Groups; Other: Alzheimer's secured unit, Adult day care Home health care.

Vancouver

Fort Vancouver Convalescent Center
8507 NE 8th Way, Vancouver, WA 98664, (360) 254-5335; Facility type: Skilled care, Alzheimer's; Beds: 90; Certified: Medicare; Owner: Nonprofit/Religious; License: state; Activities: Arts & Crafts; Dances; Pet therapy; Group exercise; Outings; Support Groups; Other: Alzheimer's secured unit, Adult day care.

Rose Vista Nursing Center
5001 Columbia View Dr., Vancouver, WA 98661, (360) 696-0161; Facility type: Skilled care, Alzheimer's; Beds: 60; Certified: Medicaid, Medicare, Veterans; Owner: Prestige Care Co; License: state; Activities: Arts & Crafts; Dances; Pet therapy; Outings; Support Groups; Other: Alzheimer's secured unit.

Walla Walla

Park Manor Rehabilitation Center
1710 Plaza Way, Walla Walla, WA 99362, (509) 529-4218; Facility type: Skilled care, Alzheimer's; Beds: 80; Certified: Medicaid, Medicare, Veterans; Owner: Vencor, Inc.; License: state; Activities: Arts & Crafts; Dances; Pet therapy; Group exercise; Support Groups; Other: Alzheimer's secured unit.

Wapato

Emerald Circle Convalescent Center
209 N Ahtanum Ave., Wapato, WA 98951, (509) 877-3175; Facility type: Skilled care, Alzheimer's; Beds: 80; Certified: Medicaid, Medicare, Veterans; Owner: Nonprofit/Religious; License: state; Activities: Arts & Crafts; Dances; Pet therapy; Group exercise; Outings; Support Groups; Other: Alzheimer's secured unit; Languages: Spanish, Filipino, Native American.

Wenatchee

Parkside Rehabilitation & Care Center
1230 Monitor Ave., Wenatchee, WA 98801, (509) 663-1628; Facility type: Skilled care, Alzheimer's; Beds: 140; Certified: Medicaid, Medicare, Veterans; Owner: Triple C Convalescent Co; License: state; Activities: Arts & Crafts; Dances; Pet therapy; Group exercise; Outings; Support Groups; Other: Alzheimer's secured unit.

Yakima

Heritage Garden Care Center
115 N 10th St., Yakima, WA 98901, (509) 248-4173; Facility type: Skilled care, Alzheimer's; Beds: 100; Certified: Medicaid; Owner: Proprietary/Public; License: state; Activities: Arts & Crafts; Dances; Pet therapy; Group exercise; Outings; Support Groups; Other: Alzheimer's secured unit.

Landmark Care Center
710 N 39th Ave., Yakima, WA 98902, (509) 248-4102; Facility type: Skilled care, Alzheimer's; Beds: 90; Certified: Medicaid, Medicare; Owner: Proprietary/Public; License: state; Activities: Arts & Crafts; Dances; Pet therapy; Group exercise; Outings; Support Groups; Other: Alzheimer's secured unit.

Summitview Healthcare Center
3905 Knobel Ave., Yakima, WA 98902, (509) 966-6240; Facility type: Skilled care, Alzheimer's; Beds: 140; Certified: Medicaid, Medicare; Owner: Nonprofit/Religious; License: state; Activities: Arts & Crafts; Dances; Pet therapy; Group exercise; Outings; Support Groups; Other: Alzheimer's secured unit.

WEST VIRGINIA

Buchanannon

Holbrook Nursing Home
346 S Florida St., Buckhannon, WV 26201, (304) 472-3280; Facility type: Skilled care, Alzheimer's; Beds: 120; Certified: Medicaid, Medicare; Owner: Proprietary/Public; License: state; Activities: Arts & Crafts; Dances; Pet therapy; Group exercise; Outings; Support Groups.

Charleston

Arthur B Hodges Center
500 Morris St., Charleston, WV 25301, (304) 435-6560; Facility type: Skilled care, Alzheimer's; Beds: 120; Certified: Medicaid, Medicare; Owner: Private; License: state; Activities: Arts &

Crafts; Dances; Pet therapy; Group exercise; Outings; Support Groups; Other: Alzheimer's secured unit.

Cowen

Webster Continuous Care Center
1 Black Oak Dr., Cowen, WV 26206, (304) 226-5301; Facility type: Skilled care, Alzheimer's; Beds: 60; Certified: Medicaid, Medicare, Veterans; Owner: American Medical Facility Mgt; License: state; Activities: Arts & Crafts; Dances; Pet therapy; Group exercise; Support Groups; Other: Adult day care.

Fairmont

Wishing Well Health Center
1539 Country Club Rd., Fairmont, WV 26554, (304) 366-9100; Facility type: Skilled care, Alzheimer's; Beds: 120; Certified: Medicaid, Medicare; Owner: Private; License: state; Activities: Arts & Crafts; Dances; Pet therapy; Group exercise; Outings; Support Groups; Other: Alzheimer's secured unit.

Harrisville

Pine View Continuous Care Center
400 McKinley St., Harrisville, WV 26362, (304) 643-2712; Facility type: Skilled care, Alzheimer's; Beds: 70; Certified: Medicaid; Owner: Proprietary/Public; License: state; Activities: Arts & Crafts; Dances; Pet therapy; Group exercise; Support Groups; Other: Alzheimer's secured unit, Adult day care.

Morgantown

Mon Pointe Continuing Care Center
161 Bakers Bridge Rd., Morgantown, WV 26505. (304) 285-0692; Facility type: Skilled care, Alzheimer's; Beds: 120; Certified: Medicaid, Medicare; Owner: Proprietary/Public; License: state; Activities: Arts & Crafts; Dances; Pet therapy; Group exercise; Outings; Support Groups.

Moundsville

Mound View Health Center
2000 Floral St., Moundsville, WV 26041, (304) 843-1045; Facility type: Skilled care, Alzheimer's; Beds: 160; Certified: Medicaid, Medicare, Veterans; Owner: Private; License: state; Activities: Arts & Crafts; Dances; Pet therapy; Group exercise; Outings; Support Groups; Other: Adult day care.

Petersburg

Grant County Nursing Home
27 Early Ave., Petersburg, WV 26847, (304) 257-4233; Facility type: Skilled care, Alzheimer's; Beds: 120; Certified: Medicaid, Medicare; Owner: Nonprofit; License: state; Activities: Arts & Crafts; Dances; Pet therapy; Group exercise; Outings; Support Groups; Other: Alzheimer's secured unit.

Princeton

Princeton Health Care Center
315 Court House Rd., Princeton, WV 24740, (304) 487-3458; Facility type: Skilled care, Alzheimer's; Beds: 120; Certified: Medicaid, Medicare, Veterans; Owner: Private; License: state; Activities: Arts & Crafts; Dances; Pet therapy; Group exercise; Outings; Support Groups; Other: Alzheimer's secured unit.

Thomas

Courtland Acres Nursing Home
HC 60, Thomas, WV 26292, (304) 463-4181; Facility type: Skilled care, Alzheimer's; Beds: 90; Certified: Medicaid, Medicare, Veterans; Owner: Nonprofit; License: state; Activities: Arts & Crafts; Dances; Pet therapy; Group exercise; Outings; Support Groups; Other: Alzheimer's secured unit.

WISCONSIN

Arpin

Bethel Center
8014 Bethel Rd., Arpin, WI 54410, (715) 652-2103; Facility type: Skilled care, Alzheimer's; Beds: 110; Certified: Medicaid; Owner: Genesis ElderCare; License: state; Activities: Arts & Crafts; Dances; Pet therapy; Group exercise; Outings; Support Groups; Other: Alzheimer's secured unit.

Beloit

Premier Care
2121 Pioneer Dr., Beloit, WI 53511, (608) 365-

9526; Facility type: Skilled care, Alzheimer's; Beds: 50; Certified: Medicaid, Medicare, Veterans; Owner: Proprietary/Public; License: state; Activities: Arts & Crafts; Dances; Pet therapy; Group exercise; Outings; Support Groups; Other: Alzheimer's secured unit, Adult day care.

Black River Falls

Pine View
400 Pine View Rd., Black River Falls, WI 54615, (715) 284-5396; Facility type: Skilled care, Alzheimer's; Beds: 100; Certified: Medicaid, Medicare, Veterans; Owner: State & Local Gov; License: state; Activities: Arts & Crafts; Dances; Pet therapy; Group exercise; Support Groups; Other: Alzheimer's secured unit, Adult day care.

Bloomer

Hetzel Care Center
PO Box 227, Boomer, WI 54724, (715) 568-2503; Facility type: Skilled care, Alzheimer's; Beds: 120; Certified: Medicaid, Medicare, Veterans; Owner: Private; License: state; Activities: Arts & Crafts; Dances; Pet therapy; Group exercise; Outings; Support Groups; Other: Alzheimer's secured unit, Adult day care.

Boscobel

Memorial Nursing Home of Boscobel
205 Parker St., Boscobel, WI 53805, (608) 375-4112; Facility type: Skilled care, Alzheimer's; Beds: 70; Certified: Medicaid, Medicare; Owner: Private; License: state; Activities: Arts & Crafts; Dances; Pet therapy; Group exercise; Outings; Support Groups; Other: Adult day care.

Burlington

Mount Carmel Medical & Rehabilitation Center
677 E State St., Burlington, WI 53105, (262) 763-9531; Facility type: Skilled care, Alzheimer's; Beds: 120; Certified: Medicaid, Medicare; Owner: Vencor, Inc.; License: state; Activities: Arts & Crafts; Dances; Pet therapy; Outings; Support Groups; Other: Alzheimer's secured unit.

Chetek

Knapp Haven Nursing Home
725 Knapp St., Chetek, WI 54728 (715) 924-4891; Facility type: Skilled care, Alzheimer's; Beds: 100; Certified: Medicaid, Veterans; Owner: Private; State & Local Gov: state; Activities: Arts & Crafts; Dances; Pet therapy; Group exercise; Outings; Support Groups; Other: Alzheimer's secured unit.

Chippewa Falls

Lakeside Nursing & Rehabilitation
7490 156th St., Chippewa Falls, WI 54729, (715) 723-9341; Facility type: Skilled care, Alzheimer's; Beds: 120; Certified: Medicaid, Medicare, Veterans; Owner: ExtendiCare Health Services; License: state; Activities: Arts & Crafts; Dances; Pet therapy; Group exercise; Outings; Support Groups; Other: Alzheimer's secured unit.

Crandon

The Crandon Nursing Home
105 W. Pioneer, Crandon, WI 54520, (715) 478-3324; Facility type: Skilled care, Alzheimer's; Beds: 120; Certified: Medicaid, Medicare, Veterans; Owner: Arizconsin Group; License: state; Activities: Arts & Crafts; Dances; Pet therapy; Group exercise; Outings; Support Groups; Other: Alzheimer's secured unit.

Eau Claire

The Clairemont
2120 Heights Rd., Eau Claire, WI 54701, (715) 832-1681; Facility type: Skilled care, Alzheimer's; Beds: 200; Certified: Medicaid, Medicare, Veterans; Owner: Real Property Health Facilities Corp; License: state; Activities: Arts & Crafts; Dances; Pet therapy; Group exercise; Outings; Support Groups.

Dove Healthcare Nursing & Rehabilitation
1405 Truax Blvd., Eau Claire, WI 54703, (715) 552-1030; Facility type: Skilled care, Alzheimer's; Beds: 190; Certified: Medicaid, Medicare, Veterans; Owner: Private; License: state; Activities: Arts & Crafts; Dances; Pet therapy; Group exercise; Outings; Support Groups.

Elkhorn

Lakeland Nursing Home of Walworth County
W3930 County Rd. NN, Elkhorn, WI 53121, (262) 741-3600; Facility type: Skilled care, Alzheimer's; Beds: 250; Certified: Medicaid; Owner: State & Local Gov; License: state; Activities: Arts & Crafts; Dances; Pet therapy; Group exercise; Outings; Support Groups; Other: Alzheimer's secured unit, Adult day care.

Elmwood

Heritage of Elmwood Nursing Home
323 E Springer Ave., Elmwood, WI 54740, (715) 639-2911; Facility type: Skilled care, Alzheimer's; Beds: 120; Certified: Medicare; Payer mix: Medicaid—70%, Medicare—5%, Private pay—25%,

Owner: State & Local Gov; License: state; Activities: Arts & Crafts; Dances; Pet therapy; Group exercise; Outings; Support Groups; Other: Alzheimer's secured unit.

Fond Du Lac

Fond Du Lac Lutheran Home
244 N Macy St., Fond Du Lac, WI 54935, (920) 921-9502; Facility type: Skilled care, Alzheimer's; Beds: 120; Certified: Medicaid; Owner: State & Local Gov; License: state; Activities: Arts & Crafts; Dances; Pet therapy; Group exercise; Outings; Support Groups.

Manor Care Health Services
265 S National Ave., Fond Du Lac, WI 54935, Facility type: Skilled care, Alzheimer's; Beds: 150; Certified: Medicaid, Medicare; Owner: HCR Health Care; License: state; Activities: Arts & Crafts; Dances; Pet therapy; Group exercise; Outings; Support Groups; Other: Alzheimer's secured unit, Adult day care.

Saint Francis Home
33 Everett St., Fond Du Lac, WI 54935, (920) 923-7980; Facility type: Skilled care, Alzheimer's; Beds: 120; Certified: Medicaid, Medicare, Veterans; Owner: Private; License: state; Activities: Arts & Crafts; Dances; Pet therapy; Group exercise; Outings; Support Groups; Other: Affiliations: Roman Catholic Church.

Glendale

Dove Healthcare
1633 W Bender Rd., Glendale, WI 53209, (414) 228-9440; Facility type: Skilled care, Alzheimer's; Beds: 250; Certified: Medicaid, Medicare, Veterans; Owner: Senior Community Services; License: state; Activities: Arts & Crafts; Dances; Pet therapy; Group exercise; Outings; Support Groups.

The Waters of Seven Oaks
6263 N Green Bay Ave., Glendale, WI 53209-3837; Facility type: Skilled care, Alzheimer's; Beds: 90; Certified: Medicaid, Medicare, Veterans; Owner: Private; License: state; Activities: Arts & Crafts; Dances; Pet therapy; Group exercise; Outings; Support Groups; Other: Alzheimer's secured unit.

Green Bay

Brown County Mental Health Center
2900 St. Anthony Dr., Green Bay, WI 54311, (920) 468-1136; Facility type: Skilled care, Alzheimer's; Beds: 170; Certified: Medicaid, Veterans; Owner: State & Local Gov; License: state; Activities: Arts & Crafts; Dances; Pet therapy; Group exercise; Outings; Support Groups; Other: Alzheimer's secured unit.

Grancare Nursing Center
1155 Dousman St., Green Bay, WI 54303, (920) 494-4525; Facility type: Skilled care, Alzheimer's; Beds: 120; Certified: Medicaid, Medicare; Owner: Proprietary/Public; License: state; Activities: Arts & Crafts; Dances; Pet therapy; Group exercise; Outings; Support Groups.

Greenfield

Clement Manor Health Care
3939 S 92nd St., Greenfield, WI 53228; Facility type: Skilled care, Alzheimer's; Beds: 170; Certified: Medicaid, Medicare; Owner: Benedictine Health Systems; License: state; Activities: Arts & Crafts; Dances; Pet therapy; Group exercise; Outings; Support Groups; Other: Alzheimer's secured unit, Adult day care.

Southpointe Healthcare Center
4500 W Loomis Rd., Greenfield, WI 53220, (414) 325-5300; Facility type: Skilled care, Alzheimer's; Beds: 120; Certified: Medicaid, Medicare, Veterans; Mariner Post Acute Network: Private; License: state; Activities: Arts & Crafts; Dances; Pet therapy; Group exercise; Support Groups; Other: Alzheimer's secured unit.

Janesville

Rocky County Health Care Center
N Parker Dr., Janesville, WI 53547, (608) 757-5000; Facility type: Skilled care, Alzheimer's; Beds: 300; Certified: Medicaid, Medicare; Owner: State & Local Gov; License: state; Activities: Arts & Crafts; Dances; Pet therapy; Group exercise; Outings; Support Groups; Other: Alzheimer's secured unit, Adult day care; Affiliations: American Assn. of Homes & Services for the Aging.

Saint Elizabeth's Nursing Home
502 St., Lawrence, Janesville, WI 53545, (608) 752-6709; Facility type: Skilled care, Alzheimer's; Beds: 120; Certified: Medicaid, Medicare, Veterans; Owner: Private; License: state; Activities: Arts & Crafts; Dances; Pet therapy; Group exercise; Outings; Support Groups; Other: Alzheimer's secured unit.

Kenosha

Brookside Care Center
3506 Washington Rd., Kenosha, WI 53144, (262) 653-3800; Facility type: Skilled care, Alzheimer's; Beds: 120; Certified: Medicaid, Medicare;

Owner: State & Local Gov; License: state; Activities: Arts & Crafts; Dances; Pet therapy; Group exercise; Outings; Support Groups; Other: Alzheimer's secured unit.

Woodstock Health & Rehabilitation Center
3415 N Sheridan Rd., Kenosha, WI 53140, (262) 657-6175; Facility type: Skilled care, Alzheimer's; Beds: 180; Certified: Medicaid, Medicare, Veterans; Owner: Vencor, Inc.; License: state; Activities: Arts & Crafts; Dances; Pet therapy; Group exercise; Outings; Support Groups.

Kewaunee

Kewaunee Health Care Center
1308 Lincoln St., Kewaunee, WI 54216, (920) 388-4111; Facility type: Skilled care, Alzheimer's; Beds: 110; Certified: Medicaid, Medicare, Veterans; Owner: Private; License: state; Activities: Arts & Crafts; Dances; Pet therapy; Group exercise; Support Groups; Other: Alzheimer's secured unit, Adult day care.

King

Wisconsin Veterans Home
County Rd. QQ, King, WI 54946; Facility type: Skilled care, Alzheimer's; Beds: 700; Certified: Medicaid, Veterans; Owner: Private; License: state; Activities: Arts & Crafts; Dances; Pet therapy; Group exercise; Outings; Support Groups; Other: Alzheimer's secured unit.

La Crosse

Hillview Healthcare Center
3501 Park Lane Dr., La Crosse, WI 54601, (608) 789-4800; Facility type: Skilled care, Alzheimer's; Beds: 200; Certified: Medicaid, Medicare, Veterans; Owner: State & Local Gov; License: state; Activities: Arts & Crafts; Dances; Pet therapy; Group exercise; Outings; Support Groups.

Lancaster

Lancaster Care Center
2350 S Madison St., Lancaster, WI 53813, (608) 723-4143; Facility type: Skilled care, Alzheimer's; Beds: 120; Certified: Medicaid, Medicare, Veterans; Owner: Rice Health Care Facilities; License: state; Activities: Arts & Crafts; Dances; Pet therapy; Group exercise; Outings; Support Groups; Other: Alzheimer's secured unit, Adult day care.

Orchard Manor
8800 Hwy. 61 S, Lancaster, WI 53813, (608) 723-2113; Facility type: Skilled care, Alzheimer's; Beds: 90; Certified: Medicaid, Medicare; Owner: State & Local Gov; License: state; Activities: Arts & Crafts; Dances; Pet therapy; Group exercise; Outings; Support Groups; Other: Alzheimer's secured unit, Adult day care.

Laona

Nu-Roc Community Healthcare
Rte. 1, Box 230, Laona, WI 54541, (715) 674-4477; Facility type: Skilled care, Alzheimer's; Beds: 60; Certified: Medicaid, Veterans; Owner: Private; License: state; Activities: Arts & Crafts; Dances; Pet therapy; Group exercise; Outings; Support Groups; Other: Alzheimer's secured unit.

Lodi

Lodi Good Samaritan Center
700 Clark St., Lodi, WI 53555, (608) 592-3241; Facility type: Skilled care, Alzheimer's; Beds: 110; Certified: Medicaid, Medicare; Owner: Evangelical Lutheran Good Samaritan Society; License: state; Activities: Arts & Crafts; Dances; Pet therapy; Group exercise; Outings; Support Groups; Other: Alzheimer's secured unit.

Madison

Belmont Nursing & Rehabilitation Center
110 Belmont Rd., Madison, WI 53714, (608) 249-7391; Facility type: Skilled care, Alzheimer's; Beds: 120; Certified: Medicaid, Medicare, Veterans; Owner: Genesis ElderCare; License: state; Activities: Arts & Crafts; Dances; Pet therapy; Group exercise; Outings; Support Groups; Other: Alzheimer's secured unit.

Manor Care Health Services
801 Braxton Pl., Madison, WI 53715, (608) 251-1010; Facility type: Skilled care, Alzheimer's; Beds: 170; Certified: Medicaid, Medicare; Owner: HCR Manor Care; License: state; Activities: Arts & Crafts; Dances; Pet therapy; Group exercise; Outings; Support Groups; Other: Alzheimer's secured unit.

Oakwood Village Lutheran Hebron Hall
6201 Mineral Point Rd., Madison, WI 53705, (608) 231-3453; Facility type: Skilled care, Alzheimer's; Beds: 140; Certified: Medicaid, Medicare; Owner: Private; Nonprofit: state; Activities: Arts & Crafts; Dances; Pet therapy; Group exercise; Outings; Support Groups; Other: Alzheimer's secured unit.

Manitowoc

Manitowoc Health Care Center
4200 Calumet Ave., Manitowoc, WI 54220, (920) 683-4100; Facility type: Skilled care, Alz-

heimer's; Beds: 50; Certified: Medicaid, Medicare, Veterans; Owner: State & Local Gov; License: state; Activities: Arts & Crafts; Dances; Pet therapy; Group exercise; Outings; Support Groups; Other: Alzheimer's secured unit.

River's Bend Health & Rehabilitation Center
960 S Rapids Rd., Manitowoc, WI 54220, (920) 684-1144; Facility type: Skilled care, Alzheimer's; Beds: 100; Certified: Medicaid, Medicare; Owner: Wisconsin Health Services; License: state; Activities: Arts & Crafts; Dances; Pet therapy; Group exercise; Outings; Support Groups.

Shady Lane
1235 S 24th St., Manitowoc, WI 54220, (920) 682-8254; Facility type: Skilled care, Alzheimer's; Beds: 200; Certified: Medicaid, Medicare, Veterans; Owner: Nonprofit; License: state; Activities: Arts & Crafts; Dances; Pet therapy; Group exercise; Outings; Support Groups; Other: Alzheimer's secured unit.

Milwaukee

Alexian Village of Milwaukee
9301 N 76th St., Milwaukee, WI 53223, (414) 355-9300; Facility type: Skilled care, Alzheimer's; Beds: 120; Certified: Medicaid, Medicare; Owner: Private; License: state; Activities: Arts & Crafts; Dances; Pet therapy; Group exercise; Outings; Support Groups; Other: Alzheimer's secured unit, Adult day care; Affiliations: Alexian Brothers of America.

Bel Air Health Care Center & Alzheimer's
9350 W Fond Du Lac Ave., Milwaukee, WI 53225, (414) 438-4360; Facility type: Skilled care, Alzheimer's; Beds: 200; Certified: Medicaid, Medicare, Veterans; Owner: Beverly Enterprises; License: state; Activities: Arts & Crafts; Dances; Pet therapy; Group exercise; Outings; Support Groups; Other: Alzheimer's secured unit, Adult day care.

Friendship Village
7300 W Dean Rd., Milwaukee, WI 53223, (414) 354-3700; Facility type: Skilled care, Alzheimer's; Beds: 90; Certified: Medicaid, Medicare; Owner: Nonprofit; License: state; Activities: Arts & Crafts; Dances; Pet therapy; Group exercise; Outings; Support Groups; Other: Alzheimer's secured unit.

Jewish Home & Care Center
1414 N Prospect Ave., Milwaukee, WI 53202, (414) 276-4828; Facility type: Skilled care, Alzheimer's; Beds: 230; Certified: Medicaid, Medicare; Owner: Nonprofit/Religious; License: state; Activities: Arts & Crafts; Dances; Pet therapy; Group exercise; Outings; Support Groups; Other: Alzheimer's secured unit; Languages: Yiddish, Hebrew, Russian, Polish; Affiliations: Jewish.

Luther Manor
4545 N 92nd St., Milwaukee, WI 53225, (414) 464-3880; Facility type: Skilled care, Alzheimer's; Beds: 124; Certified: Medicaid, Medicare; Owner: Private; License: state; Activities: Arts & Crafts; Dances; Pet therapy; Group exercise; Outings; Support Groups; Other: Alzheimer's secured unit, Adult day care; Affiliations: ELCA.

Milwaukee Catholic Home
2462 N Prospect Ave., Milwaukee, WI 53211, (414) 224-9700; Facility type: Skilled care, Alzheimer's; Beds: 200; Certified: Medicaid, Medicare; Owner: Private; License: state; Activities: Arts & Crafts; Dances; Pet therapy; Group exercise; Outings; Support Groups; Other: Alzheimer's secured unit; Adult day care; Affiliations: Roman Catholic Church; Languages: Italian, Spanish.

Milwaukee Protestant Home for Aged Health Center
2449 N Downer Ave., Milwaukee, WI 53211, (414) 332-8610; Facility type: Skilled care, Alzheimer's; Beds: 50; Certified: Medicaid; Owner: Nonprofit Corp; License: state; Activities: Arts & Crafts; Dances; Pet therapy; Group exercise; Outings; Support Groups.

Saint John's Home of Milwaukee
1840 N Prospect Ave., Milwaukee, WI 53202, (414) 272-2022; Facility type: Skilled care, Alzheimer's; Beds: 100; Certified: Medicaid, Medicare; Owner: Private; License: state; Activities: Arts & Crafts; Dances; Pet therapy; Group exercise; Outings; Support Groups; Affiliations: Episcopal Diocese of Milwaukee.

Wisconsin Lutheran Care Center
6800 N 76th St., Milwaukee, WI 53223, (414) 3353-5000; Facility type: Skilled care, Alzheimer's; Beds: 190; Certified: Medicaid, Medicare; Owner: Private; License: state; Activities: Arts & Crafts; Dances; Pet therapy; Group exercise; Outings; Support Groups; Other: Alzheimer's secured unit.

Monroe

Pleasant View Nursing Home N
3150 Hwy., 81, Monroe, WI 53566, (608) 325-2171; Facility type: Skilled care, Alzheimer's; Beds: 130; Certified: Medicaid, Medicare; Owner: Private; License: state; Activities: Arts & Crafts; Dances; Pet therapy; Group exercise; Outings; Support Groups; Other: Alzheimer's secured unit.

New Richmond

Saint Croix Health Center
1445 N 4th St., New Richmond, WI 54017; Facility type: Skilled care, Alzheimer's; Beds: 130; Certified: Medicaid, Medicare; Owner: State & Local Gov; License: state; Activities: Arts & Crafts; Dances; Pet therapy; Group exercise; Outings; Support Groups; Other: Alzheimer's secured unit.

Oconomowoc

Shorehaven Health Center
PO Box 208, Oconomowoc, WI 53066, (262) 567-8341; Facility type: Skilled care, Alzheimer's; Beds: 240; Certified: Medicaid, Medicare; Owner: Nonprofit; License: state; Activities: Arts & Crafts; Dances; Pet therapy; Group exercise; Outings; Support Groups; Other: Alzheimer's secured unit, Adult day care.

Oconto Falls

Sharpe Care LTD
900 E Highland Dr., Oconto Falls, WI 54154, (920) 846-3272; Facility type: Skilled care, Alzheimer's; Beds: 120; Certified: Medicaid, Medicare, Veterans; Owner: Proprietary/Public; License: state; Activities: Arts & Crafts; Dances; Pet therapy; Group exercise; Outings; Other: Alzheimer's secured unit, Adult day care.

Oshkosh

Evergreen Retirement Community
1130 N Westfield St., Oshkosh, WI 54902, (920) 233-2340; Facility type: Skilled care, Alzheimer's; Beds: 110; Certified: Medicaid; Owner: Private; License: state; Activities: Arts & Crafts; Dances; Pet therapy; Group exercise; Outings; Support Groups; Other: Alzheimer's secured unit, Home health care; Affiliations: WI Conference of United Methodist Church.

Oshkosh Medical & Rehabilitation Center
1850 Bowen St., Oshkosh, WI 54901, (920) 233-4011; Facility type: Skilled care, Alzheimer's; Beds: 170; Certified: Medicaid, Medicare, Veterans; Owner: Private; License: state; Activities: Arts & Crafts; Dances; Pet therapy; Group exercise; Outings; Other: Alzheimer's secured unit, Adult day care.

Phelps

Lillian E Kerr Nursing Care & Rehabilitation Center
2383 Hwy. 17, Phelps, WI 54554, (715) 545-2589; Facility type: Skilled care, Alzheimer's; Beds: 90; Certified: Medicaid, Medicare, Veterans; Nonprofit; License: state; Activities: Arts & Crafts; Dances; Pet therapy; Group exercise; Outings; Other: Alzheimer's secured unit.

Racine

The Becker-Shoop Center
6101 16th St., Racine, WI 53406, (262) 637-7486; Facility type: Skilled care, Alzheimer's; Beds: 110; Certified: Medicaid; Owner: Private; License: state; Activities: Arts & Crafts; Dances; Pet therapy; Group exercise; Outings; Support Groups; Other: Adult day care; Affiliations: Lutheran Church.

Lincoln Lutheran Care Center
1600 Ohio St., Racine, WI 53405, (262) 637-7491; Facility type: Skilled care, Alzheimer's; Beds: 230; Certified: Medicaid, Medicare; Owner: Private; License: state; Activities: Arts & Crafts; Dances; Pet therapy; Group exercise; Outings; Support Groups; Other: Alzheimer's secured unit; Affiliations: Lincoln Lutheran of Racine Ecumenical.

Reedsburg

Sauk County Health Care Center
S4555 Hwy., CH, Reedsburg, WI 53959, (608) 524-4371; Facility type: Skilled care, Alzheimer's; Beds: 200; Certified: Medicaid, Medicare; Owner: State & Local Gov; License: state; Activities: Arts & Crafts; Dances; Pet therapy; Group exercise; Outings; Support Groups; Other: Alzheimer's secured unit.

Rhinelander

Taylor Healthcare & Rehabilitation Center
PO Box 857, Rhinelander, WI 54501, (715) 365-6900; Facility type: Skilled care, Alzheimer's; Beds: 150; Certified: Medicaid, Medicare; Owner: Private; License: state; Activities: Arts & Crafts; Dances; Pet therapy; Group exercise; Outings; Support Groups; Other: Alzheimer's secured unit.

Rice Lake

Heritage Manor
19 W Newton St., Rice Lake, WI 54868, (715) 234-2161; Facility type: Skilled care, Alzheimer's; Beds: 100; Certified: Medicaid, Medicare, Veterans; Owner: First American Care Facility; License: state; Activities: Arts & Crafts; Dances; Pet therapy; Group exercise; Outings; Support Groups; Other: Alzheimer's secured unit.

Richland Center

Pine Valley Health Care
25951 Circle View Dr., Richland Center, WI 53581, (608) 647-2138; Facility type: Skilled care, Alzheimer's; Beds: 110; Certified: Medicaid, Medicare, Veterans; Owner: State & Local Gov; License: state; Activities: Arts & Crafts; Dances; Pet therapy; Group exercise; Outings; Other: Alzheimer's secured unit, Adult day care.

Shawano

Maple Lane Health Care Facility
PO Box 534, Shawano, WI 54166, (715) 526-3158; Facility type: Skilled care, Alzheimer's; Beds: 100; Certified: Medicaid; Owner: State & Local Gov; License: state; Activities: Arts & Crafts; Dances; Pet therapy; Group exercise; Outings; Support Groups; Other: Alzheimer's secured unit.

Sheboygan

Sunny Ridge
3014 E Erie Ave., Sheboygan, WI 53081, (920) 459-3028; Facility type: Skilled care, Alzheimer's; Beds: 300; Certified: Medicaid, Medicare; Owner: Private; License: state; Activities: Arts & Crafts; Dances; Pet therapy; Group exercise; Outings; Support Groups; Other: Alzheimer's secured unit.

Sheboygan Falls

Sheboygan County Comprehensive Health Center N
3790 CTH VN, Sheboygan Falls, WI 53085, (920) 467-4648; Facility type: Skilled care, Alzheimer's; Beds: 150; Certified: Medicaid, Medicare; Owner: Nonprofit; License: state; Activities: Arts & Crafts; Dances; Pet therapy; Group exercise; Outings; Support Groups; Other: Alzheimer's secured unit.

Sister Bay

Scandia Village Good Samaritan
290 Smith Dr., Sister Bay, WI 54234, (920) 854-2317; Facility type: Skilled care, Alzheimer's; Beds: 50; Certified: Medicaid, Medicare; Owner: Evangelical Lutheran Good Samaritan Society; License: state; Activities: Arts & Crafts; Dances; Pet therapy; Group exercise; Outings; Support Groups; Other: Alzheimer's secured unit, Adult day care.

Sparta

Rolling Hills Rehabilitation Center
14345 County Hwy. B, Sparta, WI 54656, (608) 269-8800; Facility type: Skilled care, Alzheimer's; Beds: 140; Certified: Medicaid, Medicare, Veterans; Owner: Private; License: state; Activities: Arts & Crafts; Dances; Pet therapy; Group exercise; Outings; Support Groups; Other: Alzheimer's secured unit.

Superior

Colonial Health Care Services
3120 N 21st St., Superior, WI 54880, (715) 393-2922; Facility type: Skilled care, Alzheimer's; Beds: 40; Certified: Medicaid; Owner: Proprietary/Public; License: state; Activities: Arts & Crafts; Dances; Pet therapy; Group exercise; Outings; Support Groups; Other: Alzheimer's secured unit.

Waukesha

Linden Grove
425 N University Dr., Waukesha, WI 52188, (262) 524-6400; Facility type: Skilled care, Alzheimer's; Beds: 120; Certified: Medicaid, Medicare; Owner: Private; License: state; Activities: Arts & Crafts; Dances; Pet therapy; Group exercise; Outings; Support Groups; Other: Alzheimer's secured unit.

Westmoreland Health Center
1810 Kensington Dr., Waukesha, WI 53188, (262) 548-1400; Facility type: Skilled care, Alzheimer's; Beds: 300; Certified: Medicaid, Medicare; Owner: Proprietary/Public; License: state; Activities: Arts & Crafts; Dances; Pet therapy; Group exercise; Outings; Support Groups; Other: Alzheimer's secured unit.

West Allis

Mary Jude Nursing Home
9806 W Lincoln Ave., West Allis, WI 53227, (414) 543-5330; Facility type: Skilled care, Alzheimer's; Beds: 60; Certified: Medicaid, Medicare; Owner: Private; License: state; Activities: Arts & Crafts; Dances; Pet therapy; Group exercise; Outings; Support Groups; Other: Languages: Polish, Spanish.

The Village at Manor Park
8615 W Beloit Rd., West Allis, WI 53227, (414) 607-4100; Facility type: Skilled care, Alzheimer's; Beds: 110; Certified: Medicaid, Medicare; Owner: Nonprofit; License: state; Activities: Arts & Crafts; Dances; Pet therapy; Group exercise; Outings; Support Groups; Other: Alzheimer's secured unit.

West Bend

Cedar Lake Healthcare
5595 County Rd. Z, West Bend, WI 53095, (262) 334-9487; Facility type: Skilled care, Alzheimer's; Beds: 310; Certified: Medicaid, Medicare; Owner: Nonprofit/Religious; License: state; Activities: Arts & Crafts; Dances; Pet therapy; Group exercise; Outings; Support Groups; Other: Alzheimer's secured unit.

West Salem

Lakeview Health Center
902 E Garland St., West Salem, WI 54669, (608) 786-1400; Facility type: Skilled care, Alzheimer's; Beds: 120; Certified: Medicaid, Veterans; Owner: State & Local Gov; License: state; Activities: Arts & Crafts; Dances; Pet therapy; Group exercise; Support Groups; Other: Alzheimer's secured unit, Adult day care.

Whitehall

Trempealeau County Health Care Center W
20298 State Rd. 121, Whitehall, WI 54773, (715) 538-4312; Facility type: Skilled care, Alzheimer's; Beds: 50; Certified: Medicaid; Owner: State & Local Gov; License: state; Activities: Arts & Crafts; Dances; Pet therapy; Group exercise; Outings; Support Groups; Other: Alzheimer's secured unit.

WYOMING

Basin

Wyoming Retirement Center
890 Hwy. 20 S, Basin, WY 82410, (307) 568-3887; Facility type: Skilled care, Alzheimer's; Beds: 100; Certified: Medicaid, Medicare, Veterans; Owner: State & Local Gov; License: state; Activities: Arts & Crafts; Dances; Pet therapy; Group exercise; Outings; Support Groups; Other: Alzheimer's secured unit.

Cheyenne

Mountain Towers Healthcare & Rehabilitation Center
3128 Boxelder Dr., Cheyenne, WY 82001, (307) 634-7901; Facility type: Skilled care, Alzheimer's; Beds: 160; Certified: Medicaid, Medicare, Veterans; Owner: Vencor, Inc.; License: state; Activities: Arts & Crafts; Dances; Pet therapy; Group exercise; Outings; Support Groups; Other: Adult day care; Languages: Spanish.

Greybull

Bonnie Bluejacket Memorial Nursing Home
388 S US Hwy. 20, Greybull, WY 82426, (307) 568-3311; Facility type: Skilled care, Alzheimer's; Beds: 40; Certified: Medicaid, Medicare, Veterans; Owner: State & Local Gov; License: state; Activities: Arts & Crafts; Dances; Pet therapy; Group exercise; Outings; Support Groups, Chapel.

Jackson

Saint John's Living Center
625 E Broadway, Jackson, WY 8300, (307) 733-3636; Facility type: Skilled care, Alzheimer's; Beds: 60; Certified: Medicaid, Medicare; Owner: Private; License: state; Activities: Arts & Crafts; Dances; Pet therapy; Group exercise; Outings; Support Groups; Other: Languages: Spanish, German, French.

Laramie

Ivinson Memorial Hospital—Extended Care Facility
255 N 30th, Laramie, WY 82072, (307) 742-2141; Facility type: Skilled care, Alzheimer's; Beds: 50; Certified: Medicaid, Medicare; State & Local Gov: Private; License: state; Activities: Arts & Crafts; Dances; Pet therapy; Group exercise; Outings; Support Groups.

Lovell

New Horizons Care Center
1111 Lane 12, Lovell, WY 82431, (307) 548-2772; Facility type: Skilled care, Alzheimer's; Beds: 90; Certified: Medicaid, Medicare; Owner: Nonprofit/Religious; License: state; Activities: Arts & Crafts; Dances; Pet therapy; Group exercise; Outings; Support Groups; Other: Alzheimer's secured unit.

Newcastle

Weston County Manor
1124 Washington Blvd., Newcastle, WY, 82701, (307) 746-4491; Facility type: Skilled care, Alzheimer's; Beds: 50; Certified: Medicaid, Medicare, Veterans; Owner: Private; License: state; Activities: Arts & Crafts; Dances; Pet therapy; Group exercise; Support Groups; Other: Alzheimer's secured unit, Home health care.

Powell

Powell Nursing Home
999 Ave. G, Powell, WY 82435, (307) 754-1250; Facility type: Skilled care, Alzheimer's; Beds: 100; Certified: Medicaid, Medicare; Owner: Private; License: state; Activities: Arts & Crafts; Dances; Pet therapy; Group exercise; Outings; Support Groups; Other: Alzheimer's secured unit, Home health care.

Riverton

Wind River Healthcare & Rehabilitation Center
1002 Forest Dr., Riverton, WY 82501, (307) 856-9471; Facility type: Skilled care, Alzheimer's; Beds: 100; Certified: Medicaid, Medicare, Veterans; Owner: Vencor, Inc.; License: state; Activities: Arts & Crafts; Dances; Pet therapy; Group exercise; Outings; Support Groups; Other: Alzheimer's secured unit, Adult day care.

Rock Springs

Sage View Care Center
1325 Sage St., Rock Springs, WY 82901, (307) 362-3780; Facility type: Skilled care, Alzheimer's; Beds: 110; Certified: Medicaid, Medicare, Veterans; Owner: Vencor, Inc.; License: state; Activities: Arts & Crafts; Dances; Pet therapy; Group exercise; Outings; Support Groups; Other: Alzheimer's secured unit.

Worland

Community Care of America at Worland
1901 Howell Ave., Worland, WY 82401, (307) 347-4285; Facility type: Skilled care, Alzheimer's; Beds: 80; Certified: Medicaid, Medicare; Owner: Integrate Health Services, Inc.; License: state; Activities: Arts & Crafts; Dances; Pet therapy; Group exercise; Outings; Support Groups; Other: Alzheimer's secured unit.

Research Facilities

The following institutions are associated with government funded research efforts. Many of these institutions are involved in clinical trials. Information on clinical trials can be found in the Resources section following this section.

Note: The addition of ADSC next to the institution designates members of the Alzheimer's Disease Cooperative Study. The addition ADC indicates that these institutions are affiliated with and funded by the National Institute on Aging.

Alabama

University of Alabama at Birmingham ADC
Lindy E. Harrell, M.D., Director
The Sparks Research Center, Suite 454
1720 7th Avenue South
Birmingham, AL 35294-0017
(205) 934-2178 E-mail: dbaker@email.neuro.uab.edu

California

Stanford University ADCS, ADC
Jerome, A. Yesavage, M.D., Director
Alzheimer's Disease Research Center
Department of Psychiatry and Behavioral Science
Stanford, CA 94305-5550
(650) 852-3827
Fax: (650) 852-3297

University of California, Davis ADCS, ADC
Wlliam J. Jagust, M.D., Director
Alzheimer's Disease Center
Department of Neurology
4860 Y Street, Suite 3700
Sacramento, CA 95817
(925) 372-2485 ADCS Information
(916) 734-6280 ADC Information
E-mail: wjjagust@lbl.gov

University of California, Irvine ADCS, ADC
Carl W. Cotman, Ph.D., director
Alzheimer's Disease Center
Institute for Brain Aging and Dementia
1113 Gillespie Neuroscience Research Facility
Irvine, CA 92697
(949) 824-8726

University of California, Los Angeles, ADC
Jeffrey L. Cummings, M.D., Director
Alzheimer's Disease Center
Department of Neurology
University of California, Los Angeles
710 Westwood Plaza
Los Angeles, CA 90095-1769
(310) 206-5238 E-mail: adc@ucla.edu

University of California, San Diego ADCS, ADC
Leon Thal, M.D., Director
Alzheimer's Disease Center
Department of Neurosciences
UCSD School of Medicine
9500 Gilman Drive
La Jolla, CA 92093-0624
(858) 622-5820, 622-5800 ADC
E-mail ithal@ucsd.edu

University of Southern California ADCS, ADC

Caleb E. Finch, Ph.D., Director
Andrus Gerontology Center
University Park, MC 0191
3715 McClintock Avenue
Los Angeles, CA 90089-0191
(323) 442-3715, (213) 740-7777
E-mail: cfinch@almaak.usc.edu

Connecticut

Yale University School of Medicine ADCS
New Haven, CT
(203) 764-8100

Florida

Mayo Clinic, Jacksonville ADCS
Jacksonville, FL
(904) 953-7103
University of South Florida, Tampa ADCS
Tampa, FL
(813) 974-4355

Georgia

Emory University ADCS, ADC
Allan I. Levey, M.D., Director
Wesley Woods Health Center, 2nd Floor
1841 Clifton Road, NE
Atlanta, GA 30329
(404) 728-6453, ADCS; 728-6950, ADC Program E-mail: emoryadc@emory.edu

Illinois

Northwestern University ADCS, ADC
Marsel Mesulam, M.D., Director and Principal Investigator ADC Program
Cognitive Neurology and Alzheimer Disease
320 East Superior Street, Searle 11-253
Chicago, IL 60611
(312) 695-2343, ADCS; 908-9339, ADC
E-mail: mmesulam@nwu.edu

Rush-Presbyterian- St. Luke's Medical Center ADCS, ADC
Denis A. Evans, M.D., Director
Alzheimer's Disease Center, Rush Institute for Healthy Aging
1645 West Jackson Boulevard, Suite 675
Chicago, IL 60612
(312) 942-8264, ADCS; 942-4463, ADC
E-mail: radc@neuro.rpsimc.edu

Indiana

Indiana University ADCS, ADC
Bernardino Ghetti, M.D., Director
Indiana Alzheimer's Disease Center
Department of Pathology and Laboratory Medicine
635 Barnhill Drive, MS-A142
Indianapolis, IN 46202-5120
(317) 278-3934, ADCS; 278-2030, ADC
E-mail: bghetti@indyvax.iupui.edu

Kansas

University of Kansas Medical Center, ADC
Department of Neurology
Charles DeCarli, M.D., Director
3901 Rainbow Boulevard
Kansas City, KS 66160-7314
(913) 588-6979

Kentucky

University of Kentucky, Lexington ADCS, ADC
William Markesbery, M.D., Director
Sanders-Brown Research Center on Aging
101 Sanders-Brown Building
Lexington, KY 40536-0230
(859) 257-6508, ADCS; (606) 323-6040, ADC
E-mail: wmarkesbery@aging.coa.uky.edu

Maryland

The Johns Hopkins Medical Institutions, ADC
Donald L. Price, M.D., Director
Alzheimer's Disease Center
Division of Neuropathology
558 Ross Research Building
720 Rutland Avenue
Baltimore, MD 21205-2196
(410) 955-5632 E-mail: adrc@welchlink.welch.jhu.edu

Massachusetts

Memorial Veterans Hospital ADCS, ADC
Boston University
Neil W. Kowall, M.D., Director
GRECC Program (182B)
Bedford VAMC
Bedford, MA 01730
(781) 687-2845 ADCS; 687-2632, ADC
E-mail: nkowall@bu.edu

Harvard Medical School/Massachusetts General Hospital, ADC
John Growdon, M.D., Director
Alzheimer's Disease Center
Department of Neurology
Massachusetts General Hospital
15 Parkman Street

Boston, MA 02114
(617) 726-1728 E-mail: growdon@helix.mgh.harvard.edu

Michigan

University of Michigan ADCS, ADC
Sil Gilman, M.D., Director
William J. Herdman Professor and Chair
Director of Neurology
1500 E. Medical Center Drive
1914 Taubman Street
Ann Arbor, MI 48109-0316
(734) 936-8764 ADCS; 764-2190, ADC
E-mail: sgilman@umich.edu

Minnesota

Mayo Clinic, Rochester ADCS, ADC
Ronald Petersen, M.D., Director
Department of Neurology
200 First Street, SW
Rochester, MN 55905
(507) 266-8485, ADCS; 284-1324, ADC
E-mail: mayoADC@mayo.edu

Missouri

Washington University ADCS, ADC
Eugene M. Johnson, Jr., Co-Director
John C. Morris, M.D., Co-Director
Alzheimer's Disease Research Center
4488 Forest Park Avenue
St. Louis, MO 63108-2293
(314) 286-2364, ADCS; 286-2881, ADC
E-mail: adrc@neuro.ewstl.edu

New York

Columbia University ADCS, ADC
Michael L. Shelanski, M.D., Director
Alzheimer's Disease Research Center
Department of Pathology
630 West 168th Street
New York, NY 10032
(212) 305-2371, ADCS; 305-6553, ADC
E-mail: mis7@columbia.edu

Mt. Sinai School of Medicine ADCS, ADC
Kenneth L. Davis, M.D., Professor and Chair
Department of Psychiatry, Box 1230
One Gustave L. Levy Place
New York, NY 10029-6574
(212) 241-0438, ADCS; 241-8329, ADC
E-mail: k_davis@smtplink.mssm.edu

New York University, ADC
Steven H. Ferris, Ph.D., Director
Alzheimer's Disease Center
New York University School of Medicine
550 First Avenue, Room THN 312V
New York, NY 10016
(212) 241-8329 E-mail: steven.ferris@med.nyu.edu

University of Rochester Medical Center ADCS, ADC
Paul Coleman, Ph.D., Director
Alzheimer's Disease Center
Center for Aging and Developmental Biology
601 Elmwood Avenue, Box 645
Rochester, NY 14642
(716) 760-6561, ADCS; 275-2581, ADC
E-mail: paulcoleman@urmc.rochester.edu

North Carolina

Duke University, ADC
Donald Schmechel, M.D., Director
Joseph and Kathleen Bryan Alzheimer's Disease Research Center
2200 West main Street, Suite A-230
Durham, NC 27705
(919) 286-3228 E-mail: desduke@duke.edu

Ohio

University Hospitals of Cleveland ADCS, ADC
Case Western University
Karl Herrup, Ph.D., Director
12200 Fairhill Road
Cleveland, OH 44120-1013
(216) 844-6419, ADCS; 844-6400, ADC

Oregon

Oregon Health Sciences University ADCS, ADC
Jeffrey Kaye, M.D., Director
Alzheimer's Disease Center
Department of Neurology, CR 131
3181 SW Sam Jackson Park Road
Portland, OR 97201-3098
(503) 494-7615, ADCS; 494-6976, ADC
E-mail: kaye@ohsu.edu

Pennsylvania

University of Pennsylvania Medical School ADCS, ADC
John Q. Trojanowski, M.D., Director
Alzheimer's Disease Center
Center for Neurodegenerative Disease Research
3rd Floor Maloney Building
3600 Spruce Street
Philadelphia, PA 19104-4283
(215) 349-5903, ADCS; 662-4708, ADC
E-mail: trojanow@mail.med.upenn.edu

University of Pittsburgh ADCS, ADC
Steven DeKosky, M.D., Director
Alzheimer's Disease Research Center
4-West Mentefiore University Hospital
200 Lothrop Street
Pittsburgh, PA 15213
(412) 692-2705, ADCS; 692-2700, ADC
E-mail: dekosyky@vms.cls.pitt.edu

Rhode Island

Memorial Hospital of Rhode Island ADCS
Brown University
Pawtucket, RI
(401) 729-3752

South Carolina

Medical University of South Carolina ADCS
North Charleston, SC
(843) 740-1592, ext 17

Texas

Baylor College of Medicine ADCS, ADC
Stanley Appel, M.D., Director
Alzheimer's Disease Research Center
6501 Fannin Street, NB 302
Houston, TX 77030-3498
(713) 798-5325, ADCS; 798-6660, ADC
E-mail: lapel@bum.tmc.edu

Southwestern Medical Center ADCS, ADC
University of Texas
Roger Rosenberg, M.D., Director
Alzheimer's Disease Research Center
5323 Harry Hines Boulevard
Dallas, TX 75235-9036
(214) 648-7466, ADCS; 648-3198, ADC

Washington

University of Washington ADCS, ADC
Murray Rasking, M.D., Director
Alzheimer's Disease Center
Department of Psychiatry, VA Medical Center
GRECC (116A)
1660 S. Columbian Way
Seattle, WA 98108
(206) 277-1493, ADCS; (800) 317-5382, ADC

University of Washington, Department of Pathology, ADC
George A. Martin, M.D., Director
Alzheimer's Disease Research Center
Box 357470, HSB K-543
1959 NE Pacific Avenue
Seattle, WA 98195-7470
(206) 543-6761 E-mail: gmmartin@U.washington.edu
Home Page: http://weber.u.washington.edu/~adrcweb/

Washington, DC

Georgetown University Medical School ADCS
Georgetown University
Washington, DC
(202) 784-6671

Resources

Books

Becker, Robert, and Ezio Giacobini, eds. *Alzheimer Disease: From Molecular Biology to Therapy*. Boston: Birkhäuser, 1997.

Davidson, Ann. *Alzheimer's. A Love Story: One Year in My Husband's Journey*. Secacus, NJ: Carol Publishing Group, 1997.

Davidson, Frena Gray. *The Alzheimer's Sourcebook for Caregivers: A Practical Guide for Getting Through the Day*. New York: McGraw-Hill, 1996.

Davis, Helen D., and Michael P. Jensen. *Alzheimer's: The Answers You Need*. Forest Knolls, CA: Elder Books, 1998.

Davis, Robert. *My Journey into Alzheimer's Disease*. Wheaton, IL: Tyndale House Publishers, 1989.

Granet, Roger, and Eileen Fallon. *Is It Alzheimer's? What to Do When Loved Ones Can't Remember What They Should*. New York: Avon Books, 2000.

Grubbs, William M. *In Sickness & In Health: Caring for a Loved One with Alzheimer's*. Forest Knolls, CA: Elder Books, 1998.

Haisman, Pam, R.N. *Alzheimer's Disease Caregivers Speak Out*. Fort Myers, FL: Chippendale House, 1998.

Hilden, Julie. *The Bad Daughter*. Chapel Hill, NC: Algonquin Books, 1998.

Khachaturia, Zaven, and Teresa Radebaugh. *Alzheimer's Disease: Cause(s), Diagnosis, Treatment and Care*. Sanford, FL: InSync Communications, 1996.

Kuhn, Daniel, and David A. Bennett. *Alzheimer's Early Stages: First Steps in Caring and Treatment*. New York: Hunter House, 1999.

Mace, Nancy, and Peter Rabins, M.D. *The 36 Hour Day: A Family Guide to Caring for Alzheimer's Disease, for Persons with Related Dementing Illnesses and Memory Loss in Later Life*, rev. ed. New York: Warner Books, 2001.

Nolte, John. *The Human Brain, An Introduction to its Functional Anatomy*, 3rd ed. St. Louis: Mosby Year Book, 1993.

Pynoos, J. E., et al. *Strategies for Alzheimer's Caregivers*. Los Angeles: Program in Policy and Services Research, Andurs Gerontology Center, University of Southern California, (213) 743-6060, 1988.

Seegmiller, Judy. *Life with Big Al (Early Alzheimer's): A Caregivers Diary*. El Dorado Hills, CA: Alexander's Publishing, 2000.

Shenk, David. *The Forgetting: Alzheimer's: Portrait of an Epidemic*. New York: Doubleday, 2001.

Snowdon, David, Ph.D. *Aging with Grace: What the Nun Study Teaches Us About Leading Longer, Healthier and More Meaningful Lives*. New York: Bantam Books, 2001.

Tanzi, Rudolph, and Ann B. Parson. *Decoding Darkness: The Search for the Genetic Causes of Alzheimer's Disease*. Cambridge, MA: Perseus Book Group, 2000.

Terry, R.D., et al., eds. *Alzheimer's Disease*. Philadelphia: Lippincott/Williams and Wilkins, 1999.

Booklets and Pamphlets

Alzheimer's Disease: Availability of Specialized Nursing Home Programs, Intramural Research Highlights, NMES: National Medical Expenditure Survey, Number 1. AHCPR Publication

Number 91-0100, Agency for Health Care Policy and Research, free of charge by calling 1-800-358-9295, or ordering online at http://www.ahcpr.gov/gils.00000408.htm

Care for Advanced Alzheimer's Disease. Publication of the Alzheimer's Association, 919 Michigan IL 60611.

Early Alzheimer's Disease: A Guide for Patients and Families. Agency for Health Care Policy and Research, U.S. Department of Health and Human Services, free of charge by calling (800) 358-9295.

From Theory to Therapy: The Development of Drugs for Alzheimer's Disease (information kit on current drug therapies and therapies currently under testing). Publication of the Alzheimer's Association, 919 Michigan IL 60611.

Guidelines for Dignity (guidelines for specialized Alzheimer's disease care in nursing homes and other residential settings). Publication of the Alzheimer's Association, 919 Michigan.

Hospitalization Happens. Publication of the North Carolina Division of Aging; available free of charge through website, http://www.dhhs.state.nc.us/aging/ad.htm or by calling (800) 228-8738.

Janicki, M., Heller, T., et al. *Practice Guidelines for the Clinical Assessment and Care Management of Alzheimer and other Dementias among Adults with Mental Retardation.* 1995. American Association on Mental Retardation—Aging Special Interest Group, 444 Suite 846, Washington (800) 424-3668.

Lott, I. *Alzheimer's Disease and Down Syndrome.* 1995. National Down Syndrome Society, 666 Broadway, New York NY 10012, (800) 221-4602 or (212) 460-9330.

Developmental Disabilities and Alzheimer's Disease ... What You Should Know. 1995. The Arc of the Unites States, National Headquarters, 500 TX 76010, (817) 261-6003.

Living with Early-Onset Alzheimer's Disease. 1999. Brochure #ED206Z, The Alzheimer's Association, (800) 272-3900.

Living with Alzheimer's Disease. Publication of TriAD, 888-TriADHELP.

Subscription Newsletters

Early Alzheimer's: a forum for early stage dementia care. Santa Barbara, CA, Chapter of the Alzheimer's Association, Published quarterly, annual subscription $55.00, (805) 563-0020.

Perspectives: A newsletter for individuals diagnosed with Alzheimer's disease. Alzheimer's Disease Research Center, La Jolla, CA, published quarterly, annual subscription $24.00, (858) 622-5800.

Journals

Alzheimer's Care Quarterly
Aspen Publishers, Inc.

This quarterly journal describes the latest treatment advances for Alzheimer's and it has articles dealing with Alzheimer's disease and its care; http://www.aspenpublishers.com/journals/acq/inthisissue.html

Alzheimer's Disease Review
www.coa.uky.edu/ADReview

While this journal has ceased publications, it's archives are available through their website.

Journal of Alzheimer's Disease

This journal focuses on the research and treatment of Alzheimer's disease. Article abstracts and articles from many medical journals can be accessed through the following websites.

National Library of Medicine PubMed
http://www.4ncbi.nlm.nih.gov/PubMed/

Amedeo Free Medical Journals
http://www.freemedicaljournals.com

Clinical Trials

A number of organizations are involved in clinical trials for Alzheimer's disease. The purpose of clinical trials is to improve the understanding of certain conditions. Patients participating in clinical trial for neurological conditions will continue receiving medical care, routine laboratory tests and diagnostic tests from their primary physicians. Information on ongoing trials can be obtained from the following agencies.

The Alzheimer's Disease Clinical Trials Database

Joint project of the Food and Drug Administration and the National Institute on Aging; provides clinical trial information by state along with contact information. http://www.alzheimers.org/trials/index.html

The Alzheimer's Disease Cooperative Study (ADCS)
University of California, San Diego
La Jolla, CA
(323) 442-3715

The ADCS consortium is network of 83 university affiliated research facilities coordinated by the University of California, San Diego. Individual facilities are listed as ADCS centers in the resource section describing *Research Facilities.*

Alzheimer's Disease Education and Referral (ADEAR) Center
(800) 438-4380

ADEAR provides information to the public about ongoing clinical trials and opportunities for participation. http://www.alzheimers.org

CenterWatch Clinical Trials Listing Service
Center Watch lists clinical trials for Alzheimer's disease that aren't included in the Alzheimer's Disease Clinical Trials Database. http://www.centerwatch.com/studies/CAT11.htm.

Clinical Trials Service of the National Institutes of Health and the National Institute of Neurological Disorders and Stroke (NINDS)
9000 Rockville Pike
Bethesda, Maryland, 20892
(800) 411-1222
This web site, through its National Library of Medicine, shows all trials for Alzheimer's disease, including those that are no longer recruiting patients. http://www.clinicaltrials.gov

San Francisco Alzheimer's and Dementia Clinic
(415) 673-4600
http://www.sfcrc.com

University of California, Davis Alzheimer's Disease Centers
Martinez, CA (925) 372-2485 contact Joan Webb, RN
Sacramento CA (916) 734-5496 contact Bobbi Henk, RN
http://alzheimer.ucdavis.edu/adc/

Veritas Medicine
Veritas is a company that helps to link patients with clinical trials, including Alzheimer's disease trials. Veritas helps patients, their family members and physicians find National Institutes of Health (NIH) sponsored trials based on their location and medical profile through partnerships with pharmaceutical companies and research organizations. http://www.veritasmedicine.com

National, Regional and Government Organizations

The following organizations provide educational resources and support for patients with Alzheimer's disease and their families. Many of these organizations have local chapters, free newsletters, current research news, and affiliated support groups.

Administration on Aging
U. S. Department of Health and Human Services
http://www.aoa.gov/alz

Ageless Design, Smarter Safer Living for Seniors
126ee 159th Court North
Jupiter, FL 33478
(561) 745-0210
http://www.agelessdesign.com/lks-alz.htm

Alzheimer's Association National Headquarters
Member of Alzheimer's Disease International
919 North Michigan Avenue, Suite 1000
Chicago, IL 60611-1676
(800) 272-3900
http://www.alz.org
Email: info@alz.org
The Alzheimer's Association has local chapters around the country.

Alzheimer's Disease Education and Referral (ADEAR) Center
P.O. Box 8250
Silver Spring, MD 20907-8250
(800) 438-4380
http://www.alzheimers.org
Email: adear@alzheimers.org

Alzheimer's Disease International
45/46 Lower Marsh
London
SE1 7RG
United Kingdom
Tel: +44 20 7620 3011
http://www.alz.co.uk
Alzheimer's Disease International is an umbrella organization of 57 national Alzheimer Associations located around the world whose main purpose is to improve the quality of life of people with dementia and their caregivers and to raise awareness of the disease.

American Association of Retired Persons
601 E St., NW
Washington, DC 20049
(202) 434-2277

American Geriatrics Society
311 Massachusetts Ave., NE
Washington, DC 20002
(202) 543-7446

American Health Assistance Foundation
15825 Shady Grove Road, Suite 140
Rockville, Maryland 20850
(800) 437-2423
http://www.ahaf.org
This organization provides funding for Alzheimer's disease research, provides educational resources to families and caregivers and provides emergency financial support for Alzheimer's disease patients and caregivers.

American Health Care Association
http://www.ahca.org
This site has links to the organization's state associations.

American Psychiatric Association Public Information on Alzheimer's Disease
1400 K Street, N.W.
Washington, DC, 20005
http:/www.psych.org/public_info/alzheim.cfm

Clearinghouse on Aging and Developmental Disabilities
RRTC on Aging and Developmental Disabilities (M/C 626)
The University of Illinois at Chicago
7640 West Roosevelt Rd.
Chicago, IL 60608-6904
(800) 996-8845

National Alzheimer's Coordinating Center
University of Washington School for Public Health
4225 Roosevelt Way NE, Suite 301
Seattle, WA 98105
(206) 543-8637
http://ww.alz.washington.edu

This center facilitates collaborative research among the 30 Alzheimer's Disease Centers funded by the National Institute on Aging. In its scope of activities, the center provides public access to clinical trial data, information about news and events and a variety of educational resources.

National Council of Senior Citizens
8403 Colesville Rd., Suite 1200
Silver Spring, Maryland 20910
(301) 578-8800

Nation Council on the Aging
409 Third Street, SW, 2nd Floor
Washington, DC 20024
(202) 479-1200
http://www.ncoa.org

National Institute on Aging (NIA)
9000 Rockville Pike
Building 31, Room 2C-02
Bethesda, MD 20205
(301) 469-1752
http://www.nia.nih.gov/

National Institute of Neurological Disorders and Stroke
National Institutes of Health
Bethesda, MD 20892
http://wwwninds.nih.gov/health_and_medical/disorders/alzheimersdisease_doc.htm

National Senior Citizens Law Center
1101 14th Street, NW, Suite 400
Washington, DC 20005
http//www.nsclc.org

Neuroscience and Neuropsychology of Aging Program
National Institute on Aging
Gateway building, suite 3C307
7201 Wisconsin Avenue MSC 9205
Bethesda, Maryland 20892-9205
(301) 496-9350
Director, Brad Wise, M.D. email: by86y@nih.gov

North Carolina Division of Aging
Alzheimer's Association-eastern NC Chapter
4000 Oberlin Road, Suite 208
Raleigh, NC 27605
(800) 228-8738, (919) 832-3732
Duke University Family Support Program (800) 672-4213

Disability, Aging and Long-Term Care Policy
Office of the Assistant Secretary for Planning and Evaluation
Department of Health and Human Services
http://aspe.hhs.gov/daltcp/hcblist.htm

Suncoast Gerontology Center at the University of South Florida
12901 Bruce B. Down Boulevard, MDC 50
Tampa, FL 33612
(800) 633-4563 (813) 974-4355
http://wwww.med.usf.edu/suncoast/alzheimer/index.html

U.S. Department of Health and Human Services
Centers for Disease Control and Prevention
Hyattsville, MD 20782
(301) 458-4636

U.S. Department of Health and Human Services
Administration on Aging
330 Independence Ave., SW, Room 4759
Washington, DC 20201
(202) 619-0724

Caregiver Resources

Caregivers web-site
Alzheimer's Disease International

Family Caregiver Alliance (FCA)
690 Market Street, Suite 600
San Francisco, CA 94104
(415) 434-3388, (800) 438-4380
http://www.caregiver.org

National Family Caregivers Association
(800) 896-3650
http://www.nfcacares.org

Resources for Enhancing Alzheimer's Caregiver Health (REACH)
Coordinating Center
University Center for Social and Urban Research
University of Pittsburgh

121 University Place
Pittsburgh, PA 15260

TriAD
(888) TriADHELP
http://members.tripod.com/caringforothers/Health/Alzheimers/triad.htm

AoA Long-Term Care Resource Centers

National Rural Long Term Care Resource Center
University of Kansas Medical Center
University of Kansas Center on Aging
3901 Rainbow Boulevard
Kansas City, KS 66167
(913) 588-1636

This center focuses on rural long-term care issues. Its major goal is to improve the availability of and access to effective long-term care and community services for the rural elderly.

National Resource Center: Diversity and Long Term Care
Brandeis University
Brandeis University Waltham, MA 02254

This center supports the development and operation of long-term care ombudsman programs within each state; provides Stat ombudsman programs with educational support and training.

National Center on Elder Abuse (NCEA)
1225 I Street, N.W., Suite 725
Washington, DC 20005
(202) 898-2586

This center is a consortium of six partners headed by the National Association of State Units on Aging. The NDEA provides elder abuse information to professionals and the public and offers technical assistance and training to elder abuse agencies. The center also conducts short-term research and assists in policy development.

National Policy and Resource Center on Nutrition and Aging
Florida International University
Department of Dietics and Nutrition, OE200
Florida International University
Miami, FL 33190

This centers serves as a national focal point for issues related to nutrition and aging, with emphasis on the prevention of malnutrition and food insecurity.

AoA Legal Assistance for the Elderly Support Centers

National Eldercare Legal Assistance Project Members

National Senior Citizens Law Center (NSCLC)
1101 14th Street, NW, Suite 400
Washington, DC 20005
(202) 289-6976
Email: nsclc@nsclc.org

The NSCLC provides case consultation, technical assistance, training and legal assistance support services to local and state aging legal service networks for their purpose of enhancing their capabilities. This group publishes newsletters with current changes in laws affecting the elderly and training materials.

National Legal Assistance Support
American Bar Association
Commission on Legal Problems of the Elderly
1800 M Street, N.W.
Washington, DC 20036
(202) 331-2630

The National Legal Assistance Support Agency helps in developing accessible and responsible legal resources for the elderly.

Legal Counsel for the Elderly
American Association of Retired Persons
601 E Street, N.W.
Washington, DC 20049
(202) 434-2120

This group provides training and technical assistance to States on substantive law and advocacy skills, on protective services law and on the expansion of legal service programs for disability and Medicare benefits. The Legal Counsel also publishes a bi-monthly newsletter, the Elder Law Forum, which is distributed to 4,500 agencies and advocates.

Black Elderly Legal Assistance Support Project
National Bar Association
1225 11th Street, N.W.
Washington, DC 20001
(202) 842-3900

This project encourages the involvement of local chapters of the Nation Bar Association in establishing and expanding African American and other minority community care coalitions in four sites throughout the nation. The groups also works to meet the needs of low income, vulnerable African American and minority older persons.

National Legal Assistance Support and Information
National Clearinghouse for Legal Services, Inc.
205 W. Monroe St., 2nd Floor
Chicago, IL 60606-5013
(312) 263-3830

The National Clearinghouse provides legal information and research services to providers of legal assistance to older persons.

Strengthening Legal Assistance Project
The Center for Social Gerontology
2307 Shelby Avenue
Ann Arbor, MI 48103-3895
(313) 665-1126

The Center for Social Gerontology, Inc. expands and improves the delivery of legal assistance to vulnerable elderly by providing training, technical assistance and educational support in areas of law such as disabilities, self-determination and the right to refuse treatment, elder abuse, and guardianship and alternatives.

National Legal Support for Elderly People with Mental Disabilities Project
Judge David L. Bazelon Center for Mental Health Law
1101 15th Street, NW, Suite 1212
Washington, DC 20005-5730
(202) 467-5730

This project trains advocates to meet the needs of the elderly with mental disabilities, ensuring they can age at home with supports that strengthen individual capabilities. The project publishes reports dealing with legal issues facing this population and sponsors workshops on advocacy systems for the elderly with mental disabilities.

Long-Term Care and Housing Referrals

American Association of Homes and Services for the Aging
(800) 272-3900
http://www.aahsa.org/public/alzheim.htm

A Place for Mom.com—Senior Housing
http://www.aplaceformom.com

This site has resources for finding retirement and care communities.

Eldercare Locator
(800) 677-1116

Continuing Care Accreditation Commission
(202) 783-7286

Nursing Home Compare: The Health Care Financing Administration's Nursing Home Search
http://www.medicare.gov/NHCompare/home.asp

The Health Care Financing Administration's nursing home database includes information about every Medicare and Medicaid-certified nursing home in the United States and whether they have complied with nursing home regulations.

Internet Educational Resources

While most of the organizations listed in the Associations and Organizations Section list related web sites with information on Alzheimer's disease, the following web sites have also been developed to help those facing the challenge of managing Alzheimer's disease.

Action for Healthy Aging & Elder Care
http://www.healthandage.com

The Novartis Gerontology Foundation's educational support web site.

Administration on Aging
http://www.aoa.gov/alz

This site has links to state Area Agencies on Aging and federal agency consumer web sites.

Alternative Natural Medical Protocols
http://www.natmedpro.com/nmp/Refs-Alzheim.htm

This site has numerous links to research articles discussing the role of aluminum, antioxidant therapy, estrogen therapy, melatonin therapy, amalgam fillings and many other topics.

Alzheimer's disease web site at the National Institute for Neurological Disorders and Stroke
http://www.ninds.nih.gov/

Alzheimer's Disease Brain
http://www.pueblo.gsa.gov/cic_text/health/alzheim/brain.gi

This government sponsored web site includes illustrations of degenerative brain neurons, pinpointing disturbances in the areas responsible for motion, vision, sensory, speech and memory.

Alzheimer's Disease Society
www.alzheimers.org.uk/

Normal and Alzheimer Brain Comparison
http://www.ALZBRAIN.org/gallery.htm

This web site includes lateral and overhead scans of a normal brain and an Alzheimer brain with the areas of memory, understanding, hearing, speech, temper, personality and brain atrophy clearly labeled.

Alzheimer's Disease: Unraveling the Mystery
http://www.alzheimer's.org/unravel.html

This well-illustrated online booklet published by the National Institute of Health provides basic information about Alzheimer's disease and current research efforts.

Alzheimer Research Forum
http://www.alzforum.org.members/

This site provides access to the latest research articles about Alzheimer's disease, access to electronic journals and live discussions.

Alzheimer Support.com
(800) 366-5924
http://www.alzheimersupport.com
This web site provides educational resources related to Alzheimer's disease. This organization focuses on three primary objectives: reporting the latest news in Alzheimer's Disease treatment and research, making top quality nutritional supplements available at low prices, and donating profits from these supplements to Alzheimer's disease research. This site also has an affiliated chat board.

American Health Assistance Foundation
http://www.ahaf.org
This non-profit organization is dedicated to research, education and emergency financial assistance for Alzheimer's disease patients.

Center for Disease Control
National Center for Health Statistics Alzheimer's Disease
http://www.cdc.gov/nchs/fastats/alzheimr.htm

ElderWeb
http://www.elderweb.com/about.htm
This site contains information about eldercare topics and state-specific Medicaid regulations.

HealingWell.com Alzheimer's Disease Resource Center
http://www.healingwell.com/alzheimers/
This site provides information and articles as well as a directory listing organizations, support groups, chat rooms, and books on Alzheimer's disease; online support group and chat room.

Health Care Financing Administration
http://www.hcfa.gov
This site offers information about federal regulations, quality care initiatives, Medicare and Medicaid

The Massachusetts General Hospital Memory Disorder Units
http://neuro-oas.mgh.harvard.edu/sea

Mayo Clinic
http://www.mayohealth.org/home?id=5.1.1.1.8

Med Grasp
http://www.alzheimers-support.com

Medline Plus Health Information for Alzheimer's disease
http://www.nlm.nih.gov/medlineplus/alzheimersdisease.html
This site has links to latest news and studies, clinical trials, alternative therapy, caregiver information and specific problems. This site provides information in both English and Spanish.

Murphy's Unofficial Medicaid Page
http://www.geocites.com/CapitolHill/5974
This site serves as a resource guide to Medicaid. It offers information about Medicaid-specific resources and links to state-specific Medicaid informational sites.

National Aging Information Center
http://www.aoa.dhhs.gov/NAIC/Notes/default.htm
Links to major web resources on topics related to aging and available services for seniors.

National Citizens' Coalition for Nursing Home Reform
http:/www.ncnhr.org
This national advocacy group works to define and improve quality long-term care. This site offers links to state advocacy groups.

Novartis Foundation for Gerontology
http://www.halthandage.com/Home/gm=20!gc=11!=2!gid2=81.
The Novartis foundation for Gerontology is dedicated to promoting healthy aging. The Alzheimer's disease center funded by this organization provides educational support related to Alzheimer's disease.

Nursing Home Compare: The Health Care Financing Administration's Nursing Home Search
http://www.medicare.gov/NHCompare/home.asp
The Health Care Financing Administration's nursing home database includes information about every Medicare and Medicaid-certified nursing home in the United States and whether they have complied with nursing home regulations.

Partners Program of Excellence in Alzheimer's and Other Neurodegenerative Diseases
http://www.neurodegeneration.org
Array of resources in basic and clinic neurosciences with links to current research, patient and caregiver resources and scientific accomplishments.

Physicians Committee for Responsible Medicine
http://www.pcrm.org
This groups is dedicated to the responsible reporting of both conventional and alternative therapies. Their web site includes news reports, clinical research, controversies and issues, links to their journal, a resource sections and a search engine.

Psychiatry Resources
http://www.Psychiatry24x7.com/
Psychiatry24x7 offers extensive information on dementia and Alzheimer's disease.

Internet Caregiver Resources

About.com Alzheimer's Disease
http://www.alzheimers.about.com
This site includes educational resources, an online support group and a list of top nursing homes

Alzheimer's Caregivers Speak Out
http://www.chpublishers.com
This site provides resources to help answer questions about Alzheimer's disease and provides information about the book of this title, which is dedicated to the problems of caring for Alzheimer's disease patients.

Alzwell
http://www.alzwell.com

The American Geriatrics Society
The Alzheimer's Disease Caregiver
http://www.americangeriatrics.org/education/forum/alzcare.shtml

The Annals of Long-Term Care
Nursing Home Medicine
http://www.mmhc.com/nhm/
This site has articles and news highlights relating to nursing home care

ElderCare Online
http://www.ec-online.net
ElderCare is an online community for people caring for loved ones with Alzheimer's disease. This site offers a comprehensive library of practical articles, educational modules and supportive discussion groups.

The Family Caregiver's Alliance
(800) 445-8106
http://www.caregiver.org

The National Family Caregivers Association
(800) 896-3650
http://www.nfcacares.org

Support & Education for Alzheimer's Disease (S.E.A.D.)
Massachusetts General Hospital Memory Disorders Unit
http://neuro-oas.mgh.harvard.edu/sea/SWEBmanage.html

TriAD
(888) TriADHELP
http://members.tripod.com/caringforothers/Health/Alzheimers/triad.htm
This organization provides information, support and local services for patients with Alzheimer's disease and their caretakers.

Internet Support Groups

Alzheimer Research Forum
www.alzforum.org

Caregivers Forum
http://thirdage.com/family/

About.com Alzheimer's Group
http://www.alzheimers.about.com

Professional Journals

Alzheimer's Disease Review
http://coa.uky.edu/ADReview

Journal of Alzheimer's Disease
http://www.j-alz.com

Medicare and Other Health Insurance Resources

Medicare Assistance
(800) 638-6833
http://www.medicare.gov

Social Security Administration
(800) 772-1213
http://www.ssa.gov

Veterans Benefits
(800) 733-8387

Department of Regulatory Agencies
Division of Insurance
(800) 930-3745

Assistance in Finding Nursing Homes Ombudsman Programs and Licensure Programs

State Ombudsman Programs offer assistance in resolving problems with nursing homes and in helping find a suitable nursing home. Departments of Health and Human Services or Public Health provide information on certifying and licensing nursing homes by state. States who have received grants under the Alzheimer's Disease Demonstration Grants to States (ADDGS) Program are designated by the addition of ADDGS next to their name.

Alabama

State Long-Term Care Ombudsman
Alabama Department of Senior Services, ADDGS
770 Washington Avenue
RSA Plaza, Suite 470
Montgomery, Alabama 99503-5209
(334) 242-5743

Executive Director, Certification Division of Provider Services
Department of Public Health
P.O. Box 303017
Montgomery, Alabama 36130-5175
(334) 206-5175

Alaska

State Long-Term Care Ombudsman
Alaska Commission on Aging, ADDGS
3601 C Street, Suite 260
Anchorage, Alaska 99503-5209
(907) 334-4480, in Alaska (800) 730-6393

Director, Health Facilities Licensing and Certification
Department of Health and Social Services
4730 Business Park Boulevard, Suite 18
Building H
Anchorage, Alaska 50399-503
(907) 561-8081

Arizona

State Long-Term Care Ombudsman
Aging and Adult Administration
Department of Economic Security
1789 W. Jefferson Street, 950 A
Phoenix, Arizona, 85007
(602) 542-4446

Program Director, Division of Assurance and Licensure Services
Arizona Department of Human Services
1647 E. Morten Avenue, Suite 130
Phoenix, Arizona 85020-4610
(602) 674-9705

Arkansas

State Long-Term Care Ombudsman
Division of Aging and Adult Services
Arkansas Department of Human Services
P.O. Box 1437, Slot 1412
Little Rock, Arkansas 72203-1437
(501) 682-2441

Director, Division of Medical Services
Office of Long-Term Care
Arkansas Department of Human Services, ADDGS
Division of Aging and Adult Services
P. O. Box 8059, Mail Slot 400
Little Rock, Arkansas 72203-8059
(501) 682-8430

California

State Long-Term Care Ombudsman
Department of Aging, ADDGS
1600 K Street
Sacramento, California 95814
(916) 322-5290

Deputy Director, Licensing and Certification Programs
Department of Health Services
P.O. Box 942732
1800 Third Street, Suite 210
Sacramento, California 94234-7320
(916) 445-3054

Colorado

State Long-Term Care Ombudsman
The Legal Center
455 Sherman Street, Suite 130
Denver, Colorado 80203
(303) 722-0300

Director, Health Facilities Division
Colorado Department of Public Health and Environment
4300 Cherry Creek Drive S.
Denver, Colorado 80246
(303) 692-2835

Connecticut

State Long-Term Care Ombudsman
Elderly Services Division
25 Sigourney Street, 10th Floor
Hartford, Connecticut 06106-5033
(860) 424-5200

Director, State of Connecticut Department of Public Health
410 Capitol Avenue, Mail Slot 12HSR
P.O. Box 340308
Hartford, Connecticut 06134
(860) 509-7406

Delaware

State Long-Term Care Ombudsman
Division of Services for the Aging and Adults with Physical Disabilities
1901 N. DuPont Highway
New Castle, Delaware 19720
(302) 577-4791

Director, Division of Long-Term Care Residents Protection
Delaware Department of Health and Social Services
3 Mill Road, Suite 308
Wilmington, Delaware 19806
(302) 577-6672

DISTRICT OF COLUMBIA

State Long-Term Care Ombudsman
Legal Counsel for the Elderly, AARP Foundation
601 E. Street N.W.
Washington, DC 20049
(202) 434-2120

Director, Health Regulation Administration
Department of Health 825 N. Capitol Street, N.E.
Washington, DC 20002
(202) 442-5888

FLORIDA

State Long-Term Care Ombudsman
LTC Ombudsman Counsel
Department of Elder Affairs, ADDGS
600 S. Calhoun Street, Suite 270
Tallahassee, Florida 32301
(850) 488-6190

Secretary, Long-Term Care Unit
Florida Agency for Health Care
Mail Station 33
2727 Mahan Drive
Tallahassee, Florida 32308
(850) 448-5861

GEORGIA

State Long-Term Care Ombudsman
Division of Aging Services
Two Peachtree Street N.W., 36th Floor
Atlanta, Georgia 30303-3176
(404) 463-8383
(888) 454-5826

Director, Office of Regulatory Service of Long-Term Care
Department of Human Resources
Two Peachtree Street N.W., Suite 31-447
Atlanta, Georgia 30303
(404) 657-5850

HAWAII

State Long-Term Care Ombudsman
Executive Office on Aging
250 S. Hotel Street, Suite 109
Honolulu, Hawaii 96813-2831
(808) 586-0100

Director, Office of Health Care Assurance
Department of Health
P.O. Box 3378
Honolulu, Hawaii 96801
(808) 586-4080

IDAHO

State Long-Term Care Ombudsman
Commission on Aging
P.O. Box 83720
Boise, Idaho 83720-0007
(208) 334-3833

Director, Bureau of Facility Standards
P.O. Box 83720
Boise, Idaho 83720-0036
(208) 334-6626

ILLINOIS

State Long-Term Care Ombudsman
Illinois Department on Aging
421 E. Capitol Avenue, Suite 100
Springfield, Illinois 62701-1789
(217) 524-6911; in-state (800) 252-8966

Director, Office of Quality Assurance
Illinois Department of Public Health, ADDGS
525-535 W. Jefferson Street
Springfield, Illinois 62761-0001
(217) 782-5180

INDIANA

State Long-Term Care Ombudsman
Aging and Rehabilitation Services, ADDGS
P.O. Box 7083-W454
402 W. Washington Street, Room W-454
Indianapolis, Indiana 46204-7083
(317) 232-7134

Director, Bureau of Aging and In-Home Services
Mail Stop 21-10
P.O. Box 7083
402 W. Washington Street, Room W-454
Indianapolis, Indiana 46204-7083
(317) 232-7020

IOWA

State Long-Term Care Ombudsman
Department of Elder Affairs, ADDGS
200 Tenth Street, 3rd Floor
Clemens Building
Des Moines, Iowa 50309-3609
(515) 242-3328

Executive Director, Health Facilities Division
Department of Inspections and Appeals
Lucas State Office Building
Des Moines, Iowa 50319-0083
(515) 281-4115

Kansas

State Long-Term Care Ombudsman
610 S.W. Tenth Avenue, Second Floor
Topeka, Kansas 66612-1616
(785) 296-3017

Secretary, Health Facilities
Landon State Office Building
900 S.W. Jackson, Suite 1001
Topeka, Kansas 66612
(785) 296-1240

Kentucky

State Long-Term Care Ombudsman
Office of Aging Services
275 E. Main Street
Frankfort, Kentucky 40621
(502) 564-6930

Director, Licensing and Regulation
Office of the Inspector General
275 E. Main Street, Mail Stop SE
Frankfort, Kentucky 40621
(502) 564-6786

Louisiana

State Long-Term Care Ombudsman
Governor's Office of Elderly Affairs
412 N. Fourth Street, 3rd Floor
Baton Rouge, Louisiana 70802
(225) 342-7100; in-state (800) 259-4900

Director, State of Louisiana Health Standards
P.O. Box 3767
Baton Rouge, Louisiana 70821-3767
(225) 342-5292

Maine

State Long-Term Care Ombudsman
P.O. Box 128
Augusta, Maine 04332
(207) 621-1079

Director, Bureau of Medical Services
Division of Licensing and Certification
Department of Human Services, ADDGS
Bureau of Elder and Adult Services
35 Anthony Avenue
11 State House Station
Augusta, Maine 04333-0011
(207) 624-5443

Maryland

State Long-Term Care Ombudsman
Maryland Department of Aging, ADDGS
301 W. Preston Street, Room 1004
Baltimore, Maryland 21201
(410) 767-1100

Secretary, Office of Health Care Quality
Spring Grove Hospital Center
BB Building
55 Wade Avenue
Baltimore, Maryland 21228
(410) 402-8000

Massachusetts

State Long-Term Care Ombudsman
Commonwealth of Massachusetts
Executive Office of Elder Affairs, ADDGS
One Ashburton Place, 5th Floor
Boston, Massachusetts 02108-1518
(617) 727-7750

Secretary, Licensure and Certification
Division of Health Care Quality
10 West Street, 5th Floor
Boston, Massachusetts 02111
(617) 753-8000

Michigan

State Long-Term Care Ombudsman
Citizens for Better Care
4750 Woodward Avenue, Suite 410
Detroit, Michigan 48201-1308
(313) 832-6387

Director, MDCIS Bureau of Health Systems
Division of Nursing Home Monitoring
P.O. Box 30664
Lansing, Michigan 48909
(517) 241-2506

Minnesota

State Long-Term Care Ombudsman
Office of Ombudsman for Older Minnesotans
Board on Aging, ADDGS
121 E. Seventh Place, Suite 280
St. Paul, Minnesota 55101
(651) 296-0382

Executive Secretary, Long-Term Care and Certification
Division of Facility and Provider Compliance
85 E. Seventh Place, Suite 300
St. Paul, Minnesota 57101
(651) 215-8701

Mississippi

State Long-Term Care Ombudsman
Division of Aging and Adult Services
750 N. State Street

Jackson, Mississippi 39202
(601) 359-4929

Director, Licensure and Certification
570 E. Woodrow Wilson, Suite 200
Jackson, Mississippi 39215
(601) 576-7300

MISSOURI

State Long-Term Care Ombudsman
Department of Social Services, Division of Aging, ADDGS
P.O. Box 1337
Jefferson City, Missouri 65102
(573) 527-0727; (800) 309-3282

Director, Division of Aging
615 Howerton Court
P.O. Box 1337
Jefferson City, Missouri 65102
(573) 751-3082

MONTANA

State Long-Term Care Ombudsman
Office on Aging, Senior and Long-Term Care Division
Department of Public Health and Human Services
P.O. Box 4210
Helena, Montana 59604-4210
(406) 444-4077

State Aging Coordinator, Quality Assurance Division
Department of Public Health and Human Services
2401 Colonial Drive
Helena, Montana 59620
(406) 444-2031

NEBRASKA

State Long-Term Care Ombudsman
Department of Health and Human Services, ADDGS
Division of Aging and Disability Services
P.O. Box 95044
Lincoln, Nebraska 68509-5044
(402) 471-2307

Administrator, Regulation and Licensure
Credentialing Division, Department of Health and Human Services
301 Centennial Mall S.
P.O. Box 95007
Lincoln, Nebraska 68509-5007
(402) 471-2946

NEVADA

State Long-Term Care Ombudsman
Department of Human Resources, Division for Aging Services, ADDGS
340 N. Eleventh Street, Suite 203
Las Vegas, Nevada 89101
(702) 486-3545

Administrator, Bureau of Licensure and Certification
1550 E. College Parkway, Suite 158
Carson City, Nevada 89706
(775) 687-4475

NEW HAMPSHIRE

State Long-Term Care Ombudsman
Health and Human Services
129 Pleasant Street
Concord, New Hampshire 03301-6505
(603) 271-4375

Director, Office of Program Support
Health Facilities Administration
Department of Health and Human Services
Division of Elderly and Adult Services, ADDGS
129 Pleasant Street
Concord, New Hampshire 03301-3857
(603) 271-4968

NEW JERSEY

State Long-Term Care Ombudsman
Office of the Ombudsman for the Institutionalized Elderly
P.O. Box 807
Trenton, New Jersey 08625-0807
(609) 588-3614

Assistant Commissioner
Division of Long-Term Care Systems
New Jersey Department of Health Services
P.O. Box 367
Trenton, New Jersey 08625
(609) 633-9034

NEW MEXICO

State Long-Term Care Ombudsman
State Agency on Aging, ADDGS
228 E. Palace Avenue
Santa Fe, New Mexico 87501
(505) 827-7640

Director, Health Facilities Licensing and Certification Bureau
525 Camino de los Marquez, Suite 2
Santa Fe, New Mexico 78501
(505) 827-7640

New York

State Long-Term Care Ombudsman
New York State Office for the Aging
Two Empire State Plaza
Albany, New York 12223-0001
(518) 474-0108

Executive Director, Office of Continuing Care
New York State Department of Health
166 Delaware Avenue
Delmar, New York 12054
(518) 474-1000

North Carolina

State Long-Term Care Ombudsman
Division of Aging
2101 Mail Service Center
Raleigh, North Carolina 27699-2101

Director, Division of Facilities Services
Licensure and Certification Section
Department of Health and Human Services, ADDGS
2711 Mail Service Center
Raleigh, North Carolina 27699-2711
(919) 733-7461

North Dakota

State Long-Term Care Ombudsman
Department of Health and Human Services
Aging Services Division
600 S. Second Street, Suite 1C
Bismarck, North Dakota 58504
(701) 328-8910

Director, Division of Health Facilities
North Dakota Department of Health
600 E. Boulevard Avenue
Bismarck, North Dakota 58505-0200
(701) 328-2352

Ohio

State Long-Term Care Ombudsman
Ohio Department of Aging
50 W. Broad Street, 9th Floor
Columbus, Ohio 43215-3363
(614) 466-1221; (800) 282-1206

Director, Licensure Program
Ohio Department of Health
246 N. High Street
Columbus, Ohio 43215-2412
(614) 466-7713

Oklahoma

State Long-Term Care Ombudsman
Aging Services Division
Department of Human Services
312 N.E. Twenty-Eighth Street
Oklahoma City, Oklahoma 73105
(405) 521-6734

Division Administrator, Special Health Services
Oklahoma State Health Department
1000 N.E. Tenth Street
Oklahoma City, Oklahoma 73117
(405) 271-6868

Oregon

State Long-Term Care Ombudsman
3855 Wolverine N.E., Suite 6
Salem, Oregon 97305-1251
(503) 378-6533

Administrator, Long-Term Care Quality Section
Senior and Disabled Services Division
500 Summer Street N.E.
Salem, Oregon 97310
(503) 945-5853

Pennsylvania

State Long-Term Care Ombudsman
Pennsylvania Department of Aging
555 Walnut Street, 5th Floor
Harrisburg, Pennsylvania 17101-1919
(717) 783-7247

Secretary, Bureau of Facility Licensure and Certification
Division of Nursing Care Facilities
Pennsylvania Department of Health
Room 526, Health and Welfare Building
Harrisburg, Pennsylvania 17120
(717) 787-1816

Rhode Island

State Long-Term Care Ombudsman
Alliance for Better Long-Term Care
422 Post Road, Suite 204
Warwick, Rhode Island 02888
(401) 785-3340

Director, Rhode Island Department of Health
Division of Facilities Regulation
Department of Elderly Affairs, ADDGS
3 Capitol Hill, Room 306
Providence, Rhode Island 09908
(401) 222-2566

South Carolina

State Long-Term Care Ombudsman
Division on Aging

1801 Main Street
P.O. Box 8206
Columbia, South Carolina 29202-8206
(803) 898-2580

Office of Senior and Long-Term Care Services
Division of Health Licensing
Department of Health and Environmental Control
2600 Bull Street
Columbia, South Carolina 29201-8206
(803) 737-7370

South Dakota

State Long-Term Care Ombudsman
Department of Social Services
Office of Adult Services and Aging
700 Governors Drive
Pierre, South Dakota 57501-2291
(605) 773-3656

Administrator, Licensure and Certification
South Dakota Department of Health
615 E. Fourth Street
Pierre, South Dakota 57501-1700
(605) 773-3357

Tennessee

State Long-Term Care Ombudsman
Commission on Aging, ADDGS
500 Deaderic Street, 9th Floor
Nashville, Tennessee 37243-0860
(615) 741-2056

Executive Director, Office of Health Licensure and Regulation
Division of Health Care Facilities
Tennessee Department of Health
425 Fifth Avenue N.
Cordell Hull Building, 1st Floor
Nashville, Tennessee 37247
(615) 741-7221

Texas

State Long-Term Care Ombudsman
Texas Department on Aging
4900 N. Lamar Boulevard
Austin, Texas 78751
(512) 424-6875

Executive Director, Long-Term Care Regulatory
Mail Code E-342, Texas Department of Human Services, ADDGS
P.O. Box 149030
Austin, Texas 78714-9030
(512) 438-2633; in-state (800) 458-9858

Utah

State Long-Term Care Ombudsman
Aging and Adult Services
120 North 200 W., Room 325
Salt Lake City, Utah 84103
(801) 538-3910

Director, Bureau of Licensing
Department of Health
288 North 1460 West
P.O. Box 142003
Salt Lake City, Utah 84116
(801) 538-6152

Vermont

State Long-Term Care Ombudsman
Vermont Legal Aid, Inc.
P.O. Box 1367
164 N. Winooski Avenue
Burlington, Vermont 05402
(802) 863-5620

Commissioner, Division of Licensing and Protection
Department of Aging and Disabilities, ADDGS
103 S. Main Street, Ladd Hall
Waterbury, Vermont 05671-2306
(802) 241-2345

Virginia

State Long-Term Care Ombudsman
530 E. Main Street, Suite 428
Richmond, Virginia 23219
(804) 644-2923

Commissioner, Division of Long-Term Care Services
Center for Quality Health Care Services and Consumer Protection
Department for the Aging, ADDGS
Virginia State Department of Health
3600 W. Broad Street, Suite 216
Richmond, Virginia 23230-4920
(804) 367-2100

Washington

State Long-Term Care Ombudsman
South King County Multi-Services Center
P.O. Box 23699
1200 S. 336th Street
Federal Way, Washington 98093-7699
(253) 838-6810; in state (800) 562-6028

Assistant Secretary, Residential Care Services
Department of Social and Health Services

P.O. Box 45600
Olympia, Washington 98504-5600
(360) 725-2300

West Virginia

State Long-Term Care Ombudsman
West Virginia Bureau of Senior Services
Commission on Aging
1900 Kanawha Boulevard E.
Holly Grove Building 10
Charleston, West Virginia 25305-0160
(304) 558-3317

Commissioner, Licensure and Certification
Office of Health Facilities
350 Capitol Street, Room 206
Charleston, West Virginia 25301-3718
(304) 558-0050

Wisconsin

State Long-Term Care Ombudsman
Board on Aging and Long-Term Care
214 N. Hamilton Street
Madison, Wisconsin 53703-2118
(800) 815-0015

Director, Bureau of Quality Assurance
Department of Health and Family Services
Bureau of Aging and Long Term Care Resources, ADDGS
One W. Wilson Street, Room 950
Madison, Wisconsin, 53701
(608) 266-8847

Wyoming

State Long-Term Care Ombudsman
Wyoming Long-Term Care Ombudsman Program
P.O. Box 94
Wheatland, Wyoming 82201
(307) 322-5553

Administrator, Office of Health Quality
Department of Health
2020 Carey Avenue, 8th Floor
Cheyenne, Wyoming 82002
(307) 777-7123

National Long Term Care Accreditation Agencies

Continuing Care Accreditation Commission
2519 Connecticut Avenue, NW
Washington DC 20008-1520
(202) 738-7286
http://www.caconline.org

Founded in 1985 and sponsored by the American Association of Homes & Services for the Aging, this is the nation's only accrediting body for continuing care retirement communities.

Joint Commission's Home Care Accreditation Program
Joint Commission on Accreditation of Healthcare Organizations
(630) 792-5743
http://jcprdw1.jcaho.org/accred/hom/hom_intr.html

Joint Commission accreditation is widely recognized as an important seal of approval in the healthcare marketplace. Surveys are conducted by professionals with administrative and clinical experience in home care organization.

Index